FRIENDS
AND ENEMIES

TATTERED
FLAG

Tattered Flag Press · East Sussex

FRIENDS and ENEMIES

THE NATAL CAMPAIGN IN THE SOUTH AFRICAN WAR
1899–1902

HUGH RETHMAN

The Author

Hugh Rethman was born in Natal into a family of farmers and traders whose forbears were among the province's early settlers. His great grandfather commanded the Border Mounted Rifles, a volunteer colonial regiment which took part in various engagements preceding and during the siege of Ladysmith, as well as pursuing the Boers out of the province.

He was educated at St Andrew's College, Grahamstown, before reading English literature, economics, economic history, and political philosophy at the University of Natal. A keen sportsman and horseman, he later moved to England where he read law at the University of Leeds. He qualified as a Barrister and practised law in both England and South Africa, and also ran a retail business in Durban. In 1993 Nelson Mandela tried to persuade him to move to Johannesburg to assist in the formulation of a policy to combat rural poverty.

He holds a wide range of interests, but is particularly passionate about history. He has written articles on the Boer War for the journals of the Victorian Military History Society and the Military History Society of South Africa. He lives in Suffolk, England. *Friends and Enemies* is his first book.

All the photographs contained in this book have been sourced by the author or are from the author's personal collection assembled over many years, much coming from family collections and archives with permission. In some cases it has not been possible to trace the potential holders of copyright either as a result of the passage of time or because of the changes which have occurred in South Africa.

Published in Great Britain in 2015 by
Tattered Flag Press
11 Church Street
Ticehurst
East Sussex TN5 7AH
England

office@thetatteredflag.com
www.thetatteredflag.com

Tattered Flag Press is an imprint of Chevron Publishing Ltd.

Friends and Enemies
© Hugh Rethman

Design: Mark Nelson
Maps © Stephen Foster (pages xii to xvi)

British Library Cataloguing in Publication Data

A Catalogue Record for this book is available from the British Library

ISBN 978-0-9576892-3-7

Printed and bound in the United Kingdom

For more information on books published by Tattered Flag Press visit
www.thetatteredflag.com

CONTENTS

INTRODUCTION

BY the end of the 19th century the attitudes of Britain's subjects towards their Empire were changing. Informed opinion envisaged it being transformed into an alliance of independent countries which might act as a counter to any aggressive intent by other powers. Canada, Australia, and New Zealand were well on the way to achieving independence, but elsewhere more complex issues had to be solved before the bonds of empire could be disentangled.

In Southern Africa, the Cape Colony and Natal had obtained a degree of independence, but were under constant threat from the two Boer Republics lying on their northern borders. The Transvaal was particularly aggressive and its leaders made it clear that it was their intention that they, and they alone, would rule Africa from Cape Town to the Zambezi River. In 1838 and in 1881 they invaded Natal but lacked the military capacity to drive the British out of the Colony. But this all changed in 1886 when the world's largest deposit of gold was discovered on the Witwatersrand and money began to flood into the Transvaal Treasury. Now able to buy the best rifles and artillery they could once again think of driving the English out of the Cape and Natal and began arming themselves accordingly. They carefully cultivated good relations with Germany and other European countries, which might be hostile to Britain. Their cause received a huge propaganda boost at the end of 1895 by the notorious Jameson Raid.

In an attempt to provoke a coup d'état, on 29 December 1895, Dr Jameson had invaded the Transvaal with 500 men and three field guns. He believed that when the news of the raid reached Johannesburg, its citizens would rise up against the government and install a new order which would respect the rights of all people living in the country. The Boers tracked Jameson's column until it was within 14 miles of Johannesburg where it was surrounded and forced to surrender. Jameson's force had suffered 65 casualties while its opponents suffered about six. To maximize on the public relations advantage the Raid had given the Transvaal, the rank and file of Jameson's party were given permission to leave the country without punishment while the officers were sent to Britain for trial.

Having disposed of the raiders the Transvaal government turned its attention towards its critics who resided in the Transvaal. The most prominent were prosecuted, security laws tightened and the constitution altered to ensure that political control of the country would remain with the ruling elite regardless of other developments in the country. The arms build-up was accelerated.

To meet the developing crisis Britain could not have chosen two more unsuitable persons to protect her interests in Southern Africa than Sir Alfred Milner, Governor of the Cape, and General Sir William Butler, Commander in Chief of the British forces in the two Colonies. Milner, though clever and a brilliant organizer, was possessed of overweening arrogance and appears to have believed that his opinion on any issue was correct and any contrary view was therefore of no consequence and should be ignored. Gen Butler despised colonials and was anti-semitic. As many of the men who arranged the finance for the mining of gold in the Transvaal had names which might be Jewish, Sir William's sympathies lay with President Kruger's regime in the Transvaal. When told that the Transvaal was preparing for war Sir William retorted, 'England is not preparing for war, even if the Transvaal is.'

In an attempt to avoid war, a conference was held between the Presidents of the Boer Republics and Sir Alfred Milner in May/June 1899. Although the war was likely to be fought over their countries, Natal and the Cape Colony were not invited. When a number of Natal politicians requested Milner to consider the views of Colonial ministers before final decisions were made, he rejected the request with fury describing the petitioners as 'wobblers and mugwumps'. Milner believed the problem could be solved if the Republics accepted British suzerainty over their countries, while the Boers had very different plans. Not surprisingly the conference achieved nothing.

In planning their invasion of the two Colonies, the enemy the Boers feared most was the locally raised volunteer regiments. Although Britain insisted that these volunteers be armed with obsolete weapons, this was more than discounted by the facts that they would be fighting on their home ground, could shoot straight and knew Boer strengths and weaknesses. Added to this they were on good terms with the indigenous peoples and could speak their languages.

By the end of September 1899 the Republics were ready to invade. Sir William Butler had been recalled, and to strengthen the Colonies' defences infantry were transferred from India, thereby doubling the number of British soldiers in South Africa. This would not have worried the Boers as infantry were not nearly mobile enough for South African conditions. On 11 October 1899 the two Boer Republics declared war on the British Empire and their Kommandos crossed the borders of the two Colonies. Initially the British suffered a series of humiliating defeats but slowly the tide turned against the Boers who were driven out of Natal. This change of fortune was brought about in no small measure by commanders taking notice of colonial advice and capability.

After a long, drawn out guerilla war, Britain signed a Peace Treaty with the Boers in 1902. The Colonies were not consulted about the terms of the treaty which gave control of the whole of South Africa to the Boers, who now called themselves Afrikaners. In control of the present, they controlled the past and they set about obliterating from history the part played by the Colonials and the Black peoples in this conflict.

Sadly, the Boers succeeded in their ploy and for generations the British have been content to acquire facts about South Africa from Afrikaners. In the process not only has the military contribution and suffering by the Colonials and Black peoples been ignored, but also the work of many contemporary British journalists reporting on the war has been swept under the carpet. Realizing that these sources of information were in danger of being lost forever, this book has been written in the hope that future generations might have a more balanced account of this part of South African and British Imperial history.

My intention has been to provide an accurate military and social history which all readers will enjoy. Where possible I have let the participants speak for themselves. Often incidents, trivial in themselves give a remarkable insight into the lives and characters of those involved. This work does not pretend to be the definitive work on the subject, however it is hoped that it will provide a change of direction in which the subject is approached in future.

ACKNOWLEDGEMENTS

MANY years ago I took my young English bride on a tour of the Natal Battlefields. In those days there were no luxury guided tours. Instead, we would follow a rough track to the vicinity of the battlefield and there, sometimes with the aid of passing Black people, build a picture in our minds of the stirring events that had occurred at Isandhlwana, Rorke's Drift, Spion Kop, Colenso and Wagon Hill. Ann was fascinated, and, from that time, shared with me a passionate interest in the history of the peoples of Natal. When, after the trauma of going into exile, I decided to write this book, Ann offered her full support, provided she could read every word I wrote and correct the text. By this means she banished the dreadful legalese into which lawyers are prone to lapse. Her influence is present throughout the book.

It is impossible to name here all the people who have given me information and support. They have all, in their different ways, contributed to this book. Especial thanks are, however, due to the following individuals: John McKenzie, Douglas and Andrew Campbell, Keith Archibald, Denise Carrick, Mike Sparks, Robert and David Lewis, Pam McFadden, Norman Leveridge, Mark Coghlan, Official Historian of the Natal Carbineers, and Samuel Goba, descendant of one of the prominent founders of the Natal Native Congress, who gave me information which enabled me to track down documents relative to the affairs of Black people in Natal during the Boer War.

My thanks are also due to the staff of the following archives, museums and libraries:

National Archives, Kew, London.
National Army Museum, Chelsea, London
Brenthurst Library, Johannesburg
Ladysmith Siege Museum, Ladysmith
Talana Museum, Dundee
African Studies Library, Johannesburg
Killie Campbell Museum, Durban
Natal Archives, Pietermaritzburg
The South African Museum of Military History, Johannesburg
King's College, London
Natal Carbineers Museum, Pietermaritzburg
Old Fort Museum, Durban
Natal Society Library, Pietermaritzburg
Natal Mounted Rifles Museum, Durban
The Estcourt Museum, Estcourt

Finally, I would like to thank my publisher, Robert Forsyth, of Tattered Flag Press. It has been a pleasure to work with him and to observe the professional skill with which he has edited the book.

Hugh Rethman

GLOSSARY

UNLESS the context suggests otherwise, the words Boer, Voortrekker, Afrikaner, and Dutchman are interchangeable, all meaning a white South African descended from Dutch or French Huguenot settlers. In the early years of the twentieth century an attempt was made to introduce the word Afrikander to describe a white person born in South Africa. The idea failed to gain acceptance and today Afrikander refers to a breed of cattle.

Colonial is used in this work to describe those people domiciled outside the British Isles whose forebears came from the British Isles.

English has a slightly different meaning when compared with its usage in Britain. In South Africa the word is generally used to describe a person whose home language is English, regardless of whether his forebears came from England, Britain's Celtic fringes, or indeed some other European country. Failure to take note of this linguistic quirk can result in embarrassing blunders.

Hollander describes a person from the Netherlands who emigrated to the Transvaal towards the end of the nineteenth century to provide the skills which were not readily available among the agrarian Boers.

Rooinek – literally 'Redneck' – is an English South African term. The word does not have the cultural connotations that redneck has in the US.

Uitlander literally an Outlander. A non-Afrikaner who at some time in his life lived in the Transvaal. The title is hereditary.

'Afrikaans' a patois derived from Dutch. Used by Afrikaners it became an official language of South Africa in the twentieth century.

Some words with which the reader might not be familiar:

Afrikaner	A white settler whose ancestors came from Holland or France during the seventeenth and eighteenth centuries and settled at the Cape
Berg	Mountain
Biltong	Dried meat
Burg	Town
Burgher	Afrikaner citizen
Donga	Ditch caused by erosion during flooding
Dopper	Ultra conservative sect of the Boer religion
Dorp	Village
Drift	River crossing
Inspan	To harness draft animals
Kloof	Ravine or gorge
Knobkerrie or Kerrie	A nutted stick used for herding animals and sometimes for fighting
Kommando	A body of men from a particular district or country fighting for the Boers
Kop	Hill
Kopje	Hillock
Kraal	A village, a home or cattle enclosure depending on context
Krantz	Cliff

Krygsraad	Council of War
Laager	Encampment
Laagte	Plain
Landrost	Senior official in a district
Lobolo	Dowry which formed part of a marriage settlement
Mealie(s)	Maize
Nek	Saddle or dip between two hills
Outspan	To unharness
Pont	Ferry over a river
Poort	Pass between two hills
Rand	A ridge of high ground the most famous of which is the Witwatersrand, or Whitewaters Ridge on which lies the city of Johannesburg. As a reef of gold bearing ore followed the line of the Witwatersrand the whole area became known as the Rand. Subsequently the word was chosen as the name for the South African unit of currency.
Sangar	Stone breastwork erected from loose stones
Schantz	Rampart often combined with a trench
Sjambok	A leather whip traditionally made from hippopotamus hide
Spruit	Stream
Stad	Town
Stoep	Veranda
Trek	Travel (verb, adjective and noun)
Uitlander Korps	Foreign volunteer regiments who fought for the Boers
Veld(t)	African countryside
Vlei	Swamp
Volksraad	Afrikaner Parliament
Voortrekker	A Dutch/French settler who left the Cape in the second quarter of the nineteenth century and settled in the lands to the north of the Orange River establishing the Free State and Transvaal republics

[Based, by permission, on a sketch-map by Mr. W. T. Maud, published in "The Graphic."

MAP OF LADYSMITH.

THE BATTLE OF TALANA HILL,
20 OCTOBER 1899

BATTLE OF ELANDSLAAGTE, 21 OCTOBER 1899

1. Intact road bridge (mined)
2. Destroyed railway bridge
3. Royal Field Artillery (Long)
4. Royal Field Artillery (Henshaw)
5. Naval Guns
6. Fort Wylie

BATTLE OF COLENSO, 15 DECEMBER 1899

The Battle of
Spion Kop, 24 January 1900

Conical Hill

Boer Artillery Fire

Green Hill

Boer Rifle Fire (1500yds)

To Three Tree Hill

N

Boer Rifle Fire (1000yds)

Thorneycroft's Mounted Infantry

King's Own Lancs.

Spion Kop

South Lancs.

Aloe Knoll Boer Rifle Fire (400yds)

Boer Riflemen

Lancs. Fusiliers

Boer Artillery Fire from Twin Peaks

Reinforcements :
Imperial Light Infantry
Scottish Rifles
Middlesex Regiment

Route of British Advance

Yards

0   200   400   600   800   1,000

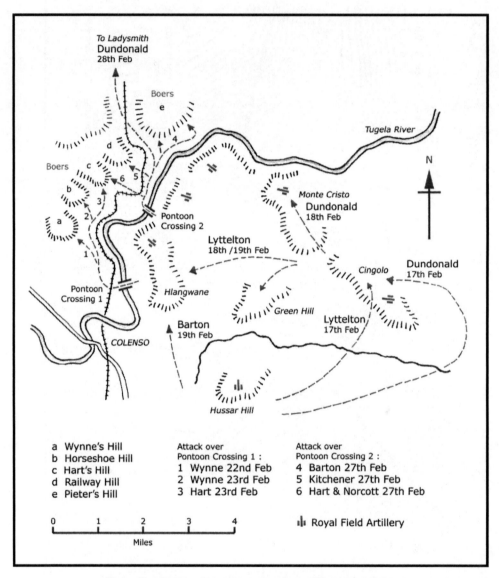

THE BREAKTHROUGH TOWARDS LADYSMITH,
14–27 FEBRUARY 1900

CHAPTER ONE

War Imminent

◆

'Always remember your friends may become your enemies,
and your enemies your friends'

FROM AN INSCRIPTION PLACED BY WALTER KARRI DAVIES ON THE BREECHBLOCK
OF A GUN CAPTURED AT LADYSMITH, NATAL, ON 7 DECEMBER 1899

MONDAY, 9 OCTOBER 1899

AS GREAT BRITAIN and the Boer Republics drifted steadily towards war, six young Boer policemen were amusing themselves with some target practice next to the Natal road on the flat, treeless plain of the Eastern Transvaal, South Africa. Watching were 7,000 young Zulu miners and their two colonial guides, Sidney Marwick and Guy Wheelwright. As all trains had been commandeered by the Boer military, the miners, escorted by the policemen, were attempting to walk the two hundred miles and more from Johannesburg to their homes in Natal and Zululand.

The marksmanship of the Boers was impressive and one of their number, Trooper Bretz, could hit the distant target almost every time he fired. After a while he handed his rifle to Wheelwright so that the Natalian could show what he could do. It was a superb new Mauser, better than any firearm Wheelwright had ever handled. As he raised the rifle and looked down the sights, there was quiet. Gently he squeezed the trigger and for a moment after the shot, there was dead silence. Then 7,000 faces broke into big smiles. Wheelwright handed the rifle back to the now thoughtful young Boer. Perhaps it was not going to be quite so easy to drive the Natalians into the sea.[1]

In 1895 the Department of Native Affairs of the Natal Colonial Government had opened agencies in Johannesburg and the nearby town of Germiston. Mindful of the fact that many Black migrant workers from the Colony were illiterate and spoke neither English nor Dutch, making them vulnerable to the wiles of the unscrupulous, these offices were set up to help them. Most of the migrant workers were employed in the gold mines.

Marwick had been appointed head of the agency in Johannesburg and Wheelwright to a similar position in Germiston. Apart from competence in their administrative duties, the agents were expected to have a deep knowledge of the Zulu language and customs. Absolute integrity was presumed.

Long hours were worked and much was achieved. They acted as a conduit through which the workers could maintain contact with their families. Finances were looked after and monies remitted to those in need at home. Claims were successfully pursued on behalf of those who had been cheated or injured at work. Zulus have a great talent for bestowing nicknames which say a great deal about a person's character. Marwick was given the name '*Muhle*' which is the Zulu word for things that are good. He was just twenty years-old when he was appointed to the post in Johannesburg in 1895.

In September 1899 Marwick arranged rail tickets for those miners who, because of the impending threat of war, wished to return to Zululand or Natal. However Blacks had to have passes to travel in the Transvaal and State Secretary, FW Reitz, refused to issue these passes. Marwick then went over Reitz's head to the Commandant-General, PJ Joubert, commander of the Boer army then preparing to invade Natal. The General agreed to the issue of the passes subject to their being stamped by the Natal Agent.

On 1 October about a thousand men were able to take advantage of this concession. The next day passenger traffic to Natal was suspended as all trains were required by the military. At the time those who had been able to get on the last train were regarded as the lucky ones.

General Joubert having left for the front, Marwick approached his Secretary, Mr Louis de Souza, with a proposal that the remaining miners be given leave to walk to Natal. If the proposal had been rejected, the Transvaal would have had thousands of hostile, unemployed and hungry Zulus prowling around behind their lines, a situation which would have done nothing to assist their war effort. And so it was agreed that Marwick, his staff, and about 5,000 Blacks should have permission to travel from Johannesburg to the Natal Border, provided they walked in one group. Strict discipline was to be maintained, and they were to be accompanied by six mounted Transvaal policemen, the charge for which would be sixty pounds.

Approval from the Native Affairs Department in Natal was sought and promptly given, the Prime Minister taking the trouble to telegraph his own support for the operation. New Heriot Mine benevolently loaned to them, free of charge, two Cape carts and a four-wheeled trap, vehicles which were to prove invaluable on the long march. In an astonishing feat of organisation, Marwick and Wheelwright were able to assemble the refugees for their march by 6 October and on the 7th they were on their way. They were to witness the demonstration of Boer and Natalian shooting skills, and have many other adventures before completing their long journey home.

The miners walking to Natal were among the last refugees to leave Johannesburg. The exodus had already begun four months earlier when talks between Britain and the Boer Republics broke down and war became not a possibility, but a virtual certainty. Tens of thousands fled to the British Colonies of the Cape and Natal; some because they feared internment, others because they did not relish the prospect of being conscripted to fight for the Boers, and yet others because the imminent war had cost them their livelihood.

Among these refugees were two men determined to resist Boer oppression and expansion and to assert what they believed to be right – Walter David 'Karri' Davies and Aubrey Woolls Sampson. At the beginning of September 1899 they were in the Natal capital, Pietermaritzburg, organising a regiment to oppose the Boers. Recruits had to be of good character, fine shots and excellent horsemen. The Regiment would be called the Imperial Light Horse.

Davies was an Australian. His father Maurice had emigrated from London with his parents to Tasmania in 1840. After seven years the family moved to Victoria. Maurice had a successful period working on the Victorian goldfields after which he moved to Adelaide to start a business as a contractor and builders' merchant. He had married and in due course six sons were born. Walter, their second son, was born in 1867.

In 1875 the family moved to Western Australia where Maurice intended to establish a sawmill. In 1878 he acquired shares in the timber industry near Karridale with access to the port facilities at Barrack Point. The business expanded rapidly. Further mills were opened, bridges were built over rivers and jetties built at different points along the coast to facilitate the export around the world of the timber from the famous Karri and Jarrah trees. When Maurice Davies arrived in this South West corner of Western Australia it was almost uninhabited and by his efforts and imagination he transformed it into a thriving community. However his interests extended beyond his timber enterprise. He still worked as a contractor, being involved in such diverse projects as the construction of the Cape Leeuwin Lighthouse and jetties from Freemantle to Eucla near the South Australian border.

His son Walter was educated at Winhames College, Adelaide and Scotch College, Melbourne. The Davies boys were encouraged to become an integral part of the family business and, in order that they might understand the industry thoroughly, they started as labourers and had to work their way up from there.

While retaining his interest in the timber industry, Walter also studied engineering and was a brilliant student, rapidly making a name for himself and being involved in several major engineering projects around Australia. He was highly articulate and, as a student, such was his promise as a public speaker that he was chosen to meet the well-known orator Lord Rosebury in a public debate in the Melbourne Town Hall. Unfortunately he broke his collarbone playing cricket on the day before the debate and had to withdraw from the contest. A few years later Lord Rosebury became Prime Minister of Great Britain.

In 1893 Walter contracted blood poisoning, which incapacitated him and to restore his health it was suggested that he take a sea cruise. He chose to go to South Africa and, once there, his curiosity ensured that he visited the new 'boom town' of Johannesburg and the gold mines of the Rand. He realised, immediately, that the rapid development of the gold mines and the linked construction of new railways and harbours provided a great opportunity for the family firm. He set up business as a timber merchant and in no time ships were plying from Australia to South Africa laden with Karri and Jarrah timber for the new mines, railways and harbours. He was given the nickname 'Karri', a not inappropriate name for a big man with an intellect and character to match. To distinguish himself from the other Davies in the Transvaal he changed his name to Walter Karri Davies.

Coming from Australia it was a matter of astonishment to him that those people in the Transvaal who contributed 97.5 per cent to the State's revenue (the mining community provided 92.5 per cent and the Black peoples 5 per cent) had no say as to how such money should be spent, all power being vested in a minority of the population who contributed a mere 2.5 per cent of the revenue. The dominant minority appeared to have every intention of maintaining the status quo. Inevitably he was drawn towards the Reform Movement and there he met Aubrey Woolls Sampson who was to become a lifelong friend. On Woolls-Sampson, Karri bestowed the nickname 'Sambo'.

Woolls Sampson, like President Kruger of the Transvaal, had been born in the Cape Colony and like the President, Aubrey also had an iron will. His father was a judge, however it was from his mother that he inherited his character. She was known in Cape Society as a strong, uncompromising personality who was implacable in what she considered to be right.

The Sampson children led an idyllic life at the Cape. Their father leased a small farm just outside Cape Town, close to both the sea and the lofty Devil's Peak. The boys were able to lead a very active life swimming, exploring and climbing all over the mountain. Their neighbour and landlord was a Dutch farmer and as the two families were frequently in each other's company, the children grew up as fluent in Dutch as they were in English. When their father employed a Zulu groom, Sam, he taught them Zulu, the first of a number of indigenous languages Aubrey was to master. Sam also taught the boys veldcraft and in particular how to find a beehive. This entailed following a bee back to the hive, an exercise which required not only an ability to move quickly across country, coupled with great concentration, but also very sharp vision. This was to serve Aubrey in great stead in later years when as a military scout he was able to see things invisible to others.

The boys learnt to read and write at home and Aubrey only went to school when he was eleven. School was not really to his liking – it was adventure he craved so he decided to run away. Hearing of his plan his mother confronted young Aubrey, 'I hear you are planning to run away,' she said, 'don't do that, just pack your bags and say goodbye.' This took the wind out of his sails and he remained at home, but the adventurous spirit remained.

When he was fifteen his father, who was to preside over the Circuit Court at the Diamond Fields, decided that Aubrey should accompany him. It was a strange decision, as Kimberley at that time was far from being the respectable place it was later to become. Perhaps the judge thought it would toughen him up. For Aubrey, the life of adventure had begun. He took any work he could get, acting as a messenger and labouring on other men's claims. At the same time in Kimberley, Cecil Rhodes was working in his little mineral water factory trying to raise sufficient money to study at Oxford, in order to obtain the education which he believed necessary to be successful.

Young Aubrey looked at the people about him and absorbed a wide knowledge of human nature in all its diversity. Alcohol was a problem and he, though never a total abstainer, hardly ever drank and throughout his life he despised drunkenness. He read voraciously, and building on his little formal education, he made a careful study of all those matters with which he came in contact, be they technical such as mining, or the languages and customs of black peoples.

He added his mother's maiden name, Woolls, to his surname and thereafter he was Aubrey Woolls Sampson. Not long after he arrived in Kimberley, the Diamond Fields revolt broke out and though only fifteen, he joined it and impressed all with his courage. This revolt, which had been sparked by maladministration, was settled amicably enabling Kimberley and the Diamond Fields to settle down to a more orderly existence. In 1873 he went with his father to Barberton in the eastern Transvaal. The next few years were spent gold prospecting and big game hunting.

After the British annexed the Transvaal in 1877 he took part in a campaign which brought an end to the Sikukuni war and also took part in the Zulu War of 1879. In the Transvaal a rebellion against the new British rule was being carefully prepared. In December 1880 the rebels proclaimed a republic and the country was plunged into war.

Aubrey joined a commando of South African-born volunteers fighting on behalf of the British. When its commandant fell ill, Aubrey took his place at its head. It was one of the units defending Pretoria, then the centre of the British administration. And so it came about that when battle was joined with a Boer *Kommando* led by one Hans Botha, a most desperate shoot-out occurred between the two leaders, each having taken cover behind an anthill with no more than 50 yards between them. Both men were superb marksmen and the slightest exposure by either was instantaneously pierced by a bullet. Thus the duel continued like some medieval contest with the champions of each side fighting to the death. From time to time, one, thinking perhaps the other had been killed, would raise himself a little only to receive yet another wound. Gradually the two champions, weakened by their many injuries, lapsed into silence behind their respective anthills and the men on both sides fell back, leaving the field to the wounded.

Aubrey had been shot in the arm and shoulder and most seriously in the neck, a wound which exposed his jugular vein. Hans Botha had been shot seven times through the body. At this point, a future mining magnate, Harry Struben, appeared on the scene with an ambulance and despite their protests, the two men were taken to hospital where they were placed in adjacent beds.

Pretoria being besieged, no definite news could be obtained in the outside world, but such were Aubrey's wounds that word went out that he had been killed and obituaries were published. Only his mother refused to believe that he was dead and announced that Aubrey would never allow himself to die while he was needed, and she was right. Miraculously, the thin membrane enclosing his jugular vein held and, slowly but surely, his wound healed.

Equally surprising, none of the seven bullets which went through Hans Botha had hit a vital organ and he too survived. In hospital there was much banter between the two men, and a lifelong friendship was formed which was to survive the troubled times which lay ahead.

As soon as the wounds had healed sufficiently, Aubrey went to the family home in the Cape to recuperate. Once again he could walk along the beach at Kalk Bay, swim in the surf, or climb mountains. With his wounds completely healed, his vibrant health returned; the once scruffy youth had now matured into a confident young man with an optimistic and charismatic personality which ensured his company would be sought and enjoyed by one and all. Women could not help but notice his extraordinary good looks, and it was said that Aubrey, 'had a great way with the ladies and that many were generally inclined to go a great way with him.'

Life was pleasant at the Cape, but Aubrey needed a challenge. He joined the Cape Infantry, a regular unit and received a commission. In due course he was appointed commander of Fort Donald, situated at the juncture of the Cape Colony, Natal and Pondoland, an independent and extensive country wedged between the Cape and Natal. Fort Donald was out in the wilds, the nearest settlement being the little Natal village of Harding, three or four hours ride away. The Fort was not really a fort but a hill. There were no permanent buildings and the garrison consisted of a few orderlies. On a clear day one can see over the rolling green hills of Pondoland to the sea, fifty or so miles away. The wild and beautiful coast of Pondoland with its romantic tales of treasure-laden ships being wrecked was an irresistible attraction for Aubrey. He did not find much treasure, but he did acquire considerable knowledge of the people, their rulers, culture and language.

When the Cape Government decided to disband the Cape Infantry, Aubrey decided against joining another regiment and instead to go prospecting in the Transvaal. In 1886 when disputes between various tribes threatened to bring chaos to Pondoland, someone remembered Aubrey, and he was selected by the Cape Government to be one of a four member delegation, under Walter Stanford, the Chief magistrate in Kokstad, tasked with restoring peace to the area. The Pondos under Chief Umqikela had long running disputes with the Xesibe and Baca peoples. Stanford was able to rely on Aubrey to negotiate with the opposing parties in a situation where one word out of place could have spelt the end of the peace process. The negotiations were a success and war averted. The official report on the matter stated: '*Mr. Sampson would appear to have conducted a delicate and difficult matter with firmness and discretion.*'

Over the following years Aubrey travelled in Rhodesia and explored unknown areas north of the Zambezi River in what is now known as Zambia. In 1895 he returned to Johannesburg to find the place in ferment. Relations between the Transvaal Government and the inhabitants of Johannesburg had reached a critical point.

To understand this crisis, the events which followed, and their effect on the people involved, it is necessary to give a brief account of the country's history.

CHAPTER TWO

The Boer Republics

• ◆ •

'The South African Flag shall yet wave from Table Bay to the Zambezi,
be that end accomplished by blood or by ink. If blood it is to be,
we shall not lack men to spill it.'

STATEMENT BY THE REV SJ DU TOIT, AT A BANQUET IN AMSTERDAM IN 1884,
IN WHICH HE SET OUT THE FOREIGN POLICY OF THE SOUTH AFRICAN REPUBLIC
(A.K.A. THE TRANSVAAL)

I N 1652 Cromwell ruled England, but the Dutch ruled the seas. In the religious wars which wracked Europe during the previous century, the Dutch had emerged as the champions of the Protestant cause, and, with Britain preoccupied with internal disputes, they became the leading trading nation of Europe. In the East, the Dutch East India Company had acquired a pre-eminent position, which brought much prosperity to Holland. However, the journey by sea around Africa took many months, and there were no ports at which the Company could call to effect essential repairs to ships and to obtain fresh provisions for passengers and crew. So in that year the Company established a station at the Cape with a small fort and adjacent gardens to be cultivated by its employees.

Though not uninhabited, the land appeared to be only sparsely populated by nomadic herdsmen, the Khoikhoi, generally known as Hottentots, who, because of their appearance, were thought to be of Chinese origin. Indeed many of the early explorers referred to them as Chinese although their language and customs had no similarity to those of the Orient. The Company encouraged intermarriage, hoping by this means to breed out the locals. This, probably Europe's first attempt at social engineering in Africa, was a failure. However the idea of a halfway house where ships could call on their way to and from the East met with instant success. The Company's gardens were unable to keep up with demand for fruit and vegetables. People were allowed to establish privately owned farms and in 1658 slaves were brought from the East Indies to help work the land and to do other manual work. A substantial stone castle was built, not to protect the settlement from the locals, but as a defence against jealous European rivals. In 1688, Huguenots fleeing from religious persecution in France were permitted to settle at the Cape, provided they broke off all links with France and adopted the Dutch language and culture. The Huguenots brought many skills to the Cape, but they also re-enforced hostility towards Roman Catholicism and gave credence to the idea that the local Dutch population could decide the cultural norms and language of the country.

The Khoikhoi, being few in number and now ravaged by new diseases brought in by the Europeans against which they had no resistance or immunity, could do little to resist the invaders. They retreated to the fringes of the expanding settlement. Some worked as servants to the Dutch. To get by they learnt Dutch and in the course of time their language was almost lost, only existing today in some remote areas of Namibia.

Over the next one hundred and fifty years what became 'Cape Town' grew steadily in size and importance and, in its immediate hinterland, towns and villages were laid out where a settled and comfortable way of life was established. Beyond this settled area the mountainous terrain impeded but did not stop further expansion of the colony. Dutch pioneers crossed the mountains, and, adopting a semi nomadic lifestyle, trekked ever northwards and eastwards.

By the end of the eighteenth century, the area of land nominally under the control of the Company was about the size of England. From the beginning the colonists had chafed under the rule of the Company and nowhere was its rule more resented than in its outlying districts. Necessity required that these pioneers be self-reliant, which in turn bred an independence of spirit. Education was often limited to learning to read the Bible, which for many was the only book they ever read. Gradually their cultural ties with Europe became ever more tenuous and what remained was firmly anchored in the religious ideas of the seventeenth century. They called themselves 'Boers', that is to say farmers, though this might perhaps be a misnomer.

While the Boers were struggling to subsist in the dry interior of the Cape, momentous changes were taking place in eighteenth century Europe. Trade, in its wake, had brought prosperity and a great flowering of scientific discovery accompanied by equally important changes in the way people thought. The industrial revolution was beginning. The American Colonies had rebelled and acquired independence, while the French had suffered a bloody revolution. The frontier Boers envied the Americans their independence, but other changes in the outside world had little effect on the way they lived their lives.

Holland had lost its pre-eminent position as a trading power and the Dutch East India Company was no longer the force it once was. When Napoleon Bonaparte conquered the Low Countries, the Dutch Government fled to Britain and requested Britain to take over the defence of the Cape. It was not a situation that appealed to the British, however they could not let Napoleon control the sea route round the Cape and in 1785 they sent troops to garrison it. In 1803 it was handed back to the Dutch, only for the British to re-occupy it in 1806. Finally in 1815, by the Treaty of Vienna, which brought a formal end to the Napoleonic wars, the Dutch ceded the Cape to Britain. No one in Britain could have realised the burden they had taken on.

The change of Governors in Cape Town was only one of the new problems facing the frontier Boers. Towards the end of the eighteenth century they clashed with a new force on the Eastern Frontier, the amaXhosa. These people were numerous, strong and warlike. The Xhosa were not going to be brushed aside easily and the Boers on their scattered farms began to feel their very existence threatened. Into this cauldron on the Frontier there arrived in 1820 nearly 5,000 British settlers at Algoa Bay, now generally known as Port Elizabeth.

On the whole, with similar trials and dangers to endure, the new settlers' relationship with the Boers was cordial, but they had come from a very different culture. Many were educated and regarded themselves as enlightened, modern people. Education was important and schools were established. The rights of individuals were to be respected and slavery was regarded with abhorrence. They were not prepared to give up their Anglo Saxon heritage, but were tolerant of the customs of others.

With tact and common sense the conflicting interests of all three very different cultures might have been reconciled. This was not to be. In 1834 slavery was abolished in the Cape Colony. This the frontier Boers were prepared to tolerate, however the demonization of them by 'interested and dishonest persons under the name of religion,'[1] caused such hurt among the religious Boers that it burned into their very being a bitter and lasting hatred of all things British. This, combined with the refusal of Lord Glenelg, the Colonial Secretary, to have any regard for local opinion, convinced many Boers that life in the Colony would be intolerable.

In their travail, they turned to their Bibles for inspiration and in particular to the Book of Exodus. From 1835 to 1837 a great migration known as the Great Trek took place. From all over the Cape interior groups of families and friends came together, loaded their few possessions onto their wagons, and set off northwards to the lands beyond the Orange River, beyond the furthest reaches of British influence. They called themselves 'Voortrekkers' and numbered somewhere between six and ten thousand. Among the migrants was a 12 year-old boy, Paul Kruger.

When the Voortrekkers crossed the Cape's northern border at the Orange River they entered a land of wide, grassy plains teeming with game and yet sparsely populated, truly the promised land. They pegged out their farms and formed the republic which became the Orange Free State. To the north the nascent state was bounded by the Vaal River.

Latecomers, and perhaps, those who hated Britain most, crossed the Vaal in search of their paradise and there founded four further republics. Life was harder here. There were constant wars with the Black people they encountered and the little republics squabbled endlessly among themselves. So quarrelsome were they that in 1857 Paul Kruger, now a Kommandant in the Potchefstroom Republic, went so far as to make an unsuccessful raid into the Orange Free State in an attempt to overthrow its government. In 1860 the Transvaal Republics agreed to unite, but shortly thereafter, war broke out between them. It was not until 1864 that unity was finally achieved, with the formation of the South African Republic, colloquially known as the Transvaal.

The first years of this new Republic were not edifying. Many of its citizens were too poor to pay taxes and the wealthier burghers simply refused to pay. The result was that there was no money in the Treasury to pay the salaries of the few civil servants, thereby encouraging the development of the corruption which was to become a striking feature of Transvaal officialdom. The state was lapsing into chaos, a situation which was not improved by a disastrous war against the tribal chief, Sikukuni, and ongoing disputes with the Zulus. In the Transvaal the idea that the country should seek protection from Britain began to find favour. At the end of 1876, Sir Theophilus Shepstone, as British Agent, travelled to the Transvaal, and demanded that the government introduce certain reforms immediately lest the whole region be plunged into war.

The reforms were not carried out and on 12 April 1877, Shepstone announced the annexation of the Transvaal by Britain. Shepstone had no authority to do this but as it was done peacefully and appeared to be supported by the locals, Britain did not repudiate his action. A leading Boer newspaper stated that 96 per cent of the country's citizens supported the annexation. Among the four per cent opposing it was Paul Kruger, though he was subtle enough to tone down his hostility for the time being.

Annexation brought prosperity to the Transvaal. The state finances were put onto a sound footing, a transformation which was achieved by the British taxpayer paying the country's not inconsiderable debts. The Sikukuni dispute was settled, and in 1879 Britain fought and subdued the Zulus while at the same time showing she was not invincible. For the Boers those factors which had favoured annexation had disappeared: the economy was on a sound footing and the fear of attack from the natives much reduced. There had also been a change of Government in England.

For those who wished to drive the English out of the Transvaal, the time had come to act. On 15 December 1880, a Republic was formally proclaimed, and on 20 December, two companies of the 94th Regiment were ambushed at Bronkhorstspruit, resulting in 56 British soldiers being killed and 101 wounded. Other British garrisons in the Transvaal were surrounded and besieged until the end of the war. Nourse's Horse, with Aubrey Woolls Sampson, was one of the regiments besieged in Pretoria.

Having neutralised the British units in the Transvaal, the Boers invaded Natal. The small British force sent to stop them suffered three defeats in quick succession at Laing's Nek, Ingogo Heights and Majuba, the mountain passes it was thought would protect Natal. The British hastily sued for peace and the Transvaal again became an independent republic. Paul Kruger, with majority support in the Transvaal legislature, the *Volksraad*, became President.

In 1873 gold had been discovered in the eastern Transvaal. To these fields, centred on the town of Barberton, gold prospectors and camp followers came from all over the world hoping to make or mend their fortunes. Many were pick-and-shovel men, uncouth, unsophisticated, uneducated and often unscrupulous, who led hard-drinking, irresponsible lives. The pious Boers and their straight-laced President looked on in horror. In 1884 President Kruger visited Europe and at a sumptuous reception, the French President,

Cockney Liz, the belle of Barberton.

seeking a compliment, asked Kruger if he had ever seen such a magnificent sight. The old Boer looked at the ladies in their décolleté gowns. 'Not since I was weaned,' he dryly commented. No wonder he looked with some disfavour on the rip-roaring mining communities of the Barberton goldfields, where the highlight of the day was the auction of the favours of 'Cockney Liz' and 'Trixie the Golden Dane'. But the state needed money and the mines did provide some revenue. Also, as the goldfields were far away, near the border of the Portuguese Colony, it might be possible to avoid contamination until such time as the gold petered out and the miners went away.

The Barberton goldfields were not the success they had promised to be. Gold strikes there were aplenty, but too often the gold-bearing seams ran out before expenses had been recovered, and by 1886 people were beginning to drift away to seek their fortunes elsewhere.

Against the trend, an Aussie battler, George Harrison, was on his way to Barberton. Indeed, he should never have been in South Africa at all. Flush with money after six months prospecting in the American West, he decided to have a night out in New York. He overdid the party and when he woke up, he was penniless and on a sailing ship bound for Cape Town. Disembarking there, he set out to walk the five hundred miles to the diamond fields at Kimberley, supporting himself by doing odd jobs along the way. In Kimberley all the claims had been bought up by wealthy financiers, and there was no room for the small man. He hitched a ride on a wagon going to Pretoria, hoping to find his way from there to the goldfields of the eastern Transvaal. When he reached the Witwatersrand, that range of hills just south of Pretoria, he was desperately short of cash and it was still a long way to Barberton. Hearing that the widow Oosthuizen was looking for someone to build a house on the farm Langlaagte, ten miles to the east, he jumped at the opportunity to earn some cash.

On the first Sunday in March, 1886, George and a friend were sitting on a *kopje* looking over the half-finished house towards the plain beyond. To complete this idyll they needed a drink, so George set off down the hill to get what was required. Near the bottom he tripped over a small boulder and fell headlong. In anger, he picked up the rock and smashed it to the ground. Looking at the broken pieces he could hardly believe what he saw. He called his friend over and together they picked up all the pieces of the offending rock and took them to the house where they found a big old bolt and a ploughshare. The pieces of rock were placed on the ploughshare and beaten into a mixture of sand and gravel by the bolt. This was placed in a frying pan, still greasy from the breakfast George had cooked that morning. The pan was filled with water and the men began the age old process of swirling the pan round and round, occasionally pouring off superfluous muck, then adding more water and repeating the process. Eventually all the sand and gravel was gone. The two men stared at the pan. They had never seen anything like this. Not in Ballarat, nor California, nor in any of the many other diggings they had visited. The world's greatest goldfield had been discovered.

In 1884 at a Convention in London, the Transvaal delegation, led by Kruger, with many pious utterances expressing gratitude to Her Majesty's Government and their love of peace in their time, obtained further concessions from the British government. A week later at a banquet in Amsterdam, the Rev. SJ du Toit, Superintendent of Education, a signatory of the Convention and speaking with the full knowledge and consent of his colleagues from the Transvaal delegation said, 'The South African flag shall yet wave from Table Bay to the Zambezi, be that end accomplished by blood or by ink. If blood it is to be, we shall not lack men to spill it.'

This would seem to be a fair summary of the foreign policy pursued by the Kruger government over the next fifteen years. The flag would, of course, be that of the Transvaal. To execute such an aggressive policy a vast amount of money was required and Digger George Harrison had just discovered where it could be found.

When news of the find got out, men of all types and conditions came to the Witwatersrand from all over the world. A shanty town, Johannesburg, came into being and rapidly expanded. To the dismay of many, the surface gold soon ran out and the place might have become yet another nineteenth century ghost town, a monument to a gold rush which had been and gone. But this gold reef was different. The gold–bearing conglomerate ran down and down, deep into the bowels of the earth, further down than man had ever been before. The ore was low grade, but unlike other goldfields it was consistent so once the reef was found it was possible to calculate the value of the gold which could be extracted.

To establish a mine, substantial capital was required and this could only be raised abroad by financiers in whom investors felt they could place their trust. Further, given the low grade of ore, for a mine to survive its management had to be super efficient. Mining is a dangerous occupation, particularly when operating at great depths, and the mines therefore required engineers and geologists who were more than competent – they had to be the best. When the colourful financier, Barney Barnato, wanted a mining engineer, he sought the best in the world. John Hays Hammond had built a reputation in the United States that he was without peer as a mining engineer. Barnato sought him out and persuaded him to come to Johannesburg. Hammond's father had won fame as a Texas ranger in the Mexican War, had taken part in the Californian gold rush of 1849 and became the first mayor of San Francisco. Having grown up in a gold mining town, it is not surprising that young John Hays Hammond became a mining engineer. He also had the advantage of growing up in a family which had played such a major part in the conversion of a wild mining settlement into one of America's great cities.

When Hays Hammond eventually left South Africa he was employed by Presidents Teddy Roosevelt, Coolidge and Taft as a presidential advisor. Bob Taft even tried to persuade him to accept nomination as vice-president, an offer which Hays Hammond refused as he did not seek political office.

With the mining personnel, there came to Johannesburg all those people necessary for a settled society – doctors, dentists, architects, builders, tradesmen of all descriptions and many others. Thus many highly skilled men from colonial South Africa, Britain, Australia, the United States and indeed the rest of the world came to Johannesburg. In typical colonial fashion it was not long before patches of *veld* were cleared for rugby, soccer and cricket. Of course there had to be horse racing, which required a one-and-a-half mile track. This was not easy to find as claims were pegged out all over the place. As a result, at the initial meetings, the horses had to run over a zigzag course between the claims, which must have been a nightmare for the stewards and a source of frequent arguments.

The town had started off as a rough mining camp and it still had some rough edges, but by the middle of the 1890s it was well on its way to becoming one of the world's more sophisticated cities.

President Kruger and his followers in the Volksraad viewed the developments on the Witwatersrand with extreme distaste. It was bad enough having miners at Barberton, but to have all these foreigners so close to the heart of the Republic was, indeed, dreadful. Perhaps because of its association with the East India Company or perhaps because Britain was a trading nation, the conservative Boers looked on all forms of trade and commerce as essentially evil and dishonest. Thus on one of his rare visits to the Witwatersrand, Kruger opened his address to the assembled crowd with the words, 'Burghers, friends, thieves, murderers, newcomers, and others'. But he needed the revenue from the mines.

Kruger's foreign policy had suffered a few reverses. An attempt to overrun Bechuanaland had failed when Britain stepped in to assist the locals and made the country a Protectorate. His plan to extend the Republic northwards to the Zambezi was frustrated when Cecil Rhodes annexed for Britain the country now known as Zimbabwe. In the east, parties of Boers disregarding protests from Natal and Britain, had moved into northern Zululand and formed a republic which they called the New Republic. If the Germans had not threatened to annex St. Lucia Bay in northern Zululand, Britain would probably have permitted the Boers to overrun the whole of the region. Frightened that Germany might cut off the route to the East, Britain promptly annexed what was left of Zululand. Thus are empires collected.

In Europe Kruger decided to swim with the crocodiles and sought alliances with the Kaiser's Germany and other powers which might be hostile to Britain. However, beyond a willingness to spread anti-British propaganda, no real assistance came from this quarter.

Kruger's foreign policy did have one major success. In 1888, the wise and capable President Brand of the Orange Free State died and the Anglophobe FW Reitz succeeded to the presidency. From then on the Orange Free State fell increasingly under the influence of the Transvaal.

In a strange corollary to the belief that all commerce was in its very nature dishonest, some Boers appeared to believe that in their own commercial dealings, it was right and proper to be dishonest. Paul Kruger was prepared to overlook the taking of bribes by his officials on the grounds that they should be able to set aside something for their old age! Also, although the consumption of alcohol was regarded as sinful, the Liquor Laws of the Republic virtually encouraged excessive drinking, particularly among the Blacks. This Kruger justified on the grounds that it enabled farmers to get higher prices for their grain.

To the inhabitants of Johannesburg, be they colonials or immigrants from Britain, this attitude was repugnant. They had worked hard to establish a mining industry whose technical achievements were truly remarkable. To finance this they had invested not only their own money, but also that of tens of thousands of shareholders from around the world. They had smiled when the *Volksraad* debated whether it was shooting at God to send exploding rockets into clouds to bring rain, or when Paul Kruger opened a Synagogue with the words, 'In the name of our Lord Jesus Christ. Amen.' But they were seriously concerned by the corrupt nature of the state which was being run for the benefit of a small oligarchy to the detriment of the rest of its inhabitants. In addition it was impossible to effect any change through the ballot box, as Kruger constantly manipulated the franchise so as to ensure that control would never pass from his faction. In an attempt to redress their grievances, a pressure group, labelled Reformists, came into being. It was not a political party and had as its supporters such diverse figures as the republican Hays Hammond and the imperialist Cecil Rhodes.

CHAPTER THREE

Dissent in the Transvaal

● ◆ ●

'What is the use of protesting? You have not got the guns, I have.'

PRESIDENT PAUL KRUGER.

NEITHER the discovery of gold on the Witwatersrand, nor the growth of the burgeoning town of Johannesburg, prompted the government to make any administrative changes which would take into account the development taking place. As there was no local authority, the miners, being practical men, set up a Digger's Committee to attend to such matters as drains, demarcating streets and other tasks which would normally fall within the ambit of the powers of a local authority. Out of this committee was to evolve the Reform Committee.

From the start relations with the Pretoria government were strained, a situation which did not improve with time. The *Uitlanders*, as Paul Kruger contemptuously referred to the more recent arrivals in the country, felt they were being unfairly exploited by a corrupt and incompetent regime. Among their complaints were the following:

1. The ill-treatment of Black peoples and the callous disregard of their rights caused constant friction, and did not bode well for the future.
2. Permanent residents not of Boer origin were denied voting rights, a restriction that applied to their children even though they were born in the Republic.
3. Monopolies and concessions granted to the ruling elite and their coterie not only resulted in inefficiencies but also brought much hardship to the general public. Particularly irksome was the dynamite monopoly and the concession granted to the inefficient Netherlands Railway syndicate. The former raised concerns about safety and obliged the mines to use dynamite which was not only expensive but also of poor quality. The railway monopoly greatly hindered the development of a modern transport system which was so badly needed by the country.
4. Residents with no voting rights were subject to military service.
5. Many of the necessities of life were taxed, causing hardship to the poor.
6. Johannesburg had no local authority to manage its affairs.
7. The Police were not properly supervised, and no serious effort was made to control crime.
8. Children from English-speaking families did not have the same rights to education as Boer children. The Government spent eight pounds six shillings per child per annum on

the education of Boer children while a paltry one shilling and ten pence per child per annum was spent on *Uitlander* children. In other words, the government spent more than eighty times as much on the education of a Boer child than it did on the education of an *Uitlander* child. This, in a situation where the *Uitlanders* provided more than ninety per cent of the state revenue.

9. Little or nothing was done about corruption in the civil service.
10. Delays in the criminal justice system resulted in prisoners having to spend up to eighteen months in gaol before being brought to trial. In one group of 63 men, 31 died before being -brought to trial. The deaths were attributed to the absence of vegetable foods.

As the year 1895 drew to a close, the citizens of Johannesburg, having had no success in their attempts to ameliorate their grievances by consultation, were becoming desperate. Kruger's attitude was succinctly expressed in a statement by him to an *Uitlander* delegation, 'Protest! Protest! What is the good of protesting? You have not got the guns, I have.'

And he did have the guns. With revenue pouring in from the goldfields, the country was stockpiling arms and ammunition far beyond what would normally be required for its defence and the Government had built a fort overlooking Johannesburg, which seemed to indicate that an attack against the town might be planned. Further, as it made no secret of its intention to throw the British out of Southern Africa, the residents did wonder what was planned for them.

In their everyday dealings with the Boers the *Uitlanders* found there were many who were practical, intelligent men with whom they could reason and they knew that in the *Volksraad* there was a progressive faction which opposed Kruger. However they also knew of Kruger's

President Paul Kruger and his wife.

ability to manipulate the franchise in his favour, and how deftly he used the system of monopolies and state concessions to shore up his support. In this atmosphere the idea of a *coup d'etat* was born.

One of the more fanciful schemes was that residents would arm themselves with whatever weapons they had, storm the fort, thereby supplementing their arms, and then march on Pretoria, where Kruger would be deposed and a more progressive Boer administration installed. Free and fair elections would then be held.

Some had wanted Britain to annex the country, but there was strong opposition to this led by the republican American, John Hays Hammond, whose views prevailed.

Cecil Rhodes, now Prime Minister of the Cape Colony and resident in Cape Town, arranged for some rifles to be smuggled into Johannesburg so that its citizens might be able to defend themselves. Rhodes also arranged for a force from the British Chartered

Company's territory (now known as Zimbabwe) to be stationed on the western border of the Transvaal. This contingent, of five hundred mounted men and three field guns, was led by a certain Dr Jameson, and was to provide assistance should the Reformists request their help. Kruger, fully aware of Jameson's movements, made his preparations and waited. To use his own metaphor, he would wait until the tortoise stuck its head out and then chop it off.

Aubrey Woolls Sampson could not have chosen a more tumultuous time to arrive back in Johannesburg. He fully sympathised with the motives of the Reformers and the need for the changes they sought. However he was also fully aware of the military strength of the Boers and how rapidly their *Kommando* system functioned to meet any threat. Having heard the plans of the

Maj Walter Karri Davies, ILH.

proposed coup, he asked to see the arms they had collected and what he saw horrified him. They had scarcely enough rifles for the leading reformists and a few of their friends. He knew the degree of loyalty which the backveld Boers felt for their President. He knew how Kruger had outwitted the British by his apparent complaisance in annexation, and had seen the efficacy of his campaign to regain independence in 1880. To Aubrey, the plans to overthrow Kruger were sheer folly. Passionately he argued for, at the very least, a postponement of any coup. To his relief it was decided that Mr. Charles Leonard should go to Cape Town immediately to enlist the aid of Cecil Rhodes in stopping any attempt to invade.

Any satisfaction which might have been felt by the prevention of the coup was dispelled when the horrifying news reached Johannesburg that Jameson, ignoring requests not to invade the Transvaal, had crossed the border on 29 December 1895, and was on his way to Johannesburg. The tortoise had stuck its head out.

Kruger, having successfully divided the opposition, decided to deal first with Jameson and then give the people of Johannesburg his full attention. In the meantime, he sent an emissary to the Reformers to indicate a willingness on the part of the President to discuss *Uitlander* grievances. Johannesburg's communications with the outside world were cut, and the Transvaal Police were quietly withdrawn from the town.

At a meeting of many prominent men of Johannesburg on Monday, 30 December 1895, the Reform Committee was formed. Karri Davies and Aubrey Woolls Sampson were among those elected. This Committee was faced with some serious dilemmas:

Firstly, most were furious with Jameson and would have been quite happy to disown him and leave him to stew in his own juice. As Hays Hammond said, 'Without any consent on their own part the reformers were made partners in an attempt at conquest, instead of reformation.'

Unfortunately *The Star* newspaper had got hold of the news that Jameson had crossed the border and was on the way to Johannesburg. Jameson became an instantly popular hero against whom the Committee dare not act.

Secondly, law and order had to be established and maintained. It was known that there were criminal gangs operating, the most notorious being the Irish Brigade. Composed of sweepings from the streets of Dublin, their behaviour in Barberton was such that even that permissive town had found them intolerable and had chased them out. They were thought to be in Johannesburg. The Committee assigned to one Andrew Trimble, a former sergeant in the Inniskilling Dragoons, the task of organising a citizen's police force. Most of the men chosen by Trimble were Australians and in due course arms were issued to them.

Thirdly, the Reformers intercepted a telegram from the Kommandant-General in Pretoria to the Heidelberg *Kommando* ordering them to ride through Johannesburg shooting right and left indiscriminately so that any idea of a revolution could be crushed before it started. A few hours later another telegram was sent by General Joubert cancelling the order. These telegrams reinforced the idea that the Government was planning to attack Johannesburg and to protect the unarmed population it was decided to fortify the perimeter of the town with as many men as the Reformers' limited supply of arms permitted.

Karri Davies and other Australians were charged with guarding the Robinson Mine on the western fringe of the town. On the afternoon of Tuesday, 1 January 1896, they received orders from the Committee to have food and drink available for Jameson's men. Next morning, trestle tables were laid out with bread, meat and crates of beer, but Jameson never arrived.

The Boers had been tracking Jameson's column from the time it crossed the border, but it was not until it was within 14 miles of Johannesburg that the Boer *Kommandos* surrounded and attacked the raiders. The outcome was never in doubt. At 9.15 a.m. on Thursday, 2 January 1896, Jameson surrendered, after receiving a guarantee of safe conduct out of the country for every member of his force. They were taken to the Pretoria gaol pending their extradition.

In Johannesburg the sounds of battle had been heard, and later news of the surrender reached a shocked populace, who, looking for scapegoats, blamed the disaster on the leading Reformers. No mention of the offer of safe conduct leaked out.

With Jameson his hostage, Kruger gave his attention to the subjugation of Johannesburg. He invited the British High Commissioner in Cape Town, Sir Hercules Robinson, to Pretoria to discuss the crisis. Though old and ill, Sir Hercules at once set off on the long train journey to Pretoria, and on the morning of 6 January he had an hour-long discussion with Kruger. Sir Hercules was told that the Government would not open negotiations or consider any *Uitlander* grievances until Johannesburg surrendered its arms. It was pointed out to him that there were eight thousand Burghers under arms who were anxious to finish the matter and they might at any time shoot the raiders and attack Johannesburg. The Reform Committee was to have twenty-four hours to accept or reject the ultimatum. Kruger, knowing both Sir Hercules and the Reformers were unaware of the promise of safe conduct given to Jameson, made no mention of it.

A telegram was promptly sent to the Committee advising it of the terms of the ultimatum and all its members were summoned to a meeting that afternoon. The leaders believed the Committee had no choice but to accept the terms, however the majority were not convinced and argument continued until late in the afternoon when another telegram arrived from the British Agent, Sir Jacobus de Wet, stating he was coming to see them.

They met early the next morning. Sir Jacobus said the lives of Jameson and the other prisoners were in their hands, and Kruger had assured him that once the arms were surrendered, Jameson and his men would be handed over to the British Government. This was fine as far as Jameson was concerned but what about the grievances of Johannesburg, the Reform Committee, and the *Uitlanders*? Sir Jacobus gave the assurance that not a hair on the head of any man in Johannesburg would be touched and as far as the Committee was concerned, 'Not one among you will lose his liberty for a single hour. John Bull would never allow it.' He added that the *Uitlander* grievances were being considered.

The conditions of the ultimatum were accepted and it was arranged that a public meeting be held at noon outside the Rand Club. Word of the meeting quickly spread and by noon a sizable crowd had assembled. Sir Jacobus told them that Johannesburg could not defend itself against the Boers, an argument which was not only rejected, but seemed to make the populace aggressive and determined to fight. It was only when they were told that if they did not immediately surrender their arms, Jameson and all his men would be shot, that they abandoned their aggressive stance and agreed to hand their arms in. The process of collecting the arms began immediately and by the next morning all weapons issued by the Reform Committee had been handed over to the Boers. On Wednesday evening the Transvaal Police emerged from seclusion and took over police duties from Trimble's men as unobtrusively as the interchange which had occurred eight days previously. During those eight days Johannesburg had been virtually crime free for the first time in its short history. Karri Davies, Aubrey Woolls Sampson and the others accepted at face value the assurances given by Sir Jacobus de Wet, the Queen's agent in the Transvaal.

On Thursday, 9 January a Government proclamation stated that the leaders of the revolt would be prosecuted, and that night the arrest of the members of the Reform Committee began. For a while they all thought it a bit of a joke. Bags were packed as if they were going on a picnic, but the smiles vanished when they reached Pretoria. A large ill-tempered mob had gathered at the station to meet them. When the prisoners began their walk to the prison they were set upon. In vain did their small police escort attempt control the mob, but in the end the prisoners had to make a dash for the protection of the gaol, while the escort attempted to hold back their pursuers. Some of the slower prisoners were roughly manhandled, spat on and severely beaten. Littered along the road to the prison were the shattered remnants of the suitcases and parcels of those little luxuries which it was thought would make life in prison tolerable for the few days they might be there.

The prison had been built by the British during their brief occupation of the Transvaal and was designed to hold no more than twenty criminals of the rougher class. It now had to hold more than sixty of Johannesburg's most prominent citizens. Four – Lionel Phillips, George Farrar, Frank Rhodes and Hays Hammond who was suffering from severe dysentery – were put together in a cell ten feet by ten. There were four filthy canvas stretchers for them to sleep on and the only ventilation was a narrow iron grille above the door. The other prisoners were split up into small groups and herded into cells in which there were no beds, and barely enough room for them to lie side by side on a floor covered in excrement, fleas and lice. Many could not bring themselves to lie down, eventually collapsing from exhaustion. The doors of the cells were locked at six o'clock in the evening and not re-opened until six o'clock the next morning. Although Jameson and five of his officers were in the same gaol no contact between the two groups was possible.

The prisoners made the best of their miserable surroundings. They were permitted to purchase meals from the Pretoria Club, they cleaned up their cells and were allowed visits

John Hays Hammond.

from wives and relations. By the end of the month all members of the Reform Committee except the alleged ringleaders, Phillips, Farrar, Frank Rhodes, Hammond and Percy Fitzpatrick, were released on bail of £2,000 each.

The Raid had left Johannesburg stunned, but not for long. Lord Hawke arrived with an English cricket team and for a time it was cricket and not politics which dominated conversation. Thousands flocked to see the matches and though the visitors took some time to get used to the light, matting wicket, and grassless field, they were able to beat the local side. Boers watching this strange game were puzzled. Obviously the *Uitlanders* were up to something evil, but they were not quite sure what it was. One who could not be there was the mining magnate Abe Bailey. He was in gaol in Pretoria with the rest of the Reform Committee. A keen cricketer, he was a great patron of the sport and spent considerable time and money on the promotion of all sport in South Africa. Some years later his son was to marry Diana, daughter of Winston Churchill.

January turned to February and it seemed everything was getting back to normal. On Sunday, 16 February 1896, eight railway trucks loaded with more than 60 tons of dynamite and detonators were shunted into the goods siding at Braamfontein, on the edge of the city. The representative of the concessionary dynamite company refused to accept the consignment, claiming their magazines were full. The trucks were left at the siding to be unloaded at a time more convenient than a hot Sunday afternoon. For three days the trucks stood in the hot sun and just after 3:00 p.m. on the following Wednesday, a gang of labourers with their mule wagons arrived to unload the dynamite.

A kilometre away in Government Square the Circuit Court was in session. The accused took the Bible in his right hand and promised to tell the truth, the whole truth, and nothing but the truth. At that moment the building shook, a glass chandelier crashed down on the bench while at the same time there was the roar of an explosion as a blast of air shattered the windows. The Judge, despite his gown, leapt over the Bench and was first into the street. The accused, still clutching the Bible, was seen running towards the open *veld* promising never to tell another lie. People rushed into the streets and after the initial panic it was realised that something had happened at Braamfontein.

A great crowd headed in the direction of that part of the town and there, where once the station had stood, was a huge hole 250 feet long, 60 feet wide and about 40 feet deep. Of engine, trucks, wagons, mules and men there was no sign, save for a few pieces of twisted metal and charred flesh.

The station had been located in a poor neighbourhood which had its houses flattened by the blast. A rescue operation began immediately. The hospital was soon overflowing so the Wanderers Club, which a few weeks before had hosted the English cricketers, was turned into a second infirmary. That night the Rand Club held a meeting to form a relief committee and over £4,000 was immediately subscribed. The next day the Stock Exchange boosted it to above £100,000. The concessionaire, The Netherlands Railway Co., donated £10,000, a gift regarded in Johannesburg as conscience money. Subsequently the Government donated a further £25,000 and announced that a Commission of Enquiry would enquire into the cause of the disaster.

The explosion had shaken the whole of Johannesburg, both physically and mentally. On that fateful Wednesday afternoon, young Jackie Hays Hammond, no doubt keen to become a miner, was digging in the garden when suddenly the earth shook and there followed the great noise of the explosion. The child rushed into the house shouting, '*Mommy, Mommy, I've dug up hell…*' Mrs. Natalie Hays Hammond thought she had been there for some time already.

The trial of the Reform Committee was set down for hearing at the Market Hall, Pretoria, on 24 April 1896. There were four charges;

1) Inviting Jameson to invade.
2) Inciting the people of Johannesburg to assist him.
3) Distributing arms and ammunition.
4) Forming and arming a police force.

Kruger appointed the State Attorney of the Orange Free State, a Mr. Gregorowski, to preside over the trial. Judge Gregorowski made no attempt to conceal where his sympathies lay, and before the trial made enquiries as to where he might obtain a black cap for use when passing sentence. About a week before the trial, the State Attorney approached Advocate Wessels, who represented the accused, with an offer; if Phillips, Farrar, Frank Rhodes and Hays Hammond pleaded guilty to the first two charges, he would withdraw the other two charges against them, provided the remaining sixty-three pleaded guilty to counts three and four. In which case, counts one and two would be withdrawn against the sixty-three, who would only receive a nominal punishment. Some suspected another trap and many were innocent of all charges, but, as the offer demanded unanimous acceptance, and rejection might prejudice the position of the leaders, it was accepted. The State withdrew charges and the accused pleaded guilty as agreed. For the sixty-three the trial appeared a mere formality, but for the others – Phillips, Farrar, Frank Rhodes and Hays Hammond – the matter was more complex. There was no doubt that there had been a plot to overthrow the regime and this could be treason.

The Transvaal legal system was based on Roman Dutch Law which had been developed by Dutch jurists during the period between the Renaissance and the imposition of the Napoleonic code on the Netherlands. The penalties for treason in Roman Dutch Law were, as one would expect from laws developed in those far off times, brutal. However, the Transvaal legislature, the *Volksraad*, had in the early days of the republic repudiated these penalties, and laid down that the penalty for conspiring with a foreign power to overthrow the state would be a fine and banishment. Did they perhaps remember that raid by the Transvaal into the Free State in 1859, or anticipate the revolution of 1880? Be that as it may, it was trite law that if there was a conflict between Roman Dutch Law and Local Law, the latter would prevail. Further, if the law provided differing penalties for an offence, the Court should impose the lesser penalty.

Advocate Wessels, one of southern Africa's great jurists, had every reason to believe that the four leaders faced no more than a fine and banishment, though even this might not be imposed in its entirety as they had not conspired with a foreign power, (unless the freebooter Jameson could be described as a foreign power) and no one had been shot or injured as a result of any action by them. However he was to be disappointed.

The Judge found, without there being any evidence to support the finding, that the Reformers had conspired with Britain to overthrow the government. He also gave to himself the power to decide whether to apply Roman Dutch Law or Local Law and chose the former. The four leaders he found guilty of high treason and proceeded to pass sentence.

Lionel Phillips was brought forward. The judge placed a black cap on his head and sentenced him to death. George Farrar and Frank Rhodes followed and were in turn also sentenced to death.

When the time came for the seriously ill Hays Hammond to be led forward, the Court Interpreter, who had shown mounting distress, broke down sobbing and had to be comforted by the condemned man's doctor. There was a disturbance among the public as a woman collapsed in a dead faint. The Judge ignored it all and went on in a monotone, informing the prisoner that he would be taken to a place of execution and there hung by the neck until he was dead. The four were led out.

While they were being led away, the Judge busied himself writing and when he was ready he asked the remaining prisoners to stand up. Smiling benevolently, he carefully looked them

Barney Barnato: Cockney Prizefighter, flamboyant financier and friend of Paul Kruger.

over, then, wiping the smile off his face with a deft movement of his hand, he pronounced the sentence. They would each go to gaol for two years and pay a fine of two thousand pounds sterling. In addition, after the expiration of their gaol sentence, they would be banished from the Republic for three years. By no stretch of the imagination could this be called a nominal sentence.

As the Judge was about to leave a voice called out, '*Just a minute Judge!*' and a man strode into the well of the court, as the stunned lawyers moved out of his way. Both the lawyers and the Judge knew who he was: Barney Barnato, the cockney prize fighter from the East End of London who had gone to Kimberley and made a fortune which had been considerably increased by wise investment in Johannesburg. Barney prided himself on his lack of interest in politics and regarded himself as a personal friend of Paul Kruger. When his nephew, Solly Joel, joined the Reformers he was disappointed, but when Solly was arrested, Barney, always loyal, attended the trial. Now he stood in the well of the court, and told the Judge just what he thought of him and his judgment. Transfixed, the Judge listened until Advocate Wessels distracted Barney and the Judge shuffled out of court. Of course Barnato should have been arrested for contempt of court, but in the old Transvaal one did not readily arrest friends of the President.

As the prisoners were led out, Barney told them not to worry – he would have them out in no time. In the street outside the court, Barney continued his diatribe against Kruger and his judicial lackey, much to the delight of an assembled crowd of *Uitlanders*. From there he went to the Pretoria Club where a few drinks did nothing to quell his fury. He was still holding forth on the subject, when who should come into the bar but Judge Gregorowski, who should have known better. Barney had abused the Judge in court, and now on his own turf he was in no mood to exercise restraint. In response to further invective, Gregorowski shouted out, '*Mr. Barnato, you are no gentleman.*'

'*And you, Mr. Gregorowski, are no judge…*' replied Barney, who had never pretended to be a gentleman.

In London, news of the sentences was read to a concerned House of Commons. In Washington, the U.S. Congress requested the Secretary of State to intervene on behalf of Hays Hammond and the other condemned men. In Johannesburg, the Reformers, once reviled by the populace for failing to support Jameson, now had the sympathy of the people. The battle for the release of the prisoners had begun.

One cannot leave the trial without mentioning that while awaiting trial, Hays Hammond had been released on bail of twenty thousand pounds sterling so that he might receive medical attention in Cape Town. This bail was provided by Barney Barnato. After the trial, Barnato asked Hammond why he did not skip bail and leave the country, rather than risk being sentenced to death. Hammond replied that if he had done so he would have broken his undertaking to present himself for trial, and also the bail money would have been forfeited, a loss he could not inflict on a loyal friend.

The next day Barnato decided to see Kruger, but first he would call on Mrs Hays Hammond. Natalie Hammond and Mrs Phillips had just returned from a visit to Pretoria where they had seen Mrs. Kruger in the hope of getting her to intercede on behalf of the condemned men.

The President's wife sat in stony silence, knitting, while the women made their tearful pleas for their husband's lives. When they had finished, Mrs. Kruger replied coldly, 'If the Raid had succeeded, my husband would have had to get out the white horse he has not ridden for years and join the fighting. Would you have thought of me then, ladies? Would you?'

When Barney arrived at the Hammond home he found Natalie in a very distraught state. For once, he was lost for words and could only hold her hand in silence. As he rose to leave he said gently, 'Don't fret my dear. I brought your husband to Africa and I'll stand by him until he's safely out of the country. That's a promise.'

Kruger gave his erstwhile friend a very frosty reception. The President declined to shake his hand or to remove his stovepipe top hat, but sat behind his desk, in his buttoned-up, tight frock coat bedecked with the broad sash of the Republic, and glowered at his visitor.

Barney apologised for his behaviour in court and the offence he might have given, but would make no concessions with respect to the sentences. He told the President that unless the death sentences were commuted and the Reform Committee released he would close down all his companies, thereby putting one hundred and twenty thousand people out of work; the country would lose one of its principal sources of income, and the economy would be ruined. A slight exaggeration, but flamboyance always comes with some exaggeration. The next day the principle South African newspapers carried a Preliminary Notice of the intended sale of all the Barnato properties.

Barnato was not the only one in the Transvaal to take action. The Mercantile Association held an emergency meeting on the day following the sentencing and decided unanimously to close all premises the next day. The Stock Exchange suspended business as a protest against the sentences. Johannesburg was tense but restrained.

It began to look as if another tortoise was in trouble, but this was a wily old tortoise who knew when and how to retreat into his shell. On that Wednesday morning, two days after the passing of the death sentences, it was announced that they had been commuted. However, nothing further was done and a few weeks later one of the little known prisoners, unable to stand the prison conditions any longer, cut his throat. Ten thousand people attended his funeral and the clergyman officiating described his death as judicial murder.

Shocked into action, the government announced new sentences. The ringleaders were to undergo 15 years imprisonment followed by banishment and the others to serve terms varying between three and twelve months. These others could be released if they signed a petition for clemency, and gave an undertaking not to interfere in the politics of the country for a period of 3 years, on pain of banishment. In addition, they were to pay a fine of £2,000 sterling. In consequence of the unhygienic conditions in the prison, many of the prisoners were seriously ill on their release.

But agitation for the release of the ringleaders continued and on 11 June, one hundred mayors from all over South Africa including the first citizens of every major town assembled in Pretoria to plead for their release. They were discussing the matter when a messenger arrived with the news that the four had been released after they had each paid a fine of £25,000 sterling. Three had also signed an undertaking that they would not interfere in the internal or external politics of the country, a breach of which would result in lifelong banishment. Frank Rhodes did not sign and left the country immediately.

Frank was the elder brother of the empire builder, Cecil Rhodes, but had a very different personality. Whereas Cecil was terrified of women, Frank rather enjoyed their company. Cecil possessed a burning ambition to empower Africa to adopt a British lifestyle, to which end he acquired enormous wealth. Frank appears to have sought no more than a comfortable living surrounded by friends. Born in 1851, Frank entered the 1st Dragoons in 1873 and by 1889 held the rank of Colonel. He seems to have been a competent and loyal officer. To supplement his army pay he acted as a reporter for *The Times* on various occasions. A severe attack of blackwater fever resulted in his retirement from the army in 1893. On his recovery, he went to Africa and Cecil appointed him representative of Consolidated Goldfields in Johannesburg. He was loyal to his younger brother, who had provided him with an income to supplement his army pension. Not unnaturally many of his friends were Reformers. No doubt the Boers would have preferred to prosecute Cecil, but being unable to do so, Frank was a convenient substitute. When Frank died in 1905, the net value of his estate was a modest £102,139. We shall hear more of this amiable and kind man.

With their minds occupied by the trial, few noticed the publication of the report by the Commission into the Braamfontein explosion. It was found that it might have been caused by a box of dynamite falling off a truck onto the rails and no one could be blamed for that!

Not all the prisoners had been released. Walter Karri Davies and Aubrey Woolls Sampson were still in gaol. They refused to pay the fine or to sign the petition. To do so would, in their opinion, amount to an admission that they had been correctly prosecuted and sentenced. As they felt this was not the case, they refused to compromise their personal integrity and accept the terms for their release. In July, 1896, they wrote to the Acting British Agent giving reasons for their failure to pay the fine or sign the required undertaking. The reasons given were:

a) They had been deceived by Sir Hercules Robinson's statement that Jameson and his party might be shot if Kruger's terms were not accepted.
b) Sir Jacobus de Wet had deceived them, when he told them that the Reform Committee would be fully protected by the British Government and that not one of the Reform Committee would, 'lose his liberty for a single hour. John Bull would never allow it.'
c) The Transvaal State Attorney had stated that if they pleaded guilty to the lesser charges (3&4) they would only receive a nominal sentence.[1]

It is true that the trial Judge was not bound by the agreement, but the Transvaal Government was bound by the undertaking of its State Attorney. It should have ensured immediate compliance with the agreement and set aside the sentences, while Britain, and perhaps Western Australia, should not have turned a blind eye to the manner in which they had been tricked into pleading guilty.

Chamberlain subsequently denied that Sir Hercules Robinson and Sir Jacobus de Wet had made the statements attributed to them. This denial may have carried some weight in Britain, but to those most affected Chamberlain's denial was an obvious lie.

If Karri and Aubrey had heavy hearts when they began their sentences, it was not the prospect of two years in jail that disturbed them as they had no fear of hardship, but the disdainful deceit of the British officials. They knew life in prison would be hard, and it was. The head gaoler, one du Plessis, never lost an opportunity to insult them or to make their lives as unpleasant as he possibly could. However, the two were kept apart from the common criminals and some of the staff did treat them decently. One of the clerks, Matthys Human, became a friend, a friendship which was to stand Karri in good stead some years later.

Making the best of their situation, Karri and Aubrey worked out an exercise routine which they followed meticulously and which ensured they maintained their physical fitness. Using their knowledge of mining they dug an escape tunnel under the prison wall, which could be used in an emergency, though they had no intention of escaping.

Their families, knowing the appalling conditions in the Pretoria gaol, were worried about their welfare. Mrs. Sampson wrote from the Cape begging Aubrey to pay the fine and sign whatever was necessary to get out of prison. Maurice Davies travelled from Australia and from

Durban sent a petition in Dutch to the President, begging that his son might be released. Kruger was unmoved.

Initially the public took little interest in the fate of the two in prison, but after a time people began to consider the matter more carefully. The Cape Colony sent a delegation to Pretoria to plead for their release. Their friends in the old Reform Committee collected money which was given to them to pay the fine. The gift was appreciated but instead of being used to pay the fine it was put into trust. Every week the *Cape Times* published a notice in the following terms: '*Today Messrs. Sampson and Davies complete the ... week of their imprisonment in Pretoria gaol for the crime of not signing a petition.*'

Many Boers called for their release and none was more pressing in his entreaties to the President than old Hans Botha who had been so badly wounded by Aubrey fifteen years before. Karri and Aubrey became a major talking point and the longer they stayed in prison, the more Jameson and his raid slipped from public consciousness, to be replaced by concern over the way the country was governed. Kruger was embarrassed and did not know what to do. It would be humiliating to release them and at the same time their presence in prison gave the lie to the carefully nurtured belief that the *Uitlanders* were a bunch of unprincipled, money grabbing, cowardly scoundrels. At last, in 1897, after Karri and Aubrey had served fourteen months of their sentence, relief came for Kruger in the form of Queen Victoria's Diamond Jubilee. He used the occasion to release them in what he hoped would be regarded as a magnanimous act of clemency. In submitting to imprisonment they had sought to expose injustice and the absence of integrity in public life. They had succeeded in this objective but their sacrifice brought no amelioration to the manner in which the Transvaal was governed.

Karri Davies and Woolls Sampson are generally recognized as being the first prisoners of conscience in the modern world. The idea of going to prison for one's beliefs was a strategy subsequently used very effectively by the suffragettes in England and Mr MK Gandhi in India.

Kruger did effect some changes. Johannesburg was given a Town Council but it was so constituted that 2,000 Boers would have a permanent majority over the rest of the residents who numbered well over 100,000. It was decreed that the decisions of the *Volksraad* would take precedence over the law. When Chief Justice Kotze protested that this would destroy the independence of the judiciary, Kruger sacked him, appointing Judge Gregorowski in his place. Powers to expel aliens were widened, the conditions enabling immigrants to obtain citizenship were made even more difficult and Press restrictions increased.

A slump in the economy caused President Kruger to appoint an Industrial Commission to inquire into the gold mining industry. Perhaps it would show how the Rand's mining magnates had by their greed and inefficiency brought about the current economic depression!

Mr. Schalk Burger, a respected member of the Government's Executive Council, was to chair the Commission which conducted a thorough and detailed investigation into the gold mining industry. Its Report was not quite what President Kruger had expected. It stated:

'*at present there exist all the indications of an honest administration, and the State, as well as the mining industry, must be congratulated upon the fact that most of the mines are controlled and directed by financial and practical men who devote their time, energy and knowledge to the mining industry...*'

The Report went on to criticise the application of the Liquor Law and the Gold Law relating to the theft of gold. Ten per cent of the gold extracted was being stolen and nothing was being done about this, the philosophy being that as it was the Boer's country, they owned the gold, and they could not steal their own property. The Report also recommended a reduction in railway rates and import tariffs and an investigation into the dynamite monopoly. It went on to recommend the formation of a joint mining board to be composed of nominees of the

Government and mining industry, '*so that the Government should have the benefit of the experience of men whose daily occupation it is to look closely into all the affairs appertaining to the mines.*'

For Kruger it was a bitter blow. A *Volksraad* committee was appointed to study the Report and in due course dutifully rejected it. Meanwhile in the Cape, Sir Alfred Milner had replaced Sir Hercules Robinson as High Commissioner. Though a competent and intelligent administrator, Sir Alfred was unfortunately a self-opinionated and arrogant man, unsuited to the task ahead of him which required tact and not a little humility. His reaction to the Mining Report was typical. He was surprised by the Report – he had not realised any Boers were capable of such breadth of understanding.

Before the Jameson Raid, the Boers had been arming themselves stealthily but after it preparations began in earnest. By 1899 they had built up their military strength to the point where they should have been able to sweep all before them. The old Boer dream of conquering Natal began once more to surface.

Between 31 May and 5 June 1899, a conference was held in Bloemfontein attended by the Presidents of the Boer Republics and Sir Alfred Milner. The purpose of the conference was to prevent war. Although the war was likely to be fought over their countries, Natal and the Cape Colony were not invited. A number of Natal politicians, including the former Prime Minister Sir Harry Escombe, requested Milner to consider the views of Colonial ministers before any final decisions were made. This suggestion was rejected with fury by Milner, who regarded it as an unjustified interference in Imperial Affairs. The petitioners he described as 'wobblers and mugwumps.' In London, Lord Wolseley, Commander-in-Chief of the British army, requested a similar exclusion of the Colonial governments from military decisions and information.

Sir Alfred and the British Colonial Secretary, Sir Joseph Chamberlain, appear to have come to the conclusion that there would be no peace in the region until the Kruger regime was removed from power. The major threat to peace was the danger of the Boer Republics attempting to annex the Cape and Natal. The Transvaal had never made any secret of its intention to conquer Natal, and Britain may well have permitted them to do so but for one important fact. British goods were increasingly being carried around the world in steamships which needed coal and Durban was the principal port where ships travelling between Britain and the East via the Cape could fill their bunkers. The British could not let this port fall into the hands of a hostile power.

There was no question of Britain launching a military attack against the Boer Republics. She had made no preparations for any military campaign against them, indeed, she had made no adequate arrangements to defend the Cape Colony or Natal. Outside a small circle of people with relatives in South Africa, the British public did not care one iota what happened there. Their knowledge of the country was slight and probably limited to the fact that gold had been discovered in the Transvaal. Of the strategic importance of the South African colonies they knew nothing, and would never have condoned an unprovoked attack against those distant Republics. For all practical purposes it was the Boer Republics who would decide whether or not there would be war.

Milner believed that some sort of suzerainty agreement with the Boers might solve the crisis. Britain would control the foreign relations of the Boer Republics who in turn would have a wide discretion in their internal affairs. This Milner believed would protect British interests and avert war. The Boers on the other hand were not going to surrender any part of their independence. Not surprisingly no agreement was reached at the 1899 Bloemfontein Conference.

Over the next few months a campaign in the *Uitlander* press, criticising the treatment of coloured people by the Transvaal Government, exacerbated the worsening relationship between the Boers and the other inhabitants of the Transvaal, while Milner continued to seek acceptance of his feudal idea that Britain should have suzerainty over the Transvaal and Free State.

We have seen how in 1884 the Rev. S. J. du Toit had spelt out Boer ambitions in Southern Africa, and that these ambitions had not died is dramatically illustrated by a memorandum written by the Transvaal State Attorney, Jan Smuts, in September, 1899. In it he stated that if the Boers were victors in the coming war, they would be 'founders of a United South Africa, one of the great empires of the world, an Afrikaner republic stretching from Table Bay to the Zambezi.'

Knowing how the *Voortrekkers* had behaved towards civilians in their abortive attempt to take over Natal between 1838 and 1842, and being aware of the treatment meted out to the *Uitlanders* in the Transvaal, the Natalians were not going to consent to the Boers taking over their well-ordered little Colony and expressed their support for the *Uitlander's* struggle.

When Karri Davies and Aubrey Woolls Sampson were released from prison, Aubrey joined his family in the Cape while Karri went back to his business, journeying to England, Egypt and China, seeking new markets for its timber. In June 1899 he was in Cairo on business when news reached him of the deteriorating situation in South Africa. He returned and after discussions with Aubrey and others, the idea of forming a volunteer mounted regiment was conceived. They initially sought permission from the Army Commander in the Cape, Sir William Butler. An anti-Semite, Sir William believed that the political situation in South Africa was being manipulated by a colossal syndicate of Jewish capitalists in Johannesburg which he referred to derisively as 'Jewburg.'

This anti-Semitism was not peculiar to Sir William. In the final decade of the 19th century there had developed in Britain a philosophy which believed that a coterie of Jewish capitalists sought to dominate the world. As many of the prominent personalities involved in the development of the gold mines in the Transvaal had names which were, or could be Jewish, it was but a small step to persuade the gullible that Jewish goldbugs were leading the country into war in order to enhance the power of Jewish financiers. The 'Jew-Jingo' owners of the *Daily Telegraph* were portrayed as 'gold-greedy ghouls thirsting for blood', and the Trade Unions Congress denounced the spending of a hundred million pounds of taxpayers' money to secure the goldfields of South Africa for cosmopolitan Jews, most of whom had no patriotism and no country. Cecil Rhodes was denounced as a mere puppet of the Jewish conspiracy.[2] It was not only in the labour movement that this theory found support. In the military establishment there were some who had more than a little sympathy for anti-Jewish sentiments.

The British Prime Minister, Lord Salisbury, was another who shared the distaste for the threatening war in South Africa. In a memorandum to Lord Landsdowne, Secretary for War, he wrote, '*I see before us the necessity for considerable military effort – and all for a people whom we despise, and for territory which will bring no profit and no power to England.*'

When Aubrey Woolls Sampson and Karri Davies saw General Sir William Butler, he refused point blank to sanction the raising of a regiment of volunteers stating, 'England is not preparing for war, even if the Transvaal is.'

However, in Natal, Aubrey and Karri were made welcome.

Chapter Four

The Colony of Natal

British administration at Port Natal would be '...a powerful aid towards abolishing the East African slave trade' and 'a colony based upon sound principals of political and social liberty, guaranteed to all denominations of men, and properly guarded against abuse and license ... will lead to a profitable investment of money, and obtain for free laborers of all classes and colors ample remuneration, with the prospect of steadily bettering their conditions.'

EXTRACT FROM A PETITION, DATED 22 MARCH 1839, BY THE MERCHANTS OF PORT NATAL TO THE HOUSE OF COMMONS REQUESTING THAT BRITAIN ESTABLISH AN ADMINISTRATION AT PORT NATAL. SEE APPENDIX 4.

NATAL was named by the Portuguese navigator and explorer, Vasco da Gama, who had made landfall near Durban on Christmas day, 1497. Three centuries were to pass before it attracted any lasting interest by European travellers. Following the success of their settlement at Cape Town, the Dutch wondered whether a similar port of call might be practical on the Natal coast and in October 1688 the Cape Governor ordered one of their vessels, the *Noord*, to survey the east coast and search for any survivors of shipwrecks. At Port Natal the *Noord* found two survivors from the wreck of a Dutch ship, the *Stavenisse,* which had run ashore on the Natal south coast on 16 February 1686. Though pleased to see their countrymen, they had been well treated by the locals who were 'friendly, and there was an abundance of food and fresh water to be had.'[1] On their return to the Cape the report by the crew of the *Noord* seems to have impressed the Governor who sent the vessel back to Port Natal with instructions to buy the Bay of Natal and adjacent land. The *Noord* was welcomed on its return to Natal and the local chieftain put his mark to an agreement selling the land to the Dutch East India Company.[2] On 11 January 1690, the *Noord* left Port Natal for Cape Town with the Deed of Sale on board. Five days later she ran aground near Algoa Bay. Out of her original complement of eighteen, only four were able, after much suffering, to survive the shipwreck and the overland journey to the Cape. The Deed of Sale was lost to the sea.[3]

In 1705 there was a shortage of timber at the Cape and the Governor ordered another vessel, the *Postlooper* under Johannes Gerbrantzer, one of the survivors from the *Noord*, to investigate whether Natal might be able to supply timber. On arrival he found that the old chief had died and had been succeeded by his son. The son expressed complete disinterest in any agreement purportedly made by his father, saying he now ruled the district and only his own decisions had any validity. Gerbrantzer was wise enough not to argue with the chief. He reported unfavourably on the harbour and though he found an abundance of timber, its quality was no better than that grown in the Cape.[4] So ended Dutch interest in Natal for almost 150 years.

Over the centuries many ships were wrecked on the eastern seaboard of southern Africa. Most of the survivors attempted to walk to Delagoa Bay (now Maputo) or the Cape. Many died en route, some were murdered, and some were absorbed into the local native tribes. To these early reluctant travellers Natal appeared to be a veritable Garden of Eden with a superabundance of wild birds and animals, and many exotic fruits growing wild on the fringes of the forests where the trees grew tall and straight. The inhabitants near Port Natal were described as being of 'middle stature, with very good limbs and graceful'. A Captain Rogers who called at Port Natal in the 1690s found they were '…very just and extraordinarily civil to Strangers,'[5] and 'in their intercourse with each other they are very civil, polite, and talkative, saluting each other, whether young or old, male or female, wherever they meet; asking whence they come and whither they are going, what is their news, and whether they have learned any new dances or songs.'[6]

The country was ruled by a number of petty chiefs until early in the nineteenth century when a man of exceptional ability, Dingiswayo, united many of the Zulu clans. To ensure security he re-organized the country's defences. All young men were obliged to serve in his army which was divided into regiments, and these in turn were divided into companies. The companies were named and distinguished by the colour of their shields. Regimental and company commanders were recognisable by their imposing dress.

Unfortunately in a campaign against a recalcitrant tribe in 1817, Dingiswayo was captured and executed. Shaka, the leader of one of the smaller tribes who paid tribute to Dingiswayo, came forward to claim the vacant throne. Brave, intelligent, ambitious, and ruthless, he was nonetheless capable at times of great kindness and loyalty. Shaka soon consolidated his position as successor to Dingiswayo. He retained the military structure established by his predecessor and tightened discipline. However, the method of fighting was drastically altered. Previously, warriors had thrown long spears at each other. Shaka abolished the long spear and equipped his men with a large shield and a short stabbing spear. In battle his impis, like the Greek and Roman phalanxes, would advance in close formation, using their large shields as protection from missiles. The enemy would then be engaged at close quarters where the short spear was deadly.

Having secured his position as ruler of Zululand, Shaka turned his attention to the neighbouring peoples. To ensure they would no longer pose any threat to him or the Zulus, they were attacked and those who escaped the slaughter of battle were driven from the land, their *kraals* and crops destroyed and their cattle expropriated. From the Tugela River in the north, to the Mzimvubu River in the south, and from the sea to the Drakensberg mountains in the west, the land was almost emptied of inhabitants. At this time, when nations trembled at the mere mention of his name, such was the complexity of his character that he insisted on personally attending to the needs of his venerated and frail old grandmother, even cutting her toenails.

After the Dutch had ceded the Cape to the British in 1815, a group of Cape merchants decided to explore the possibility of trading with the Zulu people. They knew that Zululand was ruled by a mighty monarch, Shaka, whose military genius had resulted in vast tracts of land being subjugated by the Zulus. However as it was not their intention to conquer the Zulus but to trade with them, in 1823 they fitted out a brig, the *Salisbury*, under the command of James Saunders King, who was tasked with finding a suitable site for the establishment of a trading post in Natal. King had been born in Canada in 1795, joined the Royal Navy as a ship's boy in 1805, and left the Navy in 1815 with the rank of midshipman. Assisting King was Lieutenant George Francis Farewell who had served on a naval vessel conducting a survey of the South East African coast. They sailed first to St. Lucia Bay on the Natal north coast. Here three of a landing party drowned in the surf, while at the same time the Salisbury was blown many miles out to sea. It was five weeks before the winds permitted the Salisbury to return to St. Lucia to pick up the survivors of the landing party. After visiting Algoa Bay for supplies, the Salisbury returned to Natal where King charted the sheltered estuary at Port Natal (now known as Durban Bay) in detail before the party returned to Cape Town in December 1823. King went to England on an unsuccessful mission to obtain a commission, while Farewell concentrated on persuading merchants that Port Natal was a suitable place for a trading site. At the beginning of 1824 it was decided to go ahead with the venture. Like merchants of all times and in all places, they sought customers who were prosperous and content.

To reconnoitre the locality prior to the arrival of the main group, an advance party, under the leadership of a young man, Henry Francis Fynn, was sent ahead. On or about 10 May 1824, they arrived safely at the Bay on the sloop *Julia*. This land, which the writer Alan Paton described as '…beautiful beyond the telling', was found to be almost deserted. The only locals they saw were a few wretched people hiding in the coastal bush and subsisting on such shellfish as they could scavenge on the shore.

Having established a camp, Fynn, accompanied by an interpreter and one of the locals, set out northwards to find Shaka. They had not travelled far before they were overtaken by a Zulu Impi many thousands strong, returning from an expedition against the Pondos whose lands lay some 100 miles to the south. At the first hint of the presence of the Zulus his companions bolted, but Fynn stood his ground. Though later to become a pre-eminent authority on the Zulu language, he knew no Zulu and could only repeat the name 'Shaka' when approached. This was enough. The Zulus accepted him as a friend, and placed him in the care of one of Shaka's uncles while instructions were sought from Shaka, who was at his capital, Bulawayo, 125 miles to the north.

Shaka had heard of the English, whose arrival seems to have pleased him, for he immediately sent a present of forty cattle and several tusks of ivory as a gift. Later, when Farewell arrived in Natal, he and Fynn set off directly to visit Shaka, from whom they received a most cordial welcome with dancing, feasting and the interchange of presents. Shaka gave permission for the establishment of the trading station as well as making a grant of land (Appendix 1) which included the coast of the future colony and extended about 60 miles inland.

To Fynn must go much of the credit for the success of the visit, and the establishment of the trading station. His personality was such that he won the friendship and trust not only of Shaka but of all Zulus. This bond was strengthened when Fynn, using knowledge gained while working as a loblollyboy at Christ's Hospital, successfully treated wounds suffered by Shaka in an assassination attempt. Shaka appointed him chief of the Blacks living in Natal. This included those destitute souls living near the coast and several small clans near the mountains. Many were refugees from Zululand, who would have been hunted down and killed by Shaka but for the influence of Fynn. When the escape and flight of these people to Port Natal was reported to the monarch he is reputed to have said, 'They have gone to my friends and not my enemies.' Thus it came about that several thousand Zulus collected at Port Natal and Fynn noted, 'the fate of the natives became identified with our own, and could scarcely be separated.'[7]

Many years later it was written of Fynn,

> *'His intimacy with the Zulu language, his travels on foot amongst the Native people, his warm hearted disposition, his unfailing humanity to those in distress, and in these times they were very numerous and everywhere in hiding, especially in Natal, were such that even in these days a century later, his name is held in honour throughout the length and breadth of the land. In these things he was always first.'*

Because of his concern for them, those people over whom he was chief came to venerate him almost as a god.[8]

Fynn was given the name Mbuyasi, and when a son was born to Shaka's nephew, Mpande, the baby was named Mbuyazi, presumably in honour of the visitor who had arrived among them.

While Farewell and his party were establishing their little settlement, King had not been idle. In Britain he acquired a two-masted, square-rigged vessel, the *Mary*, for use at Port Natal. He sailed via St. Helena where he delivered a consignment of goods to a merchant on the island. The merchant's 16 year-old nephew, Nathaniel Isaacs, persuaded King to take him to Natal. Isaacs was an intelligent young man with a good command of English and fine powers of observation. They arrived at Port Natal on 30 September 1825. A strong onshore wind and heavy seas caused the ship to run aground at the harbour entrance. Fortunately no lives were lost, but the ship was irretrievably damaged. Over the next two years the foundations of the settlement were laid. Of necessity dwellings were at first primitive and designed to do no more than to provide protection from wild animals and shelter from the elements. Isaacs found the climate healthy and congenial and delighted in the lush vegetation and the abundance of wild fruits and vegetables.

The little settlement had its vicissitudes. Wild animals, particularly leopards and snakes were a constant threat. When, in 1827, medical supplies ran out, a fifteen year-old boy, John Ross, was given the task of walking 300 miles north to the Portuguese post at Delagoa Bay, to obtain fresh supplies. Shaka provided a bodyguard of warriors and the medicines were duly obtained. In spite of difficulties, the beauty and promise of the land was such that the settlement continued to grow steadily.

Good relations were maintained with Shaka, but at a price. Some were obliged to assist Shaka in his military campaigns. On one such campaign Isaacs was wounded. All food was withheld from him until he drank a concoction made from some roots and the gall and entrails of a heifer. The smell of the potion was so vile that Isaacs wondered whether death might not be a better alternative to drinking it. Perhaps their greatest trial was being obliged, on visits to Shaka, to witness the purposeless slaughter of his subjects, a form of entertainment to which Shaka was becoming addicted.

March 1828 saw the launching of the first ocean-going vessel built in Port Natal. Using timbers from the wrecked brig *Mary* and local trees, Hatton, chief officer of the *Mary*, and four crew members had taken two years to build the ship, which was named the *Elizabeth and Susan* in honour of the wife of Farewell and the mother of King. On 30 April 1828, the vessel left for Algoa Bay. On board were Lt and Mrs Farewell, King, Isaacs, Hatton, and two of Shaka's headmen who were to negotiate a friendly alliance with King George. (see Appendix 2.)

So anxious was Shaka to form an alliance with the British that he conceived the idea of obliterating the tribes which lay between the southern border of his domain and the Cape Colony. He was persuaded to give his emissaries two months' grace before embarking on any such campaign, however the *Elizabeth and Susan* had no sooner set off on her maiden voyage, than his impis attacked the Pondos on his southern border. In support of his army, Shaka came south with his entourage and visited Fynn at his home near the Mzimkulu River. Fortunately, Fynn was able to persuade Shaka to take his impis back to Zululand. The Zulus retired with ten thousand captured cattle.

The mission of the Zulu chiefs to Algoa Bay was an abject failure. British officials treated them as spies or criminals and subjected them to lengthy interrogation while keeping them under virtual house arrest. They were also refused permission to see the Lieutenant Governor at Grahamstown. After three months the British decided to send Shaka's men back to Natal on HMS *Helicon*. They refused to board the ship without King, who returned with them to

Natal. Farewell, Isaacs and Hatton returned at the same time on the *Susan and Elizabeth*. King was deeply affected by the failure of the mission and afflicted by severe depression, he fell ill and died on 7 September 1828. He was buried near his home on the Bluff, the promontory which shelters the bay from the ocean. Isaacs left a moving description of his funeral: 'The whole of the vicinity was crowded by natives from the surrounding districts, all lamenting the death of our friend. Their lamentations were sincere, their tears genuine drops of sorrow, that fell involuntarily from their streaming eyes.'

Shaka was infuriated by the treatment that his emissaries had received, and believed that King had been poisoned by the British. With Shaka in such a bad mood, all had to walk on eggshells; however he went no further than directing abuse at the whites. Indeed, such was his unpredictable nature at the time, that he made grants of land to Isaacs and Fynn without any regard for the fact that the same land had already been granted to Farewell and King.

Perhaps because he had exercised absolute power for so long, Shaka was becoming ever more brutal and cruel towards his subjects. His many military campaigns had exhausted his army, whose men longed for the day when they could marry and settle down to a more peaceful existence. Dingane, Shaka's half-brother, noticed the monarch's waning popularity, and when an opportune moment occurred on 23 September 1828, he assassinated Shaka, and usurped the throne.

Dingane appears to have had a genuine desire to rule humanely, and his accession was welcomed by most Zulus. He sent a reassuring message to the settlers at Port Natal.

In December, 1828, the *Elizabeth and Susan* again sailed from Natal to Algoa Bay. On board were Farewell and Isaacs. On arrival at Algoa Bay, the Port Authorities seized the vessel because she had no register. This was despite the fact that there was no shipping registrar at Port Natal, the vessel had lain in Algoa Bay for three months earlier in the year, and had been given written clearance. The ship was sold and the proceeds divided between the seizing officers and the crown. It was simple bureaucratic piracy. Deprived of the *Elizabeth and Susan*, Farewell decided to wait until his wife had been delivered of a child she was expecting, before returning to Natal by the overland route. In September 1829, Farewell and two companions set off for Natal. Near the Mzimvubu River they met a Zulu clan which had fled south after the accession of Dingane. Their chief, Queto, invited Farewell's party to visit him and on their arrival at his *kraal*, Queto gave them a warm welcome and a gift of cattle. That night, 6 October 1829, the guy ropes of Farewell's tent were cut and Farewell and his companions were stabbed to death through the canvas. The Pondos subsequently drove Queto back to Zululand where he was executed by Dingane.

On the whole, relations between Dingane and the settlement at Durban were cordial. Isaacs, who had been to St. Helena, returned in 1830 and noticed that all had gone well in his absence. On his visits to the Royal Kraal, he had long talks with Dingane as they watched the sun go down and his host amused himself by displaying his magnificent herd of 3,000 snow white Nguni cattle.

A traveller from the Eastern Cape, a Dr. Cowie, visited Dingane whom he found to be '…anxious to anticipate their wants, hospitable without ostentation' and displaying, '…a magnanimity and capacity befitting the chief of a great people.' Dingane told Cowie that his conduct would be of an opposite character to that of his predecessor and that his only ambition was 'to make his subjects free and happy.' Cowie noticed their huts were 'clean and commodious, the country was fertile and cultivation was extensively practised.'[9]

Isaacs noted that, unlike Shaka, Dingane did tend to vacillate in his opinions and lacked constancy. However, when he spoke his language was fluent, impressive and to the point. He expressed a desire for education both for himself and his people and thought this might be obtained from missionaries. On one of their visits to Dingane the immigrants appeared on horses. Dingane had never seen a horse before and immediately realised that foot soldiers would be no match for mounted men in Natal.

In 1830 Dingane sent two residents at the port, Cane and Holstead, on a mission of friendship to the Cape with two great tusks of ivory as a gift. The Cape government refused to see the emissaries, a rejection which bitterly offended Dingane. In just two years, British officials had treated the representatives of two Zulu monarchs with contempt and in so doing insulted the whole Zulu nation. This behaviour by the British authorities should have spelt the end of the settlement at Port Natal, but this did not happen. Because of the good relationship between the residents and the Zulus, the latter made no attempt to drive them out of the country.

The next few years were a period of steady growth and stability at Port Natal. New people arrived and although trade was still the principal source of revenue, farms were being established. In establishing the settlement, the founders believed they were advancing British commercial interests, while at the same time bringing stability to the region, including the Cape's eastern border, and providing a base to combat the slave trade further north along the East African coast. They also knew that nature abhors a vacuum and if Britain did not act, other European powers would. Repeated requests to Britain to establish an administration at Port Natal were ignored. Among those anxious for the governance of Natal to be placed on a proper footing was a former Attorney General of New South Wales, Mr Saxe Bannister. On 12 May 1829, he sent a detailed submission to the Secretary of State for the Colonies pointing out the advantages of bringing the settlement under the jurisdiction of the Crown and the dangers of not doing so. He met with no more success than other petitioners.

One issue had become a cause of friction between the new Zulu monarch and the settlement. Zulus who had fallen foul of Dingane would flee to Natal, where they were given sanctuary. Dingane, unlike Shaka, felt these emigrants should be returned to Zululand.

A former naval commander turned missionary, the Reverend Captain Allen Francis Gardiner, arrived in Natal in 1834. He left an account of his experiences from which he emerges as an absurd figure in which the comic wrestled with the tragic. His safari overland from the Cape was filled with a series of self-induced calamities. One of his happier experiences on this journey was the discovery that the people of Pondoland were remarkably honest and theft appeared to be almost unknown, a characteristic which survived in Pondoland until at least the middle of the 20th century. On Gardiner's arrival in Natal, such was the fierce heat of his religious fervour that he immediately set off to convert Dingane, who was much changed from the man Cowie had met a few years before. He had put on weight and much of his time was spent with his numerous wives. Attempts to engage him in religious discussion achieved no more than to demonstrate that in philosophical argument Gardiner was no match for the wily Zulu monarch.

Undeterred, Gardiner took it upon himself to negotiate a treaty with Dingane, wherein the latter agreed, 'never to molest any of his subjects now at Natal for past offences.' In exchange Gardiner agreed, '…never more to receive any deserter from his dominions.'[10] By this means Gardiner obtained temporary consent to undertake missionary work in Zululand. Back at Port Natal, and anxious to comply with his treaty, he arrested two men and two women who had recently fled from Zululand. He handcuffed the fugitives and took them back to Dingane, who promised not to kill them. Dingane kept his promise but denied the prisoners any food. Hearing what had happened, Gardiner, in full naval uniform, returned to Dingane to plead for the lives of the prisoners. Neither the plea nor the uniform impressed the king who remained unmoved. Gardiner concluded the interview by measuring Dingane for a new pair of boots that he intended to have made for the monarch. In order to recover his handcuffs, which he thought might be needed at some future date, he visited the poor starving prisoners, removed their handcuffs, and recommended a prayer to them. They thanked him, and wished him a happy journey. On the way back he chose the site for his mission station in Zululand. It would be called 'Culoola' ('To set free')!

Worse was to follow. One of the women had three children and Dingane demanded that they be delivered to him. A relative of the children offered to take their place but Gardiner refused, commenting, 'of course it could not be permitted.' So the children were sent off to suffer the same fate as their parents, while Gardiner wrote a letter to Dingane in which he stated, 'If deserters must be killed, let them be killed at once; but if they are to be starved to death, we are resolved that not another individual shall be sent back.'[11]

Dingane responded with a decree that all traders wishing to trade in Zululand needed a permit from Gardiner, who would be responsible for ensuring compliance with the treaty. Gardiner now attempted to lay out a township for Port Natal. Because there was no executive authority to enforce decisions, nothing was to come of this enterprise except that the township was named d'Urban after a successful governor at the Cape. Realising the need for a civil authority at the settlement, Gardiner decided to visit England in the hope of obtaining an official position for himself.

He arrived in England in May 1836, and shortly thereafter gave evidence to a Select Committee of the House of Commons on the treatment of aborigines in the British Colonies. His was the only evidence given to the Committee about Natal. He repeatedly stressed that the settlers were in grave danger of being slaughtered by Dingane, and in this he was correct, for they were indeed in much greater danger of being attacked and murdered by the Zulus than the Zulus were of being injured by them. However he had not gone to England to represent the white residents. He accused them of irritating Dingane by encouraging Zulu women to go to the Port, and of harbouring deserters from the kingdom. Some were 'notoriously living in a very immoral state' and many lived in a disgraceful way without chairs or tables. They persuaded villagers to sell them cattle by pretending it was the King's orders. On one occasion a Hottentot told him he had heard a shot being fired and Gardiner was amazed that they had not cut each other's throats a long time ago.

The Committee questioned him about the immigrants' behaviour towards the locals:

Question: 'Did the English residents at Natal instigate the natives of the settlement to annoy their Chief Dingana?'
Answer: 'Not in the least.'
Question: 'Then according to your knowledge the English residents at Natal had conducted themselves with propriety as far as relates to the natives?'
Answer: 'As far as relates to the natives.'[12]

The Preamble of the Cape Punishment Act, which followed the Report of the Select Committee stated: 'Whereas the inhabitants of the country north of the Cape Colony were uncivilised, and offences against them were frequently committed by British subjects with impunity....'[13]

No matter how reprehensible was the absence of household furniture, however scandalous it was that some settlers lived with women to whom they were not married, however frightening the sound of a gunshot might be to sensitive souls, and however miraculous the fact that the settlers had failed for years to sever each other's jugular veins, none of this can justify the Committee's assertion that crimes against natives were frequently committed with impunity.

The Report of the Select Committee of the House of Commons with respect to Natal is contained in Appendix 3. The Committee clearly regarded the settlers as high principled clerics who, from time to time, were tempted to neglect their pastoral duties for a little barter on the side. One wonders what the hunters and traders who had settled in Natal would have thought of the role that had been assigned to them. No doubt the Committee and the Commons meant well and we can laugh at their naivety, however, like a persistent computer virus, the Preamble burnt into many British minds an attitude towards Colonials which persists to this day.

While Gardiner was away, refugees from Zululand continued to seek sanctuary in Natal. The residents, lacking the physical capacity to prevent the entry of these immigrants, and believing it would be inhumane to send them back to certain death, ignored Gardiner's treaty. In April, 1837, two tribes fled from Zululand to Natal causing Dingane to suspend all trade. Fearing that they might be attacked, they with Black immigrants took steps to defend themselves by forming several companies of militia, which they called the 'Port Natal Volunteers.' On 26 May they received a message form Dingane who swore that he never had the slightest intention of attacking or destroying the settlement, and that he would never kill a white man. He said Gardiner had recommended that he should stop the trade and had also suggested he should have nothing to do with white men who were all rascals. The Volunteers were disbanded and trade with Zululand resumed. On his return to Natal, Gardiner received a hostile reception and moved to a site on the Tongaat River, 20 miles north of Durban. He visited Dingane, who was so delighted with the boots Gardiner had brought him, that he made yet another grant of Natal, this time to the British monarch. Gardiner failed to obtain permission to establish a mission station in Zululand.

In 1837 a pass from the Free State through the Drakensberg was found, and a group of *Voortrekkers* under Piet Retief descended into Natal. Retief immediately rode on to Port Natal, and in the course of his journey of 200 miles to the sea, did not see one living soul. On arrival he was given a cordial welcome, and told the residents he would report further after seeing Dingane.

Retief told the monarch how the *Voortrekkers* had defeated Mzilikase and his Matabele warriors and chased them across the Limpopo River into what is now known as Zimbabwe.[14] Dingane listened to this boast without making any comment. Instead he expressed a willingness to cede land to the *Voortrekkers*,[15] provided Retief and his principal lieutenants came to his *kraal* unarmed so that the matter might be finalised. Retief accepted the proposal and in February1838, he and his party went unarmed to Dingane's *kraal* where they were murdered. At the same time, Zulu impis crossed the Tugela and fell upon the *Voortrekkers*, who were camped in laagers over an area of about 45 miles by 25 miles near the present town of Weenen. Some groups were able to defend themselves but 281 were killed, as well as 531 camp followers.[16]

Under pressure from Zulu refugees, and believing in the friendly intentions of the Boers, some residents at Port Natal unwisely got together a force consisting of 16 whites, 30 Hottentots, and 800 Zulus drawn from those who had fled to Natal following the death of Shaka. This contingent crossed the Tugela into Zululand on 16 April 1838. The next day they were surrounded by Dingane's warriors who quickly overwhelmed them. Only four whites and about two hundred Zulu immigrants escaped the massacre.[17] One of the survivors, Dick King, known to the Zulus as uDiki, was to become a legendary figure in Natal colonial history.

To follow up their victory, the Zulus crossed into Natal and arrived at Durban on 24 April. The residents took refuge on an island in the middle of the Bay while the Zulus wreaked havoc on the settlement, destroying everything – houses, furniture, clothing, cattle, poultry, dogs, cats – nothing was spared. Presumably satisfied that they had inflicted sufficient punishment on the settlers, after nine days they re-crossed the Tugela into Zululand.[18]

After the massacres around Weenen the Boers, led by a Transvaler Andries Pretorius regrouped, obtained reinforcements from the Highveld, and comprehensively defeated Dingane's warriors at Blood River on 16 December 1838.

On 27 March 1839 yet another petition to annex Natal was addressed to the British Parliament on behalf of the English settlers, (Appendix 4). An interesting document, it displays an enlightened and practical approach to the region's problems, the implementation of which would have burdened the British government with little expense, while at the same time it would have avoided many of the difficulties which were later to arise. However, practical suggestions from Colonials were not going to disturb the equanimity of British opinion, which continued to be guided by the Preamble to the Cape Punishment Act. The Petition was ignored.

After the defeat of Dingane, the *Voortrekkers* purported to establish a republic which they called Natalia and had as its capital the nascent town of Pietermaritzburg, named after the *Voortrekker* leaders Piet Retief and Gert Maritz. About 30 Boers went down to the coast and laid out a village at Congela, on Durban Bay some distance from the English settlement.[19]

The Boers and the residents of Durban were soon on a collision course. The Boers believed that they, and they alone, would decide who could or could not live in Natal, and who would govern the land. The worsening relationship between the two groups was observed by a young Zulu, Ndongeni. He was of royal Zulu blood, and was born in 1826. While still a toddler, his father was put to death by Dingane, so mother and child fled to Port Natal, where they were given sanctuary by Dick King. He later wrote a memoir in Zulu describing the events of those times. In 1905 it was translated into English. About the dispute between the Boers and the English settlers, Ndongeni wrote, 'It became evident that the Boer attitude towards the English living in Durban was one of hostility. They said the country had been given to them by Dingane, and yet the English had been given it some time before by Shaka.'[20]

It is often suggested that the Grants made by the Zulu monarchs to the English immigrants should be ignored because they were illiterate and would not have understood the full implications of the documents. In these matters intention is everything. When William the Conqueror made grants of land to his barons in 1066, neither he nor they were learned people, and none of them could have anticipated the rights and duties imposed on both the state and the citizen by modern land law, and yet ownership of almost every acre of land in England can be traced back to a bequest made by William. When Shaka made a grant to the English, his clear intention was to grant them the right to live in Natal according to their customs. He also believed that he retained certain rights over the land. He did, for example, move his armies across Natal to attack the Pondos, and he appointed Fynn chief of the Black people living in Natal, rights which were not disputed. No doubt there were other issues that still needed agreement, but this does not detract from his intention to give the English traders the right to live and trade in Natal, which was never challenged by him.

The offer made by Dingane to the *Voortrekkers* was different. He had no intention of permitting them to live in Natal, and when making the offer, had already made plans to kill Retief and expel the *Voortrekkers*. Besides, as Ndongeni stated, neither Dingane nor his successor, Mpande, could give that which had already been granted to someone else.

The British Government believed the *Voortrekkers* still owed allegiance to the Crown, and this obligation was not altered by their emigration. The Republic of Natalia was not recognized, and the dispute with the Settlers was regarded as a quarrel between two groups of British citizens. Nonetheless, Sir George Napier, the Governor at the Cape, decided to send 80 men and some artillery under Major Charters to 'Fort Victoria' at Port Natal to keep an eye on things. They landed without opposition on 4 December.[21] They found there was no such place as Fort Victoria, so Charters commandeered Maynard's Store belonging to a Mr Dunn and a warehouse owned by Mr J. Owen Smith. To comply with orders, a small fort called Fort Victoria was built near the northern entrance to the harbour. On 16 December

1838 the British flag was hoisted amidst scenes of jubilation among the residents.[22] The following month Charters left for the Cape leaving Major Jervis in command.

In July 1838 the fortunes of the *Voortrekkers* had received an unexpected boost. Dingane had quarrelled with his brother, Mpande, who arrived in Natal with over 15,000 followers. The Boers immediately took him under their protection. Full of confidence, they told Major Jervis he and his troops had to leave. Jervis felt he had no choice but to comply and left with his small force on 24 December 1839.[23] The British had decided to await events.

The *Voortrekkers* now became much more aggressive towards the residents of the Port. All people in Natal would have to submit to the jurisdiction of the *Volksraad* and British residents wishing to travel were required to obtain a pass. One of the first to fall foul of the new 'pass law' was Henry Ogle. One of the original pioneers, he had brokered a peace deal between the *Voortrekkers* and Dingane in which the Zulu monarch agreed to return the cattle and arms his impis had captured in February, 1838. In order that he might help the Boers collect the cattle, Ogle travelled to Pietermaritzburg where he was promptly put in gaol for not having a pass.[24]

Dingane was unable to make immediate payment of the full amount due under the settlement resulting in the *Volksraad* deciding, in January 1840, to invade Zululand and destroy Dingane.[25] A *Kommando* under Andries Pretorius was assembled and set off for Zululand. Just before they left, emissaries arrived from Dingane. Despite being diplomats, they were promptly arrested and subsequently shot.[26] Mpande had meanwhile taken his impis into Zululand by a different route, and had met and routed Dingane's force. Dingane fled to Swaziland where he was murdered. Having triumphed without firing a single shot, Pretorius annexed to the new republic a substantial slice of north-western Zululand,[27] proclaimed Mpande king of the now reduced Zululand, and appropriated some 22,000 cattle to stock the *Voortrekker*'s new farms.[28]

While Pretorius was away hunting down Dingane, the *Volksraad* was busy establishing its administration. On 6 February 1840, it published Port Regulations for Natal. Of particular interest to the English settlers at Port Natal was Regulation 14 which stated, 'That a licence of 20 Rds. per annum be taken out for every boat used for the purpose of landing or shipping goods, and that *no such licence is to be granted to any person not being a burgher under this government.'*[29] (Italics inserted by the writer)

In terms of this edict, all trade was to be controlled by the Boers while the British, who by their labour, courage, and enterprise had created and built up that trade, were to be deprived of their livelihood.

During this period a Dutch ship, the *Brazilia*, called at Durban. Though the visit was to have no immediate effect on South Africa, it did create in Boer minds the idea that they might receive support from European powers, while at the same time it alerted the British to the possibility that Port Natal might prove a valuable asset to Britain's European rivals.

Towards the end of 1840, the Boers suspected that the Baca people, who lived to the south of Natal near the source of the Mmzimvubu River, might have stolen some of their cattle. They attacked the Baca, killing about 40 tribesmen and appropriating 3,000 head of cattle.[30] Paramount Chief Faku, the ruler of neighbouring Pondoland, was alarmed by this aggressive action by the Boers and requested assistance from Britain. Sir George Napier responded by sending Captain Thomas Charlton Smith with two companies of the 27th Foot (the Inniskillings), some guns, a few Cape Mounted Riflemen and Engineers plus 250 civilian workers to Mgazi in Pondoland.

In August 1841, the *Volksraad* passed a resolution that all wandering or detribalised Blacks were to be expelled and settled south of Natal, in the land between the Mzimkulu and Mzimvubu rivers.[31] The possible domino effect of this action posed a direct threat to the

Cape border and this could not be ignored by Britain. In December 1841, Captain Smith was ordered to proceed overland to Port Natal to protect Britain's interests. Camp was struck, and soldiers and civilians with sixty wagons and six hundred oxen to provide transport and food, set off on the long and tortuous journey to Natal.

Several women went with the party. Among them were the wives of Captain Lonsdale and the Reverend Archbell, both of whom had three children. A few days into the journey, a Mrs. Gilligan was delivered of a son and the next day the wife of the Commissariet Issuer gave birth to a 'beautiful daughter.' It was a difficult journey, and when they reached the Mkomazi River thirty miles south of Durban, a private soldier collapsed and died of exhaustion. After a brief rest the column moved on towards Durban. About 25 miles from the port they met four heavily armed Englishmen who stated that the Boers had threatened to hang them if they did not fight against the advancing column.[32] The following day they met a larger group of English residents, also heavily armed, who gave the troops a great welcome. No armed Boers were seen as Captain Smith led his column through Durban to the little fort at the northern entrance to the harbour. The *Voortrekker* flag was lowered and the Union flag raised once more.[33] For his base camp Smith chose a site about a mile away from Fort Victoria, near the present day Kingsmead cricket ground. Two ships, the ninety ton schooner, *Mazeppa*, and the *Pilot* arrived and anchored in the harbour. They brought with them supplies of salt beef, pork and biscuits. Also on board were nine would-be immigrants who must have been wondering why they had decided to come to Natal. The English troops were confined to camp and at night they could hear wagons arriving with Boer reinforcements, some coming from as far away as the Transvaal and the Free State.

The Boers assembled a *Kommando* at a camp about three miles south of Durban. An ultimatum was sent to Smith demanding his withdrawal from *Voortrekker* territory and on 23 May 1842, the Boers appropriated most of the cattle which the troops had brought with them.[34] That night Smith launched an attack on the Boer camp, the line of advance being along the edge of the Bay. He failed to take into account the effect of the tides, the difficulty of maintaining silence, and the impossibility of manhandling the guns through the tangled roots of mangrove trees abutting the bay. The result was that a howitzer, which was sent by boat, stuck on a sand bank before it could get within range. The commotion caused by the attempt to bring up the two guns along the water's edge alerted the Boers who were able to take up concealed positions from which they directed 'heavy and well directed fire' on the British. Smith had no option but to call off the attack and retire to his base camp. The two guns were abandoned.[35] The Boers followed the retreating soldiers and attacked the British camp from three sides. The camp might have been overrun had the Boers not been subjected to unexpected cannon fire from the rear. A resident, George Cato, and some friends had taken two cannon behind the Boer lines and at the opportune moment opened fire.[36] Thrown into confusion by this new development, the Boers beat a hasty retreat. In the engagement, which terminated just before dawn, the British suffered 34 killed, 63 wounded and 6 missing.[37] Heavy losses for so small a force.

The next day Smith set about fortifying the camp by forming a 'laager' with his wagons, building earthworks and digging trenches. Not knowing how to send a request for help to Grahamstown, Smith asked Cato for advice. Cato offered to take the dispatch himself, but Smith felt Cato's services were needed 'on the spot'. Cato suggested that if he was given two troop horses, he would find someone to carry the dispatch to Grahamstown. Suitable horses were found and he decided to entrust the task to the settler Richard (Dick) King. Sixteen year old Ndongeni was to accompany King.

On the night of 25 May 1842 two boats manned by Cato and his brother, Christopher, quietly rowed the two men, with their horses swimming behind, across the Bay to begin their epic ride. Ahead of them lay 600 miles of uncharted land, much of it ruled by Black chiefs whose cooperation was essential. They had to cross hundreds of rivers, traverse forests and wide, deep valleys, which had over millennia been gouged out of the land by rivers. Even today these are wild and inaccessible places.

Their first great challenge was to elude the Boers, who had picked up their trail and were in hot pursuit, chasing them as far as the Mkomazi River. Near the Mzimkulu River, they were stopped by some Baca, who thought they were Boers. Knowing their language, King persuaded them that this was not the case and they were allowed to continue. They now had to face the natural hazards of leopards, crocodiles, hippos and the venomous snakes that abounded along the coast and in the river valleys. With the most difficult part of the journey completed, Ndongeni fell ill and King was obliged to leave him at the Mission hospital at Buntingville.[38]

The day after after King's departure, the Boers attacked and captured Fort Victoria, killing two soldiers and taking prisoner sixteen of Smith's men. Among the residents who had fought alongside the soldiers one, Charlie Adams, was killed, while ten others were captured. In this group was George Cato. The Boers seized and plundered the two ships in the harbour and in the process captured several cannon and a large quantity of stores. Though the ballast was removed from the *Mazeppa* and the Master was taken into custody, they did not remove the rudder and permitted ten of the crew and two ship's boys to remain on board. They failed to notice that Christopher Cato, an experienced seaman, had passed himself off as a member of the crew. The settlement's civilians were incarcerated in an enclosure near the Boer camp – the first concentration camp! One who attempted to escape was shot dead. The ten civilians who had been captured fighting alongside the British were to receive special treatment.

On 31 May the Boers again attacked the British camp. With better fortifications, the attack – which lasted most of the day – was beaten off. During the day the women and children in the camp were constantly exposed to enemy fire. Subsequently, under a flag of truce, it was arranged that seven women and eighteen children be transferred to the *Mazeppa*.

Without the stores from the two ships, the lifting of the siege acquired greater urgency. Lest King should fail to reach Grahamstown, it was now vital to arrange an alternative plea for help. On the *Mazeppa* food was surreptitiously saved from the rations supplied by the Boers. Citing laundry needs, extra fresh water was taken on. The women adopted the routine of hanging their washing over the bulwarks. So meticulous were they in their household chores, that they even took out the sails and dried the dew off them. The ship's longboat floated idly astern. An air of peaceful domesticity pervaded the scene. Ever cautious, the Boers had placed an eighteen-pounder cannon about fifty yards away, sighted on the bulwarks of the the vessel.

On 10 June, the wind changed to the south-west. That day the women washed the blankets and hung them out to dry over the port bulwark. Of a sudden the Boers noticed the sails were going up and the ship was underway. They rushed to the cannon, but before it could be fired, the ship had rounded a corner and was heading down the channel towards the harbour entrance.

Christopher Cato, assisted by Isaac Craig, the ship's carpenter, had led the ropes, which raised the sails, below decks. On command, the anchor was slipped while below decks every available man, woman and child hauled frantically on the ropes to raise the sails. Cato stationed himself on the bow while Craig steered.

Though clear of the big cannon, the ship still had to pass, on her port side, about 80 Boers at the harbour entrance who were armed with elephant guns and a four-pounder cannon. At point-blank range the Boers opened fire on the ship. The cannon fired ball after ball at the ship and there was a continuous roar of fire from the elephant guns, but the ship sailed on, out of the harbour and into the open sea. Once out of range of the shore guns, she hove to. The women, when hanging the blankets out to dry over the port bulwarks, had placed mattresses behind them which absorbed the Boer's fire.

Having reached the safety of the open sea, the damage to the ship was assessed. When leaving the harbour the longboat had been swamped and sank. The sails were riddled with holes, the rigging torn and the mattresses and other padding filled with bullets. Ballast-free, the ship rolled about, resulting in almost everyone on board suffering appalling bouts of seasickness. Nonetheless, the men and women immediately set to repairing the sails and rigging, while the children picked the bullets out of the mattresses. In five hours, much of the damage had been repaired and it was decided to sail before the wind to Delagoa Bay where they might meet a British warship.

They had food and water for four days. If the wind changed they would rapidly die of thirst and starvation. If the wind increased, the ship, without its ballast, would probably founder and all would drown. Luckily, the wind held fair and by the night of 13 June they had reached Delagoa Bay. There were no British ships in port and none arrived over the next few days so, but nothing daunted, they took on food, water and ballast and then set sail for Algoa Bay a thousand miles away. When they reached Port Natal the siege was over.[39]

Dick King had ridden the six hundred miles to Grahamstown in just eleven days and on 24 June 1842, the first warship had arrived at Durban to be followed by another the following day. On 26 June, British troops disembarked and in the skirmish which followed two men were killed. One, Private McCaffrey, when struck in the breast, refused medical attention uttering the immortal last words, 'Sure, never mind me. Attend to the man that's kilt.'[40]

The Boers offered little resistance and soon melted away; the siege had been raised. The conditions at the British camp were appalling. Twenty-six sick and wounded, many with arms and legs missing and suffering from dysentery, lay in a trench four to five feet deep with uncured horse hides providing the only shelter. The stench from the hides and rotting offal was horrible. Sanitation was absent. Captain Lonsdale, who had been wounded and whose wife was on the *Mazeppa*, had lain there for twenty-seven days '...without so much as a jacket on.' One woman, who refused to leave her husband when the siege began, told a relieving officer that, because of the incessant fire from the Boers, she had not dared to stand up for nearly a month.

When the siege began Captain Smith ordered that all cattle in the camp be killed and following local practice their meat was salted and dried in the sun. By preserving their meat in this way ensured that its shelf life was considerably extended. When this source of food was exhausted, they were forced to eat their horses. After the loss of the *Mazeppa* and the *Pilot*, daily rations were reduced to 6 oz. meat and 4 oz. biscuit dust. When relief came, all but one of the horses had been killed and eaten. The sole surviving horse was found sitting on his haunches, too weak to get up.[41] Captain Bell, commander of one of the two relieving ships, left a quaint description of Captain Smith: '...he was very much reduced by the hardships he had endured; his rigging much chafed and out of order, but his interior remained sterling steel.'[42]

Christopher Cato and Isaac Craig have never received the recognition that was due to them, a comment which applies equally to the women and children on the *Mazeppa*. These tough pioneer women, two of whom were nursing six week-old babies, displayed courage, determination, and stamina which today is difficult even to imagine. The same can be said of the discipline and fortitude of the children.

Those residents who were captured by the Boers while fighting with the British, were H. Parkins, D. Toohey, B. Schwikkard, H. Ogle, J. Hogg, J. Douglas, G.C. Cato, F. McCabe, S. Benningfield and F. Armstrong. They were kept in stocks at Congela for a week, after which they were sent to Pietermaritzburg, where, during the day, they were chained two by two and exhibited to the public as objects of abuse and vilification. Their nights were spent chained together with their feet in stocks in a locked room 8 feet by 9 feet. On 7 June 1842 they sent a petition to the *Voortrekker* leader, Andries Pretorius, in which they pointed out that they had committed no crime and continued:

> '*We humbly submit to you and hope you will take into consideration and kindly ease us of being chained during the day and of the intolerable stench caused by our being obliged to ease ourselves inside the Tronk (cell), this with being confined with closed windows which may soon cause a disease fatal to us and spread through the whole town.*

> '*We sincerely hope you will ease us of the above grievances and we hereby promise you with the help of God to submit patiently to His will and your orders and you will have no cause to repent of your kind indulgence. We are your humble Petitioners...*'[43]

But nothing was done to relieve their suffering until British troops landed at Port Natal on 26 June 1842.

During the siege, the homes and businesses of the British residents were looted by the Boers. By their own admission they had removed 70 to 80 wagon-loads of goods from Durban to Pietermaritzburg plus all the residents' cattle and horses.[44]

A few days after King had left him at the Buntingville Mission, Ndongeni saw the British warships making their way up the coast, and he knew uDiki must have succeeded in his mission. He duly recovered from his illness and made his way back to Durban to receive an emotional welcome from King and his friends. After the epic ride, Dick King was given the further name Mlamulankunzi – literally, the 'separator of fighting bulls' (i.e. the peacemaker). In later years Ndongeni was given a farm by the Natal government to mark the appreciation they felt for his contribution to Dick King's ride.

Three weeks after the relief, the Pietermaritzburg *Volksraad*, despite vigorous opposition from their women folk, decided to submit to British rule.[45] Colonel Cloete, a Cape Afrikaner

One of the stocks used in 1842 to exhibit Natal residents who objected to the invading Voortrekkers taking over their settlement at Port Natal.

and commander of the relief force, negotiated a treaty with the *Voortrekkers* who immediately began to search for ways of avoiding their obligations under the treaty. They declined to return the horses, cattle and goods they had stolen and troubles were fermenting between them and the Blacks. The result was that in 1843, Britain annexed Natal. Though the paramount British official in South Africa remained the Governor in Cape Town, a Lieutenant-Governor was appointed to administer Natal. The first person to hold this post was Martin West, an Indian.

Although there was no pressure on them to do so, most of the Boers went back over the Drakensberg to join their compatriots in the Free State and Transvaal. By 1848 there were about sixty Boer families in Natal, and those who stayed were given the same rights as the English settlers, and in addition were permitted to keep their farms which were usually about 6,000 acres in extent.

When Britain annexed Natal the British made it clear that the Colony should become self-supporting as soon as possible. It was expensive to administer a colony so, in the hope that the country might become self-sufficient and able to defend itself, it was decided to encourage immigration to Natal. Various schemes were set up with the principal groups arriving between 1849 and 1852, though further immigrants from Britain and its Colonies continued to arrive throughout the nineteenth century.

One such scheme was set up by Joseph Charles Byrne, a Dubliner, who, although not known for his honesty, was a persuasive speaker and opportunist. He had never been to Natal, yet he toured Great Britain giving glowing accounts of the land and in the process persuaded 2,500 people to emigrate there. They were promised that each family would receive a 20-acre farm plus 5 acres for each child and a half acre in the local village. Each of these farms would have water, arable land, pasturage and timber and be close to markets.

The voyage, which was supposed to take six weeks, took three months in slow, heavily laden ships. At the end of this long and uncomfortable voyage, in which people died and babies were born, the immigrants found that their trials, far from being over, were just beginning. Because there was no jetty in Durban, they had to wade ashore. Those who had difficulty, especially the women in their long skirts, had to be carried ashore.

To get their possessions ashore proved most difficult and much was lost or damaged – the most serious catastrophe being the sinking of one of the larger ships, the *Minerva*, on rocks near the anchorage. Though the passengers were saved, much of what they had brought with them was lost. These were not luxury goods but such vital items as tools, cooking utensils, clothing and so on. One woman, having been saved from the sinking *Minerva*, went into labour shortly after getting ashore and gave birth to her second son under a tarpaulin on the beach. The landing place was just over a mile from Durban. Another immigrant left this record of his first sighting of that town: 'I landed with my father in 1850. After landing, we walked a mile or so when we came to a man standing alongside the road with a flour-sack apron on. My mother said, "*Can you tell me, sir, how far is it to the town of Durban?*" He replied, "*God bless you, mum, you're in the middle of Durban now.*"'[46]

Among those whom Byrne persuaded to come to Natal was a young tenant farmer from Scotland, Duncan McKenzie, and his wife, Margaret. Like so many others, they had lost nearly all their possessions to the sea at Durban. They had been allocated land at Richmond, approximately 65 miles from the port. There was no road to Richmond and the wagon journey there was long and difficult. One glance at the allocated land was sufficient to convince them that there was no prospect of earning a living from it. The holding was too small, there was no infrastructure and the place was too far from potential markets. They had no choice but to move back to Pinetown, near Durban, where Duncan was able to obtain work as a pick-and-shovel man on the road being built to Pietermaritzburg. He increased his income by doing piecework and with hard work it was not long before he was made a superintendent over a section of the road. By the exercise of strict economy, he and Margaret saved every penny they could, and after seven years they had £300, enough to buy a farm Lion's Bush in the Natal Midlands.

This farm, which was sold to them by a *Voortrekker* returning to the High Veldt, had a wattle and daub thatched cottage but was otherwise undeveloped. To buy the necessary livestock and equipment to make the farm viable, Duncan continued to work on the roads. Children came along at regular intervals, their first son Donald being born in February 1851 followed by two daughters and a second son, Archibald, in 1858. A third son, Duncan, was born at Lion's Bush in August 1859, followed by two more boys. Not only was Margaret responsible for bringing up the children, but in the absence of her husband much of the day to day work on the farm was done by her.

Once he had raised sufficient capital, Duncan left the roads department and went into business transporting goods to the Free State and the Transvaal by ox wagon, the only viable means of transporting goods in those days. Virtually all the exports and imports for the Free State and Transvaal were shipped through Durban so there was plenty of business. But this was no sinecure and many were the difficulties and dangers. Anyone who has tried to plough a straight furrow with two oxen will know how difficult it must be to control a team of 16 pulling a wagon. Great skill and nerve was a prerequisite for all drivers. The oxen had at all times to be fit and strong, and each one had a name and a particular position in the team. The driver had to know the name of each ox, its position and what was required of each animal while at the same time navigating the wagon across country where there were no roads or bridges and rivers frequently came down in flood. Swollen rivers would require that the oxen should first swim across the river and once on the far bank they would be inspanned and as many as three spans (48 oxen) might be used to pull the wagon across, all the time care being taken to ensure there was no water damage to the goods. Any mistake could mean loss or damage to the goods or wagon. As always, those receiving the goods were in a hurry to receive the consignment, so any delay could be expensive. In these tough competitive conditions McKenzie thrived. The discovery of the Barberton goldfields brought more work and more challenges as heavy machinery had to be transported over very difficult terrain. However McKenzie was up to the task and established a reputation as a transport rider without peer. But it was not only the wagon trains that were doing well: the farm, with astute and enlightened management, was also prospering.

The eldest son, Donald, received little formal education. In his younger years he had to help his mother on the farm and by the time he was fifteen he had joined his father transport-riding and trading. The other children were able to have more formal schooling, which of necessity required going to a boarding school. The boys went to the newly established Hilton College near Pietermaritzburg which, apart from teaching academic subjects, placed great emphasis on the importance of integrity in all things. Archibald, after showing considerable promise at school, studied medicine in Edinburgh and on his return to Durban achieved great renown as a surgeon, general practitioner and public benefactor. In the Boer War he served as a major in the Natal Medical Corps and in the Great War as a Colonel in the South African Medical Corps.

Duncan junior (references to Duncan McKenzie will from now on refer to the son) was a good rugby player but it was as a horseman that he was really talented. He took part in the various equestrian competitions which were then popular among the rural communities. He was from his schooldays an excellent polo player and at country race meetings rode in steeplechases and on the flat. He was able to kick a rugby ball over the posts while mounted! Like other colonial children, he learnt to swim at an early age and became a strong swimmer. It should be borne in mind that in the early days of the Colony, people had of necessity to

Brigadier General Sir Duncan McKenzie:
a portrait taken after his successful campaign
in German South West Africa in 1915.

wash in rivers and there being no bridges, often the only way of crossing a river was to swim.

Duncan left school when he was sixteen and decided to follow his father and elder brother into farming. Like other members of the family, he went transport riding to acquire the necessary capital to enable him to farm. Though railways were beginning to make their presence felt in South Africa, there were still opportunities for the wagon trains. Like his father and brother before him, Duncan soon became known for the speed and reliability of his wagon trains and his ability to transport the heaviest and most difficult loads. Goods were carried not only to Bloemfontein, Johannesburg and Barberton but as far afield as Rhodesia. For his services, customers were prepared to pay a premium, and after six years transport riding, he was able to go farming on his own account in 1881. He brought to farming the same meticulous attention to detail and striving for excellence that he had employed with his wagon trains. He married a local girl, Katherine Agnes McArthur, in 1883. He bred cattle, sheep and horses as well as selling timber, hay and dairy products. He always sought to improve his stock and did not hesitate to import the best for breeding. Because of its altitude, his farm was ideally suited to the breeding of horses and many of South Africa's best racehorses were bred by him. He never took any interest in politics.

Living in the Natal Midlands, Duncan was invited to join the volunteer regiment, the Natal Carbineers, and did so as a trooper in 1880. In 1885 he became a lieutenant, in 1887 a captain, and in 1897 he was promoted to major. Of medium build, he had a commanding appearance which impressed all who met him. It was not only his appearance which drew respect. Characteristically, his soldiering had the same qualities of attention to detail and striving for excellence which marked his farming and transport-riding. In addition he had learnt from the latter how to read the lie of the land ahead, an essential skill when no maps were available, and the long hours in the saddle had taught him just what could be expected of men and horses. He was a strict disciplinarian and some of his men gave him the nickname 'Shaka,' a reference to the stern discipline which that monarch had imposed on his impis. However they knew of his absolute fairness, his strict sense of duty and loyalty to them. In return he received their affection and respect.

In 1899 he and his wife visited Britain where he bought thoroughbred breeding stock and South Devon cattle. While there he received a telegram stating that war with the Boers was imminent and he was to report for duty as soon as possible. He caught the first available ship home. It was fortunate that he arrived back too late to be incarcerated by the Boers in Ladysmith with the rest of his unit.[47]

Apart from the immigrants from Britain, other groups came to Natal, one such being 35 families from Germany who arrived at Port Natal in 1848 under a scheme to grow cotton. Unfortunately, the cotton seed they brought was infected with boll weevil which resulted in the collapse of the enterprise. Among these immigrants was a blacksmith, Georg Friedrich

Rethmann, with his wife and child. His wife died shortly after they arrived in Natal and his child a couple of years later. However, in 1851 he married Barbara Field, an English schoolteacher. Like many of the new arrivals, Georg found it difficult to obtain regular employment and at various times worked as a blacksmith, farmer, professor of music, labourer, musician, engineer, piano tuner and turner. To provide for a growing family, Barbara taught, often having to create the school where she was to teach. Their eldest son John Frederick 'Jack' Rethman was born in 1852. As was the case for most settlers, life was not easy for the family. Lack of funds resulted in Jack having to leave school at an early age and take work as a messenger for a firm in Durban.

When he was sixteen he and a friend took mules loaded with goods into Pondoland, then an independent country south of Natal, intending to barter them for cattle. They were able to exchange the goods, but just before they set out for home, the cattle were looted in fighting which had broken out between the Mzizi and Madiba (Mandela's people) clans. Though his companion returned to Natal, Jack pursued the spoor of the cattle until he found them in the Xesebe country. There Chief Jojo made the raiders return the cattle and in addition gave the young man a horse as a gift. Using the contacts made, Jack (known as Mxhakaza – 'Confounder') went on to build up an extensive trading business in Pondoland which continued until the apartheid government expelled whites from the territory a hundred years later. He was also one of the pioneer farmers in southern Natal and in 1890 was elected to the Natal Legislative Assembly. He had joined the local Volunteers in 1884 and rose, step by step, until he was appointed to the command of the Border Mounted Rifles in 1895 with the rank of major.

In 1824, when Lt Farewell established his little trading post, Natal was an unpopulated land approximately half the size of England. Seventy-five years later it was a well ordered little country whose short history had been packed with incident.

The assassination of King Shaka and the accession of Dingane was to bring an influx of Black people seeking sanctuary. The *Voortrekkers* had come and gone and the arrival in mid-century of approximately 5,000 European immigrants brought not only more people, but with them, the demand for the creation of schools, hospitals, roads, piped water and other infrastructure which the modern world takes for granted but which did not exist in Natal in 1850. Agriculture also changed and meant more than just living on a farm and shooting what game was available. Crops and livestock had to be efficiently produced and marketed.

On its northern frontier, a dispute as to who should succeed Mpande, the Zulu monarch, resulted in a bloody civil war in 1856, in which the half brothers, Cetshwayo and Mbuyazi, fought for paramountcy in the Kingdom. Cetshwayo emerged victorious, defeating his opponent in a battle fought near the lower Tugela River. The bodies of many of those killed were washed down the river and into the sea from whence they were carried south by the Mozambique current to be deposited on the beaches of Natal.

The year 1879 saw the trauma of the Zulu War, which included the famous battles of Isandlwana and Rorke's Drift. Natal had never sought to acquire Zulu territory and lived on good terms with its northern neighbour. In contrast, there was constant friction between the Transvaal and Zululand. When in 1876 the Transvaal attempted to impose taxes on Zulus in disputed territories, the Zulu king Cetshwayo began to prepare for war.

As we have seen, in April 1877 Britain took over the administration of the Transvaal. At the same time a new governor arrived at the Cape, Sir Bartle Frere, who was also appointed Commissioner of Native Affairs for the whole of southern Africa. He had had a distinguished career in India and had acquired, in his opinion at any rate, some experience of Africa, having four years previously visited the Sultan of the Island of Zanzibar. Sir Bartle believed that it was his duty to create a Federation in South Africa. It seems that he had come to the conclusion that war with Zululand was necessary if the desired Federation was to come into being. The prospect of war delighted many British officers anxious to distinguish themselves and thereby gain promotion.[48]

To the people of Natal this talk of war was alarming. In an attempt to settle the matter peacefully, the Governor, Sir Henry Bulwer, suggested that an enquiry be held into the boundary dispute between the Transvaal and Zululand. The proposal was accepted by the British and the Zulus. Michael Gallwey, the Natal Attorney General, was appointed Chairman of the Commission, the other members being John Shepstone, and Lt Col A. Durnford. In Britain, in the Transvaal, and in the Cape it was assumed that the Commission would find in favour of the Boers, but they did not take into account the integrity of the Commissioners. In their report submitted on 20 June 1878, their main conclusions were in favour of the Zulus. The finding does not appear to have had any influence on Sir Bartle. Nonetheless he took the precaution of not releasing its findings until war was inevitable.

A few weeks later, two wives of a Zulu chief, Sirayo, fled to Natal with their lovers. The adulterers were pursued by two of Sirayo's sons, Mehlokazulu and Mkumbikazulu, who captured them, and took them back to Zululand where they were executed. This violation of the Colony's frontier coupled with the brutal penalty, did much to quell criticism of Frere's policies and to foster the belief that perhaps the proposed campaign might bring future security. One should not forget that King Henry VIII had two of his wives beheaded because they committed adultery.

It was not disclosed to the public that Sirayo was visiting King Cetshwayo at the time of the raid into Natal, neither had prior knowledge of it, and both recognised that the violation of the border was wrong. Initially the British demanded the return of the culprits, but subsequently agreed that a fine of 500 cattle be paid. When Cetshwayo asked for time to collect the cattle from Sirayo's tribe, Frere ignored the request.

By the beginning of December 1879, Sir Bartle felt the army was ready to act and on 11 December, he served an ultimatum on the Zulus. The terms of the ultimatum were insulting and compliance impossible. The inevitable non-compliance provided Sir Bartle with an excuse for the invasion of Zululand. Now that the findings of the Boundaries Commission were irrelevant Frere released their report.

Despite British attempts to spread alarm among Natal residents, their attitude towards the war was often ambivalent as can be seen from the diary of a volunteer, Fred Symons, who describes how one day during the campaign, while his troop was resting on a hill, an officer came up to him and said, "'Well, Symons! Wouldn't you like to see this slope covered with dead Zulus?" I replied, "No Sir, I wouldn't!" "Why not?" said he. "Because we have no quarrel with the Zulus and I consider this war an unjust one." He turned and walked away without a word.'[49]

Cetshwayo said after the war:

'This war was forced on me and the Zulus. We never desired to fight against the English. The Boers were the real cause of that war. They were continually worrying the Zulus about their land, and threatening to invade the country if we did not give them land, and this forced us to get our forces ready to resist, and consequently the land became disturbed, and the Natal people, mistakenly, believed we were preparing against them.'[50]

Robert Samuelson, who knew Cetshwayo well, said of him, '…he was a great friend of all white people, except the Boers, who were always filibustering in Zululand. He was kind and liberal to a degree.'[51]

Though eventually victorious, the war proved humiliating for Britain, and certainly did nothing to promote the federation Sir Bartle sought. While these events were occupying the

British, the wily old tortoise, Kruger, was biding his time in the Transvaal. *Let the British secure the Transvaal borders and then perhaps another Federation with another ruler.*

The Zulu War and other disturbances in neighbouring states had resulted in a flood of further refugees into Natal, which the government accommodated by allocating land to the different clans or tribes while at the same time granting corridors of land to white farmers to separate potential warring factions.

Many Indians had come to Natal under three-year contracts of service, and, liking the country, they stayed on after their contracts had expired. The discovery of gold in the Transvaal provided a big economic boost for Natal as well as drawing more immigrants to to the Colony from Great Britain and its colonies. Railways were built to the Free State and the Transvaal and, despite the obstructionist attitude of the Kruger government, it was through Durban that much of their trade passed.

When the first pioneers arrived, the entrance to the harbour was little more than four feet deep. By 1854 this had been increased to six and a half feet. This, however, was not sufficient for most ocean-going ships, goods and passengers having to be transported to the shore in lighters. In the 1860s, after a north-easterly gale, young boys would run down to the beach to see which ships had been blown ashore and to swim out to any wrecks. Over the years, harbour works steadily increased the depth of the harbour entrance until, by the 1890s, the depth had been increased at high tide to nineteen feet, deep enough to take all but the largest ships. By 1908 the entrance was deep enough to take any ship and Durban was southern Africa's premier harbour, handling more cargo than all the others combined. It had become one of the great ports of the world.

Durban was also the largest town in Natal and in July 1899 its population was 41,259 of whom 19,762 were of European descent, 9,562 were of Indian descent and there were 11,935 Blacks, most of whom were Zulus and among whom there were only 601 women.

The capital, Pietermaritzburg, was about 50 miles inland from Durban and though much smaller than Durban, it was the only other substantial town in the Colony. One hundred miles north of Pietermaritzburg, on the Klip River, and at the junction of the railways from the Transvaal and the Free State, was the little town of Ladysmith. The construction of the railways to the Free State and the Transvaal had brought a mini boom to Ladysmith, which was reinforced by the British establishing an army base near the town. North of Ladysmith, an extensive coalfield had been discovered, which not only created little communities around the mines, but breathed life into the pretty little towns of Dundee and Newcastle nearer the Transvaal border.

Elsewhere in the Natal hinterland, villages had come into being to serve the needs of the local farmers who all the while were making the land more productive. Sport provided the principal recreation in the Colony and almost everyone either played or took an interest in rugby, cricket and tennis. As horses played such a key role in their lives, horse racing was popular and equestrian sports such as polo had a substantial following without the elitist connotations found elsewhere.

In 1899 the threat of invasion by the Boer Republics hung over the Colony. It had built up an efficient and disciplined corps of Volunteers, but this force was tiny compared with the superbly armed and equipped Kommandos which now threatened to drive them into the sea. It is not surprising that they welcomed their friends Karri Davies and Woolls Sampson's decision to form a mounted regiment to assist in the defence of their Country.

CHAPTER FIVE

The Opposing Forces

◆

The Weigh-In. The Boer War is often depicted as a struggle between a mighty empire, anxious to extend its domains, and a handful of simple farmers wanting no more than to be left in peace. But was this really the position?

THE BOER REPUBLICS

IN the course of their many wars, the Boers had developed a form of conscription, known as the *Kommando* system, which ensured that a formidable army could be rapidly mobilised. All men between the ages of 16 and 60 were obliged to join their local *Kommando* and on a call to arms had to assemble immediately at a prearranged place with a horse, a rifle and food for eight days. They were unpaid, had no uniforms, and wore whatever took their fancy. Apart from attending occasional shooting competitions they received no military training, but they had a lifestyle which made them formidable foes. The ability to shoot game was an essential survival skill, and this made them superb marksmen, able to hit a moving target, gauge distance and adjust their sights appropriately. They were able to conceal themselves from approaching prey, or approach their target without being seen or heard. Because much of their life was spent in the saddle, they were good horsemen who also understood what their horses needed by way of water, food and rest. Their horses were trained not to wander off when dismounted, which avoided the detailing of a substantial number of men to act as horse-holders whenever they went into action. When it was necessary for the men to stay in one place for any length of time, family and friends would visit in their wagons bringing with them servants and provisions. However, when deployed against an enemy they could move quickly without a burdensome commissariat.

The command structure was simple. The smallest unit was the Corporalship of about 25 men. Five or six of these units would combine into a Field-Cornetcy, a similar number of which would constitute the District *Kommando*. A *Korporaal*, a *Veldt Kornet* and a *Kommandant* in the Boer army were roughly the equivalent of a Lieutenant, a Major and a Colonel in the Imperial army. In command of the whole army was the *Kommandant*-General, who was assisted by a number of Combat-Generals. The men elected their officers and all had a right to be heard in a *Krygsraad* or War Council. This was very democratic but not good for discipline. The problem was aggravated by the individualism of the burghers, who, while they could be trusted to exploit opportunities in battle without waiting for orders, would also refuse to obey orders with which they disagreed. There was no legal penalty for refusing to obey.

When the Boer forces mobilised in September 1899, the Transvaal *Kommandos* mustered about 32,000 men and the Free State about 22,000. In addition to these, the uniformed Transvaal Police supplied 300 mounted officers and men, and 600 officers and men on foot.

Approximately 2,000 foreign mercenaries, known as the *Uitlander Korps*, served in the Boer army and formed themselves into appropriately named units; the Legion of France, the Hollander Corps, the American Volunteers, the Irish Brigade, the Russian Scouts, the German Corps, the Italian Corps and the Scandinavian Corps. The Boers did not have a high opinion of their *Uitlander Korps*. The diary of a young Boer girl, Freda Schlosberg, gives a description of a visit by these warriors to the family farm:

'Members of the *Uitlander Korps* have been arriving all day, carrying bundles of luggage, rifles and ammunition. The detachment consists of two or three hundred mercenaries – Hollanders, Germans, Frenchmen, Americans, Italians, Hungarians – all rough-looking, common men, evidently from the lowest classes. They are armed not only with the usual rifles and revolvers, but also with swords, daggers, etc., the Italians especially with homemade stilettos. Some of the *Korps* were *Uitlanders* from the Transvaal; others had come from abroad through Delagoa Bay.

'The first thing they did after settling down was to steal some of our fowls, geese and ducks; then they took most of the wood lying in our yard without even asking permission. They are undisciplined and unprincipled, and under no control whatever by their officers. Later in the day they broke into the cattle camp of one of our neighbouring Boers, Mr Erasmus, on the excuse that tents must be pitched there. When Mr Erasmus, who is also acting Field Cornet of the district, remonstrated with them, they answered, 'We are our own masters and do what we please.' In the afternoon some of them went to the river to practice shooting and they nearly shot the old Boer guarding the bridge.

'Next morning they went out in groups to the neighbouring farms, stealing poultry, pigs, sheep, and whatever they could lay their hands on. A few who remained in the camp had a terrible quarrel about a stolen rifle. A German was about to shoot an Italian but was stopped by the others. They all behave outrageously and declare repeatedly that they can do whatever they wish. Their presence near our farm is terrifying.'[1]

Unfortunately some modern writers seem to have confused the *Uitlander Korps* with Imperial Volunteer regiments such as the Imperial Light Horse and the South African Light Horse who fought on the other side and were formed from a very different type of person.

Though almost all the burghers had their own rifles, which they could use if they so chose, the government was willing to sell them the latest new rifles at cost. If a burgher was too poor to buy a rifle, one was given to him. Most chose to arm themselves with the 1898 *Gewehr* pattern German Mauser. Having a 0.275-inch calibre, it fired a bullet smaller than the .303-inch British rifles, used smokeless cartridges, had better sights and a longer effective range (about 1,500 yds.) than any other rifle. To these advantages it added the innovation of having its cartridges inserted into the magazine in clips of five. This gave it a significantly quicker firing rate than other rifles which required that cartridges be inserted into the magazine one by one. At that time the Mauser was the best rifle in the world. It is estimated that in September 1899, there were about 43,000 Mausers in South Africa, 38,000 being in the Transvaal and 5,000 in the Free State. As most of the Free State burghers used Mausers it must be assumed that they were supplied from Transvaal stocks. In addition, the Transvaal had approximately 34,000 Martini-Henri and other rifles. This over-supply of rifles appears to have been intended for the arming of rebels in the Cape Colony.

The Republics took care to acquire plentiful supplies of small arms ammunition, and it is estimated that by October 1899, they had upwards of 70 million rounds in stock, including at least 25 million rounds of Mauser ammunition which the British had allowed to pass through their blockade at Delagoa Bay in September!

In their preparations for war, the Republics did not neglect the artillery. German instructors were brought out to train what was to become a disciplined and efficient uniformed unit firing the best guns in the world. The Transvaal trained a corps of 800 artillerymen and the Free State 400. Their recent gun imports were:

By the Transvaal:
   Four 155 mm (6-inch) Creusot fortress guns which threw a 94 lb shell up to 11,000 yds. These were the famous 'Long Toms'.
   Four 120 mm (4.7 inch) Krupp howitzers.
   Six 75 mm Creusot quick-firing field guns.
   Eight 75 mm Krupp quick-firing, high velocity field guns.
   Five 75 mm Vickers-Maxim quick-firing mountain guns
   At least twenty-two Vickers-Maxim automatic guns (pom-poms) firing a 1 lb shell with a bursting charge.
   At least thirty-one Maxim machine guns of .303 or .45 calibre.

By the Free State,
   Fourteen 75 mm Krupp quick-firing, high velocity field guns. Whereas the Transvaal used smokeless powder the Free State used black powder.

Both Republics had other guns which were obsolescent in varying degrees. All in all they had about 60 or 70 pieces of modern artillery and about 30 older guns, and they had not neglected to buy ammunition for the guns at the time of purchase. In addition, a factory was set up in the Transvaal to manufacture shells under the supervision of two members of the Creusot company.

An effective Intelligence Department was organised and experts were employed to prepare detailed maps of the areas where the war was likely to be fought. As a result when the Boers went to war they had the benefit of excellent intelligence and good maps.[2]

The Boers were well mounted on locally bred horses. For the best part of 200 years the Dutch had been importing Arab horses into the Cape. Their progeny developed over the years into a distinct type later known as the '*Boereperd*' – tough, sure-footed, possessed of almost limitless stamina, and were fast over country. They were, however, smaller than English horses and for this reason they were often described as ponies. They bore no resemblance to the British native pony breeds.

But the Boers did have their weaknesses. Their discipline was poor. In Natal they would be fighting in country that was strange to many of them. They could expect hostility from the Black population and, because of their belief that everyone should speak Dutch, few could speak Zulu or any of the other Black languages. There were some who, having become urbanised, were initially poor marksmen, though this could be corrected. Past victories over poorly armed tribesmen, as well as their easy victory over the British in the War of 1879/1880, had resulted in over-confidence.

NATAL

Though Britain had granted the Colony responsible government in 1893, any decision by the colonial government required the consent of the British government. This inevitably resulted in the British being not a little arrogant in their dealings with the Colonials, as can be seen from Alfred Milner's refusal to permit the Colonial Governments to take any part in negotiations with the Boer Republics.

The Prime Minister of Natal from June 1899 to August 1903 was Lt Col Albert Hime. He had studied engineering at Edinburgh University and on qualifying joined the Royal Engineers. His ability was soon noticed and shortly before the Zulu War (1879) he was appointed Colonial Engineer to Natal, a position he filled with distinction. When Natal was granted Responsible Government he was elected to the Legislature, and in 1897 became Minister of Lands and Works, a portfolio he retained when he became Prime Minister. After the outbreak of war and the imposition of Martial Law, the British abandoned any pretence of regard for colonial opinion. In spite of this, and many other difficulties facing them, the Natal government was able to keep the machinery of state running efficiently throughout the war.

From its earliest days Natal had relied on volunteers for its defence. With its small tax base, and needing every penny it could get to build up the infrastructure of the Colony, there was no question of the Natal government being able to maintain a regular army, or to spend lavishly on armaments.

In September 1899, the commander of the Natal Volunteers was Col. William Royston, and his chief staff officer was Lt Col Bru-de-Wold. Willie Royston came to Natal with his parents in 1872 and joined the Natal Carbineers as a trumpeter when he was 16. His ability as a soldier was soon recognised and by 1881 he was in command of that regiment. In 1889 he was appointed Commandant of Volunteers. An intelligent and reliable man, he was respected by all, one contemporary describing him as a 'fine Christian gentleman.'[3]

His Chief of Staff, Hilmar Bru de Wold, never swore on Sundays. Born in Trondheim, he had arrived at Natal as a 20 year-old in 1862, not on an immigrant ship, but on a Norwegian naval vessel. Following a quarrel with an officer, he decided to desert, and swam ashore when the ship anchored off Durban. He walked down the coast seeking work as a labourer in the sugar fields. At Ifafa he had the good fortune to be offered work by John Bazley, a pioneer sugar farmer. He fell in love with his employer's daughter Sarah and they were married in 1871. By 1882 he was farming on his own account. A short, wiry man, he never lost his seaman's rolling gait or his strong Nordic accent. His choice of words and expressions was quaint and unconsciously humorous even when serious. When reprimanding a delinquent he added to his speech a collection of imaginative and colourful swear words, which were delivered with a furtive smile flickering about his face. The result was that the offender, though thoroughly chastened, would have difficulty suppressing his mirth and would bear no ill will for the telling-off. Bru de Wold joined the Volunteers in 1865, saw service in the Zulu War, being mentioned in despatches, was commissioned in 1880 and in 1894 became commander of the Border Mounted Rifles. He resigned from this post in 1895 when he was appointed District Adjutant for southern Natal.[4] The Colony was fortunate in having these two excellent officers in charge of its Volunteers, one entirely conventional and the other entirely the opposite.

Apart from regular local parades, the volunteers were required to attend an annual training camp lasting at least ten days. They had to pay for their uniforms, and each mounted volunteer had to provide himself with a horse, saddlery and top boots. They were given rifles and were paid while on duty. When ordered to mobilise on 28 September the Volunteers numbered just over 2,000, comprising the following Corps:

The Natal Carbineers

The Carbineers had been in existence since 1855 and drew their recruits from Pietermaritzburg, the Natal Midlands and Northern Natal and from the beginning were a mounted regiment. Their commander in 1899 was Lieutenant Colonel EM Greene and its strength 508 (all ranks).

The regiment had achieved great renown in the Zulu War of 1879. It formed part of the column which Lord Chelmsford led into Zululand in January of that year. On 20 January the Carbineers had camped with the British troops at the foot of Isandlwana Mountain and the following day Chelmsford, with about half his troops, pushed on into Zululand taking with him, as scouts, 27 Carbineers. The remaining 28 Carbineers, under a Lieutenant Frederick Scott, remained at Isandlwana. This troop was detailed to keep a lookout from a small hill a few miles to the north-east of the main camp. On the morning of the 22nd, they spotted a large force of Zulus approaching and immediately set off back to base. When still about a mile from the main camp, they joined Colonel Durnford of the Natal Native Contingent who had with him about 100 men. This group of Durnford's men and Carbineers now came under attack by the Zulus. In an attempt to protect the British right flank, they tried to make a stand in a dried water course but, faced by repeated and determined attacks by the Zulus, they were slowly driven back. The Zulus had meanwhile broken through the British defences leaving Durnford's group surrounded. Against overwhelming odds they fought on. A Zulu leader, Mehlokazulu, described their final stand: 'They threw down their guns when their ammunition was done, and then commenced with their pistols… and then they formed a line, shoulder to shoulder, back to back, and fought with their knives.'

Overcome with assegai and bullet wounds, they collapsed and died where they had fought. Lieutenant Scott was among the 18 Carbineers who died with Durnford and his Natal Natives. They could have mounted their horses and escaped, but instead stayed to help Durnford. For two and a half hours they had fought and by so doing enabled others to escape.

Elsewhere on the field, five other Carbineers died and five were able to escape. During the flight from Isandlwana, one of the survivors, William Barker, repeatedly risked his life to save others fleeing the battlefield, including giving his horse to an exhausted British officer, Lieutenant Higginson. Barker was recommended for a Victoria Cross, but it was refused by the British authorities, although a British regular soldier was given the award for a similar deed.[6]

When Chelmsford's column heard the sound of the battle at Isandlwana, it immediately retraced its steps back to the doomed camp. Four scouts from the local Buffalo Border Guards rode ahead and that evening were the first to arrive at the camp site. That morning they had breakfasted with comrades whose mutilated corpses were now scattered over the campsite. In charge of these scouts was Sergeant-Major Charles George Willson, who by 1899 had been promoted to Captain in command of the Dundee Squadron of the Natal Carbineers.

The Natal Mounted Rifles

This regiment had been formed in 1873 and drew its members from the Durban area. It succeeded other militia groups which had been raised from time to time to meet crises in the history of the settlement. During the Zulu War the regiment was required to guard the Natal Border and was not involved in any of the major battles of that war.

In September 1899, it was commanded by Major Robert W Evans and its strength on mobilisation, inclusive of all ranks, was 220 – surprisingly few for a fairly large town, but Durban provided other military units and not all of its urbanised citizens were horsemen.

In the latter part of the nineteenth century a substantial number of Australians settled in Natal. With a similar pioneering and cultural background, they integrated well with the locals who were able to make full use of their skill as horsemen. A NMR veteran recalled an incident when trying to break-in two big thoroughbreds which had just been commandeered. About 90% of the men present at the camp attempted to ride the horses but none lasted more than a few seconds. Then a new recruit,

'…a lean Australian, who looked like a Sunday school teacher, mild face and eyeglasses, said he would like to try. Everybody laughed, as the man looked so unlike the job, but he swung into the saddle, yelled, 'Let go!' and boy could he ride! That horse tried everything, even attempting to get among the seats on the grandstand, but in a very short and exciting time Le Mesurier (for that was his name) had that horse gentled, sweating and obeying his commands. He rested a little, and did the same with the other one. I have seen many good men with horses, but have yet to see one better than him.'[7]

The Border Mounted Rifles

Its members, who were farmers or traders, came from the south of the Colony. Like other Natalians, most of them could speak Zulu but being far from the Boer Republics few had ever heard Dutch spoken. The regiment came into being in 1884 as part of a rationalisation of the existing volunteer units. Its commanding officer in 1899 was Major JF Rethman MLA and its strength on mobilisation was 286.

In March 1899, the Governor, Sir Walter Hely-Hutchinson, made his annual visit to the training camps of the Volunteer regiments. Having wined and dined with the officers of the Natal Carbineers whose table was adorned with the glittering trophies of that illustrious Regiment, he came to the much simpler mess of the Border Mounted Rifles. Glancing at the table before him he said, 'This is very Spartan, Rethman, and what I like to see.' 'We are Rough but Ready,' was the reply. The Regimental Medical Officer, Captain HT Platt then placed a top boot complete with spur on the table and said, 'This is all the plate we have.' The Governor suggested the Regiment should adopt 'Rough but Ready' as its motto, and the Boot and Spur as its badge.[8] This was done and in later years, when the regiment amalgamated with the Natal Mounted Rifles, the motto and badge followed them.

The regiment was divided into four squadrons. No. 1 Squadron was led by Captain John Robinson (Galloping Jack) Royston who, later in the Boer War and in the First World War, was to serve with Australian units, ending his military service as a Brigadier-General.

The Umvoti Mounted Rifles

Founded in 1864, it was the smallest of the mounted regiments, its strength on mobilisation being only 89. On this little regiment, with its headquarters in Greytown, fell the duty of protecting the Colony against attack from the north-east. It was commanded by Major George Leuchars, an experienced officer with a profound knowledge of the difficult terrain which he had to protect.

All these regiments were armed with the obsolete .303 Martini-Enfield or Martini-Metford rifles without magazines giving them a much slower rate of fire than the Boer Mausers and British rifles. Their officers were elected, resulting in a good relationship between officers and men. Their fighting skills were more than a match for the Boers, and to this they added good discipline and local knowledge. They had the support of:

The Natal Police

Commanded by a Canadian, Col JG Dartnell, the Natal Police were usually mounted, and were scattered over the whole of Natal. At the start of the war they numbered 317. John Dartnell was born in Canada in 1838 and joined the British army when he was seventeen. He was posted to India, and served with great distinction in the Mutiny. He retired from the army with the rank of major in 1869 and moved to Natal where he intended to farm. In 1874 he was persuaded to accept an appointment as commander of the newly formed Natal Mounted Police. The Chief of Police and the Prime Minister in 1899, Albert Hime, were old friends. In their portraits they display all the gravitas one would expect from people of their standing in the late Victorian era, however they had quite a mischievous sense of humour. In 1880 work had begun on the construction of a harbour at Port Shepstone on the mouth of the Mzimkulu River in southern Natal. The then Governor, having embarked on a tour of inspection of southern Natal, decided to visit the harbour works at Port Shepstone. Included in his entourage were Dartnell, whose Police formed the Governor's guard, and Hime the Colonial Engineer. The construction of the harbour had been entrusted to one William Bazley who was one of those marvellous self-taught Victorian engineers who so often achieved the impossible. With this there came a degree of eccentricity. Where the estuary flowed into the sea there was an underwater reef that had to be removed by blasting. Wearing the diving suit provided by nature, Bazley would dive down to the reef, place the dynamite charges, and after the blast he would go down again to clear away the debris. He spent long hours underwater. His only aids in these diving operations were a tube which brought him oxygen from a primitive hand operated pump, and a long pole at the end of which was a large gaff hook. The pole he used as a prodder to drive away inquisitive sharks and, from time to time, to wake up the operator of the pump. When he was not diving he habitually carried sticks of dynamite in his pockets, which he would sometimes use as giant firecrackers, to enliven proceedings. The Governor, a nervous and delicate man, had been very frugal in the arrangements he made for his escort who were a little peeved by the lack of consideration shown towards them. It had been arranged that the Governor would be rowed in a barge from a river crossing several miles upstream, down to the river mouth where he would inspect the harbour works.

Dartnell and Hime felt that it would not do to have a naked Bazley emerging like Neptune from the sea to welcome the Governor, so they sent a message to Bazley that he should wear a frock coat and top hat. They also added that the Governor was very deaf, which was not true, and that Bazley should take care to speak up. The Governor was told that Bazley was a little eccentric and always carried in his pockets sticks of dynamite and detonators along with his pipe, tobacco and matches. Somehow Bazley achieved the impossible and obtained a frock coat and top hat in Port Shepstone.

With due pomp and ceremony the official party in the barge was rowed down to the harbour and when His Excellency stepped ashore, he was confronted by a strange figure dressed in a frock coat and top hat carrying a long pole at the end of which was a large hook. Bazley, never shy, closed in on the Governor and leaning forward, began shouting out in minute detail how he was constructing the harbour. Startled, and no doubt anxious about the dynamite, the Governor stepped back but Bazley followed, shouting even louder. This was too much for His Excellency who turned and fled back to the barge.[9]

Subsequently the expenditure on the harbour works at Port Shepstone was approved without query by the Governor. William Bazley was Bru de Wold's brother-in-law and his son George served as a trooper in the Border Mounted Rifles. As such he was incarcerated with his regiment in Ladysmith during the siege.

Natal Field Artillery
Led by Captain Dan Taylor, it had six obsolete 2.5 inch guns manned by 123 men. It was well trained and could be relied on to hit a target within the limited range of its guns.

The Natal Naval Volunteers
This unit had come into being in 1885. Britain had quarrelled with Russia about Afghanistan, and feared that the Russian navy might attack Durban! Heavy guns were therefore installed to protect the harbour. For some reason the Russian fleet remained in the Baltic and the attack did not materialise, but the unit remained, and by adapting the naval guns, it was able to play a significant role in the coming conflict.

The Durban Light Infantry

This regiment, which could trace its origins to the earliest days of the settlement, numbered 416 on mobilisation. Realising the importance of mounted men, it applied to be converted to a mounted unit but the British would not consent to the request.

The Natal Volunteer Medical Corps

A Volunteer Medical Corps with doctors, nurses and orderlies had been organised and on mobilisation accompanied the volunteers to the front. It was led by Dr James Hyslop who had trained in Edinburgh, Berlin, Vienna and Munich. He was a psychiatrist. This Corps provided the Volunteers with medical attention, which was not only better than that provided to the Regular army, but probably better than that which had ever been provided to any army in the field. Two of the doctors in the corps were Australians, Rupert Hornabrook from Adelaide and Robert Buntine from Melbourne. They were to achieve great distinction during the war.

The Natal Bridge Guards and Natal Royal Rifles

With a strength of 150 and 61 respectively these units were absorbed into other units in the first few months of the start of the war.

Scouts

Various scouting units, manned by the peoples of Natal, were formed during the war. They will be dealt with on an ad hoc basis.

The citizens of Natal hoped and prayed that war could be avoided, but if the Boers decided to go ahead with the invasion, they would defend themselves. It would not be for the glory of the Empire, nor to avenge Majuba, nor to show that they were better men than the Boers, nor for any British strategic interest. For them, it would be a struggle for survival. However, excellent as their Volunteers might be, because they were so heavily outnumbered, and because Britain was not prepared to permit them to raise further units, they were going to need some assistance.

GREAT BRITAIN

By June, 1899, it was obvious to the Natal government that the Transvaal intended to invade the country and it begged for help, but Britain, doubtless anxious not to get involved in a war, initially hesitated. However the British could not turn a blind eye to the events unfolding in Southern Africa forever. In July they sent two companies of engineers to South Africa. By 15 August they had 6,000 men in Natal. Following further representations by Natal, the British cabinet agreed on 8 September to double the strength of the Natal contingent by sending reinforcements from the army in India, which was achieved with remarkable efficiency. The result was that when war was declared, Britain had approximately 11,000 men in Natal aside from the 2,000 Colonial Volunteers. On that same day in September, the War Office gave its approval for the formation of the Imperial Light Horse, which would add a further 500 men to those preparing to defend the Colony. On 22 September, the War Office decided to call up an Army Corps of 42,000 men for service in South Africa, but this Corps had still to be raised, equipped and shipped, and it would therefore be a few months before they could provide any protection for the Colony.

However, although no one doubted the courage of the British, they did seem to have some serious weaknesses. Many of the Colonials having close relatives in Britain regarded the British as allies, whereas the British regarded the Colonials as subordinates whose opinions were not sought and who should do as they were told without question. It was not long before friction began to surface. Early in September, Major Rethman of the Border Mounted Rifles received from a friend in Johannesburg, details of the preparations being made by the Boers to invade Natal and the armaments including machine guns they were importing right under the noses of the British. Feeling the information was important, he immediately travelled to Pietermaritzburg and passed the report on to his Commandant, Col W. Royston. Royston, realizing the gravity of the intelligence, arranged a meeting with the Governor. The Governor requested the newly arrived commander of the British army in Natal, General Penn Symons, to join them. The General jeered at the information, making caustic comments as to the usual Colonial exaggerations. The Major, stung to the quick, expressed himself 'very forthrightly', and the Governor had to intervene several times.[10] The information turned out to be correct, and the grave of General Penn Symons is to be found in Dundee, near the site of the first battle of the War.

Apart from this unfortunate attitude to the Colonials, the training the British troops received did not teach them the skills they would need in the coming war. Their experience of warfare had been gained in the confined spaces of Europe or against poorly armed tribesmen. Now they had to contend with a mobile, unseen enemy, equipped with weapons superior to their own. Much of their training was done on the barrack square and on the parade ground, where they learnt how to perform various drill movements with clockwork precision. Much of the rest of their time was spent cleaning their uniforms, polishing buttons, scrubbing floors and other menial tasks. Very little effort was made to improve their marksmanship, their shooting being limited to firing, annually, 200 rounds at a fixed target at a known distance. No attempt was made to teach them the art of camouflage, or to impress upon them the importance of ensuring they should not be seen by the enemy. They were, in the words of a contemporary, '...indifferent shots, careless of cover, slow to comprehend what was taking place, or to grasp the whereabouts of the enemy, always getting surprised or lost, helpless without their officers. In a word, the British soldier was well disciplined but ill-trained.' Their regimental officers, though capable, also lacked the training which would have enabled them to improve the effectiveness of their units, and what applied to these officers applied in an even more marked degree to their generals. The army had to learn on the battlefield what it should have learnt in training.[11]

Serious as it was, lack of proper training was not the only difficulty the British faced. Their intelligence department had been starved of funds, the budget for the whole Empire being smaller than that of the same department in the Transvaal Republic, with the obvious result that British commanders often lacked the information they needed to make informed decisions. Counter-intelligence was virtually non-existent and Boer spies were able to operate unhindered. Furthermore, no proper maps had been prepared of the country over which the war was likely to be fought. The excuse given for this omission was that such activity might be dangerous as it might offend Boer farmers![12] There *were* some Dutch farmers in northern Natal, but they were in a minority and they could not have prevented the country being mapped by the British army's survey section which would have had the full protection of the Natal Police had this been necessary.

Even if they chose to ignore Colonial advice, the British should have noticed that apart from a few policemen and the artillery, the entire Boer army was mounted. Informed opinion was that one mounted man was worth at least three men on foot. Three quarters of the British troops in Natal were infantry. If this was not bad enough, British numbers were inflated by a substantial number of non-combatants attached to each unit, whereas the numbers given for Boers referred to men with rifles.

The training of the cavalry also left much to be desired. Each day the men would take the horses out of their stables for a couple of hours exercise, which generally involved schooling to execute various parade ground manoeuvres, after which they were returned to their stables to be fed and groomed. Leo Amery of *The Times* commented: 'Of the things that are vital in war – the limit of a horse's capacity to cover long distances and to carry heavy weights, the minimum of food, water and rest it requires for continuous effort, the precautions by which its strength can be husbanded – they had no inkling.'[13] Their horses also tended to be too large and heavy for the conditions on the South African *veld*, and they were burdened with much heavy and largely unnecessary equipment. Once again they made no attempt to obtain local advice and imported into South Africa many unsuitable horses thereby wasting money and severely restricting and sometimes endangering mounted units.

Duncan McKenzie was one of the best mounted men on either side. He chose as his mount 'Inspector' a part-bred (seven eighths thoroughbred) entire, who had already covered his book of mares for the 1899 season. At 15.3 hands high, he was a little taller than most of the Volunteers' horses. Close coupled, he was tough, endowed with both speed and stamina, and to these characteristics he added a wonderful temperament. As an entire he would be able to maintain condition and fitness, where a gelding might need extra feeding and rest. Obviously the whole army could not have been mounted on such a horse, however he was the type of horse which the British should have sought, and by so doing they would have avoided such blunders as buying thousands of Argentinian heavy cobs which were, for all practical purposes, useless in South African conditions.

The artillery, though well-trained and disciplined, was in danger of being out-ranged by the Boer guns.

The Imperial Light Horse

In granting its consent to the raising of the Imperial Light Horse (ILH), the War Office limited the numbers to 500, and required that the regiment be commanded by an Imperial officer. Col Scott Chisholme of the 5th Lancers was appointed its first commander.

In a few days 3,500 applications to join the regiment had been received at its recruiting office in Pietermaritzburg. Karri Davies and Aubrey Woolls Sampson were now in the fortunate position of being able to choose their men, and they took care to choose the best. Since the recruiting took place in Pietermaritzburg many of the applicants were locals, however from the start the regiment attracted men from many different backgrounds and countries, including Australia, Canada, New Zealand, Britain and Ireland. Some had worked in Johannesburg and others had only just arrived in South Africa, however all were determined to resist Kruger's desire to chase the British out of southern Africa. Despite their diverse origins they blended well together and relations between all ranks was excellent. They were divided into six squadrons, each with 86 men including NCOs. They were armed with second-hand, single-shot, obsolete rifles which had a Lee-Metford bore and Martini-Henri action. These were supplied from stock by the Natal government. No bayonets were issued, and they were only to receive modern rifles with magazines after the relief of Ladysmith.

The Imperial government agreed to pay members of the regiment at the same rate as other Volunteers, but it was up to the regiment itself to fund its establishment costs, the principal items being the provision of horses, saddlery and uniforms for the men.[15] It should be remembered that the Natal Volunteers had also to provide their own horses, saddlery and buy their uniforms, but many of the ILH recruits lacked the means to equip themselves. The £4,000 which the Reform Committee had given to Karri Davies and Aubrey Woolls Samson to pay their fines after the Jameson Raid was donated to a fund

Officers of the Imperial Light Horse. Standing: Lt C Webb, Lt PH Normand, Capt RW Barnes, Capt JE Orr, Capt CH Mullins, Lt MW Curry, Lt D Campbell, Lt R Johnstone, Lt AE Brabant. Seated: Surgeon Maj WTF Davies, Maj A Woolls Sampson, Col J Scott Chisholme, Maj W Karri Davies, Capt JC Knapp, Lt J Donaldson. Front: Lt WL Forbes, Lt DH Huntley, Capt CH Fowler, Lt FHP Cresswell, Lt AD Shore.

to meet establishment costs. However more money was needed. The horses alone would cost about £10,000. So Woolls Sampson approached his friends Percy Fitzpatrick and Lionel Phillips for help, and through them received an offer from the German mining house, Wernher Beit & Co., to pay the balance of the establishment costs of the 500 strong regiment.[16]

The money given by Wernher, Beit & Co. was a single donation given unconditionally. When, after the Relief of Ladysmith, the company was asked for another donation to replace horses which had died or been eaten, it responded that in making its original contribution it did not intend to assume the position of sponsors of the British Empire![17] It did however agree to lend money for the purchase of the replacement horses. When, after audit, the British government repaid this loan of approximately £25,000, Wernher, Beit & Co. donated the money to a fund formed to assist members of the regiment who had been disabled by wounds and the widows of those who had been killed.[18]

In Pietermaritzburg Karri and Sambo were reunited with an old friend, Charlie Mullins. Charles Herbert Mullins was born in Grahamstown in the Eastern Cape in 1869. I doubt if there is any person who knows the Mullins clan of Grahamstown who would not agree that this family can truly be described as 'the salt of the earth' – an overworked expression perhaps, but nonetheless very apt. Over the generations their contribution to education in that part of the world has been enormous. However, in all things, this family has always contributed much to the society in which they lived. For example, Charlie's brother was a surgeon and served as such throughout the Boer War with the British forces, and later with the South African Medical Corps in France in 1917/18.

Charlie Mullins, on completing his schooling in Grahamstown, went to Keble College, Oxford, read law, and in due course was called to the Bar by the Inner Temple, and practised as a barrister. In 1894 he moved to Johannesburg where he practised as a solicitor in the firm Bell and Mullins. He was appalled by what would today be described as the human rights abuses of the Kruger government. He joined the Reform movement and became a close friend of Karri and Sambo, and he was among those reformists who were arrested and imprisoned after the Jameson Raid. He paid the fine imposed, and on his release went to Pietermaritzburg, where he became a partner in the firm of solicitors, Hudson, Hutchinson and Mullins. When war appeared inevitable, Charlie Mullins, though by nature a man of peace, gave Karri and Aubrey his full support and along with them is regarded as one of the driving forces behind the formation of the Imperial Light Horse.

Horses for the Regiment were bought in Natal, Pondoland, Basutoland (now Lesotho) and, cheekily, in the Transvaal. They cost between £20 and £50 each and were generally of good quality. Some were unschooled, but after a few days under Australian Rough-riders they were ready for duty. The purchase of saddlery virtually exhausted stocks in Pietermaritzburg and some was of poor quality.

In the British army it usually took six months to train a mounted man to the stage where he would be fit to take the field. With war imminent, that which would normally take months had to be achieved in weeks. Training began immediately. In the morning there was mounted drill and the grooming of horses. In the afternoon the troopers drilled on foot and practised shooting. Mounted training was sited at Foxhill on Pietermaritzburg's southern outskirts.

Charles Herbert Mullins VC.

The Colonel began by requiring the squadrons to advance in parallel lines across the *veld*. 'F' Squadron unexpectedly encountered a donga (dry water course), and in the process of negotiating it, got themselves hopelessly jumbled up. Scott Chisholme, not knowing what had caused the problem, saw the squadron disintegrate into a disorganised tangle of men and galloped across to them.

'Who commands this squadron?' he demanded.

'I do, Sir!' answered the Squadron-Leader while extricating himself from the others.

Chisholme looked at the shambles for a second or two before galloping back to his original position. As he did so he was heard to mutter, 'poor bloody men.'

The attitude of the Colonel soon mellowed. The men were capable, intelligent and enthusiastic – perhaps a bit too enthusiastic, and he was even moved to warn a group at work: 'Look here, you men, there is such a thing as being over-keen. If you are not careful half of you will be killed in your first fight.'

When the Colonel went to the shooting range to see how the recruits were getting on, he could hardly believe his eyes. Turning to Regimental Sergeant-Major M Dryden, who had also been in the 5th Lancers, the crack shots of the army in India, he said, 'Surely this is remarkable shooting!' and received the answer, 'Yes Sir, we never saw shooting like that in the 5th'.[20]

The Chief of Staff designate in Natal, General Sir Archibald Hunter, in evidence given to the War Commission after the war, described his first meeting with the Regiment which Karri and Sambo had founded:

'The first time I ever saw them was on the first day I arrived at Pietermaritzburg. It was the first day they had ever been on parade as a regiment; up to that time they had only paraded as squadrons under their squadron leaders; it was the first day that Colonel Chisholme had ever had them under his command. Sir Walter Hely Hutchinson drove up to the ground, as he wanted to see them, and he asked me to go round and look at them. I had not long come from a tour abroad, where I had seen nothing but the picked guards of Sweden, Denmark, Russia, Prussia, and Saxony, and there was nothing I saw on the Continent then, and nothing I have ever seen here, except the Irish Constabulary, that could put a patch on them. You can tell men when you look at them. Every man was a picture of manhood; he was beaming with intelligence. They were a great success, a most undoubted success. They were the finest corps I have ever seen anywhere in my life.'

When war was declared on 13 October 1899, they were still in Pietermaritzburg but were taken to the front within the next few days. The senior officers under Col. Scott Chisholme were Maj Woolls Sampson, Maj Karri Davies, Capt Charles Mullins, Maj Doveton and Lt Bottomley. Over the next few months there were promotions and other officers came to the fore.

The Imperial Light Horse was the prototype of scores of mounted regiments which were raised in South Africa during the war. The most prominent in the Natal Campaign being The South African Light Horse, Thornycroft's Mounted Infantry, Bethune's Mounted Infantry, the Imperial Light Infantry, as well as various scouting units and the Natal Volunteer Ambulance Corps. Shortly before hostilities broke out, Col W Royston heard that a ship carrying members of the British Indian Army back to England on leave would be calling at Durban. He persuaded many of these men to disembark at the southern Africa port, with the result that they provided the leavening of British officers which the British authorities required before they would consent to the raising of the volunteer regiments which were to make a contribution to the defence of Natal out of all proportion to their numbers.

The Imperial Light Horse on parade in Pietermaritzburg.

A serious mistake made by the British was to disregard those thousands of Natalians who, though not members of one of the established regiments, were keen to contribute to the defence of their homeland. Duncan McKenzie has this to say about them:

'If the Colonists had been called out, they would have formed some of the best irregular Cavalry in the world. They were good shots, and would have been well mounted on their own horses. They would have consisted mostly of farmers who understood the Boer ways, and would have been equal in every respect to the Boers themselves. Had this been done, and five or six thousand Colonials been brigaded under their own officers, the Boers would have been driven beyond the Tugela in a very short time, and I feel quite sure there would have been no siege of Ladysmith.'[21]

Lord Milner discouraged the recruitment of volunteers in South Africa, it being his opinion that the arming of such volunteers would achieve no more than provide additional arms for the enemy. This prejudice might explain why the arms made available to the Volunteers were obsolete and would have been of little interest to the Boers.

It was also unfortunate that the British treated lightly the offer made in June 1899 by Australia, New Zealand and Canada to send mounted troops to South Africa. These countries realised before Britain that the Boer Republics had every intention of going to war and also that it would be mounted men who could best thwart Boer ambitions.

Despite Boer superiority in numbers and equipment, they were going to struggle to drive the 'Rooineks' into the sea, and it was not only because thousands of British soldiers would, in a few months, be on their way to South Africa from England.

CHAPTER SIX

Invasion of Northern Natal

• ◆ •

'May the Vierkleur soon wave over a free harbour.'

TELEGRAM SENT BY GEN LOUIS BOTHA TO PRESIDENT KRUGER,
10 OCTOBER 1899

ON Monday 9 October 1899, the Colonial Secretary in London received a telegram from
the State Secretary of the Transvaal Republic, FW Reitz. It demanded that troops on the
borders of the Republic be instantly withdrawn, that all reinforcements which had arrived
within the last year should leave South Africa, and that those upon the sea should be
sent back without landing. Failure to make a satisfactory response to the demand within forty-
eight hours would be regarded by the Transvaal Government as a declaration of war by
Her Majesty's Government.

FW Reitz disliked the English with a passion which at times made even Paul Kruger
look pro-British. He had been a judge in the Orange Free State and on the death of President
Brand in 1887, was elected President. In 1895 he became ill and resigned, the Presidency
being taken over by President Steyn. On his recovery, Reitz went to the Transvaal and was
appointed State Secretary. Long before gold was discovered on the Witwatersrand
or Cecil Rhodes had made his fortune, and at a time when Britain had recognized the
independence of the Transvaal, Reitz was working for the expulsion of the English from
Southern Africa. His message was spread by every possible means; in the press, the pulpit,
schools and colleges and in the *Volksraad*. One prominent Afrikaner wrote, '*Believe me, the day
on which FW Reitz sat down to pen his ultimatum to Britain was the proudest and happiest moment
of his life, and one which had for long years been looked forward to by him with eager longing
and expectation.*'[2]

Reitz knew the British could not and would not comply with the demand, and the
following day, the Colonial Office advised him that it was not prepared to comply with the
ultimatum. So it was that at 5 p.m. on the afternoon of Wednesday, 11 October 1899, the
Boer Republics went to war with the British Empire.

As we have seen, the invasion and conquest of Natal had long formed part of the strategy
of the Transvaal government. Revenue from the gold mines had provided the money to
purchase the necessary arms, however the timing of the invasion was governed by a more
mundane issue. If thirty to fifty thousand mounted men were to invade Natal, they would take
with them thirty to fifty thousand horses, which had to be fed each day. As the Boers carried
no feed as such for their horses, they had to rely on grazing the *veld* and this would only be
possible after the first spring rains. They therefore had no choice but to wait until the spring

of 1899 before launching the invasion. By 27 September it was felt the time to act had arrived, and the Transvaal called out its *Kommandos*.

Trains leaving the Transvaal were packed with refugees fleeing to the British Colonies. On 29 September, the railways were taken over by the state and all civilian rail traffic to Natal was stopped. The trains were now packed with *Kommandos* travelling to the Natal border. On the 30th alone twenty-six military trains left Johannesburg and Pretoria for the Natal frontier. In response to events in the Transvaal, all the Natal Volunteers were ordered to mobilise on 29 September, ostensibly for 10 days training.

Among the first *Kommandos* leaving Pretoria for the Natal border that day was seventeen year-old Deneys Reitz, son of the Secretary of State. Heavy traffic on the railway resulted in the train taking three days to reach Sandspruit, 10 miles from the Natal border. Here was mustered the largest body of mounted men ever seen in South Africa and what a confident crowd they were. Writing after the war, Deneys, loyal to his father, describes the British Government as the chief culprit and then continued, '*but the Transvaalers were also spoiling for a fight, and from what I saw in Pretoria during the weeks that preceded the ultimatum, I feel sure that the Boers would in any case have insisted on a rupture.*'[3]

Deneys Reitz was not the only observer of events in Pretoria. Teise Ndhlovu came from the Ladysmith district and was fluent in Zulu, Sotho, English and Dutch. For some time prior to 1899 he had worked as special groom to Kommandant General Piet Joubert. As such Teise would regularly accompany the General and hold his horse when he was visiting. Prior to the ultimatum they went to Kruger's residence in Pretoria where Joubert found Kruger seated on his veranda. Quietly holding Joubert's horse, Teise listened to the conversation on the veranda and later reported its content:

'Kruger urged that they should get everything ready to fight the English, but General Joubert replied that he had better arrange matters peacefully; that he had been in England and knew the power of England. The Boers might succeed for a time but end in being beaten. There then came onto the scene Mrs. Kruger, who it appears, had been listening to the conversation, and said, 'Kruger, do you agree that we should not fight the English? You had better put on my clothes, stay at home and do my work, and I will put on your clothes and lead the Burgers to fight against the fordermde English.' This speech altered his mind and he decided to fight.'[4]

Teise abandoned his employment with Joubert, and made his way to Natal where he arrived on 8 October 1899. Here he immediately enlisted as a scout. We shall come across him again.

While Teise was on his way to Natal and the *Kommandos* were waiting for the spring rains, young Reitz and his friends were enjoying camping on the *veld* at Sandspruit and looking forward to the expected excitement of the coming weeks. In Pretoria the Attorney General, Jan Smuts, and the State Secretary Reitz were frustrated by the delay and deplored the lack of action. But then neither was familiar with conditions in Natal.

Young Freda Schlosberg went with her family to see their local *Kommando* leave for the Front. Before the train steamed off, their Field Cornet, holding the Transvaal flag, made a long speech which was loudly applauded. She noted, 'Few, very few tears were shed by the women at the station. Why should they weep? The war would not last long and their men would soon return triumphant, after having driven the English into the sea and taken over their farms and homes.'[5]

On 2 October, President Steyn called out the Free State *Kommandos* and a few days later it rained. By the 9th the grass was sprouting and at long last the Secretary of State could sign the ultimatum.

At Sandspruit on 10 October, a great parade was held to honour Paul Kruger's birthday and great was the excitement when General Joubert told them of the ultimatum. Deneys Reitz wrote, '*The great throng stood in its stirrups and shouted itself hoarse, and it was not until long after the Kommandant General and his retinue had fought their way through the crowd that the Kommandos began to disperse.*'[6]

Each Boer was issued with rations for five days and early on the morning of the 12th they moved off – '*As far as the eye could see the plain was alive with horsemen, guns, and cattle all steadily going forward to the frontier. The scene was a stirring one, and I shall never forget riding to war with that great host.*'[6]

Deneys Reitz had a fairly accurate idea of the troops which opposed them, believing about seven thousand troops were at Dundee 60 miles away, and 40 miles further on at Ladysmith, were a further six or seven thousand. The Boers knew Britain had no troops to withdraw from the Natal frontier, and that with such a disposition, it was highly unlikely that there were any plans to invade the Transvaal. Indeed, Britain had no clear idea as to how its Colonies could be defended.

When the probability of war was finally realised, the British military establishment at last began to seriously consider how the Colony might be protected. Northern Natal is in the shape of a triangle, at the northern apex of which is the hamlet of Charlestown. To the west are the Drakensberg Mountains and the Free State, and in the east the Buffalo River formed the boundary with the Transvaal. Between Charlestown and Newcastle, the first substantial town in Northern Natal, are three mountain passes – Laing's Nek, Majuba and Ingogo Heights. General Sir William Penn Symons, who in May had been appointed commander of the army in Natal, rejected these passes as possible defensive positions as the defenders could easily be cut off and surrounded by the Boers invading from east and west. By 13 September, he had devised a plan. Once the additional troops arrived from India, Natal should be occupied as far as Newcastle, where his troops would have no trouble beating off any attack.

As Britain had doubled the strength of the army in Natal, it was decided that a more senior general should assume command. On 6 September, General Sir George White VC, formerly Commander-in-Chief in India, was appointed commander in Natal. He had shown himself to be a brave, cautious and able leader and, though 63 and a little lame from a riding accident, was thought to be eminently suitable for the task ahead. He was given no clear directives by the War Office.

Sir George hastened to South Africa and arrived in Durban on 7 October 1899. He spent one day in Durban, acquainting himself with the latest developments with respect to the troops from India and making arrangements for their transfer upcountry. The next day he travelled to Pietermaritzburg to meet the Governor, Sir Walter Hely-Hutchinson, and Penn Symons. During the sea voyage to South Africa, the old General had spent many hours trying to work out where the British forces should draw their defensive line. Given that most of his troops were slow-moving infantry, it appeared to Sir George that the border at Charlestown, the three mountain passes, Newcastle and the coalfields extending down to Dundee were all indefensible against the highly mobile Boer forces. At Ladysmith, the railway from the coast divided, with one line going west to the Free State and the other north east to the Transvaal. At this road and rail junction the British army had a camp and had accumulated a considerable quantity of stores. There were also railway workshops at Ladysmith which could be useful to the military. Initially, Sir George thought the Biggarsberg range of hills between Ladysmith and Dundee might form a suitable defensive line, but the absence of a reliable supply of water caused him to abandon this idea. It seemed he would have to make a stand at Ladysmith. At his meeting with the Governor and Penn Symons, his plan was turned on its head.

Before Sir George arrived in Natal, Penn Symons had already taken 4,000 men from Ladysmith to Dundee, thereby splitting the army in two. In addition, the Governor begged Sir George not to abandon northern Natal – firstly, because of the importance of its coalfields, access to which was vital to British interests as both naval and mercantile ships relied on the bunkering facilities at Durban for their coal-fired steam engines. Secondly, if Britain appeared weak and unable to maintain order, conflict might break out between various groups of Zulus. The Boers were adept at exploiting tribal rivalries to acquire land for themselves, as had occurred in northern Zululand in 1877 (see Chapter Four). He must have known that from the border at Charlestown to the sea lived British subjects of all colours, who looked to Britain for protection, and who in an invasion, would lose everything. We shall see that Sir George White, throughout the time he was in Natal, took into account the interests of the civilian residents when making military decisions. Penn Symons was adamant that with a few more troops in Dundee he would have no trouble dealing with the Boers. Sir George was not entirely convinced, but being new to the country he bowed to pressure and agreed to leave Penn Symons and his troops in Dundee. In addition, he despatched to Dundee the 1st Royal Irish Fusiliers which had only just arrived from India. On 11 October, the day the ultimatum expired, General White arrived in Ladysmith.

Two days before, there had occurred the display of Boer and Colonial shooting skills described in Chapter One. This great humanitarian exercise to rescue 7,000 men from behind enemy lines was conceived and executed by officials of the Natal Government. Neither Lord Milner nor Chamberlain had anything to do with the plan. The official who carried ultimate responsibility for the venture was SO Samuelson, the Natal Under-Secretary of Native Affairs and Marwick's immediate superior. Samuelson has been described as Marwick's 'bosses.' However valid such terminology might be in some trade union circles, it is completely inappropriate in a society which did not have British class distinctions and prejudices. Marwick and Wheelwright would have had the same regard for Samuelson as they would have had for a competent captain of a sports team of which they were members.

Samuel Olaf Samuelson was an extraordinary man. The son of an early Zululand missionary, he grew up in that country during the reign of King Cetshwayo. In due course he went to school in Cape Town, where apart from other achievements he mastered Latin, Greek, Xhosa, Sesotho, Portuguese, Norwegian, Dutch, Italian and Hebrew. However it was in his knowledge of Zulu customs and the classical Zulu language that he was pre-eminent, and it is a tragedy that so little of his knowledge was recorded for posterity.[7]

Marwick was born in Richmond, Natal, to a family with Scottish antecedents. As a local he knew how Zulu society was organised and how disciplined its people were. His achievement during the walk was to get the Zulus themselves to organise and control the 7,000 people moving to Natal. His and Wheelwright's main function was to decide on the route to be followed and to liaise with the Boers along the way.

Much of the culture of the Black peoples of Natal has been destroyed over the past 100 years, so it might be appropriate to mention a little about them as they were a century ago.

When Henry Francis Fynn arrived at the *kraal* of King Shaka, he found a people who were content with their own civilisation and culture, which was perfectly adapted to the world in which they lived. Central to their society was the family or *Kraal*. It was a patriarchal society in which the head of each family was the eldest male. A wife was expected to always treat her husband with respect and to obey his commands. She managed the household, looked after the children and prepared the meals. In return, the husband was expected to treat her courteously at all times and to thank her for her efforts on behalf of the family. The husband was expected to perform those duties imposed on the family by the king or the local chief, to maintain the fabric of the family buildings and stock enclosures, as well as to oversee the care of the family's livestock. All dealings with the outside world were carried out by him and, except for a few exceptions, he owned all family property.

Children were taught at an early age to respect their parents and elders and to carry out their instructions promptly and without demur. From about the age of seven a young boy would begin his training for life in Zulu society. He would start with some simple task such as looking after the calves, and graduate from there to looking after larger animals, then to hunting and finally came his military training. Boys learned strict codes of behaviour. As examples, the elderly were treated with deference, and strangers were always to be greeted and treated courteously. They would be taught songs and many of their tasks would be performed while singing. They heard their history and learned the stories of their national heroes. In this way they were taught how to be brave and loyal citizens of their country. Girls would help their mothers with household chores and as they got older they would help with the more difficult tasks such as hoeing the fields and cooking. Women lived lives separate from the men, and girls, like boys, were taught their duties to society. Complex rules governed courtship procedures.

Governing family relations was the custom of lobolo. Often described as a dowry paid to buy a wife, it was much more complex than that. It ensured that everyone had a place in society and were part of a family. No one starved. If a young Zulu wished to marry, he would first discuss the matter with his family, who would then send messengers bearing gifts to the family of the proposed bride. Negotiations would decide how many lobolo cattle would be paid. Once this had been done, the local chieftain would indicate where the new family might build their home and what land they might cultivate. Communal grazing was available for any cattle the young suitor may acquire. If a husband ill-treated his wife she would, with her children, return to her father and his care. The husband would lose all rights over his children, including the right to receive lobolo when his daughters married. If the wife misbehaved, the husband would not only keep the children but could demand the return of lobolo from his father-in-law. Both the groom's and the bride's families therefore had a strong interest in ensuring the union was successful.

Wealth was measured in cattle and it was some time before the early settlers were able to persuade the Zulus that money had value. It was considered ridiculous that a coin or piece of paper with an image of some unknown stranger should have value. Initially all trade was by barter.

Inevitably there were some tribesmen who, attracted by the perceived advantages of western civilisation, went to Durban and elsewhere to work. Generally they did not regard this as a permanent change of lifestyle and retained their tribal links. They kept their homes in Zululand where the women and children continued to live a traditional rural life. This explains why in 1899 there were 11,935 Zulu men in Durban and only 601 women. (see Chapter Four).

The developing goldmines in Johannesburg needed labour badly, but they were faced with two difficulties. Firstly, the Transvaal government was not prepared to allow additional Blacks to settle in the country; however, they were prepared to issue a short-term work permit on the expiry of which the worker would have to leave the country. Secondly, the Black people from the rural areas were not seeking permanent employment. The gold mines therefore had no choice but to employ short-term migrant labour. This was not a situation created by them, neither was it in their interests. The recruits came into an environment completely foreign to them. They did not understand Dutch or English and could not read or write. To impart to them the necessary skills and knowledge to enable them to function properly was a costly process, and no sooner had it been achieved, than the men would leave to be replaced by a batch of fresh recruits. This made their labour expensive. Further, if the mines were to recruit any workers from Zululand or Natal, they had to tempt them with wages which would persuade them to give up, for a time, their pleasant lifestyle.

One factor did assist the mines in recruiting labour: a young Zulu had not only to obtain the consent of his father to his marriage, but he had also to rely on his father to provide lobolo. It was the father, as kraalhead, who would decide when the son would marry and have children. In the nineteenth century a Zulu woman would be considered ready for marriage at 25 and a man at 30 or older. Into this world came the gold mines seeking labour. If a man worked on the gold mines for six months and managed his affairs prudently, he was able to save enough money to buy the lobolo cattle himself. No longer would he be beholden to his father. The long term effect on their society was profound and not always for the better.

In 1899 the gold mines offered recruits a package which included travelling from their homes and back, full board and lodging, sport and other entertainment at weekends and a salary of three pounds and six shillings a month. To put this in perspective, in 1922, when the value of the pound had sunk significantly below its 1899 value, the writer's father started work in Pondoland just south of the Natal border. He could read, write and speak English, Zulu and Pondo. His employer gave him full board during the week, his annual subscription to the local cricket club, and a monthly salary of one pound and ten shillings; i.e. less than half the salary which a Zulu or Pondo recruit on the mines would have received 23 years earlier. In 1900 a young man in rural England, seeking work on a farm, could expect to receive by way of remuneration his board and lodging, boots and clothing, and a sovereign at Christmas.

The gold mines had given to young Zulu men the power to marry soon after reaching maturity. In contrast, in those times, most young Colonials had to work for many years before they could afford to marry.[8]

When Marwick's group settled down for the night on their great walk to Natal, the miners would no doubt have sung their songs, which would have included passages about their adventures on the mines and their walk home. Marwick, Wheelwright, and the six policemen would have had the privilege of listening to a unique and awesome choral concert.

Before leaving Johannesburg, Marwick and Wheelwright, on behalf of the miners, transmitted £9,500 to the their families. An additional £10,000 was entrusted by the miners to them for safe-keeping until they reached Natal. The miners had sufficient money on them to buy food during the journey, and because of the disciplined manner in which they conducted themselves, Boer farmers and traders were only too pleased to sell them food. There were a few minor incidents along the way which were sorted out by the Zulus themselves.

The delivery of the Ultimatum put considerable pressure on the walkers to get through Boer lines before the hostilities began. On 10 October 1899, they were close to Standerton where Marwick was able to get some of the stragglers onto a train going to the Natal border. On the 11th they were advised by the *Landrost* (magistrate) at Standerton that the Ultimatum would expire in a few hours and that a state of war was imminent. They pressed on towards the Boer camp at Sandspruit where they found the Boer army had already left. Only the Irish *Kommando* remained. They were said to be tidying up the camp. Marwick, somewhat naively it must be said, tried to send a telegram from the Sandspruit post office. The postal official pointed out that he was an enemy who should be shot and he was only saved by the intervention of their police guard. Marwick was able to get some further stragglers onto a train and the main group set off hot foot for Volksrust and the border.

At Volksrust they were challenged but once again luck was with them. Marwick recognised an officer in the Transvaal Artillery who, although Dutch, had previously lived in Natal, where he had been a member of the Umvoti Mounted Rifles. He was able to smooth things over and see them on their way. They followed a detachment of the Transvaal artillery through the mountain passes, but after passing Majuba they were again stopped by a Boer *Kommando*. Once again the artillery officer came to their rescue and persuaded the Kommandant to let them through.

On 14 October, they set off before dawn, passed through the Boer lines, and marched without stopping to Newcastle. Here they received rations from the Magistrate, who, as the district representative of the Natal government, had authority to give food to the indigent. As they were leaving the town, the vanguard of the Boer *Kommandos* was entering it. They only had time for a brief rest that night before setting off again. They were able to keep ahead of the Boers and during the day groups would split off to take different routes to their homes.

At about 5 o'clock on the afternoon of Sunday, 15 October, Marwick and the remaining marchers, who now numbered about 1,000, arrived at Hattingh's Spruit station where they were able to entrain for home. Most of these remaining refugees would have been Pondos whose homes lay to the south of Natal and who would use Natal's transport system to travel to and from Johannesburg.

Marwick arrived in Pietermaritzburg the following day to a hero's welcome and much praise in the local press. The Prime Minister telegraphed his congratulations. To pluck 7,000 people out of enemy territory was indeed a remarkable achievement by the two young Natal officials. However, all those participating in this long walk deserve praise. For nine days and nights, without shelter and in all weathers, this great throng of people had by their orderly and disciplined behaviour succeeded in reaching the safety of Natal. Samuelson and the Natal government also deserve credit for the part they played. On 5 October 1899, when Marwick advised Samuelson by telegram of his plan to walk with the miners to Natal, telegrams were taking up to four hours to get through. Samuelson had to consider the safety of the walkers for whom he was responsible, and as the proposed walk was to take place in a foreign country, it was necessary to consult the Governor before taking action. The Prime Minister therefore saw the Governor, who raised no objection to the plan. Samuelson telegraphed approval through to Marwick, who received the consent that same day. Samuelson also confirmed the arrangements for the journey and gave Marwick some useful advice which contributed much to the success of the enterprise. On one point Marwick was unable to comply precisely with his instructions. Only Zulus and other Blacks from Natal were supposed to be part of the group. There were some Pondos and Swazis following the same route and in practice it was impossible to exclude them.

As we have seen, the Prime Minister had sent a telegram of support to Marwick before the march. Both the Prime Minister and Samuelson urged Marwick not to incur unnecessary expenditure, an instruction which has been portrayed as meanness. In colonial Natal this was regarded as good governance and with war imminent money was tight. Another criticism is that neither sent a telegram wishing Marwick 'good luck'. Reliance on luck was never a feature of the Natal administration.

Very few bureaucrats would make such a bold decision as that made by Samuelson in authorising the walk. Certainly there was no one in the Cape who was prepared to do so. The migrant workers from the Cape were left to find their own way home and what happened to them no one will ever know. The £10 000 entrusted to Marwick and Wheelwright was duly paid to the correct recipients shortly after their arrival in Natal. No one expected anything else.

Marwick was asked by Samuelson to write a full report of the rescue of the migrant workers and when it was completed, a copy was despatched to the Colonial Office in London, where Chamberlain commented, 'Mr Marwick and others responsible for carrying out the arrangements for the return of the natives deserve great credit for its success.' The expense incurred in the rescue was paid by Natal not Britain.

Among those congratulating Marwick, was Joseph Baynes, a member of the Natal Legislative Assembly, who farmed in Marwick's home district of Richmond. In a letter to Marwick he said, '*We have reason to be proud of the stand taken by our Colony in this serious crisis and proud, very proud of our Volunteers, but I think there is no act greater than your achievement.*'[9]

The first two weeks in October 1899, were very traumatic for the people of Natal. Many found it difficult to believe that they were about to be attacked by the Boer Republics. After all, President Kruger had stated at the June conference with Milner, '…we shall never be the attacking party on another man's land.' Kruger was subtle enough to avoid stating that he regarded the whole of Southern Africa as his land.

While Marwick and the miners were on their walk, a former Prime Minister of Natal, Sir Harry Escombe, was touring the northern part of the Colony telling people there was no immediate danger of war. In the end, to avoid Boer patrols, he had to make an undignified escape in a post cart disguised as an old woman.

The volunteer unit in northern Natal, initially known as the Buffalo Guards, was absorbed by the Natal Carbineers. At the beginning of September 1899 the squadron of the Carbineers, based in Dundee and who numbered about 40, were the only military force guarding Natal north of Ladysmith. The citizens of Dundee, alarmed by reports of Boer *Kommandos* assembling on Natal's borders, decided to form a Town Guard and 150 men enrolled. The proprietor of the Masonic Hotel was elected commandant and to assist him six lieutenants were also elected. For two weeks they drilled, built fortifications and had rifle practice. Many were crack shots.

On 25 September, the first of General Penn Symons' Imperial troops arrived. Into Dundee came the 18th Hussars, the Royal Dublin Fusiliers, the Leicester Regiment, the King's Royal Rifles (the 60th) and finally, on 16 October, the Royal Inniskillings, who had been sent on from Ladysmith by Sir George White. There were some mounted infantry attached to the Leicesters, the Rifles and the Dublins. With them were three batteries of artillery, and two hospital corps. Completing the military were some Natal Police under Col. Dartnell and of course the local Carbineers. All in all just over 4,000 men, fewer than Reitz expected, but nonetheless a substantial force.

Fleeing before the advancing Boers, many of Newcastle's residents headed for Dundee. The rain which ensured adequate grazing for the Boers only added to the misery of the refugees. Gerard Bailey, the Anglican vicar of St. James church kept a diary, in which he described the plight of the civilians on Northern Natal. He was particularly moved by the misery of the women and children. On 1 October his wife had left for Durban the couple thinking they would only be parted for a few weeks. Alone in his house, Gerard took in as many refugees as he could and formed a Relief Committee.

Among the refugees met by Gerard were two stonemasons who had walked unmolested through the Boer lines. They had noticed that the Transvaal railway carriages had written on them in Dutch their intended destinations '*Durban*' or '*Pietermaritzburg*'. The Boers also had plenty to say for themselves. They told the masons that they were truly sorry for the British soldiers who were coming to South Africa only to be shot. They boasted that they were going to walk through Natal, and drive the rooineks into the sea. They even offered to employ the stonemasons to build their houses in Durban.

Bailey found Penn Symons to be bright, affable, genial and popular with the townspeople. No doubt they found his self-confidence reassuring. It was not his first visit to Dundee. As a young man in 1879 he was with Chelmsford's column when it discovered the slaughter and destruction at Isandhlwana. Penn Symons was shocked and unnerved by the experience and took a few weeks recuperative leave at Talana, the home of Peter and Ann Smith. Ann Smith mothered the young man until, with his confidence restored, he returned to his regiment.[10] When Penn Symons arrived at Dundee in 1899 he called at the farm, but Peter and Ann were away, visiting their daughter and son-in-law, James Grey, who farmed near Ladysmith.

Gerard Bailey's Relief Committee never had a chance to carry out their good works. On Monday, 16 October, all women and children were requested to leave Dundee on the train, which had just brought the Inniskillings from Ladysmith. The Vicar helped his guests carry their few belongings to the station and watched them, packed like sardines, depart. Returning to his empty home he reflected on the plight of the refugees, who did not know where fate was taking them or how long their ordeal would last. Over the following two days further trainloads left Dundee.

The fate of many of the refugees was to be worse than Gerard could have imagined. Most went to Durban where local authority facilities and charities were overwhelmed by the thousands of destitute people fleeing from the Transvaal and Northern Natal. Where possible, local families gave them shelter but this was only able to benefit a small proportion of the refugees. Land was set aside for them where they might set up tents which cost between £1 10s and £4 10s. Those who were unable to afford the tents made shelters from tins and boxes. Few had money to buy food. Local charities attempted to provide food, but the task was beyond their resources. Mr. Haggar of the YMCA wrote to the Natal Mercury describing some of the problems he faced on a typical day:

'*Woman with two children, husband's whereabouts unknown; no money, not a change of clothing. Brings me a note from a gentleman who knows her to be respectable. My funds are exhausted, and all the clothing left was an old black skirt – that was better than nothing, and she took it.*

'*Women with four children; husband supposed to be in Johannesburg; rent and relief stopped; could get work but who is to look after the children? Besides, what can a woman do with four children and only £2 per month (pay) at most.*

'*Very delicate woman; no shamming about her; has two children; her husband went to Ladysmith with a convoy before the siege; has heard nothing since; all relief stopped, and is in arrears for rent; needs a prolonged course of medical treatment. All I could do was to express sympathy and give her a little clothing for her boy. She had no money; neither had I, and the poor woman has to live on hope – a very cruel protector.*

'*A poor woman stood at the door of my room, unable to speak because of the lump in her throat. After some minutes, she said, 'I have never asked for help before, and it will be too cruel for me to go and perhaps be told, there is no money. I have come to you because I come from Australia. My husband is dead.*'[11]

Although almost all the refugees were British subjects, the British government showed no interest in their welfare. When word of the appalling conditions under which they were living reached London, the Lord Mayor set up an emergency fund to provide basic necessities. People contributed generously and the money was sent to Lord Milner for distribution in South Africa. The Durban Relief Fund received £11,000 without which many of the refugees would have died of starvation.

CHAPTER SEVEN

Border Patrol

◆

With quiet determination the Volunteers prepared to resist the invaders.

VOLUNTEER REACTION TO THE DECLARATION OF WAR.

THE Natal Volunteers responded promptly to the order to mobilise. At 6 a.m. on 1 October 1899, those Natal Carbineer squadrons which were based in Pietermaritzburg paraded in the Market Square, and then marched to the station accompanied by a band playing 'Soldiers of the Queen'. Along the route they were cheered by a large crowd. They entrained at 8.15 a.m. and arrived at Ladysmith that evening. The Natal Mounted Rifles reached Ladysmith on the morning of 2 October and the Border Mounted Rifles (BMR), many of whose members had a long ride to their nearest railway station, assembled in Ladysmith at 7 p.m. that same evening. The Natal Field Artillery and the Natal Naval Volunteers were also sent to Ladysmith. The Estcourt squadron of the Carbineers assembled at Estcourt, and from Greytown the Umvoti Mounted Rifles moved north towards Helpmekaar to patrol the crossings of the Tugela near the Transvaal border. The Durban Light Infantry, who mustered 430 men, went ten miles south of Ladysmith to the hamlet of Colenso, the site of important road and rail bridges across the Tugela River. The Dundee squadron of the Natal Carbineers remained in Dundee.

As the mounted regiments required veterinary surgeons, a Volunteer Veterinary Corps was recruited and most of its ten members went to Ladysmith. Their senior officer was Major Herbert Watkins-Pitchford, who had been in charge of the Natal Government's veterinary research station at Allerton, Pietermaritzburg. Over the years, their research had many successes in the fight to control animal diseases, which threatened stock all over Africa.

Doctors and nurses of the Natal Volunteer Medical Corps accompanied their regiments to Ladysmith. Three doctors went out on patrol with their units, namely Robert Buntine with the Carbineers, Rupert Hornebrook with the Natal Mounted Rifles, and Dr HT Platt with the Border Mounted Rifles. The other doctors manned the tented Volunteer hospital in Ladysmith. Included in the Corps were eighteen qualified nurses.

Despite the refusal on 28 July 1899 by the then British Commander in Chief in South Africa, Major General Sir William Butler, to authorise the enlistment of armed or unarmed native scouts in case of causing offence to the Boers, the Natal authorities decided in September 1899, to defy the order and to enlist a corps of Native Scouts. Among the Carbineers in Ladysmith was Robert Samuelson, a practising solicitor and brother of SO Samuelson, the Natal official whose prompt action and expert advice were to play such an

Scout Teise Ndlovu with Lt Robert Samuelson.
Teise arranged for the photograph to be taken
and paid for it.

important part in the rescue of the 7,000 Zulus who were in danger of being trapped in the Transvaal. Colonel Royston knew Robert Samuelson and felt he would be the ideal person to raise and command the Scouts. Apart from his professional career, Robert like many Colonials was a keen sportsman, and in more peaceful times had established a reputation as a decent cricketer.

On 3 October, Robert Samuelson was appointed OC of the Natal Native Scouts and ordered to raise 150 men to cover the Drakensberg from Tintwa Pass in the west, to the Biggarsberg mountains to the north of Ladysmith. He was given full discretion with respect to their recruitment and deployment. On receiving the orders, Samuelson, accompanied by the magistrate, immediately rode out to the home of Chief Khumalo which was some twenty miles north of Ladysmith near a place called Driefontein. The magistrate introduced Samuelson to the Chief and then returned to Ladysmith. At that time the Chief was over 100 years-old and somewhat frail but was still in full possession of all his mental faculties.

Organizers of the Driefontein Scouts. Back Row: S. Gule, R. Mdaweni, L. Kumalo, T. Gule, N. Kumalo, A. Msimang, P. Malinga, N.Silgee. Middle Row: E. Msimang, A. Mtimkulu, Chief Johannes Kumalo, Rev L. Msimang, Rev J. Msimang. Front: S. Kambule and Assistant Chief Khumalo.

With invasion imminent the Natal Carbineers leave Ladysmith to patrol the Frontier.

The next day he summoned his people whom he addressed thus:

'My children this is the day of days; an impudent foe, the Boers, are preparing to fight against her Majesty the Queen, our Sovereign and Mother, who has for so many years spread her wings over us to protect us, and who is minded to continue spreading her wings like an Angel over us till they touch the earth; That Queen requires your services, go and serve her till death.'

A chorus of approval was shouted by all present, whereupon the Chief instructed them to get everything ready. Horses, bridles and saddles were collected. As there were not enough saddles to go round, some of the scouts had to ride bareback. Samuelson decided to adopt the Zulu system of scouting; men were stationed at intervals along the border and gallopers went to and fro between the different scout groups bringing back to Samuelson the information which had been gathered. He kept several scouts with him who would take such information he thought important to Colonel Willie Royston in Ladysmith. Much of the activity, including feeding the scouts was undertaken at night so as to avoid detection by the Boers. Samuelson also sent men, fluent in Sotho and Dutch, across the border, where they would mix with the Boer servants and gain much useful information in the process. One such scout even fell into conversation with some Boers and, among other things, learnt that if they caught old Chief Khumalo they would gouge his eyes out. Samuelson immediately arranged for a Cape cart to take the Chief to the home of Simeon Khambule, a hero on the British side of the Battles of Isandlwana and Ulundi. Simeon was head of the body of scouts working in Ladysmith. Because of his extreme age the old chief delegated many of his duties to his grandson, Joseph Khumalo, and it was with Joseph that Samuelson arranged much of the day to day work of the scouts.[1]

Although war had not yet been declared, the Volunteers went out on patrol as soon as they arrived in Ladysmith. The Carbineers, the Border Mounted Rifles and the Natal Mounted Rifles patrolled the area covering the mountain passes, through which the Free State might launch a surprise attack. It was very hard work. They would rise well before dawn, breakfast, saddle up and be on their way before first light. In the evening they would unsaddle and have something to eat. As soon as it was dark they would strike camp, saddle up and ride to another site about 10 miles away. On arrival, which was generally at about 1 a.m., they would unsaddle and get what sleep they could before repeating the routine the next day. This procedure ensured that they would not be surprised by a night attack, however the many hours in the saddle and sleep deprivation was exhausting.

A Field Day was held in which the various corps in Ladysmith put on a display. The Colonel in charge complimented the Border Mounted Rifles on the manner in which they were able to get over rough, stony ground. The Natal Carbineers showed how their horses had been schooled to lie down and stay down in action. The highlight of the day was a charge by the full complement of the 5th Lancers. It was a magnificent sight as they charged across the plain, lances at the ready and bugles sounding to disappear in clouds of dust. When the dust cleared it was seen that about a dozen horses had come down and the riders were busy picking themselves up. Fortunately only one rider was injured, and he not too seriously.[2]

On 12 October 1899, Mrs Portsmouth, whose family had a farm and shop near van Reenen's Pass, noticed men and guns coming over the passes into Natal.

On that same day, the Natal Volunteers were told that war had been declared. In contrast to the invading Boers, who stood in their stirrups and cheered themselves hoarse when they heard of the ultimatum, the Volunteers greeted the news with quiet determination to resist the invaders. No one stood in their stirrups or cheered. As usual they were ordered out on patrol. The Natal Mounted Rifles patrolled north of Ladysmith in the direction of Dundee, the Border Mounted Rifles watched the border between Mont aux Sources and Tintwa Mountain and the Carbineers from Tintwa to van Reenen's Pass. It was not long before Major Taunton of the Carbineers reported signs of enemy activity. Headquarters doubted the validity of the information.

The following day the Carbineers again reported Boers descending into Natal and the Border Mounted Rifles reported a strong column of Boers coming into the Colony by the Tintwa Pass. That day a rumour was circulated in Ladysmith that the Border Mounted Rifles had been surrounded and all had been killed. Whether it was for this or some other reason, a column of about 4,000 Imperial troops marched out along the road towards van Reenen's Pass. Showing a complete lack of sporting spirit, the Free Staters declined to show themselves.

At a Field Day in Ladysmith prior to the Declaration of War, a Natal Carbineer demonstrates how the regiment's horses had been schooled to lie down on command and remain lying down despite rifle fire.

Staff Officers of the Natal Volunteers in Ladysmith. Col W. Royston seated in the centre with Col Bru de Wold on his right.

After marching about 8 miles, and discovering that the rumour of the destruction of the BMR was false, the troops returned to Ladysmith.

That night it was cold and poured with rain, nonetheless the exhausted Border Mounted Riflemen went to sleep in the mud. At about 9.30 p.m. the alarm sounded. Scouts reported that a large body of Boers was approaching. In seven minutes, the men were saddled up with packs and ammunition ready, and all fallen in. Captain Jack Royston was delegated to investigate and found it was not Boers who were approaching, but a large body of civilian refugees. They had come from Harrismith in the Free State, having been told by the Boers to leave immediately. They had no choice but to attempt to walk the 50 miles to Ladysmith in freezing cold over a high mountain pass, where it was likely they would encounter snow and blizzards. They were fortunate to survive.

For the next few days the cat-and-mouse tactics continued. The Volunteers would see a group of Boers approaching, there would be an exchange of fire and the Boers would retreat. After one such skirmish, a group of Hussars and Lancers under a Major Adye came out from Ladysmith. Major Rethman pointed out the position of the Boers. Major Adye surveyed the scene and announced there were no Boers there and proceeded to lead his men forward. They immediately came under rifle fire and had to beat a hasty retreat to their original position. Major Rethman asked whether they were about to attack the Boers and was told by Adye that he had merely come out to check the Volunteer's report.[3]

On 16 October, Regimental Sergeant Major Bowen of the Carbineers, together with a sergeant and twelve troopers, visited Robert Samuelson at his outpost. They found everything in order and were given an excellent and much appreciated meal prepared by Mrs Joseph Khumalo. The next day, the Carbineers came under heavy fire from a Boer commando. In response, the regiment's Maxim gun went forward with Lt Gallwey and opened fire.

Col Greene, in command, then noticed that the Boers were attempting to outflank him, so he ordered the Maxim group to return which they did with the Maxim, but without Gallwey; he had been captured after receiving a kick from his horse which prevented his withdrawing with the others.

Outnumbered and in danger of being surrounded, Col Greene decided that any attempt to rescue Gallwey would put the whole regiment at risk, and accordingly ordered that they retire. As they did so, one of their horses fell, throwing its rider heavily. Seeing what had happened, Dr Buntine immediately rode back, under fire, to assist the injured trooper who had been stunned. He tried to get the injured man onto his horse but was unable to do so until his orderly, F Duke, joined him. Together they were able to get the trooper mounted and, with Buntine running alongside the injured man, they arrived back safely to their comrades. Despite their Red Cross badges, Buntine and Duke were under persistent fire from the Boers while attending to the injured man.[4]

Capt Dr Robert Buntine NVMC.
An Australian who settled in Natal, he performed the first act of conspicuous gallantry of the War, and in the fighting around Ladysmith he performed complex medical operations on the field.

Robert Andrew Buntine was born near Melbourne, Victoria, in 1869 and attended Scotch College from 1884 to 1886. He received a Queen's College scholarship and studied medicine at Melbourne University, graduating M.B. in 1891 and B.Sc. in March 1892. Several subjects were passed with honours. He excelled as a sportsman, being the University champion athlete. In 1892 he was appointed resident surgeon at Melbourne Hospital. He married the daughter of Henry Pinson who had moved from Australia to Natal. Perhaps because of this family connection, Robert Buntine moved to Pietermaritzburg in 1893. Afterwards he spent a year in England; however, when he was offered the post of resident surgeon at Grey's Hospital in Pietermaritzburg, he returned to Natal.

The rescue of the injured trooper by Buntine and Duke was the first conspicuous act of bravery in the war, though it was never officially recognised as such because Headquarters had not authorised the action. The Volunteer's orders were to report on the enemy's movements but not to engage them, so strictly speaking, the action by the Carbineers exceeded their orders. However it is difficult to see how this logic can be applied to giving medical attention to an injured soldier. We shall come across Buntine again. His orderly, Duke, died during the siege.

On 18 October, both the Carbineers and the Border Mounted Rifles came into contact with the Boers, and after an exchange of fire, the Boers occupied the railway siding at Besters on the Ladysmith/Harrismith line. In the course of the action Trooper J Surgeson of the Carbineers lost his horse but was able to hide from the Boers until he was found by a group of Samuelson's scouts who were on their way to report the movements of the enemy. As a result of their report Samuelson ordered the whole line of Scouts to hold fast while at the same time retiring towards Ladysmith where they would receive further orders. The scouts successfully completed their retirement over the next few days.

A horse was found for Surgeson who, with Samuelson, rode into Ladysmith to resume duty with the Carbineers.

After they had withdrawn from Besters, the Volunteers received orders to retire to Ladysmith, coupled with advice that, as the enemy had penetrated between the Volunteers and Ladysmith, it was no longer practicable to return by the direct road.

The order to retire was brought to the BMR by a veteran Carbineer, W Leathern, owner of the farm where the BMR was temporarily camped. Major Rethman decided to send his commissariat wagons back to Ladysmith via the main road, telling the drivers that if they saw Boers, they were to advise them that the regiment would be following an hour later. Immediately they were out of sight, the rest of the regiment, guided by Leathern, set off on a circuitous route back to base. Riding hard with scouts out, they were able to reach Ladysmith at 2.30 a.m. Rethman immediately went to Col Willie Royston to advise him that he had had to sacrifice his wagons, only to find that the wagons had arrived safely in Ladysmith, without having seen any Boers. The men were exhausted, having been in the saddle almost continuously for 24 hours and the horses had had no rest for 36 hours. They fed the horses, put their saddle blankets down on the road and fell asleep instantly. But not for long.

At daylight they were called upon to sort out their lines and get everything in order. The next day they were called out at 4.30 a.m., as Headquarters urgently wanted information as to the movements of the Free State commandos. Although it was pouring with rain and they had had nothing to eat, the troopers nevertheless saddled up and rode out on patrol. They found the Boers near Besters Station and tracked their movements through the day, returning to Ladysmith at 5 p.m., Major Rethman reporting his losses as being one hat.

One of the most severe tests of stamina of man and horse during this period was carried out by C Squadron of the Natal Mounted Rifles led by Captain LT Wales. This troop was out for five days during which it covered about 200 miles over varied terrain. They gained and transmitted to Headquarters much valuable information regarding nests of Boers who were awaiting the arrival of the main commandos. It is estimated that on one stretch they covered more than seventy miles in 24 hours. On their return to camp in Ladysmith, men and horses were so exhausted that some had to be assisted out of their saddles, while others, half asleep, simply tumbled out and, refusing food, slept for a day and a night without a move. The horses lay down in the lines for several days, getting up only to eat. In the long history of equestrian warfare, this must rank as one of the most remarkable displays of stamina by man and horse.

The outbreak of war did not change the attitude of many in the British army towards the Colonials. One junior British artillery officer, more perceptive than most, complained in his diary, of the '*criminal ignorance and negligence of our Intelligence Department, who are above acting on news received from Colonial troops (who prove a jolly sight better scouters than our regular cavalry).*'[5]

One man who had begun to recognise the capabilities of the colonial Volunteers was General White. On 18 October he selected Captain FS Tatham of the Natal Carbineers and 21 NCOs and men of the Natal Mounted Rifles to be his personal bodyguard.

CHAPTER EIGHT

Battle of Talana Hill

•—◆—•

'Where's Charlie? Where's Willson?'

O N Sunday, 8 October 1899, in Dundee, the Reverend Gerard Bailey chose as the text for his sermon, Psalm 121: '*I will lift up mine eyes unto the hills, from whence cometh my help.*' Less than two weeks later, the Vicar, when visiting the hospital, was told by a wounded officer that it was not help that came from the hills, but the Boers.

If one stands in Dundee and looks north towards Newcastle the view is of a broad shallow valley dominated by two hills. On the left is the massive bulk of Mpati. This hill, which in many places would be called a mountain, is about 3 miles from Dundee and rises about 1,500 feet above the valley floor. On the right, about one and a half miles from Dundee, is a longer, lower hill generally known as Talana but sometimes as Smith's Hill. Further still to the right (or the east) and connected to Talana by a saddle known as Smith's Nek, is another eminence called Lennox Hill. In the shallow valley between Dundee and Talana is a stream known as the Sandspruit.

In the 1850s Thomas Smith emigrated from Scotland to Australia and after spending five years on the Australian goldfields, moved to Natal where he purchased a farm which he called Dundee after his home town in Scotland. On the farm was Talana Hill and it was on the slopes of this hill that the farmhouse and other buildings were sited. Thomas worked as a building contractor and small-time farmer. In 1864 he persuaded his brother Peter and family to join him. They burnt their own bricks for building and built up fine herds of South Devon cattle and Merino sheep. Shortly after his arrival in 1864, Peter Smith found coal on the farm. The coal turned out to be of high quality and a small mining community gradually developed. In due course Peter inherited the farm from his brother.

In 1882 it was decided to lay out a township to accommodate the growing population. This new town was called, not surprisingly, Dundee. Its founders were Peter Smith, his son William Craighead Smith, his son–in–law, Dugald MacPhail, and Charles George Willson.

William Craighead Smith had served with the Buffalo Border Guards in the Anglo–Zulu war and in 1899 was a member of the Dundee squadron of the Natal Carbineers. William's son also served with the Carbineers and was to be killed by shellfire during the siege of Ladysmith.

Dugald MacPhail owned a neighbouring farm, had served in the Anglo- Zulu war and was one of the few survivors of the Battle of Isandlwana. In 1940 he enrolled with the police reserve, the oldest reservist and the oldest ex-serviceman in the Empire. He died in 1941 aged 100. In 1899 he was a member of the Dundee Town Guard.

Charles George Willson was born in London in 1850 and came to Natal with his parents in 1852. In 1873 William Smith persuaded him to open a business in Dundee to serve the growing community. He joined the Buffalo Border Guards and served as a sergeant major in the Anglo-Zulu war. He was the leader of the scouts sent out by Lord Chelmsford to ascertain what was happening at the Isandlwana base camp, and was the first person to reach that stricken battlefield. In the Carbineers he was appointed Lieutenant in 1888 and Captain in 1895. In 1899 he was the senior officer of the Dundee squadron of the Carbineers.

Charlie Willson was a man of prodigious energy who had a long record of public service. Not only was he one of the founders of Dundee, but he was mayor of the town for many years. His drive and initiative was primarily responsible for the construction of the town's waterworks and electricity power station and it was he who persuaded the railway authority, which had planned to bypass Glencoe and Dundee, to route their mainline through Glencoe with a branch to Dundee. He was president of the local building society from its foundation to his death, and as a prominent man in agricultural circles, he was one of the founders of the Natal Wool Company. He played a leading role in the development of coal mining in the district, an industry which was to contribute much to the development of South Africa. A keen sportsman, he was president or vice-president of a number of sports clubs. He and his wife were two of the most popular and respected people in northern Natal which he had represented in the Legislative Assembly for four years from 1893.

When British troops arrived at Dundee on 25 September, there was of course a military presence there already, namely the Natal Carbineers commanded by Captain CG Willson. On arrival, General Sir William Penn Symons, as a matter of courtesy, ought to have sought out the commander of the Carbineers, explained what he was doing in Dundee, and asked for Willson's assistance and advice. With his knowledge of the district and its people, no one was in a better position to advise the General than Charlie Willson, and no one was more in need of such advice than Penn Symons. Sadly, Penn Symons appears to have taken little or no interest in the assistance he could have obtained from the local Carbineers or their commander. A possible reason for this attitude might be that both he and Sir Archibald Hunter, Chief of Staff in Ladysmith, would have been fully aware of Sir Garnet Wolseley's directive that military information should not be passed on to Colonials.

Even before they received the order to mobilise, the Carbineers would have been anxiously watching developments across the nearby Transvaal border. After mobilisation, they and some members of the Town Guard patrolled the district so as to detect immediately the presence of any Boers.

During the initial stages of their invasion of Natal, the Boers advanced very cautiously as General Piet Joubert, the Transvaal Commandant-General, feared the British had laid minefields. It took their army from 12 to 16 October 1899, to cover the 30 unopposed miles from the border to Newcastle. While Joubert was searching for landmines, another peril was threatening the Transvaal. In Pretoria there was considerable concern that Britain was about to invade the Republic with a great fleet of war balloons! Telegraph stations were ordered to report any sightings immediately and many reports of balloons with coloured searchlights were reported daily from every corner of the Transvaal. Freda Schlosberg noted in her diary, 'Several balloons are rumoured to have been seen over Johannesburg, Pretoria and Standerton, and it is said that the government has given orders to shoot at them; so several stars have been shot at.'[1]

When the Boer army crossed the last mountain pass before Newcastle and reached the crossing of the Buffalo River, one of their leaders was moved to make a speech. Deneys Reitz recalled:

'General "Maroola", with a quick eye to the occasion, faced round and made a speech telling us that Natal was a heritage filched from our forefathers, which must now be recovered from the usurper. Amid enthusiastic cries we began to ford the stream. It took nearly an hour for all to cross, during this time the cheering and singing of the Volkslied was continuous, and we rode into the smiling land of Natal full of hope and courage.'[2]

Of the reception of the Boers in Newcastle, Deneys wrote, '…such of the inhabitants as sympathized with us waving encouragement, and the rest looking on in sullen resentment, as the long lines of horsemen went by.'[3] Of course 'the rest' did not include those train-loads of refugees who had already fled Newcastle. At Newcastle General Joubert decided on his tactics for the invasion. One column of about 5,000 men under General Lukas Meyer would cross the border at a point east of Dundee. The centre column, with another 5,000 men, including young Reitz and commanded by General Erasmus, an older brother of 'Maroola', would continue along the main route south and link up with Meyer at Dundee. A third, smaller column under General Kock would move west, link up with the Free State Kommandos, then the combined force would turn south and cut the railway line between Ladysmith and Dundee, thereby isolating the latter.

By the evening of 19 October, the Boer Kommandos were closing in on Dundee. General Kock had succeeded in cutting the rail and telegraph link with Ladysmith at Elandslaagte, though the telegraph link through Greytown remained open. General Erasmus had reached the northern slopes of Mpati and in the east, Lukus Meyer had crossed the Buffalo River and was well on his way to Talana. It was from these two hills that the Boers planned to launch their attack on Dundee,

The British camp lay in the valley to the west of Dundee, and not only was it overlooked by both Mpati and Talana, but it was also within the range of artillery placed on either. Penn Symons, for some inexplicable reason, had decided not to occupy either of the hills. He paid no regard to the reports by scouts warning of the approach of the Boers, and when on the morning of the 19th the manager of the Navigation Colliery, which is on the northern slope of Mpati, rode in and reported the Boers were bringing up guns with the intention of shelling Dundee, the General retorted that this was ridiculous.[4] Furthermore, initially, he made no attempt to guard Smith's Nek, a natural doorway from the Transvaal to Natal. However on the evening of 19 October, a picket of mounted infantry drawn from the Dublin Fusiliers was sent there.

At 3.30 a.m. on 20 October, the now dismounted Fusiliers on Smith's Nek were fired on by scouts from Lucas Meyer's Kommando. Lt Grimshaw, in charge of the picket, wisely decided to retire. The gunfire had stampeded their horses but shielded by mist and the dark they were able to withdraw on foot. A sergeant was sent back to the camp with the news and, in response, two companies of the Dublin Fusiliers were sent out to support their comrades. The picket was able to find their horses and, with their reinforcements they dug in along the Sandspruit at the bottom of Talana Hill.

Apart from this little incident, it was just the start of another day in the British camp, and what better way to welcome the cold dawn than to have a cup of good, hot, English tea. As the officers looked at the dawn breaking over Talana, through the swirling mist they could see little black dots moving about on the top of the hill. *Could it be? No, impossible, what a laugh! Better check through the field glasses. It was.* The Boers in some numbers had occupied Talana. No one paid much attention to Mpati, which was still shrouded in mist.

The Reverend Bailey had heard the rifle shots just after 3.00 a.m., got up and he too had a cup of tea. At 5.00 a.m. he and a friend went down to the market place, where they met some members of the Town Guard, who were going home after a night patrolling the town.

They told Bailey that the picket at Smith's Nek had been fired on. The parson had a look at Talana through his field glasses. He could see people moving around but concluded they must be British troops investigating the attack on the picket. He did not entertain this illusion for long. Suddenly a big gun boomed, followed by a rushing sound as a shell came over the town, pitching somewhere to the north-west. The spectators concluded that the British had placed a gun on Talana and were shelling a target near Mpati. The next landed just past the British camp. The third landed in the camp and thereafter, shell after shell crashed into the camp. The townsmen hurriedly sought shelter though for the time being they were safe as the Boers concentrated all their fire on the army.

The first shell to hit the British camp landed a few feet from the tent of General Penn Symons and would surely have killed him had it exploded. But, like most of the other shells sent over by the Boers that day, it failed to explode as the percussion caps were set incorrectly, resulting in the shells burrowing into the soft, wet ground rather than exploding. If the arrival of the Boer shells surprised the General, they certainly did not fluster or intimidate him. Within a few minutes, his artillery had attempted to return the Boer fire and the General had formed his plan of action.

The infantry, backed by the artillery, would make a frontal assault on Talana, thereby dislodging the Boers from the hill, while the cavalry would go round to the back of the hill, and, cutting off the Boer retreat, deliver the *coup de grâce*. The Dublin Fusiliers would assault on the left and the King's Royal Rifles on the right. The Royal Irish Fusiliers would provide support for the other two regiments. The 1st Leicester Regiment, supported by 67th Field Battery, were ordered out to protect the western approaches to the town. Brigadier-General Yule, Penn Symons' second in command, suggested that to support the main thrust a flank attack be made on the northern shoulder of Talana. Such an attack would not only assist the main thrust but would have been sheltered from flanking fire from Lennox Hill. Penn Symons rejected Yule's proposal out of hand, but he did not forget the Natal Carbineers. They were given the task of guarding the base camp, something which could have been done quite effectively by some of the less able members of the Town Guard.

The first salvo of shells from the Royal Artillery fell well short of the target on Talana. They quickly moved forward to within 3,000 yards of the target, only to find that they were still outranged. Finally at 2,300 yards they were able to reach the target and silence the Boer guns on Talana and Lennox Hill. Not long afterwards the Boers removed their guns from the battlefield. Meanwhile the infantry, cheered on by the civilians, marched through the town, and successfully made their way across the open ground to the Sandspruit. Though rifle fire was directed at them, because of the extreme range, they were able to make the safety of the banks of the stream without any serious casualties. The Boers now knew precisely where to expect the attack.

British officers surveying the scene saw that from the stream stretched 875 to 1,095 yards of open grassland before the farm and its buildings were reached. Here there was a band of trees roughly parallel to the stream and the summit of the hill. Beyond the trees was another stretch of open grassland above which was a stone wall, again approximately parallel to the trees and the summit. Beyond the stone wall the slope of the hill to the top became progressively more precipitous though just how steep, rocky and awkward the final climb would be, was not readily apparent from afar.

Down in the bed of the stream, Penn Symons sorted out his infantry regiments into the proposed attack formations and at 7.30 a.m. they broke cover and charged in open order towards the trees. A withering fire from the Boers greeted this move and men began to fall. On reaching the trees it was found that they provided but little cover, compelling the men to go to ground. Fortunately, it was found that there was another stone wall running along the upper edge of the wood and this provided some shelter. At right angles to these two walls was yet another which ran straight up the hill. Later that morning, this third wall was to provide valuable shelter from flanking fire coming from Lennox Hill.

At about 9.00 a.m. Penn Symons, apparently concerned that the attack might have stalled, sent two staff officers to Yule, the commander in the wood, instructing him to proceed with the assault. Yule replied that he would do so as soon as possible.[5] Apparently not satisfied with this response, the General decided to go to the wood himself. His horse was brought to him and accompanied by Col Dartnell and Majors Hattersley and Murray, galloped under heavy fire across the open grassland towards the wood. At the edge of the wood was a fence and seeing it, the General kicked on and soared over it and into the wood. Once there he dismounted, and ignoring enemy fire, walked through the trees urging the men forward in readiness for the final assault. As they approached the further edge, Major Hattersley was wounded and shortly afterwards the General, seeing a gap in the low wall, stepped across to look at the position. A moment later he turned to Murray and said, 'I'm severely, mortally, wounded in the stomach.'

Murray helped him back across the wall and to his horse. Riding back through the wood the General gave no sign of being injured, until, having passed out of sight of his men, he collapsed.

Brigadier General Yule, now in overall command, ordered the assault on the summit to proceed. Using the wall going straight up the hill to give some protection from flanking fire, the attackers extricated themselves from the wood and under heavy fire gained the upper stone wall. Here they were pinned down for almost two hours during which time they were constantly under fire, not only from the Boers on the summit, but also from snipers on Lennox Hill. Meanwhile, the Royal Artillery had continued its bombardment of the Boers occupying the summits of Talana and Lennox Hill.

At about midday there was a lull in the artillery fire, which was taken as the signal for the final rush to the summit. It must have seemed an almost impossible task to climb that precipitous slope. Nothing daunted, the attackers jumped over the wall, to be met by a barrage of rifle fire. Despite heavy losses they scrambled ever upwards, over the rocks and through thorn bushes. As they reached the crest, their own artillery re-opened fire on the summit, and before the blunder could be corrected, more losses were inflicted, and they had to retreat down the rocks. However, as soon as the artillery fire ceased they climbed back and the Boers were driven from the summit. Forty-one officers and men had been killed and 203 wounded in the attack.

Now that the British were in possession of the top of the hill, the Boers retreated not only down the reverse slope of Talana but also from Lennox Hill. As soon as this was realised, two Artillery batteries under Col Pickwoad immediately pushed up the hill and unlimbered on Smith's Nek. Though it was drizzling, the gunners had a fine view of the retreating Boers and could have wrought havoc amongst them. Instead they held their fire.

The mounted troops who were to deliver the *coup de grâce* consisted of three squadrons of the 18th Hussars, and some mounted infantry from the Dublin Fusiliers and the King's Royal Rifles. Commanded by Col BD Moller, they left the camp at about 7.00 a.m. with orders to work round the north of Talana and take up a concealed position while awaiting an opportunity to strike at the enemy. It seems that these rather vague orders were considered adequate and the details were left to the discretion of Col Moller. As they rode up the Sandspruit valley between Talana and the mist-covered Mpati, they were spotted by the Boers on Talana who sent some machine gun fire in their direction, but because of the long range no damage was suffered. They continued north until well past Talana and then turned right, crossed the stream, and took up an excellent concealed position on the right rear of the Boers on Talana.

A golden opportunity to influence the day's proceedings now presented itself. The British had discovered the Boer ponies. Majors Knox and Marling of the 18th Hussars begged for permission to fire on them with a machine gun so as to drive them away and leave the Boers stranded on the hill. However Col Moller would have none of it and forbad any interference with the ponies. Instead they were ordered to take two squadrons to the rear of Lennox Hill so as to discover what the Boers were doing. The two squadrons made their way in gathering mist towards the back of Lennox Hill. They met several parties of Boers, some of whom they charged and struck with their swords. Whether it was because the swords were blunt or the homespun jackets of the Boers were very tough is not known, but what is known is that the swords failed to cut through the Boers' coats. Nevertheless 30 or 40 prisoners with rather bruised shoulders were taken by these cavalrymen as they galloped to and fro in the mist.

By midday this escapade had taken them to a point some distance behind the Boer lines and to the east of Smith's Nek. Col Moller now arrived with the rest of the mounted men. He ordered Knox and Marling to take the two squadrons to the south so as to reconnoitre the land in that direction. Knox handed over the prisoners to Moller, and he and his squadrons departed on their venture of discovery. In the course of the afternoon Knox and Marling were at various times in contact with large groups of Boers, but were able to extricate themselves from danger and arrived back in Dundee at 7.00 p.m.

The remainder of the mounted force, including the Hussars' Maxim detachment, were ordered by Moller to take up positions across the anticipated Boer line of retreat. About 200 men armed with rifles and one machine gun planned to stop nearly 4,000 Boers on an open plain. When the Boers began their retirement off Talana and Lennox Hill, Moller realised what he was up against and hastily attempted to get his men away. The prisoners were abandoned and when the Maxim gun became bogged down in the Sandspruit, it and its crew were also abandoned. Subsequently, four of the crew were killed and the fifth was wounded and taken prisoner. Instead of returning the way he had come, Moller drifted steadily northwards past the back of Mpati. There the mist was beginning to clear and Deneys Reitz with some of his friends were admiring the view northwards from the back of that hill when they were astonished to see a troop of English horsemen, pursued by Boers, riding in a northerly direction up the valley. They quickly saddled up and set off down the steep hill to join the turkey shoot.

Moller appears to have become completely disorientated because every move he made took him further from his base and deeper into Boer territory. Finally, with his men exhausted and night approaching, he decided to make a stand at Adelaide Farm about 8 miles from Dundee whose buildings and stone walls might provide some protection. The Boers quickly surrounded the farm, and though the defenders fought bravely, they were running out of ammunition. When the Boers brought their artillery to bear on the farm, Moller felt he had no alternative but to surrender. He had lost eight men killed and had eighteen wounded. Nine officers and 200 men were captured.

From the moment Moller set out that morning, he was doomed. Coming from the northern hemisphere his sense of direction would have sent him all the wrong signals, and because of the iron in the hills, compass readings would have been inaccurate. If he had been accompanied by some Natal Carbineers, these difficulties might have been overcome, but nothing could have saved his command from his failure to seek good advice.

In Dundee, Gerard Bailey had watched the progress of the battle. By the time the infantry had reached the wood at Smith's farm, '…the rifle firing was continuous and incessant. To us at a distance it sounded like bubbling boiling water; no rests, no pauses, no intervals. The maxims augmented the din, and the artillery pounded away.'

Soon the wounded began to arrive, carried in by the bearers which the army had brought with them from India. These men, from Major Donegan's 18th Field Hospital, showed great courage on this day and continued to do so throughout the Natal campaign. A warehouse in the town was converted into a temporary hospital and the vicar noted how among all the horrors of war, 'everything was done so quietly and orderly.' He was amazed at the fortitude and cheerfulness of the wounded. He asked one young lad with a bandaged head about his wound and received the reply, 'I've got one in my head, and one in my chest, there's nothing like being greedy.'

Looking through his field glasses, the vicar noticed how crowded together the men were. Later he saw some of the infantry leave the shelter of the stone wall and climb to the crest of the hill, only to return to the wall. He added, 'They probably found that they were too near to the shells.' He was probably twice as far from the hilltop as the artillery, which failed to recognize its own troops. Once the crest had been gained the vicar saw 12 guns unlimber on Smith's Nek. He knew that behind the hills lay many miles of open country. The Boers were at their mercy and should surely have been compelled to surrender. And yet nothing happened. Subsequently, GB Fyfe, a refugee from Newcastle, told the vicar of a conversation he had had with an army officer on that day. Fyfe had followed the artillery up onto Smith's Nek and was looking at the retreating Boers when an officer asked him, 'Are those the enemy?' 'They most certainly are,' was the reply. The officer then said he had no orders to fire.[6]

A posed photograph taken during the Boer occupation of Dundee, showing three Boers standing on top of Talana Hill. In the distance can be seen Dundee and in the middle distance the stream from which the attack was launched. Below the Boers is the belt of trees and the stone wall which provided the only cover as the infantry attacked up the ever more precipitous slope against the enemy concealed among the rocks on the summit.

The courage and sacrifice of the infantry had placed the British in a position where they could have annihilated a substantial portion of the invading army, and possibly brought the war to a speedy end. Instead they turned victory into defeat, which was achieved by the failure of the artillery to press home the advantage gained, and the purposeless galloping around of the mounted men.

Responsibility for the failure by the artillery rests with General Yule, and it was not the only example of his erratic behaviour that day. In the weeks leading up to the battle he would, as second-in-command, have been aware of the great danger which was being created by Penn Symons' over-confidence and no doubt he was becoming increasingly nervous about the situation. When Penn Symons announced his plan of attack early in the morning, Yule had made the eminently sensible suggestion of an attack on the Boer's right flank at Talana. This proposal was, as we have seen, rejected out of hand. Yule nonetheless loyally led the assault from the Sandspruit up into the wood at Smith's farm. Once in the wood, he found there was inadequate shelter and that the men were crowded far too closely together. Any further advance would require the troops to cross open *veld* in which they would be exposed to fire not only from the crest of the hill, where concealed Boers were waiting for them, but also to flanking fire from Lennox Hill. He seems to have been reluctant to submit his men to the certain slaughter which the proposed attack would inevitably bring. When Penn Symons ordered an immediate attack, his reply that he would attack when ready, came as close to defiance as one could reasonably go without actually refusing to obey orders.

The arrival of Penn Symons in the wood, his suffering a mortal wound, and the assumption of overall command, seems to have changed Yule. He casually ordered the assault up the hill to commence immediately. He made no attempt to get the men into a more open order. There was no attempt at a flanking attack, or to co-ordinate the actions of the cavalry, artillery and the infantry. He simply let the battle run according to Penn Symons' plan. When the Boers had completed their retirement he withdrew the British regiments from the hill.

The capture of mounted men under Moller, and the purposeless galloping around of the squadrons under Majors Knox and Marling, should be attributed to the arrogance of Penn Symons. Captain Willson and his Carbineers should have been with the British cavalry commanders who ought to have consulted them regularly on all matters.

After the withdrawal from the battlefield, Yule's inertia continued. Lieutenant Crum, a mounted member of the King's Royal Rifles, was severely wounded shortly after the Boers began their retreat. He was found by a Dr Hardy who applied a dressing to his wound and arranged for Crum and other wounded to be taken to the farm at Talana, where a field hospital had been set up. After a long and painful night, dawn at last came and with it the hope that ambulance carts would come and collect them. Crum recorded his experiences at Talana on the day after the battle:

'There were about 60 Boers and a few English… Many of the wounded Boers came in and looked at us. They shook their heads when they saw Masters, who seemed to be very near dying. Some came and talked to me. All were kind and sympathetic. Our shrapnel seemed to have done terrible work among them, and we all agreed that modern warfare was not "goot". We had taken the hill, but no guard was left there, and those slightly wounded, with their rifles, ponies, and wagons were allowed to go off as they pleased! They kept leaving in large numbers with rifles, ponies and wagons, and all seemed agreed that they did not intend to fight any more… The time dragged on and we seem to have been forgotten. The thought of being dressed and the feeling that something ought to be done for my arm made me fret.

'About 12 o'clock some of the Dundee Town Guard came up and found us. I told them how we stood and one of them rode back to get an ambulance. It was great relief when these good fellows came and gave us drinks. The Boers had nearly all cleared. About 1 o'clock the ambulance turned up and at last we got away.'[7]

For Charlie Willson and the Carbineers it had been a very disappointing and frustrating couple of days. They were well trained, experienced and knew the country intimately, and had volunteered in order that they might contribute to the defence of their town and country. The Carbineers knew the Boers had gone on an orgy of destruction, looting and pillaging after crossing the border. The farms, businesses and homes being destroyed or appropriated by the invaders belonged to them and their friends and had been created over many years by hard work. Now, when they were most needed, they were required to look after the tents and baggage of the newly arrived British troops.

It was not only the British commanders who had failed so miserably at Dundee. The Boers too had their problems. They had permitted their force to be split in two, with one half under General Erasmus sitting in the mists on top of Mpati, able to contribute nothing more to the battle than listen to the sound of firing. They had failed to ensure that their retreat was safe from artillery attack and had failed to take adequate precautions to guard their ponies, without which they would have been helpless. Finally because they were unfamiliar with conditions in Natal, the Staatsartillerie had failed to take into account the fact that the soils in Natal were softer than the hard ground of the Transvaal Highveld, with the result that in spite of being able to outrange the British artillery, they were ineffective.

On 21 October, the British moved their camp southwards, hoping thereby to be beyond the range of the Boer guns believed to be on Mpati. However at 4.00 p.m. that afternoon, Boer shells arrived in the new camp causing casualties. In the pouring rain it was moved that night two miles further south. On the following day came the cheering news of a British victory at Elandslaagte, a hamlet and rail siding a few miles north of Ladysmith. This lifted spirits and the British contingent marched out along the Glencoe road to intercept Boers fleeing from Elandslaagte. The hopes turned out to be illusory as the Boers were moving towards Ladysmith rather than fleeing. The column had no choice but to march back to its camp. General Yule now wished to move his men to the top of Talana and hold out there until relief came. It was with some difficulty that Col Dartnell and others persuaded him that he had no alternative but to retire to Ladysmith by the more circuitous southerly route along the Helpmekaar road. Only a few senior officers knew of this plan. From about this time contemporary writers make frequent references to General Yule being ill, though the nature of his illness is never stated.

Major Marling has left an account of the British camp on the evening of 22 October:

'…there was the most awful confusion: regiments without their commanding officers, and commanding officers without their regiments. No one knew where the General was, and all the Staff but two had been knocked over. The Headquarters telegraph clerk came and asked me where the General was, as he had been hunting for him with a most important message for an hour. It was to this effect: "From GOC Ladysmith. I cannot reinforce you without sacrificing Ladysmith and the Colony behind. You must try and fall back on Ladysmith. I will do what I may to help when nearer." Cheery under the circumstances, I couldn't find General Yule so gave it to old Pickwood in the RA, the next senior officer, who nearly fell off his horse when he read it. It had been drizzling since 5 p.m., and now rained in a steady downpour… We got no orders at all, and none of us had any idea what we were to do in the morning.'

It had been decided to leave Dundee that night. The troops were told to leave the candles burning in their tents but were not told what they were to do or where they were going, with the result that when the men fell in and were marched through Dundee, few would have guessed they were leaving for good. That was only realised when they had covered some considerable distance out of town.

Meanwhile, the Town Guard had been ordered out to Talana to guard the eastern approaches to the town. No one mentioned the proposed flight from Dundee to them.

On the night of 22 October, Gerard Bailey accepted an invitation from Father Murray to sleep in the Roman Catholic church as it was felt that, in the event of the Boers shelling the town, it would be safer there than in the Anglican vicarage which was in the centre of town. The sisters of the convent had left them blankets and pillows so the Anglican and Roman priests made up their beds behind the altar. Before he fell asleep, Gerard Bailey thought of the psalmist, '*I will lay me down in peace and take my rest; for it is Thou, Lord, only, that makes me dwell in safety.*' He awoke at about 11.00 p.m. Outside there was a noise of horses tramping by. He looked out of a window and saw infantry quietly marching along at a steady pace. The cavalry had apparently already passed. After the infantry came the supply wagons, which somehow created a traffic jam and which an officer was endeavouring to clear'. Overcome with tiredness, he fell asleep before the last wagon had passed.

Monday, 23 October, was Gerard's birthday. He awoke to find that the British troops had left Dundee. Where they had gone no one knew. Some civilians had set off, on foot and by horse, for Greytown or along the railway to Ladysmith. At about 10 o'clock Gerard went to the local grocer to find he, too, was about to leave. He bought all the groceries he could carry and saw the erstwhile proprietor of the Masonic Hotel and commandant of the Town Guard driving away in a cart. The commandant had left no orders for his men for whom he appeared to have no concern. To make matters worse, he failed to destroy the list of Town Guard Members, a document which the Boers were to find most interesting. Serious as this misdemeanour was, it was nothing like as bad as that perpetrated by the British. They had left two of their code books in Dundee.

The Town Guard had helped with the wounded on the day of the battle, and on the days which followed they were employed on arduous guard duties by the British. Notwithstanding the subsequent poor conduct of their commandant, the Vicar had no doubt that they had been treated very badly, and the manner in which the British army had sneaked away, abandoning the Guard, created much resentment in Natal at that time.

At about 11.00 a.m., the Magistrate released seventeen Boer prisoners, having extracted from them a promise not to take up arms against the British. At about 1.00 p.m. the Boers rode into town. Gerard Bailey watched them riding in. They came in cautiously as if expecting a trap and seemed puzzled by the absence of any troops. Once they had satisfied themselves that they were safe they rode round town enquiring, 'Where's Charlie? Where's Willson?'[8] Of all the Queen's horses and all the Queen's men who had defended Dundee, the one who concerned the Boers most was Captain CG Willson of the Natal Carbineers.

CHAPTER NINE

Battle of Elandslaagte

•◆•

'Don't shoot! It's Karri Davies.'

A WOUNDED BOER, DURING THE BATTLE OF ELANDSLAAGTE.

WITH an establishment of four officers and 86 other ranks, 'A' Squadron of the Imperial Light Horse was the first in the regiment to be armed and equipped. Shortly after war was declared, the squadron entrained for Estcourt, a small town about two thirds of the way between Pietermaritzburg and Ladysmith. Under Major DE Doveton, its duty was to scout the area from Weenen to Oliviershoek Pass, the most westerly pass over the Drakensberg into Natal. As the distance between these two places is about 80 miles as the crow flies and the countryside is very hilly, it was quite a formidable task. Fortunately, it would patrol in conjunction with the Estcourt squadron of the Natal Carbineers, which knew the country well, and both regiments could rely on the support of local civilians.

The remaining five squadrons were armed and equipped by 16 October and immediately entrained for Ladysmith. Col Scott Chisholme was in command, and had as his senior officers, Majors Aubrey Woolls Sampson and Walter Karri Davies. With a Boer attack on Ladysmith expected at any time, they knew it would not be long before they would be in action, and that they would be singled out for special treatment. The Colonel had received a letter from the Krugersdorp *Kommando* requesting details of their distinguishing pennant so that they could be easily recognized.[1] They also knew that the *Kommandant* of the Johannesburg *Kommando*, one Ben Viljoen, was responsible for an order that anyone who had ever lived in Johannesburg and was now fighting against the Boers should, on capture, be shot immediately.[2]

While General Joubert's central and eastern columns were held up at Dundee, his western column under General Kock was making good progress towards Ladysmith. Aware of the fact that their very existence caused such great offence to the Boers, the local civilian population fled before the invaders and joined the refugee trail to Ladysmith. Among those who were able to get away just in time was farmer James Grey and his family, which included his father-in-law, Peter Smith, the owner of the farm near Dundee on which the battle of Talana was to be fought.

On 19 October, Kock's forward scouts reached Elandslaagte, a railway station about 12 miles north of Ladysmith. As they approached, the Boers saw a train at the station apparently about to leave for Dundee. No doubt sensing the possibility of acquiring some loot, the Boers raced to the station. However, an alert stationmaster had seen them coming and was able to get the train away just in time. The Boers galloped after it in a vain attempt to stop it and in an exchange of fire, one Boer was wounded and one of their horses killed. This infuriated them, so they immediately arrested the stationmaster and his staff. Not long afterwards a second train loaded with supplies for the army at Dundee steamed into the station and was promptly captured. The telegraph wires to Ladysmith were then cut and Black mineworkers from the nearby coalmine commandeered to pull up the railway line. The Boers now set about examining the contents of the goods trucks standing in the station. They were amazed at some of the paraphernalia, such as sporting equipment which the British carried about with them on a military campaign. However, speculation about the lifestyle of the British ceased when liquor was found. Soon jovial, but drunken, Boers were staggering about the platform of the Elandslaagte railway station. It was at this point that Colonel Adolf Schiel, commander of the German Commando in the Boer Army, arrived.

Col Schiel had served in the Prussian Army, probably as a sergeant, before coming to the Transvaal in 1878. He had become a friend of Paul Kruger and had done much work developing the German-trained Transvaal Artillery (*Staatsartillerie*) into the disciplined and effective force it was in 1899. Karri Davies and Aubrey Woolls Sampson were well known to him as he was Superintendent of Prisons when they were imprisoned in Pretoria. Schiel possessed in full measure the Germanic passion for order and discipline, and was often frustrated by the ways of the Boers and complained about 'the disorder and complete lack of discipline amongst the burgher commandos.' He found the Boers viewed with 'distrust, even aversion, any military innovation' and would meet any representations in this regard with 'a supercilious smile.'[3]

For their part, the Boer military leaders often found Schiel exasperating and resented his lack of respect for their African experience. On one occasion, an irritated General Piet Joubert dismissed a suggestion from Schiel with the comment, 'Schiel you always bother me with your European military ideas.'

Colonel Adolf Schiel, commander of the German Kommando.

Schiel had brought with him into Natal 150 members of the German *Uitlander Korps*, no doubt the pick of that corps, and probably the best of the foreign units fighting for the Boer Republics. His Adjutant was the German aristocrat, Count Zeppelin. Attached to General Kock's western column, they crossed the Biggarsburg range early on the morning of 19 October, and later that morning stopped at a farm which seemed a suitable campsite. On the approach of the Boers, the owner and his family fled, leaving a manager in charge. From this man, potatoes and a fat beast were requisitioned and thus a fine barbeque was in prospect. However this was not the only reason for Schiel calling a halt.

Field Cornet Potgieter had been scouting ahead and Schiel felt his *Kommando* should not proceed further until Potgieter's report had been received and considered. Also he was not happy with the manner in which the advance was proceeding and wanted to discuss the matter with General Kock. In a book published after the war Schiel wrote:

'Our advance was again unplanned and to put it mildly, quite careless. General Kock did not keep his units together and every Field Cornet went his own way which means he advanced without concerning himself with keeping in touch with other detachments… It seemed inevitable that this unplanned riding would sooner or later have disastrous results. Nobody seemed to be concerned that we found ourselves in enemy country and that we could be attacked at any moment.'[4]

Schiel sent a message to the General expressing his concerns and requesting a meeting. To his surprise, Kock agreed with the Colonel's comments and said he would see him that afternoon.

The smell of the roasting meat must have filled the men with eager anticipation for the feast to come, but just as the food was ready, a message arrived from *Veld Kornet* Potgieter saying that he had captured two heavily laden trains and two of his men had been wounded; he urgently needed reinforcement as otherwise he could not hold the trains. Schiel ordered 100 men to saddle up immediately, and after sending a message advising Kock of the position, the barbeque was abandoned and they set off for Elandslaagte about 17 miles from Ladysmith.

The sight of drunken Boers staggering around Elandslaagte station would have done nothing to strengthen the Colonel's confidence, however the position had to be defended so he took his unit out to a small hill from which he could cover both the road and the railway line from Ladysmith. From the train they took oats for their horses and a case of whisky for themselves. As darkness fell it began to rain in torrents. Cold, wet and hungry, the Germans kept vigil through the night.

Late that evening Schiel went to the Hotel at Elandslaagte to check the condition of the wounded men. He found the hotel full to bursting with a party in full swing. *Kommandant* Ben Viljoen had arrived with his Johannesburg *Kommando*. However it was not only Boers who were present; their prisoners and local residents had also been invited. A Boer, in a wet raincoat with his carbine slung over his back, sat at the piano and played popular songs, which were sung lustily by the men gathered around him. Schiel considered himself fortunate to obtain a cup of tea laced with a liberal shot of rum, which gave him some warmth as he went back in the rain to his unit. It is said that the proceedings at the hotel that night closed with everyone singing the Transvaal anthem, *Die Volkslied*, and God Save the Queen.

Early the following morning, General Kock arrived with the rest of his detachment plus two 75mm. field guns and a Maxim.

Despite the joviality of the previous evening, the Boers arrested the General Manager of the Elandslaagte Colliery, David Harris, along with his management staff, and took them to the local hotel for trial. The presiding officer was General Kock's son who conducted proceedings while having a breakfast of grilled goat ribs. At the conclusion of the trial, Harris and his fellow employees were released on parole. The Boers permitted him to remove 100 bags of rice from the train as this was part of the rations to be given to Indian workers at the mine. One of the trucks contained some fine furniture which Harris had imported as a gift for his newly-wedded bride. The furniture remained on the train.

When Schiel arrived that morning he was disgusted to find broken boxes of liquor, food, musical instruments, regimental records, private luggage and all manner of other goods littered across the muddy station platform. Fearing a drunken orgy, he ordered that all liquor be destroyed. A Hollander, Captain de Witt-Hammer, was entrusted with this task. The order was only partially obeyed.

Acting on his own initiative, Schiel decided to patrol in the direction of Ladysmith. After his men had ridden for about an hour, Count Zeppelin, whose troop provided the vanguard of the patrol, reported a strong enemy force approaching from Ladysmith.

On receiving the report, Schiel immediately returned to Elandslaagte. At the station he found the trains being looted by Indian mineworkers, many of whose fellows were lying about drunk. Presumably they had found the leftovers in the smashed liquor bottles. Elsewhere Boers were preparing for the coming battle, building sangars and getting the artillery into place. Other burghers visited the nearby coal mine. Apart from ransacking the offices and breaking open empty safes they found 200 lbs of dynamite as well as 3,000 rounds of ammunition which had been intended for use by the local rifle club.

Schiel met General Kock at the station and was surprised by his lack of interest in the chaos and looting. Instead the General pointed out a line of hills, about a mile south of the railway, and said that it was there he would meet the enemy attack. Schiel then drew Kock's attention to the fact that their task was to cut the track and establish contact with the Free Staters, not to provoke a battle in which they would be outnumbered. He suggested they retreat to the Biggarsberg where they could easily hold off a British attack. The General was unmoved and replied, 'I am a general myself – I take instructions from no one. This is not only where I shall await the enemy, this is where I shall defeat him. This will not be the first time I have done that. You come with me to the hill and take up your position!'[5] Schiel saluted and withdrew to collect his unit. On returning to his men, Schiel found that Zeppelin had returned with a report that the enemy had withdrawn to Ladysmith, the immediate danger had passed. He now called a meeting of his officers and it was decided to make one final effort to persuade Kock to change his mind and burn the trains, break up the railway track, and return to the protective cover of the mountains. Schiel added that if the general was not prepared to change his mind, he would place pickets along the Ladysmith road that coming

Leading men of Gen JHM Kock's Kommandos.

night. A messenger took the suggestion to Kock and half an hour later returned to report: 'The general says he did not come to guard mountains, but to fight, and directs you to place pickets on the road to Ladysmith at night as suggested by you, but with the break of dawn you shall fall back on the position already allocated to you.'[6]

Before dawn the next day, forward pickets reported the approach of an enemy detachment with artillery. Schiel ordered the pickets not to fire, but to fall back on him. In the dark Schiel's unit, which now included about a hundred Free Staters, saddled up and readied themselves for the return to the main Boer position as directed by Kock.

When the telegraph line was cut at Elandslaagte on 19 October, General White in Ladysmith sent the Natal Carbineers to scout along the Newcastle road as far as the Modderspruit, approximately half way between Ladysmith and Elandslaagte. No contact was made with the enemy. The following day the Carbineers, accompanied by the 5th Hussars, were again sent out scouting in the same direction. This time contact was made with the enemy and four prisoners were taken.[7] It would seem that these prisoners were part of the patrol which Schiel had sent out under Count Zeppelin. On arrival in Ladysmith, they were interrogated and from information gathered, General White was able to get some idea of the force camped at Elandslaagte. He decided to attack before further reinforcements arrived.

The next day, Saturday, 21 October, Major General Sir John French was ordered to clear Elandslaagte, repair the railway line, and restore telegraph contact with Dundee. The Chief Staff Officer under General French was Major Douglas Haig. Five squadrons of the Imperial Light Horse, a couple of squadrons of the Natal Mounted Rifles, and the Natal Field Artillery with their six obsolete 2.5-inch muzzle-loading guns were to go by road. Infantry, consisting of half a battalion of the Manchester Regiment, were to travel by train. They were to be accompanied by the Royal Engineers Railway and Telegraph sections.

The mounted men set off at 4.00 a.m. and by dawn they had reached a vantage point about one and a half miles from the railway station. The rain had stopped and before him French saw a broad valley along which ran the road and railway line to Dundee and Newcastle. The railway was on his right and was fenced on both sides with barbed wire. To the right of the station could be seen a line of hills which rose a couple of hundred feet above the valley floor and which were at right angles to the railway. On his left was the towering peak of Jonono's Kop at the foot of which were some smaller hills. Though the day promised to be fair, patches of mist still hung about the higher ground. Concealed in these hills were Schiel and his men, watching.

'E' Squadron of the Imperial Light Horse under Captain Knapp was sent ahead to see if it was possible to outflank the Boers. Possibly a fortuitous patch of mist concealed their departure, as Schiel was unaware that they had left the main group. Without waiting for the Infantry to arrive by train, French decided to test the enemy defences. The Artillery unlimbered and fired a salvo at the station. Schiel, having been associated with Transvaal *Staatsartillerie* and its professional soldiers with their modern guns, was rather scornful of their effort. However their gunnery was not too bad. One shell struck a shed, another killed a mule, another hit an inadequately marked empty ambulance wagon, thereby disturbing a pharmacist's morning toilet without injuring him, while yet another hit the truck in which Mine Manager Harris' furniture was stored. The furniture was blown to smithereens. Apart from the damage to the ambulance, the Boers were unscathed. They now sent their reply.

Firing from a position well beyond the range of the little Natal guns and near the hills to the right of the station, the Boer artillery almost immediately disabled the Volunteers' ammunition wagon and would have caused much more damage had their shells been properly primed. It was now apparent to French that the main Boer force was located on the hills to the right of the railway. Realising his guns were outranged, he withdrew to a position beyond the range of the Boer guns. The arrival of the train with the Manchesters and Engineers enabled him to telegraph Ladysmith with a request for reinforcements.

While withdrawing, Karri Davies noticed that the squadron of the Imperial Light Horse under Knapp was continuing down the valley getting further and further away from the main column with every passing minute. He realised that Knapp did not know of the order to retire and his squadron was heading straight for the Boers' main camp where they would be annihilated. A sergeant and a trooper were sent to warn Knapp to fall back on the main column immediately. Karri watched the two through his field glasses as they galloped down the valley. Suddenly, a number of shots were heard, the trooper fell from his horse, the Sergeant stopped, dismounted, helped the wounded man back into the saddle, and led the horse back towards his own lines.

Watching the incident, Schiel recognised that the two men were from the ILH and, being impressed by the heroic action of the sergeant, was pleased when his own men shouted, 'Don't shoot that man – let him go.'[8]

Through his glasses Karri saw Knapp's squadron beginning to disappear behind Elandslaagte station and Boers moving in the same direction, apparently with the intention of cutting them off. When the sergeant returned and reported their failure to get through, Karri, without showing any regard for his own personal safety, immediately charged down the hill and galloped down the wide valley in full view of the enemy. Heavy fire was opened on him. To those watching, it seemed that there was only a chance in a million that he would get through, but, by a miracle, neither horse nor rider was hit. Once through the danger zone, Karri was able to locate Knapp and, by taking a wide detour, lead the squadron back to the main column.[9]

Though they played no further part in the day's proceedings, the Natal Artillery had caused sufficient chaos at the station to enable Harris and other mine employees to make off across the *veld* to British lines. Although his wife would probably be infuriated by the loss of her furniture, Harris must have been very relieved that he had got away. He was chairman of the local Rifle Association and once the Boers linked him to the 3,000 rounds of ammunition found at the mine he would have been in big trouble. The railway employees who had been locked up in the station escaped through the ticket office window, taking their guard with them as a prisoner. These two groups of escapees were able to provide French with valuable information regarding the disposition of the Boer forces.

In Ladysmith White responded immediately to French's request. By road he sent:

> Two squadrons of the 5th Lancers
> A squadron of the 5th Dragoon Guards
> Three squadrons of the Natal Mounted Rifles
> The 21st and 42nd Batteries of the Royal Field Artillery with 18 guns between them.

By train came:

> Seven companies of the Devonshire Regiment
> Five companies of the Gordon Highlanders
> Members of the Natal Volunteer Medical Corps

Stretcher bearers who had accompanied the British regiments from India must also have come on the train as they later helped with the wounded.

As a precaution against an attack from the west by the Free Staters, the Border Mounted Rifles and Carbineers were ordered to guard the western approaches to Ladysmith, while General White and his guard of twenty-two men from the Natal Mounted Rifles joined the mounted men en route to Elandslaagte.

Earlier French had asked Col Scott Chisholme what the ILH would like to do. The Colonel replied that they would like to take the hill on the Boer's left flank. French gave him permission to do just that. The ILH therefore, with one squadron of the 5th Lancers in reserve, rode south to engage the left flank of the Boers who had positioned themselves some way forward of the Boer main position. Before the ILH went into action, Scott Chisholme called a meeting of his officers, at which he told them that the Boers were a disorganised bunch of simple farmers from whom they had little to fear.[10] By mid-morning the Light Horse had made contact with the Boer *Kommando*, and began to drive them back.

During the day two Carbineer messengers arrived from Dundee with news of the battle at Talana and the mortal wound suffered by General Penn Symons. For his part, sensing that the coming day might see him taking part in an historic event, General Kock donned a black frock coat and top hat. Later that morning an alert observer would have noticed banks of cumulus clouds building up over the mountains, a sure sign of an impending storm.

The withdrawal by French after the early morning abortive attack lifted the spirits of General Kock. Seeing Schiel had complied with orders and placed his men on the chosen hill, Kock strode over to the Prussian and with a friendly greeting said, 'Do you see now our position is not as bad as you tried to make it?' By 12.00 p.m. Kock had changed his mind and ordered Schiel, with 100 of his men, to go back to a position to the north-west of the Elandslaagte station, where they were joined by some men from a Free State *Kommando*.

It took some time for the train from Ladysmith to arrive with the reinforcements, however by 3.00 p.m. the British forces were all present. On the left facing Schiel were the Dragoons and a squadron of Lancers supported by the 42nd Battery, with the Natal Mounted Rifles in reserve. In the centre were the infantry, which were positioned from left to right, the Devons, the Gordons and the Manchesters, who were to attack the Boer's main position on the hills lying to the right of the station. With them were two batteries of the Royal Artillery. On the right the Imperial Light Horse continued to drive back the *Kommando* which was guarding the Boer left flank.

When General White arrived, French offered to hand over command to him, however White insisted that French should direct the coming battle. To defeat a force of approximately 850 Boers with two guns and one Maxim, French now had under his command 1,630 infantry, 1,314 mounted men and eighteen modern guns. Although it would only be a couple of hours before darkness descended, he decided to attack at once. All the while those banks of cloud over the mountains were becoming larger and blacker.

Col Ian Hamilton, who was to lead the infantry attack, began by getting his troops into open order, an almost unknown practice in the British army of that time. The *veld* which the British had to traverse appeared from a distance to be flat but there were in fact a number of low ridges and hollows which would provide some cover for the advancing men. Nonetheless for much of the advance they would be exposed to enemy fire.

The British opened their attack with a barrage of fire from their artillery directed at the Boer guns in an attempt to put them out of action, an objective they were never quite able to achieve. The Boer guns replied and the artillery duel continued for some time before fire from the Boers died down. The British artillery now switched to shrapnel and raked the hills occupied by the Boers. At about 4.30 p.m. the Devons began the infantry advance towards the Boer centre while at the same time the Manchesters and Gordons worked round to the right so as to attack the Boer left flank.

Hamilton had spread the firing line of the infantry over approximately 1,000 yards with successive lines of reserves each set a further 400 yards back. This gave them a depth of almost a mile. The Boer artillery sent shell after shell into the advancing infantry but this was completely ineffectual against the widely dispersed men. After the Devons had advanced to within 1,000 yards of the Boers, intense rifle fire forced them to take cover and await the development of the attack on the Boer left flank.

By 5.00 p.m. the Manchesters and Gordons had linked up with the Imperial Light Horse and were ready to attack the Boer's left. Between them and the crest of the hill occupied by the Boers, lay about 800 yards of *veld* exposed to fire from virtually the entire Boer front. The dismounted ILH took up a position on the right of the infantry. In front of them the ground was covered by boulders, and rose steadily, becoming steeper near the crest.

The storm which had been building up for hours now broke and the men of both sides felt its fury. The crash of thunder and lightning added to the cacophony of artillery and rifle fire, while torrential rain drenched everyone and everything and the ground underfoot turned to slippery mud. As the rain-soaked Infantry and the Light Horse rose to advance, they were met by a veritable hail of bullets. Nonetheless by advancing in rushes, the tide of attackers moved steadily up the hill. A barbed wire fence temporarily slowed the advance and men fell. The wire was cut and the forward surge continued.

Col Ian Hamilton, disregarding the storm and enemy fire, rode back and forth on the battlefield exhorting and encouraging all to maintain the momentum of the advance. One who did not need encouragement was Col Scott Chisholme. Appointing Major Woolls Sampson to lead on the left and Major Karri Davies on the right, Chisholme placed himself in the centre of the ILH. Instructing his men to follow, he held aloft a walking stick to which was attached a little flag, and set off up the rocky slope towards the hidden enemy. Though the Artillery continued to rake the summit with shrapnel, rifle fire from the crest never slackened for a second. Fierce as it was, it failed to check the inexorable advance of the ILH. Hamilton left this description of the gallant Colonel leading his regiment up that slope, 'To see that little red rag going on and on and on without a falter was the bravest sight I have ever seen in my life.'[11]

Hamilton also saw Major Woolls Sampson at the head of his men. Exposed to enemy fire and seemingly oblivious to danger, he was twirling the stick he always carried, while at the same time, pouring out a torrent of curses at his men for not taking cover between rushes forward. In one such advance, one man failed to rise and told Woolls Sampson he was so paralysed with fear that he could not move. The Major went on, but had not gone far before a bullet found its mark and Sambo was down. His thigh had been shattered by a soft-nosed bullet. As he lay there unable to move, he saw a trooper with blood flowing from a wound to his face, leading the charge, shouting curses and yelling defiance at the enemy. It was that same individual who, a few moments before, had been paralysed with fear.[12]

On the right, Karri Davies and his men were not so much going up the hill as going round the end of the hill towards the rear of the Boer position.

Though the approach to the summit was not as precipitous as that scaled by the Dublins and Irish Fusiliers at Dundee, it was sufficiently steep to compel the defenders to look over the edge. Not wishing to be silhouetted against the sky, their fire slackened. A piper with the Gordon Highlanders played out the call to 'Charge.' Far away on the left, the call was repeated by the bugles of the Devons, who with Manchesters and Gordons, fixed bayonets and charged towards the crest. The Imperial Light Horse, not having bayonets and relying solely on its single shot rifles, went with the infantry and stormed over the crest in the expectation that victory was only moments away.

With the British steadily advancing up the hills occupied by his *Kommandos*, General Kock sent an order to Schiel to bring his men back immediately. As soon as they received the order, the Germans and Free Staters set off at a gallop to join Kock. At the railway they had to stop to cut their way through the barbed wire fences. This gave their horses a breather and the men an opportunity to drink a toast to their 'Most Gracious Kaiser.' Having established where their loyalties lay, the *Kommando* galloped on. While crossing a flooded stream, Schiel's horse sank up to its saddle in the mud, and though Schiel jumped off, it was unable to extricate itself. His men quickly came to his assistance, pulled the horse out, and on they rode. Schiel noticed groups of Boers leaving the battlefield and could not resist saying to one of his lieutenants, 'If only we had a gun, instead of firing at the British I would let those bastards have it.'[13]

As they made their way towards the left of the Boer line, they came under artillery fire. Count Zeppelin died instantly when hit by shrapnel. On reaching the place where they had been that morning, they dismounted and began to climb the hill. As they neared the top, Schiel was horrified to find Scottish infantry were in the process of outflanking them. They raced onto the summit and with no more than 100 yards separating them, the two sides poured a murderous fire into each other. Then in the Colonel's words:

'A new disaster struck. A detachment of Imperial Light Horse appeared on the flank of the enemy... Next to me knelt a certain Ludwig von Borries; I admired the calmness with which he fired. Every one of his shots found its mark. He jumped up to advance a few paces, then he fell back right at my feet with a bullet through his forehead. Field Cornet Potgieter knelt two paces to my half right. He used a big rock for cover. I saw him lift his rifle to take aim then suddenly his head jerked to the right and he too sank to the ground ('we never saw shooting like that in the 5th'). Left and right my poor boys lay on the ground but no help was in sight.

'In pressing forward I called to Captain Weiss to send an orderly to the General to tell him that we had been overtaken and to advise him that if he could make no further change in his front we would endeavour to delay the enemy to cover the retreat.

'My rifle became so hot that I could scarcely hold it. All of a sudden I felt a jab just below the heel of one foot as if someone had prodded me with a red hot poker and I was convinced that I had been struck by a bullet. My magazine was again empty; I took a fresh clip of cartridges from my bandolier and fired another three shots towards the enemy who was already so close that we could discern the whites of their eyes. The air was thick with bullets. I intended taking a pace forward, but felt all of a sudden as if I had been dispossessed of my left leg; I fell and blacked out.'[14]

Along the whole length of their line the Boers were being pushed back and were making their way down the reverse slope of the hill. Their guns were captured and it seemed that the British hold on the hills was secure. In the course of the advance a disproportionately high number of British officers had been killed or wounded with the result that when the summit was reached not only were Devons, Manchesters, Gordon Highlanders and Imperial Light Horse all mixed inexorably together, but the chain of command had become very blurred, many of the men being uncertain to whom they should look for orders.

Some time after 5.00 p.m., Hamilton noticed a white flag in the Boer camp. In spite of the fact that Boers could be seen riding away from the battlefield, he ordered the trumpeter to sound 'Cease Fire.' This was done.

Down in the Boer camp, Dr Coster, who had been State Attorney at the time of the trial of the Reformers in 1896, tore down the white flag saying, '*Liever sterven!*' (Rather Die!). At the same time General Kock and a party of about fifty Boers who were concealed just over the reverse slope of the hill launched a vigorous counter-attack, storming back onto the summit and firing at point blank range into the British. One of the first hit was Col Scott Chisholme. He was shot in the ankle while bandaging a wounded trooper. Clifford (Dick) Turpin from Grahamstown and C. Lamb attempted to carry him to cover but he was struck by two further bullets which killed him. His last words were, 'My Boys are doing well. My Boys are First.'[15]

For a time it looked as if the counter-attack might succeed. Bewildered by the call to 'Cease Fire' and the vicious enemy attack which followed, the British infantry began to retire down the hill. The Boers recaptured their guns and immediately brought them back into action. Their success was short lived however. Led by Ian Hamilton and officers from the Imperial Light Horse, order was restored among the British troops, who rapidly turned the tables on the Boers, causing them to race down the reverse slope to their ponies and flight.

In turning the potential disaster into the final successful rout of the enemy, three officers of the Light Horse played a particularly important role – Captain Charles Mullins, Lieutenant Robert Johnstone and Lieutenant AE Brabant. Seeing the predicament in which some of the Regulars found themselves, they instantly rushed to their aid, assumed leadership, rallied them and reformed their lines. For their courage and leadership at a critical moment of the action all three were recommended for the Victoria Cross.[16]

Throughout the advance General French had been among the men rallying and urging his troops forward. General White too did not limit his role to that of a mere spectator. He rode in amongst the troops encouraging them. Twice, both he and his bodyguard narrowly escaped death when shells failed to explode.

We left Karri Davies and his squadron rounding the hill on the Boer's left flank. Here lay a farm with several outbuildings. As the Light Horse approached, heavy fire emanating from the farmhouse was opened on them. Realising that the Boers holding the farm constituted a threat to the British flank and rear, Karri ordered it to be taken. Through a curtain of Mauser bullets the ILH rushed towards the farmhouse and as they did so the man next to Karri fell, shot in the leg. Lying in that exposed position he would almost certainly have been killed. The big man did not hesitate. He picked up the wounded trooper and carrying him, made for the nearest shelter – one of the farm's outbuildings. Upon reaching it, Karri put his shoulder to the door and pushed into the darkened room. As he was putting the wounded man on the

V.C. HEROES – BOER WAR
N°61.

Captain R. Johnstone, V.C.
(Imperial Light Horse) awarded the Victoria Cross
in connection with Captain Mullins great
gallantry at Elandslaagte, Oct 21 99. He is also
famous in the world of football

Captain Robert Johnstone VC.

ground, something made him look round. A yard away stood a big Boer with a Mauser pointing straight at his head. 'Drop your gun or I'll blow your brains out!' shouted Karri. From across the room another voice cried, 'Don't shoot! It's Karri Davies.'

The Boer lowered his rifle and a big smile spread over his face as he saw the cane Karri was pointing at him. It was the only weapon Karri ever carried. Looking across the room Karri saw a wounded Boer whom he recognized at once. It was Matthys Human, the Clerk at the Pretoria gaol who had befriended Karri and Sambo. For a few moments the bedlam of war was forgotten, to be replaced by smiles, friendly greetings and handshakes as introductions were made all round.[17]

By this time the ILH had surrounded and taken the farmhouse. Twenty-three prisoners were captured, among whom was General Kock.

During the day the farmhouse and its outbuildings had been used by the Boers not only as a fortified strongpoint, but also as a temporary shelter for their wounded. Given the extraordinary way Kock dressed that day, it is not surprising that when he launched his final counter-attack he was one of the first to fall, seriously wounded. A Dutch lawyer named Tindell saw the general fall and carried him to the nearest shelter, which was the farmhouse now under attack from the ILH, who were about 100 yards away. Seeing what was happening and realizing Tindell's courage, the ILH held their fire until the two had passed into the safety of the house.[18]

When firing between the two sides finally ceased, Kock was carried back to the Boer campsite where a tarpaulin shelter was made for him. A mattress was found (probably in one of the station houses) and he was made as comfortable as possible. Throughout the night, the British cared for the old General as if he was one of their own. A nephew of Kock asked if he could remain with him and this request was granted. In describing the treatment of Kock, Ian Hamilton wrote, '*a deadly poison was injected by the black mamba snake called Propaganda into the body politic of South Africa.*'[19] A metaphor which was to apply to far more than the treatment of the old Boer General.

Having captured the Boer position, the British did not direct artillery or rifle fire at the fleeing enemy. It was now the turn of the British cavalry to show what they could do and to deliver the *coup de grâce* by cutting off the Boer retreat. The Cavalry assigned with this task were commanded by a Major Gore and consisted of a squadron of the 5th Lancers and a squadron of the 5th Dragoon Guards each having about 100 men. During the afternoon they were positioned near the station and to the north of the railway line, where the shafts and slag heaps of a coal mine concealed them from the enemy, whose anticipated line of retreat was about two miles away from their position. They were not on the green swards of the Curragh or Windsor Great Park, but on the rough South African *veld*. Visibility was poor, the grass was, by British standards, long and it concealed rocks and holes, which like the ubiquitous anthills, could bring down horse and rider. It was also raining, making the ground wet and slippery. Barbed wire fences and flooded streams would add to their difficulties. At Dundee the day before, Majors Knox and Marling had, in far better conditions, achieved no more with their cavalry than the bruising and the capturing of some prisoners. At 5.30 p.m. Major Gore gave the order to advance. Because of the conditions, Gore decided to abandon the usual knee to knee formation and gave the order to proceed in extended files.

Many are the gory tales which have been written about what happened next. Propagandists had a field day. Their reports of helpless unarmed men and women being skewered by brutal Lancers, egged on by blood-thirsty officers, were readily accepted by those who were either disposed to think ill of Britain, or whose lifeblood was the waging of the British class war. Tales even came from the Cavalry itself; some rather crude boasting from the ranks, and some hearsay of reputed statements by officers, in which irony was probably misunderstood. These lurid stories have one thing in common, they are all highly suspect and a cursory examination of each will show fundamental flaws. Many of the eyewitnesses can easily be proved to have been many miles away at the time of the action, while others describe acts which it would be impossible to execute. These tales were met with some scepticism by the Natal Volunteers.

With General Kock at Elandslaagte was the Johannesburg *Kommando*. Many of its members had been conscripted into the Boer army, and were very reluctant to fight against the British. As a refusal to join the *Kommando* would have meant imprisonment or possibly being shot, an opportunity to be taken as a prisoner of war was an attractive option. In the first few months of the war there were many 'soft' captures of prisoners, who chose to surrender in this way.

As the heat of the battle intensified on that momentous day, many men quietly slipped away from the battlefield. Among the early leavers was General Ben Viljoen also of the Johannesburg *Kommando*. With the collapse of the Boer resistance more Boers joined those fleeing. Instead of retreating in an orderly fashion with scouts out, the Boers gathered in a hollow where they could not see the approaching cavalry whose appearance came as a complete surprise. The Boer's reaction was to scatter, galloping off as hard as they could in different directions. Viljoen was among those who escaped in this manner by the simple process of outdistancing their pursuers who could not keep up on their unwieldy horses.

However, there were some in the *Kommando* who chose not to ride away but instead to surrender. Sadly, before it was realised that they were surrendering some were attacked and wounded with lances, swords and pistols. Major Gore, in a rather vague report gives no figures for the number of enemy dead or wounded, admitting only to taking 30 or 40 prisoners. Neither does he mention any falls or casualties suffered by the Lancers or Dragoons. It would have been quite a simple matter to count the dead and wounded. After more than a hundred years and the spread of much misinformation it is impossible to say how many Boers were wounded by the Lancers or how many, if any, were killed.

The attempt by the cavalry to cut off the retreat of the enemy had been a dismal failure, and the engagement had shown quite conclusively that lance and sword were now obsolete weapons of war.

For the Boers, the incident was a godsend. Instead of having to explain the folly of engaging in the battle and why they had run away at a crucial stage of the engagement, they were able to harangue the listener with tales of atrocities committed against them by the English. In recent times another variation has appeared on this theme: 'The Lancers and Dragoons swept on leaving dozens of Boers and some of their African retainers, spiked and slashed on the ground.'[20]

No authority has been given for this statement. The men who were attacked by the cavalry came almost exclusively from the Johannesburg *Kommando* who would not have taken retainers on campaign. Any retainers at Elandslaagte would have stayed with Kock's wagons at the Boer camp, instead of wandering about the *veld* in the pouring rain several miles away. Further, there is no reason whatsoever why the British cavalry should have attacked unarmed civilians in this manner. Such unfounded statements fuel racial resentment.

As darkness fell, the ceasefire sounded and the violence of the storm was replaced by steady drizzle. On the battlefield at Elandslaagte lay the dead and wounded of both sides. That day the total Boer casualties were 45 killed and 110 wounded. On those hills where General Kock made his stand, the defenders had been subjected to two hours of intensive artillery fire in which almost 500 shells had landed on the confined space where they had stood. The British infantry had fired 61,000 rifle bullets at the defenders and over 1,500 men attacked them with bayonets. It was a miracle the Boer losses were so small. With the exception of General Ben Viljoen, every Boer leader on the field that day was either killed or wounded. There is no room in these statistics for the propaganda slaughter of Boers and their retainers by the Cavalry.

The British casualties were 50 killed and 213 wounded. These figures include the losses of the Imperial Light Horse who suffered 14 killed and 34 wounded. The regiment's commanding officer had been killed and its second-in-command had been seriously wounded and lay somewhere on the battlefield. Karri, with only a few weeks training behind him, now found himself in command of a regiment described by an officer of the Gordons who had seen them in action that day, as 'the finest regiment in the world.' From the battlefield could be heard the piteous cries and groans of the wounded and dying from both sides. Volunteers were sent out to assist in finding and bringing in the wounded.

It is said that General White had sent only one doctor to Elandslaagte. This might be true if one only counts doctors attached to British regiments; however, Dr Rupert Hornabrook went to Elandslaagte with the Natal Mounted Rifles and Surgeon-Major WTF Davies and Sergeant Dr C Ligertwood accompanied the Imperial Light Horse. In addition, there were doctors serving as troopers in the ranks of the ILH, orderlies from the Natal Volunteer Medical Corps and the Indian stretcher bearers who carried the wounded on stretchers (called *dhoolies*) fitted with a shelter to protect the patient from sun or rain. Throughout the day and throughout the night, ignoring the vagaries of the weather and danger to themselves, these men, together with the Boer doctors, worked to ease the suffering of the wounded and dying. No distinction was made between friend and foe. Makeshift first aid posts were established at the railway station and the farmhouse. Urgent and delicate operations, including a tracheotomy, were carried out in the field by lamplight in the pouring rain. And all the while that mamba was gliding over the field spreading his poison. Included among the tales which were told was one which said that General Kock had his money, rings, and watch stolen. He had apparently been stripped of all his clothes except for his trousers; and thus, wounded as he was, had to lie out in the cold all night, half naked.

While these cruelties were supposedly being inflicted on Kock, lying on the battlefield was that doughty opponent of Britain and the *Uitlanders*, Col Schiel. When he regained consciousness, the tide of battle had passed over him. Looking around he saw a trooper approaching and realized he was a member of the Imperial Light Horse. He called out to the trooper, 'Hello! You are one of the ILH. Please give my regards to Woolls Sampson and Karri Davies.'[21] Then, as an afterthought, he gave his rifle to the trooper to keep as a memento. The trooper, M Greathead, was later killed at the battle of Wagon Hill. Schiel gave this description of the battlefield that night:

'How dreadful was the sight that met my eyes. All around me my brave lads were lying on the ground; only a few had made it. Scottish soldiers and our own lay intermingled. To my left lay the dead body of Herr von Borries, a pace in front of me Field Cornet Potgieter on his back: his pale face with a black beard and his large wide-open eyes presented a dreadful aspect. His eyes were turned towards me as if he was on the point of speaking to me. Three paces behind me sat Potgieter's youngest brother with a bullet through both shoulders. Close by, two paces to my right, lay an Afrikaner. Groaning, he turned towards me, saw me and said, 'Is the commandant not dead?'

'Notwithstanding my pain I could not help but smile at this naïve question. The poor fellow had a bullet through the chest and a shattered arm. A little further on lay Schmidt, a former Prussian Artillery NCO, obviously dead.

'A Light Horse who was collecting rifles approached me. "Great Scot!" he said, "That is Colonel Schiel!" He was an acquaintance from Johannesburg. "Who won?" I asked, as we shook hands. "We," he said hesitatingly, "We won, but a large number of your chaps got away!" Thank heavens for that, I thought to myself.

'I wanted to say something, but darkness again overcame me and I fell over. The friendly Light Horse took his field flask and held it to my lips. That worked wonders; his cognac sent the blood coursing through my veins again, but I could feel the blood still running from my wound. Another Light Horse turned up. "Have you any arms?" "Yes, two," I said, "but only one leg!" "No," he said, "That's not what I mean." Now I understood. I thought he had enquired as to whether I had been shot through the arms. My rifle was gone, my revolver as well. When he saw that I still had my binoculars he took them away. I must say I would rather have given them to his friendlier comrade who later came back, after it had started to rain heavily, to give me his raincoat for protection and as a souvenir.

'As darkness fell, some other Light Horse came along to carry me to the First Aid Post. I requested them, however, to attend rather to those of my men who were more seriously wounded. I must admit that it was not only compassion for the other wounded which prompted me to turn down the friendly offer of help, but rather the hope that during the night Weiss or von Albedyll would come with their men to look for me... My brother Max told me later that he had heard that I had been killed. Some men had seen me fall down on my side and had reported this fact to him. He spent the whole night walking around and towards midnight had come upon a few Gordon Highlanders. He asked one of them if he had seen me, giving him as detailed a description of me as he could. "He is dead," said the Gordon, "I blew his brains out!" (It was not only cavalrymen who indulged in imaginative boasting to make themselves appear fearsome!)

'The rain began to fall heavily; the night was bitterly cold. Fortunately I still had a little cognac in my flask. I crept up to poor Potgieter who could not lie still for agony of his wound. The poor fellow moaned pitifully; only a few paces away lay the corpse of his brother. A few paces further on lay a Gordon, also with a bullet his leg. We shared the brandy. He still had some tobacco and some dry matches, so we smoked a pipe of peace together. The raincoat which the friendly Light Horse had given me I passed on to Potgieter. Soon after the Gordon was carried away. A few paces from me lay one of our lads. He must have been close to death for his breath rattled, almost like a snoring man, and continued until midnight when all of a sudden it stopped.

'The English soldiers, particularly the Light Horse, helped our wounded wherever they could, and when darkness fell many had already been taken to the First Aid Post. I asked one of them to give Potgieter a little water. They gave us all they had....A Sergeant, a musician or piper, sat himself next to me and offered me his help. When he saw I had not yet been bandaged and that my riding breeches were soaked in blood, he took his knife out of his pocket and without hesitation cut my left trouser leg from top to bottom through breeches, underpants and riding boots, to dress the wound. I was grateful for his well-meant assistance, but wished, however, he had not cut my clothes in this manner because, notwithstanding my severe pain, I had remained warm. Now, however, the cold rain struck my naked leg and I began to shiver until my teeth chattered. The sergeant stayed with me for a long while and told me about his little daughter who was, as he said, his one and only joy. I thought of my little girls whom I had not seen for a whole year. When this good fellow saw how I shivered from the cold he went away to fetch help to carry me away; his own raincoat he had already given away long ago. Later on he visited me in hospital in Ladysmith and told me that he had gone to fetch two Gordons but was unable to find me again in the dark.'[22]

Aubrey Woolls Sampson was one of the last wounded brought in. He was found by a group of Light Horsemen led by Karri Davies. To carry Sambo they constructed a rough litter out of three rifles and in that way they were able to convey him over the rocky ground to the First Aid post at the Station. It must have been an agonising journey for him. One of those who helped carry him left this account:

'He was cheerful when I first saw him and was merely solicitous on behalf of other wounded men in his more immediate neighbourhood and anxious that a Gordon Highlander, who had been killed in close proximity, should have decent carriage to his own lines... Major Sampson bore his wounds with great fortitude and during the six hours it took us to carry him to the station he uttered no word of complaint though undoubtedly suffering the acutest of agony.'[23]

Early the next morning General Kock, Col Schiel, Woolls Sampson and other wounded from both sides were taken by hospital train to Ladysmith. Late that night an officer with the telegraph section went to the Elandslaagte Hotel and noted with a hint of disapproval that Boer prisoners who were having their wounds dressed appeared to be having a good time. They were eating and drinking with their opponents as if nothing had occurred. Among those present were Douglas Haig and Karri Davies. The officer was invited to take a seat and despite the unusual circumstances he had a 'jolly time' and was disappointed when, at 4.30 a.m., his orderly arrived with a message that the horses were ready for the trip back to Ladysmith.[24]

Perhaps Col Schiel should have the last word on the battle: 'How easy it would have been for the English to surround us completely. If they had done this instead of launching a frontal attack they could have achieved victory due to their artillery superiority without losing hardly a man.'

Chapter Ten

Fall-out from Elandslaagte

◆

'As each man received his measure of beer, he carried it across to a comrade in the Imperial Light Horse.'

Gesture by the rank and file of the Gordon Highlanders after the battle of Elandslaagte

I N Pietermaritzburg on the morning of Sunday, 22 October 1899, an excited 24 year-old nurse, Kate Driver, was up early. She was going to Ladysmith. Kate's grandparents had come to South Africa with the 1820 settlers and she had grown up in Queenstown in the Eastern Cape. On her leaving school, the family moved to Pietermaritzburg, where Kate trained as a nurse at Grey's Hospital, which was already acquiring a reputation for excellence. On completion of her training she stayed on in Pietermaritzburg, working as a private nurse.

At Grey's she had worked under the guidance of an outstanding doctor, Dr OJ Currie, who had spent some years in India, specialising in the prevention of malaria, after which he came to Natal, where, amongst other things, he contributed much to the fight against the spread of that debilitating disease. When war threatened, Dr Currie joined the Natal Carbineers as a Surgeon Captain and asked Kate if she would be willing to serve as his surgical nurse. She readily agreed.

Kate's uncle, Clement Webb, was an officer in the Imperial Light Horse and while the regiment was undergoing its initial training in Pietermaritzburg, he would most certainly have spent some time with his sister and niece. Also in the regiment was a young trooper, Guthrie Smith, who came from Kingwilliamstown in the Eastern Cape. The Webb and Guthrie Smith families had many friends in common and no doubt the trooper would have attended one or more of these social meetings of family and friends.

When the Carbineers were ordered to Ladysmith, Kate was not among the nurses selected to go with them and she was devastated. She could have nursed at the Military Hospital being set up in Pietermaritzburg, but it was to Ladysmith that she wanted to go. Kate's mother did not like the idea of her daughter leaving home to go to the town and, unknown to Kate, wrote to the Principal Medical Officer of the Volunteers saying her daughter was not strong enough to endure the hardships which she would have to suffer on the campaign. Noticing how distraught Kate was, her mother confessed to what she had done and promptly wrote to the Medical Officer withdrawing her earlier letter.

And so it came about that at 9.a.m. on the day after the battle at Elandslaagte, Kate Driver, now possessed with 'wild gaiety and energy' after saying goodbye to her tearful and anxious mother, caught the train to Ladysmith. She has left a description of that journey:

'We had not gone far on our journey before we learnt that a train previous to ours had been fired upon. People up the line were in a great state of excitement. Boers had been sighted in groups about the *veld*. At every station there were men in khaki. Some of them, noticing my red cross arm badge, saluted, and suddenly I remembered I too was wearing a uniform. I smiled and returned the greetings of those who passed near my window, and then I found myself watching a very tall young man with red hair, carrying a cup of tea with great concentration so as not to spill it. He stopped as he reached my compartment and took his eyes off the tea. "This is yours, Nurse. We may not be able to get tea at every station." I thanked him warmly. "I saw your red cross. My sister is a nurse too. She is coming from Australia to nurse in this war."

"A long way to come!" I said.

"Some girls nowadays will come a long way for this job," he replied.

'At the next station I saw some men of the Imperial Light Horse, an irregular regiment formed in Johannesburg and destined to become quite famous. I had many friends and relations in it. I already felt a pride in it, a kind of belonging. I scanned their faces eagerly in case there should be some I knew. My heart was beating faster for the joy and pride of being part of all this.

'During our slow progress of the next few hours, trains crammed with soldiers came champing past us – our slower wheels, their quicker wheels all pounding out the forceful rhythm of war....

'The war was in khaki and I was in the surge of it all now, and I did not know what I felt, save excitement and a kind of proud thankfulness that I too could help. At about five o'clock our train stopped just outside Ladysmith. By now it was raining heavily.'[1]

For a long time Kate waited patiently on the train but in the end decided to walk through the rain to the station where she found the platform and yard were packed with rows of dhoolies from under the covers of which she heard moans of agony. She began to realise what war meant and to struggle with a paralysing fear that beneath the green covers she might see a face she knew.

At the station she was directed to the Town Hall which had been converted into the Military Hospital while the adjacent Public Library held the operating theatres. Next to these buildings were a collection of marquees which formed the headquarters of the Natal Volunteer Hospital. Although the Volunteers had suffered no casualties on the previous day, she found the staff up to their eyes in work: 'Night nurses as well as day nurses were on duty to cope with all the operations, and men were being brought in as fast as possible.'[2]

Kate was welcomed by the matron, an old friend from Greys, who took her to the Nurses' marquee so she could take off her wet clothes, while the matron fetched her some tea. In a few minutes all thoughts of tea or dry clothes disappeared when it was realised that the Nurse's Tent was needed for patients and Nurse Driver began work: 'As fast as beds were put up and made, men were brought in, some waiting in great pain, while the more urgent cases were taken to the operating theatre first.'[3] It was midnight before she and the other nurses were able to have something to eat.

It had been arranged that Kate and another nurse should stay in a private house in the town. They were given directions and the two young women set out into the night to find the house where they had been billeted: 'As we made our way through the dark, muddy square, suddenly there was a flash of steel and we were challenged by a big Indian doing sentry duty. After a little discussion we showed him our Red Cross badges. This time there was a flash of white teeth as he smiled and let us pass.'[3]

Their hosts were not pleased at being woken in the middle of the night but as soon as they realised the girls were Volunteer nurses they were welcomed. Weary beyond words, Kate was at last able to go to bed and steal a few hours sleep. She had travelled a long way that day.

Among the first batch of wounded to arrive in Ladysmith was General Kock. His condition was desperate and this, combined with his age and status, made it desirable that he should have the best possible care. The medical authorities should not have had any worries on this point. As soon as it became known that General Kock had been seriously wounded, the correspondent of the London *Times* made available his bed and blankets to the old General, so that he might be as comfortable as possible. The person who chose to sleep on the floor so that a wounded Boer General might be comfortable was Colonel Frank Rhodes.[4]

It had been an exhausting couple of days for all the medical personnel at Ladysmith. Surgeon Captain Rupert Hornabrook had ridden out with the Natal Mounted Rifles when they were ordered to join French's force at Elandslaagte. Hornabrook had followed a similar route to Natal as Dr Currie. After qualifying as a doctor, he also went to India where he took part in the campaign to eradicate malaria and other tropical diseases and from there he moved to South Africa to help prevent the spread of disease among mineworkers. When war threatened he moved to Natal and became the medical officer of the Natal Mounted Rifles.

Although the Natal Mounted Rifles were in reserve throughout the battle, as soon as the British troops began to suffer casualties in the afternoon, Hornabrook, with the other Natal Medical Volunteers, immediately went to the assistance of the wounded. We have seen that as afternoon turned to evening, the number of casualties on both sides increased and as darkness fell, the overburdened medical staff not only had to attend to the wounded in temporary first aid posts, but also had to go out into the rain to give emergency treatment to those who had yet to be brought in from the battlefield. It was not until the early hours of the next morning that the young doctor was able to saddle up his horse for the ride back to Ladysmith.

After Hornabrook had ridden a couple of miles he spotted a group of twenty-five armed Boers. He rode up to them and told them they were surrounded and should surrender immediately! Three of the Boers were directed by him to collect their colleague's rifles. They complied with his directions and were led back to Elandslaagte where the prisoners and their arms were handed over to the British Regulars.[5] It had been a very brave action by the young Australian to approach these enemy fighters and demand that they surrender. However their behaviour indicates that this might have been a 'soft' capture and that this group of 'Boers' was actually seeking captivity (see Chapter Nine). The arrival of the Boer prisoners in Ladysmith caused quite a stir as they were marched through the town on their way to the train which would take them to the coast and a prisoner of war camp on the island of St. Helena.

Living close to the Transvaal and Free State borders, the Zulus working in Ladysmith were fully aware of the manner in which the Boers behaved towards other Black peoples. In addition they had seen and heard what happened to those refugee mineworkers from the Reef who had thought themselves fortunate to catch a train home from Johannesburg. Once on the train, these refugees were required to hand over all their money to Transvaal officials. As a general rule no receipts were issued, neither were records kept of the money so confiscated. Many who failed to hand over their money or attempted to hide it were beaten with a *sjambok*. Mineworkers usually kept their money in a knot tied in one of their garments. If the Boers found the money, the refugee not only lost it but often his garment as well. One refugee, S Msimang, stitched five sovereigns into both his shirt collar and the shoulder padding. The sovereigns in his shirt collar were discovered and expropriated. With only half his savings purloined he was fortunate. When the Boer prisoners arrived in Ladysmith, the Zulus took the opportunity to deride and taunt them as they marched through the town.

The battle at Elandslaagte had convinced General White that his force there would not be strong enough to hold that position once the main Boer army arrived. He therefore decided to withdraw all units to Ladysmith immediately.

When the worn and weary Imperial Light Horse reached Ladysmith, they dismounted alongside the lines of the Gordon Highlanders, where the men were lining up to receive their daily beer ration. They had missed this little luxury the previous day and no doubt were looking forward to their pint. There then occurred a spontaneous act, splendid in its simplicity and immense in its significance. As each man received his measure of beer he carried it across to a comrade in the ILH, a generous self-denying tribute from those in the ranks of a famous old regiment to their colonial brothers-in-arms.[6]

On that same Sunday, General French sent for the new de facto commander of the Imperial Light Horse, Major Karri Davies. French told Karri that he knew not only of his brave ride which had rescued Captain Knapp and 'E' Squadron, but also how, later in the day, in the face of terrific fire and at point blank range, he had picked up a wounded man and carried him to safety. Because of his great courage in saving these lives, the General told Karri that it was his intention to recommend that he be awarded the Victoria Cross. Karri's reply must have astonished General French. He thanked him for offering to put his name forward, but asked him not to do so. Karri said that on signing up he had given an undertaking to General Penn Symons that he would serve throughout the war without pay, promotion or decoration, and that the only reward he sought was to serve Queen and Country.[7]

The circumstances under which he gave the undertaking are not recorded, however Penn Symons, alone among British senior officers, was unimpressed by the ILH while they were in Pietermaritzburg. We also know of his low opinion of colonials, and no doubt he possessed, in full measure, the disdain which some of the military caste felt for those involved in trade. It is not difficult to imagine the type of comment which would have goaded Karri into making the undertaking. To some his reaction might appear to be overly pedantic. After all, Penn Symons was dying and no one else would know about the undertaking given by Karri. The award would have been the first Victoria Cross presented to an Australian and his countrymen would no doubt have been immensely proud of such an honour, as would the Imperial Light Horse. However, Karri knew he had given the undertaking and for him his word must be his bond.

Captain Knapp, in his report on the battle, described how his squadron had been saved by Karri Davies whose prompt and heroic action saved them from annihilation. The report was submitted to his commanding officer, who happened to be Karri, with the result that this part of the report went no further.

Subsequently it was recommended that four members of the ILH be awarded the Victoria Cross. They were Major Aubrey Woolls Sampson, Captain Charles Herbert Mullins, Captain Robert Johnstone, and Lieutenant A.E. Brabant.

In due course a reply was received from the War Office in London stating '…*while Colonel Woolls Sampson evidently led his men with much gallantry, Lord Wolseley does not feel that his conduct was sufficiently exceptional to call for the bestowal of the great favour of the Victoria Cross.*' With respect to the other three, the War Office apparently felt all three deserved the award but were only prepared to award two to the regiment. The responsibility of deciding on whom these much prized decorations should be conferred fell on the ILH Adjutant, Captain Barnes. Barnes consulted with the regiment and it was decided that the award should go to Mullins and Johnstone, though all felt that Brabant had also deserved it.

Robert Johnstone was a well known international rugby player, having played many games for Ireland. Shortly before the war he toured South Africa with the 1896 British Lions rugby team. With war clouds gathering, he stayed on and subsequently joined the ILH. After the war he returned to his home in Ireland.

Lt Brabant, the son of a General, was born in the Cape Colony. Less than a fortnight after Elandslaagte, this talented and unassuming young officer was to die of wounds suffered in an engagement on 3 November. He was killed before the decision of the War Office was received in Ladysmith.

Robert Johnstone was not the only Irish international rugby player at Elandslaagte. Dr Tommy Crean was also a member of the 1896 Lions team. A big, brawny man with a perpetual smile on his face, he loved the rough and tumble of rugby. After a game he would challenge his team mates to a fight, individually or the whole lot together. He survived the tour and settled down to practice medicine in Johannesburg. Despite his sometimes unusual behaviour, or perhaps because of it, he soon acquired a substantial practice. On one occasion a patient barged into a room where Tommy, dressed only in a short shirt, was shaving. Tommy glared at the man: 'Is it no manners that ye have intruding on the privacy of a gentleman? And your face is a cruel one; it

Surgeon Captain TJ Crean
VC DSO.

needs hitting. Will ye fight with me?' The patient was out of the house in a flash, running down the street with Tommy after him. On reaching his home the man rushed inside and bolted the door, leaving Tommy on the mat, demanding that he 'come out and fight.' A crowd soon collected and in due course a policeman arrived. Tommy, unabashed, offered to fight the policeman for his trousers. Somehow the law melted away, and Tommy was able to borrow a jacket and completely unperturbed by the morning's events, walked home.

Tommy gave the 'Uitlanders unqualified support in their struggle against the Kruger regime, and was one of the first to join the ILH at Pietermaritzburg. Because the Regiment already had its full compliment of doctors he, with other medical men, chose to serve as troopers. Tommy was among those wounded at Elandslaagte.

In addition to those awarded to Mullins and Johnstone, Captain Meikeljohn and Sergeant Major W Robertson, both of the 2nd Gordon Highlanders, were awarded Victoria Crosses for their gallantry at Elandslaagte.

Also arriving in Ladysmith that Sunday, 22 October 1899, was Captain C.G. Willson with the Dundee squadron of the Natal Carbineers. They were accompanied by four Boer prisoners whom they had captured in the course of their ride from Dundee. On arrival, Charlie Willson was promptly arrested and relieved of his duties.[8] Quite what he had done to deserve such treatment was not known. One rumour was that he had failed to obey orders, another that he was charged with cowardice. Bearing in mind that the Carbineers in Dundee were not billeted in the British camp and the chaos which existed in Dundee at the time, one does wonder what the orders were that he failed to obey. Similarly it is hard to imagine what act of cowardice could have been attributed to him while his squadron was guarding the British camp during the battle of Talana.

Not surprisingly, there was some dissatisfaction among the Carbineers regarding the treatment which Charlie had received. He had after all brought his squadron to Ladysmith without losing any men, while at the same time taking prisoners.

There were officers among the Carbineers who could have taken over leadership of the Dundee squadron, however the military did not follow this route. Instead, to replace Charlie, Lieutenant Archibald Wales of the Natal Mounted Rifles was moved across to the Carbineers and promoted Captain.

CHAPTER ELEVEN

Retreat of Dundee column to Ladysmith

•◆•

*'All farmers and transport riders from the northern frontier, lean, bearded,
sun-dried, framed of steel and whipcord, sitting their horses like the riders
of the Elgin marbles, swift and cunning as the Boers, and far braver,
they are the heaven-sent type of irregular troopers.'*

BRITISH JOURNALIST, GW STEEVENS, ON THE BORDER MOUNTED RIFLES

GENERAL WHITE had never liked the idea of sending a substantial number of his troops to northern Natal, and now the situation he feared most had come to pass: his army was split in two. During the battle at Elandslaagte he received news of the inconclusive engagement at Dundee and the serious wound suffered by General Penn Symons. The next day he received a telegram from the Dundee column to say it was falling back on Helpmekaar, a village about 25 miles due south of Dundee. White replied with an order that it should retire to Ladysmith immediately.

The result was that the Dundee column under Col Yule would go south along the Helpmekaar road for about 15 miles to the hamlet of Beith and there turn right and follow the track to Ladysmith which lay about 45 miles to the west. The column would be vulnerable during the entire march and particularly so while crossing some hills near Beith in an area known as van Tonder's Pass.

It was decided to send a squadron of Volunteers – the Dundee Troop of the Natal Carbineers – out along the Beith road to make contact with Yule. The Troop had arrived from Dundee on the afternoon of 22 October and no doubt both men and horses were exhausted. Added to this, the new senior officer, Captain Wales, came from the coast and was not familiar with northern Natal. This plan did have the advantage that they would be out of Ladysmith until such time as Yule's column arrived and the arrest of Captain Willson would be kept firmly under the carpet for the time being.

On Monday, 23 October 1899, Martial Law was extended over the whole of Natal, which strengthened the control of the military over civilians. Free State Boers re-occupied Elandslaagte station and the *Kommando* under General Erasmus entered Dundee. Lieutenant Brooking of the ILH was ordered to take twelve men to Elandslaagte to collect the bodies of the Colonel and other regimental dead. With them were burial parties from the Gordons, Devons and Manchesters. They set off on a train bedecked with white flags, but had travelled only about 5 miles before Boer fire compelled them to turn back. They had just begun the return journey when alongside the train came a troop of Hussars, 'riding a finish'. They had been racing the enemy from Dundee and their horses were exhausted. Two of the horses were 'cooked' and they and their riders were taken onto the train. The rest rode alongside the train as it steamed back to Ladysmith.[1]

Brooking reported to headquarters, and was told to try again. He was given a letter of introduction from a Boer prisoner. This time they were stopped, not by enemy fire, but by stones across the railway line. Boers rode up and an '*indaba*' (conference) was held. The burial party was told by the Boers that the rails had been ripped up and a bridge burnt, so they had no choice but to walk the rest of the way under escort. Arriving after dark, they were invited to spend the night at the Station Master's house. Under the watchful eye of a sentry, they spent an uncomfortable night attempting to sleep in station chairs.

The next morning they discovered that all the bodies had been buried, so the Gordons, Manchesters and Devons immediately returned to Ladysmith, leaving behind a Chaplain, Major Grant of the Royal Engineers, and the ILH. They exhumed the body of Colonel Scott-Chisholme and the Chaplain read the burial service over the other graves. The Boers asked if they would exhume the body of Dr Coster as his wife wished to bury him elsewhere. So they set to and exhumed his body and handed it over to the Boers.

During the day sounds of battle were heard, which was frustrating, however they had no choice but to continue with the task in hand until it was completed. The Boers lent them two wagons, one to carry the body of the Colonel, the other the burial party. They set off in the evening, Brooking recording that they, '... had a quiet night on the road back, but the Dutch Doctor driving our fellows was in such a desperate hurry to get through, most of our fellows got out and walked. Collared a real good Dutch pony, but it was collared again from me the same night.'[2]

During the flight from Dundee, Yule was so incapacitated by his curious illness that the task of leading the column fell on Col Dartnell of the Natal Police. Although a Canadian, as a former British Army officer, Dartnell was given more credence than would normally be given to a colonial officer. To this advantage he added knowledge of northern Natal. When dawn came on 23 October, the column was twelve miles from Dundee. By midday it had passed Beith and was resting in the hills of van Tonder's Pass. It was here that it was met by Captain Wales and his troop of Carbineers. That night they marched through the hills into the comparative safety of the Sundays River valley.

Concerned that the Free State *Kommandos* might cut off the retreat of the Dundee column, General White decided a show of force against them might persuade them to remain where they were, in the hills to the north of Ladysmith. On the 23rd he ordered five men from his bodyguard to scout along the Newcastle road to find out the position and strength of these *Kommandos*. In charge of the party was Corporal CJ Landsberg; the other members being Troopers LV Ash, AC Brandon, GJL Golding and AW Evans, the son of the OC the Natal Mounted Rifles. They rode out along the Newcastle road until they reached a dry water course which led up to the hills which were thought to be occupied by the Boers. Concealed from anyone on the hills, they were able to ride a considerable way before Landsberg decided it was time to dismount.

Leaving their horses in the care of the other three members of the squad, Landsberg and Golding crept forward through the tall grass and rocks until they were within 500 yards of Boers. Here they were able to note the disposition of the enemy and watch them as they went about their daily routine. Eventually they perceived a movement among the enemy which threatened to cut them off, so they decided to break cover and run for it. As they rose from their sheltered position, they were spotted by the sentries and, as they raced a zigzag course down the hill over rocks and through long grass, they could hear hundreds of Mauser bullets whistling past them. Fortune was with them and they reached the shelter of the riverbed unscathed. The rest of the squad were anxiously waiting with their horses, and as the fugitives arrived they were given them and they all galloped off. All, that is, except Trooper Golding. As he was about to mount, his horse shied, and breaking loose, galloped after the others. Exhausted by his hard run, Golding could only stagger along the riverbed as Boer bullets threw up spouts of sand around his feet. He was about to give up when he heard his name called. This produced just enough adrenalin to enable him to make it round the next bend. There he found a dismounted Trooper Evans holding the runaway horse. Evans called, 'Jump up smartly – it's too hot in this quarter – let's get out of it.' Muttering his thanks, Golding scrambled into the saddle and together they raced back to the rest of the squad and safety. Golding subsequently learned that while the squad was under fire, Evans saw the loose horse, caught it and turned back to find out what had happened to the rider. By this time the Boers were pouring heavy fire into the watercourse, forcing Evans to dismount and continue his search on foot. Evans was the youngest trooper in the Natal Mounted Rifles and his action was much applauded by all in Ladysmith. He received the DCM for so courageously returning to save Golding.[3] With the information gained from this sortie and from the Natal Native Scouts, General White now knew where to launch a diversionary attack.

At 1.30 a.m. on Tuesday, 24 October, 5,300 men were roused from their slumbers and by 2.30 a.m. they had assembled and set off along the Newcastle road. It was a mixed group of Volunteers and Regulars – the Imperial Light Horse, the Natal Mounted Rifles, the Natal Carbineers, the Border Mounted Rifles, the 5th Lancers and the 19th Hussars constituted the mounted contingent. The infantry were represented by the Devons, Gloucesters, Liverpools and the Kings Royal Rifles. In support were two Batteries of Field Artillery and one Mountain Battery,

The rains of the past few weeks had abated leaving the promise of a glorious morning. After they had travelled about 8 miles, the expected rifle fire was received from the Tintwanyoni hills on their left. Reaction to the enemy fire was prompt. The Hussars, the Lancers and some squadrons of the ILH immediately went forward along the Newcastle road, thereby securing the right flank of the British force. When the Boer guns fired on the column they were rapidly silenced by the Artillery. The infantry, with a detachment of the Imperial Light Horse, swung left, crossed the railway and took up a position about 800 to 1,000 yards from the Boers. The two sides began an exchange of rifle fire which lasted about 4 hours.

The Volunteers were delegated the task of protecting the British left. At 10.00 a.m. it was noticed that Boers on a hill to the west of Tintwanyoni were attempting to circumvent the British left. The Volunteers were ordered forward. With the Border Mounted Rifles and the Natal Mounted Rifles in the van, the Volunteers pushed up a valley and occupied a kopje to the west of the British infantry. Robert Samuelson, who was acting as galloper between Col Royston and the regimental commanders, watched the Volunteers move up to a ridge and bring their machine guns into action: '….a hail of projectiles, great and small, were hurled at them, but they went on as coolly as if they were at an ordinary parade, and returned the compliment.'[4]

Fighting in rocky, broken country the Volunteers were not only able to check the Boer attempt to outflank the British, but also to drive them back. The result was that when General White decided to call off the action it was no longer the British left flank which was threatened but the Boer's right flank. But at 11:00 a.m. an unfortunate incident occurred. The Gloucesters broke cover and proceeded to advance towards the enemy, apparently with the intention of driving the Boers off the secure position they occupied on the hills. They were immediately subjected to heavy fire. Their commander, Colonel Wilford, and six men were killed and forty wounded before they could crawl back to cover. The ILH who joined them in this escapade were fortunate not to suffer any casualties. At noon General White received a heliograph message that the Dundee column had reached the Waschbank River, 18 miles away. He decided it was no longer necessary to continue the engagement and gave the order to retire to Ladysmith. The artillery successfully covered the retreat of the infantry off the hills and during the retirement along the Newcastle road, the Volunteers formed a defensive shield at the rear of the column. All were back in town by 3.30 p.m. In the engagement the Border Mounted Rifles lost two men killed (Troopers S Brown from Harding and P Nilsen from Port Shepstone) and 9 were wounded; the Carbineers lost two men killed (Sgt AE Colville and Trooper W Cleaver) and had 9 wounded; the Natal Mounted Rifles had 3 men wounded. In his despatch of 2 December 1899, General White mentioned the gallant manner in which Major Sangmeister (BMR) and Major Taunton (Carbineers) seized a *kopje*, and by speedily bringing a Maxim gun into action, cleared out the enemy. Surgeon Captains R. Buntine and HT Platt were also mentioned in the same despatch for the courage displayed when, under heavy fire, they tended the wounded.[6]

The effect of the smaller, high-speed Mauser bullet was dramatically illustrated by the wound suffered by one NMR trooper. During the fighting he felt a sharp pain and cried out, 'I'm hit!' 'Nonsense, man, it's only your horse,' said a comrade. Accepting the assurance, he went on fighting. That night he suffered a great deal from what he called 'spasms'. The next morning it was found that he had been shot through the body. He collapsed and was taken to hospital.[7]

The following day Major Herbert Watkins-Pitchford and Surgeon Major James Hyslop were ordered to take a detail of 10 men with a mule-wagon, to recover the bodies of those who had been killed on the previous day. As they neared the scene of the battle, they could see clumps of Boers scouring the hills. Uncertain of the reception they might receive from the Free State Boers, Hyslop and Watkins-Pitchford took off their tunics bedecked with badges, and put on trooper's coats. With each holding a Red Cross flag they rode over to the Boers. Their flags were respected, the Boer general having left a message that they were to be given 'every assistance'. A signal was sent to the Volunteers' wagon to come up.

Vultures were already circling in the air above each corpse so there was no difficulty locating the bodies. The bodies lay where they had fallen. Their boots had been taken and their pockets rifled, but they were otherwise undisturbed. When the Volunteer dead had been collected, the Boers told them there were nine more bodies on the hill which had been occupied by the Gloucesters. While climbing this hill the officers and men somehow separated, with the result that when the bodies of nine Gloucesters were found, the burial party consisted of the two officers and a Father Ford, a Roman Catholic priest. As no Imperial troops were to be seen, Father Ford said prayers over the deceased and the three men set about digging a grave. Before they had finished a squad from the Gloucesters arrived who took over the task.

On the way back they called at the now vacated farm of the local member of the Natal Legislative Assembly, Mr Pepworth. The Boers had been through the place but had not taken anything of value. The detail loaded some of the more valuable items in the house onto the wagon for safekeeping in Ladysmith. On arrival the bodies were unloaded for burial and Pepworth's belongings were left in the custody of the Police.[8]

In Dundee on that same Wednesday, 25 October 1899, the Reverend Gerard Bailey and Father Murray, the Roman Catholic chaplain to the Dublin Fusiliers, attended to the burial at Smith's farm of thirty-five men who had been killed during the battle the previous Friday. They were laid to rest near the Smith family graveyard, which is in the wood and a little higher than the farmhouse. The farmhouse, graveyard and much else beside, now form part of the excellent Talana Museum. The funerals were to have taken place at 6.00 p.m. on Saturday on 21 October. However, as Gerard was about to set off to walk to Talana, Boer Artillery opened fire on the British camp and in the Vicar's words '… it was soon clear that they had more powerful guns than we had.' Having created havoc in the British camp the Boer gunners decided to deliver 'a dose all round'. Gerard was walking along the path from the vicarage to the church,

'...when I heard the Boer gun again and this time very distinctly, and in a moment I realised that a shell was about to strike near me. Before I had time for another thought I found myself full length on the ground. "Thank goodness I am lying down," was the flash thought which came to me. There was a heavy thud and a shower of mud played on and about me. The shell had missed striking the house by a few feet, and had landed half way between the house and the church. Fortunately the ground was very soft, as there had been a good deal of rain, and so the shell buried itself and the force of the explosion was confined.'

He hurried on down to the drift to cross the Sandspruit which he found was in flood. There was no sign of a burial party at Smith's farm so he decided the funerals must, of necessity, be postponed. The following days were so packed with incident that it was not until the 25th that an opportunity arose to attend to the burials at Talana.

On Sunday, 22nd the Vicar and Father Murray conducted the funerals of eight men in the grounds of the hospital and in the afternoon four more were buried in the churchyard of St. James' church. In the course of the day Gerard and Father Murray struck up a friendship which from that time resulted in their being constantly in each other's company. Unlike the Boer Republics, where there existed strong anti-Catholic sentiment, in Natal there was no hostility between Catholics and Protestants and the fact that the two men became friends would have caused no surprise. Natalians did, however, find it bewildering that some Irish Catholics, in America and elsewhere, should support the Boer attempt to subjugate their country.

On Monday, 23 October the Boers entered Dundee and that evening General Penn Symons died. The next day Gerard conducted the burial of the General in the churchyard of St. James. Only a handful of people were present.

Dundee had a peacetime population of approximately 1,000 souls. This had swelled with the arrival of refugees but had shrunk again as the Boers approached. In the days which followed the battle at Talana many of the residents fled, some to Greytown, others towards Weenen and Estcourt. Every wheeled vehicle was pressed into service. Those who did not have a vehicle rode, and those who did not have a horse walked. When it was discovered that the army had sneaked off, many citizens chased after it and walked with the column to Ladysmith. It seems that all those who attempted to get away succeeded. They, like the British column, could have been intercepted and captured, if the Boers had not been otherwise engaged.

Deneys Reitz was among the triumphant Boers who rode into Dundee on 23 October 1899 and left this description of their entry into the town:

'...soon 1,500 men were whooping through the streets, and behaving in a very undisciplined manner. Officers tried to stem the rush, but we were not to be denied, and we plundered shops and dwelling-houses, and did considerable damage before the Kommandants and Field-Cornets were able to restore some semblance of order. It was not what we got out of it, for we knew we could carry little or nothing away with us, but the joy of ransacking other people's property is hard to resist, and we gave way to impulse.'[9]

Reitz was ordered to remain in the Dundee area when the rest of his *Kommando* moved south. At Glencoe station he saw the wife of General Kock searching for her husband, the memory of her tear-stained face impressing on the young man the first hint of what women suffer in time of war.

Not all the residents of Dundee had joined the exodus. When the Boers rode in, some 250 still remained in the town, as well as the sick, wounded and medical personnel of the military camp. The majority of those who remained were men and they had different reasons for staying. Some such as the doctors, nurses and medical orderlies, stayed on because they felt they had a duty to continue to do the best they could for those in their care; others had been so overwhelmed by the swift turn of events that they did not know what to do and so did nothing, while still others, such as the magistrate, felt they should not desert their posts. There were even some who believed that they had nothing to fear from the Boers.

General Joubert had issued a widely publicised proclamation addressed to the inhabitants of the Cape Colony and Natal in which he stated:

'...the Government and people of this Republic have been forced into war by evil disposed capitalists and war-like British ministers; and they must now stand up and fight in the true interest of the whole of the South African people irrespective of place or origin. It is not the intention of officers and burghers to molest or injure any individual or private property of those who are friendly disposed towards, and desist from all hostilities against us. If it should happen, which is not desired, that any inhabitant is harmed by circumstances or by casualties, the officers and war council will be prepared to lend a willing ear to all complaints or objections reasonably brought before them. No persons will be allowed to commit a culpable act without coming under severe punishment. We will, however, carry on this war, forced upon us, according to civilised and humane usages and under the guidance of an all-directing God in heaven.'

'All very nice,' was the comment on the Proclamation by Gerard Bailey, who was soon to learn how the Boers interpreted, 'the guidance of an all-directing God in heaven' – an interpretation to which the people of Dundee had perforce to submit. Gerard wrote:

'I was in the streets of Dundee constantly during the first week so I had ample opportunities of witnessing the work of destruction. Out of all the stores, including Arab stores, only two escaped. The rest were wrecked. The owners or their representatives, of stores and offices were many of them in town, but the work of destruction was so rapid and violent that it was of little use protesting. One of our townsmen who kept a restaurant told me that his was one of the first places the invaders came to. They helped themselves wholesale to the liquor, and then turned their attention to the cigars. He began dealing them out one by one, but they demanded boxes and ignoring him altogether seized his whole stock. They then went into another room, here they smashed up a new cinematograph, wrenched the action out of a piano, and demolished several musical instruments. I myself went through the rooms with the proprietor and saw how they served him.

'I visited a bookseller's store where I had left my camera. Books, stationery, pictures, ornaments, etc. all lay on the floor. The camera may have been buried beneath the debris. The Boers as they came in trampled everything underfoot. The safe I found forced open. This was the case pretty well in every office. I do not suppose the burglars were rewarded for their pains. You can be sure all moneys were removed. A Dutch photographer came to me, anxious to get plates, chemicals, etc. I told him there was a studio in town. He came back to tell me everything had been destroyed, even the printing papers torn open and exposed. A watchmaker, who had remained in town, and was helping at the hospital, lost everything. He found watch glasses, main-springs etc. strewn about and crushed and spoilt in the most reckless manner, likewise all his valuable tools gone, and everything in the shape of silver and electroplate. But the same fate awaited every store and office. The only two that resisted the looters were Messrs Oldacre's and Handley's and these only to a limited extent, as later on they were taken over by the Transvaal authorities and then looting was done in a more genteel manner. [The Magistrate had persuaded Oldacre and Handley not to leave so as to provide some continuity of normal civilian life.] The Boer in his looting had his own particular fancies. Macintoshes were eagerly snapped up, sardines never passed over, and Dutch Bibles taken as godsends. I found one Boer gloating over a heavy well bound one. "Hullo, got a Bible?" I said. His eyes beamed with satisfaction. If he survives the war, he will read it every night to his vrou and kinders [wife and children] and tell them how the Lord gave him the Bible when the burghers took Dundee, and *smote the English hip and thigh. I said to one Boer, "I think we shall have to start a new set of commandments. The eighth seems a bit out of date just now."*[10]

At that time in rural Natal the only way many clergyman could visit parts of their parish was to ride. Indeed it was not until the second half of the twentieth century that an ability to ride a horse ceased to be a necessary accomplishment for a priest in some parishes. The Baileys had three horses. One was his wife's much loved pony which had taken first prize at the Weenen show. The other two horses were used by the Vicar to get around the parish, visit mission stations and so on. The Boers lost no time appropriating the three horses, all their tack and Gerard's saddle. They knew his wife had a saddle, a much prized wedding present, however it had been hidden by Gerard and they were never able to find it. Gerard consoled himself with the thought that the Boers generally treated their horses well.

While the Boers were thus occupied in Dundee, the British column, nominally under Yule, was struggling on towards Ladysmith. After the engagement at Tintwanyoni, a report was received from Native Scouts that the Free Staters were preparing to cut off the Dundee column. Colonel W Royston persuaded General White to permit him to take all the Natal Volunteers to meet the column, and hurry it back to Ladysmith. He found the column about 15 miles out on the Helpmekaar road, about to set up camp in an extremely vulnerable position. With difficulty he persuaded the men to break camp and resume their march. The correspondent of the London *Daily Mail*, George W Steevens, gave this account of the meeting of the two groups.

"'Come to meet us!' cried the staff officer with amazement in his voice. "What on earth for?" It was on October 25th, about five miles out along the Helpmekaar road, which runs east from Ladysmith… The staff officer could not make out what in the world it meant. He had pushed on from the Dundee column, but it was a childish superstition to imagine that the Dundee column could possibly need assistance. They had only marched thirty odd miles on Monday and Tuesday; starting at four in the morning, they would by two o'clock or so have covered the seventeen miles that would take them into camp, fifteen miles outside Ladysmith. They were coming to help Ladysmith, if you like; but the idea of Ladysmith helping them! Eight miles or so along the road I came upon the Border Mounted Rifles, saddles off, and lolling on the grass. All farmers and transport riders from the northern frontier, lean, bearded, sun-dried, framed of steel and whipcord, sitting their horses like the riders of the Elgin marbles, swift and cunning as Boers, and far braver, they are the heaven-sent type of irregular troopers. It was they who had ridden out and made connection with the returning column an hour before."[11]

Except that the BMR came from the southern border, Steevens' description rings true.

It had been a glorious morning on 24 October, when General White's troops marched out to engage the Free Staters on the Tintwanyoni hills, but by the night of the 25th the rains had returned. As the rain poured down, the men, horses, guns, cattle, wagons and mules turned the track into a quagmire. Horses, sometimes up to their hocks in mud, struggled to drag the guns along. By the time they reached Ladysmith the next morning, everything – men, animals and equipment – was caked in mud. However they had reached base, when they could so easily have been in a prison in Pretoria.

Chapter Twelve

Situation in Ladysmith

•→•

'Natal grows fat on war.'

HW Nevinson, English War Correspondent.

A
S gold prospectors flock to remote corners of the globe at the first hint of a gold strike, so journalists, war artists and photographers came to Ladysmith. The town had acquired 'celebrity' status' with all the minutiae of its daily life being reported to the world. Neither this status nor the war had been sought by its residents.

No newly established town is beautiful. It takes time for trees to grow and an infrastructure to be created, however from its founding, the townspeople had striven hard to create their little bit of paradise. Ladysmith enjoyed a fine setting and a healthy climate. Its residents were proud of their Town Hall and adjacent Library. The Roman Catholic Convent and small Government School provided, in all important things, an excellent and inexpensive education. Various denominations had built churches which were well supported and there were cricket, rugby, hockey, and tennis clubs. It even had a racecourse. As in other country towns of the period, its businessmen, craftsmen and professional men offered a range of services which today would be difficult to find in a town ten or twenty times its size.

But the residents of Ladysmith soon found out what happened when 12,000 soldiers with 8,000 retainers arrive in a little town. Added to this, the newcomers brought with them approximately 10,000 horses, 2,500 cattle, several hundred mules, hundreds of sheep, innumerable wagons and carts and all the other impedimenta of an army. Not surprisingly grass and other vegetation rapidly disappeared, and when the rains came the bare soil turned to mud, churned up into a soup by thousands of animal and human feet. When the sun came out the mud turned to fine dust which permeated everything. The smell of horse manure and cow dung was everywhere. Trench latrines were dug for the troops and the town was soon infested with swarms of flies.

So when the Paparazzi arrived, this badly bruised little town was not at its best. Obviously in coming to Ladysmith, they hoped to improve their own personal fortunes and when submitting their reports they took into account the views of their employers and the characteristics of their potential readership. For example, British reporters thought it very important that their readers should know that the houses in Ladysmith had corrugated iron roofs, while the correspondent of the *Melbourne Argus*, Donald Macdonald, did not think this worth a mention. One expects such differences. Most made a genuine attempt to give an accurate report on the war. Unfortunately there were some whose primary concern was to promote a cause in their homeland, and if the facts did not suit their purposes, adjustments had to be made.

HW Nevinson was employed by the *Daily Chronicle*, a London newspaper which was a staunch opponent of the ruling Conservative Party. If it could be shown that it was wrong to resist the Boers, or that the war was improperly conducted, the British government would be embarrassed and its standing with the electorate severely damaged. Nevinson empathised with his employers, but was unable to send them regular reports while in Ladysmith. He did, however, make up for this deficiency in 1900 by publishing a book about his experiences in South Africa. This book was one of the first to be published on the War and was to be influential in creating sympathy for the Boers and in demonising the peoples of Natal and their allies.

Henry Woodd Nevinson, though a socialist, came from a privileged English background and had served in one of the more fashionable regiments of the British army. In many ways he resembled Sir Alfred Milner for he never doubted his own superiority, had already formed his opinions about South Africa before leaving England, and would never consult with Colonials, or seek their opinion on anything. He arrived in Cape Town before hostilities began, and immediately set off overland through the Boer Republics, to the British base at Ladysmith. Though he was to stay in hotels which provided full board, he hired two manservants to attend to his personal comfort. While passing through the Republics he took the trouble to acquire some knowledge of the character of the Boers. He noted that the Boer '…like the English poorer classes has large quantities of relations and one of them is always dying.'[1] He observed with satisfaction the neatness of their homes and their attempts to beautify them with little gardens. He found them hospitable and noticed they had little libraries of English books, Greek coins, and other evidence of advancing culture. However, their broad brimmed hats were often stained and dirty. His observation was that in South Africa corrugated iron was practically the sole building material and there were 'few architectural features to boast of.' Thus informed, he was able to tell his readers that the Boers were 'armed and mounted peasants.'[2] Given that many of their farms comprised at least 6,000 acres of good farmland, they were quite unusual peasants, and one does wonder what the Boers thought of his patronage.

Shortly after his arrival in Ladysmith, Nevinson travelled to the top of van Reneen's Pass which crossed the mountains into the Free State. There, in the crisp clear mountain air, he saw spread before him a vast panoramic view of the Colony. Where Winston Churchill saw smooth slopes of the richest verdure broken only at intervals by lofty bluffs crowned with forests, with wide tracts of fertile soil watered by abundant rains and young Deneys Reitz saw a smiling land, Henry Nevinson saw something different. This is how he described Natal:

'…a parched, brown land like the desert beyond the Dead Sea, dusty bits of plain broken up by line upon line of bare red mountains. It seemed a poor country to make a fuss about, yet as South Africa goes, it is rich and even fertile in its way. Indeed on the reddest granite mountain one never fails to find multitudes of flowering plants and pasturage for thinnish sheep.'[3]

The readers of the *Daily Chronicle* knew nothing about Natal and when reading this description they would not have challenged its veracity. They must have thought their government either evil or stupid to even consider going to war and risking British lives, just to prevent some of those nice peasants from keeping a few thinnish sheep in this barren desert. On 21 October, Nevinson and other correspondents rode to Elandslaagte to witness the anticipated battle. In the darkness and 'blinding rain' after the battle, they walked around the field. Nevinson subsequently wrote: '*I was two hours on the ground moving about. The wounded lay very thick, groaning and appealing for help. In coming down I nearly trod on the up-turned white face of an old white-bearded man. He was lying quite silent with a kind of dignity. We asked who he was. He said, "I am Kock, father of the commandant." But the old man was wrong. He himself had been in command."*[4]

When writing this, Nevinson had no doubt already heard the propaganda that the seriously wounded Kock had been stripped of most of his clothes, and then left out all night in the cold rain. We know that when the general fell he was carried by his men to the shelter of the farmhouse as described in Chapter Nine. After the ceasefire he was brought to the first aid post near the Boer camp.[5] It is not even remotely possible that the Boer doctors, medical orderlies and other non-combatants would have carried him out into the rain and there abandoned him. Another question arises from Nevinson's statement. If these media personnel did find the old general on the battlefield, why did they not do something to help him? They could have covered him up, or carried him to a first aid station, or fetched stretcher bearers, or reported his presence to the doctors or the military. Instead they returned to Ladysmith, supper and a comfortable bed. It is a shame that Nevinson did not go out with one of Karri's search parties. That would really have given him something to write about. He might even have had a drink and a bite to eat with Karri Davies, Douglas Haig and the Boers.

South Africa is a complex society, and one can understand how a person new to a country can fail to pick up subtle nuances and as a result come to an incorrect conclusion. Nevinson has, however, gone much further than this. In the two passages quoted above he deliberately misinformed his readers. He knew Natal was not a desert and even he must have realised that this land, from its golden beaches along the warm Indian Ocean to its high mountains, is one of nature's glories. His tale about General Kock is so improbable that it must be rejected as pure invention designed to create sympathy for the Boers and hostility against their opponents. This lack of integrity requires that a reader should be sceptical about everything he wrote. However he should not be ignored, not only because of the influence he has had on many modern British historians, but also because he possessed, to a remarkable degree, those characteristics which, over the years, have bedevilled relations between the British and Colonials everywhere.

On arrival in Natal, Nevinson was presented with another difficulty which had to be accommodated if the desired perception was to be created: people were already living in the country. The discovery that most of the town's residents and the district's farmers were of British origin was a direct threat to his and his employers' policy to use the war to embarrass the English government. In an apparent attempt to discredit the locals, Nevinson tells us that a loaf of bread, '…costs a shilling. Everything costs a shilling here, unless it costs half-a-crown; and Natal grows fat on war. A shilling for a bit of bread! What is the good of Christianity?'[6]

The price of bread in Natal was always high, because wheat was one of the few crops which did not flourish in the Colony, resulting in it having to be brought half-way around the world before it could be milled in Ladysmith. This situation was exacerbated by the declaration of war. The high price of imported wheaten products was the subject of much debate in the Colony and is a complex subject beyond the scope of this work. For the people living in Natal, bread was a luxury and for most, maize products were their staple food. Farmers would begin their day with a plate of unrefined yellow mealie (maize) meal porridge and many, including the writer's grandparents, would include it in all their meals. To suggest that 'Natal grows fat on war', because a hawker was attempting to sell bread at the railway station in Ladysmith, is as ludicrous as to suggest that Britain grew fat on war in 1940, because avocado pears were expensive in London. This clumsy attempt to defame the Colonials is appalling, however, the manner in which Nevinson, with his crude Darwinism, describes the

Zulus and other blacks is even more repugnant. Although he had a low opinion of them, the blacks soon had his measure.

While Nevinson was attempting to put the world to rights by abusing the peoples of Natal, the residents of Ladysmith had other matters to occupy their minds. For many years, George Tatham, a solicitor and land surveyor, had been a member of the Natal Carbineers. In 1899 he was a captain and senior officer in the Ladysmith squadron of the regiment, and had been selected to command General White's personal bodyguard. A number of letters written by his wife Francis have survived. These letters, while concerned principally with family matters, provide valuable insights into the feelings, fears and fortunes of those women who chose stay in the town, no matter how dangerous life became. On 10 October, Francis wrote to her sister Polly in England:

'*The Boers are such cruel brutes. Just fancy, in one truckload of women and children there were six births and one death* [the death was of a woman who died in childbirth leaving the new born baby alone in the world]. *The Boers would not allow the poor refugee creatures even a drink of water at any of the Transvaal stations. Maggie and her two daughters and two grand daughters are still in Harrismith. They did not manage to get away before the commandeering began and so Artie Smith, Jessie's husband, has been commandeered. He refused to fight against the English, so they have taken his four horses, saddles and bridles and fined him £60. He now has to do work in the town but is exempt from fighting…*

'*Oh dear Polly, it is all so sad to see people wandering about homeless who had nice homes and were doing well before all this began. The Boers take possession of everything they can lay their hands on and destroy what they don't want. Poor old Sarah, it is hard for her. She has had to scatter all her things and leave her farm to the mercy of these rebels. Their crops will be destroyed. She had to get rid of poultry, pigs and everything. It will be like starting again. My Willie is in the same case. I had six destitute refugees here in my laundry for some time, but had to put them on the Relief Committee when Sarah came, as we had no room for them. You will think this a very selfish letter, all about ourselves, and our anxieties, but one can think of little else. I am determined to leave this Colony, if I am spared, after this war is over. I have arranged that if Maritzburg is in danger, the girls are to be sent to Ada who can easily get on board a steamer and be off. We have made our Wills and done all that is necessary. Our children are doing so well. Dolly had taken two certificates for Music during the last term, and Georgie a class 1st Prize and an Oxford Certificate.*

'*Does Richard ever think of us and the perils we are threatened with? I wonder if Will would like to be here and go with George? All the young men here are anxious to go to the front. We have completed our Ambulance classes, and are now competent to stop a bleeding wound and dress it, put on bandages properly, turn, lift and wash a patient. When the worst comes I am going to turn four large rooms into hospital wards and our class will nurse Volunteers. The Regulars will be provided for. I must close now. With much love to you and hoping to hear from you. And with warm love to Richard and the girls and boys.*'[7]

The Tatham family had some choices open to them, however others were less fortunate and had to accept what fate sent their way. William Watson was born in Yorkshire and came to Natal as a seventeen year-old in 1851. In 1854 he moved to Ladysmith and established a successful business selling goods sent out from Yorkshire by his father. He married, but sadly his wife died in 1879, leaving him with five young children to bring up. On his being appointed Town Constable and Foreman in 1882, he closed his business. In his younger days he had found time to serve as a sergeant major in the Natal Frontier Guards. His eldest daughter, Annie, married a dentist from Edinburgh and the young couple went to live in Paarl near Cape Town. Tragically, after three children had been born, the young dentist suffered a stroke which left him paralysed. Unable to manage on her own, Annie, with three young daughters and a paralysed husband, moved back to her father's home in Ladysmith. In 1899 William Watson was retired and, outside his family, his pride and joy was his garden with its orchard and copse of trees which he had carefully nurtured over more than 30 years. This doughty old Yorkshireman kept a diary laced with irony during the period 30 October 1899 to 2 March 1990. As one would expect he had very decided opinions and little respect for the political correctness of the time. He believed that the war had come about as a result of a combination of British premier Gladstone's feeble response to the Transvaal's attempt to subjugate Natal in 1881 and the machinations of 'old Barabbus at Pretoria' with his selective biblical quotations. Though he believed the Boers were 'by no means Sybarites', they were accustomed to rough substantial comfort and because 'a few volleys from their deadly rifles exterminated a tribe, or laid a regiment low', they had become overconfident.[8]

Though their future appeared bleak, the people of Ladysmith put on a brave face and did their best to to lead a normal life: women continued to chat to each other and sometimes even indulged in the custom of drinking tea together. Some brave souls rode out on their bicycles to view military emplacements and even rode out of town to watch the fighting at Tintwanyoni.

Meanwhile, the losses at Elandslaagte had compelled the Imperial Light Horse to make some changes. Aubrey Woolls Sampson was promoted to Lieutenant Colonel and, in theory, commanded the regiment. But he was in a very poor state. His femur had been so badly shattered that the doctors believed that amputation of the limb was absolutely necessary. This he would not allow, and the doctors had no choice but to accept his decision. To achieve any mobility he would have to undergo an operation which could not be done in Ladysmith. It was to be many months before he would be mobile again. Command in the field therefore passed to the next ranking officer, Major Karri Davies. With Scott Chisholme dead and Aubrey

A section of the Ladysmith Town Guard. A total of 176 men had enrolled with the Town Guard who despite their civilian clothes and obsolete rifles would, in all probability, have been more than a match for the Boers.

incapacitated, Major Doveton came over from Estcourt, leaving Lt Herbert Bottomley in charge of 'A' Squadron in Estcourt. Bottomley proved to be a very capable officer and it was not long before he had been promoted to major.

For their part, the Natal Volunteers continued their patrols in the hills near Ladysmith, which enabled them to keep Headquarters advised of Boer troop movements. In the east of the Colony, Major Leuchars of the Umvoti Mounted Rifles withdrew from Pomeroy and fell back on Tugela Ferry. The Boers occupied Pomeroy, where they went on another spree of looting and destruction of civilian property.

With the Dundee column now re-united with the rest of his force, General White set about formulating a plan to drive the Boers back into their Republics. He was one of the first to realise the strength of the Boer artillery, and on 24 October, he sent a telegram to the British naval base at Simonstown in the Cape with an urgent request for some long-range naval guns.[9] He has never been given full credit for his enterprise in taking this step, which despite being greeted without any enthusiasm by some senior officers on his staff, was to prove vital for the defence of the town. White had decided to stand firm in Ladysmith and plans were made for its defence. But first he hoped to inflict a stunning defeat on the Boers, which would send them scuttling back across the Border.

The plan devised by the British to inflict this defeat bore all the hallmarks of contemporary military thinking. An attack would be launched against the Transvaal burghers who had been assembling in some numbers in the hills to the north-east of the town. Once the enemy had been dislodged from their positions, they would be driven west into the hills to the north of Ladysmith, where another British column would hold the Free Staters in check and be ready to deliver the knockout blow against any fleeing Transvaalers. Monday, 30 October was chosen as the date for the attack. It was all to go horribly wrong.

On 28 October, the cruiser HMS *Powerful* had arrived in Durban carrying guns destined for Ladysmith. There were two quick-firing 4.7-inch guns, three long 12-pounders (weight 12 cwt.), one 12-pounder naval field gun and four Maxims. Captain Percy Scott RN had, on receipt of White's telegram, designed, constructed, and tested wheels and platforms for these guns which the *Powerful* had brought in. By the next day, they had been transferred from the cruiser to a train and were on their way to Ladysmith accompanied by a Naval Brigade, commanded by Captain H Lambton RN, comprising 18 officers and 267 men. Travelling as fast as it could, by dawn on 30 October the train had reached Estcourt, and by 8.30 a.m. it was at Colenso. Those on board could hear the sound of almost continuous firing including the roar of big cannon. As the rail track was still intact, they pressed on.

At 10 p.m. the previous night, a column, commanded by Lt Col Carleton, comprising the Royal Irish Fusiliers, the Gloucesters and a Mountain Battery, had marched out of Ladysmith intending to take up a position on Nicholson's Nek about 7 miles north of the town. They were to be guided by a Major Adye whom we met in Chapter Seven. The Major had no doubt about his ability to guide the column. The plan required that they hold the Free Staters in check while the attack was being launched against the Transvaal commandos by the rest of the Ladysmith garrison. It was a dark, moonless night and the track they had to follow was rough and not always easy to see. The success of the manoeuvre depended on absolute silence being maintained throughout the march, something which the column had no hope of achieving as it stumbled along in the inky blackness.

While the British were preparing their attack a significant change occurred in the Boer camp. Sick and exhausted, General Lucas Meyer surrendered the command of his 4,000 commandos to Louis Botha, an ambitious and capable man anxious to display his powers of leadership. Botha was born in Greytown, Natal. However, while still a toddler, his family moved to the Vryheid district which the Transvaal had expropriated from Zululand. His success

A converted Naval gun on the quayside in Durban.

as a General in Natal is attributed by many British writers to his knowledge of the country, which he is said to have acquired as a youth while hunting buck over the various battlefields. This is not so. As will be seen, nearly all the farms over which the war in Natal was fought, were owned by people with good Anglo Saxon or Scottish names. Given that Louis Botha grew up in a society dedicated to driving these farmers into the sea, it is highly unlikely that they would have invited him to hunt buck on their farms. It was in the Transvaal that Botha learnt the capabilities of the long-range rifle and the importance of concealment.

For some days the Boers had been gathering on Long Hill and Pepworth's Hill to the north-east of Ladysmith and at Lombard's Kop and Bulwana in the east. It was against the Boers at Long Hill and Pepworth's Hill that the main British attack would fall. A brigade, under the command of Col Grimwood, consisting of five battalions of infantry with supporting artillery, was to dislodge the Boers from Long Hill. A second brigade under Col Ian Hamilton, consisting of four infantry battalions, artillery and some regular cavalry was to attack Pepworth Hill once Long Hill had been cleared. The Border Mounted Rifles and the Natal Mounted Rifles were to protect the British right by covering Lombard's Kop and Bulwana. This whole force moved off from camp at 12 a.m. on Monday, 30 October, and most were in position before dawn. In the darkness two of the infantry battalions and the artillery wandered off course and contact with the regular cavalry was lost.

At first light Grimwood launched his attack against Long Hill only to discover the Boers were not there. Possibly forewarned by spies, they had withdrawn from the hill, and established themselves across the Modderspruit in the rough, bushy country on the eastern bank of that stream. From concealed positions they opened a withering fire on Grimwood's infantry as they crossed the open ground leading to Long Hill, obliging the British to go to ground behind whatever shelter they could find. To add to their misery, Boer guns on Pepworth Hill, which included a big Creuzot Long Tom cannon, opened fire on them. Hamilton had no choice but to abandon any thoughts of capturing Pepworth Hill and to concentrate instead on assisting Grimwood. His infantry went forward to reinforce Grimwood's left and the artillery attempted to put the Boer guns out of action. Initially they were outranged, but by courageously going forward under fire, they brought the enemy guns within range and succeeded in scoring some hits, however the fire from the Boer guns was only temporally stilled and the artillery had to disperse to avoid being annihilated.

Having neutralised the attack by the infantry, Louis Botha, in an apparent attempt to break into Ladysmith, launched an attack against the British right flank, a section of the line held by the Border Mounted Rifles and the Natal Mounted Rifles. Despite repeated attacks by a more numerous enemy, by clever use of available cover the Colonials not only held their line, but by advancing in rushes, they steadily drove the Boers back.

While all this activity was taking place, the Boer Long Tom on Pepworth found time to send four of its 96 lb shells towards Ladysmith. These shells were apparently aimed at the railway station where a train had just arrived with the guns from HMS *Powerful* and Lambton's men. Luckily the Boers had yet to find the range, with the result that the shells flew harmlessly overhead. Army personnel helped the sailors detrain the guns, and after a quick breakfast, three 12 pounders were lashed to ox wagons and, under the command of Lieutenant Michael Hodges, they set off for the battlefield. Leading them was a young local boy on a bicycle who was to show the way.[10] On reaching Limit Hill they came under fire from the Boer Artillery. Hodges unlimbered his guns and was about to fire when orders came through that they should withdraw. Shellfire had already wounded three of his men, knocked a wheel off one of the guns and the oxen had bolted. Nothing daunted, the sailors rounded up the oxen, found a spare wheel and were able to get back to the safety of their new base at Gordon Hill. Here Hodges unlimbered and opened fire on Long Tom at a range of 6,000 yards and with only his third shell, he silenced it for the day.[11] Unfortunately Long Tom was back in action the next day.

At midday Colonel Knox, commander of the small reserve in Ladysmith, sent a message to White advising that the Free State commandos appeared to be gathering to launch an attack on the town from the west. With Grimwood's infantry in disarray, White felt he had no alternative but to call off the attack and to order the immediate return to base. The Artillery came forward to cover the retirement of the infantry, thereby considerably reducing their casualties. Once the infantry had reached safety, the Artillery batteries successfully covered each other in alternate retirements. Once the guns were safely back in Ladysmith, the Natal Volunteers retired, being among the last to leave the battlefield.

During the day General White had heard gunfire coming from the north, so he knew that Carleton's column must have engaged the enemy. He would have realised that as a result of the failure to defeat the Transvaal commandos, Carleton was in danger of being surrounded and there was nothing he could do to help.

After Carleton and his column had travelled about 5 miles along the track to Nicholson's Nek, he noticed a large hill on his left and decided it should be occupied. In the pitch dark the men climbed up in single file. As the leading men reached the top, someone dislodged a rock which, as it tumbled down the hill, dislodged other rocks, some shots went off and for a few seconds there was general pandemonium. Some said a Boer picket had been disturbed and, panic stricken, its members had run down the hill adding to the tumult. All of this was too much for the column's 200 mules who bolted into the night, taking with them the guns of the Mountain Battery, the water kegs, almost all the reserve ammunition and the two heliographs which provided the only means of communication with headquarters.

The men climbed to the top of the hill to await the dawn which was to bring them no joy. As the dawn light spread over the hill it was obvious to all that they were surrounded. They fought courageously, although there was never any doubt what would be the outcome. With ammunition running out, they surrendered. Forty-four men were killed, 150 wounded, and 843 taken prisoner. About 70 men escaped back to Ladysmith with news of the defeat. Two men from the Mountain Battery were found by some of Chief Khumalo's men from Driefontein. They were taken to Joseph Khumalo, who was acting chief in his grandfather's absence. He was able to care for them and to hide them from the Boers until, in March 1900, he was able to bring them safely back to Ladysmith.[12]

General White was devastated by the day's events and accepted full responsibility for the disaster, saying that it was he and he alone who was to blame. The Imperial Light Horse, with Karri Davies in command, had gone out with Hamilton, but had a quiet day acting in support throughout. Lt Brooking recorded in his diary with Austenesque irony, the feelings of many in the regiment:

> 'When at last we got back to camp we heard that the Glosters & Royal Irish Fusiliers were all taken prisoners. Then was the day called "Black Monday" and nobody seemed a bit pleased with the day's fight, until we were told that we had achieved our object and made a Reconnaissance in Force. No doubt the Glosters and RIF were delighted at the idea of having such a nice long rest in Pretoria.'[13]

On a day when little went right for the British, Sir George White was able to state in his despatch:

> 'The services, which Colonel Royston and the forces under his command have rendered to the State and the Colony, have been of the very highest value. In him I have found a bold and successful leader, and an advisor whose experience of the Colony and of the enemy has been of great value to me. Employed on arduous duty from the commencement of the campaign, in touch with the enemy, I have found him prompt and ready for any emergency; he and his force reflect the greatest credit on the colony of Natal."[14]
> During the engagement Lt WJ Clapham of the Natal Mounted Rifles died instantly when he was shot through the heart, and Lt D Brown, Cpl P Lloyd and Trooper AF Sander were wounded. Sgt EF Gibbens and Cpl A Stuart of the Border Mounted Rifles were wounded.'

It had been a bad day for Britain, but it was not without a silver lining. The Boer attempt to break into the town had been frustrated. The big naval guns had arrived in Ladysmith,

A Naval 4.7-inch Gun at Ladysmith, waiting for the word to Fire.

providing cannons which could challenge the Boer Long Toms. In spite of the fact that they were outranged, the regular artillery had also done well and with help from the Navy, there was every reason to suppose the dominance of the Boer Artillery was at an end. The amazing efficiency and speed with which the naval guns had been adapted for use on land and transported to the battlefield showed what Britain could do if pushed into a corner. Perhaps the most important consequence of the humiliation was that British public opinion began to swing against the Boers. And of course it should be remembered that this was the first time Britain had sent its mightiest cannons into battle with a young colonial boy on a bicycle showing the way.

Chapter Thirteen

Investment of Ladysmith

•—◆—•

*'The ghastly wound and the face that showed the shocked
and sudden crumpling up of life.'*

KATE DRIVER REMEMBERING THE DEATH OF THE FIRST CIVILIAN
KILLED IN LADYSMITH.

THOUGH the medical staff in Ladysmith did everything they could to save him, General Kock died of his wounds on 31 October 1899. General Sir George White gave permission to his widow to remove his body for burial in the Transvaal. His nephew, who had been with him since Elandslaagte, was permitted to leave with the bereaved widow. While in Ladysmith, she went out of her way to thank General White for the courtesy and kindness which both she and her late husband had received from the British. The body of the Boer General was taken to Pretoria where he was given a State Funeral.

While Mrs. Kock was engaged in the sad task of collecting her husband's body, the troops in Ladysmith were frantically building fortifications on the defensive perimeter approved by General White. Over the years he has been much censured for his decision to stand firm in Ladysmith. It is said that because the town lay in a valley surrounded by hills it was indefensible. In 1902 Sir George said in his evidence in London to the Commission on the War in South Africa, 'I defended it for 118 days against the headquarters and united armies of the South African Republics…' – a succinct and complete answer to this criticism.

In deciding to remain north of the Tugela, General White took into account another factor. The flow of rivers in Natal is determined by the level of the subterranean water table. During the dry season from May to September this level gradually falls as does the flow in rivers. Apart from localised flash floods, when the rains come in spring, the water table does not rise immediately, and generally it is only in January that the flow of water in the rivers begins to rise substantially. Sir George was quite correct when he told the London Commission that in November 1899, the Tugela could have been 'crossed on foot almost anywhere. Against an enemy with more than double my numbers, and three times my mobility, I could not hope to maintain such a line with my small force.' Added to this the topography of Natal is such that the major rivers which the Boers would have crossed on their way to the coast had high hills on their northern bank and gently sloping hills on their southern bank, thereby providing a natural fortress against any relieving army trying to fight its way from the coast into the interior.

He has also been criticised for failing to blow up the railway lines leading to the Boer Republics. As these lines ran roughly parallel to the Border, which was never far away, their destruction would have been no more than an irritation for the Boers. The railways were an important part of the Colony's infrastructure and would become vital when the time came to drive the invaders out of Natal.

Finally Sir George is criticised for permitting non-combatants to remain in Ladysmith until it was too late to get rid of their 'useless mouths.' Many of the civilians in the town were employed by the army and no doubt they remained because the army still needed their services. Some of the residents, like the Watson family, had no choice but to stay in the town, either because they were physically incapable of leaving, or because they had nowhere else to go. Others chose to remain because they wished to contribute to the defence of their homes and businesses. For example, the nursing home created by Fanny Tatham in her house provided a much needed contribution to the care of the sick and wounded. Almost all the men joined the Town Guard and with a little training they could have become one of the key units defending it. Before the war there were not many resident Blacks in the town. There were some employers who provided temporary accommodation for their employees, however most Zulus chose to live at their *kraals* in the country and to ride or walk into town to work or attend to their affairs. Once the Boers invaded Natal, Blacks such as Samuelson's Scouts sought shelter in Ladysmith, while Indian nationals employed by the Natal coal mines were herded into the town by the Boers. Colonial refugees from northern Natal also congregated in Ladysmith and having nowhere else to go, stayed on in the town. Finally, we should not forget the war correspondents, their manservants and horses, all of whom would require feeding.

Short of shooting all these people, or arresting them and sending them under guard to Durban, it was impossible for General White to 'get rid of these useless mouths', however inconvenient their presence might be. But White never even considered such things. He believed it was his duty to do everything in his power to protect the civilians who were in Ladysmith, and though he made mistakes, his consideration for these unfortunate people adds a dimension to his character often missing from that of his detractors. It was not only the residents of Ladysmith for whom White felt responsible. Throughout Northern Natal there were Zulus who had gone there for protection and who, as a result of the Boer advance into Natal, faced a very uncertain future. If Ladysmith was to be abandoned, not only would further Colonials have had their farms, businesses and homes looted and destroyed, but also thousands of Zulus would have been forced to submit to Boer government and face the possibility of having their land confiscated

Though his decision to stand firm at Ladysmith was undoubtedly correct, General White does appear to have made mistakes with regard to the disposition of his forces. It was a mistake to send the Durban Light Infantry to Colenso where their lack of numbers and mobility rendered them almost useless. They should have been brought to Ladysmith where they could have made a substantial contribution to the defence of the town. The Natal Field Artillery with their obsolete muzzle loading guns were also sent to Colenso. They should have been sent back to Durban and equipped with modern guns, or, if this was not permitted, discharged. Different considerations applied to the mounted Volunteers however. They were highly mobile, knew the country and were able to detect and track Boers while remaining concealed. They owned their horses which were suited to the conditions in which they were to operate. Though equipped with obsolete rifles, such was their marksmanship that they were the opponents most feared by the Boers. In addition they spoke Zulu and their relationship with the Black people was good. To keep these units in Ladysmith was to fail to make full use of their potential.

On 27 October, the Natal Governor, Sir Walter Hely Hutchinson, wrote to the Colonial Secretary advising him that should the Boers raid Pietermaritzburg or Durban the populace would hold the Volunteers responsible. The Volunteers were fully aware of the reliance placed on them by the people of Natal. Once it appeared inevitable that Ladysmith would be besieged, officers in the Volunteer regiments were concerned that while they were shut up in the town, the invading Boers would have a free hand to loot and destroy throughout the country. Major Rethman of the Border Mounted Rifles drafted a letter to General White requesting permission for the mounted Volunteer regiments to leave Ladysmith before the Boers closed the door. He knew that as a major in a Volunteer regiment he had no right to make any such suggestion to a senior British officer, so he wrote the letter in his capacity as an elected Member of the Natal Legislative Assembly. He discussed the letter with some of his officers and it was decided to send it to the local army headquarters. The result was predictable. Headquarters refused to consider the suggestion and he was given a terrific dressing down. Having failed to persuade his headquarters to permit the Mounted Volunteers to leave Ladysmith, the Major requested permission for his regiment to cultivate a kitchen garden. This was also refused on the ground that it was alarmist. Frustrated by the lack of cooperation they received, Major Rethman and Captain Sparks from the Natal Mounted Rifles went to see a Dutch farmer whose land lay within the defensive perimeter chosen by General White. They persuaded the farmer to plant as much of his land as possible to maize. Over the next few weeks, the farmer and his labourers were seen ploughing, preparing and planting their fields, apparently oblivious to the war being waged around them. Even when the Boers sent some shells in their direction, they were not distracted from their work. The maize turned out to be a godsend during the later stages of the siege, providing fresh corn for those besieged. In addition the cobs and maize stalks provided much needed food for the Volunteer's horses. The Dutch farmer did well out of his maize that season.[1]

Subsequently the officer in command of the infantry regiments in Ladysmith, Colonel Ian Hamilton, noted in his diary, 'The cavalry ought, beyond doubt, to have been cleared out of here as soon as it was clear we were going to be invested.'[2]

When Kate Driver reported for duty on the day after her arrival in Ladysmith, she was told that she had been assigned night duty. The Volunteer hospital had five marquees, each being a separate ward. Four nurses would be on duty at any one time. In Kate's ward were several Gordon Highlanders, one of whom had been shot in the head while climbing through a fence at Elandslaagte. During her first night on duty this man became delirious and began singing, 'Yes please, Sirs! Yes please, Sirs!' to the tune of 'Three Blind Mice.' When she came on duty the following evening she found that he, with two other delirious men with bad head wounds, had been placed in a separate marquee. She was made responsible for this ward as well as her original one. She would often sit outside between her two tents and listen, 'For nearly two weeks this poor shattered piper of the Gordon Highlanders screamed and moaned and sang his scrap of song more and more out of tune. Morphia seemed to have little effect upon him. Most of the men in most of the tents were kept awake, and some were badly affected by the noise. When, quite suddenly, the noise stopped and he was dead.'[3]

During her first ten days in Ladysmith the post did much to relieve the stress Kate and her colleagues felt. It brought little luxuries for the nurses as Natal friends had sent boxes of good things for the Hospital. Kate had the comfort of being able to send letters describing her experiences to her mother. She told her about 'my dear Gordon Highlander' and about her friends from Pietermaritzburg: 'Nurse Otto nursed one of the officers, Lieutenant Campbell, until he died. She tells me how heart-rending it was. Poor Nurse Early lost one of her boys this morning and was terribly cut up, a friend of her friends. Every two or three minutes I can hear some young fellow with fever calling out in his delirium, and on the other side, Nurse Thompson has a man with a very badly broken leg, he keeps calling out too.'[4]

Very early on the morning of 31 October the Boer Artillery began their bombardment of the town. This was the first time Kate had heard the sound of oncoming shells and seen them explode. Possibly because she had yet to realise the danger, she felt no fear, only excitement. When the night nurses went off duty in the morning they went up Convent Hill to see from whence the shells came. They were shown around by the soldiers and allowed to look through a telescope and field glasses at the various gun emplacements including the newly arrived naval guns. Their curiosity aroused, they walked to Gordon's Hill to have a closer look at the new arrivals. Here the gunnery Officer permitted them to look through his glasses at the great gun the Boers had placed on Bulwana Hill, after which they were introduced to Captain Lambton, commander of the naval squadron. Dressed in full uniform including a cocked hat, he made a great impression on the girls. Presumably he was on his way to introduce himself to General White.

On arriving back at base, Kate received a message that she was wanted by Dr. Currie. At the operating theatre a Zulu had just been brought in. He had been looking after some mules, when a shell hit his thigh causing a horrendous wound. Before anything could be done for him, he died. Sixty years later Kate could still picture '...the ghastly wound and the face that showed the shocked and sudden crumpling up of life.'[5] He was the first civilian to be killed in Ladysmith.

On this same day, 31 October, Commandant General Joubert demonstrated why he was known as 'Slim Piet' (Sly or Cunning Pete). A Boer ambulance wagon was sent into Ladysmith with wounded British prisoners, the Boers stating that they wished to exchange these men for wounded Boers, and a 24-hour truce was suggested to enable women and children to leave. The British not only agreed to the request but permitted the wagon to enter Ladysmith accompanied by their escort of twenty men, all with Red Cross badges prominently displayed. No attempt was made to blindfold any of this group who were permitted to wander around Ladysmith without any restriction and unaccompanied. They were permitted to talk to unwounded Boer prisoners and known Boer sympathisers. They drank at public bars and one of their number asked to have Frank Rhodes, Dr Jameson and Sir John Willoughby pointed out to him. This behaviour did not appear to have raised any suspicions among the British military. The local residents noticed among the escort several well known Boers who were neither doctors nor in any other way qualified to attend to wounded men. Of those recognized, one Mattey was a well known member of the Boer Artillery corps.[6] They were permitted to take an inordinately long time collecting the wounded exchange prisoners and no doubt were also able to obtain all the information they wanted about Ladysmith's defences. For the Boers it was a great intelligence coup. It was no coincidence that in the days which followed, the Boer artillery were able to shell with pinpoint accuracy the camp of the Imperial Light Horse, important military stores and places known to be frequented by officers. The ILH was obliged to hastily move its camp to a more sheltered position and dye its tents with mud, while the stores had to be moved and some imperial officers had their social life severely disturbed.

Quite what Jameson and Willoughby thought they were doing in Ladysmith is a mystery. Jameson was ill, and because he had provided Kruger with an excuse to build up Boer armaments, he was not popular in Natal. In Ladysmith he presented a picture of abject misery and loneliness. Sir John Willoughby was an Englishman who had served in the Royal Horse Guards. He was the senior officer under Jameson during the Raid and was sentenced to 10 months imprisonment in England. He was of no consequence in Natal, though he was regarded as important by the Boers and latterly by conspiracy theorists. Willoughby left South Africa in 1900.

Among the prisoners exchanged was Major CS Kincaid of the Irish Fusiliers who reported that the prisoners had all been well treated. One does wonder whether the depositing of sick and wounded men in a town, with the intention of either killing them with shellfire or starving them to death is good treatment! The Major obviously thought so, but then he probably expected the siege to be raised within a few weeks. While in captivity he had the opportunity of observing the Irish Brigade and discovered that almost all its members were Americans and those who were not Americans were English. There was not an Irishman among them!

In the days following Black Monday, the Natal Volunteers, the ILH and the British cavalry continued to patrol the countryside around Ladysmith. In a few desultory exchanges of fire they were able to harass the enemy but, as they were always outnumbered and the Boers were able to call on artillery support, they were unable to halt the inexorable drift towards complete encirclement of the town.

During one of his brief periods off duty, Captain George Tatham was asked by his wife to leave an order for a few weeks supplies at Sparks Bros. When delivering the order, George told the shopkeeper to double the quantity of all items requested.[7] Events were to show whether he was an alarmist or a realist. Old William Watson noted in his diary that General Buller, who had boasted that he would be in Pretoria in a month, had landed in Cape Town. He wryly commented that now Buller was in the country, '…he will have the satisfaction of knowing that a very considerable body of our troops, horse, foot and artillery are already in Pretoria, as prisoners of war.'[8]

All over Natal the families and friends of the Volunteers were, of course, very concerned about their loved ones. Just before the siege closed in, Lieutenant George Archibald of the Border Mounted Rifles received from his sweetheart and future wife Rosie, a letter expressing some of the concerns they felt:

'*Mother heard that there are 20,000 refugees in Durban; is it not sad, so many homeless people, whatever will become of them all? … When Sir Redvers Buller does come, do you think there will be any chance of you all coming home, or will they still keep you away? It is exactly a month since that day you came to tell us you had to go to the front – that Friday so long ago. Are you in more danger from those horrid Boers? Of course no one would like to go to shoot a man, even though he be a Boer, for the sake of shooting, but why have they come down and attacked us? Natal is not quarrelling with them. We cannot pity them when it is through them, all you brave Volunteers have to be taken away… I wish you were all at home, the Boers too, if only they could have a good beating first… [and about the horses] Sultan and Chick will not understand such hard times – is there grass enough for them?*'[9]

During the last days of October the Boers were seen placing their big Creusot Long Tom gun on Bulwana, a massive hill about four miles south-east of Ladysmith. Once the gun was in place, men could be seen building fortifications to protect it. It was apparent to all that from this hill the Boer artillery would command much of the town. It therefore came as a surprise to many that the military took no steps to prevent the gun being placed there or to stop the building of the fortifications. Some even thought the British should have included Bulwana within their defensive perimeter. The 1902 London Commission questioned Gen White's Chief of Staff, Sir Archibald Hunter, about these matters. Sir Archibald in his evidence admitted, 'I do not know the country well, except from maps. I only passed up once from Pietermaritzburg, and down again in the dark.' Perhaps relying on the fact that he had spent more than four months in Ladysmith, the Commission asked him about the defences of the town :-

Chairman: 'And there had been no preparations for defence in Ladysmith?'

Hunter: 'None whatever, and the conditions of the life of the garrison there were such with the local farmers, and so on, that you dare not go off the roads. The cavalry officers were supposed to do reconnaissances every year, and to send sketch maps to show what work in this respect they had been doing. But there were simple sketches of the line of the track: they dare not go off it.'

'Every farmer was a Boer or a Dutchman with Boer sympathies; and there was not a single man (Briton) who had been on top of Bulwana, except one and he is dead now – Captain Valentin of the Somersetshire Light Infantry. He had been asked by one of these young farmers to go out for a day's shooting, and in the course of the day he crossed over the top of Bulwana Hill and down the other side, and he was the only man who had ever been on top. Nobody knew whether there was water on the other side or whether there was not.'

Chairman: (incredulously) 'Do you mean that before the war, in our own colony, a British officer could not sketch the country? I mean that in our own colony in the neighbourhood of Ladysmith, that is to say within a girdle of ground that would be naturally occupied in any system of defence for the town, covering stores and so on, there was not a single officer except this Captain Valentin who had been on the main feature or any of the features that dominated a position that had to be held?'

Hunter: 'Not one.'

Chairman: 'Because the farmers would have offered violence?'

Hunter: 'No, they would have summoned them before the magistrate for trespass, and the magistrate would have given a decision against them, and they would have been bound by the magistrate's order.'
Chairman: 'Did it ever happen?'

Hunter: 'It was threatened.'[10]

General Hunter can be forgiven for being unfamiliar with the local terrain and his ignorance of the law of trespass as applied in Natal. However he did look at maps and those maps, inadequate as they might have been, did mention the names of farmers. On one contemporary map of the environs of Ladysmith appear the following names of farmers, Farquhar, Pepworth, Bell, Tatham, Nicholson, Hobbs, Walker, Kirk O'Tulloch and Smith. On the same map appear only three names of Boer farmers, Bester, Potgieter and de Waal. This map does not pretend to give a comprehensive list of the farmers but clearly most of them were of British descent. The proportion of British to Dutch near the borders of the Boer Republics was about five to one, a difference which increased dramatically south of Ladysmith.

One name not mentioned on that particular map is WW Willis, a former mayor of Ladysmith and in 1899 the owner of the farm on which Bulwana Hill was situated. He was in Ladysmith throughout the siege and begged the military to attack the Boers on Bulwana, and was able and willing to give the British any information they might want. All his offers of help were spurned.

With the confidence of ignorance Hunter went on to tell the Commission about the attitude of the Zulus at the start of the War, '… on the one side was this big force of savages waiting to see what we were going to do, and of course the Boers would have sent their agents among them, and have pointed out that we had run before we had been hit, which would have had a very disastrous effect – it might even have led to the massacre of every white man, woman and child they could get at, and the whole of the eastern part of the colony, in Natal, at the foot of their mountains would have been absolutely at their mercy, and also it would have had a very exhilarating effect to say the least, upon the Boers themselves.'[11]

Curiously, those Colonials in Natal who spent much of their daily lives in the company of Zulus, seem to have been blithely unaware of the terrible fate hanging over their heads. The Commissioners questioned Hunter about this issue.

Sir George Taubman-Goldie: 'Just going back to the argument used about the 70,000 Zulus sitting on the fence in case we withdrew from the northern apex of Natal: as a matter of fact, nothing did happen when we were driven out of the northern apex by the Boers?'

Hunter: 'No. But then of course we were driven out as a result of a fight. It was not as if we had turned tail before we were hit, and the result of the fight was an acknowledged British success'

Taubman-Goldie: 'And the 70,000 Zulus were aware of that fact?'

Hunter: 'Yes they were, and they saw us always holding out. And I think it is an acknowledged thing throughout the whole of South Africa that the fall of Ladysmith was to be accepted as the promised sign. They are very biblical in their ways of thinking, and so on, and the Cape Colony, and the Zulus and everyone else, who were watching to see who was going to be master, were practically asked whether they would accept the fall of Ladysmith as a sign. Therefore if Ladysmith had fallen, I believe all the Dutch in the Cape Colony would have risen, the Zulus and everyone else. They would have plumped then for the Boers as their future masters.'[12]

In reality, this was a sad lot of nonsense. When speaking about matters with which he was familiar, General Hunter had said such positive things about the Imperial Light Horse, so we should perhaps try to understand how he came to give this extraordinary evidence.

From the earliest days of the British trading settlement, a substantial and influential group of intellectuals in England, who had never been near Natal, believed that a terrible mutual animosity existed between the English settlers and the Zulu. In addition, Boer propaganda carefully nurtured the belief that Natal was a country occupied by Dutch farmers. In spite of the inherent contradictions, Hunter appears to have accepted the veracity of these propositions in their entirety. One can understand how Hunter possessed these opinions on arrival in Natal, but how did they survive his four-month stay in Ladysmith? The answer to this question lies in the customs and traditions of the British army.

The Regular units tended to look down on Volunteers and perhaps for this reason, Volunteer officers were not welcomed into the officer's mess of regiments in the Regular army. The result was that contact between the two groups was generally restricted to the giving and receiving of orders. The informal contact and discourse which would have come as a result of eating and drinking with the Volunteers would have been of inestimable value to the British and would have prevented many of their blunders. Though Hunter and his colleagues appear to have stuck religiously to the prevailing custom while in Ladysmith, there was, on his way to South Africa, a British officer who was prepared to break the mould.

Meanwhile during these busy days before the siege began, an enquiry was held into the health of Brigadier General Yule and it was decided that he was no longer fit for duty and should be shipped back to England immediately. An enquiry was also held into the conduct of Captain CG Willson of the Natal Carbineers, and it was decided that he should be court martialed. The writer has been unable to trace any record of these proceedings either in London or Natal.

Realising that Ladysmith might be besieged for some time, Herbert Watkins-Pitchford felt that he should make a quick journey to Pietermaritzburg to ensure that matters at the Veterinary Research Station would be properly managed while he was away. To this end on 1 November he went down to the Ladysmith station:

> 'Two long trains were standing full to overflowing with women and children, the men struggling with the luggage which blocked the way everywhere. So I sent my bag back and rode back to camp again. It was midnight before they got the last women away in trucks. The next afternoon I saw Leumann at the station for a few minutes looking absolutely thin and pinched. He was taking down a trainload of men wounded at Tinta Inyoni and the poor chaps were brought from the hospital in dhoolies or square hammocks with green coverings slung on a long bamboo and carried by four dhoolie bearers. Some of the poor fellows were badly hit and groaned loudly as they were lifted into the carriage, but it was imperative to empty the hospitals as it was expected that they would be overflowing again shortly. So Leumann went off after a few minutes' chat, and a special train carrying General French and Major Haig followed immediately. This train was the last to get through and only just managed to run the blockade, being heavily fired upon. We heard that night that the wires were down, and natives reported the line cut and held by large bodies of Boers just above Colenso.'[13]

During the journey of that last train, the Boer fire was so intense that the two future Field Marshals, John French and Douglas Haig, were obliged to lie on the floor and even there they were far from safe, one bullet hitting a suitcase which Haig had with him.

The following day it was decided that General Brocklehurst should make a reconnaissance in force to the south-west of the town in order to ascertain the number of the enemy in that locality as well as the number and calibre of their guns. Brocklehurst took with him the British cavalry, the Imperial Light Horse and a brigade of artillery. The action which followed has been described as 'hopeless in its inception and bad in its execution.'[14]

Outside the defended perimeter to the west of Ladysmith lay a broad plain, called Long Valley, beyond which were a number of hills on which the Boers had placed guns. Due west was Rifleman's Ridge and south of it another eminence, Lancer's Hill. To the south-east of them were three flat-topped hills: Mounted Infantry Hill, Middle Hill and End Hill. On arrival in Long Valley the 18th Hussars were ordered to guard the right flank while the 19th Hussars attacked Rifleman's Ridge. A Mounted Infantry company occupied the appropriately named Mounted Infantry Hill to protect the left rear. The 5th Dragoon Guards with the 21st Battery moved south down Long Valley. When Karri approached the new cavalry commander, General Brocklehurst, for orders, he was told, 'I've heard your men are very fine fellows Major, do what you like.'[15]

It was less than two months since Karri and the rest of the ILH began their training, which was received from British instructors following traditional British principles. At Elandslaagte the ILH had shown its ability and courage and the British had witnessed the gallant manner in which Colonel Scott Chisholme led the regiment. No one mentioned that the brave colonel, by setting off up the rocky slope towards a hidden enemy, with walking stick and flag held aloft, was setting an appalling example. It was the virtues of stealth and surprise which should have been emphasised. When General French asked Col Scott Chisholme at Elandslaagte what he would like to do, the Colonel replied that they would like to take the hill on the Boer left flank. Having received carte blanche from General Brocklehurst, Karri, following Scott Chisholme's example, looked for a target which could be attacked. The artillery had been shelling Lancer's Hill and the Boer gun there had been silenced, causing Karri to believe quite erroneously that the enemy was vacating it. He decided to attack Lancer's Hill. He sent two squadrons to Middle Hill to protect his left flank, and then turning towards the remaining two squadrons said, 'Load your guns. You see that kopje, that's the Boer laager, we're going to take it. Right squadron go on. Left in support.'[16]

To reach the hill they had to cross one and a half miles of flat, open country. After they had covered about half a mile they were met by surprisingly heavy rifle fire. Fortunately a donga offered them some shelter where the horses could be left while they went forward on foot. They were able to get within 800 yards of the enemy before the fire became so intense that they had to shelter in another donga. Major Doveton led a charge towards the hill, but half the men failed to follow him, and he and his group were forced to go to ground hiding behind anthills and whatever other cover they might find. During their advance, Captain Knapp was killed instantly when he was hit in the head. To add to their problems they were now receiving flanking fire from the Boers on Middle Hill, where they had checked the ILH attack. In the attempt to take this hill, Lieutenant Brabant was mortally wounded. Unable to advance or retreat and with substantial numbers of Boers arriving from the east, Karri called for reinforcements.

In fighting which lasted several hours, the dismounted 5th Dragoons, with artillery support, were able to cover the retreat of the ILH from Lancer's Hill. The Natal Volunteers were called out and secured the left by clearing the Boers off Middle Hill and End Hill. In driving the Boers off those hills two Carbineers, Major Taunton and Sergeant Mapstone, were killed and four men were wounded. Corporal Silburn of the Natal Mounted Rifles was wounded. No Border Mounted Riflemen were killed but the Adjutant, Captain Arnott, and three troopers, GL Edmunds, AG Goldstone and FJ Thomas, were wounded. Captain Arnott was shot through both legs while leading his men on the left flank. He had fallen in an exposed position and seeing him, Major Evans of the NMR, with a complete disregard for his own safety, bandaged Arnott's wounds and after making him as comfortable as possible, sent for an ambulance. The rifle fire became so intense that Arnott struggled back to cover, crawling from stone to stone until he joined his men. Noticing more ammunition was needed, and seeing Surgeon Lieutenant Platt and Lieutenant JR (Galloping Jack) Royston approaching, Arnott shouted, 'Go back and fetch more ammunition.' Royston hurried the ammunition mules forward and went along the lines serving it out, while Platt, under heavy fire, stayed with the wounded man until the stretcher bearers arrived.[17]

Major Rethman and Lieutenant Andreason had a narrow escape when a shell burst within a couple of yards of them. Such was the severity of the explosion that onlookers thought they must have been killed, however both were unscathed. Over the next few months there were many instances where individuals narrowly missed being killed, but surely none can surpass the experience of Trooper GL Edmunds. A Mauser bullet hit him in the centre of his chest, passing through his lungs and back. As he fell, a second bullet hit him a little lower down passing through his lower abdomen and coming out in the thigh without breaking a bone. For several days the doctors thought he had no hope of surviving and his bed was allotted to another wounded man. However he gradually gained strength until an attack of pleurisy in the wounded lung again brought him to death's door. Once more he rallied and was almost convalescent when, in a violent thunderstorm, lightning struck his tent. At the time he was holding the tent-pole and should have been killed instantly but survived, suffering a severe electric shock.[18]

Once the ILH had been extricated from their dangerous position, General Brocklehurst, noting the steady build up of Boer forces, decided to call off the engagement and return to base. The withdrawal was completed without incident.

The engagement did confirm that the encirclement of Ladysmith was complete, and some information was gained about the number and calibre of the enemy guns. The Imperial Light Horse lost seven killed including two of its best officers, and ten men. Among their wounded was Trooper Guthrie Smith who had been shot through the liver. When Karri was asked by one of his officers for an explanation of his headlong interpretation of his orders, he replied, 'Well Jimmy, as the Regiment was formed to fight the Boers, I went for them.' General Brocklehurst was the party principally to blame for the fiasco as he should never have granted carte blanche to an inexperienced officer and he should have explained to Karri and his officers what their objectives were and what was required of them. But Karri did recognise that he too was at fault and wrote to General White stating that because of his lack of experience and training a more experienced officer should be appointed to lead the regiment. In due course the following order was promulgated:

'At the request of Major Karri Davies and the officers of the ILH, Major AHM Edwards, 5th Dragoon Guards, is appointed to the command of the ILH during the absence of Lieutenant-Colonel Woolls Sampson, and is granted the local rank of Lieutenant-Colonel while so employed.'[19]

The choice of Lt Col Edwards to lead the Regiment was a happy one. He got on well with the Regiment and they with him. About Karri he wrote, 'He promised me that he would give me every assistance and support. This I have no hesitation in saying he always did. As I got to know him I found him to be a straight-forward, warm-hearted, generous man. A most extraordinary character.'

While Gen. Brocklehurst was carrying out his reconnaissance in force, the Boer artillery made use of some of the information which they had gained in the course of the prisoner exchange. A shell hit the Royal Hotel at lunchtime causing extensive destruction in the dining room. Although many British officers and members of the press corps were present no one was hurt. Another shell burst in the back yard of Dr Rouillard's house, an event which might have been of no great significance had the army not stored their ammunition on either side of it. Unaware of these dramas, William Watson noted in his diary, 'Waterworks destroyed, reservoir dry. I have the pleasure of carrying water in buckets from the river, which is half a mile distant. It is hard work for an ancient Briton like me.'

CHAPTER FOURTEEN

Defence of Natal Midlands

• ◆ •

*'They taught me more about conducting a reconnaissance than I
had learnt in over ten years service in the Cavalry! They moved by bounds
like a wild animal carefully approaching his prey.'*

THE FUTURE GENERAL SIR HUBERT GOUGH AFTER A DAY'S SCOUTING
WITH THE NATAL CARBINEERS

O NCE Ladysmith was invested, the Boers had to decide whether to attempt to take the
town by storm or to continue their drive south towards Durban and the sea. At a meeting
of their war council on 9 November 1899, a compromise solution was reached. It was
decided that a portion of their army should maintain the siege while the balance should
continue the advance southwards.

The main road to the south and the sea crossed the Tugela River near the village of
Colenso, about 18 miles from Ladysmith. The Durban Light Infantry, the Natal Field Battery
and the 2nd Battalion Royal Dublin Fusiliers with its 100 Mounted Infantry had been sent
to Colenso to guard the road and rail bridges across the Tugela. When on patrol, the Mounted
Infantry were assisted by the Estcourt Squadron of the Natal Carbineers under Captain
Mackay. The whole force was under the command of Col Cooper of the Dublin Fusiliers.

On 1 November, the Mounted Infantry and the Carbineers exchanged fire with a strong
force of Boers scouting towards Colenso. After losing several men, killed or wounded, the
Boers retired. One man from the Mounted Infantry was killed in the engagement. On that
same day the Durban Light Infantry at Colenso were shelled by the Boers. Col Cooper,
fearing that his small force might be overwhelmed, decided to withdraw to Chieveley, about
5 miles south of Colenso.

The following day at Nottingham Road, Major Duncan McKenzie, who had just arrived
back from England, boarded the train to Ladysmith. At Chieveley the train was stopped
pending the arrival of a train from Ladysmith. After a considerable delay the train from
Ladysmith came through bearing the marks of the gauntlet it had run through shell and rifle
fire. It was, of course, the last train from Ladysmith and was carrying General French and
Major Douglas Haig on the first leg of their journey to the Cape front.

Uncertain what course he should follow in the rapidly changing circumstances,
Col Cooper decided to seek the opinions of the other officers, and invited the newly arrived
Duncan McKenzie to join the discussion. When Col Cooper asked for his opinion, McKenzie
replied, 'Well, Sir, if your information is correct, and there are 6,000 Boers advancing on
Colenso, the wisest thing you can do is fall back on Estcourt, for the river is not full, and they
can easily cross higher up and so cut off your force from Estcourt, and so hem you in against
the Tugela River.'[1]

After further discussion, Col Cooper decided to heed McKenzie's advice and fall back on Estcourt. During the night the infantry entrained for Estcourt, the last train leaving at 3.00 a.m. The Natal Field Battery marched by road, setting off at 9.00 p.m. Though Captain Mackay was an excellent officer, McKenzie decided to assume command of the Carbineer squadron immediately.

When the last batch of infantry had left, Duncan moved the mounted men back a mile or two and after following his usual practice of sending out patrols to the right and left, they waited for dawn. When daylight came, there was no sign of the enemy, and it seemed the Boers had yet to cross the Tugela. Nonetheless the Carbineers remained in position until the evening, when they retired to Estcourt.[2]

The senior officer in Estcourt was a Colonel Long who instituted the practice of sending an armoured train to Colenso from time to time, presumably to scout or show the flag. The engine pulled a number of open trucks, the sides of which were reinforced with steel plates through which firing holes had been cut. With no sign of activity from the Boers, the train was able to make a number of these excursions without being molested.

Initially the British took no steps to call up the rifle associations, which existed in most country districts. However a British visitor, the Hon TK Murray, saw the value of tapping into this resource of mounted men who could shoot straight, and obtained permission to recruit a unit which would be known as Murray's Horse. By 2 November, Murray had 80 men at Mooi River, a small village approximately halfway between Ladysmith and Pietermaritzburg. Within the next few days the strength of the unit had increased to 150 men.[3]

All the while ships were bringing out further men and supplies which were rushed to the Natal front. One of the first of the new arrivals was a young Winston Churchill, who arrived in Estcourt on 6 November. He had gained some military experience in India and the Sudan before abandoning the army in favour of a career in politics. After defeat in his first attempt to be elected to Parliament, he had persuaded the *London Morning Post* to appoint him as a special correspondent to cover the war in South Africa. His employers paid him a salary which made him the highest paid correspondent in South Africa and it is easy to see why. His grandfather was a Duke, his father a prominent Victorian politician and his mother an American heiress – connections which should ensure that he would obtain access to the best stories. In addition, he was already well known to the English public, had a great command of English and his writing was always entertaining. For Churchill the appointment gave him financial security and a wonderful opportunity to promote his political career. Sometimes his reports were woefully inaccurate and influenced by his personal prejudices and a desire to place himself at the centre of events.

The little coaster which had brought Churchill from East London in the Cape Colony to Durban, arrived at midnight on 4 November 1899. He caught the 7.00 a.m. train to Pietermaritzburg. In those few hours he had visited the hospital ship Sumatra where he found several friends. One who had been badly wounded at Elandslaagte, told the budding member of parliament, 'I never felt safe with those politicians.'[4]

Pietermaritzburg he found to be a 'sleepy, dead-alive place' which might account for the nickname 'Sleepy Hollow' so often applied to the town. In spite of their rather laid back approach to life, Churchill could not be effusive enough in his praise of its inhabitants and wrote, '*I wish it were within the power of my poor pen to bring home to the people of England how excellently the colonists of Natal have deserved of the State.*'[5] And again,

'*...they knew that if war should come, on them would fall the first fury of the storm. Nevertheless, they courageously supported and acclaimed the action of the Ministry. Now at last there is war. It means a good* deal to all of us, but more than to any it comes home to the Natalian. He is invaded; his cattle have been seized by the Boer; his towns are shelled or captured; the most powerful force on which he relies for protection is isolated in Ladysmith; his capital is being loopholed and entrenched; Newcastle has been abandoned, Colenso has fallen, Estcourt is threatened; the possibility that the whole province will be overrun stares him in the face. From the beginning he asked for protection. From the beginning he was promised complete protection, but scarcely a word of complaint is heard. The townsfolk are calm and orderly, the Press dignified and sober. The men capable of bearing arms have responded nobly. Boys of sixteen march with men of fifty to war – to no easy light war. All the Volunteers are in the field bearing their full share of the fighting like men.'[6]

And yet again,

'Viewed in quieter days, the patient, trustful attitude of this colony of Natal will impress the historian. The devotion of its people to their Sovereign and to their motherland should endear them to all good Englishmen, and win them sympathy and respect.'[7]

Although he spent only one day in Pietermaritzburg, Winston set about acquiring as much local knowledge as possible, and even found time to visit the wounded in hospital and to speak to some of the men: 'I talked with a wounded Gordon Highlander – one of those who had dashed across the famous causeway of Dargai and breasted the still more glorious slope of Elandslaagte. "We had the Imperial Horse with us," he said, "They're the best I've ever seen."'

The unsolicited praise which was heaped on the ILH by those of all ranks and classes on first meeting them is interesting. No doubt they were, in every way, a fine body of men, but the reaction hints strongly that there had existed in the minds of many people in Britain, certain misconceptions about the character of the Johannesburg *Uitlanders*. Churchill refers to one such misconception when, speaking of the part played by the ILH at Elandslaagte, he states, 'After this who will call the Outlanders cowards?'[8]

Soon after his arrival in Estcourt, Churchill let it be known that he would pay £200 to anyone who would guide him into Ladysmith. A nineteen year-old trooper in the Carbineers, W Park Gray, heard of the offer which seemed to him to promise almost unbelievable riches. His family farmed in the foothills of the Drakensberg and being thoroughly conversant with the locality, he was confidant that he could guide this generous benefactor through Boer lines and into Ladysmith. So he went to see Churchill in his quarters near the station. He was surprised at how young, pink and white Churchill looked; however he also noticed how carefully Churchill was weighing him up. Park Gray thought it would take three days to complete the mission and after some discussion he went to see Major McKenzie to ask for three days leave. At the time, the mounted men in Estcourt were very busy and Park Gray was recognised as the best shot in the Regiment. So when McKenzie heard that he required the leave to escort a war correspondent, the request was indignantly refused, McKenzie stating that he was not prepared to lose one of his best men for some 'bloody war correspondent.'[9] Unfortunately when Park Gray told Churchill that leave had been refused, he quoted McKenzie a little too fully. Churchill never forgave this lack of deference to the grandson of a Duke.

With his plans for the visit to Ladysmith frustrated, Churchill accepted an offer of a ride to Colenso on the armoured train. At Colenso they found the village looted and deserted, the bridge intact, a section of the railway line ripped up and telegraph wires cut. The inspection complete, the train steamed back to Estcourt without incident. On the return journey Churchill fell into conversation with a trooper from Durban who was a builder by trade and serving with the Durban Light Infantry. Before the war he had employed nine men, whom he had had to discharge when called up. Although he did not know how he would be able to reestablish his business after the war, he bore no resentment for being required to defend his country, believing it was no more than his duty.

On 9 November most of the troops in Estcourt made a reconnaissance towards Colenso, without the train. Churchill, as expected, was not going to be left out:

'Galloping over the beautiful grassy hills to the north of the town, I soon reached a spot whence the column could be seen. First of all came a cyclist – a Natal Volunteer pedalling leisurely along with his rifle slung across his back – then two more, then about twenty. Next after an interval of a quarter of a mile, rode the cavalry – the squadron of the Imperial Light Horse, sixty Natal Carbineers, a company of Mounted Infantry, and about forty of the Natal Mounted Police. This is the total cavalry force in Natal, all the rest is bottled up in Ladysmith, and scarcely three hundred horsemen are available for the defence of the colony against a hostile army entirely composed of mounted men. Small were their numbers, but the quality was good. The Imperial Light Horse have shown their courage, and have only to display their discipline to equal advantage, to be considered first class soldiers. The Natal Carbineers are excellent volunteer cavalry: the police an alert and reliable troop.'[10]

After the mounted men came the infantry – on this occasion the Dublin Fusiliers and the newly arrived Border Regiment. When the force had 'passed in review' Churchill, with two companions, set off for a high, flat-topped hill to the north-west which promised a view of the country towards Ladysmith. It took them an hour to climb the hill and from the top they could see the roofs of the houses of Colenso set out in neat squares and oblongs. Beyond the village, hills obscured Ladysmith, but the long black outline of Bulwana Hill could be seen. From time to time a white flash was visible on the hill. Long Tom was at work. The owner of the farm, a tall red-bearded man, joined them. Absorbed by the distant drama, their conversation was suddenly interrupted:

'Over the crest of the hill to the rear, two horsemen trotted swiftly into view. A hundred yards to the left, three or four more were dismounting among the rocks. Three other figures appeared on the other side. We were surrounded – but by the Natal Carbineers. "Got you, I think," said the sergeant, who now arrived, "Will you kindly tell us about who you are?" We introduced ourselves as President Kruger and General Joubert, and presented the farmer as Mr. Schreiner, who had come to a secret conference, and having produced our passes, satisfied the patrol that we were not eligible for capture. The sergeant looked disappointed. "It took us half an hour to stalk you, but if you had only been Dutchmen we'd have fixed you up properly." Indeed the whole manoeuvre had been neatly and cleverly executed, and showed the smartness and efficiency of these irregular forces in all matters of scouting and reconnaissance. The patrol was then appeased by being photographed "for the London papers", and we hastened to accept the farmer's invitation to lunch. "Only plain fare," said he, "but perhaps you are used to roughing it."

'The farm stood in a sheltered angle of the hill at no great distance from its summit. It was a good-sized house, with stonewalls and a corrugated iron roof. A few sheds and outhouses surrounded it, four or five blue gums afforded a little shade from the sun and a little relief to the grassy smoothness of the landscape. Two women met us at the door, one the wife the other, I think, the sister of our host. Neither was young, but their smiling faces showed the invigorating effects of this delicious air. "These are anxious times," said the older; "we hear cannonading every morning at breakfast. What will come of it all?" Over a most excellent luncheon we discussed many things with these kind people, and spoke of how the nation was this time resolved to make an end of the long quarrel with the Boers, so that there should be no uncertainty and alarm among loyal subjects of the Queen. "We have always known," said the farmer, "that it must end in war, and I cannot say I am sorry it has come at last. But it falls heavily on us. I am the only man for twenty miles who has not left his farm. Of course we are defenceless here. Any day the Dutchmen may come. They wouldn't kill us, but they would burn or plunder everything, and it's all I've got in the world. Fifteen years have I worked at this place, and I said to myself we may as well stay and face it out, whatever happens." Indeed it was an anxious time for such a man."[11]

Over the years General Joubert has been much criticised for failing to press on into southern Natal immediately after Ladysmith had been invested. Ten days were to pass before the Boers crossed the Tugela and began their drive south, by which time reinforcements had arrived to strengthen the British force. Whether an earlier start would have enabled the Boers to advance further into Natal, is by no means certain.

Joubert, as we know, was opposed to the war. In an article written by him, which was published in German journals before the declaration of war, he expressed the opinion that the Boer's foreign friends would not intervene, and that the Boers would not succeed in driving the British into the sea. He conceded that, '…in Natal and the south we have to deal with unfamiliar conditions. In contrast, on the high plains of the Transvaal and the Orange Free State we shall be at home, and the British will meet opposition from us and from Nature every step of the way, and at all times be prepared for action on two or three fronts. In this way will be developed a guerrilla warfare of a most inconceivably bloody character, such as the British will be unable to endure for more than a few months.'[12]

In anticipation of this guerrilla war, lines of depots had been constructed and communications systems set up between them. It seems his heart was not in the Natal campaign and besides he had other difficulties.

As the Boer commandos would come and go as they pleased, no one knew how many men would be available for any particular operation. The Free State had annexed northern Natal and with Boers pegging out farms for themselves, an administration had to be set up. His Generals had let him down badly by failing to obey their instructions. In Dundee, Generals Meyer and Erasmus had failed to coordinate their actions, with the result that the British column at Dundee had been able to escape. At Elandslaagte, General Kock had failed to wait for the main Boer force to arrive before provoking a battle, with the result that the *Kommandos* had been badly mauled. He was infuriated by reports that Blacks had been ill-treated by his Kommandos, something which he believed threatened the very existence of the Boer people and thought such conduct deserved the death penalty. His edict against looting and the harassment of civilians was almost everywhere ignored.

His dislike of the foreign contingents fighting on behalf of the Boers had intensified. Commandant Ben Viljoen, whom it will be remembered was in command during the retreat from Elandslaagte, felt the full force of a tongue-lashing from Joubert: 'As for those Germans and Hollanders with you,' he told him, 'they may go back to Johannesburg. I won't have them here anymore.'[13] Though this outburst was perhaps unfair on the Germans, who had fought bravely at Elandslaagte, Joubert had clearly lost patience with the various Boer *Uitlander Korps*, who had shown more interest in looting than fighting.

A man known only as 'Jim, son of Antoni', who lived near Port Elizabeth, made a statement to the Natal Police at the end of November, 1899. He describes an incident which provides an interesting insight into some of the problems the Boers faced and how they dealt with them. Jim was probably a Fingo, a people who had been granted land near Port Elizabeth after one of the wars with the Xhosa. The statement appears to be genuine as many of the facts stated were subsequently found to be correct and would not have been known in Natal at the time:

'1. About eight months ago I left home and went to Port Elizabeth from where I left, accompanying a labour Agent, to Johannesburg.

2. I was employed at Rooipoort Mines until about three months ago when we were informed by the Manager that war had broken out and that we had better go home.

3. I left Rooipoort Station by rail and on arriving at Elandsfontein (not to be confused with Elandslaagte in Natal) station with twenty one others also from Port Elizabeth, we were arrested and taken to Pretoria Gaol. After being in gaol for three days we were taken out and divided amongst the Boers as servants, and I so happened to be made General Joubert's servant.

4. We left Pretoria by rail as far as Volksrust when we left the train and proceeded by ox wagon to Newcastle. The commando remained there a few days, during which time they burnt a few of the big stores down, as they said they were going to destroy all Englishmen's property and drive them into the sea.

5. After leaving Newcastle we went to Dundee, and just before reaching it we captured, I think, about 174 English soldiers, who were at the time going towards the Buffalo River, they were surrounded and captured by the Boers.

6. We then moved towards Dundee and about two or three days after they had captured the 174 soldiers, they caught four more, dressed in khaki, one of whom was tied to a tree by a lot of the Burghers, among whom I knew four, as follows: Joseph Foree of Pretoria, De Lang, son-in-law to General Joubert, John Joubert, and Joseph Joubert.

7. After tying this man to the tree, they went about 100 yards away and shot him, this was done by Joseph Foree who was to fire first.

8. The man who was shot like this, was not dressed like the others. He had brown leggings with straps round them; he was about five feet in height; middle aged; moustache, but no beard. He had two small yellow things on his shoulders; on his hat, which is like the hats the soldiers wear, was a puggaree on which was a little piece of red.

9. The Boers say they shot him because he was the oldest of the four and an old scoundrel. The other three were dressed in putties and black boots and had long knives.

10. We then left for Ladysmith and on our way we met some men that took part in the Elandslaagte fight who were running away at the time and the General made them go back again.

11. After we reached Ladysmith a few days the English blew off the mouth of the big gun that was placed on the big hill by Ladysmith and few days afterwards blew it all to pieces; then Joubert said it is no use staying there we will move on to Estcourt, which we did and we crossed the Tugela, and there they had a fight with a train and took a lot of English prisoners, I saw three English killed and three Dutch and a lot of English were killed falling under the trucks. The Boers then moved to Ulundi, and then to Mooi River, from where I ran away.

(Sd.) Jim
Witness to Interpretation (Sd) A.R. Brandon, Tr. NP.'[14]

Three of the prisoners appear to have been captured with Col. Moller near Dundee, in which case they would have been sent to a prisoner-of-war camp. The identity of the man executed is not known. His description does not fit that of a member of the British forces, or the Volunteers. The Irish Brigade fighting with the Boers had adopted a red flag as their banner which raises the possibility that he belonged to that unit. Members of the Irish Brigade had attempted to persuade Dublin Fusiliers captured with Moller to join the Boers, an act which might have resulted in those Fusiliers being executed as traitors, had they subsequently fallen into British hands. The Boers were infuriated by this attempted manipulation of their prisoners.

By 14 November General Joubert was finally ready to begin his incursion into southern Natal. With Louis Botha and his *Kommando* leading, Joubert and his army of three to six thousand Boers crossed the Tugela. It had been decided that the main force should bypass Chieveley, Frere and Escourt on the west, while a smaller force of six hundred men under David Joubert, nephew of the Commandant-General, was to advance via Weenen in the east. The two columns would then meet in a pincer movement near Mooi River, and thereby cut Estcourt off from the south. Scouts from the Volunteers quickly picked up the movements of the enemy, and the news was conveyed to Col Long, who, unimpressed, decided that on the following day, 15 November, the armoured train, under the command of a Captain Haldane, should as usual carry out its reconnaissance to Colenso.[15]

Haldane was far from delighted by the prospect of a ride in the armoured train which almost everyone, with the notable exception of Col Long, regarded as a dangerous and useless contraption which could not do the job half as well as a single mounted scout. Haldane was to be accompanied by a company of the ninety Dublin Fusiliers, eighty men from the Durban Light Infantry and an obsolete 7-pounder gun with ten Naval gunners.[16] Haldane invited three newspaper correspondents, Winston Churchill, Leo Amery and John Atkins to join the venture. Churchill, despite having reservations, accepted the invitation. Atkins declined, stating he was being paid to cover the war, not to become a prisoner of war, while Leo Amery gave as his excuse for not going, the possibility of rain, a strange excuse for an Englishman.

At 5.30 a.m. the train steamed out of Estcourt bound for Colenso with 180 men and a number of civilians aboard. The foremost truck had placed on it the Naval gun; next came an armoured truck filled with Fusiliers, then the locomotive, followed by two further trucks with the balance of the Fusiliers and the DLI, and finally a flatbed truck on which were a telegrapher with his equipment, and a group of platelayers. In the still morning air the sound of the train would have been heard many miles away. At Frere the occupants of the train met a small patrol of Natal Police who told them that there were no Boers for the next mile or two. Haldane, against his better judgment, but urged on by Churchill, decided to press on to Chieveley more than ten miles away. On arriving at Chieveley, Boers were seen riding southwards. Haldane instructed the driver to return to Escourt at once. The order of the trucks on the train was, of course, now reversed. The platelayers and telegraphist were now in front followed by trucks filled with infantry, the locomotive, more infantry, and at the rear the sailors, and the 7-pounder gun. It seemed the return journey might be uneventful until, about two miles from Frere, Boers could be seen on a hill six hundred yards away. The infantry loaded their rifles and the gun was readied to fire. Suddenly, on the crest ahead, appeared two large field guns and a rapid-firing Maxim. The engine driver slammed on full speed and as the train gathered pace it rounded a bend and crashed straight into a pile of rocks placed across the line. The leading truck with its passengers was thrown high into the air and overturned against the embankment. The second truck containing the Durban Light Infantry ploughed on for about twenty yards before falling on its side and spilling out its passengers on the leeward side. The next truck was derailed and was leaning over precariously. Miraculously, the locomotive and the rest of the train remained on the rails. In Churchill's words, 'we were not left long in the comparative peace and safety of a railway accident.'[17] The Boers opened fire on the wrecked train, but the infantry were not slow in responding and to some extent checked the enemy fire. Relying on the shelter of the train Churchill jumped off the truck at the back, and ran forward to see what had happened up front. The line was blocked by the derailed truck. To clear the line, the Durban Light Infantry under Captain Wylie pushed and heaved at the obstructing truck, while the engine acting as a battering ram made repeated attempts to knock it out of the way. It took more than an hour to clear the line during which time a shell smashed the coupling between the locomotive tender and the truck behind, thereby isolating the trucks at the rear. The wounded were placed on the locomotive which, with its wooden fitments ablaze and the platelayers clinging on where they could, steamed away towards Estcourt.[18]

Throughout the engagement the entire train had been subjected to heavy shell and rifle fire and its passengers had behaved with great courage. Churchill was indefatigable in giving encouragement to those struggling to clear the line. The sailors were able to fire three shots at the Boers before a shell struck the old muzzle-loader and put it out of action. Those Dublin Fusiliers trapped in the armoured truck at the rear maintained an effective fire through the firing holes thereby helping the DLI in their struggle to free the locomotive. When the locomotive steamed away, Churchill decided to lead the infantry to safety and set off to find them. He didn't find them. Instead the Boers found Churchill wandering about alone on the *veld* and took him prisoner. Over the years Churchill was to make a number of contradictory statements about his capture. Five days after becoming a Boer prisoner, he was able to send a despatch to the *Morning Post* which brought him fame and propelled him into Parliament.

Meanwhile, the departure of the engine left those Fusiliers trapped in the rear trucks no choice but to surrender. Louis Botha, who had initiated the attack, was delighted and cabled Pretoria, '*Our guns were ready and quickly punctured the armoured trucks. The engine broke loose and returned badly damaged. Loss of the enemy 4 dead, 14 wounded and 58 taken prisoner, also a mountain gun… Our loss 4 slightly wounded.*'[19]

It is at this point that most accounts of the armoured train incident end. However it was not the end of the affair. Louis Botha stated the British losses to be 76 and we know 180 men plus some civilians went out on the train that morning. If one allows for, say, 10 wounded on the locomotive, at least 94 men appear to be missing from the final tally. Captain Wylie, in command of the Durban Light Infantry suffered multiple wounds and was one of those who escaped on the locomotive. After the locomotive had left, the infantry who were not trapped in the train broke up into small groups and set off on foot for Estcourt. Not surprisingly the Boers followed.

When the sound of gunfire was heard in Estcourt, Major Duncan McKenzie was ordered to go to the relief of the armoured train with his squadron of the Carbineers (45 men) and a squadron of the Imperial Light Horse (80 men). Being a local regiment consisting primarily of farmers, the Carbineers knew the country well. They also knew that despite a failure by the Boers to expel the English settlers from Natal in 1842, the Boers still coveted Natal and had equipped their *Kommandos* with the latest weaponry. Anxious lest the Boers make another attempt to drive them into the sea, the local volunteers had adapted their training and strategy to meet the danger posed by mounted men who were good marksmen armed with modern long-range rifles. Although an imperial regiment paid by Britain, the ILH had been recruited in Pietermaritzburg, and were quick to learn the methods employed by the Natal Volunteers.

After riding a few miles the Volunteers met the engine with the wounded and McKenzie was told what had happened. It had begun to rain steadily, but the two squadrons pressed forward along the line of the railway as quickly as possible. Near the rail siding of Ennersdale they passed a group of infantry trying to make its way back to Estcourt and further groups were passed as they hurried on. Finally they sighted the Boers pursuing the hindmost infantry. The Boers were checked at the first indication of the presence of the Volunteers and retired in a north easterly direction until stopped by a wire fence. While they were cutting the fence, the Carbineers opened fire from concealed positions at a distance of about 800 yards, killing several Boers who were later found dead on the field (refer 'Jim's' affidavit). Once through the fence the Boers took up a position on a *kopje*. In an exchange of fire which followed they appeared to suffer several casualties. Noting the fire against them was increasing, McKenzie ordered the Carbineers to retire, while at the same time an orderly was sent to the ILH with instructions to follow suit. They retired along the railway line in extended order, with the Carbineers on the left, and the ILH on the right. Being locals and knowing the lie of the land intimately they were able to conceal their movements from the enemy, who, disconcerted by their inability to see their opponents or gauge their strength, gave up the chase after a few miles. Watching the Boers off-saddle in the open, McKenzie estimated that they numbered three to five thousand.[20]

McKenzie's small force of just over one hundred men had held in check a Boer force of at least 3,000, and in doing so had enabled half of those who had set out on the train that morning to get back to base safely. McKenzie had kept his men hidden from the Boers who never knew how many opposed them or precisely where they were located. Because the Carbineers were good shots, they were able to wait and then strike hard as soon as the Boers were vulnerable, after which they would melt back into the *veld*. The Carbineers suffered no casualties and the only casualty of the ILH was the one wounded man. Duncan McKenzie had given his first demonstration on how to defeat the invaders.

Each morning McKenzie would send patrols out towards Beacon Hill in the west, and towards Weenen in the east with instructions to obtain information from the Zulus about the enemy's activities, while being careful not to show themselves. One morning, Lt Col CG Martyr, the new commander of the mounted troops who had just arrived in Estcourt, visited the Carbineers camp. He was described by Lt Malcolm Riall of the West Yorks as a 'bloodthirsty soldier with two rows of medal ribbons.' He had served in the Egyptian Expedition of 1882, the Sudan Expedition of 1884-5, Sudan 1888-91, the Expedition to Dongola of 1896, and Uganda in 1896,[21] experience unlikely to be of value in Natal. Martyr asked McKenzie what dispositions had been made. McKenzie told him about the morning patrols, whereupon Martyr told him not to do this as they would probably be captured. McKenzie replied that it was better to have a patrol captured, than to have the whole unit surrounded before the approach of the enemy was known. Unconvinced, Martyr ordered that the patrols cease. McKenzie did not quibble but sent out the same patrols surreptitiously.[22]

On 13 November the famous West Yorkshire Regiment, commanded by Col Walter Kitchener, had arrived in Estcourt. Kitchener was six years younger than his celebrated brother Herbert, the future Field Marshal Lord Kitchener and the differences between the two brothers were almost as marked as those between Frank and Cecil Rhodes. Lord Kitchener was excessively reserved, even by Victorian standards, and was terrified of showing any emotion, preferring to be misunderstood rather than display his feelings. When doing good he did so by stealth. Disappointed in love as a young man, he concentrated his energy towards the promotion of his career in the army. His brother was far more approachable and was prepared to laugh even when the joke was on him. Not long after Walter Kitchener arrived, McKenzie went to see him and found the Colonel looking very serious. The infantry had been firing at a farmer's goats. McKenzie said he hoped the troops had killed them all. Kitchener looked horrified and asked, 'Why?' 'Well Sir,' replied Duncan, 'If they cannot kill goats, they cannot kill Boers.' Walter laughed.[23]

On 17 November, David Joubert's *Kommando* entered Weenen and set about destroying everything in the village. As was the case in Dundee, while the Boers were destroying the property of civilians, the British were given a few more days to organise themselves. General Hildyard displaced Col Long as senior British officer in Estcourt on 16 November when he arrived with the 2nd Battalion Royal West Surrey Regiment, and the 2nd Battalion East Surrey Rifles. They were followed the next day by Bethune's Mounted Infantry and the 7th Field Battery. The 2nd Royal Irish Fusiliers arrived in Mooi River, twenty miles south of Estcourt on the 16 November, to be followed two days later by General Barton with the 1st Royal Welsh Fusiliers and Thornycroft's Mounted Infantry.

It will be recalled that during General White's brief stay in Pietermaritzburg in early October, Colonels Thornycroft and Bethune had been given permission to recruit men for their volunteer regiments. Thorneycroft, who paid the establishment costs of his regiment personally, recruited in Pietermaritzburg, while Bethune recruited in Durban. Recruits had to be good horsemen and able to shoot straight. There was not the time available to teach other elementary skills. It says much about the quality of the officers and men of these regiments that they were considered fit to be on active service so soon after they had been recruited. Being Volunteers, they were armed with rifles without magazines and did not carry bayonets. They were not 'Uitlander' regiments but were drawn from all men in Natal at the time. Local rifle associations were a fertile source of good recruits as were the Australians who came to Natal with the thousands of horses being imported into Durban by the British. Alfred Ernest Henry Carrick was quite typical of these recruits. As a young man he served as a trooper with the Australian Light Horse in the Middle East in 1885. On his return to Australia he worked for his uncle who owned Warwick Farm Race Course and stables at 'Hurstville', Sydney. In 1899 he arrived in Durban as one of 40 horse-handlers on a ship with 700 horses. With no wharves available they had to swim the horses ashore. This task completed, Alf Carrick and his friends joined the volunteer regiments.[24]

On Sunday 19 October McKenzie was told that Boers had been seen at Wallace's Farm, which lay to the east of Highlands rail siding between Estcourt and Mooi River. Taking about 50 Carbineers he found the Boers, part of David Joubert's *Kommando*, encamped on the other side of a deep valley. A few desultory shots were exchanged between the two groups, but being at very long range, no damage was done. At about 4.00 p.m. a troop of Thornycroft's Mounted Infantry under a subaltern arrived and took up a position next to the Carbineers. After a while the subaltern asked if they might charge across at the Boers. 'Certainly not,' replied McKenzie. Some of Thorneycroft's regiment closed on the enemy and a few men were lost. Later the subaltern asked McKenzie if he and his men might retire to the camp at Mooi River. Once again the Major refused, telling the young officer that they could not leave until the Carbineers left, which would be after dark, so as to leave the Boers uncertain as to whether or not the position was still occupied.[25] On the way back to camp the Carbineers met Col Martyr who, with a Carbineer as a guide, had come out to meet them. Martyr told them they had to go back to the position they had occupied. McKenzie told him this was out of the question as his men had had no food all day, and Martyr then agreed to permit them to continue back to camp. At Mooi River the garrison was strengthened by the arrival on 19 November of the 14th Battery of the Royal Field Artillery and on the following day it was further reinforced by the arrival of the 2nd Devonshire Regiment.

Early on Monday, 20 November, General Hildyard moved his infantry south to Willow Grange and then marched out along the road to Mooi River hoping to find the Boers. Having failed to find them by midday, the infantry marched back to Willow Grange. Col Martyr's mounted force, which had been waiting, with saddles on, since 3.00 a.m., now rode down the same road towards Mooi River. The Carbineers were scouting in front when they saw a small Boer patrol advancing from the east where the engagement had occurred on the previous day. As a nearby plantation offered an excellent opportunity to trap the patrol, the Carbineers took care to keep out of sight. Regrettably the rest of the force made no effort to conceal themselves and were seen by the Boers who immediately cleared off. Near Highlands station McKenzie noticed mounted men lining the hills to the north of Mooi River and reported this to Col Martyr, who said they were trees. McKenzie disputed this and said he was quite sure they were Boers from Weenen attempting to join the main Boer column coming from Colenso via Ntabanhlope. Martyr insisted they were trees. When the mounted men arrived at Highlands station they found other British troops looking through field glasses at the same Boers who were still clearly visible. The Carbineers stood about for some time then received an order to unsaddle. No sooner had they done this, when they received an order to saddle up, and ride back to Willow Grange where they were ordered to retire on Estcourt without delay. McKenzie immediately went to Col Kitchener, who was in overall command, and implored him not to move until after dark. After some persuasion Kitchener agreed to this and arranged for the Carbineers to do outpost duty and form the rear guard during the retirement. The whole column arrived in Estcourt without the Boers having realised that they had left Willow Grange. That same day the two Boer columns converged. The pincers had closed and Estcourt was now cut off from Mooi River.

The next day Duncan McKenzie received a message that General Hildyard wished to see him. He hurried up to the General's headquarters at the Old Fort in Estcourt. Hildyard welcomed Duncan: 'I understand you know a good deal about the country and the Boers.' He proceeded to get out his maps. After some discussion, Duncan asked if the General wished to re-open rail contact with Mooi River. The General replied in the affirmative and asked Duncan how it could be done. Duncan was of the opinion a night attack might be the way. He told the general that there was a stone wall several miles long which ran to the top of a hill, Brynbella, where the Boers had placed guns which dominated the surrounding countryside. If the infantry followed this wall it would guide them right onto Brynbella and the Boer guns which could be captured or destroyed. Duncan emphasised the importance of silence and, in particular, that there should be no shooting as it would betray their position. Duncan with General Hildyard, Col. Kitchener, and other officers who might take part, then rode to the hill above Estcourt where Duncan pointed out the stone wall and all other features which might be important. He also expressed his belief that the guns could be taken without any casualties being sustained. However the infantry would be in real danger if caught retreating from Brynbella the next morning. Artillery cover would then be essential. General Hildyard decided to launch the attack that night and requested that the Carbineers do the scouting. Duncan McKenzie arranged that an old friend, Frick Chapman, should act as guide for the infantry.

The troops marched out from Estcourt to Willow Grange, with McKenzie and the Carbineers scouting ahead, and taking care to keep under cover of the hills so as not to be seen by the enemy. The East Surreys and the West Yorks were to carry out the night attack with a regiment on either side of the wall. The rest of Hildyard's force, the West Surreys, the Durban Light Infantry, and the Border Regiment were to keep under the cover of a high eminence, Beacon Hill, from the top of which a Naval 12-pounder and the 7th Battery were to cover any retreat in the morning. Heavy rain and hail during the afternoon, followed by dense mist created miserable conditions for the infantry. Col Kitchener was nervous about the coming engagement and was particularly concerned about the slouch hats worn by the colonials which he thought might cause confusion as they looked similar to Boer headgear.

Before even reaching the wall along which they were to approach the Boers, the East Surreys and West Yorks mistook each other for the enemy, and in the resulting shooting match and bayonet charge they suffered several casualties. These casualties would have been much higher, but for the prompt intervention of Captain Mackay of the Carbineers. McKenzie could not resist pointing out to Kitchener that no one in this fracas wore a slouch hat, and that the goats had been shot despite being hatless.

It had been decided that the Carbineers would not take part in the coming engagement but instead should return to Estcourt. Before he left, McKenzie reminded Kitchener of the necessity of having artillery to cover any possible retreat off Brynbella. Kitchener wrote out an order for the 7th Battery which he asked McKenzie to deliver. McKenzie found the Battery and explained to the officer in charge precisely where Kitchener wanted it positioned early the next morning. The officer said he was 'damned if he would take his guns up there.'

A little further on the Navy was struggling in the wet and cold to get its gun onto Beacon Hill. Its two teams of oxen were in a hopeless muddle and it seemed unlikely that the sailors would succeed in getting the gun into position before dawn. McKenzie and the Carbineers dismounted, took off their jackets and strode over to the cattle which were quickly formed up in their correct positions and on command began the ascent of the hill. With McKenzie in charge some Carbineers drove the oxen while others pushed the gun. The old transport riding skills were still there, and the big Naval gun was soon in position on top of the hill. A heavy mist had concealed these movements from the Boers, but suddenly the mist lifted and exposed some infantry on the side of Beacon Hill. Though it was getting dark the Boers sent some harmless long-range rifle fire in their direction. An appalling blunder was now made. The naval gun fired several shots at the Boers on Brynbella to which the Boer guns replied. The Boers now knew where the British were and where their Naval gun was positioned and the approximate range. But worst of all, they realised where the British would attack. As Duncan McKenzie and the Carbineers rode back in the dark to Estcourt, Duncan must have had some doubts as to the prospect of success on the following day.[26]

Early the next morning the camp in Estcourt heard that everything had gone off successfully though only two or three prisoners had been taken. The Boers had apparently retreated along the high ground which lay to their rear. Later heavy firing was heard, and ambulances began to stream into Escourt with dead and wounded. Col Kitchener had assembled his men with bayonets fixed and sent them up Brynbella on both sides of the stone wall as planned. They reached the top unperceived and as they topped the crest the Boer sentry challenged. The reply was a volley of rifle fire – strictly against orders – and a ringing cheer from the West Yorks – also against orders. The infantrymen rushed on over the dead sentry to the Boer lager. There they found some blankets, saddlery and thirty or forty ponies. But there were no Boers and no guns. The Boers had fallen back about 1,500 yards during the night, taking their artillery with them. A small contingent had been left on the eastern end of the hill, however as soon as the British appeared they fled back to their main force.

It was now about 3.30 a.m. and as soon as it became lighter Kitchener placed his firing line of the West Yorks among the boulders along the highest part of the crest. The rest he withdrew behind the wall. For a couple of hours harmless fire was exchanged between the two sides, while the Boers concentrated on creeping up on both sides of the hill. The Boer attack on the British troops clinging to the end of Brynbella now intensified. Two field guns and a pom-pom were moved in by the Boers so as to bring converging fire on the narrow position occupied by the West Yorks. The artillery support which Kitchener expected did not materialise because the Boer guns were beyond the range of the Naval gun, which could only search the northern slopes of Brynbella, and the 7th Battery was lying idle at the foot of Beacon Hill, its commanding officer claiming he had no orders. Presumably orders carried to him by a Colonial officer did not count.

Kitchener now decided to retreat off Brynbella. Half his men were to go north towards Beacon Hill, and there join the rest of the infantry, while the others were to retreat north-east towards a small plantation in the Willow Grange Valley. General Hildyard arrived on the scene, and supporting the decision that the British should withdraw, ordered the West Surreys and the Border Regiment to advance across the valley until their left converged with Kitchener's men. With some protection from the rocky terrain, and the wall which had been followed the previous night, they were able to assist the withdrawal of those retiring on Beacon Hill.

On the left flank mounted units, commanded by Col Martyr, were ordered to assist the infantry retiring on Willow Grange. They dismounted, and with the Imperial Light Horse leading, climbed to the crest of Brynbella where they found only one company of the West Yorks still on the crest. Holding the line under heavy fire, the ILH waited until the West Yorks had completed their retirement and taken the wounded to safety, before they began their move down the hill. The Artillery should have covered their retreat, but again was absent. The result was that the men of the ILH had no option but to run down the hill as fast as they could, while the Boers on the summit directed heavy fire at them. Perhaps because the Boers were excited, their fire was wild and only one Light Horsemen was killed and two wounded before safety was reached.[27] To add insult to injury, the Boers brought back into action on the eastern edge of Brynbella those very guns, the capture of which was the *raison d'être* of the whole sortie.

At the end of a frustrating day, the British retired to Estcourt. They had suffered sixteen killed, over sixty wounded and eight were taken prisoner. Among those killed was the civilian guide, Frick Chapman, who had successfully guided the West Yorks to the top of Brynbella. Next day, Friday 24 November, Duncan McKenzie and some Carbineers rode out to Willow Grange to keep an eye on the enemy's movements and to recover the body of Duncan's old friend, Chapman. Col. Kitchener asked Duncan if he would also try to recover his Regiment's mess tins which had been left behind. They duly recovered both Chapman's body and the mess tins. The Carbineers were also able to observe and report on the movements of the Boers: in the east a large group of Boers were retiring towards Weenen, while in the west a smaller group rode towards Ntabanhlope and Colenso. The Boer advance into southern Natal had petered out.

In the campaign the Boers had lobbed a number of shells into Mooi River, thereby inflicting a severe attack of inertia on General Barton, commander of the 6th Brigade. This enabled small groups of Boers to penetrate as far as Nottingham Road. Everywhere the looting and destruction continued, but things were becoming a little more difficult. Murray's Horse, together with informal groups of farmers, who had banded together to protect their farms, were causing problems for the Boers who did not know where this enemy were, the numbers involved, or when and where they might strike. Also there was the possibility that the Tugela River might rise which would result in their being cut off in hostile country, and all the while their scouts told them that more and more British troops and guns were continuing to arrive.

After the engagement at Willow Grange the Boers held a meeting to decide on their future strategy. Louis Botha was all for pressing on to Pietermaritzburg and the sea. The majority, which included Commandant General Joubert, thought it would be wiser to retreat back across the Tugela, where they would find it easier to defend the territory they had conquered. The day before this meeting, Joubert had been injured in a fall from his horse and received internal injuries which were to result in his death. However his decision to retreat across the Tugela was sound and his injury does not appear to have influenced his judgment. In pain, Joubert had to return to the Transvaal and Louis Botha became the Boer commander in Natal.

At 5.00 a.m. on the morning of 25 November, all the mounted troops in Estcourt, with the exception of the Carbineers, were ordered to move out in the direction of the

Ntabanhlope road. Four hours later the Carbineers received an order to join the rest of the mounted column. They responded promptly and had gone but a little way before they came across them. McKenzie reported to Col Martyr, who ordered the Carbineers to scout the high hills in front of them where it was thought the enemy might be found. McKenzie asked for artillery support which Martyr refused. Surprised and disappointed by the refusal, McKenzie was nonetheless flattered by the thought that this Brigade of mounted troops should be unable to move until he, with 40 Carbineers, had done the scouting for them.

Deprived of artillery cover, McKenzie ordered six Carbineers to gallop forward and climb the first hill, while he, with his men, dismounted and covered the advance with their rifles. When the scouts reached the top of the hill and waved everything clear, another troop would gallop up the hill in support and once they were in position, McKenzie followed with the remainder. Once at the top, McKenzie would scout around, and if everything was clear, he would report to base, before repeating the procedure on the next hill. Following this system, and always being careful not to show themselves, the Carbineers located the Boers who were retiring towards Colenso on the Ntabanhlope road. A galloper was sent back to Martyr advising him that the Boers, unaware of the presence of the Carbineers, were riding into a position where they could easily be trapped. The galloper returned with an order that the Cabineers were to return to the main column at once as the Boer column was too strong. McKenzie had no choice but to obey. En route he was disappointed to see many of Martyr's men on the skyline where they would have been visible to the Boers. On joining the column he reported to Col Martyr, suggesting that they should take up a position on a certain hill which had to be passed by the Boers and where they could be easily ambushed. This group was about 500 strong, and though they had come into Natal lightly equipped, they were now burdened with a long train of looted livestock and wagons filled with looted goods. The livestock contained substantial numbers of valuable pedigree breeding stock which had been acquired by the local farmers over many years. Martyr refused to consider the proposal, stating the orders were to retire to Estcourt while shepherding the Boers back to Colenso. This refusal to even consider an operation which would not only have inflicted serious losses on the Boers, but would also have compelled them to abandon vast quantities of loot, infuriated McKenzie who blurted out, 'I feel ashamed to disgrace the uniform I wear.' He then turned away and Col Martyr rode on to join the other troops retiring to Estcourt. Not long afterwards McKenzie received a despatch from Col Martyr ordering him to accompany him on a visit to General Hildyard that evening. That probably meant trouble. On arrival in camp McKenzie found the order had been countermanded, and he was instead requested to write a report stating what he had seen that day.[28]

When he attended the Brigade Headquarters the next morning there was no sign of Col Martyr, who was never seen again by the Natal Volunteers. The Carbineers were ordered to scout the land to the east in the direction of Weenen. McKenzie took his regiment to the highest ridge of a line of hills between the Estcourt/Weenen and the Weenen/Colenso roads. From this high ground he had a wide view of the country and could see young Joubert's camp next to the Weenen Road, not more than a mile from him. The road which Joubert had to travel to reach Colenso had to pass through a narrow defile near the Blaaukrantz River, an ideal place for an ambush. McKenzie at once reported what he had seen, but there was no response. That night, both Boer columns with all their looted wagons, goods, and cattle reached Colenso unmolested. This wagon train of stolen goods stretched from Mooi River all the way to Weenen, a distance of more than 30 miles. Not only did the Boers plunder everything which could be taken away, they also destroyed possessions they could not move or did not want. Safes were blown open with dynamite, lamps and furniture were destroyed, doors and windows smashed with crow bars, papers, photographs and other documents were torn in pieces, orchards chopped down and vital rainwater tanks punctured. Livestock which could not be driven away was slaughtered. Fifty young turkeys were among the dead poultry found rotting on one farm. On another, 300 head of cattle and sheep were poisoned with arsenic. Businesses, farms and houses all suffered in this orgy of destruction. A German who was riding with Botha's invasion force described the raid as a *Lumpen Kreuzug* (a Tramp's Crusade). It was not Britain, or Milner, or Rhodes, or Chamberlain whom they punished, but civilians who had never done any harm to them, nor posed any threat to their Republics. After Colonel Martyr left, Duncan McKenzie was told that a Lord Dundonald was the new commander of the Cavalry Brigade. Duncan had never heard of him.

Colonel Douglas Mackinnon Bailie Hamilton Cochrane, the twelfth Earl of Dundonald, had inherited a title but not much money. His forbears had won fame and fortune at sea during the wars of the eighteenth century, a fortune which had been much reduced during the industrial revolution. His grandfather developed many improvements to the machines being used by the new industries, but refused to patent any of his inventions, believing a man's knowledge should be shared free of charge with all mankind. The result was that others profited from his work, and when the future twelfth Earl joined the Life Guards, he had difficulty maintaining the lifestyle expected of an officer in that elite Regiment. He had had the misfortune to contract malaria while campaigning in the Sudan, and that debilitating disease seriously affected his health, and caused him to suffer bouts of fever for the rest of his life.

Lord Dundonald, commander of Buller's Mounted Brigade.

Possibly because of his health, he was not among those originally selected to go to South Africa. However as a soldier he believed that he should, in time of war, serve his country, so he paid his fare to Cape Town, where he went to see the newly appointed Commander in Chief in South Africa, General Sir Redvers Buller. General Buller knew Dundonald and asked him to take on the command of the Mounted Brigade in Natal. Lord Dundonald would have under his command:

The Royal Dragoons
The 13th Hussars
Thorneycroft's Mounted Infantry
Bethune's Mounted Infantry
A squadron of the Natal Carbineers (which included some men from the BMR and NMR)
A squadron of the Imperial Light Horse
A Naval Brigade with two 4.7inch guns and fourteen 12 cwt guns

In all about 1,800 men and Dundonald's appointment was an unexpected but wise choice for the vital post. Dundonald realised how vulnerable the British army had become, and in particular that the standard of shooting was very poor. On taking command of the 2nd Life Guards in 1895, he set about improving matters. At that time, if a regiment wished to use in target practice more than the allotted number of rounds per annum, the officers of the regiment had to pay, out of their own pockets, for extra ammunition, hire of the range and the men's rail fares. Dundonald could not afford this, so he organised a shooting club and wrote to all old officers of the regiment, asking them to subscribe to the fund. This helped, but obviously only to a limited extent and, of course, it was only his Regiment which benefited. Later he was to write, '...during the South African War, I used to talk with first-class rifle shots such as men in the Border Mounted Rifles – who when they fired killed – and the consensus was that to keep up first-class marksmanship a man required much practice and would have to expend 400 to 500 cartridges a year.'[29]

Marksmanship was not his only concern. He believed that the non-commissioned ranks should receive more information as to what was required of them. To this end he drafted and had printed, a map to be distributed to all ranks, entitled 'To Find the Way'. This map gave instructions on how to find the way over a trackless country by day, and at night by compass or by stars. He had prepared, printed and had posted in every barrack room, large placards giving information on such subjects as Field Engineering, Reconnaissance, Map-reading, and Outpost Duty, which he believed every cavalry soldier should know. He was also concerned about the divide which existed between Regular units and Volunteer regiments. When the Colonel of one such Regiment wrote to Dundonald asking if he would 'allow the officers the use of the Officers' Mess of the 2nd Life Guards; to mix with your officers on terms of equality would be something they would never forget,' Dundonald had no hesitation in issuing an invitation to them. The Volunteers came and everyone liked them. It was the first time Volunteer officers were made honorary members of an Officers' Mess of a Household Cavalry Regiment.[30] Not only was he willing to dine with Volunteers, he was willing to listen to them and to have regard for their opinions. These concepts were revolutionary ideas in the British army of that time. To these attributes, he added loyalty both to those in authority over him, and those under his command.

On arrival in Natal he went to Mooi River and from there he was ordered to take those of his command at Mooi River to join General Hildyard at Estcourt. He arrived at Estcourt just as Hildyard and his column were about to set off for Frere in pursuit of the retreating Boers. Dundonald has left a description of what they found on arrival:

'The Boers had destroyed the iron railway bridge at Frere and a very complete destructive effort they had made; the Natal railwaymen with us said that they would soon erect a temporary bridge of wood, which they did in a very short time. Frere had been occupied by the Boers in their advance in Natal. [.....] We were all of us furious to see the cruel havoc they had made in the houses of this small town; it looked as if it had been devastated by savages. The first house we entered was Bartle Cottage; it belonged to two maiden ladies, The whole place was a wreck, little mementoes of home scattered on the ground, photographs torn up; the beds were ripped up, and one walked knee-deep in the fluff from them. All the other houses were treated in the same way but none were destroyed by fire, showing that the Boers had set a limit to their work of destruction. I heard that the better class of Boer did not approve of this work.'[31]

On his sea voyage to South Africa on board the Carisbrooke Castle, Dundonald had met an ambitious young officer of the 16th Lancers, Captain Hubert Gough. Gough wrote to Dundonald telling him that he was with a squadron guarding a railway, work he did not like. Dundonald invited him to Frere and appointed him to his Staff as Intelligence Officer. On arrival in Natal, Gough joined the Mounted Brigade and this is how he described his first reconnaissance with a Natal Volunteer unit:

'I found them a friendly, practical body, prepared to fight when required, but not at all inclined to gallop thoughtlessly into danger. My military experience of this war began at once. At dawn the next morning we set forth on a reconnaissance to the east of the railway. Riding with these Natal farmers we covered about thirty miles out and back in a day, and returned to Nottingham Road that same evening. We did not encounter any Boers, but in that long ride they taught me more about conducting a reconnaissance than I had learnt in over ten years service in the Cavalry! They moved by bounds – like a wild animal carefully approaching his prey, which has now become the classic method of advance for scouts.'[32]

While the principal Boer invasion south from the Tugela had followed the main road and rail route from Ladysmith to Pieternaritzburg, a smaller force of 300 to 400 Boers was making its way south on a more easterly route closer to the Zululand border via Helpmekaar, Pomeroy, and Tugela Ferry. From there it was to press on to Greytown, Pietermaritzburg and the coast. To bar its drive south were about seventy men of the Umvoti Mounted Rifles who had dug themselves in along the southern bank of the Tugela River.

On 18 November, General Sir Francis Clery, temporarily in overall command in Natal, instructed Major Leuchars of the Umvoti Mounted Rifles to destroy the punts at Tugela Ferry and Keat's Drift and thereafter withdraw to Greytown. Leuchars started his withdrawal, leaving a detachment at the river crossing, which was to destroy the punt and road on receipt of instructions. The following day General Clery amended his orders to Leuchars stating he should watch the road between Tugela Ferry and Mooi River, while at the same time he was to use his discretion as to the destruction of the punts and further retirement. Leuchars wired back to say he would delay the destruction until the last moment. On 23 November, the Boers attacked the detachment Leuchars had left at Tugela Ferry. Assisted by a full river, they were able to hold their own until Major Leuchars arrived with the rest of his small force. After an exchange of fire lasting several hours the Boers withdrew, and made no further attempt to pursue their invasion of Natal along this route.[33]

As the Boer threat to southern Natal had been contained, Murray's Horse was disbanded at the end of November.

CHAPTER FIFTEEN

Inside Ladysmith

• ➤ •

'What is the use of shelling them? They just go on playing cricket.'

A BOER ARTILLERYMAN COMMENTING ON THE EFFECTIVENESS
OF BOER ARTILLERY

AFTER his capture, Churchill and his fellow prisoners were marched to the railhead near Elandslaagte. As they neared Ladysmith they could see the smoke of Boer artillery fire from Bulwana. The Boers were happy to converse with their prisoners. Writing shortly after escaping from captivity, Churchill left us this account of their conversation:

"That goes on always," said a Boer. "Can any soldiers bear that long? Oh, you will find all the English army at Pretoria. Indeed, if it were not for sea-sickness we would take England. Besides, do you think the European Powers will allow you to bully us?"

I said, "Why bully if you are so strong?"

"Well, why should you come and invade our country?"

"Your country? I thought this was Natal."

So it is but Natal is ours. You stole it from us. Now we take it back again. That's all."

A hum of approval ran round the grinning circle. An old Boer came up. He did not understand what induced the soldiers to go in an armoured train. Frankland (an English prisoner) replied, "Ordered to. Don't you have to obey your orders?"

The old man shook his head in bewilderment, then he observed, "I fight to kill: I do not fight to be killed. If the Field Cornet was to order me to go in an armoured train, I would say to him 'Field Cornet, go to hell.'"

"Ah, you are not soldiers."

"But we catch soldiers and kill soldiers and make soldiers run away."

There was a general chorus of "Yaw, yaw, yaw", and grunts of amusement.

"You English," said a well-dressed man, "die for your country: We Afrikanders live for ours."

I said, "Surely you don't think you will win this war?"

"Oh yes; we will win all right this time, just the same as before."

"But it is not the same as before. Gladstone is dead, they are determined at home. If necessary they will send three hundred thousand men and spend a hundred millions."

"We are not afraid; no matter how many penny soldiers you send," an English Boer added, "Let 'em all come.'"

After about ten hours marching the prisoners reached the camp site where they were to spend the night. An exhausted Churchill complained that during the march the prisoners had received '…no food except for toasted ox, a disgusting form of nourishment." It seems that barbeques had yet to become fashionable among the British aristocracy. The Field Cornet gave them some tea and bully beef and invited the British officers and Churchill to share his tent. Refreshed by food much more to his liking, Churchill was ready for further argument. The Boers crowded into the small tent.

"'Will you tell us why there is this war?"
I said that it was because they wanted to beat us out of South Africa and we did not like the idea.
"Oh no, that is not the reason." Now that the war had begun they would drive the British into the sea; but if we had been content with what we had they would not have interfered with us – except to get a port and have their full independence recognised.
"I will tell you what is the real cause of this war. It's all those damned capitalists. They want to steal our country, and they have bought Chamberlain, and now these three, Rhodes, Beit, and Chamberlain, think they will have the Rand to divide between them afterwards."
"Don't you know that the gold mines are the property of the shareholders, many of whom are foreigners – Frenchmen and Germans and others? After the war, whatever government rules, they will still belong to these people."
"What are we fighting for then?"
"Because you hate us bitterly, and have armed yourselves in order to attack us and we naturally chose to fight when we are not occupied elsewhere." Agree with thine adversary whilst thou art in the way with him.
"Don't you think it is wicked to try to steal our country?"
"We only protect ourselves and our own interests. We didn't want your country."
"No, but the damned capitalists do."
"If you had tried to keep on friendly terms with us there would have been no war. But you want to drive us out of South Africa. Think of a great Afrikander Republic – all South Africa speaking Dutch – A United States under your President and your Flag, sovereign and international."
Their eyes glittered. "That's what we want," said one. "Yaw, Yaw," said the others, "and that's what we are going to have."
"Well, that's the reason of the war."
"No, no. You know it's those damned capitalists and Jews who have caused the war."
And the argument recommenced its orbit.'[1]

Winston had let the cat out of the bag. There runs a deep skein of anti-semitism through Boer philosophy of the period, and as many of the men who arranged finance for the goldmines were Jews, the Boers lost no time in exploiting this prejudice in their campaign against the *Uitlanders*. Johannesburg was given the disparaging nickname of Jewburg. Modern apologists for the Boers leave out the anti-semitic component of their philosophy and have even gone so far as to substitute Judasburg as the nickname for Johannesburg. The writer has on very many occasions heard Afrikaners refer to Jewburg, but never once to Judasburg.

Churchill was to receive further illumination of Boer attitudes, when a Boer asked him, 'Is it right that a dirty Kaffir should walk on the pavement – without a pass too? That's what they do in your British Colonies.' [2]

Churchill was taken to the Model School in Pretoria, which had been converted into a prisoner-of-war camp for British officers. On the night of 12 December 1899, Churchill escaped and after some exciting adventures reached Delagoa Bay in Portuguese territory. He caught a ship to Durban, arriving there on 23 December and within a day or two was at Frere where the British had set up their headquarters. On his return to Natal the Relieving Force was no nearer Ladysmith than when he was captured and Ladysmith was just as firmly besieged.

Early in the morning of Friday, 3 November 1899, Kate Driver was making her patient's beds and clearing up before going off duty when there was a tremendous explosion: 'The ground I stood on seemed to heave, the trees swayed violently. Then in the comparative quiet that followed came the sound of shouts and of running feet and of shell fragments rattling on the pavements and on the tents.'

A Boer shell had hit the Town Hall hospital. Fortunately there were no serious injuries, however the psychological damage was considerable. Kate recorded her feelings: 'The possibility that a shell should come right into the Hospital, flying the Hospital flag, had never for an instant come to my mind. In a flash, in a burst of noise, the red cross that had seemed to me an infallible symbol of protection for the sick and wounded everywhere, lost its power. The ruthlessness of war overwhelmed me.'[3]

And her anguish was to continue. News came through that Guthrie Smith had been badly wounded. Being a member of the ILH his care was not the responsibility of the Natal Volunteers, however it was arranged that he would be nursed by Kate in the Volunteer Hospital under the supervision of Dr. Currie. When he was brought into the hospital that evening the seriousness of the wound was immediately apparent. He had been shot through the liver and there seemed to be little hope of his survival.

When she came off duty the following morning she was unable to sleep, so Kate and some of the other nurses went shopping. They were surprised to find the army had commandeered the leading shops and Kate was able to obtain a large raincoat which was to prove very valuable in the months ahead. That night she noticed that Guthrie Smith had begun to show signs of improvement. When Dr. Currie confirmed this improvement, her hopes began to rise.

Meanwhile the Town Council had decided to urge Sir George White to ask General Joubert to permit civilians and the wounded to leave for the South. The request was sent to Joubert, who turned it down. He did however suggest an alternative; that a camp for non-combatants and a hospital be set up in no man's land at a place known as Intombi, which lay about four miles to the south of Ladysmith. The site lay near the railway so patients, medical personnel and supplies could be brought by rail or by wagon from Ladysmith. The move was to begin at noon on Sunday, 5 November from which time there was to be a twenty-four hour ceasefire. General White accepted the offer.

When Kate came off duty that Sunday morning she was immediately plunged into the task of arranging the transfer of the patients to Intombi. She was able to obtain mattresses for Guthrie Smith and another seriously ill patient. The nurses were to travel on the train with the wounded and they did their best to make the men as comfortable as possible in the cramped coaches. Before boarding the train, Kate noticed a nurse had brought a cooler of water with her. A civilian seeing Kate eyeing the cooler, told her there would be no water at the place where they were going. Kate looked up and down the platform until her eyes lighted on a Fire Bucket. The civilian read her thoughts, ran down the platform, grabbed the Fire Bucket, and after filling it with clean water brought it back to the train. This bucket of water and that in the cooler was the only water the nurses and their patients had for the whole of that day and the following night.

The British Military were responsible for setting up the camp and conveying patients, medical staff, civilians and goods to Intombi. One tented camp was to be the hospital and

Northern Natal.

Left to Right: Col I Hamilton (OC Cavalry), Gen Sir Archibald Hunter (Staff), Gen Sir George White (GOC Ladysmith), Col JF Brocklehurst (OC Cavalry). A sketch taken from 'The Leaguer of Ladysmith – Nov 2nd 1899 to Feb 28th 1900' by Capt Clive Dixon of the 16th Lancers, who was ADC to Gen Sir George White VC (1900).

A Sergeant-Major of the Imperial Light Horse (review order). Like all horses used by mounted men recruited in Natal, this particular horse appears to have had its mane hogged and the tail trimmed and cut short. The often wet and muddy conditions in Natal necessitated this practice which considerably reduced the time grooming the horses. The hogging or pulling of the horses' manes also ensured the rider's hands would not get caught in horsehair. In the drier conditions prevailing in the Transvaal and Free State this practice was not followed. Boer horses had flowing manes and long tails. This made it a simple matter to recognize at a considerable distance whether a body of horsemen was friend or foe.

Some Regiments recruited in Natal. Rear (mounted) from left: Natal Mounted Police, Trooper, Review Order; Natal Carbineers, Officer, Review Order. Front from left: Officer, Durban Light Infantry, Review Order; Officer, Natal Police, Service Kit; Officer, Imperial Light Horse, Service Kit; Trooper (mounted), Natal Carbineers, Service Kit.

The First Shell
Ladysmith   November 1899

CMD.

Sketches taken from 'The Leaguer of Ladysmith – Nov 2nd 1899 to Feb 28th 1900' by Capt Clive Dixon of the 16th Lancers, who was ADC to Gen Sir George White VC (1900).

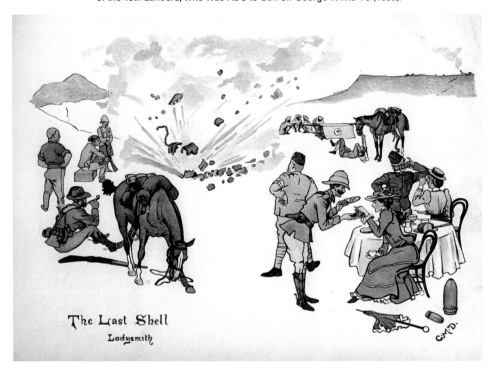

The Last Shell
Ladysmith

CMD.

about 400 yards away another was to be set up for civilians. There were delays in setting it up and it was well into the afternoon before the nurses and their patients set off for the new hospital. It did not take long for the train to cover the few miles to the selected site. In dismay the nurses looked at the bare *veld* on which the camp was being set up. Two bell tents and a marquee constituted their new home and hospital. It was placed in a hollow which would fill with water when it rained. There was no platform so the nurses had to jump from the train. Being young and fit, they did this easily, though they did struggle manhandling their bags and parcels. Having alighted, they were confronted by a barbed wire fence. By helping each other they were able to scramble through and make their way over to their tents.

The military brought over all the hospital equipment, medicines, bedding and so on in a completely haphazard manner, resulting in chaotic conditions, which became worse once darkness descended. Somehow the nurses had to reduce the muddle to some sort of order. Captain Murray, Chaplain to the Gordons, found them some candles which provided the only light as they set to work. Kate later wrote that if she lived to be a hundred she would never forget those first few days at Intombi. She had been without sleep for almost three days and nights:

'It began to rain. The wind got up with a roar. The patient's mattresses were right up against each other, and to get to a man one had to step onto his bed. At one corner of the tent the wind was blowing the rain in. As I stooped to try and fasten it down I seemed to lose myself for a moment. The dread of falling on the poor wounded boy whose bed I knelt on made me give a little scream. In a second, Nurse Otto had helped me onto an empty mattress. She thought I had fainted, but in a few moments I was myself again.

There was a brief pause. We had a quick meal. By now it was said all the men had been brought into the tents, but we saw a number of our patients had not arrived. "Oh, they'll have been taken to the Military Hospital tents," said the soldiers who had been helping the d'hoolie-bearers to bring in the men. "They'll be quite all right, you needn't worry."

We did worry. Nurse Ruiter decided to go and investigate. Off she went in the darkness towards the barbed wire and the standing train. About twenty minutes later I heard some shouts from that direction and we guessed Nurse Ruiter had found some patients and was having difficulty in getting them brought to the hospital tents in the pitch darkness. I was too busy, however, to know what was happening, and shortly afterwards was sent off duty for the first half of what remained of the night.

In the nurses' tent the mattresses were packed like sardines. No sooner did I put my head on the pillow than I had a violent attack of toothache. Nurse Otto again came to my rescue. Climbing through the tent ropes she went and fetched me a cup of stout. In ordinary life I detest stout. I drank it now as much for the kind thoughtfulness as for the hope it would cure my toothache. However, in a few moments I was asleep, and when after a couple of hours we were called up, I felt somewhat refreshed.

As day came on I was told the whole story of what had happened when Nurse Ruiter went off to search for the missing patients. As she neared the train she heard someone calling. In the van were my two most seriously injured patients waiting to be taken out. She shouted at some d'hoolie bearers at the other end of the train, and the sick men were lifted out. Guiding them as well as she could in the pitch dark, she led them towards our tents.

"As we got near the marquee," she said, "one of the stretcher poles broke and the patient fell out. We could see nothing but when we called two men came running to our help, bringing a lantern."

"Who was the patient?" I asked, my heart standing still." "Guthrie Smith," she said sadly, pointing to the far corner of the marquee. I hurried to him. He lay quietly in great pain. I stood and looked down at him. Only the day before the doctor had said he thought now there was very good hope of recovery.

He opened his eyes and recognised me. "Oh my little nursie, I'm a gonner," he said.

There was not much to do just then as many of my patients were sleeping. I sat on the ground next to him. I could see too that he was "a gonner." I tried to persuade him otherwise. We had mutual friends in the Cape. I talked of these, and I tried to get knowledge of his relations. "In case I kick the bucket?" he said looking at me. I could not tell him "yes." He pointed to his tunic that lay near him. "In that little purse in the top pocket – it's all in there," he said. "In another pocket are my badges. I wanted you to have those." Then we talked of other things for a few minutes until I was called away.

When the light came it was clear for all to see what a desolate place we had come to. It was time to wash the patients. Where was there any water? I hunted round for my fire bucket in case I should find water, but neither water nor bucket could I find, and in those few moments of frustration the image of that red bucket with the black letters FIRE painted on it became indelibly associated for me with the inhospitable *veld* on which we had been dumped.'[4]

Kate's mood did not improve when she found that although it was 10 a.m. the patients had not yet received any food. She saw Dr Currie who went to see the Military Hospital authorities and arrangements were made for the food to be sent over to the Volunteers Hospital. She nearly quarrelled with one of the Military nurses but checked herself. Finally she took Dr Currie round to see all the men and then at last she could make her way to bed:

'When I got to our nurses' tent, the other night nurses asked me where I had been and what I was doing and why on earth did I not come to bed? I tried to explain, standing in the hot tent taking off my apron. Suddenly the feeling of anger and pity that had filled me during the last busy hours overwhelmed me and I burst into tears. They comforted me and I went off to sleep…

After a long day's rest we got up to find that a new marquee of enormous size had been put up, and all the men comfortably arranged in it, each of the four nurses having a quarter of it as her responsibility. We were, however, disappointed to find we did not have our own patients in our own quarter. I talked with the matron and she kindly moved Guthrie Smith into my corner of the ward as an extra patient. He was very bad indeed and had a special day nurse. Nurse Otto and I had been trained in the same hospital in Maritzburg where one of the unwritten rules was; the patients who are the most ill must be the only ones petted or spoiled. One of her worst cases was also in my quarter of the ward but several beds lower down than Guthrie Smith unfortunately. Neither of these two patients slept well, and I hardly seemed to get to the one before the other poor man wanted me.

Webber, Nurse Otto's patient, said, "I believe, Nurse, if you would let me put my head on your lap, I'd go to sleep." Perching beside him, I lifted his head on to my lap and before long he was sleeping calmly. Nurse Thompson attended to my patient for me. After some time the boy woke and did not take long to fall deeply asleep on his own pillow again.

By the next night Guthrie Smith had been moved into another tent alone, and with him sat Nurse Mary watching over him. She said he had been calling for me during the day, but now when I spoke to him he did not recognise me. Up to now he had been so glad to see me when I came on duty at night. He was near the end and soon became unconscious. Of all my patients he was the only one I had nursed from the beginning. I felt stunned and sick at heart at losing him. His was the first death that occurred in our camp, and it was indeed a pitiful case, for having begun to recover from his severe wound in the liver, he died from peritonitis as a result of a fall.

I looked for the badges he had wanted me to have but they were gone. After crosses were put up to all the first casualties, I asked our orderly to photograph the cemetery so that his name could be seen.'[5] Oh Kate!

To set up the hospital and civilian camp in the time permitted was an impossible task and the British should have made it clear to Joubert and his staff that their demands were inhumane. They did not make the task easier for themselves by requiring that at all times their medical units should carry medical supplies which might be needed in any part of the Empire. A unit in a tropical jungle would therefore have medicines available to treat frostbite. The result was that the British army carried around with it vast quantities of medical supplies which were not always relevant to the campaign they were fighting. At Intombi they drafted civilian orderlies to work in the camp who were not suited to the tasks they had to perform. Some consultation with the locals would have helped. Another difficulty lay in the personality of the Principal Medical Officer, Colonel R. Exham, who believed a doctor's primary duty was to comply with Regulations. These set out the minimum quantities of drugs and medicines which a medical unit should hold. Once the supply of a medicine had dropped to this minimum level, Dr. Exham would refuse to permit its further use as that might result in a breach of the Regulations. How many died as a result of this policy cannot be accurately assessed but it certainly caused much suffering and distress which could have been avoided. He was also pompous and unable to get along with either the British or Volunteer doctors.

Initially, at Intombi, there were 300 beds divided between two British military hospitals and the one hospital for the Volunteers. To man these three hospitals there were 30 doctors, 120 trained medical personnel which included the nurses and 56 Indian bearers whom the army had brought from India. Dr. Currie was in charge at the Volunteer hospital. The civilian refugee camp fell under the authority of Mr. Bennett, the Resident Magistrate of Ladysmith.

In the town, hospitals were still necessary, so the Town Hall and the Convent continued to fly the Red Cross flag, and residents made their houses available as nursing homes for recuperating soldiers. As time wore on and conditions at Intombi deteriorated, more and more of the wounded and sick chose to remain in Ladysmith. Unfortunately the records of civilians at Intombi were destroyed in a comparatively recent fire, however, it does seem that most were refugees and not many were residents of the town.

At the start of the siege the principal stores announced that they would not increase their prices while the siege lasted. They complied with this undertaking. However, the army commandeered their stock in any case. No fewer than 1,700 slaughter cattle, 14,000 tins of condensed milk and many hundreds of thousand pounds of mealies (maize) were among other items taken by the army. The town's weekly market was discontinued, so for the time being, the local auctioneers decided to provide twice weekly sales, where people could sell produce and surplus food.

As soon as the ceasefire expired on 6 November the Boers recommenced their artillery bombardment of the town. The Roman Catholic Convent was on a hill near the centre of the town and had been converted into a hospital. A large Red Cross had been hoisted on the highest part of the ground. Ignoring the flag, the Boers directed their fire at the Convent, scoring several hits. Luckily there was no loss of life as the terrified nuns had crammed themselves into a cellar with a few wounded officers. To avert a potential tragedy it was decided that the sixteen Sisters and Nurses should go at once to Intombi camp. They gathered together their few possessions, and with some of their patients in dhoolies, they set off for the camp where they thought they would only remain a few days. They were about to experience 'holy poverty' beyond anything they had ever imagined.

Although not young, and dressed in voluminous habits, they somehow clambered off the train and through the barbed wire fence, and made their way to the site which had been allocated to them. Here they found three tents. The Reverend Mother, Marie des Anges, wrote,

'One was needed for Rev. Father Saby, one for our four secular nurses, and the third to shelter our provisions, and be used as a kitchen and sleeping room for two of our sisters. The difficult question was where to lodge the other ten Sisters. Fortunately an old pupil brought her father, who was an engineer to see us, and he very kindly sacrificed a kind of hut which he had made with branches of trees. It was also he who improvised for us a kind of stove with a few stones. That "tent", we used as a Chapel, a Refectory and a Community Room during the day, and as a dormitory at night for two of the Sisters. Towards evening two of our doctors came to ask if we were in need of anything. The most essential thing was a tent for the other six Sisters without shelter.'[6]

The doctor was able to arrange a tent for the exhausted Sisters, who at long last were able to get some rest, though the tent only had room for three small mattresses. The Reverend Mother was grateful that they were a little isolated from the main crowd, and even this one consolation was taken away the following day, when two hundred men were lodged next to them. These men had been taken prisoner by the Boers and were, because of their wounds or for other reasons, no longer considered a threat to their captors. Then, as today, the sending of prisoners of war into a situation of great peril would be regarded as a War Crime. To the Sisters it meant a loss of their peace and quiet, however there were compensations: 'All night we could hear them and sometimes they held concerts. However, we had not much to complain of regarding them. They were always ready to help us. Amongst them were several Catholics who increased the number of those who attended Mass.'[7]

There were also problems in Ladysmith. Henry Nevinson's two manservants wanted to leave, and if this was not bad enough, he was arrested by the 5th Lancers when he failed to produce a pass. To prevent spies operating in the town, the army had, on 29 October, issued a directive that everyone in the town should carry a pass. Nevinson made such a fuss when required to produce one, that he ended up being escorted to the General Staff by the Colonel himself, three privates armed with rifles and a mounted orderly with a lance. He was eventually able to persuade the army to let him go, but not before Zulus and Indians had had some fun pouring 'derision' on him in a manner they normally reserved for the Boers.[8]

Once the town was besieged the most urgent task facing the military was to strengthen its 14-mile defensive perimeter. Each unit was allocated a section of the perimeter which it had to defend. The Natal Volunteers, with some help from the Ladysmith Town Guard, were to protect the town from an attack on a front of about two miles, across the flat plain in the Klip River valley between Ladysmith and Bulwana Mountain. The Volunteers lost no time constructing trenches and sangars which were constantly improved, making this one of the best defended sections on the whole perimeter. At night selected Volunteers would quietly sneak up to the Boer lines and watch and listen, before silently going back to their own lines before dawn.

On the Volunteers' right was a flat-topped hill known as Caesar's Camp, joined at its western end to Wagon Hill. It is about two and a half miles from the eastern end of Caesar's camp to the western extremity of Wagon Hill. The Manchesters were responsible for the defence of Caesar's Camp and Wagon Hill. The ILH were to provide back up for them. On 7 November Col Edwards, of the ILH, went to Caesar's Camp to look at the defences and noted that Wagon Hill had not been occupied, although the ground beyond it was 'dead' and might well have been used by the enemy as a place of assembly prior to an attack. He realised the danger it presented and took it upon himself to occupy the far end of Wagon Hill with a detachment of the ILH. From that time until the end of the siege it was never left unoccupied.

On 9 November, artillery fire from the Boers began at 5.00 a.m. followed by probing attacks on various positions on the perimeter. None of these attacks were persisted with for any length of time. Finally their guns began to rake the Manchesters position on Caesar's Camp, and Boers were seen attempting to cross the valley in front of them. They were however beaten back by the Manchesters, who, with their flanks protected, were able to concentrate their fire on the attackers. At noon the Naval guns slowly fired twenty-one rounds at regular intervals. Not surprisingly the Boers were puzzled by this turn of events and for a time their fire died down. It was a 21-gun salute to commemorate the Prince of Wales' birthday! In due course the Boers resumed their fire on the Manchesters which continued until sunset. Lieutenant Fisher described in his report some curious manoeuvres by the enemy:

'*One contingent, apparently some foreign legion, showing traces of elementary discipline and evidently not numbering in its' ranks many Boers of the old school, advanced boldly across ground that afforded them little cover, and there began to "front form" in fairly good order. They were well within range of Lee-Enfield rifles, and a few well-directed volleys sent them to right-about in anything but good order. Soon after, a second column advanced with even more bravado, headed by a standard–bearer, who carried a red flag. These were said to be Irishmen, who, having elected to serve a republic, and being debarred from fighting under the green banner of their own country, yet not quite ready to acknowledge the supremacy of another race, may have flaunted the emblem of liberty by way of compromise. More probably, however, they were a mixed lot owning no common country, but willing or unwilling to serve under any colours with equal impartiality. [After] two or three shrapnels bursting in front of them to a vibrato accompaniment of rifle fire, many were seen to fall, but whether badly hit or not, nobody on our side could say. At any rate, these adventurous auxiliaries are likely to learn discretion from the wily Boer after such an experience.*'[9]

As night approached the rifle fire between the two sides died down. The British had lost four killed and twenty-seven wounded, mostly by shells, in twelve hours of intermittent fighting. An Irish American, who had deserted from the Boers, arrived in Ladysmith a few days later and claimed the Irish Brigade had suffered heavy losses, one shell alone killing ten of his erstwhile colleagues. This story, it is said, should only be swallowed with salt.

At Intombi the nuns never lost faith despite their miserable lot:

'When it rained heavily it was impossible to light a fire. We had to go to bed without supper. At other times the strong winds tore the ropes of the tents. Rain filled the trenches which overflowed and inundated the interior, soaked our beds and forced us to climb on the boxes to avoid sinking in the liquid mud. Oh! The miserable nights, when it thundered unexpectedly and awakened us with a start. We had to get up to see that our luggage was safe. Many a time we could not help laughing at our good Mother Assistant trying to sleep under an open umbrella while the storm was raging. The next morning our goods had to be put out to dry. After a heavy rain undesirable visitors swarmed in, mosquitoes, scorpions, frogs, snakes and the rest... Imagine three mattresses for six people, no sheets, no pillows. Each one wrapped herself in her blanket and went to sleep, all the feet tending to the central part of the tent and the heads to the circumference of the circles. When everybody was lying down it was impossible to move without disturbing the whole colony.'[10]

They were only able to celebrate Holy Mass when the weather was fine.

'What a lesson to us to see Our Divine Master come down in such poor habitation on an Altar made of wooden boxes, covered with sheets, and a quilt as Altar Cloth. The tent was too low to allow us to stand, the seats were most primitive, trunks of trees, wooden boxes and big stones. We were not quite out of danger in the neutral camps. More than once stray bullets hit people in their tents or within the enclosure.'[11]

When the Boers' supply of chlorodyne ran out a few days later, General White supplied the medicine without query or condition.

Except on Sundays, when they limited their martial actions to preparing for the next day's fighting, the Boers continued to send a steady stream of shells into Ladysmith. As a defence against the bombardment, the ILH came up with the idea of burrowing into the banks of the Klip River to create bomb shelters. At first they cut mere niches into the bank where a group of men could huddle during a bombardment. When it was found that it was relatively easy to tunnel into the banks, the mining engineers in the regiment created a labyrinth of interconnecting tunnels with substantial caves which could house a whole regiment and its ammunition. The excavations were deep enough to ensure safety even in the event of a direct hit and were so constructed that they did not even require supporting timbers.

Seeing how successful the ILH had been, many of the residents began to dig out shelters for their families in the river bank. These shelters, though by no means as accommodating as those created by the ILH, were nonetheless quite adequate. In these early days of the siege, the men could be seen with picks and shovels constructing caves for their families, while their wives would be looking after the children, ensuring that they took shelter when a bombardment threatened.

A Mr. Brockbank, realising the difficulties under which the family of William Watson, the retired Town Constable, laboured, excavated a shelter in the river bank for them. At daybreak William, his daughter accompanied by her children, and with his disabled son-in-law on a stretcher, would go down to the river and return home to sleep at nightfall.

When white smoke was spotted spouting from the barrel of Long Tom on Bulwana it would take 23 seconds before the shell arrived in Ladysmith. To warn all of the approach of one of these shells, the army erected a platform on which was stationed an orderly who waved a flag to warn of the approach of a shell before he himself retreated to the shelter at the base of the platform. To carry out this duty the military chose two reliable men from the auxiliary units which had accompanied the soldiers from India.

In spite of these precautions, shellfire still provided a constant threat, but such is human nature that many learned to live with it and were prepared to take chances rather than let the Boer Artillery dominate their lives. On 12 November 1899 Mrs Moor gave birth to a baby on the family farm which was in the centre of defensive works. The Moor family had tried living in a dugout by the river, but Mrs. Moor did not like the damp atmosphere, so she, with her husband and other children, moved back to their farm for the birth of the first siege baby.

In those early days of the siege George Steevens, correspondent of the *Daily Mail*, amused himself by observing the ILH:

'They were a curious regiment. They appeared to consider that it rested with themselves when they rose in the morning, and remonstrated loudly with the non-commissioned officers when, as rarely befell, they were ordered on fatigue. They grumbled about everything, especially their food, being accustomed to eat twenty-four hours' rations at a meal. They considered no Imperial Officer knew anything. No Imperial troops could do anything. They considered that they alone won Elandslaagte, and alone averted disaster at Lombard's Kop. As for talk… never was there such a corps to talk… Withal, they were an honest, sober and well-behaved lot of men. They were conspicuously clean in camp, as they were consistently brave in action. And when a few Regular Officers and Sergeants were imported among them, their discipline improved every hour.'[12]

On 14 November, General Brocklehurst took out a mounted patrol, comprising the ILH and the Natal Volunteers, into the area to the west of the town lying between the British and Boer lines. One of their objectives was to clear the area of snipers and to destroy places such as farm buildings and deserted native *kraals* which might provide cover for them. It should be mentioned here that modern accounts of the war often leave out the word 'deserted' when describing native *kraals* being destroyed by the British army in such circumstances. This gives a completely different and erroneous impression of the purpose of such sorties. The British army had faults enough, but a desire to inflict unnecessary suffering on native peoples was not one of them. As the patrol was coming in, the Boer artillery opened fire on them and though shells exploded next to and among them, no one was hit. Staff watching saw a shell burst between Dr Hornabrook and Dr Platt. The smoke momentarily hid them from view and the watchers said they must be killed. Yet when the smoke cleared they were quietly riding on. Trooper Schram of the NMR said to a comrade as he rode into camp, 'You missed nothing. It was a wasted day. Let us go and have a sleep.' He went to his tent, and as he slept a shell almost severed his head, killing him instantly. He was the first soldier killed by a shell pitched at random into the town.

As previously mentioned, one of the first things the Boers did on investing the town was to cut off the water supply, leaving the town dependant on the Klip River for its water. The spring rains, and overgrazing of the river valley, resulted in the water carrying a lot of mud. In addition, dead animals were being washed into, or perhaps placed in, the river, polluting the water further. Mr Binnie, a civil engineer employed by the Natal Government, and Chief Engineer C.C. Sheen of the Navy, created between them three condensers capable of producing daily 12,000 gallons of potable water, for as long as supplies of coal lasted. At Intombi purified water was obtained by sinking barrels into the sand of the river. This supply was supplemented early in December by the discovery of a spring within carrying distance. Indian inhabitants were permitted to cultivate kitchen gardens, and by their horticultural diligence they raised a substantial crop of seasonable vegetables which they sold at great profit to themselves and to benefit the general health of the troops. Colonel Ward was in charge of the food stocks in the town and at the beginning of the siege, it was calculated that the food should last for approximately two and a half months. The initial daily ration per person was:

Bread one and a quarter pounds, or, one pound of biscuits
Coffee, one ounce, or tea, half an ounce
Sugar, three ounces
Pepper, one and a third ounces
Potatoes, half a pound, or compressed vegetables, one ounce.

Whatever food was available, the flies in Ladysmith at that time would have ensured eating was never very pleasant. The vast quantities of horse and cattle dung in the town, plus the trench latrines used by the troops, resulted in a plague of flies. To ease the situation a mixture of Cooper's dip powder and water was spread out. This killed countless millions of flies and special fatigues were employed to sweep them up and carry them away in wheelbarrows.

Throughout the siege, both civilians and the military relied on black runners to carry letters and other documents through to the outside world, and to bring letters and even newspapers into Ladysmith. Generally £15 was charged for this service, which of course would be doubled if there was a return trip. The work was dangerous but obviously profitable. Apart from physical fitness, it required knowledge of the country to be traversed, the habits of the Boers, and careful planning. The Boers employed great ingenuity in their endeavours to trap these runners. Their paths were carefully watched, and bell wires set. One would be placed close to the ground and the next at about head height, so that the runner, in keeping a sharp lookout for one was almost certain to strike the other. This would set off an electric bell which would bring the Boer guards swarming down like bees from their camp. The runners matched cunning with cunning, and were equal to every emergency. When they were put through the outer line of pickets they flitted away silently like shadows into the night to a nearby Zulu *kraal*. Here the documents would be passed on to one of the women who would surreptitiously take them to an agreed place where another girl would collect them and carry them on to the next agreed spot, and so on, until they were finally handed over to General Buller's Staff. If the runner was stopped and searched no papers would be found on him. The plan was expensive, since so many had to be paid for their labour; but it was effective. It also required great courage and audacity by all concerned.[13] Henry Nevinson had difficulty obtaining runners to carry his despatches. On 16 November he was able to obtain a runner and celebrated with another insulting racist comment.[14]

When war was declared a new cricket season was just starting. In Ladysmith, rugby posts would have been taken down, and the cricket pitch prepared for the new season. The field bore but little resemblance to the luxurious fields and pitches which were the norm in England. Because of the warmer climate and cold dry winters, the fine grasses which grew in England could not survive in South Africa without constant irrigation. The pitch therefore was plain earth, rolled flat and smooth. In the first years of its existence the energies of a club would be devoted to obtaining funds to buy a coir mat which would cover the pitch from batting-crease to batting-crease. This would provide a true wicket with a regular bounce which always took some spin. Fast bowlers found that their best deliveries bounced over the wickets and batsmen found they acquired a lot of bruises. A big advantage of such a wicket was that it could be used day after day with minimal repairs. With the number of grazing animals in the town it is unlikely that it was ever necessary to cut the *veld* grass which constituted the outfield. Equipment, such as bats, balls, pads, and gloves, would have been in short supply. As always in Natal, rain was a problem, but when the sun shone, out came the cricketers. The townspeople played against the military, and the regiments played each other. The Boers watched these strange rituals and from time to time directed shells at the field. On one occasion, warning was given that a shell was on its way, and the players scurried from the field to find shelter. The batsman, his mind still wrapped up in the game, dallied, and as batsmen so often do, played a phantom shot at an imaginary ball. Only it was not an imaginary ball that landed in front of him, but a shell. He was knocked down but suffered no injury.

Karri Davies was active in the organisation of all sport during the siege and in particular successful athletic competitions. There were a number of top-rate athletes among the besieged including some who had competed internationally, so competition was fierce. This was so despite the meetings being held on rough ground with occasional thorn bushes and cacti. The athletes, most of whom would have competed barefoot, accepted the conditions as simply adding to the challenge.

In spite of the heat some soccer matches were organised. In a game between the Gordon Highlanders and the ILH, a shell landed on the field. In the dust, smoke and confusion caused by the explosion, the Gordons scored a goal, much to the indignation of the ILH whose belief in the integrity of the Scots was severely dented.

One Boer Artilleryman, when asked how effective the shelling of Ladysmith had been, commented, 'What is the use of shelling them? They just go on playing cricket.'

On 23 November, the Boers sent 230 Indians, who had been living in the Transvaal, into Ladysmith. Realising, at last, that these non-combatants were being sent to the town to consume the garrison's supplies, General White hardened his heart and refused to accept them, telling the Boers that they should be handed over to the British forces south of the Tugela. The Boers, who must have been surprised by the unexpected resolution shown by the British, had no choice but to take the Indians to the British army south of the Tugela. As if in spite, that day a splinter from a shell killed a dhoolie bearer near the Town Hall. He appears to have been the first such bearer killed, although from the beginning of the invasion of Natal, they were prominently exposed on the battlefields when collecting the wounded.

That evening an attempt was made to destroy the only locomotive the Boers had on the Harrismith line. An old engine was selected and once it had built up a full head of steam, it was sent, driverless, along the line to Harrismith and the Free State. Even the best plans sometimes go wrong. In this case the Boers had anticipated the ploy, and had destroyed a section of the line just before their terminus. When the engine hit the damaged line, it fell on its side and lay hissing and steaming on the *veld* like some wounded monster. Fearing it might be filled with explosives, the Boers did not approach until the next morning, when their artillery fired some shells into it. Later Boers were seen cautiously approaching the still steaming and hissing locomotive, and poking and prodding it with their rifles.

On 24 November, slaughter cattle, belonging to the military and herded by unmounted Zulus guarded by a British Mounted Infantry unit, were permitted to stray beyond the town's defences. Quick to grasp the opportunity presented to them, the Boers fired shells onto the town side of the cattle, causing them to hasten towards their lines. Not surprisingly, the unarmed herdsmen abandoned the cattle and sought shelter. Belatedly the Mounted Infantry attempted to recover the herd, but it was too late and 228 cattle were lost to the Boers. It was a humiliating incident for the British and an attempt was made to blame the herdsmen. However the real blame rested with those who had placed the Mounted Infantry in charge, when they knew these troops had no experience of herding cattle or knowledge of the Zulu language. After this incident, a detail of Natal Volunteers or the Imperial Light Horse went out with the cattle.

Three days later the Boers attempted to repeat their success and capture some horses that were grazing on the *veld* towards Bulwana. Henry Pearse of the *Daily News* described what happened next:

'But they have to do now with the Natal Carbineers, many of whom, like themselves, are *veld* farmers, familiar with every trick of rounding up horses and oxen. In vain do the gunners of "Puffing Billy" (a Boer cannon) throw percussion shells to drive the herd towards their lines. In vain is shrapnel timed to burst in a shower where Carbineers sweep round like Indian scouts to herd the startled horses back. The Volunteers do their work neatly, coolly, quickly, to the chagrin of Boers who wait in kloofs beyond the Klip River for a chance of carrying off some valuable horses. In their disappointment the Bulwaan battery tries to get some consolation by shelling the camp of the Carbineers.'[15]

On 30 November 1899, another Boer shell hit the Town Hall hospital, killing one patient and wounding ten others. In contravention of international usage the Boers had persistently shelled this building, and to protests they replied that all patients should be moved to Intombi. After this incident, patients at the Town Hall Hospital were moved to another site in town, however the Boers should have been told in no uncertain terms that it was not up to them to decide where British field hospitals and dressing stations were to be sited, and that failure to respect the Red Cross flag would have dire consequences. This was not done and as a result the Red Cross flag was not respected.

During these last days of November, the occupants of Ladysmith saw travelling to the railhead at Elandslaagte, long wagon trains, loaded with vast quantities of loot which the Boers had plundered in southern Natal. On 28 November, Donald Macdonald counted 160 loaded wagons on their way to Elandslaagte. Great herds of cattle were also seen being driven from the south, along the roads leading to van Reenen's Pass.

On 1 December an early bombardment resulted in four men being killed before breakfast. Two Gordons were ripped to pieces while standing in their lines and a driver with the artillery died when a shell took off both his legs. At the other end of town, nineteen year-old Trooper Crickmore of the Natal Mounted Rifles was hit by a shell as he rode past the Town Hall. His horse was reduced to pulp and a piece of one of Crickmore's lungs was torn away leaving part of the shell protruding under his left arm. He should have died instantly but lived for several hours. He saw many of his friends and cheerfully told them that in spite of all he would pull through, and then, at the height of his good spirits, his head fell forward and he was dead.

It had been noticed that for some days the Boers had been carrying out works on a hill (now known as Gun Hill) due west of Lombard's Kop. On 2 December a 6-inch Long Tom opened fire from this hill at various targets near the Convent. Also on this day heliograph contact was re-established with Weenen.

The long hours spent on patrol by the mounted men were exhausting and when Lt Douglas Campbell of the ILH led his squadron back into camp on the afternoon of 6 December, he was looking forward to a few hours of undisturbed sleep. He had just dozed off when a shell came through his tent and burrowed into the ground by his feet without exploding. He stalked out of the tent cursing the Boers and saying it was criminal that they should be able to disturb a man's sleep. Nonetheless, his was one of many lucky escapes since the start of the siege. From to the beginning of November to 6 December, shellfire had killed 13 men in Ladysmith and injured another 148. Whether these figures include civilians is not clear.

A concert was held in the ILH camp on the evening of 7 December. The proceedings were in full swing, when at 9:00 p.m. the ILH, the Carbineers and the Border Mounted Rifles were ordered to assemble immediately at Devonshire Post on the eastern edge of the town. They were requested to wear soft-soled shoes. The Volunteers had already acquired a reputation for the speed at which they could assemble, so it came as no surprise when they were assembled and ready to march at 10.15 p.m. The force consisted of 500 Natal Volunteers under Col W. Royston, 100 men of the ILH under Col Edwards, a detachment of Engineers under Captain Fowke and some guides under Major Henderson. General Hunter was the senior officer present. They marched for a couple of miles along the Helpmekaar road and then turned left and made their way through scrub to the foot of Gun Hill, which was about a mile from the road. Silence was maintained.

On reaching the foot of Gun Hill, the 100 Imperial Light Horsemen and 100 Natal Carbineers under Major Addison, accompanied by the engineers, were instructed to destroy the guns on the summit. The Border Mounted Rifles, under Major Rethman, were detailed to protect the left flank of the assault party, while the balance of the Carbineers, under Col Royston, would protect the right. Slowly and steadily, the assault force began the

250-foot ascent of the steep, boulder-strewn slope. It seems they passed the first picket without, at first, being noticed. When the sentry realised something was amiss, he shouted several times in an ever more anxious voice, '*Wie kom daar?*' ('Who comes there?') then, '*So waar as God, hier is hulle.*' ('As true as God, here are they'). A shot rang out, followed by some ragged firing from the crest of the hill. The attackers pressed ever upwards, clambering over the boulders and into the dead ground near the summit where the enemy's fire went over their heads. Someone shouted 'Fix Bayonets' and another, 'Give them cold steel.' In a few seconds they were over the crest, just in time to see the defenders disappearing down the other side of the hill. The ILH and the Carbineers moved across the top of the hill and took up defensive positions on the crest while the Engineers prepared charges to destroy the Long Tom and a Howitzer. Then followed the explosion of the charges which wrecked the guns. General Hunter called for three cheers for the Queen. The order to retire was given and the Volunteers were able to get back to base before dawn and without further incident. Seven men were wounded in the action, the most serious being Trooper RG Nicol who had been shot through the spine. Ambulance Sergeant Dr Charles E Ligertwood dressed his wounds and stayed with him and the non-walking wounded. Sergeant Ligertwood was a well known medical practitioner in Johannesburg and during the First World War became a combatant Lieutenant Colonel and commanded the ILH in the German South West Africa campaign.

The troops brought back with them an automatic Maxim gun found on the summit, as well as other trophies, the principal one being the breech block of the Long Tom. Karri Davies was solely responsible for the removal of the breech block, which although regarded as his property, was for many years placed on the table at any dinner or function given by the ILH. Karri subsequently presented it to General Smuts with a view to it being placed in the War Museum in Pretoria. At the time of writing it is in the Siege Museum at Ladysmith.

Col Royston had been pressing for many weeks for such an attack to be made, and in the Volunteers' camp he was credited with conceiving and planning it. With the exception of the 'Cheers for the Queen' incident, the sortie carries all the hallmarks of a Colonial operation. Some British historians believe General Hunter conceived, planned and organised the raid. Given his apparent dislike of night-time operations and his complete ignorance of local conditions and people, as evidenced by his statements to the Boer War Commission, it is difficult to imagine that he was the driving force behind this raid. Other British historians give the credit to Lt Col Sir Henry Rawlinson, while yet others believe Col WG Knox was the instigator of the sortie. That night Col Knox did take out three companies of the Liverpools, a company of mounted infantry and the 19th Hussars in what was thought to be a diversionary action. The cavalry burnt down Pepworth's Farm where the Boers had established a commissariat, but committed the elementary error of failing to get back to Ladysmith before dawn broke. They were subjected to vigorous shell and rifle fire which resulted in them losing three killed and fifteen wounded.

At daylight on the following day, Surgeon-Major Davies of the ILH returned to Gun Hill with an ambulance to bring in the wounded. Dr Davies and Sergeant Ligertwood were arrested and taken to General Schalk Burger. Burger was in no mood to let the doctors go and made various false charges against them, all of which Davies refuted. Finally he accused Davies of having been a member of the Reform Committee who had once been sent to gaol and was only released on giving an undertaking not to fight against the Transvaal again. Davies admitted being a member of the Committee and being sent to gaol, but said his undertaking was not to interfere in Transvaal politics for three years. At this point a Landrost (Magistrate), who was present, felt he should intervene and told Burger that the Doctor was correct. The Landrost told Davies and Ligertwood that they could go back to Ladysmith and take back with them the wounded men, the ambulance and their horses. Davies did not think Trooper

Nicol would survive the journey, so it was decided to leave him in the Boer hospital. Nicol died the next day. His body was sent under a white flag to Ladysmith, together with £16 cash which he had with him and his watch. Everything possible had been done to save him.

Anxious to emulate the Volunteers, the Regulars went out on a sortie on the night of 10/11 December, intending to destroy a howitzer which the Boers had placed on Surprise Hill. They did not bother to wear soft shoes. Initially luck was with them. The Boers had not put out their forward pickets, resulting in the British reaching the brow of the hill before they were challenged. After a sharp exchange of rifle fire the Boers were driven off the summit and an explosive charge was placed on the gun. Nothing happened. Another charge was prepared and placed in position. This time there was a suitable explosion followed by traditional cheering. The troops hurried down the hill, at the foot of which, a line of Boers was waiting for them. With bayonets fixed, they charged the Boers and by sheer weight of numbers they were able to break through and make their way back to Ladysmith. The British lost fourteen killed and fifty wounded. One howitzer and some ammunition had been destroyed.

As the Volunteers did not carry bayonets the call to 'Fix Bayonets' near the summit of Gun Hill had been a bluff. Many attributed this ruse to Karri Davies and so the position might have remained but for the intervention of Karri himself. In 1904 a dinner was given in Johannesburg for Field Marshal Lord Roberts by the officers of the Imperial Light Horse. When the Field Marshal was returning thanks, he turned to Karri Davies and pointing to the breechblock which was on the table, congratulated him on his timely bluff in calling to his men to 'Fix Bayonets'. Karri at once corrected him: 'It was not me, Sir, it was Colonel Edwards.' Today Edwards is generally given credit for the bluff and Karri credit for the reference to cold steel.

A letter was found at Gun Hill, which a Burgher had been writing to his wife; it gives some idea of the feelings of one young Boer:

'It is one month and seven days since we besieged Ladysmith, and don't know what will happen further. The English we see every day walking about the town, and we bombard thetown every day with our cannon. They have erected plenty of breastworks outside the town. It is very dangerous to take the town. Near the town they have two naval guns from which we receive very heavy fire, which we cannot stand. I think there will be much blood spilt before they surrender, as Mr. Englishman fights hard and well, and our burghers are a bit frightened.'

After perusal by Headquarters, Karri posted it to the addressee with a covering letter:

'Dear Madam,
Enclosed please find a letter addressed to you which we found in a tent on Lombard's Kop on the morning of 8 December when we captured some guns from the Boers. Duty necessitated my handing it to the military authorities whom I asked to return it to me to enable me to forward it to you. I regret the unavoidable delay, but hope it will reach you safely. Trusting your husband will return to you safely after the war.

I remain, dear Madam, W. Karri Davies, Major, ILH'

On 6 of December, a baby boy, Harry Buller Siege Willis was born in Ladysmith. Had he been born a fortnight later his parents might have named him differently.

CHAPTER SIXTEEN

Battle of Colenso

•—◆—•

*'We felt very down on our luck, for we realised what a terrible hash
our Commanders had made of everything.'*

MAJOR DUNCAN MCKENZIE, AFTER THE BATTLE OF COLENSO,
DECEMBER 1899

IN those early months of the war when disaster followed disaster, one thought consoled the British; General Sir Redvers Buller VC was on his way to take command of the army. On 8 August 1899, the anti-semitic, pro-Boer Commander in Chief in South Africa, Sir William Butler, resigned. General Buller, who for the past few years had held the powerful position of Adjutant-General at the War Office, was regarded by most people as the obvious choice as a successor to Butler, and it came as no surprise when he received the appointment. On 14 October, Buller boarded the S.S. *Dunottar Castle* bound for Cape Town.

Redvers Buller was the second of seven sons of a wealthy landowning family from Downes in Devon. He went to Harrow, but had to leave after an incident in which some doors were painted red, and completed his schooling at Eton. His holidays were spent on the family estate where young Redvers would undertake any work which might be required of him, whether it was in the smithy, carpentry shop or stables. The family had always taken a keen interest in the welfare of the tenants and workers at Downes, and Redvers inherited this characteristic.

On leaving school he decided to join the army and in 1858 became an Ensign in the 60th Rifles. His family paid for his commission. His fellow subalterns tended to regard him as a country bumpkin, but were nonetheless a little in awe of him, not only because he had grown into a phenomenally strong man with flashes of bad temper, but also because he was forthright and constant in his opinions.

His bouts of ill-temper would pass rapidly and those who knew him soon discovered that he was, by nature, a very kind man. His upbringing at Downes led him to identify with his men and there was no barrier of class distinction between them. The rank and file adored him. He served in many of the small wars in which Britain was engaged in Victorian times and showed himself to be a man of great courage, being awarded the Victoria Cross in the Zulu War. He always worked hard and it was not surprising that he was noticed by General Wolseley, who made Buller his Intelligence Officer in the Ashanti War of 1873. He was loyal to Wolseley, and as the latter rose in power, so did Buller rise up the army ladder. When his elder brother died he inherited the family estate and could have retired to a comfortable life as a country squire, instead he decided to continue with his army career. In 1886 he was sent to Ireland to deal with a group of nationalist peasants known as the Moonlighters who were stealing cattle and collecting arms. He was reasonably successful in checking the Moonlighters but was appalled by the manner in which many landlords treated their tenants. In his report to the Chief Secretary for Ireland he stated, '*For 120 years British bayonets have backed up landlords in extracting excessive rents, and have supported them in grossly neglecting their tenants.*' Such statements might have spelt the end of his career but as Wolesley's star rose, Buller continued his upward climb. Queen Victoria liked his bluff manner and with his patron Sir Garnet Wolesley now Commander-in-Chief, the goodwill surrounding him when he left for South Africa was almost tangible.

One of the few persons who were not moved by this adulation was Redvers Buller himself. He had never held an independent command and doubted whether he was suited to do so. He saw himself as an able administrator who could carry out other men's ideas but as he confessed to his wife, 'I never credited myself with much ability on the inventive side.' Early in his career he found that war, despite its excitement, was 'wicked and brutal', a feeling which would only have grown stronger with the passing of time. The years working long hours at an office desk in Whitehall had resulted in his putting on weight and losing much of his former physical vigour, while the duty of having to attend an endless round of functions resulted in his acquiring a taste for fine champagne. He never sought the posting to South Africa, did not want to fight the Boers, and fervently hoped the war would soon be over, so that he could return home.

To have fulfilled the expectations which rested on him would have required an imaginative military genius of almost supernatural power and foresight. Like his army, Buller was to follow the tried and tested solutions to problems which, in other places and at other times, had been successful. However if the Boers were to be defeated a new way of fighting was required, and the British habit of not listening to other opinions ensured that the lessons were to be learnt the hard way.

When the bad days came, his detractors were quick to draw attention to his love of champagne and other small luxuries, but the men he commanded knew that General Buller would not touch his food until every man in the ranks had been fed. Indeed, one of his greatest weaknesses was the large commissariat he required to accompany his army. He insisted that everything which might possibly be required to ensure the wellbeing of the troops was available. Also, in the same manner that the once gauche West Country subaltern had awed his peers by his sheer persistence, so the older Buller was able to infuse into his army that same determination to fight on and never to give in.

Buller was given no specific instructions as to how the campaign in South Africa was to be conducted. It was, however, decided that he would go to the northern Cape and from there advance through the Free State via Bloemfontein and then on to Pretoria to accept the surrender of the Boer forces. During the voyage to Cape Town he received a report that the Boers had been defeated in three battles and Penn Symons had been killed. On 31 October 1899, he arrived in Cape Town where he received news of the capture of the British soldiers at Nicholson's Nek. Over the next few days he received nothing but bad news from all fronts.

He spent three weeks in Cape Town. During this period he decided to split the Army Corps which had followed him out from England: one half would join Lord Methuen in the northern Cape and relieve Kimberley, while the other half would accompany him to Natal where the first priority would be the relief of Ladysmith. With only a scratch staff he displayed his great powers of organisation, sending troops off to their appropriate fronts and arranging all their transport and supplies. He also authorised the raising of the South African Light Horse and several other groups of Colonial troops. He embarked for Durban on 22 November, and on arrival he sent General Clery to Frere to organise the troops already there, while he remained in Pietermaritzburg organising various supplies. In addition, he had conceived the idea of a large field hospital, erected as close as possible to the front line to enable wounded troops to receive early treatment. He now set about organising it. He also arranged the creation of a Field Canteen, where little luxuries not normally included in army rations, could be purchased. The profits from the Canteen went to the next-of-kin of those killed in action or dying of wounds.

While Buller was in Pietermaritzburg, the mounted troops under Lord Dundonald were on constant patrol monitoring the Boer movements. In the early hours of 28 November, Dundonald led a force of mounted men on a reconnaissance in the direction of Colenso. With him were the Natal Carbineers, a squadron of the Imperial Light Horse, Bethune's Mounted Infantry, Thornycroft's Mounted Infantry, a company of Regular Mounted Infantry, some Natal Police and a battery of Field Artillery. At dawn Boer scouts were seen ahead, but they disappeared without a shot being fired. When they reached the crest from which they could see the land sloping down to Colenso and the Tugela River, McKenzie pointed out to Dundonald the trenches the Boers were digging on Robinson's farm across the river from Colenso. To obtain a better view of the Boer defences, McKenzie advised that they could advance to the next patch of shelter, as the Boers would be reluctant to use their big guns since this would give away their position. Dundonald then ordered the column to advance and as they did so, McKenzie glanced round and noticed the whole mounted brigade was in close order. As he was only a volunteer and a major, he should perhaps have kept quiet, but he felt it was his duty to say something as the men made a most tempting shot for the enemy's guns, 'I think, Sir, you have not noticed, that the men are not in extended order.' Dundonald at once told McKenzie to give the order to extend, which was promptly done. The Boer's guns now opened fire but because the troops were extended, no damage was done. The British Artillery unlimbered and attempted to return fire but were outranged. Meanwhile the Natal Police, who had formed the advance guard of the column, had reached a position with little cover. McKenzie, noticing this, asked that they should be given leave to retire, as it served no purpose to have the Police in this forward position. Dundonald agreed, and McKenzie rode forward with the order to retire. When they arrived back at the guns they found the other mounted men had already retired. McKenzie told the Officer in Command of the guns to follow him. This was the same officer, Major Henshaw, who had been so uncooperative at Willow Grange, but this time he followed McKenzie who led them through a little valley which hid them from the enemy's view until they were out of effective range. The column returned to Frere having obtained useful information about the Boer's defences. The only damage suffered was an injury to one horse's hoof.

General Buller arrived at Frere on Wednesday, 6 December 1899, and immediately set off with his staff, including Dundonald, to inspect the position at Colenso. Dundonald had brought along Duncan McKenzie whom he introduced to Buller. On reaching the high ground a few miles south of Colenso, General Buller was able to look over the gently sloping *veld* to the village beyond which could be seen the Tugela River. North of the river was Fort Wylie and a line of hills, which provided an even more formidable natural fortress. McKenzie pointed out where the Boers had dug their trenches and also drew attention to a hill, Hlangwane, which lay to the east of Colenso and which appeared to be situated to the north of the river, whereas in fact it lay south of it. From Hlangwane it would be possible to bring flanking fire to bear on the main Boer position as well as providing protection for troops crossing the river. Buller thanked McKenzie for his help and the party returned to Frere to consider how to break through the Boer line.[1]

It was during this period that one of the more significant conversations of the campaign took place. For centuries European armies had placed great store on intimidating their opponents with a show of force. Having recently come from Britain and being fully aware of Britain's heroic past, Dundonald asked McKenzie whether the Boers would fight 'when they saw Her Majesty's troops'. McKenzie replied that the Boers, far from being overawed, would fight. From that time Dundonald abandoned the old idea of intimidating the enemy and followed the Volunteers creed of keeping his position, strength and intentions hidden from the enemy.[2]

While Buller and his staff were preparing an attack on the Boer positions along the Tugela, the newly recruited mounted regiments, Thornycroft's Mounted Infantry, the South African Light Horse, and Bethune's Mounted Infantry were able to get in some essential training. Initially, Dundonald was disappointed with these regiments commenting, 'What a formidable force they would have been if they could have shot as well as the Border Mounted Rifles, but a novice with any tool – more especially a rifle or a revolver – cannot use it with efficiency until after much practice.' It was soon Dundonald's turn to be amazed at how quickly they learned and he soon noted the 'astonishing progress in the direction of efficiency.'

Meanwhile Duncan McKenzie, with the assistance of some of his Zulu-speaking officers, built up a small Native Intelligence Corps to assist Dundonald's Brigade. This Corps was able to furnish a great deal of information for the Natal army, many were to show great courage in the face of the enemy and several were to lose their lives. On 14 December, Dundonald had approximately 1,150 mounted men under his command, all but the 13th Hussars being Volunteers.

One of the big difficulties faced by Buller and his Staff was that they did not have any reliable maps. The Tugela had for a long time been considered by the British as a possible line of defence and the area should have been properly surveyed and mapped before the war. Even after the ultimatum had been sent such an important survey should have been made. The owner of the land across the river from Colenso, one Robinson, would, if approached, have given the army every possible assistance. As was the case around Ladysmith, the army spurned what could have been a very valuable source of information. Without the maps, Buller relied on his own observation and by 12 December, he had come to the conclusion that it would be too costly to relieve Ladysmith by means of an attack on the enemy positions at Colenso. With his army now 18,000 strong, he decided instead to use his numerical advantage over the Boers and to attempt to bypass the Boer right flank by a rapid night march to Potgieter's Drift some eighteen miles upstream from Colenso. He heliographed General White in Ladysmith to say that he would start his advance to Potgieter's Drift on the 12th and hoped to be in Ladysmith five days later.

On the evening of 12 December, Major-General Barton's 6th Brigade was ordered to take up a position in front of Colenso and act as a distraction, while the rest of the army began its preparations for the move to Potgieters Drift. The following day General Buller changed his mind. He would instead attack the Boers at Colenso, something which a mere 24 hours before he had thought would be too costly. It is, of course, impossible to state precisely what brought about the change in plan, though receipt of the news of the defeat and death of General Wauchope at Maggersfontein, and the reverse suffered a few days before by General Gatacre at Stormberg must have weighed heavily with him. In abandoning his sensible plan, he displayed his own lack of self-confidence and his indecisiveness. He heliographed White to say that the plan had changed and he was now coming through via Colenso and Onderbroek Spruit (the literal translation is Underpants Stream!). Buller omitted this time to say when he would arrive in Ladysmith.

On the afternoon of 14 December 1899, Sir Redvers Buller advised his senior officers that he intended to attack Colenso the following day. At about midnight they received their orders. On the left, a brigade under General Fitzroy Hart was to advance down to the river which would be crossed at a place known as Bridle Drift, and then move along the northern bank attacking the Boer right flank. They were to be supported by two artillery batteries.

In the centre, Hildyard's Brigade, supported by two artillery batteries and six naval guns, was to advance down past the village, cross the still intact road bridge before driving the Boers off the *kopjes* which they occupied. It should be mentioned that the Boers had destroyed the rail bridge, which lay about half a mile downstream from the road bridge. On the right Lord Dundonald and his Mounted Brigade with the support of one artillery battery, were to occupy Hlangwane Hill and from there direct flanking fire at the Boers. General Lyttelton's and Barton's brigades were to remain in reserve to render support where required. Placed between Hildyard and Barton were some Naval 4.7 and 12 pounder guns which were available to support either advance. Buller stationed himself near these guns. Included in the Naval Brigade were 47 men of the Natal Naval Volunteers under Lieutenants Anderson and Chiazarri. Officers were instructed not to carry swords to prevent identification by the enemy.

The Boers too had made plans for the coming battle. They had mined the road bridge with explosives but did not detonate the charges. There was of course a reason for this — it was the route they wished the British to follow. Louis Botha's plan was to permit the British to cross the river unchallenged, and only when they were in the open on the northern bank, would his concealed riflemen and artillery open fire and the bridge be blown up. Trapped in the open against the river the British force would be annihilated. Because possession of Hlangwane Hill would present an opportunity for the British to outflank his forces, Botha was concerned that every effort should be made to ensure the retention of the Hill. However the individualistic Boers did not like the idea of fighting on Hlangwane as they could easily be trapped on the wrong side of the river. On 13 December, they deserted the position and nothing Botha could say would persuade them to go back across the river. Botha telegraphed Joubert in Pretoria who replied that Hlangwane must be re-occupied at all costs. Still Botha's commandos refused to move. Finally Botha resorted to the biblical method of selection: lots were drawn. The 800-strong Wakkerstroom *Kommando* was selected and at 3 a.m. on 15 December it crossed the river and took up its positions on Hlangwane.

On the 15th the British troops had their breakfast at 3 a.m. and fell in at 3.30 a.m. General Hart, who had the nickname 'No-Bobs' because he never ducked while under fire, began the day by subjecting his command to half an hour of parade ground drill. This preliminary over, he and his men joined the rest of the British force just before dawn as they marched towards the Tugela River. Hart rode at the head of his Brigade who followed in tight columns of four. First came the Dublin Fusiliers, then the Inniskillings, the Connaught Rangers and the Border Regiment. Hart insisted that the men remain in close order. At 5.30 they heard the big Naval guns firing at the Boers. The Boers made no reply. Hart rode on to the river where a Zulu, apparently under the impression that Hart was seeking a punt to cross the river, advised him to follow the river as it turned northwards to form a loop before turning south. Though the Boers would have removed the punt, Hart seems to have been

Maj Gen Fitzroy 'No-Bobs' Hart, Commanding Officer of the Irish Brigade.

A Naval 40-pounder being hauled into position at Colenso.

persuaded that the crossing was at the northern end of the tongue of land formed by the loop and led his men into the salient. The Boers were unable to resist the bait any longer and opened close-range rifle fire from three sides on the Irishmen. Hart's response was to bring even more men into the salient while, sword in hand, he urged them ever forward. Some men made it into the water where they were either shot or drowned. Despite the Boers having hidden barbed wire in the water, a few men made it to the other side, only to find they had no support and had no choice but to attempt the hazardous crossing back. Hart appeared to have become completely irrational and men were beginning to disobey his commands even though he threatened to shoot them.

Scorning cover and waving his sword around, No-Bobs must have provided a tempting target and few would have been willing to be in his vicinity. One colonial ignored the exceptional danger of being near Hart, who had this to say about him, 'Mr Norgate, a civilian gentleman, not called upon by his engagement to risk his life, kept near me under that heavy fire, in case he could be of any use to me; very gallant, patriotic conduct that I hope will be recognised well.' An hour or so later Norgate was injured while carrying a wounded man from the field.

Buller, from his vantage point had seen the trap into which Hart had led his men and before 7.00 a.m. sent a messenger down with an order for immediate retirement. He then rode down to the salient and personally confirmed his order, before riding over to General Lyttelton, who was acting as reserve for Hart's Brigade, telling him, 'Hart has got into a devil of a mess down there, get him out of it as best you can.' There was nothing Lyttleton could do other than cover Hart's retreat which was conducted in piecemeal fashion throughout the day.

In the centre the British had fared no better. Col Long's orders were to move forward and cover Hildyard's advance. It was not indicated precisely how far he should advance, or that he should not get ahead of the attacking infantry, or indeed that he should not bring his guns within rifle range without adequate cover. Perhaps General Buller thought these were matters for common sense. Col Long had other ideas. He was going to smash up the Boers. Before 6.00 a.m. twelve 15-pounder horse-drawn field guns had formed up in drill formation and with Col Long and his officers riding abreast, trotted forward down the long slope towards Colenso. Six 12-pounder Naval guns followed but because they were drawn by oxen they were slower and were soon some distance behind the field guns. On and on went the guns. When their scouts reached the river, the guns unlimbered and prepared to 'smash up the Boers'. Estimates as to precisely how far they were from the Boers vary between 500 and 1,000 yards. They were certainly well within the range of the Boer riflemen.

The Boers had watched, with some amazement, the steady approach of the Artillery. They held their fire until the British guns unlimbered before opening withering rifle and artillery fire on the unfortunate gunners. Showing tremendous courage, the British artillery stuck to their guns, though the slaughter of men and horses was terrible. Because the Boers had cunningly disguised their positions and used smokeless powder, the British artillery could not discover precisely where they should direct their fire. Nonetheless they kept firing for almost an hour until a shortage of ammunition and men to serve the guns forced them to abandon them and seek shelter with the dead and wounded in a donga a few hundred yards further back. Col Long was one of the first men wounded and was carried to shelter in the donga.

The Naval guns which had set off early that morning with Col Long were some way behind when the firing started. They were, however, within range of the Boer Artillery whose shellfire killed some of their oxen. In the resulting general chaos the rest of the oxen stampeded. With difficulty, the sailors unlimbered their guns and manhandled them into position and began a bombardment of the Boers. A gun was spotted near Fort Wylie, so they concentrated their fire on it and were delighted to see it topple over. However the Boer gunfire, instead of abating, intensified. In response the sailors set to work pulling the guns back into a safer position in another donga. The heavily laden ammunition wagons proved a difficult proposition and required that every available man lend a hand in hauling them to shelter. General Buller, who happened to be nearby, saw what was happening. He dismounted, and putting his shoulder to the wheel heaved and shoved with the sailors until the wagons had reached safety.

During this process, a spare wagon, owned by a Mr Pringle, a local farmer, had been left behind. Pringle, ignoring the enemy fire, calmly rounded up a few oxen, inspanned them to the wagon, and single-handedly brought it to safety. Following Boer looting, it would have been very difficult to replace.

Buller had been so preoccupied with the calamity which had befallen his forces on the left, that it was only after receiving a report from one of Long's staff officers that he rode to see what could be done for the artillery. He seems to have instantly formed the opinion that the engagement should be broken off. The Naval guns were in a position to withdraw but what could be done about the twelve deserted field guns?

Hildyard had explicit instructions to move out with his infantry at 4.00 a.m. to attack the Boers at the bridge and form a bridgehead where the army could cross the river and begin the advance to Ladysmith. He and Long had failed to coordinate their movements and when Buller arrived at about 7.00 a.m., Hildyard's infantry had yet to begin their attack. Buller ordered them to advance to the left of the abandoned guns so as to provide covering fire for an attempt to extricate them. The infantry now advanced in exemplary fashion with a widely extended line. They passed the deserted guns and occupied the ruined houses and sheds in Colenso. Here they were able to counter Boer fire, but were unable to advance any further.

Buller instructed a Captain Schofield to try to get the guns away. Schofield called for volunteers. Two officers were among them, Capt Congreve and Lt Freddie Roberts, only son of Field Marshal Lord Roberts. Buller had been at considerable pains to protect the over-enthusiastic young Roberts and had placed him on General Clery's Staff but could do nothing to save him now. When Schofield and his volunteers, with two teams of horses, galloped out to retrieve the guns they were met by fire as fierce as any which had been directed at the British that day. Captain Reed and two teams from the 7th Battery also joined the rescue operation. Two of the twelve guns were recovered before ever-increasing Boer fire made further sorties impossible. The slaughter of men and horses during the attempt to save guns was appalling. One of those killed was Freddie Roberts who rode towards the guns laughing and waving a whip in the air. When he fell, Captain Congreve, who was also wounded badly and Major Babtie of the Medical Corps, at great risk to themselves, crawled out to the unconscious Roberts and brought him to the sheltering donga. He died the next day without regaining consciousness.

By 11.00 a.m. Buller could stand the slaughter no longer and decided on a general withdrawal and to abandon the 10 field guns. He sent a message to Hildyard to withdraw from Colenso, then rode over to the Naval guns and told their unit to withdraw. Finally he rode across to Dundonald with instructions that he too should disengage all his men.

From the time McKenzie had drawn his attention to Hlangwane, Dundonald had felt that here lay the key to success of an attack against the Boers on the Colenso front. As we have seen, Louis Botha and General Joubert were very anxious to prevent the British from gaining control of this hill and had risked 800 men from one of their best *Kommandos* to defend it. Dundonald had been obliged to withdraw from his Brigade Bethune's Mounted Infantry for baggage and other duties, and if account is taken of the men required to look after the horses, he had no more than 600 men with rifles to carry out the attack. Not only was he outnumbered, but the majority of his men were green recruits. The Boers were ensconced on a boulder-strewn hill which made an ideal defensive position and which could not easily be carried by a frontal assault. While at Frere and at a time when Buller had yet to finalise his plans, Dundonald had met a Major Elliot of the Royal Engineers who was the Railway Staff Officer at the nearby station. Elliot asked if he might accompany a reconnaissance, which gave Dundonald an opportunity to point out to him Hlangwane and the neighbouring hills of Monte Christo and Cingolo. Elliot was impressed by the opportunity this configuration of the land offered, and drew a map of the area, while Dundonald wrote out a report on the subject. The map and report were then presented to General Buller who, apart from showing annoyance, indicated no interest in the suggested plan of attack.

The Mounted Brigade had moved out towards Hlangwane at 4 a.m. on 15 December. The Native Intelligence Unit recruited by McKenzie reported that the Boers had occupied the Hill during the night. Dundonald decided that Duncan McKenzie should remain with him, resulting in Captain MacKay taking over command of the Carbineers. Dundonald placed his portion of the Royal Artillery's 7th Battery, commanded by Major Henshaw, on a small hill south of Hlangwane, where it was hoped it would be able to assist the Mounted Brigade on Hlangwane and if required Hildyard's advance.

Thornycroft's Mounted Infantry and a Composite Regiment (comprising the Carbineers, the ILH, the Natal Police, some Mounted Infantry from the King's Royal Rifles and the Dublin Fusiliers), were to attack the south eastern slopes of the hill, while the South African Light Horse simultaneously attacked the southern slopes. The 13th Hussars were placed in support on the small hill with the 7th Battery.

Thornycroft's MI and the Composite Regiment in their attack from the south-east had only advanced about half a mile before they were checked by heavy fire from Boers among boulders on the hill. At 7.40 a.m. Thornycroft sent a message to say that the Boers held very strong positions and that not only had the advance been held up, but that his right might also be threatened. Dundonald and McKenzie went to see for themselves what was happening. They found that Thornycroft's MI, the Composite Regiment and the SA Light Horse had all been checked by heavy rifle fire. Though they could hold the Boers, it was impossible to advance further without reinforcements. McKenzie noticed the recurring problem caused by the British being unable to see things readily apparent to locals. He could see the Boer positions on Hlangwane but found they were invisible to Dundonald.[3] It takes time to learn how to notice things on the *veld*. This phenomenon can be seen on modern safaris where tourists generally fail to see animals until they are pointed out by a guide.

Dundonald's orders clearly stated that the 6th Brigade under General Barton should if necessary support the Mounted Brigade as they moved towards Hlangwane. With all his men committed, Dundonald asked General Barton for a battalion of infantry to go round to the northern side of Hlangwane and thereby threaten the Boer's retreat. Using as an excuse the fact that he did not have specific orders to do this, Barton turned down the request. Added to this, the artillery with Dundonald fired 530 rounds which were concentrated almost exclusively on assisting Long and Hildyard. Thus was lost the one opportunity the British had of compensating for the losses they suffered elsewhere on the field.

Concerned about the Carbineers, McKenzie persuaded Dundonald to let him return to his regiment and he immediately set off to locate them. He had not gone far when he discovered the Hussars had retired and had formed up behind a ridge and were sitting on their horses. The Carbineers, the ILH and a few other details were still out, so McKenzie sent a request to Dundonald asking that the Hussars cover the retreat of the Volunteers. Dundonald agreed and sent an order to that effect to the Major in command of the Hussars. '*Damn the Carbineers,*' was the curt response of that officer, who ignored the order.[4]

With no help coming from that quarter, McKenzie and two companions set off to find the Carbineers, their guide being the sound of firing. They found the Carbineer horses in a donga with three men in charge of them. When asked where the Carbineers were, they pointed out the direction in which their comrades had gone. McKenzie and his companions had not gone far before they met and had a brief chat with a wounded friend, Captain Otto from Greytown, who had enlisted with Thornycroft's MI and was now being carried from the field. A little further on McKenzie was hailed by Captain Bottomley of the ILH who said, 'Hullo, Mac, where are you going?' to which McKenzie replied, 'I am looking for the Carbineers. Can you tell me where they are?' 'They are all right. I sent an orderly to tell them to retire. You had better not go on, or you won't get back,' responded Bottomley.

McKenzie now found himself alone, his companions having evidently gone towards a donga on his right. To get to the donga McKenzie had to cross some clear ground which he was able to do with only a few shots being sent his way. In the donga he found footprints but no men and received no response to calls for the Carbineers. He decided to return to the spot where the Regiment's horses had been. He was to have an exciting few minutes:

'Immediately I started I came under a very hot fire, and am not ashamed to say I ran as hard as I could. The heat was so great I soon got pumped and lay behind a thorn tree for a short time before going off again at full tilt. I had another rest behind an ant-heap, and then got clean out. Just as I neared the horses I saw the Carbineers coming out of the donga with their horses: they told me Capt Mackay was badly wounded in the face and Troopers Warren, Gray, Jenner and Adie had been killed, and some others were wounded, besides several missing, but these men gradually came in, and whenever we saw anyone on foot a mounted man galloped out with a horse and picked him up, and we were fortunate in picking up all our missing and wounded, and accounting for all our men before moving. Captain Briscoe of the Medical Corps got them into camp in a very short time. The Boers did not follow up, otherwise we should have had to "get" pretty quickly, as all the other troops had moved off, and the Estcourt squadron of the Carbineers were the only mounted men left.'[5]

Captain Mackay was shot through the cheeks just below the eyes and was given little chance of survival. He did, however, make a remarkable recovery and was back with his regiment by 21 February 1900. When Mackay was hit, 19-year old Trooper Frederick Charles Farmer of Weenen braved fierce rifle fire to bring him back to safety. For this Farmer was awarded the Distinguished Conduct Medal.

In the course of their withdrawal the Carbineers passed the ridge where Long's guns were standing deserted. They met an Artillery man who told them what had happened. McKenzie sought out Dundonald but found out that he had already left though he did find his CSO, Major Graham. McKenzie told Graham of a plan to save the guns which he was confident the Carbineers would be only too willing to undertake.

The plan was to follow the donga as far as it provided good cover, and then send forward about a dozen men, in extended order, who would crawl towards the guns trailing long ropes which they would secure to the guns before crawling back. In the donga other men would haul the guns off their elevated position into a little valley where there was sufficient cover to take off the ropes and hitch them to mules or horses who could gallop away with them. Artillery, with infantry lying down in extended order, would have provided covering fire at very little risk. Graham replied that he could do nothing as both Buller and Dundonald had left the field. Presumably they could not be disturbed. McKenzie's plan had nothing of the dash and glamour of earlier schemes to rescue the guns, but it would have ensured that with little loss, the guns did not fall into the hands of the Boers, who were later able to cross the Tugela without opposition and collect them.

McKenzie recorded the feelings of his men after the engagement: '...we felt very down on our luck, for we realised what a terrible hash our commanders had made of everything.'[6]

The day was marked by the great courage and sacrifice of the Irish Regiments under General Hart and the equal heroism of the Royal Artillery. The British suffered 1,139 casualties of whom 145 were killed, 755 wounded and 239 missing, most of whom were captured. Almost half these casualties were suffered by the Irish Regiments under Hart and most of the others were suffered by the Artillery. Of the 175 Artillery horses, 111 were killed and of the remaining 64, only 38 were unwounded. Seven Victoria Crosses were awarded, the recipients being Captain Congreve, Corporal Nurse, Major Babtie, Captain Reed, Private Ravenhill, Captain Schofield and posthumously, Lt F. Roberts. Initially there was some opposition to Captain Schofield receiving the award because Buller had told him to try to rescue the guns, which was regarded as less meritorious than volunteering to do so!

Unknown to Buller and his staff an important figure in the history of the British Empire was on his way to Colenso. On 16 October 1899, a meeting of wealthy Indian merchants and professional men decided in Durban to provide unconditionally a non-combatant unit drawn from the Indian community in Natal. Mohandas K. Gandhi wrote to the Natal government telling them about the offer and stating that although they did not know how to handle arms, there were other duties they might be able to perform on the battlefield. The Natal government was favourably impressed by the offer but not having the power to raise such a unit, it was referred to the Imperial authorities. Early in December, Sir Redvers Buller responded and a corps of 600 bearers and 25 leaders was rapidly assembled. At 3.00 p.m. on 14 December the corps arrived safely at Estcourt. The following day they travelled by train to Chieveley station where they were given their Red Cross badges, and ordered to march to the field hospital nearly 6 miles away. During the day they could hear the sound of the battle being waged at Colenso. On arrival at the field hospital they were asked to carry wounded officers and men from the field hospital to the base hospital at the Station.

Without having anything to eat, they set about the task and with three men to a stretcher they carried nearly 50 men to the hospital. It was nearly midnight before they were able to

An artist's impression of guns firing at Colenso.

Men of the Natal Volunteer Ambulance Corps carrying the wounded from the Colenso battlefield.

have their evening meal. The following day they carried patients from the hospital to the Red Cross train. After a couple of uncomfortable days at Chieveley they entrained for Estcourt where on 19 December, they received orders to disband temporarily. They were thanked for their services and told that they would probably be called upon again.[7]

Although Boer figures of their losses at Colenso are unreliable, probably about 10 were killed and 20 wounded. During the engagement the Boers received assistance from the *Uitlander Korps*. One Boer left a description of one of these men:

'I notices in the laager, an American, the most vicious looking human being I have ever seen. He glitters with knives, bayonets and revolvers; belts and ammunition were wound round him hither and thither in coils. His many weapons flashed in the morning and afternoon sun all over the camp. To look at him was terrifying. I was pleased to think he was on our side. Yet I was told that during the fighting at Colenso this glittering Hector hid in an antbear hole for three days.'[8] (An antbear is also known as a pangolin.)

The events of the day came as a great shock to Buller who seemed to lose his nerve completely. Though Hart and Long had let him down badly, he had in fact been quite fortunate. Long, by his reckless advance, had tempted the Boers into firing on them prematurely, and thereby destroyed Louis Botha's plan to entice the British force across the river via the still intact road bridge. Despite the foolhardy manner in which Hart had carried out his attack, he did engage a substantial portion of the Boer army, which could not have easily been moved elsewhere. Hildyard's Brigade, having finally been stirred into action, could more than hold its own. With his substantial reserves, Buller could have surrounded Hlangwane and pounded it into submission with his artillery. The Boers on the other side of the river, if there were any, could have done little to help their compatriots, and any intervention by their artillery would have put the lives of the Boer defenders at risk. In March 1900, General Botha's headquarters published a letter in the Boer press in the following terms:

'An important point, and where the main attack was expected was the Langweni Hill, on the southern bank of the Tugela, which was occupied by only some 800 Boers, who were selected from the best shots. 'Had the British made themselves masters of this position, they would have commanded all the Boer positions on the flank. A couple of cannon there would mean a flight to us, and victory to the British. As they were unacquainted with this position, we watched it with the greatest anxiety.'

Having by his loss of nerve turned the engagement into a disaster, Buller now compounded his misfortunes by sending a series of unfortunate cables on his return to Chieveley. To the War Office he reported that he had suffered a serious reverse, followed an hour later by another telegram where he stated, 'I am not strong enough to relieve Ladysmith... I do not think either a gun or a Boer was seen by us all day... I consider I ought to let Ladysmith go and to occupy a good position for the defence of south Natal and so let time help us.'

He heliographed White in Ladysmith advising him that he had suffered a reverse and said it would take at least one month for him to gather a force together to cross the Tugela. He asked White how many days he could hold on and continued, 'After which I suggest your firing away as much ammunition as you can, and making best terms you can. I can remain here if you have an alternative suggestion, but unaided I cannot break in.' He went on to suggest that White should burn his cipher, decipher and code books, and all deciphered messages. White, no doubt wondering if Buller had taken leave of his senses, sent a very firm response. 'I can make food last for much longer than a month, and will not think of making terms unless I am forced to... the loss of 12,000 men here would be a heavy blow to England. We must not yet think of it.'

London reacted promptly and immediately telegraphed Buller:

> '*The prosecution of the campaign in Natal is being carried on under quite unexpected difficulties, and in the opinion of Her Majesty's Government it will require your presence and whole attention. It has been decided by her Majesty's Government under these circumstances to appoint Field-Marshal Lord Roberts as Commander-in-Chief, South Africa, his Chief of Staff being Lord Kitchener.*'

What a tactful way to demote Buller who accepted the situation with good grace. On the same day that Roberts received the appointment, he received the news of the death of his only son.

Whatever London might have thought of Buller, the rank and file of his army never lost faith in him for an instant. They had witnessed his courage and complete lack of concern for his own safety, and knew that at all times his prime concern was the welfare of his men. At camp in Chieveley and Frere, Buller gradually recovered his self-confidence and began to plan his next move.

The week of 10-17 December 1899, in which the British had suffered defeats at Stormberg and Magersfontein in the Cape as well as the disaster at Colenso, became known as 'Black Week.' Bad as it might have been for the British, it was not an auspicious week for the Boers either. Britain decided to start recruiting Volunteers and changing original policy, asked the Australian Colonies, New Zealand and Canada to supply mounted troops. The Colonies responded generously, and the Boers soon found themselves facing an enemy very different from the British Army they thought could be driven into the sea in a few weeks.

Black people also observed the events unfolding. Their reaction was not quite what General Hunter imagined it might be. Prior to the war, Mr. Walter Stanford had been Chief Magistrate in East Griqualand, which abutted the southern border of Natal. When Buller arrived in Cape Town it was arranged that all military questions touching the predominately Black Transkeian Territories be channelled through Stanford, who effectively became a member of Buller's Staff. These Territories, which included East Griqualand, stretched about 250 miles down the east coast and extended about 150 miles inland to the Lesotho Border. They were strategically important because they lay between the Boer forces occupying the North-Eastern Cape and Natal. After the disasters of 'Black Week', Walter Stanford received this letter from a man who had been a member of his staff at Mount Fletcher:

> '…But, oh, it has grieved me very much to hear of the way brave English soldiers losing so many of their valuable lives which need not be lost. May I give some advice in my poor little opinion of what ought to be done. I am only a native but I know something or two about the Boers; and you are, in your position, able to consult with all the Heads of Departments, and might pass on what I say. I have a tearing fury in my heart and feel throttled in my eager wish to see this plan carried fully out against the Boers. I wish I were a bird with wings to fly just now to you and go to the English chiefs and urge them to what I think the best plan. The Boers are strongly entrenched in their schanzes and defended behind loopholes – good: let them starve and stew there and let the English army just watch them to keep them from any advance. And there is the Stormberg commando of the Boers in a strong position in a country they know well. Let General Gatacre watch them there: no more. Then march another army along to Bloemfontein; in full sight of the Boers; they will say, "What is it? To get behind us? or to get to Bloemfontein?" Then they must leave, not to be enclosed or to defend the home at its centre and Gatacre will be free to march on and join his forces to the other and then the Boers in Natal will begin to shake, and one morning their camps will be empty, for all men love their wives and their children, and the oxen and the sheep, and wish not an enemy to reap their fields, and they will go to support the Free State, or to fight for their own centre at Pretoria. Why do the English try to drive straight on against the Boers where they are now in their mountain*

fastnesses? The wild cat is in the hole and the bull dogs get their nose torn to pieces and their eyes scratched out, and their paws mauled and get weak losing blood, and out of breath. Watch the wild cat in the hole and dig in behind him.

'*That is the plan I would like to see carried out; and the Boers would have to melt away from the borders of our colonies, when they saw us doing to them in their own country what they are doing down here; and the English would win, for round Colesberg or about there, is open country on to Bloemfontein and the English swordsmen and the Lancers would have full play and work the lyddite.*
'*I very much wish I could see the English chiefs and tell them what is in my heart and my throat is dry and tight and my mind feels a warrior's fury to see all the Boers smashed up, for they do not treat us well and we have peace and equal justice under English rule.*'[9]

As Buller had moved to Natal, Stanford sent the letter to headquarters in Cape Town.

The two weeks following the battle at Colenso were a period of inaction as both sides attempted to digest the lessons learned. Buller awaited the arrival of reinforcements, in the form of General Sir Charles Warren and his 5th Division. At Chieveley and Frere, Christmas was a time for festivities and sports. Among these scenes of jollity one important event appears to have passed unnoticed.

Mabizala's and Silwane's men from the Weenen district had presented themselves fully armed at Buller's headquarters and asked to join the column at Chieveley as they wished to take part in the defence of Natal. Buller's predecessor as Commander-in-Chief in South Africa, Sir William Butler, had issued an order that in the event of hostilities against the Boers, no native peoples should be permitted to bear arms against them. Buller felt bound by this order and refused to permit them to join his force. They were told to take their rifles home and come back when they would be given work as labourers. The Zulus explained that they had not come to seek work as labourers but to fight. They were then told that if they carried rifles the Boers would fire on them, which produced the riposte that that was just what they wanted! The men had no choice but to return to Weenen. Until this time Natal Zulus and the Colonials had fought together when threatened, and this action by the British army would have caused considerable resentment. Once back at Weenen, the Zulus went to see the local Natal Magistrate, Maynard Matthews, who reported to the Governor and complained bitterly at having thrust on him the unpleasant task of attempting to explain to these men why they were not permitted to join the fighting ranks.[10] Maynard Matthews would have understood the insult which had been directed at them and he also knew that when the war was over and all the British soldiers were back in England, he and his fellows would have to live with the resentment which had been created.

CHAPTER SEVENTEEN

Boer attack on
Ladysmith Defences

◦—◆—◦

'They kept me in on every side, they kept me in, I say, on every side;
but in the Name of the Lord will I destroy them.'

PSALM FOR CHRISTMAS EVE QUOTED BY DONALD MACDONALD

A FTER the night sorties against the Boer gun positions around Ladysmith it was felt that the Boers might attempt a reprisal. At the start of the siege the Town Guard had been disbanded, but with more manpower needed General White embodied the Town Guard and two Rifle Associations into one unit which provided a further 200 men who were required to defend the Klip River bank facing Bulwana. Despite their unmilitary appearance they were, in all likelihood, a very effective fighting force, and recognised as such by the Boers who made no attempt to attack this section of the line.

On 11 December, a colonial woman was killed while washing clothes in the river. She was the first woman killed by shellfire, though some had died in childbirth.

When early on the morning of 15 December, the people in Ladysmith heard Buller's naval guns begin their bombardment, their hearts must have leapt with joy – salvation was at hand! Full of optimism they listened all morning to the artillery and even when the firing died down, their spirits remained high. Buller had crushed the Boers and relief was on its way. However, strain as they might, they could see no sign of the relief column. Perhaps it might arrive on the morrow.

At dawn the next day, the Boers subjected the town to one of the heaviest bombardments so far. This increase was attributed to the Boers' tactless celebration of their defeat of the Zulus on 16 December 1838. However, it is more likely that they were simply trying to hurry along the capitulation of the garrison. Two British soldiers were killed. One, while exercising his horse, was struck in the back by a shell which mutilated him terribly. The Boers scored another hit on the Town Hall and several houses were badly damaged. Henry Pearse, correspondent for the *London Daily News* gave this description of the 'Blitz' on Ladysmith.

'They have tried their hardest – though not successfully – to make every house in the place untenable between sunrise and sunset, doing infinitely more damage to private property than to military defences; and they have thrown shells about some parts of the long open town with a persistence that would seem petty in its spitefulness if we could be that the shots strike near what they are aimed at. So long as the Boers do not violate any laws of civilised warfare nobody has the right to blame them for trying the methods that may seem most likely to bring about the fall of Ladysmith. They have, however, simply wrecked a few houses, disfigured pretty gardens, mutilated public buildings, destroyed private property, and disabled by death

or wounds a small percentage of our troops without producing the smallest effect on the materiadefences, or weakening the garrison's powers of endurance in any appreciable degree. Such a bombardment day after day for seven weeks would doubtless get on the nerves if we allowed ourselves to think about it too much; but happily the civilians – men and women – who resolved to "stick it out" here rather than accept from their country's enemies the questionable benefits of a comparatively peaceful existence under the white flag at Intombi Spruit, have shown a fortitude and cheerfulness that wins respect from every soldier. Shelters are provided for them and their children, but they do not always take advantage of these, even when a bugle or whistle from the look-out post warns them a shell is coming. Ladies still go their daily round of shopping just as they did in the early days of bombardment, indeed more regularly, and with a cool disregard of danger that brave men might envy.'[1]

The women did, of course, have as an example, the courage of those pioneer women who were so brave and suffered so much after the first invasion of Natal by the Boers in 1838.

On Sunday, 17 December, the Boers, showing respect for the Sabbath, did not shell the town. Newspaper correspondents were invited to the intelligence office, where they were informed that General Buller had suffered a reverse having 'failed to make good his footing.' They were requested when writing their reports not to dwell on the fever and sickness in the town. That day notices were displayed in prominent places so that the cryptic message given to the correspondents should be known to all. For more than six weeks the discomforts of the siege had been endured in the sure expectation that relief was on its way, and now hope itself seemed to be destroyed. Sickness was becoming an even greater enemy than the Boers. Over 50 members of the Imperial Light Horse had been invalided, the Carbineers had 106 men on the sick list, and 96 men of the 19th Hussars were down with enteric. Enteric was another word for typhoid. The doctors found that if they told a patient that he had typhoid it was regarded as a death sentence. On the other hand patients tended to believe they might recover from enteric. Thus, by calling it another name, typhoid was thus 'banished' from Ladysmith.

Monday, 18 December 1899, was a sad day for the Natal Volunteers. The Carbineers had just returned from outpost duty and were attending to their horses when a shell from Bulwana hit one of the horses and exploded. As the smoke cleared four men lay dead or dying and another eight badly wounded. Eleven horses were dead or so badly injured that they had to be destroyed. One was plunging wildly among the tents with one leg shot away. Troopers Billy Buxton and RMM Miller from Pietermaritzburg lay dead together, one with his legs missing. A few paces away lay two troopers from Dundee. Sixteen-year old T Elliott had both his legs cut off at the thigh, and lying there, he begged the orderly to pour cold water over his legs as they felt so hot. In a few minutes his life had ebbed away. Being so young, comrades had always tried to shield him from danger, keeping him in camp on one pretext or another when they went out to fight. Partly over him lay the body of Craig Smith. A couple of years older than Elliot, Craig was the grandson of Peter Smith, on whose farm the Battle of Talana had been fought. He was beginning to show real promise as a rugby player. The fathers of both boys were in Ladysmith. Craig's father was serving with the Carbineers while Elliot's father had been sent to Intombi. Also among the wounded was Trooper A Nicholson, one of whose legs was hanging on by a piece of tendon. When the Carbineers veterinary surgeon, Major Watkins-Pritchard, arrived at the scene one man was putting five human legs in a sack.

There were, however, some lucky escapes among the Carbineers. Trooper HA Craig, also from Dundee, had three holes through his breeches, but did not receive a scratch. Another, Saddler Sergeant Lyle, was sitting on a box outside his tent talking to some friends when the shell exploded. A piece of it passed through the box on which he was sitting, smashed four

A lucky escape. On 18 December 1899, Saddler Sergeant Lyle of the Natal Carbineers was sitting on a box reading. In front lay his rifle and behind were three companions standing and chatting. A shell hit the rifle, smashing it to smithereens, went through the box on which Lyle was sitting and then into the tent where clothing and bedding was shredded. None of the men were injured. The photograph shows the men in the positions they were in when the shell struck.

rifles strapped to a pole, and then went through Sergeant Major Mitchell's kit and blankets, tearing his possessions to pieces. None of the group was injured.

A couple of hundred yards from the Carbineer's camp and across the river, an engineer had just come off duty and was lying down to rest when he was struck and killed by the base of the shell which had caused such carnage in the Carbineer's camp. A shell also killed three Zulus and a colonial who were digging a trench. Another pitched among the Manchesters, killing one man and seriously wounding another and at the other end of town, a Zulu woman was blown to pieces by yet another shell.

The Boers continued to shell the residential section of the town, and again there were some lucky escapes. Col Hamilton and Major Ludlow were resting in the bedroom of a requisitioned house, when a shell came through the roof and though a large splinter from it hit the Major's bed, neither was injured. In another house a civilian named Marchant was sleeping in his room when, 'a shell came through the window, passed between his feet, carried on to the end of the bed and burst beneath the floor. There was not a foot of that room which was not shot torn: the floor was mostly sticking to the ceiling, yet its occupant came out unhurt – came out at the window, bringing the sash with him, as the door was blocked with debris.'[2]

To avoid enemy fire, funerals were held after dark. It was not necessary to wait for graves to be dug as there were always seven or eight already prepared. As darkness descended that evening, it was the turn of the Carbineers to make their way up the hill to the cemetery. Accompanying them were details from the Natal Mounted Rifles and the Border Mounted

Rifles. Trooper Elliot's father was forbidden to leave Intombi to attend his son's funeral, as this might be considered a breach of the agreement with the Boers that residents were not permitted to leave the camp. There was no gun carriage, no band playing, no coffin, and no last volley. Instead each of the deceased was brought to the graveside on a field stretcher, wrapped in a brown blanket which was both shroud and coffin. By the faint light of a darkened lamp the funeral service was read, the dignified simplicity contributing to the poignancy of the burial. Many of the Volunteers were saddened to see among the dead horses in the Carbineers camp a grey thoroughbred, Auld Robin Gray. For years he had been a great favourite of race goers around the Colony.

On 22 December, a shell from Bulwana fell in the camp of the Gloucesters while the men were eating breakfast. Six men were killed and nine wounded, three of them seriously.[2]

Two very capable men, Colonel Ward and his second in command, Colonel Stoneman, had been placed in charge of supplies in the town. They not only carried out a comprehensive survey of the stores which the army had accumulated in Ladysmith, but also of other food which was available. Though the leading shops maintained prices at pre-siege levels, the army requisitioned all stock they thought they might need, leaving little choice for civilians. At the auctions, prices were often too high for the locals, the principal buyers being mess-presidents of regiments. It was not long before most of the residents had used all their supplies and had perforce to submit to army rations.

The reverse suffered by Gen Buller created new problems for Colonels Ward and Stoneman. Initially it was thought that the siege was bound to be raised within two months, but now rations had to be reduced to cater for a longer period, and the careful accounting by Ward and Stoneman now paid off. Rations were reduced and would have to be constantly reviewed. Whites, Indians and Blacks were given different rations. This was not because the authorities sought to favour one group above the others, but because they had to take into account cultural differences and the type of food to which the people were accustomed. In their basic rations Whites received fresh meat, biscuits and maize meal. Blacks received 25 per cent more meat than the whites and almost three times as much maize meal, but no biscuits. Indians received the same amount of maize meal as the blacks and some rice. The Indians did not receive any meat because they did not eat beef or horseflesh, the only meat available in Ladysmith, where there were no sheep, thinnish or otherwise. The Indians seem to have had the worst deal and the blacks the best. The Regular troops probably had not acquired the taste for maize meal and this might account for them being given the not very appetising Army biscuits. Zulu runners carrying messages through the Boer lines would probably have taken with them *ukota*, a meal ground from roasted maize with salt and honey (or sugar) added. This mixture had great sustaining qualities, was easily carried and could be eaten dry or mixed with water.

As Christmas approached, Australian journalist Donald Macdonald reflected on how the horrors of war, flies and disease had, '…converted this town by the Klip River from a jewel set in the midst of the *veldt* into a den of horrors.' When fellow Australian Dr. Robert Buntine called on Donald for a chat it was inevitable that their conversation should turn to home: 'How would you like to be taking a header off the springboard at St. Kilda now?' 'Or riding out to Keilor on a bicycle,' suggested Donald, 'for a quiet tea at Hassed's in the evening?' 'Or sitting in the Melbourne pavilion, watching Bruce and Trumble bat?'[3] That was all part of the world outside. Perhaps the Season of Goodwill might connect them to the rest of the world and lift the air of despondency which was beginning to hang over the town.

In no-man's-land to the south of Caesar's Camp was a farm owned by the Bester family, who were known supporters of the Boers. The young men had joined the *Kommandos* investing Ladysmith and their parents were notorious spies. The British were very tardy in taking any action against them and even after they had arrested father Bester, his wife was permitted for some time to cycle into Ladysmith where she could obtain much useful information for the Boer artillery. From time to time the Boers were seen making nocturnal visits to the farm.

At the camp of the Imperial Light Horse it was thought that, 'the military situation clearly required that the nocturnal comings and goings of the enemy in and about the homestead should be investigated, and a night raid was planned accordingly.' Details were carefully worked out. Just before daylight, the party stole out with the utmost caution and quietness. On reaching their objective, the advance guard hurriedly but thoroughly searched the farmyard and buildings for enemy scouts and patrols, and satisfied that all was in order went about 250 yards ahead, opened out fanwise, and took cover.

So far the raid had proved disappointing: not a single prisoner, not a sign of the enemy, but as dawn broke the main body followed up, armed to the teeth – with grain bags and *kerries*. They dashed in with élan, and surrenders were instant and numerous, though the captured turkeys, geese, fowls, and pigs raised a pandemonium which threatened to stir the whole of the investing army into reprisals. With prisoners well guarded and shepherded with loving care, the main body withdrew to Wagon Hill, their retirement being skilfully covered by what had earlier been the advance guard. About a dozen geese and some pigs, too mobile to be caught, were driven in military formation, before the raiding party. As they passed the officer in command of the hill, the NCO in charge reported 'All present and correct, Sir!' and the geese and pigs were duly 'taken on strength.'

Looting was frowned upon. It was thought that the High Command would not enquire too closely into the raid, but nevertheless, some sea lawyer, of cautionary habit, suggested that a fat turkey be sent to headquarters. It was not returned, nor was enquiry made regarding its next-of-kin, religion, or place of birth. The ILH not only sent the turkey to the High Command but also distributed their largesse among other regiments, gifts which were appreciated, the ILH acquiring the nickname 'The Friendlies.'[4]

For a week or so before Christmas, Karri Davies had been touring the town and buying up every toy he could find. He and Colonel John Dartnell were anxious to provide a treat for the children, whose life during the siege must have been pretty wretched. They came up with the idea of holding a Christmas tree party. Frank Rhodes and Major Doveton were roped in to assist with the organisation. The Walton and Tatham Hall was made available for the occasion and four trees were set up in it. A eucalyptus tree represented Australia, an acacia thorn tree South Africa, a fir tree Canada and another fir Great Britain. Regimental Sergeant Major Bill Perrin of the ILH was appointed Father Christmas. Some in the ILH did wonder about the choice of Perrin as the RSM was a robust martinet with Olympian aloofness and natural ferocity. The women of Ladysmith decorated the trees and the hall, and wrapped the presents.

General White instructed Col Ward to issue full rations on Christmas Day and if possible to supply regiments with such little luxuries as raisins which would assist in giving the men something approaching Christmas fare. An auction was held in the town where some fruit, butter, eggs, poultry and other items were sold. The goods barely covered one long table but did enable the regimental cooks to acquire further ingredients with which to introduce some variety into their cooking.

On Christmas Eve someone borrowed a harmonium from the Dutch church, and played songs which made many Englishmen miserable with recollections of Christmas in England, so utterly different from this one. The Natal Mounted Rifles amused everyone with a burlesque of a cavalry band: 'The drums, swung across the withers of the gaudiest horse in camp, were a pair of empty carbolic oil drums. The cymbals were the ends of a kerosene tin, the triangles the work of a local blacksmith, and the only instruments that by any stretch of the imagination could be called musical were the tin whistles.' Their uniform was made from gauze and tinsel, the most 'magnificent' being that of the drum major. His baton was surmounted by a boy's spinning top. All those who heard them play were surprised that the music produced by such makeshift instruments was quite good.

Early on Christmas Day the Boers sent some shells into Ladysmith which failed to explode on landing. On examination it was found that they had scratched on them, 'With the Complements of the Season' and were filled with something not unlike plum pudding which had been partially cooked by the heat generated by the flight of the shells. Having wasted a few shells playing this practical joke, the Boers concentrated their fire for the rest of the day on the residential part of the town. A Mrs Kennedy was fortunate to suffer only minor injuries when a shell struck her home and burst in the room in which she was standing. The windows were blown out and the furniture reduced to a heap of wood. Fortunately her children were away at the time.

All the churches were filled to capacity that morning, and despite the difficulties, the cooks were able to produce Christmas dinners which created an illusion of high living.

The Volunteer Regiments challenged the Regulars to various sporting contests and mule races were organised, care always being taken to remain out of sight of the Boer gunners. The mules gave a fine display of their legendary stubbornness and appeared to delight in destroying their jockeys' reputations as horsemen.

That evening nearly 250 excited children emerged from the caves by the river and made their way over to the Walton and Tatham Hall. Here they met Father Christmas who had enormous whiskers and wore a coat of white swansdown designed to keep out the Arctic chill. It had been 103 degrees Fahrenheit in Ladysmith that day. Bill Perrin 'radiated a bland benevolence,' and had become an 'unbelievably genial, rollicking, and realistic' Father Christmas. To avoid confusion presents were numbered to correspond with the child's ticket. As they followed Santa round the room, presents were plucked from the trees and given to the children amidst much humour and laughter. Karri and Nurse Yeatman officiated at Australia, Frank Rhodes and Ada Craw at Great Britain, John Dartnell and Olive Barker at South Africa, and Bella Craw with Major Doveton at Canada. Mrs Kennedy, showing no effects of her narrow escape in the morning was there with her children. Sir George White and his Staff attended and joined in the fun. The General seemed delighted by the innocent joy of the children. He had not realized there were so many in the town. Some noted with sadness how thin and pale their happy little faces looked.

Henry Pearse of the Daily News noted how Karri's '...long imprisonment with his brother officer Sampson in Pretoria, far from embittering him against humanity in general, has only made him more sympathetic with the trials and sufferings of others; just as heavy fines and a death sentence seemed to bring out the most lovable characteristics of Colonel Rhodes.... In days to come we may look back to our Christmas under siege in Ladysmith, and think that after all we had not a very bad time.'[5]

After the presents had been distributed the trees were taken out, the floor was swept, and a dance held. As was the custom in the Colony, the older children participated in the dancing for the first part of the evening. The party broke up at 11 o'clock.

At Intombi the medical staff were struggling to treat the rapidly increasing number of people falling ill with enteric and dysentery. Many of the wounded, having recovered from their wounds went down with one of the infectious fevers. Orderlies were becoming ill and by the middle of December the nurses were beginning to break down. Of the Volunteer nurses, Nurse Ruiter was in bed with a sore throat, Nurse Mary had enteric and appeared to be hallucinating, and shortly before Christmas, Nurse Early's temperature was 105 degrees and she was sent to bed with enteric. At night Kate Driver was the only nurse on duty in a fever ward with fifty patients and was near to breaking point:

'The heat had become nearly unbearable and the storms were many. The whole camp reeked of dysentery and enteric, for our water supply was always erratic, and disinfectants were very scarce. The flies were black on the canvas of the tents. Over our heads from daylight till dark the continual roar of the big guns was exhausting to all.

Day after day our hopes were raised by rumours of General Buller's coming 'within three days' – till the very sound of his name irritated one.

A day or two before Christmas there came a welcome diversion. An African carrier staggered exhausted into the Camp and dropped from his shoulders two heavy sacks, out of which rolled – oh wonderful sight – tins of condensed milk!

"Pelindaba!" he gasped, straightening himself up and wiping his forehead with his arm. I understood enough Xhosa to know what he meant. Pelindaba, the end of the story. Many of the tins were dented and dirty, and the man was obviously at the end of his tether. We made him sit down and someone got him a mug of soup, and bit by bit he told his story. He and two other Africans had been sent from a nearby town to try and get through the Boer lines and deliver three sacks of tins of condensed milk for the sick and wounded in Intombi. As they approached the encircling Boers they were seen, and sniped at so hotly that one of them dropped his sack and fled. The others kept going in spurts until they were very near to the Camp. There was a burst of rifle fire and the second carrier suddenly panicked and careered back down the hill they had just climbed, his sack rolling after him. The third, this staunch man, lay waiting behind rocks. At last darkness came and the firing died down. He crawled down and retrieved the sack of his deserting fellow-carrier, and laboriously lugged the two sacks into camp at last. We were full of admiration for his courage and persistence and commended him warmly.

The milk was put into use immediately, the issue being one tin for twenty-five men for twenty-four hours. It was added to the biscuit pulp....

Sir George White had remembered us nurses, and on Christmas day had sent each of us a parcel of good things. Among these gifts were some bottles of Port Wine, some bottles of lime juice, some currants, some cornflower and a tin of tongue. The matron, without asking if we approved, put all the things into a common fund for use throughout the hospital, most of the Port wine, for instance, being used for the orderlies' Christmas dinner. At the time we merely thought she should have asked us first, as each parcel had a nurse's name on it. Later when our sick nurses were in great need of such things, we wished we had all taken our parcels! Nurse Otto, however, had had the sense to ask for her Port wine. "It may come in useful," she said. That bottle of Port wine was long to be remembered by me.'[5]

On New Year's Day Kate began to ache all over and had difficulty getting through her round of patients. On going off duty and eating what passed for breakfast, she and Nurse Otto made their way to their tent. Too tired to change, Kate lay on the hard dirty ground. Nurse Otto produced her Port and the two girls had a drink, which revived their spirits, but when she tried to get up the world was spinning round and the tent was going up and down. When Kate tried to tell Nurse Otto how ill she felt, she found Otto appeared to be suffering from the same malady. Suddenly Kate realised that they were quite drunk, which the girls found hugely amusing and laughed themselves to sleep. When Kate awoke she could hear people singing the familiar hymn, *Hark the herald angels sing*. Listening to the hymn she thought of her mother, and wondered what had happened to her brother who had enlisted with the Volunteers. She thought of 'the wives and sisters and sweethearts of men dying because of war, and of all the sad eyes of dying men.' The full force of their 'deplorable circumstances' overwhelmed her and she climbed onto her bed choking with great sobs. Nurse Otto was also sobbing. They heard a pause in the service and then the start of the sermon. Another pause and the girls fell asleep. When they awoke the service was over. The Volunteer Chaplain had fainted while delivering his sermon.

When it was time for Kate to go on duty she felt giddy and weak. Otto called the Matron who took Kate's temperature and instructed her not to go on duty. A little later Dr Currie came to see her and told her that it had been arranged that Nurse Ruiter would be doing her night duty. Nurse Kate Driver had joined the sick list.

After Christmas the Boers continued their bombardment, further damaging houses and other buildings and from time to time killing or seriously wounding their inhabitants. It seemed the bombardments were becoming more intense after the New Year and scouts reported that the Boers were planning an attack on the town.

On 30 December, heavy rains caused the Klip river to come down in flood. At about 1.00 a.m. the horse guard for the ILH reported the water was rising rapidly and had almost reached the horses who were led out in batches and by the time the last one was led out the water was rising so rapidly that it was up to their bellies. All of them were saved but only just in time, as the river continued to rise before subsiding almost as quickly as it had risen.

Karri Davies, always seeking a solution to any problem, developed a dye from permanganate of potash which turned the coats of grey horses into a shade of brown, an excellent camouflage on the *veld*. Noticing that his breeches had faded to a very light shade, he decided to darken them with the new product. However the dye did not react in the same way with the fabric which turned bright pink and when hung out to dry, it ran to create pink stripes.

To the south of Ladysmith, and within the British perimeter, was a high ridge running from west to east which the Boers called '*die Platrand*' (the Flathill). Rising about 600 feet above the Klip River plain, the ridge was about three miles long and consisted of three conjoined hills. At the western extremity was a boulder-strewn rise known as Wagon Point. A dip known as Howitzer Nek linked it to Wagon Hill, also boulder strewn but with a much

The Imperial Light Horse dugout in the banks of the Klip River. Maj Woolls Sampson is seated in the centre with his crutches next to him.

larger area. Finally another dip led to Caesar's Camp, much the largest area on the ridge, being several hundreds yards wide and about two miles long and possessing less natural cover. These hills were a key element in the defence of the town, with a commanding view of the country to the south. Were they to fall into the hands of the Boers, their proximity to the town would have provided the enemy with a position from which they could have wreaked havoc, making further resistance almost impossible. The defence of Wagon Point, Howitzer Nek and the western portion of Wagon Hill was entrusted to the Imperial Light Horse. To their left on Wagon Hill were some companies of the 1st 60th King's Royal Rifles. The Rifles, who had lost much of their kit at Dundee, were suffering from exposure and many were sick. One of their officers was of the opinion that they were not fit for active service.

Caesar's Camp to the east of Wagon Hill was defended by the Manchester Regiment, assisted by the 42nd Battery of the Royal Field Artillery. Three companies of the Gordons stationed at the north-eastern foot of Caesar's Camp at a place known as Fly Kraal, were to act as reserves. Forty Natal Police and twenty Carbineers were stationed among the boulders and thorn trees on the flat land lying to the east of Caesar's Camp. Because the terrain at Wagon Point and Wagon Hill provided some natural cover between boulders, it was decided to rely principally on this, rather than digging trenches or constructing complex forts for protection. At Caesar's Camp the Manchesters had to construct more complex fortifications. Because the plateau at Caesar's Camp sloped slightly downwards from north to south, Colonel Ian Hamilton, who commanded this section of the line, had sangars and a fort built along the northern edge. This meant that any attackers coming over the southern edge of the hill would be exposed against the skyline.

On the evening of 5 January 1900, the British and Colonial units took up their allotted positions along the ridge. That night 'C' and 'D' Squadrons of the ILH were on duty. Sickness had reduced them to a combined strength of 70 men, each squadron having approximately 35 members. 'C' Squadron was led by Captain Mathias and was stationed on Wagon Hill. 'D' Squadron was positioned on Wagon Point and was under the temporary command of Captain Richardson, on loan from the 11th Hussars. Advance posts were created on both hills and each was manned by a Corporal with three to five men, placed over the southern crest facing the Boers. On Wagon Point the three advance posts were manned by 'D' Squadron while the rest of the squadron, which was to provide support, was positioned in a sangar near the northern crest. The defences on Wagon Hill were similar. 'C' Squadron manned three advanced posts while the balance of the squadron remained in reserve at a sangar again near the northern crest. On their left the Rifles had three further advance posts with the balance of their men in a redoubt near the north-eastern corner of the hill.

That night 'townguard' was the password for the British forces. Like the Volunteers, the Boers probably sent men forward to the British lines to listen to the conversations of the enemy sentries. If they did so they would have heard the word 'townguard' used frequently.

At nightfall Capt Richardson carried out a personal reconnaissance in the direction of Middle Hill where the Harrismith *Kommando* had their camp. Although he passed through their lines on both his outward and return journeys, he did not see any Boers. Whether the Boers saw him is not known, however in passing through the British lines he would have used the word 'townguard.'

Headquarters had decided to place a naval 4.7 inch gun and a Hotchkiss in position on the extreme western end of Wagon Point, and this night was chosen for the task. At about 11.30 p.m. the Naval gun arrived with an escort of Gordon Highlanders, a Navy gun crew of 10, and about 30 Sappers who were to build the gun emplacement on Wagon Point. The Hotchkiss, manned by the Natal Naval Volunteers, was placed on Howitzer Nek. The sappers and sailors set about building the emplacement for the gun. When hostilities were threatened, the gun was taken back to a wagon at the foot of the hill.

At 2.30 a.m. Corporal Dunn at one of the ILH advance posts on Wagon Hill reported that Boers could be heard approaching. The report was received by Lieutenant Patrick Normand who immediately sent a message to Captain Mathias advising that an attack was expected, and without waiting for further instructions he at once put the rest of the Squadron on alert and sent the off-duty men forward to support the picket. At 3.15 a.m. a voice called from below, 'Don't fire, we are the Ladysmith Town Guard!' Unconvinced by the ruse, the advanced posts fired a volley in the direction of the call, which seemed to check the advancing Boers, but it was not long before they heard the voice of a Boer Kommandant urging his men on. The outposts soon came under heavy rifle fire, the Boers pressing home the attack with all the men and means at their disposal. The advance posts tenaciously held their original positions, firing in the dark at the flashes from the attacker's rifles, which grew ever closer. After half an hour, with the majority of those at the advanced posts either killed or wounded, they were ordered to retire to the sangar higher up the hill.

On Wagon Point Captain Richardson heard the firing and decided to get in touch with 'C' Squadron. As he crossed the dip to Wagon Hill he heard voices and realised the Boers had established a footing between the two hills. To warn the others he shouted out, 'The Boers are here,' and was promptly knocked down by bullet which shattered his right elbow joint. In the darkness he was able to make his way back to his squadron for medical attention.[7]

In order to move silently, most of the Boers had climbed the steep boulder-strewn hills barefoot. The Harrismith *Kommando* from the Free State was at the forefront of the attack. Meantime Captain Mathias, with the remainder of 'C' Squadron and the Naval Volunteers, was able to bring the Hotchkiss into action. This checked the Boers who were trying to break through the defence line via Howitzer Nek. Though the defence line was thin, and was steadily driven back, it remained intact and they were able to withdraw with the Hotchkiss in good order to the comparative safety of their sangar. Both sides had at one time become so mixed up that Mathias found himself among the Boers. Able to speak Dutch fluently, he played the part of a firebrand until darkness afforded him an opportunity to slip ahead of the attack and rejoin the remnants of his squadron in the sangar. During his stay among the Boers he heard some of the more enterprising Boers urging, '*Kom kerels, laat ons die plek dadelik bestorm.*' ('Come men let us storm the place at once.') While the more cautious said: '*Nee! Die kannone sal ons koppe afskiet, ons moet liewer wag vir meer manskappe.*' ('No! the cannons will blow our heads off, it would be better to wait for more men.')[8]

Lt Normand was holding Wagon Hill with determination, but was concerned about his left flank. He sent for reinforcements and received a Sergeant and 30 men of the Gordons. He extended them to his left but when he went to check on the position, he found only the Sergeant (the Gordons being required elsewhere on the field). A further request for additional reinforcements obtained another Sergeant and three men from the King's Royal Rifles. Out-flanked and hard pressed in front, Normand decided to retire his small force. Captain Mathias joined them and together they retired to the sangar where they were united with the rest of 'C' Squadron. Troopers F Rogers and TC Chadwick were killed while attempting to recover a box of much needed ammunition from their original forward post. During the withdrawal Troopers Gorton and Shed were hit.

On Wagon Point 'D' Squadron was holding the attack but was subjected to flanking fire which caused several casualties. Lt Adams was killed, and with Capt Richardson out of action, Lieutenant Tom Yockney took command.[9]

From the start the men of the ILH knew from the flashes of rifle fire around them that they were hopelessly outnumbered and that their single loading rifles placed them at a grave disadvantage in close range fighting. Yet for two nightmare hours these two depleted squadrons had held at bay six or seven hundred of the Boer's best men. As dawn broke Normand took four or five men to occupy a rocky outcrop to the east of 'C' Squadron's sangar. While disposing his men he saw, to his great relief, Col Edwards arriving with reinforcements. At 4.30 a.m. Col Edwards had been awoken by the arrival of General Hunter's ADC with orders that the remainder of the Regiment proceed immediately to Wagon Hill which was under attack.

In accordance with their usual practice 'E' and 'F' Squadrons were already 'standing to' ready to start for Wagon Hill to relieve the squadrons on night duty. Edwards left orders for 'B' Squadron to follow as soon as possible and then set off with 'E' and 'F' Squadrons.[10] On arrival at the foot of Wagon Hill, Edwards dismounted and, after leaving instructions that the other squadrons should follow him, began the climb up the hill towards the sound of gunfire, which led him to the redoubt of the Rifles. Shortly afterwards 'E' Squadron, commanded by Capt Codrington, arrived. Realising that Lt Normand needed assistance on Howitzer Nek, Edwards led them to the rocky outcrop occupied by Normand, who was delighted to see them. When Normand attempted to point out the Boers, he was immediately hit in the right arm. Codrington's 'E' Squadron moved into the rocks which had previously occupied by Normand's men and opened fire on the Boers. The weight of their fire forced the Boers to leave the top of the hill and take cover under its southern slope. From this position they returned the fire of 'E' Squadron, the distance between the two groups being about 80 yards. 'F' Squadron, commanded by Captain Fowler, arrived hard on the heels of 'E' Squadron and was ordered into the gap between 'E' on the rocky outcrop and 'C' Squadron in their sangar overlooking Howitzer Nek. Not long afterwards, 'B' Squadron, commanded by Major Doveton, arrived and was ordered to occupy another rocky outcrop running north to south and therefore at right angles to the British line. The southern edge of this outcrop was only about 25 yards from the Boer line. So close were they that it was possible to add variety to their fighting by lobbing stones onto the rocks over the crest. Major Doveton, who did not realise how close the enemy were, exposed his arm as he raised his field glasses, and had the limb and shoulder instantly shattered by a Boer sharpshooter. Lieutenant Ned Kirk took his place as commander of 'B' Squadron.[11]

All capable members of the ILH, numbering about 200, were now in the front line defending Wagon Point and Wagon Hill. Included in their number were some who, because of illness, were excused duty but came along in any case, and even the cooks abandoned their pots and pans and joined the fray. One of these off-duty men who joined their comrades in the line was a renowned horseman, Jack Plunkett, from Roma in Queensland who did not have time to find his khaki jacket and went out in a blue jersey. He and a companion had a long duel with three Boers in a situation where the slightest exposure brought an instant response. With patience and care, each was able to get his man while the third Boer was killed by flanking fire. The sailors and engineers whose orders that night were merely to attend to the emplacement of the 4.7-inch gun enthusiastically took up positions in the defence line.

The struggle which began before dawn was to continue without break till dusk. Men from both sides lay hidden among the rocks and it was only by moving from the cover of one rock to another that either side could hope to drive the other from the hills. It was in the use of this cover and in the accuracy of snap-shooting that success or failure lay. An advance from one rock to another four feet away became a major gain. With the men on both sides moving in this way, continual concentration was vital and even then luck played a big part. A rock which had previously concealed a deadly rifle would become innocuous, while another which had been harmless all morning would suddenly spout death. Even presumed shelter did not ensure safety, as the marksmen would fire at a nearby sloping rock and rely on the ricochet to hit the concealed enemy. The tiniest mistake could be fatal. Capt Codrington of 'E' Squadron, while attempting to adjust his line was shot through the liver. Corporal W Weir at great risk to himself, dragged the captain to safety. He was subsequently awarded the DCM for his action. Lieutenant Douglas Campbell now took over the command of 'E' Squadron.

Col Edwards had, since his arrival on the hill, been in the forefront of the firing line, as he felt this would enable him to observe the enemy's every move and to counteract them promptly. This inevitably resulted in a degree of exposure to enemy fire and a consequent bullet hit him through his neck and shoulder. Shortly afterwards another bullet struck him in the buttock. He was pulled back to cover where, despite his wounds, he continued to direct operations. From his new 'headquarters' the Colonel saw a company of Gordons pass along towards Howitzer Nek but otherwise saw no attempt to strengthen the line. At about 10 a.m. a Captain Bowen and six men of the 60th King's Royal Rifles came clambering up the hill. Colonel Edwards asked where they were going and what their orders were. 'Rush the open ground in front and clear the enemy off the edge of the hill, Sir,' was the reply. Thus, one officer and six men were expected to clear from an immensely strong natural position a formidable enemy present in overwhelming numbers. The Colonel told him it was impossible to carry out such a task, but Bowen insisted that he must try. Since he was determined to carry out the order, 'E' Squadron was ordered to provide covering fire. Bowen and his men broke cover and rushed forward. They only went a few yards before all seven were down. To provide the covering fire, Douglas Campbell and his men had to momentarily expose themselves to the enemy. As they rose to fire, Campbell and several of the men were hit. Campbell, lying quite motionless with a wound at the back of his skull, was covered over and left for dead. Meanwhile Lieutenant Clem Webb of 'F' Squadron, an uncle of Kate Driver, crawled forward to see if anything could be done for Bowen and his men. He found they were all dead.[12]

All day the ILH Medical Officer, Major Billy Davies, oblivious of danger, had been tirelessly tending the wounded. A small man, it was said of him that he 'was five foot nothing but all solid guts.' He had worked his way back to Colonel Edwards and after he had examined him, ordered that the he be taken back to Ladysmith. Command of the Regiment now devolved on Major Karri Davies. Karri ordered the squadrons on Wagon Hill to hold their positions while he checked the situation at Wagon Point. He was now wearing the breeches

The Imperial Light Horse First Aid Post in Ladysmith. The donkey provided milk for the sick.

which had been dyed with permanganate of potash and as he darted from rock to rock, a Boer observed flashes of a pink object moving among the rocks. The inevitable duly happened – the Boer scored a bull's eye. Karri had been hit through the buttocks and was furious. Initially he refused to leave the field, but the wounds were bleeding profusely and he began to feel giddy. He had no choice but to submit to the indignity of being carried down the hill on a stretcher. At the dressing station he told the bearers to, '…hurry up and stop this bleeding, I want to get back!' and to some soldiers standing about at a loose end, 'Go on and give them hell!' One of the stretcher bearers could not resist commenting, 'The Major has tough luck – only one bullet but four wounds!'[13]

It was about 10.30 a.m. and with Colonel Edwards, Major Doveton and Major Karri Davies all wounded, command of the Regiment now devolved on Captain CH Fowler, who was to remain in command until the action closed at about 7.00 p.m. On taking over, Fowler also decided on a personal survey of the whole position. He found that a critical situation existed along the whole length of his weakly manned front. Some 25 per cent of his small force had been killed or wounded. In places, as little as nine yards separated the two sides between whom was a space void of cover watched so vigilantly that almost any movement was impossible. Cramped behind their rocks the men lay on their bellies all day with the sun burning down on them. The rocks were too hot to touch and they were tortured by thirst.

There were other tragic attempts by small groups of men to storm the Boer lines. On one occasion Captain Fowler had crawled back for water and came across Lieutenant Tod of the Rifles who, with twelve men, was getting ready for one of those futile charges. Tod knew he had no chance of success but was determined to go, so all Fowler could do was to advise him of the positions of the ILH and the Boers. Fowler watched them start and saw Tod drop dead before he had gone half-a-dozen paces. Many of his men suffered the same fate.[14] Two other officers in the Rifles, Major Macworth and Lieutenant Raikes, led similar futile charges and both were killed, although some survivors were able to crawl back and reinforce the ILH line.

A typical example of the manner in which this small force was able to hold at bay the much more numerous enemy was provided by a Trooper of 'F' Squadron, Ogilvie Norton, a young Natal farmer. He was able to wriggle unobserved into a position behind some boulders which protected him from the south and east, while giving him a view towards the west over an area not yet occupied. He anticipated that if the enemy were to advance they would cross that ground, so sitting behind his rocks he carefully watched for any sign of movement and patiently waited and waited. Eventually three Boers crept stealthily into his field of fire without being aware of his presence. Three successive shots accounted for all three, without them or anyone else knowing from whence the shots had come.[15]

Both sides utilised their artillery, however apart from the efforts of the sailors to carry out infantry duties, the gunners were able to contribute little to the outcome of the battle on this part of the battlefield – partly because of the nature of the land and partly because the two sides were so closely engaged. Colonel Ian Hamilton attempted to organise a movement to outflank the Boer left. This came to nothing though it did frustrate an attempt by the Boers to outflank the British right. Throughout much of the day Frank Rhodes was seen attending to the wounded.[16]

At 3.30 p.m. a violent storm broke and torrential rain provided a curtain which hid each side from the other. The Boers, believing this provided an opportunity to launch an attack, charged towards the ILH sangar on Wagon Hill. However the line held and as the rain slackened many Boers were caught in the open and provided easy targets for the Light Horsemen. Perhaps to create a diversion, 50 Free State Burghers threw themselves into a reckless rush towards the main sangar on Wagon Point. Such was the impetus of the attackers that they swept aside a detachment of the Gordons and in seconds were at the low stone walls of the sangar. Though some of the more recent arrivals in the sangar fled down the hill, bitter hand-to-hand fighting now ensued. Lieutenant Digby-Jones of the Royal Engineers shot the foremost Boer at point-blank range. Trooper Albrecht, ILH, shot a Veld Cornet and another Burgher who were about to shoot Digby-Jones. Albrecht was then shot by a Burgher who was shot by Digby-Jones who, in turn, was shot by another Boer. One sapper had his rifle wrested from him by a Boer, whom he promptly felled with a blow from a shovel. For a minute or two the desperate hand-to-hand struggle raged, but the steadfast defenders fought on, countering every move by their attackers. Unable to overcome the defence, the Boer attack faltered and they retired to the shelter of the rocks near the crest.[17]

In their sangar on Wagon Hill, 'C' Squadron had watched the whole dramatic encounter. Because of the intermingling of the enemy with the defenders it was impossible for them to fire, but when the Boer retreat began they inflicted severe losses. The Boer attack on Wagon Point and Wagon Hill had been broken and in Ian Hamilton's opinion the enemy were waiting for darkness when they would withdraw. After the failure of this final attack on the ILH line, *Kommandant* de Villiers told a clergyman, J.D. Kestell, that as he had lost at least a third of his men, killed or wounded, they would withdraw as soon as it became dark.

Over on Caesar's Camp the Manchesters had taken up their positions on the night of 5 January, and must have hoped for another peaceful night. At about 3.30 a.m. they heard the sound of firing coming from the direction of Wagon Hill, but as there was almost constant firing at some point on the defence perimeter they paid little attention to it. Unknown to them, the Boers, having stripped off their shoes, were quietly climbing the southern and eastern slopes of the hill. They reached the crest well before dawn and made their way along the southern and eastern crests apparently with the intention of attacking the picket at the extreme north-east of the hill and thereafter rolling up all the other pickets on the northern crest. They attacked the pickets but met stern resistance. The Manchesters fought back heroically and though their first picket appeared to have been overrun, the Boers could get no further.

The fighting on Caesar's Camp that day was spread over a wide area, and was between fairly small groups of men who each had a different perspective as to what was happening. It would be impossible to give an account of what each unit did and how it affected the eventual outcome. A general summary of the day's proceedings is that the Boers attacked and were driven off Caesar's Camp but clung to the southern and eastern edge until nightfall, when they retired.

At about 4.15 a.m. Colonel W Royston of the Natal Volunteers had received a telephone call advising him that the enemy was making an attack on Caesar's Camp. He immediately despatched 80 men of the Natal Mounted Rifles, under Major Evans, to assist the Natal Police, who were under attack in the broken country below the eastern end of Caesar's Camp. Although outnumbered, the Police detachment, under Sergeant Woon, who had been wounded, held out until the NMR reinforcements arrived. Thus reinforced, the defenders were able to stop any further advance by the Boers on this section of the field.

With arrangements to secure the left flank completed, Col Royston, accompanied by the balance of the Natal Mounted Rifles and the Border Mountain Rifles under Lieutenant Colonel Rethman (promoted in spite of his forthright manner and tendency to express his opinions), rode out to Caesar's Camp. Arriving at about 5.00 a.m., they could see Boers swarming over the south-eastern slope right up to the crest and it appeared they were intent on working their way round to the rear of the Manchesters. A party of Gordons could be seen among the rocks near the extreme north-eastern corner of the Hill. Two squadrons of the Border Mounted Rifles under Col Rethman were ordered to support the Gordons, while a third squadron under Captain Jack Royston was ordered to push forward on the eastern slopes. Rethman's men were able to rendezvous with the Gordons under Captain Carnegie, but

The Border Mounted Rifles receiving rations. The tedium of siege life has begun.

came under a hot fire as soon as they attempted to advance. The BMR detected a suspicious movement on their right front and a shot was sent in its direction, whereupon a man wearing a uniform similar to theirs, jumped up and shouted, 'Don't shoot, you bloody fools. We are the Townguard.' For the second time that night the Boers used the British code words 'Townguard'. The Volunteers dropped their guard for a second or two and a number of Boers showed themselves about 50 yards away shouting, 'Hands up you bastards, we've got you now,' while at the same time a volley was fired killing troopers Fox, James Gold, Jim Lawson and Percy Hulley, of the Border Mounted Rifles.

The 53rd Battery had been brought forward into a position where it had a clear view of the enemy, and opened fire on the Boers with devastating effect. The Manchesters, the Gordons, the Rifles and the BMR advanced, while the artillery, by lengthening its fire, followed the retreating Boers until they were driven off the crest. Once they had retired over the crest, the Boers were able to find cover among the boulders and rocks which covered the area, thereby checking any further advance. On the left Maj Jack Royston was able to drive the Boers back until they too were able to take shelter in the rocky terrain. An exchange of rifle and artillery fire was to continue between the two sides until darkness came and the Boers retreated back to their lines.

It was a particularly hot day and Trooper Martin of the BMR was detailed to fetch some water for the Regiment. Taking as many water bottles as he could carry he made his way to the water point on the sheltered side of Caesar's Camp. There he found a number of officers, one of whom, a major dressed in the uniform of the Gordon Highlanders, said, 'Hey, Ginger, where are you from?' Martin told him and after he had explained that the Gordons were fighting alongside the BMR he was asked to guide the officers to the front line. Martin loaded himself with the water bottles, and following a route sheltered from enemy fire, took the officers to a spot where he was able to point out the positions occupied by the Boers. One officer immediately contradicted Martin by looking in the direction indicated and announcing, 'no Boas thar', which in his opinion finalised the matter.[18]

For most of the day the only surgeons on Caesar's camp were Dr Hornabrook and Dr Wood of the Manchesters, both of whom were to be wounded before the day was over. At one point Dr Hornabrook attended to a Natal Volunteer, a King's Royal Rifleman, and a Manchester private all lying within a few yards of each other. When he went a little over the side of the hill to treat a Gordon Highlander, the wounded man said, 'Don't come here, sir, they'll knock you over.' Hornabrook nonetheless went to treat the man, and received some shots through his clothes and another in his side just above the hip. In spite of his own wound, he continued to treat the wounded until Major Hyslop, his commanding officer, ordered him back to camp.[19] Robert Buntine had by now joined the medical team on Caesar's Camp and like the others did not hesitate to treat the wounded while under fire. He was able to save one man's life by performing an emergency tracheotomy during the battle.[20]

On Wagon Point, Col Ian Hamilton received orders to clear the enemy off Wagon Hill for which task the Devonshire Regiment were being sent to assist him. Lieutenant Colonel CW Park of that regiment was about to have what he described later in a letter to his wife as '…*the most terrible experience of my life.*' At 4.00.p.m. Park had received orders to proceed at once with all available men to Wagon Hill. There were three companies in their camp and in a few minutes Park had them fallen in and marching. He had with him five officers and 184 men and arrived on the hill at about 5.00 p.m. In his letter Park gives a vivid account of the events which followed:

'*I reported to Colonel Hamilton and asked what he wanted me to do, and he said, "Well Park, there are about fifty Boers holding a small ridge of rocks just in front of the line we are holding here, and only one hundred yards off; they have been there all day and are picked shots, and we cannot get them out. We have our men on three sides of them, but they are all under cover of the rocks and pick off our men, if they show even their heads. If you turn them out we will give you anything in the world. The only way is to rush them with the bayonet; can you do it?" Of course, I could only answer that we would try. We settled details, and I then formed up the companies in column, close behind one another, as there wasn't room to form line in the little hollow in which we were. We fixed bayonets and charged magazines, and I explained to each company exactly what we had to do, and when all was ready Colonel Hamilton said, "Go on, and God Bless you", and away we went, the men cheering and shouting for all they were worth. The first few yards we were under cover, but when we reached the top of the crest line we were met by the most awful storm of bullets. I have never heard such a hot fire in my life, and can only compare it to the crackling of a dry gorse branch when thrown into a fire. We then saw for the first time what we had to do. The little ridge of rocks which the Boers held was in front of us and between us and it was 130 yards of open flat grass without the smallest cover or shelter of any kind. The men behaved most splendidly; every man went as straight and hard as he could for the enemy's ridge, and there wasn't any sign of checking or wavering, though, as I ran, I could see men falling like ninepins; and then at last, to my intense relief, when we were within about fifteen yards of them, I saw Boers suddenly jump up, turn tail, and fly down the hill for their lives, and the position was ours.*

'*After a minute or two, when we had got settled down in the position and I had time to look around, I realised that not only had we lost heavily in the charge, but that we were still exposed to a heavy cross-fire from both flanks, from which we suffered severely. Just then Lafone remarked that he wished someone would tell the Imperial Light Horse fellows, who were holding a little ridge behind us, to fire at the Boers on our left front, and without a word, Masterson jumped up and ran back across the open through the hail of bullets to give the Imperial Light Horse the message, and though he was badly hit by at least three bullets in both thighs, he managed to reach them and give them the message, before he collapsed. It was a splendidly brave thing to do, and I have strongly recommended him for the VC. Very soon after that I was watching Lafone, who had got a rifle and was sniping at Boers, when I suddenly saw a little hole come in his head just above his right ear, and he just sank down as he sat. I crawled over and found him quite dead, poor old fellow, and a little further on I found poor Field, also lying dead. Walker (of the Somersets) had been shot dead during the charge, and about fifty-two men were either killed or wounded, and I was the only officer left. It was about 5.30 or 5.45, and there was nothing for it but to hang on where we were till dark. The rain and hail had poured down all the time and I had no coat of any sort, and I lay behind a rock fairly blue with cold… The time passed somehow, and never was darkness more longed for, and when at last it came the Boers gave us a final burst of firing for about a minute, which did no harm, and then bolted down the hill finally beaten, and their attack had failed.'*[21]

The Reverend JD Kestell afterwards wrote a description of the Boer withdrawal:

'*We had been on the hill for sixteen hours under a most severe fire and now we retired; but we were not driven off by the Devons with levelled bayonets as I have read in the English book. We were not driven off the hill. We held it as long as it was light and when twilight fell Kommandant de Villiers considered it useless to remain there. He stopped there till the last man had gone then fired some shots, not however at the Devons advancing with fixed bayonets, but in the air, in order to make the English think we were still in our positions.*'[22]

Kestell, who came from Devon was pastor of the Dutch Reformed Church at Harrismith and acting as chaplain to the Free State *Kommandos*, had been on the field throughout the day tending to the wounded irrespective of their nationality. He dressed the wounds of several ILH men and by stopping the flow of blood, prevented their bleeding to death. Among those saved by him was Sergeant O'Flaherty of the ILH, a noted classical scholar and a talented writer and journalist.

The striking similarity between the tactics of the Colonial Volunteers and the Boers should be noted. Most importantly, both parties went to considerable lengths to keep their whereabouts hidden from the enemy. It will be recalled that even before hostilities began, when scouting, the Natal Volunteers would make camp in the evening, and after darkness fell would move a few miles away before bedding down for the night. The British, on the other hand, appeared to rely on intimidating the enemy by their mere presence. They now wore khaki, but mentally, many were still redcoats.

As far as the exigencies of the situation allowed, the dead and wounded were taken from the battlefield that night, though many could not be moved until the next morning. On the following day a truce was declared to enable both sides to collect their dead and wounded. With vultures circling overhead, the wounded were collected and given what emergency treatment was possible before being taken to hospital. Many had died of exposure during the night and many were to die during the following few days. Most of the Boers helped with the wounded regardless of which side they were on. But there was also evidence of other behaviour. An Imperial Light Horseman was found with a belt around his neck, having apparently been strangled. Elsewhere a Gordon Highlander was found without any gunshot or stab wounds, having been beaten or kicked to death.[23] For the burial parties it was a most gruesome experience. Many of those killed by shells were so badly mangled that it was impossible to move their bodies and they were buried where they were killed. For the others, the place chosen for their burial was a grass covered spot on the northern slope of Caesar's Camp.

The dead in each corps were laid out shoulder-to-shoulder, side-by-side in neat lines next to the long shallow graves which were being dug. They were lying on their backs, their young faces looking up into the sky where high above the vultures were circling. Friends and comrades walked down the lines making their last farewells to companions who such a short time before had been so full of life. Some stopped and cut off a button or other small item which could act as a memento of the dead man. When the graves were ready, the bodies were wrapped in blankets and placed in them. The various units formed up. Sir George White stood bareheaded with the Chaplain at the graveside. The gravediggers stood by with their shovels. The Chaplain began, 'I am the resurrection and the life, saith the Lord'. Then he stopped. He had noticed movement under one of the blankets. The body was immediately taken out of the grave. It was Lieutenant Douglas Campbell, who was in the process of regaining consciousness. It will be recalled that not long after he had assumed command of 'E' Squadron of the ILH, he had fallen while attempting to provide covering fire for one of the disastrous British charges on Wagon Hill. As he was about to fire, a bullet had hit him in the nostril and come out at the back of his skull. The high-speed Mauser bullet would have cauterized the wound as it passed through his head. He had been knocked out, but miraculously no vital organ had been damaged. This was not the first time Campbell had narrowly missed being killed. He had been wounded at Elandslaagte, and on another occasion an afternoon nap had been disturbed by a shell landing in his tent without exploding; this time he had survived a bullet through the head. He was later to joke that it would take more than a bullet through the head to kill a Scot. Though he could trace his lineage back to Scotland, his family had emigrated to Australia where they had prospered. By the middle of the nineteenth century his grandfather, Robert Campbell, was able to return to Britain and buy the Oxfordshire estate, Buscot Park. No doubt Douglas had come to Africa seeking adventure, which he had certainly found. He was taken with the other wounded to Intombi Hospital.

British and Colonial units suffered 424 casualties of whom 175 were killed and 249 wounded. Five men were awarded the Victoria Cross: Lieutenant R Digby-Jones, R. E. (posthumous); Lieutenant J Masterson, 1st Btn. Devonshire Regiment; Private J Pitts, 1st Btn. Manchester Regiment; Private R Scott, 1st Btn. Manchester Regiment; and Trooper H Albrecht, Imperial Light Horse (posthumous). After being orphaned, Herman Albrecht had been adopted by a colonial farming family in the North Eastern Cape. He grew up to be a tall, shy young man who excelled at cricket and swimming and was a fine horseman. At the age of 17 he was driving a Post Cart and supplementing this income by breaking in difficult horses. Like many other youths in that area he felt the glamour of Johannesburg calling, so off he went to the big city. A year or so later, with war threatening, he and his friends from Johannesburg travelled to Natal and joined the Imperial Light Horse which was then being formed in Pietermaritzburg. He was one of those indomitable spirits in the ILH who had repulsed the Boer attack on Wagon Point, and had played an important part in rallying other auxiliary units who showed signs of disintegrating during that attack.

In recognition of the gallantry they displayed throughout the day, four officers of the ILH received the DSO: Surgeon-Major WTF Davies, Captain CH Fowler, Lieutenant PH Normand, and Lieutenant Mathias.

The Imperial Light Horse suffered 60 casualties of whom 29 were killed or died of wounds, and 31 were wounded. Lieutenants WF Adams and JE Pakeman died on the battlefield and Major Doveton was later to die of his wounds. Trooper 'Dicky' Gorton ILH, a provincial rugby player from Pietermaritzburg, was one of the first men wounded. As he lay on the battlefield he was to receive a further 12 wounds. As he was carried away on

Herman Albrecht VC (posthumous).

a stretcher he was able to give a cheery smile and a mute wave to his comrades. He died four days later.

Colonel Edwards, Major Karri Davies and Lieutenant Normand recovered quickly from their wounds. Captain Codrington lay for some time between life and death, but he recovered eventually and was able to return to active life which included commanding the 1st Motor Machine Gun Brigade in the Great War. Douglas Campbell, now a Captain, made an incredibly rapid recovery and was back in mess six weeks later.

The Boers did not keep records of the number of Burghers killed and such information as they released on the subject always tried to play down their losses. They probably had in excess of 100 killed and 200 wounded. Their memorial on Caesar's Camp covers the remains of 310 Burghers who were re-buried there.

On 8 January, General Buller heliographed General White congratulating him on the gallant defence of Ladysmith and giving special praise to the Devons. Shortly afterwards a similar heliograph was received

Lt Douglas Campbell who rose from the dead after being shot through the head at Wagon Hill.

from the Queen in which she also expressed the nation's gratitude for the part played by the Devons. Neither message mentioned the Imperial Light Horse. In an attempt to correct the omission, Col Hamilton wrote an official letter to the commander of the regiment:

'*I write this line to let you and your brave fellows know that in my despatch it will be made clear that the Imperial Light Horse were second to none. No one realises more clearly than I do that they were the backbone of the defence during that long day's fighting. Please make this quite clear to the men. To have been associated with them I shall always feel to be the highest privilege and honour.*'[24]

Maladministration
of Dundee by Boers

• ◆ •

'But this was purely excess of emotion; and exuberance of delicious joy.'

BOER NEWSPAPER REPORT ON LOOTING IN DUNDEE.

O N the day following the battle at Wagon Hill, Sir George White sent a heliograph to General Buller: 'Troops here much played out, and a very large proportion of my officers have, up to date, been killed or wounded, or are sick. I would rather not call upon them to move out from Ladysmith to co-operate with you; but I am confident the enemy have been severely hit.' A few days later some of the men attempted to play a game of cricket, but abandoned it after 10 minutes because they all felt too weak to continue. The reduced rations were debilitating everyone, and from now on there was little to relieve the monotony of the long, hungry days as they waited for the arrival of the relief column.

For the Imperial Light Horse there was one pleasant surprise. On 11 January, Dr Davies brought Aubrey Woolls Sampson back from Intombi. He was driven into the ILH camp in an ambulance wagon and received a great reception from the men. His wound had healed, but the damage to his femur ensured that he was still unable to walk. He set up his quarters in the ILH dugout where he received a constant stream of well-wishers. Col Ian Hamilton was one of his frequent visitors as the dugout lay between his bivouac on Caesar's Camp and Sir George White's Headquarters: 'I always found time to look in upon Woolls Sampson. Usually there were two or three others present, and if, as was sometimes the case, they had come there with the idea of heartening and cheering Woolls Sampson, they found themselves walking away with the boot on the other foot: they, not he, were to get the pick-me-up; the hale and hearty were to drink freely from the wounded hero's inexhaustible cellar of that wine of victory, "The Will to Win".'[1]

The tonic he provided was desperately needed by the despondent and ailing garrison. The hospital at Intombi had been established to cater for 300 patients. At the end of November there were, in addition to the wounded, 15 cases of enteric and 72 cases of dysentery, and by the end of the following month, the cases of enteric had risen to 441 and cases of dysentery to 361. Most of the patients were compelled to lie on the bare earth and if this was not bad enough, the shortage of food, particularly of fresh vegetables, made recovery difficult for all but the strongest constitutions. During the last week of November, 5 people died of disease. By the end of December the weekly death rate had increased to 23 and was continuing to accelerate.

Journalist Henry Nevinson also had some difficulties. The empty shops could no longer sell him the luxuries to which he was accustomed; the Blacks continued to be reluctant to carry his despatches and the persistent rain was washing away his description of Natal as a desert. However his hostility towards Colonials continued unabated. Without any evidence to support his opinions, he sent out a stream of vulgar abuse directed at the locals. The Town Guard in their civilian clothes and obsolete rifles were an easy target for his sarcasm: 'Tonight the civilians of the Town Guard went on picket by the river, and bore their trials boldly, though one of them got a crick in the neck.'[2] What a nasty unfounded suggestion of cowardice this is. He must have been getting desperate for derogatory copy about Colonials, when just before Christmas, a woman made a complaint to Col Stoneman about alleged theft at Intombi Camp. Nevinson plunged in: '…the sick are robbed or murdered by a mob of cowardly Colonials of the rougher class, who had not enough courage to stay in the town, and now turn their native talent for swindling to the plunder of brave men who are suffering on their behalf.'[3] On 27 December, he continued, 'The 18th Hussar officers at Christmas gave up a lot of little luxuries, such as cakes and things, which count high in a siege, and sent them down to their sick at Intombi. Not a crumb of it all did the sick receive. Everything disappeared en route – stolen by officials, or sold to greedy Colonials for whom the sick had fought.'[4] We know from Kate Driver's diary that Christmas treats at Intombi hospital were pooled and divided among all the patients and staff. Nevinson made such a big fuss about the issue that General White sent Colonel Stoneman to Intombi to investigate what was happening. Stoneman saw no evidence of the robbery and murder of patients though he did find a general want of organisation, both in the distribution of food and in the care of patients. Colonel Exham, who as the Principal Medical Officer was responsible for these shortcomings, pointed out that it would cost money to provide a bed for each patient and that he could not use all the medicines as the regulations required that each medical facility should always have stocks of certain supplies. Stoneman was not impressed by these arguments, being of the opinion that the people of England would be happy to spend a few thousand pounds to provide a little comfort for the sick, wounded and dying. He ordered that further beds and bedding be sent to Intombi immediately. In addition he put in place a proper plan for the distribution of food and medicines.

Given the very mixed collection of people who had been press-ganged into working at Intombi, there might have been some petty thieving, however it would seem to have been of very minor importance. Kate Driver found the service provided by her orderlies on arriving at Intombi to be poor. The men had been recruited and trained in Pietermaritzburg as stretcher-bearers and resented having to work in the hospital. She set about teaching them their new tasks: 'They watched while I sponged one man. He was a malaria patient. "I'm sweatin' heavy sister," he said. The man in the next bed turned his eyes towards us and said huskily, "You don't say 'sweatin' to the sister. You say perspoirin." The laughter helped, and by now the boys had got some idea of what was required of them. I never once after that night had to ask either of them a second time to do anything, much as they hated fever work. They were splendid, these two volunteers of the Pietermaritzburg Ambulance Corps.'[5]

It seems Colonel Exham was not happy with Colonel Stoneman's response to the conditions at Intombi, so he asked his friend Henry Nevinson to visit the Camp and to give a 'fair' account of what he found. Nevinson applied to Sir George White for permission to visit Intombi, but the application was refused, it being stated that the agreement with General Joubert provided that only medical and commissariat officers should visit the camp. It was subsequently found that Exham was diverting supplies, such as bottles of brandy and sago, from the hospitals to his friends among the journalists and others whom he considered had influence. These items would be indented for use in the hospital and then passed on to Exham's friends. In this manner the hospital records gave the impression that the stolen supplies had been consumed in the hospital. Blaming the Colonials would provide an additional excuse if anything went wrong.

Among the sick sent to Intombi at this time was Lt Robert Samuelson, who it will be recalled had organised the Native Scouts during the early stages of the war. Robert was attacked by dysentery on 5 January 1900 and though he resisted the idea of being treated at Intombi, he eventually had no choice but to submit to transfer to the camp. After long, weary days in the hospital on rations which were constantly being reduced, he was able to get on his feet, toddle about and think of returning to Ladysmith. It was then that enteric struck. He had no pain, but as he lay in bed he felt he was quietly fading away. He joined the category of patients who were not expected to survive. The chief nurse occasionally came to talk to him and one day she asked him what he thought were the ingredients of the gruel he was fed. 'Bad arrowroot' was Robert's guess. The nurse smiled and said, 'It was made of violet powder and starch.'[6]

At this low point in his life, Robert was visited by a friend from the civilian camp across the railway line. This friend knew of some unsieved Amabele (millet) meal at the civilian camp which Robert was welcome to try and a quantity was secretly boiled up for him. He ate it in small quantities and in two days he began to feel life returning. He sent a message through to his old friend Lieutenant 'Ben' Sparks of the Carbineers to try to obtain some more of this meal and Sparks was indeed able to obtain a little of it. In a few days Robert began to feel much better and in due course felt strong enough to return to Ladysmith. He set off to find Dr Sam Campbell, one of the doctors with the Natal Volunteers. Robert described what happened next:

'I came across a monster in human form, and this was one of the Doctors in the camp. I hope he is still alive and will read this particular book, and shed tears of shame and remorse... The first person I met was a European male dressed in his ordinary clothes, and to him I said, "Will you please tell me where Dr Campbell is?" The answer was, "Do you know who I am?" I am Colonel So and So, Doctor So and So, here he reeled off his titles and I felt inclined to ask him the next question by applying my Bootmaker to his Tailor.'

However Robert was too weak to do anything more than turn his back on him and walk towards some tents. This rude and pompous person could only have been Col Exham who, as Principal Medical Officer (PMO), was the only doctor in Ladysmith to hold the rank of Colonel. At the tents Robert found Dr Sam Campbell, '...thin and worn, but as manly, kind and considerate as ever. He examined me and to my delight declared that I was fit enough to return to Ladysmith, giving me a certificate to that effect. He cut up some meat he had into thin slices, gave it to me to chew, and then gave me a kind handshake and a cheery 'goodbye' and the next day I returned to Siege Town.'[7]

Col Exham was permitted to continue in his post as Principle Medical Officer. This failure by the Military Authorities to take prompt action against him was to cost Britain dearly later in the war, when as PMO in Bloemfontein his maladministration resulted in even more deaths from disease than in Ladysmith.

Throughout this period Robert Samuelson's scouts had been providing valuable information both for the besieged garrison in Ladysmith and the Relieving Column. One of these scouts, Mdaweni, was sent by Samuelson with a despatch for General Buller. On his return he was seen near Spion Kop by the Boers, who set off after him. Seeing this he put his horse into a fast trot and made for a church. Before the war he had preached there, and on arrival he called for the bell to be rung while he entered the pulpit. Being a Sunday the local people hastened to church, as did the Boers, who came inside and sat there for a short while, and then left. It seems that the ruse worked and fortuitously they had decided that the preacher was late for the service and this had caused him to hurry along.[8]

One of the scouts active during the siege was Teise Ndlovu. Riding a small black Basuto pony and armed with an assegai carried in a leather sheath strapped over his shoulders, Teise would ride up to the Boer lines and despoil them of some of their cattle which he would drive back to Ladysmith and hand to the Military. He was given £5 for each batch he brought in. He was able to carry out six of these daring raids. From time to time he was sent on errands to deliver messages to people in Boer-occupied country. On one occasion he was spotted by Boer scouts and only escaped arrest by plunging into a pool and hiding among the reeds. On another he was captured by the Boers, tied up and given into the care of their Sotho servants, preparatory to his being shot the next day. That night the Sotho guards told Teise that they were not going to see their countryman shot so they loosened his bonds and thereby enabled him to escape.[9]

On the night the Volunteers made their successful attack on the Boer guns at Gun Hill, Teise and a companion, who was to act as a guide, set out on a mission to damage the railway line near Waschbank Station and thereafter establish a line of communication between Ladysmith and Pietermaritzburg with the help of Zulu leaders. Teise took with him letters written in Zulu by Robert Samuelson, which were addressed to the various Chiefs along the proposed route. While passing through the Boer lines around Ladysmith they heard Boer horses snorting and coming their way. Teise's companion bolted. The more experienced Teise lay quietly and let the Boers pass before moving on. On his return, he gave an account of what happened: 'I heard the firing on Gun Hill, but did not see my companion again. I gave up going to Waschbank and arranging communications with the Chiefs, as I did not know the country, and instead I kept near to a Boer Commando that was moving towards Weenen, and then eventually called at the *Kraal* of Chief Bande, near Mhlumayo Hill, who asked me how the Authorities were faring in Ladysmith, expressing a desire to send provisions if it could be arranged, and he gave me this man (indicating a tall Zulu who accompanied him), who is his uncle, to come and see what can be done.'

They made their way back to Ladysmith where the Chief's uncle was taken to the Military Authorities who thanked him for his efforts and asked him to thank Chief Bande for his thoughtfulness. However they thought it would be impossible to carry out the project [the sending of provisions] safely. Initially the Chief's uncle attempted to get home alone, but after narrowly avoiding capture he returned to Ladysmith the next day. It was decided that Teise should accompany the visitor on his return journey, a task which was completed successfully and Teise was back on duty in Ladysmith a few days later.[10] Chief Bande was an important Black leader in the Natal Midlands whose lands had been overrun by the Boers. This offer to attempt to smuggle supplies into Ladysmith was a courageous act, for if the Boers had found out about it, the Chief and his leading advisers would have been shot, their livestock expropriated and the people driven off the land.

When the British marched out of Dundee they had left behind 195 wounded, who were cared for in two Field Hospitals and in the buildings of the Swedish Lutheran Mission. In charge of the hospitals was Major FAB Daly, who was assisted by a local physician, Dr Galbraith. The orderlies came from the Irish regiments and were a cheerful and hardworking bunch. A number of local residents worked as volunteer orderlies, and prominent among whom was TH Brokensha, a Justice of the Peace. Shortly after the British army had left, the Field Hospitals moved to a piece of vacant land adjacent to the Swedish Mission, a sensible move which benefited both the staff and the patients. With local people helping in the hospital it became a focal point for many of the residents.

When the Boers entered the town about 250 residents remained. Included in this figure were 8 women and 32 children. Some stayed to protect their businesses or property, while others, such as WH Tatham, believed they had nothing to fear. Most were probably surprised by the speed of the Boer advance and being uncertain what they should do, did nothing. All were soon to discover what it was like to live under Kruger's rule.

To administer the town the Boers appointed a *Vrederechter* who set up his headquarters in the Town Board offices. The Transvaal flag was run up outside the building and it was announced that Dundee was now part of the Transvaal. The *Vrederechter* had wide executive and judicial powers. It was not long before Proclamations and Notices began to flow from this functionary's office. Residents were required to register with the *Vrederechter*; a permit was required to buy goods from the two shops still open; no one was allowed on the streets after 7.00 p.m. or to travel more than three miles from Dundee; even looting was prohibited, though this prohibition apparently did not apply to the Boers. The *Vrederechter* had a discretion to decide to whom a proclamation applied and how it should be interpreted and enforced.

During their first phase of looting the Boers concentrated on various businesses but after a week or two they turned their attention to houses. Reverend Gerard Bailey described the continuing despoliation of the town:

'Every house they could get into was looted… They made no distinctions. The Convent House of the Roman Catholic Sisters, and the residences of the Presbyterian and Wesleyan ministers suffered with the rest. The work of destruction and robbery was carried on in several ways. There were those who entered the houses and out of pure wickedness smashed and broke up everything they thought fit, even going so far as to wrench mantelpieces from their place and break them up. There were others who came with wagons and carted away furniture wholesale; others, who occupied houses, and on leaving carried off all they could, especially linen and clothes. At the end of January what was left in unoccupied houses was removed and placed in a large hall, the new Masonic Hall. Why this was done, I do not know, but this is certain, that the furniture was so roughly handled and so thrown about that much of it was entirely spoiled.

'After this, when new officials or would be residents arrived, they were taken to the hall and allowed to pick out the furniture they wished for the houses allotted to them. I am sorry to say that the nurses of the Boer ambulances were as big a thieves as any. Of this I have plenty of proof. The Boers, especially the women, appeared to look upon the town as legitimate spoil. A friend of mine happened upon some deliberate thieving. The woman defended herself by stating that she had a right to take what she liked as all now belonged to the government. "Well, then," said my friend, "I might come to your house and take away what I like." Few things disgusted one more than the way in which Boer women and their families were allowed to occupy houses and settle in town. The best residences were seized upon with avidity, and if one house did not suit they turned to another. I noticed one family that changed houses three times. As one may suppose the Boer families who were equal to this sort of thing were by no means of the best class.'[11]

Gerard Bailey and Father Murray took it in turns to guard the Vicarage and on a number of occasions were able to face down would-be looters. Gerard said of his companion, 'Father Murray behaved like a brick, and guarded the place as if it were his own. He is a big, burly, and formidable person to encounter.'

The '*Standard and Digger's News*', an English language propaganda sheet produced by the Boers, in its issue of 21 November 1899, had this to say about the looting: '*In Dundee town itself all has been done that human ingenuity could devise to generally wreck up the premises. Plenty of evidence that the Boers were on a little venture. I watched one loading up two trolley loads of pianos. But this was purely excess of emotion; and the exuberance of delicious joy.*'[12]

The exercise of this 'exuberance of delicious joy' changed with the passing of time, but the effects were the same. Gerard Bailey kept a cow which provided the Vicarage with milk until a Boer decided he wanted the cow. He went to the *Vrederechter* who gave him a permit to remove it. Fortunately some of the residents still had cows and Mr AJ Oldacre was able to offer Gerard and Father Murray some milk. Arthur Oldacre was a shopkeeper, and when the Boers first entered Dundee, his was one of the two shops which were permitted to remain open. No reason was given for this privilege, though the fact that he also owned a shop across the border in Vryheid, might account the dispensation granted to his business. In any event the privilege did not last for long. His shop, with all its stock, was duly expropriated by the Transvaal government.

It was not only over property that the *Vrederechter* had such wide powers. There was no Habeas Corpus Act or other inconvenient legislation to limit his powers over the residents. As they were now living in the Transvaal, any criticism by a resident of the authorities could be regarded as treason and result in the offender being shot. They might be imprisoned indefinitely without charge and new crimes were created on the spur of the moment. They could be sent anywhere at a moments notice, and be used as forced labour. On 2 November, Gerard, while walking to the hospital, was surprised to see wounded men being loaded onto a train. It transpired that 87 of them with minor wounds and an officer were being sent to Pretoria. Shortly afterwards he received another surprise. A man was walking around town ringing a bell and displaying a notice in Dutch and English stating, '*Notice is hereby given that all (male) inhabitants residing within a radius of three miles of the office of the Resident Justice of the Peace at Dundee must be present at the railway station at Dundee to leave for Pretoria at 2.30 p.m. tomorrow the 3rd inst.*'[13]

After reading the notice Gerard continued to the Hospital and discovered that apart from those residents due to go to Pretoria the next day, all the remaining patients who could possibly be moved, and most medical staff, were to be transported to the Boer camp at Elandslaagte. They would then be passed through the lines into Ladysmith. Realising that if he was to leave the following day, all his and the church's property would be stolen or destroyed, Gerard and Father Murray worked through the night hiding as much as they could. The more valuable items were hidden under the floorboards in the church and other things were buried in the garden.

The next morning they went to see the *Vrederechter* to ask for permission to stay in Dundee to help with the badly wounded. Initially their request was refused, but they insisted, stating that they were entitled to remain with the seriously wounded, many of whom were dying. Finally it was agreed that they might remain pending further orders. At 5.00 p.m. the next batch of wounded from the Field Hospitals left for Elandslaagte. Major Daly with a few of his medical staff stayed behind to take care of those who could not be moved. Among the civilians who assembled at the station at 2.30 p.m. for the transportation to Pretoria, was WH Tatham who must have wondered why he had ever thought the residents had nothing to fear from the Boers. After waiting about 8 hours on the station they finally set off for Pretoria.[14] There were 143 residents in this group and they had no idea what awaited them at the end of the line.

The two priests continued with their pastoral duties and also wrote letters for some of the illiterate Boers. Some of the wounded died and funeral services were conducted. However, like many men of that era their knowledge of housekeeping was limited. Gerard had perforce to do his own washing and ironing. He coped very well with his shirts but his clerical dog collar hung like a limp rag about his neck. The collar was vital to him as the Boers always had great respect for the clergy and without it he would lose all protection. Afterwards he found some starch which worked wonders, and when he visited the hospital wearing his newly starched collar, a wounded officer said he was the best dressed man he had seen there. Gerard was not to know that the starch he used for washing clothes was about to be employed down the road in Ladysmith to fill hungry stomachs.

There were still three officers and about thirty men being treated at the hospital. On most days the two priests would call at the hospital to see the wounded and would stay on for lunch. Major Daly had secured a small flock of sheep, which were looked after by one of the army orderlies and grazed on the wide open *veld*. Mysteriously, no matter how many sheep were eaten their numbers never declined. Commandeering was catching!

The deportation of 143 residents did not bring an end to the Boer attacks on the civilians of the town. Two weeks later TH Brokensha was arrested and charged with being a 'dangerous character', on the basis that he knew where there were arms, and was ready to head a rebellion. Major Daly went to see the *Vrederechter*, who after receiving a guarantee for Brokensha's future behaviour, released the prisoner, but the 'offender' was told he was no longer a Justice of the Peace. A couple of days later, one of the orderlies was found guilty of being 'out of bounds' and sentenced by the *Vrederechter* to the unusual penalty of 21 days in bed.[15] On 24 November, Arthur Oldacre and six other men were placed under arrest and incarcerated in Oldacre's home where the Boers kept them under guard. No one knew why they were arrested, though subsequent speculation was that this was done to ensure that they did not attend meetings scheduled for the following week, at which it was hoped to persuade the Natal Dutch to join the Boer cause. After the meetings they were released without explanation.

On 11 December, word was sent round that all residents were to present themselves at the *Vrederechter's* office at 3.00 p.m. where they were informed that they would be leaving for Pretoria at 6.00 a.m. the following day. Early the next morning, Gerard Bailey was at the station to see about 20 men leave under armed guard. That afternoon he went as usual to the hospital only to find it surrounded by armed guards. Nothing daunted he slipped through the fence but on his way out he was arrested and marched off to the *Vrederechter's* office, much to the amusement of his friends at the hospital. Gerard explained to the Boer official that he knew nothing of the new regulations and was released with an apology. On 15 December, the sound of cannon fire from the south-west began early and was distinct and continuous. It was apparent that a major battle was taking place. The next day Arthur Oldacre arrived with a telegram with details of the Battle of Colenso: '*British 2000 killed, 150 prisoners, 10 guns captured and a lot of ammunition.*' Father Murray and Oldacre were inconsolable. Gerard did not believe the report but as the day drifted on, more reports came in and it was apparent that Britain had suffered a severe loss.

Some of the residents were able to obtain permission to travel to Pretoria and from there to travel to Delagoa Bay. Others were less fortunate. One group of 10 residents was arrested for no known reason and locked in gaol where they remained throughout a December heatwave. On 19 December, they were marched out of the gaol to the station to continue their captivity in Pretoria. On Christmas Eve, Father Murray and four civilians voluntarily left Dundee. The next day the remaining patients and staff at the hospital received a Christmas present in the form of a directive that all inmates should hold themselves in readiness for removal to Pretoria. The women and children asked if they could accompany the wounded, but received a non-committal reply. On 30 December, a hospital train arrived and took patients, staff (including civilian orderlies) off to Pretoria. Dr. Galbraith, being a local doctor, remained behind as did one patient who had had a leg shortened and had difficulty walking. A week later Arthur Oldacre left voluntarily, intending to go to Pretoria and from there to Delagoa Day. In two weeks he was in Durban. He must have been a very persuasive man to have received consent for this journey, as he was in possession of much useful information as to the state of affairs in Northern Natal. On 25 January 1900, the Boers made their last arrest and deportation when two residents who had not left their houses for many weeks were sent off to Pretoria. Apart from the women and children the town had been almost emptied of its original inhabitants. Vicar Gerard Bailey stayed on. The few remaining residents hardly constituted a congregation, however at the end of November about seventy Cape Coloured people arrived from Newcastle. They were the wives and families of the wagon drivers who were employed by the British Army. Gerard found them to be a decent crowd and as some were Anglicans his tiny congregation received a boost.

During the last two months of 1899, the Boers had been trying to persuade the local Dutch farmers to join their cause. Farms were visited, the farmers told that northern Natal had been annexed by the Transvaal and that unless they took up arms for the Republican cause, they would be rebels to the Republic and dealt with as such, possibly shot. At the meetings in Dundee the local Dutch were told that if any Dutch farmer was low enough not to join the war between the Republics and Britain, any burgher would be justified in molesting that man in any way. In spite of the threats many of the more prominent farmers remained loyal to the Natal government and they were made to pay for the stand they took. Most of the smaller farmers yielded to pressure and agreed to serve, generally as non-combatants. One of the disloyal Boers, LJ de Jager of Waschbank, was told he would be a Commandant if he could raise 1,000 men. Given the limited number of Boers in the area, this was impossible so he ended up being Native Commissioner for the Dundee District, and looted cattle were sent to him.

In Newcastle, those residents who remained behind when the British retreated, received similar treatment to the inhabitants of Dundee. Many of the farmers fled before the Boers and had their farms looted and smashed up, but those who remained were left in peace for a time.

In an attempt to clean up the damage made by the looters in Dundee a large gang of Zulus was commandeered by the Boers. They were housed and fed in the gaol and appeared to be a cheerful crowd who were happy to talk to Gerard Bailey. They felt the English who had run away from Johannesburg, Newcastle and Dundee were great fools. When Gerard asked them what pay they received, they became uneasy and admitted that they received no pay and did not like this treatment. These people belonged to the tribe under Chief Sandanezwe. The Boers had been courting this chief for some time and had given him a house in Dundee and the green light to attack an old enemy, Chief Dumisa of the Amangwe, who lived in the Dundee district. Chief Sandanezwe approached Chief Bande of Weenen with a proposition that they should combine with the Boers, and launch an attack against Dumisa. This was the classic Boer tactic of siding with one of the parties to a dispute and then picking up the spoils after the fight. It will be recalled that as long ago as 1841 the Boers attacked the amaBaca in order to win favour with the Pondo chief, Faku. On that occasion they alarmed Faku who sought British aid. We have seen how in 1884, despite protests from Natal and Zululand, Britain permitted the Boers to use this tactic to annex northern Zululand. Chief Bande was not one to fall for such a ruse and declined to assist Sandanezwe. Instead he reported the matter to the British and sent a warning to Chief Dumisa. Chief Dumisa had already realised the danger facing his tribe and had sent his young men and cattle away before the Boers arrived. Though the Boers threatened to kill him, he would not be intimidated and survived the war.

Chief Mabizela, whose armed followers had tried to persuade General Buller to let them join the fight against the invading Boers, received a message from the Boers requiring him to come to them to explain why his men had attempted to join the British. Mabizela knew it would be fatal for him to attend on the Boers personally so he sent a message to them saying his men only went to Chieveley seeking work as porters. Not quite the truth, but understandable.

On 8 January 1900, the Governor of Natal sent a telegram to the Colonial Secretary:

'*Prime Minister informs me Chief Nsungulu, head of the Ntombela tribe near the Natal border at Mahlabatini, saying that he wishes to tender allegiance to British Government. I have caused Nsungulu to be informed that as Governor of Natal I have no power to accept offer of allegiance but that I will communicate it to Her Majesty's Government. Saunders reports Nsungulu is a powerful chief.*'[17]
(Saunders was a magistrate employed by the Natal Government)

Britain made no response to Chief Nsungulu's offer of allegiance, an ill omen for the future.

Chapter Nineteen

Army moves west and a successful attack on Boer right flank

• ◆ •

'Our objective is not Ladysmith'

Response by General Sir Charles Warren on 19 January 1900, to the news that squadrons of the Natal Carbineers and Imperial Light Horse had outflanked the Boers and the road to Ladysmith was clear.

IN the weeks following the Battle of Colenso, General Buller's self-confidence began to return. The arrival in Natal shortly after Christmas of General Sir Charles Warren and the 5th Division almost doubled the infantry and artillery under his command and would have strengthened the idea that it might be possible to outflank the Boer line stretched along the northern bank of the Tugela. Disappointingly, there was only one mounted regiment in the Division, the 13th Hussars, and Sir Charles Warren was not the person Buller would have chosen to be a senior commander in his force.

Charles Warren was the son of an Indian Army General and his choice of the army as a career followed the conventions of the time. Few would have guessed that he was to become one of the most eccentric figures in the British Army. At Sandhurst and Woolwich he displayed unusual talent as a mathematician, which resulted in him having no trouble obtaining a commission in the Royal Engineers. One of his first assignments was to conduct a trigometrical survey of the Rock of Gibraltar which he did to a scale of 50 feet to an inch and in addition produced two monstrous models of Gibraltar, each being over 30 feet in length. In 1876 he was sent to South Africa to survey the boundary between the Orange Free State and Griqualand West and subsequently his engineering skills were used in one of the wars on the Eastern Cape Frontier, after which he was posted to Bechuanaland (now Botswana). When the Boers provoked rebellion in that country, he led an expedition whose mere presence reasserted British authority. The scope of his career was widening and he was steadily rising in the army lists though he had never been involved in any actual fighting. On his return to England he stood for Parliament as an Independent Liberal, although as an officer on half-pay this was against army practice. Sir Garnet Wolseley, who was then Adjutant-General, urged him to withdraw from the election, but Warren refused on the grounds that he could not let the electors down. The electors however, had no qualms about letting him down and voted for his opponent. With his army career apparently over, he now devoted his talents to archaeology, forming a Lodge of Masonic Research and was elected Master. He hardly had time to settle into this post when, out of the blue, he was appointed to serve on the staff of the army in Egypt. His name had been put forward by Wolseley who it would seem admired eccentricity. After only a month in Egypt, where his principal concern was to prevent the servants poisoning the officers, he was offered and accepted the post of

Chief Commissioner of the Metropolitan Police in London. For a number of years the London Police had been the subject of scandals over corruption, illegal arrests and inefficiency. During the three years he spent as Chief Commissioner, Warren was to mire them in a series of controversies which were to cause past failures to pale into insignificance. A number of incidents created ill-feeling between him and the Home Secretary, a situation which reached its nadir late in 1887 when Socialists attempted to hold a protest meeting in Trafalgar Square.

Warren forbade the approach to the square of any 'organised procession' and to enforce his decision called out 4,000 constables, 300 Grenadiers, and 300 Life Guards. This force clashed violently with a large crowd of protesters. When the Grenadiers were about to execute a bayonet charge, a bloodbath was only averted by the officers and sergeants rushing in front of their men and ordering them to put up their arms. Over 150 people were injured and taken to hospital in the course of the fracas. Warren had issued orders in rhyming prose:

> The Commissioner has observed there are signs of wear
> On the Landseer lions in Trafalgar Square.
> Unauthorised persons are not to climb,
> On the Landseer lions at any time.

Whatever the Home Secretary might have thought of Warren's ability as a poet, he was shocked by his militancy, and when a further dispute occurred regarding the investigation into the 'Jack the Ripper' murders, the Home Secretary reproved him in public, resulting in Warren's resignation. Within a few weeks he was appointed to the command of the garrison in Singapore and given the temporary rank of Major-General. In Singapore he was responsible for constructing the fortifications for the island. He founded the Straits Philosophical Society, and in his capacity as District Grand Master of the Eastern Archipelago, he founded several Masonic Lodges. He soon quarrelled with the Governor of Singapore, however, and supplied the War Office with lengthy accounts of these disputes. Back in London, Redvers Buller was moved to write to him:

> 'We are inundated with long correspondence regarding squabbles between you and your Governor… all I want to say is, for heaven's sake leave us alone, do not write and send everything here. If you have to fight the Governor, fight him. Though I pray you fight as little as possible, surely the sun is hot enough in Singapore, trust us, let him send home what he likes. You may be assured you will have your say in due time.'

Warren spent five years in Singapore during which period his appointment as a Major-General was confirmed. On his return to England, he was unemployed for a year, and after a period in command of the troops in the Thames District, he retired. When hostilities broke out in South Africa he wrote to Wolseley asking if he could be of any service and was pleased and delighted when on 7 November 1899, he received command of the 5th Division which was shortly to leave for South Africa. He was now a Lieutenant General and had, as we have seen, little experience of warfare and such knowledge as he possessed was likely to be out of date. He was generally disliked by the officers who had to work with him and was well known for his bad temper, lack of tact, and intolerance of criticism. While on the ship to Durban he studied maps of Natal and played war games with his staff officers, so that on arrival he was confident that he knew the answer to Britain's military problems. When he met Buller at Frere he suggested that the line of advance should be via Hlangwane Hill to the east of Colenso. 'What do you know about it?' was Buller's response. Warren confessed that he had based his theory on his own general knowledge and war games! Frustrated in his attempt to dictate general strategy, Warren clung to two ideas. Firstly, that no military manoeuvre should be attempted without plenty of practice, and secondly, that it was the duty of the British soldier to show he was 'a better man' than the Boer. On arrival at Frere his men began practising bayonet charges.

Once he had recovered from the shock of the reverse at Colenso, Buller began to consider the other options open to him and decided that he would attempt to circumvent the Boer's right flank. This involved a march of between 15 and 20 miles westwards towards a hamlet, Springfield, now known as Winterton. Here there was a bridge over the Little Tugela, a tributary of the Tugela River approximately 8 miles to the north. From Springfield his force could strike northwards to the Tugela itself where a number of fords provided potential crossing points. Once the flank had been turned, the numerical superiority of the British artillery would ensure that his force could roll up the Boer line while advancing eastwards across open country to Ladysmith. Reliable maps of the area were not available so it was necessary that those in command should be both flexible and pragmatic. Speed was essential as any delay would enable the Boers to fortify their line.

Though there were only two regular cavalry regiments in his force, the 13th Hussars and the 1st Royal Dragoons, Buller nonetheless had under his overall command some very useful colonial mounted volunteers. There were squadrons of the Natal Carbineers, the Imperial Light Horse, and the Natal Police, who together were known as the Composite Regiment; Thornycroft's Mounted Infantry and Bethune's Mounted Infantry both of which had been raised in Natal, and there had recently arrived four squadrons of the South African Light Horse, which had been raised in the Eastern Cape. All in all Buller had approximately 2,500 mounted men who were brigaded under Lord Dundonald.

The Volunteers had not been idle during the weeks following the Colenso debacle. They were constantly out on patrol gathering information and taking part in several skirmishes with the enemy. Near Chieveley on 20 December, a picket of the 3rd Hussars, sheltering from the unaccustomed heat, were surprised by a party of Boers who killed two of them. Lieutenant Silburn of the Carbineers offered to set a trap for the marauding Boers. A detachment was taken out to the area where the previous attack occurred, and while some of the men lounged about in a position which could be seen by the enemy, the others concealed themselves. The Boers duly fell for the trap and in the brief skirmish which followed the Boers lost four men. The high ground where these incidents occurred was given the name Hussar Hill.[1]

In a situation where urgent messages could only be delivered by horsemen, the Volunteers' knowledge of the country was invaluable for the British. On one occasion a message had to be taken to a District Surgeon living in the foothills of the Drakensberg behind the Boer lines. Corporal H Norton and three troopers of the ILH were assigned the task of delivering the message. They passed through the Boer lines and headed north through this exquisitely beautiful and sparsely inhabited part of Natal. En route they came across a Native *kraal* where they were met by an old man with some women and wide-eyed children a respectful distance behind him. Uncertain of the extent to which the kraalhead might have been influenced by the Boers, Norton decided they should test his allegiance by posing as Boers: 'They had been living in the open for some days, had had no opportunity to shave or wash for a week, their uniforms were decidedly the worse for wear, slouch hats were the slouchiest, and to all outward seeming they were typical Boers.

Norton, a fine Zulu linguist, said to the kraalhead: 'We have been sent by President Paul Kruger to tell you, that all this land now belongs to the Boers, and all you Zulus are therefore Paul Kruger's men!'

The old man shook his head and said, 'No, No, No! Nkosi, that is not so!'

'What!' shouted Norton, working himself up into a well-simulated rage. 'If you dare to answer me like that, I will put a bullet through you!' He made great play with his rifle bolt and slipping a cartridge into the breach. The old Zulu, quite unperturbed, took out his snuff box, sniffed deliberately, and in a dignified manner said, 'No! No! Nkosi you are wrong. You see I am a very old man. I was born a Queen's man, and I will die a Queen's man.' Bearing his chest, he added, "Shoot."'[2]

There was no doubt where this man's sympathies lay and the patrol was so delighted by him that they gave him everything they could as gifts. He, not to be outdone in courtesy, provided them with a feast of chickens, sweet potatoes and milk, before seeing them on their way. The message was duly given to the District Surgeon, and the reply brought safely back to base.

Among the personalities who arrived in Natal that Christmas of 1899, was Winston Churchill. He had escaped from the prisoner-of-war camp in Pretoria, and after an adventurous journey to Delagoa Bay, was able to obtain a passage on a coaster travelling to Durban. Here he made some fine speeches in which he told his audiences of the high esteem in which he held the people of Natal. He then travelled to Pietermaritzburg, where he was the guest of Sir Walter Hely-Hutchinson, the Governor. He visited the wounded in hospital and met the Prime Minister before setting off for the front. At Frere he persuaded General Buller to grant him a commission in the South African Light Horse. It was agreed that he would receive no pay and might continue his career as a journalist. Though he had no specific military duties, his position as an army officer did enable him to get close to the action and thereby bring a sense of immediacy to his reports. He liked to create the impression that he was present at the scenes he described.

Buller had hoped to begin moving his army to Springfield on 6 January, but it rained constantly and it was not until the 10th that the British column was finally able to begin its

Churchill pictured after his escape from Pretoria standing in front of one of the carriages of the wrecked armoured train.

march. But in his preparations for the move, Buller had made two serious blunders: in his concern for the well-being of the troops the column took far too much baggage. Churchill, though often reluctant to criticize the Army, was moved to write:

> '*The vast amount of baggage this army takes with it on the march hampers its movements and utterly precludes all possibility of surprising the enemy....The consequence is that roads are crowded, drifts are blocked, marching troops are delayed, and all rapidity of movement is out of the question. Meanwhile, the enemy completes the fortification of his positions, and the cost of capturing them rises. It is a poor economy to let a brave soldier live well for three days at the price of killing him on the fourth.*'[3]

The second major mistake by Buller at this time was to place Sir Charles Warren in charge of the flanking movement. Warren now had command not only of his 5th Division with its two Brigades of infantry and supporting artillery, but also the 2nd Division under Major-General Clery with another two Brigades of infantry and artillery, and almost the entire Cavalry Division under Lord Dundonald, while General Barton's Brigade was delegated the task of defending the Colenso section of the front. Buller kept under his direct command the 10th Brigade under Major-General Coke. This brigade consisted of three regiments of Regular Infantry and one Volunteer regiment, the Imperial Light Infantry, which had only recently been raised in Pietermaritzburg. Commanded by a regular officer, Lieutenant-Colonel WF Nash, the ILI consisted of Colonials who had received a few weeks training before being sent to the front. Like the other Volunteers they were not issued with bayonets and were armed with obsolete single-shot rifles.

Buller's concern that his troops should have the best possible medical care ensured that the field hospital and medical staff would accompany the soldiers. With most of his stretcher-bearers locked up in Ladysmith, the Natal Volunteer Ambulance Corps was formed with Lt HSN Wright in command. It was recruited in Durban and Pietermaritzburg from those who had lost their employment as a result of the war and those who simply wanted to make a contribution to the war effort. As the Ambulance Corps were leaving Springfield they attracted the attention of a young doctor, Lieutenant Edward Blake Knox, who was serving with the Natal Field Force, and who kept a diary of his experiences:

> '...*they were dressed in ordinary clothes, but the Government had given them a fair amount of equipment, each man having received a couple of blankets, a waterproof sheet, a haversack, a pair of boots. They carried all their belongings with them, and truly it was a curious sight to see them marching past, four deep, not keeping step nor any kind of military formation, some of them encumbered with small portmanteaus, hand-bags, and various kinds of parcels, their white mackintosh sheets rolled around their shoulders, their haversacks bulging and hung around with bundles of various little odds and ends, including small pots and kettles. These were the men who were to make for themselves a reputation second to none in the Natal Army.*'[4]

Buller knew Warren was inexperienced and quite unsuited to command a major military operation, and yet he bestowed on this man the difficult task of getting round an enemy who had already shown an aptitude for exploiting any weakness. We shall never know precisely what caused Buller to commit this folly, though it possibly stemmed from his anxiety about his own lack of experience as overall commander. For his part, Warren had no doubts about his own abilities and what should be done. He was however concerned that his troops lacked practice fighting the Boers and felt no attack should be launched until they had such experience, though he never explained quite how this objective was to be obtained.

Buller's Army on the move along the rough track from Frere to Springfield a distance of about 20 miles, a formidable task in the prevailing conditions.

The march to Springfield turned out to be a wretched affair. The recent torrential rains brought every river and stream down in flood. The track across the *veld* was soon turned into a quagmire. For those in front it was a case of slipping and sliding along, but further back things were much worse as the mud became deeper and deeper. Wagons were mired in mud up to their axles and on occasions could not be moved, even by four teams of oxen. With sixteen oxen to a team this churned up the track even further. The British had brought along a number of steam traction engines which were most useful. It was found that one of these machines could free wagons which 48 oxen were unable to move, a hint of the mechanised warfare of the future.

On 10 January, Dundonald's orders were to accompany the infantry until they reached their overnight stop. Thereafter they were to press on to Springfield which should, if possible, be occupied and held overnight, pending the arrival of the main body of Warren's column the following day. The Regular Cavalry and Thorneycroft's MI did not ride with Dundonald, being required to accompany the Infantry Brigades. This left Dundonald with about 1,000 mounted men and an Artillery Battery of six guns under his command. After they had ridden 2 or 3 miles, Dundonald sought and was given permission by General Clery to press on to Springfield without delay. Dundonald found the bridge across the Little Tugela unguarded and intact. Being in the habit of consulting with his Colonial officers, he was able to acquire information which would not have been available to his colleagues. He wrote, '*Up to 8 January very little rain had fallen in this part of Natal, and the Tugela and other rivers were running very low, and were very easily fordable at the drifts…. On the night of the 8th, however, and during the whole of the 9th, heavy rain fell, with the result that the rivers at once came down in flood and by the morning of the 10th, few, or perhaps none of the drifts over the Tugela were fordable. Today, however (the 10th), the rain had ceased, and as the floods in the Natal rivers fall almost as quickly as they rise, the chances were that with no more rain in the next 24 hours, the drifts would be passable. It appeared to me that with the river still running high the Boers would not dare to occupy in force the southern heights at Mount Alice, and that if I were quick I could seize this important position without much opposition.*'[5]

About 8 miles north of Springfield lay Spearman's Hill, the western summit of which was called Mount Alice. Beyond Spearman's lay the Tugela. Dundonald decided to use his discretion and take the opportunity offered of capturing this high ground. Leaving 350 men and two guns to guard the bridge at Springfield, the rest of the force set out for Spearman's. With Bethune's Mounted Infantry scouting ahead the whole force quickly covered the ground, and by nightfall had not only established a camp on top of Mount Alice, but also managed to manhandle their four guns onto the summit. Dundonald was particularly impressed by the speed and efficiency with which Bethune's men scouted ahead. Many of these men were Australians who had come over to Natal at their own expense to resist the Boer invaders. No Boers were seen, but recently constructed fortifications were found indicating that they had occupied and intended to hold Mount Alice. As suspected, the Boers had withdrawn from the position when the rising river threatened to cut them off from the bulk of their forces.

When the Volunteers awoke the next morning they could see the Tugela River winding along the valley below them. On the far river bank was a large ferry, used in peacetime to ferry men and cattle across the river, and beyond the river bank Boer pickets could be seen, presumably guarding the ferry and watching the movements of Dundonald's force. Lieutenant Carlisle with Corporals Cox and Barkley and Troopers Howell, Godden and Collingwood of the South African Light Horse volunteered to attempt to bring the ferry across to the southern bank. A detachment of the same regiment was sent down to the scrub near the river bank to provide them with some cover, while Carlisle's men, keeping well out of sight, made their way to the river bank. Here they stripped off and then suddenly made a dash for the river and had swum half-way across before the enemy realised what was happening. Though heavy rifle fire was opened on the swimmers they were able to drag the barge in good order over to the southern bank. No casualties occurred though one man suffered cramp in the cold water and would have drowned had he not been rescued by a comrade. The barge was at a crossing of the river known as Potgieter's Drift and was later to play a significant role in ferrying troops across the river. In twenty-four hours the Volunteers with Dundonald had secured the bridge at Springfield, occupied Mount Alice and secured a means of crossing the Tugela at Potgieter's Drift. Lt Carlisle, who was a mining engineer from Johannesburg, was recommended for a DSO, an award which was refused much to the chagrin of Dundonald, who not only witnessed the heroism that morning, but also appreciated the importance of the achievement.[6]

The rest of that day and the night which followed passed without incident. On 12 January, General Buller arrived with a Brigade of Infantry. The summit at Mount Alice was 1,000 feet above the valley floor giving Buller a fine view of the hills on the northern bank of the Tugela. About 6 miles to the east could be seen the heights of Vaalkrantz, directly in front were the lower hills of Brakfontein and 5 miles to the west the massive bulk of Spion Kop and Twin Peaks. Boers could be seen busily entrenching themselves along the Brakfontein Hills. On 13 January the Naval guns arrived and replaced the guns from Dundonald's Brigade on Mount Alice. Over the next two days the transfer of the troops from Frere to Spearman's was almost completed. In addition a large accumulation of stores had been built up at Springfield.

On 16 January, Dundonald attended a meeting at Mount Alice of senior officers, at which Sir Redvers Buller gave a broad outline of his plans. Sir Redvers felt that it would be well nigh impossible to break through the Boer lines on the Brakfontein hills in front of Mount Alice and therefore it was his intention that only General Lyttleton's Brigade should cross the Tugela at Potgieter's Drift and occupy the kopjes lying to the north of the river in front of Mount Alice. Warren, with his two Divisions was to march west, cross the river about 5 miles upstream at Trichardt's Drift, and then execute a flanking movement, refusing his right and throwing his left forward. Clearly Buller intended that Warren's force should skirt round the west of

Spion Kop. With the exception of Bethune's MI, who were to assist Lyttleton's Brigade, the rest of Dundonald's mounted brigade numbering about 1,500 fell within Warren's command.

When Dundonald arrived at Trichardt's Drift on 17 January, Lieutenant Tom Bridges, formerly of the Royal Artillery and now with the Imperial Light Horse, offered to swim the river to discover what opposition they could expect from the Boers. With a small patrol, Bridges crossed the river and on approaching a farm on the north bank a couple of Boers fired on them before making off. Otherwise the coast appeared to be clear. While the Engineers were constructing a pontoon and bridge to enable the infantry and transport wagons to cross Trichardt's Drift, Dundonald decided his mounted men should cross the Tugela at another drift about half a mile lower downstream. Probably because their colonial horses were small compared with the big English chargers, the Carbineers were placed at the rear of the column making its way to the new crossing. Duncan McKenzie thought how splendid the cavalry looked marching in columns of four down to the river, but was very surprised to see them stop when they reached it and counter-march back up the hill. Duncan rode down to find out what was happening and was told by Dundonald that the river was too full to cross. Duncan wanted to have a closer look so he and Dundonald rode back to the drift. The river was fairly full and running swiftly. The drift was formed by a natural weir, downstream of which was deep water. Duncan rode into the drift, and though the water came up to his saddle flaps, he had no difficulty getting across and coming back again. He told Dundonald that despite their smaller horses, the Carbineers would have no difficulty crossing, but he was not so sure about the English horses which were unfamiliar with flowing water. Having seen how easily McKenzie had crossed the river, Dundonald changed his mind. The 1st Royal Dragoons were to lead the way. They were advised to keep their horses' heads facing upstream while the riders should look straight ahead. Under no circumstances should the rider look downstream as the horse would feel the rider's movement and instinctively move in that direction, causing it to shift into the deeper water, lose its footing and be swept downstream. Unfortunately the Dragoons either would not or could not control their horses properly on the drift and were swept into the deep water. Most were able to get onto a shallow bank from which they were later rescued. Others were less fortunate. Troopers David Sclanders and Fred Woods of the Carbineers plunged in and rescued several men, one of whom, Captain Tremayne, was pulled from the water unconscious. Despite the efforts of Sclanders and Wood, one of the Dragoons drowned. Realising that more men might drown, McKenzie suggested that a line of Carbineers be placed across the drift and that the mounted men cross just above them. Dundonald acquiesced, and a chain of mounted men was formed along the downstream edge of the drift. Duncan chose big men who were strong swimmers and once they were in place, the rest of the column crossed without any further untoward incident.[7] Sclanders was afterwards presented with the Royal Humane Society's silver medal.

That night the mounted brigade bivouacked on the northern bank of the river. Early the following morning it set out to put into effect Sir Redvers Buller's plan to outflank the Boers. They travelled west along the northern bank of the Tugela. In his autobiography Dundonald wrote:

'My idea was to try and get to the west of the Boer right flank before it was entrenched, and secure and hold a position commanding the Acton-Ladysmith road. All was going well and I continued my advance, feeling sure that the infantry would be following. About halfway to Acton Homes there is a stream called Venter's Spruit; here I left Thorneycroft's Mounted Infantry on a good defensive position on the *kopjes* at this important point. At Venter's Spruit *kopjes* I arranged for sketches to be prepared of the Tabanyama (Rangeworthy Hills) to the north, as they appeared from Venter's Spruit. It was most important to hold the Venter's

Spruit line of kopjes, as the infantry could deploy to the west behind them unmolested, in order to take up their position for the wheel. Shortly after leaving Thorneycroft's regiment to hold the Venter's Spruit kopjes, I was astounded by receiving the following message from Sir Charles Warren:

"To OC Mounted Troops or next senior.

The GOC as far as he can see finds that there are no Cavalry whatever round the camp, and nothing to prevent the oxen being swept away. You are to send 500 men at once to be placed round the camp.

Sgd. AH Morris AAG Col 18/1/00"

'There was nothing to do except obey the order I had received, so as the nearest approach to 500 men was the Royal Dragoons, with great regret I sent this splendid regiment back to Sir Charles Warren, hoping that Colonel Burn-Murdoch might argue matters out with him and soon return, – but this order paralysed the Mounted Brigade at the very moment it wanted strengthening. Had not Sir Charles the River Tugela behind him, and Natives to keep his oxen from straying? He also had his divisional cavalry. The situation seemed quite inexplicable and augured ill for the success of Buller's plans.'[8]

Despite the drastic reduction in its numbers, Dundonald decided his column should not retreat but instead hold its position on the Acton Homes road. When camp was formed, the Carbineers were put on outpost duty. That afternoon Duncan McKenzie saw a large body of Boers riding out from behind Spion Kop in the direction of Acton Homes. A British officer, Major Graham, who was nominally in command of the Carbineers, happened to be at the outpost when the Boers were spotted. McKenzie pointed out the enemy to him, saying at the same time, 'I can trap these men if you will let me.' Graham replied, 'Do what you like, McKenzie.' Duncan did just that. He gave the order to mount, and in seconds the men were in their saddles and off at a full gallop.[9]

Being aware that if he took the direct route the Boers on Spion Kop, or the *Kommando* itself, might see them, Duncan decided to make a wide detour and keep out of sight, as they made their way to two *kopjes* where it was intended to ambush the Boers. This meant that they had to travel twice as far as the Boers to reach the desired position in time, riding hard the whole way. Captain Herbert Bottomley and the Imperial Light Horse had noticed the sudden burst of activity by the Carbineers and, anxious not to miss any excitement, they mounted their horses and galloped after them. Ever since the incident of the armoured train the ILH had worked closely with the Carbineers who were delighted to have their help. They had to ride nearly 5 miles and in the course of the gallop four ILH troopers and one or two Carbineers had their horses brought down by holes in the *veld*. As they neared the *kopjes*, McKenzie slowed down as he was uncertain whether or not the Boers were already there. Trooper Gray of the Carbineers was ordered to gallop on as fast as he could to the nek between the *kopjes* and if the Boers were close to gallop back. If they were not yet there, he was to remain in position and wave on the Carbineers. Gray galloped to the *kopjes*, dismounted and crept up to the crest of the nek between the two *kopjes* where he had a view of the land ahead. He then drew back from the skyline and waved. McKenzie sent a message back to Dundonald for support, instructed the ILH to occupy the ground on the left, while the Carbineers made for the *kopje* on the right. All were ordered to hold their fire until McKenzie blew his whistle. They galloped over to the kopjes, dismounted and leaving their linked horses under cover, climbed up into the rocks, keeping themselves well hidden.

They had only beaten the Boer *Kommando* to the *kopjes* by a few minutes. From his concealed position McKenzie saw them riding along in the typical irregular Boer fashion with men riding four or five abreast in clumps of about 40 or 50 riders. Obviously they were not expecting any opposition, had no proper scouts out, and talked and rode as they felt inclined. There were 320 Boers in the *Kommando* riding against the Carbineers and ILH who together totalled no more than 80 men. McKenzie was almost ready to give the order to fire, when one of the ILH men could stand the tension no longer and fired. McKenzie had no choice but to blow his whistle as a general order to fire. Everyone fired as fast as they could with their single-shot rifles. Boer saddles quickly emptied as riders were either shot or jumped off to seek cover. The Boers at the rear of the *Kommando* turned tail and galloped away. Some of them found cover behind a bank and attempted to return the fire while their commander, *Kommandant* Mentz, rallied a few men and took up a position on a small stony *kopje* some 800 yards away. For about an hour the firing continued as the Volunteers steadily eliminated pockets of resistance and Boers surrendered. At one point some Boers raised a white flag, causing McKenzie to order a cease fire. When he stood up to tell them to come in, a bullet came whistling past his head. A Boer prisoner was then brought forward to tell the Boers to put down their arms and come in. The reply was another bullet which narrowly missed the prisoner. This apparent abuse of the white flag created some anger, however it was subsequently discovered that the fire came from the men with *Kommandant* Mentz from whose position the white flag would not have been visible.

As the engagement drew to a close, the 60th King's Royal Rifles arrived in response to McKenzie's request for support. Unfortunately, instead of joining the Carbineers they attempted a flank attack on the fleeing Boers and lost 2 men killed. In the engagement one Carbineer and two Imperial Light Horsemen were wounded. The 60th KRR also suffered a couple of men wounded. The Boer losses were 14 killed, about 40 wounded and nearly 40 taken prisoner. The Boer leader, Mentz, was among those killed. It is said he died holding a letter from his wife.

Duncan McKenzie, though pleased with the outcome of the engagement, was saddened by the casualties brought about by war, and described the shooting of the enemy as a 'horrible affair.'[10] That night six Carbineers escorted the Boer prisoners back to base. It seems word had got out that prisoners had been taken and when they arrived at the camp the next morning they were met by a crowd of Zulus dressed in full war paint, singing a song about the downfall of the Boers, and shouting jeering insults at them. For a moment or two it looked as if a general mêlée might break out. One Carbineer commented, 'It was a lesson to the Boers because they always ill-treat the Natives and flog them.'[11]

Dundonald rode out to Acton Homes as soon as he heard of the engagement. He was delighted by the success of the two Volunteer squadrons and fully appreciated the opportunity they had created. He sent a message to General Warren asking for some guns which could knock out any guns the Boers might bring up to block the advance. He also asked that the Royal Dragoons be returned to his command. That night Dundonald and his three squadrons bivouacked on the two *kopjes* they had secured which provided an excellent defensive position. Somewhat naively he imagined Warren would be making haste to reinforce the successful turning of the Boer flank with infantry and artillery. The next morning Dundonald received an urgent message that Sir Charles Warren wished to see him. Dundonald found Sir Charles at Venter's Spruit, actively supervising the crossing of the stream by the wagons. With pointed rudeness Warren continued supervising the wagons when approached by Dundonald who repeated his request to Warren for some guns and reinforcements only to receive the retort, 'Our objective is not Ladysmith; our objective is to effect junction with Sir R. Buller's force.'[12] This statement must have been very puzzling to Dundonald. Buller had told them at the meeting on the 16th that he could not break through the Brakfontein Hills. If the objective was to effect a junction with Buller the obvious thing would have been to turn around and go back to Mount Alice where Buller had set up his headquarters. They were certainly not going to find him on Thabanyama or Spion Kop which seemed to be where Warren's force was heading. Dundonald attempted to get clarification of his orders and left this account of what happened next:

'He said he wanted the cavalry close to him; I replied I was trying to carry out Sir Redvers Buller's orders in the only way possible. 'I want you close to me,' he repeated, – then followed a shout at the driver of a transport wagon. I repeated to him the role Buller said on 16 January his mounted men had to play. His eyes remained glued on the drift – then another shout at a wagon driver. I also spoke of the importance of the outflanking movement of the Boer right by the cavalry, and asked him for all the mounted men possible and some guns. Sir Charles Warren was obdurate and insisted on keeping the Royal Dragoons, and also requested that Thorneycroft's Mounted Infantry be sent to him.

'I did not understand then that Sir Charles Warren had any idea of abandoning the deployment outwards toward Acton Homes, preparatory to a great wheeling movement to the east, for the

An artist's sketch of the ambush of a Boer Kommando by the Natal Carbineers and Imperial Light near Acton Homes on 18 January 1900.

very place where I found him was at Venter's Spruit, seated on the ground watching the wagons fording the stream in order to proceed in the Acton Homes direction. Any difficulty in fording Venter's Spruit might have been in my opinion, soon overcome, and in the meanwhile artillery, and infantry marching light, could have made a flank march via our position on the Acton Homes/Ladysmith road, and commenced operations on the enemy's right flank.

'When I left Sir Charles Warren I was completely puzzled. One thing was, however, clear, Sir Redvers Buller's plans for a great turning movement were not being rapidly carried out, and every hour's delay meant increased opposition.

'After my conversation with Sir Charles Warren, Major Denny, Transport Officer, Mounted Brigade, told me that when he arrived at Venter's Spruit, Sir Charles said, 'Whose wagons are those?' 'Mounted Brigade, sir.' 'Can't pass,' said Sir Charles. 'If I let them go, Lord Dundonald will try and go on to Ladysmith.' But Major Denny was an old hand; he bided his time and slipped across the stream, or I do not know what we would have done without food for men and horses.'[13]

With his force weakened by the loss of two regiments (Royal Dragoons and Thorneycroft's) Dundonald spent the night at Acton Homes. The next morning (20 January) he received a message in triplicate from Sir Charles Warren directing him to come nearer the main force. He had no choice but to withdraw from a position which he felt sure he could hold against attack.

After the long and arduous march from Frere the infantry had crossed the Tugela at Trichardt's Drift and by 18 January were in position to begin the move to skirt round the hills which formed the Boer's right flank. Instead they were halted for 'some reason unknown' and spent the next few days watching the Boers fortifying their positions on those hills.[14]

Of the engagement at Acton Homes Buller had this to say: 'Dundonald's movement was a decided success, and should have been supported by artillery, while Warren's infantry should have attacked the salient which Dundonald's success had left exposed. On that night I debated with myself whether or not I should relieve Warren of his command.'[15] Tragically he failed to do so.

A Natal family returns to its home after the Boer retreat from southern Natal.

Chapter Twenty

Battle of Spion Kop

*'On 24 January 2000, a group of people were assembled on the top of a hill,
once known as Ntwananyama, and now more generally as Spion Kop.
Someone looked up and then others. High in the atmosphere above
them was a bright circle of light.'*

RECOLLECTION OF MAJOR KEITH ARCHIBALD,
ADJUTANT (RETD), NATAL CARBINEERS

THE order to retire from his position at Acton Homes was the last order that Lord Dundonald was to receive from General Warren. Possibly peeved by what he perceived as insubordination by his cavalry commander, Warren declined to communicate with him for the rest of the campaign.

After instructing the Composite Regiment to make a demonstration in the direction of Ladysmith, Dundonald set off with the remainder of his force towards Trichardt's Drift. As they rode along he pondered the meaning of his orders. Where was 'nearer' to Warren, and precisely what was he to do when he arrived there? A line of low hills kept the movement of his force hidden from the enemy, while the sound of rifle fire and artillery indicated that an attack was in progress. On his left was the massive Thabanyama plateau at the western end of which was a steep-sided buttress jutting out southwards which Dundonald named Bastion Hill. As they passed it he could see infantry attacking up the eastern slopes of Thabanyama. It was apparent to him that this promontory provided a height from which enemy artillery could dominate the infantry attack currently in progress. To prevent them making use of this natural fortress he decided to occupy it immediately.

Two squadrons of the South African Light Horse were given the task of taking the summit of Bastion Hill while the two remaining squadrons of that regiment and three machine guns were to provide covering fire. As the SALH was Winston Churchill's regiment, he was present and attached himself to the squadrons delegated the task of providing cover for the attackers. Winston watched the first two squadrons gallop across an exposed grassy plain to gain cover, dismount and begin their climb up the precipitous slope. On the summit Boers were seen moving about, however because of the hill's convex shape, the attackers would have disappeared from the sight of those on the crest once they reached the base of the hill. It was now time for the other two squadrons to play their part. They had to cross an exposed area of about a thousand yards before reaching the shelter of a wood. Winston wrote:

'We moved off at a walk, spreading into a wide open order, as wise colonial cavalry always do. And it was fortunate that our formation was dispersed, for no sooner had we moved into the open than there was a flash of a gun far away among the hills to the westward…It came swiftly, passed overhead with a sound like rending thin sheets of iron, and burst with a rather dull explosion in the ground a hundred yards behind

the squadrons, throwing up smoke and clods of earth. We broke into a gallop, and moved in a curving course towards the wood.'[1]

They crossed a number of dongas, in one of which the Colonel decided they should leave their horses and continue on foot. They reached the wood safely, but on emerging at its further edge they were subjected to long-range rifle fire. It was decided to take up a position in a donga about 100 yards ahead. Churchill described how the SALH effected this manoeuvre: '*...the troopers immediately began running across in twos and threes. In the irregular corps all appearances are sacrificed to the main object of getting where you want to be without being hurt. No one was hurt.*'[2]

Once they were in position they opened fire on the Boers and in the long-range musketry fight which ensued no casualties were suffered. Churchill commented, '*The colonial troopers, as wary as the Dutch, showed very little to shoot at, so that, though there were plenty of bullets, there was no bloodshed. Regular infantry would probably have lost thirty or forty men.*'[3]

Meanwhile the three machine guns had been brought up and, faced with this additional hazard, the Boers disappeared from view. The two squadrons tasked with taking the summit had climbed up the face of Bastion Hill with astonishing speed and on breasting the crest found that the Boers had retreated to a line about a thousand yards further back on the Thabanyama plateau. With no cover or artillery support it was impossible to advance further. Despite Boer shellfire, which killed one of their officers, Major Childe, the Colonials consolidated their position. The attack had taken the Boers by surprise and the speed of its execution had left them no time in which to reinforce the southern crest. With the promontory secured, Churchill was able to watch the battle taking place at the eastern end of Thabanyama. Things did not seem to be going quite as well there as they had on Bastion Hill. That night the South African Light Horse was replaced by men from Hildyard's Brigade.

On 17 January, General Warren's force had arrived at Trichardt's Drift. It was now time for his troops to practice fighting the Boers. He maintained that no one would play a cricket, football or golf match without practising, so why should the same principle not apply to war? Over the next three days his troops did not see any Boers but were subjected to some long-range rifle fire which Warren believed provided his force with sufficient knowledge of the enemy for the real fighting to begin. It does not seem to have occurred to him that it was the Generals who were in need of knowledge about Boer fighting methods.

On the evening of the 19th Warren held a meeting with his principal officers and told them of his intentions. It was a strange meeting. Lord Dundonald, the one senior officer who knew something of the lie of the land over which they proposed to advance, was not invited. Warren said there were two possible routes along which they might advance, one via Acton Homes and the other along a road which ran between the heights of Thabanyama and Spion Kop, serving the farms Fair View and Rosalie. The route via Acton Homes he rejected as being too long. His officers, who knew nothing of the success of Dundonald's force the previous day, or of the configuration of the land ahead, agreed. The attack would therefore proceed along the Fair View/Rosalie Road. It was a rather rough track so Warren intended to make 'special arrangements' to have it cleared. Once this was done the men would be issued with three or four days rations with which they were to fight their way across the plain behind Spion Kop to Ladysmith.[4] No one asked why, if the men were to carry their rations, it had been necessary to spend days hauling the wagons across the Tugela and Venter's Spruit. Neither did anyone query the fact that no attempt had been made to reconnoitre the land ahead. By 'special arrangements' Warren meant the clearing of the Boers off Thabanyama, and the operation was to begin the next day.

Because he was believed to be a master strategist, General Clery, who was almost crippled by varicose veins, was placed in command of the attack on Thabanyama. A number of spurs jutted out southwards from the plateau. Near its western end was Bastion Hill and at its eastern end, opposite Trichardt's Drift, was a spur crowned by a small eminence which was given the name Three Tree Hill. Gazing up at the hills, Warren and Clery decided their first move should be to capture Three Tree Hill, which would be achieved by an advance up the western slopes of the spur close to the Fair View/Rosalie Road. General Woodgate with his Lancashire regiments was detailed to lead this attack, while General 'No-Bobs' Hart with his Brigade would take up a position to their right and act as a reserve.

At 3 a.m. on 20 January 1900, the Lancastrians moved off. Woodgate, with two of his regiments, led the attack on Three Tree Hill, while his other two assaulted the adjoining spur on their left. They soon discovered that the Boers did not occupy either position, and by 6 a.m. Woodgate and his men were firmly ensconced on Three Tree Hill. Orders were given to entrench, pending the arrival of the artillery. With his varicose veins aching, Clery climbed the Hill with Warren and, joining Woodgate, they took stock of their position. Ahead of them lay about 2000 yards of open ground which rose gently to the northern edge of the plateau where Boer entrenchments could clearly be seen. The terrain offered little or no cover. Louis Botha, in forming his defence line, had followed the same principles as the British at Caesar's Camp with trenches and sangars being constructed at the rear of the position to be defended. However on Caesar's Camp there was some cover for the attacking Boers whereas it was almost non-existent on Thabanyama and the distance to be traversed was 3 or 4 times further.

Nonetheless Clery decided to attack across Thabanyama from the spur immediately to the west of Three Tree Hill. Woodgate's two companies of Lancastrians on that spur were reinforced and were also joined by Hart's Brigade, it having been decided that General Hart should lead this new attack. At 7 a.m. the batteries on Three Tree Hill opened fire on the Boer trenches and at 10 a.m. the bombardment increased in intensity when two further batteries came into action. The Boers, secure behind their thick stone walls and deep trenches, held their fire. At 11 a.m. Hart began his advance, and immediately came under fire. At first some rocky outcrops provided a little cover, but when that petered out, men began to fall. The Boers, invisible to the attackers and spread over a wide front, were firing into the exposed and crowded ranks of the infantry. By 3 p.m. the remnants of Hart's leading battalions had reached the very end of what little cover there was and still had to cross 600 yards of exposed ground before reaching the Boer trenches. General 'No-Bobs' decided it was time to rush the enemy line and gave the order to fix bayonets. No doubt with sword in hand he intended to lead this attack. However before he had time to wreak further damage, General Clery decided to intervene, and stopped the advance. This unplanned and seemingly purposeless attack had cost the British 308 casualties of whom 18 were killed and 209 wounded.

Lt Blake Knox of the Medical Corps, watching the action from a distance, saw specks moving out across the battlefield. His glasses showed these were stretcher-bearers, the majority of whom were civilians of the Natal Volunteer Ambulance Corps. He commented: 'throughout the day these stretcher-bearers… excited the utmost admiration and praise. They went forward, solidly and unflinchingly, to the very firing line, and could be seen bending over the fallen, tending and removing the wounded with devotion so faithful and a coolness so superb, amidst a hail of bullets and shells, that unfortunately many paid dearly for their self-sacrifice. The Boers fired on them without the least hesitation; either because they could not or would not see the Red Cross brassard worn on their left arm.'[5] The range of rifle fire had increased quite considerably since the Crimean War when the practice of medical units wearing the Red Cross was introduced.

It was thought that perhaps the Boers could not see the red cross brassards so the practice was introduced that the four bearers for each stretcher should be accompanied by a fifth man carrying a red cross flag. Sadly the Boers continued to shoot down the stretcher-bearers. A diarist serving with the 2nd West Yorkshire Regiment, having witnessed three out of four stretcher-bearers being deliberately shot down, expressed the opinion that '....*the devil never hated holy water with half the intensity the Boers hated the civilian stretcher bearers.*'[6]

On the following day, Sunday 21 January, Col Kitchener of Hildyard's column was given permission to launch an attack against the western section of Thabanyama near Bastion Hill. With no artillery available, the Boer line was subjected to some hours of continuous rifle and maxim fire, before the advance began. By making use of a donga they were able to make some progress towards the enemy position, but when they made a premature attempt to advance beyond their cover, 4 out of 5 officers were immediately hit. When word came through that two batteries were at last on their way, Kitchener felt confident that he could now over-run the weak defences along this western section of the Boer line, and thereby turn the whole line. An order now came through from Clery requiring that the attack be abandoned immediately. Warren had decided that before proceeding further, he would demoralize the Boers with three or four days of continuous artillery fire.

After the ambush at Acton Homes on 18 January, the Boers increased their mounted patrols in the area and from time to time they came into contact with Volunteer units. Churchill contrasted the Colonials with the Regulars, noting that a dismounted squadron of the South African Light Horse held an advanced *kopje* all day under heavy fire and never lost a man. Two hundred yards back was another *kopje* held by two companies of regular infantry who lost more than 20 men killed or wounded.[7] The incident may be apocryphal and possibly invented to boost Churchill's political career, nonetheless the message is clear and should have been heeded.

The lack of any real progress alarmed Buller who, early on the morning of Monday 22 January, visited Warren to express his dissatisfaction with the course of events. Buller wanted immediate action and suggested a whole-hearted attack on the Boer right, but Warren was not going to change his mind on this issue and insisted that the advance should be along the Fair View/Rosalie road. When told that this route could only be followed after Spion Kop had been taken, Buller incautiously said, 'Of course you must take Spion Kop.'[8] The capture of this hill, which had never before even been considered, was now taken for granted. The discussion over, Buller rode over to Bastion Hill, and that afternoon sent a note to Warren suggesting a night attack on the Boer right flank. Alarmed by Buller's suggestion, Warren called Generals Clery, Hildyard and the newly arrived Talbot Coke to a conference and asked their advice. Clery strongly opposed the idea of moving to Bastion Hill to launch the attack, and pointed out that success could result in their having to take the whole Boer position, which was, of course, what many had thought was the object of the campaign. Clery was supported by Hildyard while Talbot Coke, who had recently broken a leg and was still lame, expressed no opinion at all. By a process of elimination it was thus decided to attack Spion Kop.

It has been said that this hill is 'the highest peak in the Drakensburg Range,' and 'it was from the 460 metre summit of Spion Kop, or "Scouts Hill" that the *Voortrekkers* had first looked down on the rolling plains of Natal.' This quotation from a recent British book on the war, while complying with British folklore, does not state the true position. This hill is not part of the Drakensberg Range and though one of the larger hills in the Tugela Valley, it is not an outstanding feature of the topography of Natal and the view from it is limited to a section of that valley only. The British – then, and now – when wanting information about South Africa turn to the Boers and were comfortable with the name 'Spion Kop'. Before the arrival of the *Voortrekkers* and even before the arrival of the British settlers, these hills over which the British and Boer armies were fighting already had names. As previously mentioned, the Zulus had a knack of bestowing appropriate names. So what were their names for these hills and what did they mean? Thabanyama should be divided into two words. '*Thaba*', is the Sotho word for 'hill' (given the proximity of Lesotho it is not surprising that there was a degree of cross fertilisation of languages) and '*nyama*' which is Zulu for 'black'. Thabanyama therefore means Blackhill. There is nothing exceptional about this. The hill runs from east to west and being in the southern hemisphere, its southern face would almost always be shaded. Around the world there are hundreds of other Black Hills and Mountains so named because of the light and shade in which they are placed.

Thabanyama's eastern neighbour, the hill the British call Spion Kop, had a more interesting name – Ntwananyama. '*Ntwana*' is the Zulu word for child. The translation of the name is 'Child of the Black (Hill)'. In Zulu culture the parents occupied a dominant position in the family and that being the case, it was a major blunder to imagine that by securing a position on the 'child's hill' they would be able to dominate the 'parent'. The Generals, if they had taken advice from the locals, would surely have gathered from these names that to occupy Spion Kop, without first being in control of Thabanyama, was not a viable option. The Colonials tended to accept the indigenous names of physical features of the land, and British Intelligence was advised of the local name for Spion Kop. Because the British found Ntwananyama difficult, they decided to use the Dutch/Afrikaans name. And still they blundered. *Spioen* is the word for 'spy'; the word '*spion*' refers to a cow's udder. Because the name Spion Kop has been in general use for one hundred years, this work will refer to that hill by this name, which in no way derogates from the fact the hill's true name is Ntwananyama.

The next day, 22 January, Warren spent rearranging his command. Clery was placed in command of all troops to the west of Three Tree Hill, while Talbot Coke was given command of the 5th Division and tasked with taking Spion Kop. All that day the artillery continued its bombardment of the Boer trenches. At 4 a.m. on the following day, Warren and Talbot Coke rode out to have a good look at Spion Kop.

Later that morning Warren was again visited by Buller, who, alarmed by the delay, gave him the choice of either proceeding with the attack that night or retiring across the river. He criticised the appointment of Talbot Coke to lead the assault and suggested that General Woodgate should lead it, 'as his two sound legs were better adapted for mountain climbing.' At 55, and not in the best of health, Major-General Woodgate would now lead the column up Spion Kop. No one had any idea what the column was to do once it had taken the summit, Buller's sole comment on this subject being that, 'It has got to stay there.'[9]

Warren and Coke spent the rest of the day making preparations for the coming night attack. Woodgate selected from his own Brigade the Lancashire Fusiliers, six companies of the Royal Lancasters, and two companies of South Lancashires, plus a company of Engineers, and 180 men from Thorneycroft's Mounted Infantry who were to proceed dismounted. A mountain Battery was to accompany them, black water carriers were to take water to the summit, and arrangements were made for a dressing station at the top of Spion Kop and a hospital at its base. A spur or ridge ran down from the summit in a south westerly direction and it was proposed that the column should follow this ridge to the top. Apart from those in command, no one knew of the proposed attack.

When Lieutenant Tom Bridges of the Imperial Light Horse discovered that the British generals had no idea of the configuration of the land beyond that which could be seen from their positions at Mount Alice and Trichardt's Drift, he volunteered to go through the Boer lines to sketch and map the unknown land beyond the visible crests. The offer was accepted. As an assistant, Tom Bridges chose Stanley London, then a trooper in the ILH. This young Natal farmer had enlisted in Pietermaritzburg and was a fluent Zulu linguist familiar with the country they were about to traverse. As dusk was falling on 23 January they made their way through the Boer lines. As they went about their work they heard the sound of a battle raging on Spion Kop. That evening, with their work completed, they were making their way back to the British lines when they saw the enemy trekking away as fast as they could from the battlefield. Delighted, they pressed on, until several hours later, they came upon the British, who were also retreating. The two armies appeared to be running away from each other. On their reaching the British lines, Tom Bridges was promptly arrested and charged with being 'absent without leave.' The Court found him guilty and he was reduced 35 places in seniority on the Royal Artillery list.[10]

A couple of hours after Bridges and London had left to map and sketch the land to the north of Thabanyama and Spion Kop, 1,700 troops assembled near White's Farm in a gully below Three Tree Hill. Here they received orders to climb the southern slope of Spion Kop and eject the Boers from the summit. Most of the remaining eighteen thousand members of Buller's force were required to do little more than watch events unfold. Woodgate decided that Lt Col Alec Thorneycroft and his dismounted men should lead the assault. Standing 6 feet 2 inches, Thorneycroft was a great bull of a man, full of energy and possessed of great courage. He had reconnoitred a possible route up the hill and this, coupled with the fact that he was fit, were the probable reasons for choosing him to lead the column to the summit. However, like the other British officers, he had no idea what they would find there.

Warren's decision to send a mounted regiment up Spion Kop is, even by his standards, truly astonishing. Buller's army was desperately short of mounted men, and they should not have been called on to carry out a task more suited to infantry. It appears that Sir Charles had never understood the purpose and function of mounted troops. Further, Thorneycroft's MI with their obsolete rifles lacking bayonets would be at a considerable disadvantage when engaged in the anticipated close-range combat.

At 11 p.m. Woodgate's assault column set off, and though they originally marched in fours they were soon in single file, with Thorneycroft in front followed first by his own men, and then by the Lancashire contingents. Orders were passed forward that there was to be no shooting, and on contact with the enemy, bayonets only were to be used. Presumably Thorneycroft's colonials, who were leading the climb up the hill, were to use their rifles as clubs! For four hours they climbed. General Woodgate struggled on the climb and had to be helped by his batman up the rockier parts of the ridge. Eventually the track broadened out and those in front were able to spread out and lie down while the Lancastrians came up and joined them. With dawn about to break, a heavy mist descended on the hill, limiting vision to a couple of yards. Cautiously they rose and moved forward when out of the mist came the repeated cry '*Wie is daar?*' (Who is there?), followed by some rifle shots. On hearing the sentry's challenge the colonials had dropped to the ground and the rifle fire flew harmlessly over their heads. Thorneycroft now gave the order to charge, causing the Boer sentries to flee into the mist but not before at least one of their number had been bayoneted by a Lancastrian. After the long arduous climb Woodgate's men were at last on the summit – they had captured Spion Kop. Three cheers rang out to tell Warren of their success.[11] Of course, this also told the Boers where they were and what had happened. Louis Botha was quick to respond.

Stumbling around in the mist, the engineers chose an area where the ground sloped gently away to the north and there taped a position 300 to 400 yards long where trenches should be sited. Shaped like a boomerang, with its apex facing north, the trenches were intended to provide a clear view of any enemy counterattack. The engineers started to dig, but their spades were too fragile for the task, and after they had gone down 18 inches, they struck a solid bed of rock on which even their picks could make little impression. Hurriedly, they attempted to construct stone sangars. Sandbags would have been a big help and were available at White's farm, but they had been overlooked and left behind during the excitement at the start of the ascent.

A partial and temporary break in the mist revealed the fact that the trenches were not in the right place. North of their trench the ground sloped downwards for about 200 yards, but then fell so steeply that the Boers would be able to climb the hill unseen and remain hidden just over the crest. The British tried to bring their line forward to the northern crest, but were driven back to their original position by increasing fire. In the thick mist no one was quite sure of the location of the Boers firing on them, though General Woodgate remained confident that everything was under control. Prevented by the mist from using flags to signal, he sent a staff officer down the hill at 7.15 a.m. with a letter for Warren in which he wrote, '*I pushed on a bit quicker than I perhaps should otherwise have done, lest it (the mist) should lift before we got here. We have entrenched a position, and are, I hope secure; but fog too thick to see, so I retain Thorneycroft's men and Royal Engineers for a bit longer. Thorneycroft's men attacked in fine style.*'

On the way down the officer passed the headquarters of General Talbot Coke whose men were entrenched on the hillside to cover any possible reverse. At the foot of the hill he was able to borrow a horse and rode over to Warren's headquarters at Three Tree Hill, arriving at 9 o'clock. He delivered the letter, and told Warren a small spring had been found on top of the hill, and asked that a naval gun and some sandbags be sent up to Woodgate.[12] Warren signalled to Coke to ask if support was needed on the summit, and was told that because of the mist it had not been possible to establish contact with Woodgate. Nonetheless Warren decided to reinforce the summit with a further infantry battalion. Two companies each of the Imperial Light Infantry and the Middlesex Regiment were ordered to proceed at once to the summit. They were not to follow the westerly route chosen by Thorneycroft the previous evening, but instead to climb up the south-eastern face of Spion Kop. Perhaps because many of their members came from Natal, and despite the facts that they had only a few weeks training and were armed with the obsolete rifles without bayonets, the ILI were to lead the way.

The tops of the hills were still shrouded in mist and it was not until 9.50 a.m. that Warren received a signal from Spion Kop. The message stated, '*Colonel Crofton to GOC Force. Reinforce at once or all lost. General Dead.*'[13]

On the summit the mist suddenly cleared at 8.30 a.m. revealing nearly 1700 men crowded into a confined space on the summit. On the right (or east) were the Lancashire Fusiliers, in the centre at the apex of the main trench were Thorneycroft's MI, to their left six companies of the Royal Lancaster Regiment and on the extreme left two companies of the South Lancashire regiment. They soon realised the grim reality that the Boers were facing them on three sides. From the left (or west) they received long-range rifle fire from Conical Hill (1,000 yards) and Green Hill (1,500 yards). In the centre, the Boers had climbed to the northern crest and from concealed positions opened close-range rifle fire on the British 'trench' while at the same time working their way forward towards the British line. About 400 yards to the east was a small hill called Aloe Knoll, the existence of which had been unknown to the British a few minutes before, but which now had, concealed among its rocks, Boers who were pouring rifle fire into the exposed right of the trench. So unexpected and effective was this fire that it was found afterwards that seventy per cent of Lancashire Fusiliers who were killed had been shot in the right side of the head.

Botha only had five guns and a couple of pom-poms available to him, but they were superbly placed. In the west two guns were brought up from Acton Homes to the northern slopes of Thabanyama and opened fire on Spion Kop; to the north another gun and a pom-pom near Coventry's farm began to shell the summit, while in the east, on Twin Peaks, two guns and a pom-pom joined the bombardment. Boer signallers on Aloe Knoll were able to give precise directions to their guns. The British guns by contrast were completely ineffectual as they had no idea where the enemy were. The Boer guns soon forced the British signallers to seek shelter on the south eastern spur, where the only signal station visible to them was Buller's headquarters on Spearman's Hill, from which signals could be relayed to Warren's headquarters at Three Tree Hill. General Woodgate, uncertain what he should do, had dictated a message asking for reinforcements. The message, the wording of which might have been altered in transmission, stated: '*Am exposed to terrible cross-fire, especially near first dressing station. Can barely hold our own. Water badly needed. Help us. Woodgate.*'

In an attempt to find out where the fire into his right flank originated, General Woodgate broke cover for an instant and fell mortally wounded. His Brigade-Major, a Captain Vertue, made his way over to Colonel Crofton of the Royal Lancaster Regiment to tell him Woodgate was dead, and that as senior Colonel he was now in command. Vertue delivered the message and immediately afterwards he too was shot dead. At Warren's headquarters, Crofton's message was met with some surprise. They clung to the belief that all was well, and felt that Crofton must have lost his head. A message was sent back up the hill saying help was on its way and concluding, '*You must hold on to the last. No surrender.*'

Warren had always wanted General Talbot Coke to lead the assault and now rode over to Coke to tell him to take command on the summit. Taking with him the Dorset Regiment, whose men were carrying sandbags, Coke, aided by a walking stick, set off at 11 o'clock for his new command. Before he left, Warren told him there should be no surrender. Warren did not tell Buller that he had appointed Coke to succeed the mortally wounded Woodgate. Buller had also received the alarming messages from Spion Kop and from his position it was clear a great struggle was taking place on top of the hill. He sent a heliograph to Warren: '*Unless you put some really good hard fighting man in command on the top you will lose the hill. I suggest Thorneycroft.*'

Warren promptly sent a message to Crofton that Thorneycroft was in command on the summit. He did not inform Coke of this change, and what is more, when Coke sent messages back to base which clearly showed he thought he was in command, Warren made no attempt to advise him of the true position. While the Generals were playing this macabre game of musical chairs the desperate fight continued on the hill.

Reading of these events today, it is astonishing that any living creature could have survived the terrible onslaught of bullets and shells on Spion Kop that day. And yet in the shallow trenches, and among the rocks and their dead and wounded comrades, the men fought on. The Boers, who were also suffering casualties, clawed their way over the crest and were beginning to drive back the British line. At about 11 o'clock Thorneycroft led a charge of about 40 of his men and the Lancashire Fusiliers to clear the Boers off the crest, but the enemy fire was so intense they were forced to go to ground. Thorneycroft fell, but in a day when there was little good news, it turned out he had only twisted his ankle. It was at this stage that he received the news that he had been promoted to the local rank of Brigadier-General and was in command on the summit. The bearer of this message was killed while delivering it. For the time being all Thorneycroft's energies were devoted to holding the Boers at bay and he was unable to take any action under the new powers which had been thrust on him.

The three Lancastrian regiments and Thorneycroft's MI had arrived on Spion Kop in cold mist but now they were lying in the scorching sun. The spring, which the staff officer told Warren existed on the hill, turned out to be a pool of fetid water. All who were tempted to drink from it became ill and some died from its effects. Water bottles were soon exhausted and a raging thirst was added to the miseries being suffered. On the right the Lancashire Fusiliers had suffered more than most. Almost all their officers had been killed or seriously wounded and as they lay on the ground too terrified even to lift their heads to shoot, someone raised a white flag. The Boers rose to accept the surrender. When Thorneycroft discovered what was happening, this great giant of a man stood up, and limping over to the Boer leader said, 'I'm commandant here. Take your men back to hell, sir. There's no surrender.'[14] He then turned his back on the Boers and limped back to his trench. Nonplussed, the Boers went back to their positions and when everyone had settled down, the fighting resumed. Before Thorneycroft's intervention the Boers had taken into captivity about 150 of the Fusiliers.

Shortly after this incident the first reinforcements arrived in the shape of the Imperial Light Infantry. Thorneycroft ordered them to take up a position on the right in order to compensate for the losses of the Lancashire Fusiliers. Into this maelstrom of flying metal and death, where survival seemed but a remote possibility, these untried volunteer Colonials with only rudimentary training and obsolete rifles, were now thrust. They did not flinch, but fought their way to the shallow trench and then on into the forward firing line. Casualties were inevitable, but their resolution did not waiver for a second and the right flank held. Next up was the Middlesex Regiment which took up positions among the Light Infantry. One private of this Regular Regiment was about to peer over a rock when he was pulled back by a Natal colonial of the ILI, who told him never to put his head over the top but to fire round the rock.[15] Many of the Middlesex man's comrades were killed that day trying to fire over the sheltering rocks. Fortunately for him, this private listened to the advice and survived.

When the mist cleared from the summit of Spion Kop that morning, on Spearman's Hill General Lyttelton watched the battle unfolding. Early in the morning his troops had made a diversionary demonstration against the Brakfontein Hills. When messages arrived from the summit requesting reinforcements, Lyttelton decided on supplying more direct assistance to those embattled units on Spion Kop. The Scottish Rifles crossed the Tugela, and began making their way up the hill. At the same time a battalion of the 60th Rifles crossed the river to attack Twin Peaks lying to the east of Spion Kop. Through telescopes Boers could be seen on Aloe Knoll and they presented an obvious target for the artillery. Lyttelton ordered his eight 12-pounder naval guns and two howitzers to open fire on them. Two 4.7-inch guns from Mount Alice joined in the bombardment. At last the artillery was making an effective attack on the Boers. Unfortunately they had hardly begun the bombardment when a message came through from Warren: '*We occupy the whole summit and I fear you are shelling us seriously. Can you not turn your guns on the enemy's guns?*'[16]

The assault force only occupied the western half of the summit and Warren had no reason to believe anything to the contrary. Throughout the whole day he was convinced that the entire summit was occupied and nothing would shake this conviction. Lyttelton had no choice but to obey, and ordered the artillery to cease fire. On Mount Alice Buller could see that Warren was mistaken, but instead of correcting the error and ordering the guns to resume firing, he remained silent. Lyttelton's artillery may have stopped firing, but the 60th Rifles continued to make their way towards Twin Peaks.

On Spion Kop the men had no time to contemplate overall strategy. Subjected to continuous and intense fire, their immediate instinct was for the preservation of themselves and those around them. In the process of dodging from one rock to another, regiments had become muddled up. To prevent the Boers concentrating their fire on officers, badges of rank had been removed which added to the confusion. In the centre Thorneycroft and his Colonials were fully occupied trying to stem the tide of Boers trying to get a toehold on the summit. To their left Crofton was engaged in a similar struggle. On the right the remnants of the Fusiliers with the ILI and the Middlesex Regiment were all the while under heavy fire from Aloe Knoll and also had to deal with a Boer attempt to get round the British right flank. It was impossible for the leaders on the summit to communicate meaningfully with each other in such conditions, and the fight began to separate into sections. We have seen that

Coke, who was making his way painfully up Spion Kop, thought he was in command, as did Thorneycroft. The arrival of the Middlesex Regiment under Colonel Hill added another name to the list of those who thought they were in command. Colonel Hill, senior to both Crofton and Thorneycroft, thought that in the absence of Coke he must now be the commander on the summit.

At midday Colonel Nash of the Imperial Light Infantry received an order to reinforce the summit with every available man. By 2 p.m. he was on the summit with the remaining companies of the ILI and the balance of the Middlesex Regiment. As their comrades had done earlier in the day, these further companies of the ILI rushed fearlessly across open ground to the firing trench, where they immediately went into action. Enemy fire continued all afternoon without a break and when darkness fell they were still in position. Other reinforcements arrived which crowded the summit still further, without alleviating its problems. At 4 o'clock Coke finally arrived somewhere near the summit. He did not go into the main firing line, being content with a statement that the men were holding their own. Neither did he attempt to contact Thorneycroft whom he regarded as 'a junior brevet Lieutenant-Colonel in command of a small unit'. Coke was considerably shaken by the scenes he found near the summit. He consulted with his staff and Colonel Hill, and at 6 o'clock he sent a message to Warren asking for orders while at the same time hinting that a withdrawal was necessary. He received no reply.

Thorneycroft meanwhile had seen Colonel Crofton who confirmed his appointment as Brigadier-General. He had no doubt he was in command and sent a despatch to Warren: '*The enemy are now (6.30 p.m.) firing heavily from both flanks (rifle, shell and Nordenfelt), while a heavy rifle-fire is being kept up on the front. It is all I can do to hold my own. If my casualties go on at the present rate I shall barely hold out the night. A large number of stretcher-bearers should be sent up, and also all the water possible. The situation is critical.*'[17]

At about 7 o'clock darkness fell. The firing died down and the exhausted and thirsty men lay in their trench and waited. Nothing happened.

It will be recalled that Lyttelton had sent a battalion of the 60th Rifles to attack Twin Peaks which lay to the east of Spion Kop. The battalion divided in two, each half being assigned one of the hills. In places the hillsides were almost perpendicular and it took them some time to make the ascent. When Lyttelton told Buller what he had done, Buller was furious that the battalion had gone out without support and ordered that they return immediately. The commanders of the two half battalions pretended not to have received this order and continued up the hills. At 4.45 p.m. they reached the summit of the eastern peak and after a bayonet charge the defenders fled. At 5 p.m. the second peak was taken in similar fashion. The Boers had succeeded in getting their guns away just in time. For the remainder of the afternoon, the 60th Rifles were able to take some of the pressure off the troops on Spion Kop. When the orders to withdraw were repeated at 8 o'clock they withdrew in good order. It appears that when the assault on Twin Peaks was made, Buller had already decided Spion Kop was not worth the price which had to be paid, and was anxious to break off the action as soon as possible.

At about 8.00 p.m. Thorneycroft conferred with Crofton and Colonel Cooke of the Scottish Rifles. No orders had been received from Warren and efforts to contact Coke and Col Hill had proved fruitless and both might be dead. Crofton and Cooke felt they should withdraw. Thorneycroft agreed and at 8.15 p.m. the evacuation of Spion Kop began. Not all those on the field that night agreed with that decision, and attempts were made to stop the withdrawal, but Thorneycroft was not one to change his mind and in the end they all came down the hill.

While the British were withdrawing down one side of the hill, the Boers were withdrawing down the other. The Boers had also sustained heavy losses and after the capture of Twin Peaks by Lyttelton they felt any further attempt by them to regain Spion Kop would be doomed to failure.

Thorneycroft has been criticised for withdrawing without orders. He certainly tried to obtain orders and the failure of the lines of communication can hardly be laid at his door. Out of the 180 men in his Regiment which he led up the hill, 39 had been killed and over 60 wounded. Our diarist in the Army Medical Corps, Lt Blake Knox, saw the conditions on top of Spion Kop and left this description of what the troops had endured:

> 'It is doubtful whether, in the records of civilized warfare, troops have ever before been exposed to similar conditions. Without sleep the night before, without water, without cover, with a limited supply of food, under a blazing hot African sun, the British and Colonial infantry, unable to move forward, still held their ground. No other troops in the world would have done so. The sufferings of the wounded under these circumstances were too horrible to be described, many of them being shot over and over again, as they attempted to crawl away, and even the torpor of death did not protect their poor lifeless frames.'[18]

In the dark various groups of men joined the procession going down the hill. At about 9 o'clock Colonel Nash received a message to move off the hill. The Imperial Light Infantry formed up and began the march back. They had gone about 200 yards when an officer appeared and wanted to know where they were going. Nash explained that he had been ordered to take the regiment off the hill. The other officer then said, 'I am Colonel Hill of the Middlesex, not a man or a regiment is to leave the hill.' The Officers of the ILI then told their men that a mistake had been made and the column 'about turned' and marched back to the position they had just vacated. Pickets were put out and they settled down among the dead and wounded.[19]

Unknown to them, the other troops, including Colonel Hill and his regiment, were making their way down the hill. No one told Colonel Nash what was happening so the ILI remained in position. At 2 a.m. someone must have realised they were still on the summit and the following order was issued, 'Officer commanding Imperial Light Infantry. Withdraw at once. 2 a.m. WJ Bonus, Brigade-Major.' A staff-officer took the message up to Nash and some time between 3 a.m. and 4 a.m. the regiment assembled again and finally left the summit. Prior to the ILI leaving, no Boers had ventured back on to Spion Kop.[20] The Imperial Light Infantry casualties were originally stated as being 31 killed (including 2 officers), 113 wounded (including 3 officers), and 19 men missing. Subsequently it was found that the missing men had been either killed or wounded.[21]

Colonial volunteers were the first troops on the summit and the last to leave. The behaviour of Col Hill and some of the other British officers during the engagement betrayed the extraordinary attitude which many of them had towards volunteers, an attitude which they extended to the regular officers serving with the volunteers. Although they were fighting in close proximity to each other against a common enemy, these officers showed little or no interest in cooperating with the volunteer units. Communication might have been difficult during the height of the battle, but there was no excuse for what happened after darkness fell. It must surely have been a simple matter for the officers to have met together to decide on a coherent plan, instead of the absurd process of wrangling over seniority while doing their best to exclude the volunteer regiments from the decision making process.

Lt Blake Knox had had a very busy day. From about midday stretcher parties began to arrive at the bottom of the hill. He set up a dressing station near a stream which was sheltered from Boer fire by a bank and close to the path which ran to and fro from the plateau on top of Spion Kop. A large Red Cross flag was placed above the site. From the time the dressing station was set up, all wounded coming off the hill were checked by Blake Knox. Some had

Spion Kop. British dead lying in a shallow trench on the day after the battle.

had their wounds attended to at the dressing station further up the hill and all that was necessary was to ensure the bandages were still in place and the bleeding had stopped. Comrades had bandaged the wounds of others while some had dressed their own wounds, often using their clothing as bandages. Many had died on the way down and others were appallingly mutilated. He noticed how cheerful the wounded were and the absence of any grumbling. Though it was but little comfort, he was pleased that they had gallons of beef tea and brandy to offer the patients before they moved on to the field hospital. One patient stood out in his memory. An old, grey-bearded Colonial in Thorneycroft's MI staggered in with the help of his rifle. He was a mass of wounds, one ear was pierced by a bullet, his chin, neck and chest also shot through by others, his back and legs torn by shell fire. 'He came in saying that he had just dropped in to have a finger off. It was so shattered he could not pull a trigger, and it got in the way of the next finger which he could use.'[22] The medics of course refused to let him return to the firing line. It was exhausting work constantly bending down and treating the stretcher cases and as darkness came and the night wore on Blake Knox and his staff had to struggle against creeping tiredness, many falling asleep. The light they received from their two lanterns was inadequate and made their work more difficult. In spite of the difficult conditions in which he was working, the doctor noticed how others were coping: '*The kindness of the stretcher-bearers, many of whom belonged to the Natal Volunteer Ambulance Corps, was splendid. Many a poor man shot in the morning in the front-trenches, who could not be reached, and who had lain, as was often the case in the blazing sun all day without food and water, and then in the cold of the night without his coat, and shivering, was rolled up in the stretcher-bearers' coats, and his wound bound with the bearer's only towel or only handkerchief, which was lost to its owner when the case was passed on.*'[23]

A soldier of the Lancaster Regiment also noticed these stretcher-bearers: '…them stretcher-bearers worked 'ard too – they may be civilians, and mayn't look over and above smart, but we of the King's Own won't fergit all as they did for our men in a 'urry….Carrying men down a place as steep as a 'ouse and under 'eavy fire too. Body-snatchers, some calls em, and thinks they's being funny. But I says a man wot does that don't know is friends; and wot's more, 'e ought ter be shot. They chaps of the Volunteer Stretcher Bearers worked like 'eroes, and no mistake abaht it.'[24]

Before dawn of the next day Blake Knox arranged for the remaining patients at his dressing station to be sent on to the field hospital, and gathering together as many stretcher-bearers as he could muster, set off for the summit. On the plateau all was now silent. In the trenches lay intermingled the dead and wounded. They set to immediately, placing the dead on one side and doing what they could for the wounded. They had just started work when suddenly the silence was broken. '*Hands up,*' said a voice in a Dutch accent. They were surrounded by Boers. Being the only unwounded officer present, Blake Knox advanced to parley. He told them he was a doctor. They laughed and pointed at his sleeve. His Red Cross brassard was no longer there. More Boers approached including one wearing a brassard. Blake Knox discovered he had an Edinburgh qualification and was able to convince this man of his bona fides. Louis Botha arrived shortly afterwards, and once further proof was produced, Botha ordered his release on parole while at the same time offering him some coffee. While this was being prepared, Botha complained of British barbarity. In particular he referred to the ill-treatment of the prisoners taken at Acton Homes, that ambulances taken from the Boers were sent to Cape Town and that Boer prisoners were tied to guns and dragged along the road. On being asked if he had proof, Botha answered, 'No, but they were common reports in his lines.' Botha was assured that Blake Knox himself had attended to the Acton Homes prisoners and that they had not been ill-treated. Perhaps the doctor did not know about the unkind things the Zulus had said to the Boers on that occasion. At 10 a.m. the Boers granted permission for the removal of the wounded and within an hour all were on their way to the field hospital, which lay in a bush covered area on the northern bank of the Tugela below Spion Kop.

On the day following the battle, Dundonald went to see Thorneycroft's regiment as it marched away to bivouac: 'It was a sad sight, half of the horses were led horses with empty saddles, their riders lying dead on Spion Kop, or mangled in hospital. As to Colonel Thorneycroft's behaviour on Spion Kop, there was but one opinion, that he was the life and soul of the defence, performing acts of great gallantry.'[25]

On that morning of 25 January, Buller was at last stirred into action: Warren was relieved of the command of all but his 5th Division. Perhaps because the element of surprise had been lost, Buller abandoned the idea of outflanking the Boer right. His troops with their massive baggage train had to return to their positions south of the Tugela. Over the next few days men, animals, guns and wagons were very efficiently moved back across Trichardt's Drift. Perhaps practice does help!

When the last of the wounded left the plateau on 25 January, a burial party of four army chaplains and 25 men of the Natal Volunteer Ambulance Corps climbed up to the summit to bury the dead. Although they took advantage of the excavations of what had once been shallow trenches and now became graves, it took them three days to complete their task because of the hard rocky ground. In this failed attempt to capture Spion Kop the British and Colonials suffered 885 casualties of which 322 were killed and 563 wounded. In addition the Boers took 173 prisoners. The Boer losses were about one quarter of those suffered by the British.

Early in January, MK Gandhi's Indian Ambulance Corps was again mobilised and on 7 January the corps' men travelled by train to Estcourt. Here they received training on lifting

Col Alec W Thorneycroft whose courage and leadership saved the day at Spion Kop.

a wounded man onto a stretcher and carrying the laden stretcher. They also took part in several route marches. On 24 January at 2.00 p.m. when the battle of Spion Kop was at its height, they received orders to be ready to entrain for Frere at 6.00 p.m. that evening. The next day they marched from Frere to Spearman's Farm about 25 miles away. After a night's rest they were told that there were many wounded in a temporary field hospital at the foot of Spion Kop. These men had to be brought back to the field hospital at Spearman's and this would involve crossing a pontoon bridge which might be subjected to Boer fire. All the leaders and men in the unit expressed their willingness to take this risk. By that evening they had brought all the wounded at the dressing station at the foot of Spion Kop across the Tugela to the field hospital at Spearman's. Because the journey over the rough and dusty track in an ambulance or wagon would have caused much suffering to the wounded, it was decided that despite the distance involved, stretcher-bearers should carry the wounded from Spearman's to Frere. Gandhi's men spent approximately three weeks on this humanitarian task,[26] and thereby relieved the wounded of much pain and probably saved some lives.[27]

At Intombi, Kate Driver recovered from her bout of illness, and though far from well, returned to work. The matron had enteric, six out of the ten nurses were ill and the remaining four 'not quite so ill anymore' Many of their Natal orderlies were also ill and though they received some excellent help from refugee civil servants from Dundee, the other orderlies with whom she now had to work were not up to standard. She, like everyone else at Ladysmith, was excited when in the last week of January, Buller's guns could be heard roaring among the hills to the south:

'Oh, the joy of Buller's approach! From my uncle Clem in Ladysmith I received a bright hopeful letter, and – unbelievable luxury – a cake! It was not large, but many of us had bits of it. No one dreamed of asking what it was made of. It soon came to an end. So did that lovely boom of guns. And the reaction was terrible. Our hopes had been so high....

'Into one of my wards they brought a boy of eighteen, wounded in the spine so that he could never get better. His great eyes were seldom off me; and those eyes reminded me of my brother of eighteen who had joined up a few months ago. I kept imagining, as I tried to comfort this boy, that my brother was in a similar state, for a rumour was about that Thorneycroft's men, among whom was my brother, all – except eighty – were killed or wounded. I was in this suspense for days, and then to my great joy, a helio message was handed to me. It was from a friend and it said, 'Your brother and I en route for Ladysmith in the Imperial Light Infantry.'[28]

(Owen Driver had enlisted with Thorneycroft's Mounted Infantry but was later rejected because 'his riding was not up to standard.' He then enlisted with the Imperial Light Infantry.)

On 24 January 2000, the centenary of this famous battle, a number of people gathered at Spion Kop. One group climbed up the hill following the route taken by the British, while others followed the path taken by the Boers. They met at the summit where a memorial service was held. Someone looked up and then others. High in the atmosphere above them was a bright circle of light. When the service was over and they had driven down the hill, the circle of light remained visible over Spion Kop.[29] There is of course a scientific explanation for the phenomenon – something connected to light being reflected off frozen particles of moisture. And the coincidence – well that is another matter altogether.

Chapter Twenty-One

Battle of Vaalkrantz.
Distress of Besieged

• ◆ •

'As Byron wrote,
'Such is the aspect of this shore;
''Tis Greece, but living Greece no more.'
And I am like Marius amidst the ruins of Carthage.'

WILLIAM WATSON CONTEMPLATING THE ARMY'S DESTRUCTION OF THE ORCHARD
AND WOODLAND BIRD SANCTUARY WHICH HE HAD CREATED OVER 36 YEARS

AFTER the frustration of his plan to turn the Boer's right flank, Buller decided to launch his next attack against the Boers a few miles further downstream. The Brakfontein Hills ran east from Spion Kop terminating in a hill known as Vaalkrantz. Below Vaalkrantz a road ran through to Ladysmith and it was along this road that Buller now intended to fight his way through to the beleaguered town. On the other or eastern side of the road, was Green Hill, behind which lay a larger hill called Doorn Kop.

South of the river, Swartz Kop provided Buller with a excellent site for his artillery. From this hill his guns would be able to dominate Vaalkrantz, Green Hill and Doorn Kop. The whole operation was to be conducted by the Regulars and those ideas which had failed so spectacularly at Spion Kop would be tried again in this new attempt to effect a breakthrough to the west, Woodgate's brigade, now under the command of Major-General Wynne, crossed the Tugela via the pontoon near Potgieter's Drift and occupied, without opposition, the Maconochie Hills. It will be recalled that it was from these hills that General Lyttelton had launched his diversionary attack on the enemy's left during the battle for Spion Kop. General Wynne was to make the same diversionary attack as Lyttelton had done during the battle for Spion Kop only on this occasion it was intended to be seen as an assault on the Boer's right. Lyttelton's brigade would now attack the Boer centre and drive them off Vaalkrantz. On the right General 'No Bobs' Hart's infantry would march north along the road in the valley, while yet further to the right General Hildyard would secure Green Hill. The regular Cavalry under General Burn Murdoch would follow Hart through the hills, and then move on towards Ladysmith.

Roughly midway between Wynne's brigade on Maconochie Hills and Vaalkrantz, a new pontoon was constructed across the Tugela. Lyttelton's brigade took up a position near this pontoon while remaining on the south side of the river. The construction of the pontoon, and stationing of Lyttelton's men nearby, was intended to deceive the Boers into thinking the main attack would be against Brakfontein. At 6.00 a.m. on Monday, 5 February, the military square dance began. The guns on Mount Alice blazed away at the assumed position of the Boer trenches on the Brakfontein Hills, while Wynne's infantry began a steady advance towards those hills. Some long-range fire failed to check the advance, though they suffered a few casualties – one man killed and 30 wounded.

At the same time, Buller's guns on Swartz Kop laid down a heavy barrage on what appeared to be Boer fortifications on the top of Vaalkrantz. It later transpired that the fortifications seen on top of the hill were dummies, the Boer riflemen having taken up concealed positions just below the summit. Meanwhile Lyttelton's men abandoned all pretence that they would support the attack on Brakfontein and marched back to Vaalkrantz.

It was now the turn of the sappers to come forward and show their skill and courage by constructing a bridge across the Tugela over which the main attack could be launched. Under persistent sniper fire from those hidden positions on Vaalkrantz, they constructed a 70-yard pontoon bridge in just 50 minutes. With the bridge in place the main attack could now begin.

Once again creeping self-doubt afflicted Buller. Perhaps the attack should not start until the troops involved in the diversionary attack had returned to their strong position on the Maconochie Hills? Wynne was ordered to retire, a manoeuvre he was able to do in parade ground good order, making the guns which supported him available to assist the main attack. It was 2.00 p.m. but still Buller hesitated, and suggested to Lyttelton that it was too late to begin the attack and perhaps the whole enterprise should be called off. Lyttelton, whose men had been standing by for hours while the Boers reinforced their defences, promised Buller that if he left at once they would be on the top of Vaalkrantz by 4 o'clock. Buller reluctantly agreed and Lyttelton immediately set off. Hildyard's and Hart's brigades were about to follow when they were checked by Buller who ordered them to remain south of the river. The result was that the Boers retained control of Green Hill, nobody could travel along the road to Ladysmith, and Lyttlelton's brigade was climbing up a precipitous hill in a situation where success would achieve nothing. With great determination, the infantrymen battled up the eastern end of Vaalkrantz and at precisely 4 o'clock a young officer was seen on the crest waving his helmet before falling mortally wounded. For a few precious moments he had been King of the Castle.

Though ordered to retire, Lyttelton decided to remain on the hill that night. However Boer fire from the north and from Green Hill and Doorn Kop in the east forced them onto the western side of Vaalkrantz where they dug in. That night the Boers re-positioned their guns and brought up reinforcements.

Buller was up early the next morning. The tried and tested tactics of the British Victorian army were not working. The speed with which the Boers re-deployed their forces, their reluctance to show themselves and their deadly long-range rifle fire were factors which had never been encountered before. Buller was in a terrible quandary. Should he continue with the attack or should he order a retirement? The redeployment of the Boer forces had made the whole operation hopeless and yet he was committed to an attack which could cost two to three thousand lives. He again told Lyttelton to retire and then changed his mind and asked him to stay on the hill during the day while he 'watched developments'. In an attempt to obtain an answer to his problem he sent a telegram to Lord Roberts asking what he should do. The answer was not what Buller wanted. Roberts said he must attack even if it meant suffering the anticipated casualties. If the men were told 'the honour of the Empire was in their hands' Roberts had no doubt they would succeed. Buller could not bring himself to sacrifice his men in this manner. During the day the artillery on both sides indulged in an ineffectual duel and that afternoon Buller ordered Hildyard to relieve Lyttelton. Once off the hill, Lyttelton and his Brigade Major went to report to Buller whom they found having dinner. Buller asked how they had fared, to which Lyttelton, who was not in the best of moods, replied, 'Very bad, shot at day and night from nearly all sides.' Buller ordered two large glasses of his excellent champagne for his guests who were at least partially mollified.

The arrival of dawn on the following day brought no solution to Buller's dilemma. The Boers were still in their commanding positions in the hills and he was still uncertain whether to attack or withdraw. He called a meeting of his Generals. They met in Clery's tent that afternoon. Lyttelton, Wynne and Clery were for retirement. Hart was as usual keen to attack. Warren, who had originally opposed the Vaalkrantz operation, was in favour of continuing the action. The reason he gave for this change of mind was that he had 'taken the pulse of 20,000 men'. When asked if he favoured any other line of attack, he said, 'Hlangwane', and other Generals murmured their assent. Buller now had the decision he wanted. It had been democratically decided that they would withdraw so he was now able to give the order to withdraw from Vaalkrantz and return to Chieveley. The whole operation had cost the British 30 men killed and 350 wounded. The Boers lost 30 men killed and about 50 wounded. Though the action would appear to have achieved nothing, this was not so. There had been persistent intelligence that the Boers intended to launch another attack on Ladysmith on 5 February. When Buller's army began its move towards Vaalkrantz, the Boers had been compelled to draw men from Ladysmith to reinforce the long Tugela line. As a result the attack against the town was abandoned and no further attempt was to be made to overcome its enfeebled defences.

Dundonald's Brigade, which now consisted solely of Volunteers, played no part in the action at Vaalkrantz. They were required to cover the rear of the column as they retreated back to Chieveley. Buller sent a heliograph to General White telling of the change in plan and suggested he 'keep it dark'.

In Ladysmith they had heard the sounds of battle from the direction of Vaalkrantz followed by yet another anti-climax as the sound of the guns died down with no sign of the relieving force. On 24 January, the last of the garrison's maize went through the mill. From now on, not only was the supply of food limited, but its quality and nutritional value declined steadily. The serving out of the rations was strictly supervised. Europeans, Blacks and Indians all lined up together and each applicant was required to present himself at a barrier, and after producing his ration permit, pass down a gangway guarded on either side by barbed wire before reaching four depots where each in turn received a little packet of meat, biscuit or bread, sugar, and tea/coffee. The barbed wire entanglements indicated 'that the military authorities looked forward as a possibility to the day when they might have to guard against the rush of starving people inside the town, as well as the rush of an enemy from the outside.'[1] Mule and horsemeat had become the norm. Many of the horses had already died from starvation and those which had to be slaughtered were generally in the process of dying. Leaving aside the repugnance many felt towards the eating of horseflesh, the meat would in any normal circumstances have been considered unfit for consumption. Two classes of horses were given a slightly privileged position when it came to the selection of those to be slaughtered. The artillery horses were needed for the guns and the Volunteers were permitted a little more latitude regarding the feeding of their mounts. This was said to be because the Volunteers rode their own horses and had in many cases strong personal ties with their mounts. The Regular cavalry on the other hand rode army issue horses and would not have had the same rapport with them.

From 1 February the men were given a choice of a full pound of horseflesh as their daily ration or half a pound of tinned beef. Some, finding the thought of eating horse repulsive, initially chose the beef. This option was not only less filling but was also less nutritious and in the end hunger drove many into eating horse. On 4 February Henry Pearse of the *Daily News* had brought home to him how desperate the situation was becoming: 'I found sitting on a doorstep, apparently too weak to move, a young fellow of the Imperial Light Horse – scarcely more than a boy – his stalwart form shrunken by illness. He was toying with a spray of wild jasmine, as if its perfume brought back vague memories of home. I learned that he had been wounded at Elandslaagte and again on Wagon Hill. Then came Intombi and malaria.

He had only been discharged from hospital that morning. His appetite was not quite equal to the horseflesh test, so he had gone without food. I took him to my room and gave him such things as a scanty store could furnish, with the last dram of whisky for a stimulant.'[2]

It should be mentioned that the Black peoples of eastern South Africa have a strong aversion to eating horsemeat, and many groups will not touch pork. Most would have spurned the offer of horsemeat. Horseflesh was also the principal ingredient of an extract which was given the name Chevril, an obvious reference to the unobtainable beef extract, Bovril. Originally intended for use in the hospitals, it proved nutritious and orders were issued that a pint of soup made from Chevril should be issued daily to each man. The bread was made from *mealie* meal, a starch which was intended to hold it together, and some unknown substance. The army biscuits, though rock hard, could be eaten if soaked in water and then lightly toasted. There were no vegetables except for wild spinach which grew in neglected gardens until its value was discovered. Thereafter it became as rare as other vegetables. To combat scurvy all were required to take a daily dose of vinegar. Tea was dished out at the rate of one-sixth of an ounce per family per day. The coffee was a mixture of coffee and *mealie* meal. Unfortunately the two ingredients did not mix, the coffee settling on the bottom of the mug while the *mealie* meal floated on the surface.

Not surprisingly, relations between the residents and the new arrivals became strained. Mrs Haden, who provided accommodation for a number of War Correspondents, was driven to near collapse by certain of her guests, who believing they were entitled to live like kings, demanded that at each meal, varied and appetising dishes should be set before them. (Henry Pearse and Frank Rhodes were not among the correspondents living at the Haden house.) Residents of the town who had a surplus of some foods sold it by auction rather than hand it over to the military, and received a little extra money as a result. This brought forth from Mrs Haden's royalty, howls of righteous indignation about greedy Colonials depriving sick children and dying soldiers of the nourishment they needed to survive.

Old William Watson was one of these profiteers. Just before Christmas he sold a dozen eggs for ten shillings. With this money he was able to buy some sugar to sweeten the food of his three grandchildren. Like the members of many families in Ladysmith he kept a few hens which provided them with eggs and meat. By February, theft had reduced the number of his laying hens to two. William now received a circular requiring that all eggs be sent to the town office so as to ensure they were distributed to the sick in hospital. Failure to comply would result in the fowls being seized. William, who believed that the military had already surreptitiously seized most of his fowls by night, sent his daughter Annie to Col Stoneman with a plea that they be granted permission to keep their eggs for her three young children, and desperately ill and bed-ridden husband. The Colonel declined to exempt them from the order. Interspersed among other matters in his diary, William described some of the meals the family ate. Back in December they had for dinner a plate of boiled dried beans with a little salt and pepper. There was of course no butter or gravy but they did have a glass of clean water. The following day they had a plate of porridge with sugar, a cup of black coffee, and a slice of dry bread – all they could get that day. On Boxing Day they had a piece of dry bread and a cup of black coffee. William wrote, '*We don't go in for luxuries.*'[3] And things were only going to get worse.

Over the years most of the residents had carefully cultivated orchards. That summer soldiers stripped the trees bare of fruit even before it had ripened. William Watson hoped it gave them internal convulsions and judging from the number of dysentery cases, his hope was probably fulfilled. In the last month of the siege fuel supplies ran out and the military commandeered the timber in his precious copse. He had carefully tended those trees for 36 years. The copse had become a bird sanctuary and he believed it was the '…sweetest spot for 50 miles round

Ladysmith.' A Scottish friend told him, 'eh mon, ye'll be peed for ye're trees.' 'Damm the peement', was the response. As the Commissariat cut down the trees they permitted them to fall onto the orchard, thereby completing the destruction of the old man's garden. William recorded his feelings,

> 'It was my hobby and now it is a wreck. As Byron wrote.
> "*Such is the aspect of this shore*
> *'Tis Greece, but living Greece no more.*"
> I am like Marius amidst the ruins of Carthage. And Buller will be made a lord, and
> others will get medals and crosses, stars and garters, for their glorious achievements,
> although they have achieved nothing.'[4]

The dozen eggs William Watson sent to auction were not the only item submitted which could have been used to feed the sick. Some residents sent in their spare tins of jam. One person sent in a jar of stewed peaches. There were also some carrots, marrows and tomatoes which had been produced despite the efforts of thieves to strip the gardens of everything edible. All were sold at a price well above the normal peacetime rate, but when added together they were but a trifle. The real money was raised by other things. La Union cigars, Common cigars, Old Gold cigarettes, plug tobacco, Boer tobacco, Three Castle cigarettes, Brandy, Whisky, Port, and Rum. Were these things really to be given to dying soldiers and sick children crying for food? Or was it that some were peeved at having to pay more for their privileged lifestyle while children and sick soldiers were starving?

Alone among the journalists Donald Macdonald followed up one of these cases of alleged colonial profiteering. One woman was rumoured to have hidden away a large stock of so called luxuries when the army was seizing supplies. When the siege began to bite, she could be seen leaving her home with an old basket over her arm. She would visit families with little children and, unobserved, pass on to mothers little gifts of essential foods for the children.[5]

It was necessary to maintain discipline in the town, and one of the easiest ways for the army to do this was to make an example of one of the locals. HC Foss, a miller, and his manager, William Gradwell, were arrested and charged with speaking disrespectfully about British Generals. Gradwell was seriously ill and a night in the lock-up was more than his constitution could bear and he died. Foss was tried and sentenced to a year in prison, which one hopes was commuted after the Relief. In colonial society people were not accustomed to leaving all decision making and responsibility to 'their betters'. Foss, who after all was a civilian, would have felt he was entitled to hold and express opinions on all matters affecting his life. Given the manner in which the war had been conducted up to that time, it is difficult to imagine anything which Foss could have said which would not have reflected a degree of disrespect for some of the actions of senior British officers. This cultural difference was noticed by Donald Macdonald. Together with other newspaper correspondents, he had been waiting near an artillery battery hoping to get some copy, when a South African galloped in from a forward outpost. Upon being asked what was going on he replied,

'We are retreating'.

'You should know better, sir, than to make such a remark as that within hearing of the soldiers,' flamed out an indignant English correspondent, whose white military moustache and tall soldierly figure always led to his being mistaken for a general at least.

'I know much better than that,' retorted the Afrikander (Colonial), 'but you asked me a question, and I have answered it as far as my ability to gauge the situation goes. If you doubt the truth of what I say, go up to the firing line and have a look for yourself.'[7] The only correspondent fitting the description is Henry Nevinson.

In times of adversity, human nature always tries to find solace in humour. 11 February was the one hundred and first day of the siege. The Boers flashed a curt message to Caesar's Camp, '101 and not out yet.' With their sharp north country wit, the Manchesters replied 'Ladysmith still batting.'[7]

The Manchesters, in their exposed position on Caesar's Camp, had little more than their sense of humour to provide consolation. If it was not raining, the sun beat down on their pale skins adding sunburn to their other miseries. The clothes, which should have protected them from rain and sun, were not only covered in red clay, but were now collapsing into holes and splits. Their boots had worn out, and most had been discarded, forcing the men to walk barefoot among the rocks and thorns; very hard on those who had worn shoes or boots all their lives. Even in the Carbineer's camp, the sorry state of their clothes was causing concern. An order was issued that they should change their shirts. A sergeant saw an officer and explained that the men did not have any other shirts. 'I can't help that', retorted the officer, 'the order is that they change shirts. Let them change with each other.'

It will be recalled that in the early days of the siege Major Rethman of the BMR and Captain Sparks of the NMR persuaded a Dutch farmer to plant mealies, and that the farmer worked day and night planting the crop. With the good rains, a fine crop of maize was produced for which the military were happy to pay a high price. Closer to Bulwana and within the range of Boer riflemen, 10 acres of the mealies remained untouched. One night some volunteers slipped quietly into the mealie field and collected bags of fresh green mealie cobs. The following night a larger group went out and stripped the rest of the mealie cobs from the plants. The next night the volunteers went out yet again, and quietly cut down all the stalks, which they brought back to Ladysmith to provide a wonderful treat for their horses. When morning came, the Boers on Bulwana were astonished to see 10 acres of bare ground where only a few hours before had stood a fine stand of green mealies. In another attempt to supplement the feed for the horses still in work, a corps of Indian grass-cutters was organised. They went out by day and night, cutting the grass which was often found near or beyond the defended perimeter. Though frequently subjected to enemy fire and suffering casualties, they continued to bring in feed for the starving animals.

One piece of colonial initiative nearly had an unfortunate ending. Aleck Macpherson, a skilled hunter, noticed some wild duck on a patch of water midway between the Boer and British lines. He crept out one day and was able to bring back three ducks. The next day he went out to the same spot and no sooner had he fired his first shot, than Mauser bullets came whistling past him, compelling him to run home as fast as he could, with Boer fire chasing him the whole way.

Towards the end of the siege it became apparent that there existed a hidden source for the supply of cigars. The provost-sergeant decided to search the stores. At one Indian store the sergeant ordered his corporal to slit the canvas ceiling and put his head through. Ten bags of rice and two bales of tobacco were found which were promptly commandeered. For those unfortunate Indians existing on their meagre rations of rice it was probably a lifesaver. The same cannot be said for the tobacco, however it was enjoyed by Donald Macdonald and his friends. He recalled: 'It was a happy lot of men who sat round, while Mr. "Arty" Spring, a Natal farmer, and an expert in Boer tobacco, chopped up the leaf – chaffed it would be a better word – damped and sweated it, mixed in a little saltpetre, and then – well, it was good to smoke it, better even to be able to give one's friends a pipe.'[8]

As the siege wore on, more and more use was made of the Tatham's home to treat convalescent patients until it was virtually a fully-fledged hospital staffed by women from the town supervised by one of the Volunteer nurses and doctors from the Natal Volunteer Medical Corps. One of the patients they cared for was the Norwegian Major Bru de Wold, Chief of Staff to the Natal Volunteers. On 18 January the major had been hit by a piece of shrapnel which struck him just under the eye and came out at the back of the neck. Bella Craw, a young woman in Ladysmith, was one of the carers who looked after him from the time he was brought in. Whether it was the Nordic curses of the injured and frustrated major, or a desire to prove to future generations that there is nothing new under the sun, Bella was inspired to kick over the traces. She confessed: 'I did an awful thing today which I am afraid I will many a time regret, and that is to have my arm tattooed, "1899 Ladysmith Pro Patria 1900." No one knows of it yet. I hardly know how to break it to Mama and the boys for I know they will say I am very foolish, as a good many have already told me, Dr.Buntine and Dr. Currie, Bert and others. However, it can't be helped now, it is done.'[9]

Bru de Wold received excellent care and made a remarkable recovery from the wound, which could so easily have been fatal. He was back in harness by the end of the siege.

Major Doveton of the ILH had suffered a serious shoulder wound at Wagon Hill and was taken to Intombi with the other wounded. With his condition deteriorating he was moved to Fanny Tatham's nursing home on 30 January. By 7 February doctors felt it was impossible to save his arm and amputation was necessary. A heliograph was sent to Mrs. Doveton in Pietermaritzburg telling her about the proposed amputation. Someone, who was said to be anonymous, arranged that she should pass through the Boer lines and come into Ladysmith to nurse her husband. On 12 February Karri Davies accompanied by Dr Rogers went out to the Boer lines in an ambulance and collected her. That same day the arm was amputated. Karri rigged up a tent for Mrs Doveton next to her husband's ward so that she could be as close to him as possible. The amputation proved to be more than Doveton could bear and on the 13th his condition deteriorated. Bella Craw wrote, 'Major Doveton very bad tonight. They are afraid he will not live through the night. Poor Mrs. Doveton came in just now to change and put her dressing gown on. She walks and looks in a dream. We are all feeling so miserable and sorry for her, and so helpless and unable to comfort her.'

The next day Bella wrote, 'Poor Major Doveton passed a dreadful night, but passed quietly away at half past ten this morning. The funeral was large and left here at 7.30 tonight.'[10] Karri was able to find a trap and horse to drive Mrs. Doveton to the funeral. The Generals and all the important people attended. Doveton had been a mine manager in Johannesburg before the war and was loved by all who knew him. Perhaps because Doveton was a professional engineer, Henry Nevinson had been prepared to converse with him, and even he could think no ill of the deceased. After the funeral Mrs. Doveton spent the night with the Lines family, Mr. Lines being the Secretary and Treasurer of the Town Guard. The next day Karri took her back to the Boer lines for her sad journey to Pietermaritzburg.

The Boers were much praised for allowing Mrs. Doveton to visit her dying husband, which is of course as it should be. It would however have been pleasant to hear one word of appreciation from the Boer side, of the kindness shown by Sir George White in permitting Mrs. Kock to nurse her dying husband after the battle of Elandslaagte.

It was not only the soldiers who were sick and dying in Ladysmith. The Coventry family, whose farm lay on the northern slopes of Spion Kop, had moved into Ladysmith when the Boers invaded Natal. Mrs. Coventry was heavily pregnant and the baby was born in a cellar during one of the first bombardments. Never quite able to overcome its poor start in life, the infant died on 21 February. She was one of many babies to die during the siege. That disease respected neither age nor gender is illustrated by the deaths of two young women. Mary Carbutt on 5 January and her sister, Evelyn, on 17 February. On 27 January Commandant Willie Royston, who had seemed to have an iron constitution, began to show the first signs of illness.

Despite the efforts of Colonel Stoneman, conditions at Intombi Hospital continued to deteriorate. The death rate was creeping up to 20 a day and new patients to the hospital would pass lines of bodies waiting to be buried, while gravediggers struggled to keep up with the demand. Doctors, nurses and orderlies were all being struck down with one or other of the infectious diseases and the rise in patient numbers far outstripped the capacity to expand the hospital's facilities. The supply of beds, which consisted of three planks suspended a few inches above the ground, had again failed to meet demand and many patients had to lie on cut grass put over the bare earth. Many of the orderlies were now drawn from men whom the Boers had sent into Ladysmith during the early days of the siege. On the outbreak of hostilities the Transvaal authorities emptied their prisons by sending the inmates to Natal as refugees. In this manner they were able to get rid of their undesirables, and to pass on to the besieged garrison the duty of feeding them. We have seen it took some time for the British to counter this ploy.

Out in the rural areas of Natal, the people were aware of what was happening in Ladysmith. Without being asked, and acting spontaneously, various communities sent in donations to the Department of Native Affairs early in 1900. By modern standards many of the donations might appear to be small. Often these people had yet to embrace a western style money economy, and the money donated probably represented all they had. Like the donation of their beer ration by the Gordon Highlanders to the Imperial Light Horse, the monetary value of the gifts was as nothing when compared with the concern, kindness and support displayed.

These are the donations which were made and they are listed under the following columns, Donor, Amount, and for whom the gift was intended. Values are given in the old money of pounds, shillings and pence.

Donor	Amount	For whom intended
Ndaleni Community per P.M. Majosi	£3. 0. 0	Sick and Wounded
Ndwedwe Chiefs Mbozane, Goba, Sotobe, Cshani, Mbango, Rodoba, Mdiya, and Deliweyo		
	£36. 13. 0	Volunteers in Ladysmith
Chief Ndungwe, Ifafa	£7. 0. 0	Soldiers fighting in Natal
Pinetown Mission	£8. 0. 0	Sick and wounded
Chief Henuhemu	£10. 0. 0	Soldiers who defended Ladysmith
Chief Mzingelwa	£5. 0. 0	Any relief made necessary by present war.
Christian communities at Inanda, Cato Ridge, Umzumbe, Verulam, and Mapumulo.		
	£15. 0. 0	Relief of sufferers
Church of Scotland Mission PMB.	£9.05.06	Sick and Wounded
Chief Laduma	£8. 0. 0	Sick and wounded
Chief Ncitshuise, Ifafa	£7.15. 3	For Artillery who fought at Colenso. Token of appreciation of bravery attempting to retake lost guns.
Mpolweni Mission	£3.17. 4	Sick and wounded
J.H. Kumalo, Lions River	£3.18. 0	Sick and Wounded
Chief Gayede	£6. 0. 0	Sick and Wounded
Chief Mdungazwe ka Makongolo	£8. 9.10	Sick and wounded
Christian Natives at New Hanover	£3. 5. 0	Any Native requiring relief
Chief Xegwana, Estcourt	£1. 10. 0	Sick and Wounded
Amangwane tribe, Estcourt	£140. 0. 0	Sick and Wounded Soldiers

In addition to the gift of £140, Chief Ncwadi of the Amangwane, accompanied by his brother Nyanda and other senior members of his people whose lands lay near the source of the Tugela and the Free State border, called on Samuel Samuelson of the Native Affairs Department in Pietermaritzburg, and handed to him a bag of money which had been collected by his people. For a time during the incursion of the Boers towards southern Natal, they had been cut off from the rest of the Colony. When handing over the gift the Chief said:

> 'In this bag you will find a small token of the gratitude of myself and my people for the protection afforded us by the Government and the Army of Her Majesty the Queen. We were told to stay at home and we have done so. The Queen's soldiers have fought, have been wounded and have died for us whilst we remained unscathed in our homes. Many of them are wounded and sick. This small gift from me and my people may furnish some needful comforts for them and for this purpose I have brought it. We have just paid our hut tax and dog tax, we have had anxiety and much expense to provide for ourselves and families, my people have not been able to work and earn money as they might have done. If it were not for these things your table would be red with Amangwane money for the use of the sick and wounded soldiers of Her Majesty the Queen.'

The contents of the bag were emptied onto the table, and found to contain £219.6.00.[11] (the total sum given by the Amangwane people was therefore £359.06.00). This was not a token donation and says a great deal about the feelings of the Black people and yet British and Irish writers ignore it. Why? Fear of offending the Boers, or perhaps upsetting some carefully cultivated illusions about Natal?

Many educated Black people (the Amakolwa), who had abandoned their traditional way of life, in May 1900 formed an association to represent their interests. Mr George Hulett, a successful Natal sugar farmer and Member of the Legislative Assembly, played a leading part in the formation of this association which was called the Natal Native Congress and was subsequently to develop into the African National Congress. Chief Isaac Mkize was elected President, Mr. HHC Matiwane Secretary, and Chief Majozi from Ndaleni, Treasurer. They hoped that when the war was over any peace terms would ensure 1) They would not be denied education; 2) A degree of direct representation in the Legislature; 3) They would have freedom to trade; 4) They would be entitled to acquire land.

In Natal they already enjoyed the rights referred to in 1, 3 and 4. The representation issue was more complex. All prospective voters in Natal had to show they had abandoned any previous domicile and now lived according to the laws of the Colony. For a member of the Amakolwa to be registered as a voter he had to show that he was no longer subject to the jurisdiction of a Zulu chief and was living according to the laws of Natal. Because they would constitute a minority of the electorate, few bothered to register. Their attitude on this issue was replicated by many white voters in Natal throughout the twentieth century. Being a small minority and knowing the Zulu leaders would be reluctant to surrender their traditional powers, the Amakolwa did not seek universal franchise. Instead they decided to act as a pressure group like the Farmer's Association.

Their resolutions are interesting. They expressed their gratitude to Joseph Chamberlain for the firm stand he took against the Transvaal; they expressed their admiration for the services rendered by Sir Alfred Milner; and they expressed their thanks to the Natal Government for sending troops to repel the invaders and thereby frustrate the Boers' 'design to conquer the whole of Natal'. Also passed was a resolution proposed by Chief Goba, 'That this meeting places on record its sincere sympathy with the relatives and friends of those who have fallen in the cause of freedom during the present war.'[12]

One delegate expressed concern that the Natal Government tended to place the interests of Blacks living according to traditional Zulu custom above the interests of the educated Amakolwa. And yet, two of the most senior positions in the Congress were filled by Chiefs who would in all probability have opposed any reduction in their power. To add a further complication, Chief Majozi of Ndaleni had been elected to the chieftainship by his people, possibly the first democratically elected Black leader in sub Saharan Africa.[13]

The Natal Government noted the formation of the Native Congress. The Secretary of Native Affairs, Mr Moor, believed that James Hulett was the driving force behind the formation of the Congress and it was uncertain whether it would garner much support among the Blacks without the support of the Chiefs. However in his report to the Governor he stated, 'that they cannot permanently be kept in a state of tutelage.'[14]

CHAPTER TWENTY-TWO

Boer Line breached.
Siege Raised

•—◆—•

*'Never this side of heaven can I hope to see such a scene of happiness,
and it was all impromptu.'*

A NATAL CARBINEER DESCRIBING THE RELIEF OF LADYSMITH

AFTER the British withdrew from Vaalkrantz, Buller sent his Regular Cavalry west to Springfield. This was to protect his left, and in the hope that the Boers would believe that the next attack could be expected somewhere near Spion Kop. The Boers were not fooled by this manoeuvre and hastened to reinforce their defensive line along the hills lying to the east of Colenso.

After passing Colenso, the Tugela River sweeps round to the left and flows in a northerly direction for about 6 miles before swinging to the right to resume its flow eastwards. Like other stretches of the upper Tugela, a series of hills lies to the north of this stretch of the river. The railway crosses the river near Colenso, and then travels north along its bank for about 6 miles before turning away from the river and passing through a gap in the hills to make its way across the plain which leads to Ladysmith. It was along this route that Buller intended to relieve the siege.

The hills to the north of the river had been cleverly fortified by the Boers who took care to ensure that their trenches and other fortifications were virtually invisible to any would-be attackers. This however was only their second line of defence. To the south of the river and east of Colenso lies Hlangwane, the hill whose strategic importance had been so sadly neglected by the British commanders during the battle on 15 December. Moving east from Hlangwane is Green Hill (the third hill so named by the British army) and then Cingolo. North of Cingolo is a long section of high ground called Monte Cristo, which runs north for about 4 miles to the Tugela. It is near the northern tip of Monte Cristo that the river resumes its easterly course and the railway leaves the river to pass between the hills on its way to Ladysmith. Because artillery on Hlangwane, Green Hill, Cingolo and Monte Cristo would provide considerable assistance to any attempt to establish a bridgehead across the river anywhere from Colenso to Monte Cristo, these hills were occupied in some force by the Boers. To supply these *Kommandos* a pontoon bridge was constructed a couple of miles downstream of Colenso. The Boers considered the land to the east of Monte Cristo and Cingolo too broken for the British to be able to mount an attack via that route.

On 11 February, Lord Dundonald received orders to occupy Hussar Hill, which lies about 3 miles south of Hlangwane. It will be recalled that on 20 December 1899, the Boers had ambushed a detachment of Hussars on this hill, and that when they returned for a second helping a few days later, they themselves were ambushed by the Carbineers. From that time this high ground was known as Hussar Hill. Early on the morning of 12 February, the Volunteers went out with Dundonald to the hill, which they found was occupied by the Boers. After a brief skirmish the Boers retired, enabling General Buller to make a detailed telescopic reconnaissance of the Boer positions he proposed to attack. The reconnaissance completed, the Volunteers were ordered to retire. When this began, the Boers attempted to attack the retreating colonials. However the Volunteers withdrew in alternate sections, one section maintaining a hot fire on the Boers from a concealed position, while the other withdrew, and then the roles would be reversed. In this way the manoeuvre was completed without any casualties. Following the withdrawal, the Boers resumed occupation of Hussar Hill. The next day Buller issued the following order: 'It is intended to seize Hussar Hill to-morrow, and the spurs to the east of it north of Moord Kraal, and to occupy this position with artillery. Lord Dundonald's Brigade will cover the movement. It will strike its camp and bivouac on a site which will be pointed out to it.'[1]

So on Wednesday, 14 February, the Volunteers again set out to take Hussar Hill and yet again the Boers defended it. However the South African Light Horse, by advancing quickly, had secured a commanding ridge, and bringing up four Colt machine guns, compelled the enemy to retire, leaving two wounded. The infantry occupied the hill and the Naval and other guns were soon on the summit.

While the SALH were engaged at Hussar Hill, McKenzie, who was scouting on the right, took the Carbineers northwards into the inhospitable terrain east of Cingolo and Monte Cristo. They had to traverse boulder-strewn land covered with thick bush and in these dangerous places they really were bearding the lion in his den. They found and climbed a steep path to the summit of Monte Cristo which was covered in hoof marks indicating it was being used by the Boers. On the summit they received a heliograph message to return to base, which was achieved without incident.[2] The information gathered in the course of this foray was to prove of inestimable advantage in the coming advance.

General Sir Charles Warren had been out of the limelight for some time when, on 15 February, he joined his infantry on top of Hussar Hill. Enemy shell fire appeared to be causing the men to be a little edgy, so Sir Charles decided something had to be done to give them confidence. He ordered his bath to be brought up to the top of the hill and that it be filled with hot water, a task that was achieved despite the continuing shellfire. Warren stripped off and climbed into the bath and began soaping himself. The troops 'at a respectful distance' watched in silence. As luck would have it, at this moment General Buller and his Staff rode up with the Division's orders for the following day. Warren got out of the bath, wrapped himself in a towel and, still dripping wet, was given his instructions. Buller and his Staff then rode off. Of this meeting Warren said, 'I felt like an eastern potentate receiving homage.' What Buller thought is not recorded. Warren thought the escapade had been a great success: 'I felt that I had done what I could for the day to amuse the men.'[3] When they were subjected to shellfire on the following day, Warren commented, 'the men must get used to it. There should be no grousing now that I have had my bath in the midst of it, with the Commander-in-Chief's Staff all closing round.'[4]

On 15 February, there was a general advance towards Cingolo and Monte Cristo supported by the artillery on Hussar Hill. By nightfall General Lyttelton's Division was about 2 miles from Cingolo with Dundonald's Volunteers covering the left and right flanks. In the course of the advance they passed a farm looted by the Boers. Lt Blake Knox noted, 'The place was a perfect wreck, all the furniture broken, and the floor littered with torn books, letters and photographs belonging to some recent loyal Natalian; amongst the debris lay the family Bible, torn and desecrated.'[5]

Far away to the west in the northern Cape, the siege of Kimberley was raised.

The next day the heat was intense and Buller decided his troops could not be expected to advance against the enemy in such conditions. Captain William Birdwood (later Sir William Birdwood of ANZAC fame) who had been made Chief Staff Officer to Lord Dundonald, approached McKenzie and asked if he would put in writing his ideas on the best way to relieve Ladysmith. If McKenzie would do this Birdwood would see to it that the document was placed before General Buller. Unfortunately McKenzie had to go out on patrol and was unable to write the memorandum there and then, but Birdwood was fully aware of McKenzie's opinions,[6] as no doubt was Dundonald. On the 16th Dundonald received his orders for the following day:

'You will divide your command, half will be on the right and, advancing in the rear of the Infantry, will endeavour, as soon as opportunity offers, to gain ground to the right and outflank any detachment of the enemy that may appear on the Nek. The other half, less one strong troop, will operate on our left up the Gomba Valley (between Green Hill and Cingolo), taking such opportunities as may offer.'[7]

Dundonald recorded his response to these orders:

'During the night of 16-17 February, I heard that the enemy was still in occupation of Cingolo; I made up my mind to use some discretion with regard to the orders I had received, and therefore sent one regiment to the left of the infantry, keeping two regiments (some 650 men) for work on the right flank. I also used further discretion with regard to these orders, and instead of advancing behind the right of the infantry, waiting for an opportunity to occur, in the early hours of the morning I took the two regiments which were with me, by a circuitous route to the southern end of Cingolo. My idea was to assist the operations in the most effective manner possible, viz., by ascending the hill, getting behind the enemy, and clearing him off it.'[8]

In embarking on this enterprise, Dundonald was disobeying the order to remain behind the infantry. Failure would not only have been calamitous for his own career but might also have severely prejudiced the British advance. The regiments Dundonald took with him were the Composite Regiment (comprising the Carbineers and the I.L.H.) and the South African Light Horse. Winston Churchill was there and wrote this description of the sortie:

'By daybreak all were moving, and as the Irregular Cavalry forded the Blue Krantz stream on their enveloping march, we heard the boom of the first gun. The usual leisurely bombardment had begun, and I counted only thirty shells in the first ten minutes, which was not very hard work for the gunners considering nearly seventy guns were in action. But the artillery never hurry themselves, and indeed I do not remember to have heard in this war a really good cannonade, such as we had at Omdurman, except for a few minutes at Vaal Krantz.

'The Cavalry marched ten miles eastward through most broken and difficult country, all rock, high grass, and dense thickets, which made it imperative to move in single file, and the sound of the general action grew fainter and fainter. Gradually we began to turn again towards it. The slope of the ground rose against us. The scrub became more dense. To ride further was impossible. We dismounted and led our horses, who scrambled and blundered painfully among the trees and boulders. So scattered was our formation that I did not care to imagine what would have happened had the enemy put in an appearance. But our safety lay in these same natural difficulties. The Boers doubtless reflected, "No one will ever try to go through such ground as that" – besides which war cannot be made without running risks. The soldier must chance his life.

'The general must not be afraid to brave disaster. But how tolerant the arm-chair critics should be of men who try daring coups and fail! You must put your head in the lion's mouth if the performance is to be a success…

'At length we reached the foot of the hill and halted to reconnoitre the slopes as far as was possible. After half an hour, since nothing could be seen, the advance was resumed up the side of a precipice and through a jungle so thick we had to cut our road. It was eleven o'clock before we reached the summit of the ridge and emerged on a more or less open plateau, diversified with patches of wood and heaps of great boulders. Two squadrons had re-formed on the top and deployed to cover the others. The troopers of the remaining seven squadrons were making their way up four to the minute. Suddenly there was a rifle shot.'[9]

The Boers had discovered that they were not the only ones on the summit. They thought the British would launch their attack up the western slope of Cingolo, and as expected Lyttelton's 2nd Division did just that. All morning the Boers behind their fortifications fought back repeated attacks by Lyttelton's infantry. But now with their fortifications providing no cover from the attack from the east, and not relishing the prospect of being sandwiched between the two forces, the Boers abandoned their positions and fled towards Monte Cristo. A running fight ensued in which a Carbineer, Trooper Goldstein, was killed. The terrain with its cover of bushes, boulders, and high grass made pursuit difficult. Added to this the Volunteers were obliged to work on the eastern side of the crest to avoid being shot by Lyttelton's infantry advancing from the west. With the Composite Regiment near the crest, and the South African Light Horse on their right to prevent any attempt at a flanking movement, the Boers were steadily driven back towards Monte Cristo. When Buller called a halt to the action that evening, the Boers had been cleared off Cingolo, and though they still occupied Monte Cristo and part of the Nek between it and Cingolo, it had been a good day for his army. That night the gunners of the 64th Battery, assisted by the Devons, dragged their guns and ammunition onto the newly captured high ground and worked through the night placing the guns in suitable positions and erecting cover.[10] Before the dawn of the new day they were ready for action, and for once it was the Boers who were not quite sure what was going on.

Losses on both sides had been few. The Carbineers had lost one man killed, several Boers had been killed and a number of their horses captured. But for the danger posed by the friendly fire of Lyttelton's infantry, the Volunteers would, in all probability, have killed or captured all the Boers on Cingolo. After the Volunteers had reached the summit Dundonald attempted to advise Lyttelton that his men were now on it, but it was some time before they could get the heliograph to work. Of course, he could have told Lyttelton of his plans the previous evening and would, by so doing, have prevented the friendly fire hampering the Volunteers.[11] But Dundonald would have remembered what had happened at Acton Homes and his decision to keep the plan to himself seems to have been the correct one.

From his account of the sortie, Churchill betrays not a little anxiety, and well might he have been anxious. It is very easy to get lost in the dense bush found in the valleys of many Natal rivers. Constantly one is confronted by a dense wall of bush. On peering through the vegetation one might see what appears to be open grassland ahead, which on getting through the undergrowth turns out to be nothing more than a patch of grass surrounded by yet more dense bush. In the unfenced land of the period this process could have gone on for days. What Churchill did not know was that McKenzie had visited the area on 14 February, and with his customary care, had scouted the route which Dundonald's men were to follow. In disregarding his orders and leading his men away from the battlefield for 10 miles over difficult terrain, Dundonald displayed the extraordinary confidence he had in McKenzie. The venture could only have originated from McKenzie, and in its execution, he and the Carbineers had demonstrated once again how the invading Boers could be defeated without incurring heavy losses.

At dawn on Sunday, 18 February, the attack on the Boer positions resumed. With Dundonald's Volunteers on the right and Hildyard's infantry on the left, Dundonald's men steadily pushed the Boers towards the northern extremity of Monte Cristo and the Tugela. The Boers on Green Hill, realising their position was enfiladed by guns on Hussar Hill and Cingolo, offered only token resistance to the infantry before fleeing across the Tugela. By the evening of the 18th, only Hlangwane of the Boer's fortress hills across the Tugela was still in their hands. Buller was able to report that from the time he commenced the action on the 15th to the evening of the 18th, he had lost one officer and 13 men killed, 155 wounded and 2 missing.[12]

The next day the British infantry advanced towards Hlangwane from both the south-west and the north-east. The sight of this formidable host bearing down on them was too much for the defenders, who chose to hasten back across the Tugela while the opportunity was available to them. At the same time the Boers evacuated Colenso leaving the British in exclusive control of all the land south of the Tugela. It had all seemed so easy – so easy in fact that Buller was convinced that only a rearguard remained between him and Ladysmith. Perhaps the Boers had realised their folly in invading Natal and had begun their long retreat back to their Republics, in which case there would be no point in risking further lives! The fleeing Boers were permitted to cross the river almost unscathed. In the lull which followed the engagement south of the river, Lt Dr Blake Knox, went for a stroll round Colenso:

> 'The village had been shamefully looted and polluted. What had once been a peaceful and picturesque little hamlet was now a mass of foetid ruins. In anticipation of our occupation, the enemy had dragged their dead horses into the interior of the houses, and they lay in rooms among broken furniture and debris. The corrugated zinc roofs had been torn from the buildings, all available woodwork had been removed for fuel, windows and doors were wantonly smashed.'[13]

Buller spent the following days preparing for the final advance to Ladysmith. Though he had the opportunity to construct bridges at various places on the Tugela, he decided that one bridge would suffice and that it should be constructed about a mile west of Hlangwane. This pontoon bridge led into a valley surrounded at a distance by steep hills, a natural amphitheatre. The Boers could not have picked a better site for their opponents to begin their campaign north of the Tugela. Unobserved, they could sit in their hidden trenches and watch every move by the British. By 21 February, eleven battalions and 40 guns had crossed the river and moved onto this natural stage. The following day four more battalions joined them. Some British officers were appalled at Buller's choice of the site for the crossing, and even more appalled by the massing of troops on a crowded plain where they could be subjected to enemy fire from three sides. Warren, whose troops had taken no part in the fighting over the past few days, thought Buller's idea a 'masterly tactical stroke'. Another who was pleased by the turn of events was General 'No-Bobs' Hart. He and his Irish regiments had been cooling their heels at Chieveley, but now they were back at Colenso, and the fearless old General would soon have an opportunity to show the Boers a thing or two. So confident was Buller of the weakness of the force confronting him, that he moved his headquarters across the river.

The Volunteers spent several days on Monte Cristo guarding the right flank while the Boers were being shepherded across the river. Then they too were ordered to cross on the pontoon bridge and bivouac on the northern bank of the Tugela. Dundonald had always impressed on McKenzie that he should tell him when he thought a forward move should not be made. On this occasion McKenzie told Dundonald that he thought the move was premature, as they would be hemmed in behind the infantry. Dundonald understood the validity of McKenzie's argument but felt that they had no choice but to obey orders.[14] So they crossed on the pontoon, and finding the best cover they could, spent three uncomfortable days being shelled and shot at, before being ordered back to their old position on Monte Cristo.

As the Boers showed no signs of going away, Buller decided it was time to implement his plan to advance along the railway line to Ladysmith. Looking north along the intended route was the small stream, Onderbroek Spruit, beyond which were two hills lying to the left of the railway line. General Wynne, with the Lancashire Regiments who had suffered so terribly at Spion Kop, was ordered to take these hills. On the 22nd they moved against the first hill and despite being subjected to heavy rifle fire were able to take it. Buller's headquarters was badly damaged by shellfire, but Buller as usual impressed all by his quiet courage. On the 21st and 22nd his force suffered over 500 casualties.

It had been a busy time for Lt Blake Knox. On the 22nd his dressing station came under heavy fire and several Natal stretcher bearers were wounded. He decided to move the station to a safer place under a railway culvert. To convert the culvert into a dressing station required a little labour:

> 'I accordingly got a number of Natal stretcher bearers to accompany me, and with borrowed shovels and picks, constructed a fairly smooth path from the railway embankment down to the culvert and removed the barbed wire fences on both sides of the line. Although all the time under brisk rifle fire the men set to their task cheerfully and energetically. Never can I look back on these men, who went by the name of 'body snatchers' without thinking how much we all owe to them.'[15]

The following morning, Gen Wynne attacked the second hill in the line and was successful in driving the Boers off it. The capture of these two hills turned out to be a Pyrrhic victory as they were enfiladed on three sides by the Boers and taking them provided little advantage.

At midday General Hart was ordered to take the next hill in the range, Hart's Hill (which is sometimes called Inniskilling Hill). In addition to the Irish regiments, Hart had with him the Colonials of the Imperial Light Infantry. At 12.30 p.m. they moved off along the railway line and for part of the way they were sheltered from Boer fire by the river bank and the hills recently taken by Wynne, but once they left this cover they came under fire from the Boers. Two particularly dangerous areas were the railway bridges over Onderbroek Spruit and another stream, Langerwachte Spruit, which lay beyond Wynne's Hill. The Royal Engineers had very courageously begun to place sandbags on the ironwork along the sides of the bridges. Until this was done the men were obliged to run the gauntlet one at a time. Sixty men, including several stretcher-bearers, were to fall crossing these bridges. It was not only soldiers who had to face this peril. A Black driver was knocked off an ammunition wagon and with his head covered in blood was taken to a dressing station grinning, laughing, chattering and abusing Dutchmen. A Mauser bullet was extracted from a wound just above one of his ears. The wound was dressed and bandaged, and before anyone could stop him he had made off back to his wagon.[16]

It was 5 o'clock before the infantry reached the base of Hart's Hill. During the day the artillery had subjected the summit to a tremendous cannonade without eliciting any response from the Boers, leaving their opponents uncertain where they were, or how strongly the hill was defended. Neither of these difficulties, nor the lateness of the hour, intimidated General 'No-Bobs' Hart. He ordered the attack to proceed at once. With the Inniskillings in the lead, his men clambered up the hill into a wall of fire. With men falling regularly they reached the trenches on the crest about 300 feet above the Tugela only to find it was a false crest and the Boers had retreated to other trenches higher up. Fully exposed to enemy fire, the infantry attempted to continue the advance, but before they reached the enemy, the attack had petered out. There were no longer enough men left standing to carry it through. Sensing that they were gaining the ascendancy, the Boer fire increased and from the rapidity of their fire many thought they must have loaders with spare rifles to hand up from the trenches. In the gathering darkness the survivors were driven back down the hill. In the assault 450 men had been killed or wounded, half of the casualties coming from the Inniskilling Fusiliers.

Apart from the Inniskillings, no other regiment suffered greater losses that day than the Imperial Light Infantry. With its obsolete rifles and without the protection of bayonets the regiment had lost 19 men killed and 105 wounded. A further 8 were missing, presumed killed. Major Hay, its commanding officer, was badly wounded. Throughout the engagement the men of this regiment behaved with great courage. Mentioned in despatches were Private R Hunter, who under heavy fire, twice built sangars round wounded comrades; and Private G Reed, who also under heavy fire, carried in a wounded Connaught Ranger to a place of safety, and remained with him after the other men retired.[17]

At about midnight General Hart called at Doctor Blake Knox's dressing station with a request that stretcher parties be sent out to attend to a number of wounded men lying on the hill unattended. Although extremely busy, the Doctor called for volunteers. A dozen stretcher squads manned by the Natal Volunteer Ambulance Corps plus some regulars came forward, and went with the Doctor onto the hill. In the dark they succeeded in carrying back a good many of the more severe cases. Blake Knox thought all was going well, '...until an unfortunate incident occurred. I had to delay over one case which was lying out some distance from the lower crest of the hill. This patient I thought was unconscious, though he was in reality dead. I had handed my dark lantern, with its shutter closed, to one of my party, to enable me to determine by nearer examination whether there was any sign of life in the motionless form, which was still warm. The man holding the lantern, either by accident or thinking to help me, released the shutter, when a broad beam of light flashed out, and this was immediately followed by a volley from the enemy's trenches in our direction.. The holder of the lantern was shot dead, and two more stretcher-bearers were wounded. Had not the bullets gone for the most part high, and the lantern extinguished by its fall, more casualties might have occurred. As it was, we had all to lie close behind what scanty cover we could crawl to for over an hour, and make our way back as quietly as we could, for it was impossible to recover any more wounded, the enemy being thenceforward on the alert. On our way down towards the Langerwachte Spruit, we heard some groaning, and, proceeding in the direction of the sound, one of the party stumbled over a stretcher on the ground. On that stretcher lay an unconscious man. His head was partially bandaged, and beside the stretcher lay the two bearers. One of these had been shot dead, and the other was lying in a pool of blood groaning. He had been struck by a bullet through the thigh, the bone being badly broken, which rendered him helpless. We removed both cases, and the poor fellow, who was conscious, told me that he and a comrade had been shot down while dressing the unconscious man's head.'[18]

During the night the Irish built sangars all along their line on Hart's Hill. When dawn broke they discovered that the Boers had dug fresh trenches which, in places, were less than

300 yards away. On the open ground between the two combatants lay many of the wounded, dead and dying of the previous day's carnage. There was some desultory firing between the two groups before a further unfortunate incident occurred. The Boers, near whom most of the wounded lay, came out with a Red Cross flag and firing on that section of the line ceased. After collecting their own wounded, they gave their opponents some water, while taking away their rifles, and began despoiling the dead and wounded. They pulled the boots off them, and began undressing them as they rifled pockets and searched for valuables. This was too much for the Irish who fired on the Boers. The Boers believed that this was a breach of the Geneva Convention, though the Convention was intended to cover people rendering medical assistance, not those conducting pillage and robbery. The first shots sent the Boers scuttling back to their trenches, and general firing broke out. The Boers' passions were so inflamed by the Irish troops' reaction to their robbery of the dead and wounded, that any slight movement by the wounded resulted in heavy fire being directed at them.[19]

All through the day the rifle and artillery fire between the two sides continued, while at the same time the exhausted troops at Hart's Hill were replaced by fresh regiments from Warren's Division. General 'No-Bobs' was keen to have another go at taking the hill, but no such order came through from Buller who was, as usual, distressed by the casualties which had been suffered – the old uncertainty was still there. His plan required that after securing Hart's Hill, the next hill down the line, Railway Hill, should be captured. He did not believe General Hart was the ideal leader for such an operation, and as the 5th Division should lead this attack, he sent for Warren.

Warren found Buller and his Staff pinned down by shellfire. After finding a safe spot for himself Warren was seen by Buller to be shaking with laughter. Buller sent a message to enquire why he was laughing, to which he received the reply, 'Come over and see.' Under fire, Buller crawled over to him and was told, 'look at your Staff' and Warren pointed out that as each shell came over, the senior Staff members did not move, but the others would duck, the most junior members lowering their heads the most. This produced the effect of a wave passing through the group. Buller was neither pleased nor amused. He gave Warren his orders and crawled back to his staff and told them to try and keep their heads steady. Warren reflected, 'A good laugh does one's inside so much good.'[20]

Warren went over to Hart and it was arranged that General 'No-Bobs' himself should lead the attack on Railway Hill, while Colonel Cooper of the Dublin Fusiliers should lead the new attack on Hart's Hill. However as it was now 4 o'clock, it was decided that the attack should be postponed until the following day, Sunday, 25 February. Through the night the British clung to their positions on the hills, while above them the Boers remained in their hidden trenches.

Whatever his subordinates may have decided, Buller was not prepared to authorise this proposed attack on the Sabbath. Many of the wounded had lain on those hillsides for two days and two nights without food, water, shelter or medical attention. As a result many, whose wounds would not normally have been fatal, had died. It was imperative that a ceasefire be arranged for the removal of the wounded from the battlefield and burying of the dead. The Boers were persuaded to permit the removal of seriously wounded soldiers, but insisted that those men who were not badly wounded should become their prisoners of war. Rather surprisingly, the British agreed to these somewhat harsh terms. By noon all the wounded had been taken off the battlefield and the dead buried.

That Sunday those close to Buller had noticed a change in him. Energy and a sense of purpose had returned. Colonel a'Court on his Staff noted, 'He had suddenly become the old War Office Buller, and dictated so rapidly that I could scarcely keep pace with him, but as he went on I saw that he had a complete grasp of the operation.'

The next day, the Boers saw the British artillery and army baggage going back across the river and men could be seen gathering on the northern bank of the Tugela near the pontoon bridge. Louis Botha advised Pretoria that because of the heavy losses they had suffered, the British appeared to be retiring. The long cherished dream of chasing the *rooineks* out of Natal and into the sea had once again begun to look achievable.

And still there were no orders from Buller to attack. Instead he rode out along the heights from Hlangwane to Monte Cristo making sure the artillery was in place; 76 guns over a distance of about four and a half miles. The infantry, presently entrenched across the Tugela, were instructed to hold their positions while the remainder were marched back across the pontoon bridge to take up positions on the southern bank. That night the bridge was dismantled and reassembled at a new site about four miles downstream opposite Hart's Hill, and Buller gave his commanders their orders. Barton's brigade would attack Pieter's Hill, Kitchener's would assault Railway Hill, and Hart's, assisted by Norcott's brigade, would assault Hart's Hill. Lord Dundonald's Mounted Brigade was to be deployed to the right of the main attack to provide flank protection and covering fire.[21] When General Lyttelton heard the details of Buller's orders he commented that the ideas behind it 'appeared so sound that I doubted if they were his own.' Perhaps they were not, in which case Buller should be given credit for listening to sound advice, a rare virtue among British commanders.

When dawn came on Tuesday, 27 February 1900, the Boers in their trenches on the hills above the northern bank of the Tugela looked south expecting to see the British army in full retreat. Instead they saw a new bridge snaking across the river, while at the same time the Royal Artillery opened a terrific barrage on the Boer positions along the whole four and a half miles of the front making it well nigh impossible for the Boers to rapidly redeploy men to threatened areas. Barton's brigade, consisting of the Scots, Irish and Dublin Fusiliers, were first across the new bridge and on reaching the northern bank hurried along eastwards in single file, using the river bank to hide their movement from the enemy. At Pieter's Hill they left the shelter of the river bank and climbed the precipitous 500 feet up onto the plateau where the Irish Fusiliers were able to rush and capture the nearest *kopjes*. On their right the Scots were checked by heavy fire from the defenders and were forced to take shelter in a donga. For a while the brigade's forward movement was checked, however it had gained a footing on the plateau and was able to direct rifle fire not only at the Boers confronting it, but also those attempting to hold Railway Hill.

Kitchener and his brigade of Lancastrians and Yorkshiremen were next into the fray charging up Railway Hill. The Boers offered little resistance as the infantrymen stormed into their trenches, bayoneting several of the occupants and taking over 50 prisoners. So intent were they on fleeing down the reverse slope of the hill that they did not bother to shoot the British soldier who stood on the highest point of the hill waving his helmet. It was now the turn of Hart and Norcott to attack Hart's Hill. Suffering under heavy artillery fire, the sight of reinforcements arriving to back up the Irish already on the hill was too much for the Boers who 'ran like hunted rats from their trenches.'

As evening approached Barton brought three companies of his Irishmen round from the left of Pieter's Hill to clear a *kopje* on the right where the Boers had stubbornly resisted the Scots throughout the day. A charge by the Irish Fusiliers drove the last of the Boers off the hill but at a heavy price. They lost a third of their number and every one of their officers was either killed or wounded.

The enemy had been cleared off all three hills and Buller had at last broken through the Boers' defensive line along the Tugela. The British losses during the two weeks of this extended battle for 'Tugela Heights' were 26 officers and 347 men killed and 99 officers and 1,710 men wounded. The Red Cross calculated that the Boers suffered 81 killed and 343 wounded.

Dundonald's men had spent the day on the rough, rocky ground on the southern bank of the Tugela where, with the assistance of a machine gun, they kept up a continuous fire on the Boers on Pieter's Hill. This covering fire enabled Barton's force to deploy along the river and advance for a considerable distance up the hill without serious molestation.

Winston Churchill was with the mounted brigade on that day, though both he and the South African Light Horse had been away from the Tugela Front for a few days having been ordered to drive off some Boers who were threatening lines of communication near Frere. This they did and were able rejoin the Brigade on 26 February. It must have been very frustrating for young Winston to be away from the centre of things at such a crucial time. On the evening of the 26th he told his commanding officer, Col. Byng, that he 'wanted to get the DSO, as it would look so nice on the robes of the Chancellor of the Exchequer.' Byng replied, that he 'must first get into Parliament, if he could get any constituency to have him!'[22]

For a time General Buller toyed with the idea of sending his cavalry in pursuit of the Boers but fortunately abandoned this idea which could very easily have resulted in the destruction of his entire Regular Cavalry. Instead he decided to concentrate on the relief of Ladysmith. Late on the night of 27 February, Dundonald received the orders for the following day; these were: 'To cross the pontoon tomorrow morning and reconnoitre the enemy.'[23]

At dawn on that momentous day, 28 February 1900, Dundonald's brigade saddled up, crossed the river and rode down the valley between Pieter's Hill and Railway Hill, following the railway towards Ladysmith. Forward patrols from Thorneycroft's MI reported the enemy were ensconced in rocky ground near Pieter's Station. Despite coming under heavy fire, the brigade, assisted by their machine guns, drove the Boers from this position, Thorneycroft's regiment suffering a few casualties. The brigade now fanned out with the SALH on the right moving towards the Klip River and the Carbineers under McKenzie on the left.

Though subjected to occasional sniping from the Boer rear guard, the Carbineers made steady progress as they scouted towards Ladysmith. A Boer commando was seen travelling down a road making for the bridge over the Klip River presenting an ideal opportunity for an ambush. The Carbineers concealed themselves behind a ridge watching their unsuspecting prey approach. They were about to spring the trap when a distant Maxim gun opened fire on the Boers who wheeled around and rode off. McKenzie was furious and when Major Gough arrived a short while later, McKenzie wanted to know 'what fool had fired the Maxims?' Gough blamed a Capt Hill and Dundonald.[24]

Gough returned to Brigade headquarters, while the Carbineers continued to scout towards Ladysmith, keeping well to the left of the railway line, while the other regiments worked down towards the right. They passed through a looted farm, owned by one Woodhouse, and pressed on towards Caesar's Camp. Coming over a rise they could see below them Intombi Camp and a few miles across the plain lay Ladysmith. They could have ridden straight into Ladysmith, which the men were keen to do, but McKenzie called a halt, so that he could ensure that such action would not prejudice any other unit. In due course Major Gough arrived with the Imperial Light Horse following some distance behind. Greeting him McKenzie said, 'Now, Gough, there is Ladysmith, let us ride in.'[25]

Gough asked for an orderly to take a note back to Dundonald. While Gough was writing out the note, McKenzie instructed the sergeant major to ensure that the ILH did not sneak past them. With the message on its' way to Dundonald, the Carbineers moved down the stony path off the hill and when they reached the level ground McKenzie had to check his men to prevent them embarking on a wild gallop into the town. It was at this stage that a message came from Captain Bottomley of the ILH asking if they might ride into Ladysmith with the Carbineers. Throughout the campaign the Imperial Light Horse had fought alongside

Gun of 7th Battery in action clearing the road to Ladysmith.

the Carbineers, shared its vicissitudes, and rendered help without being asked. Without hesitating McKenzie agreed to the request. So the two regiments lined up in half sections making a column of fours with Duncan McKenzie and Capt DW Mackay leading the Carbineers, while Herbert Bottomley with Lt Bridges led the ILH.[26] Hubert Gough was of course somewhere thereabouts. The scene was set for a dignified entry into Ladysmith.

They crossed the defended perimeter at an outpost manned by the Border Mounted Rifles. Captain Vause was in charge that day and it was appropriate that the Natal Volunteers should be the first to welcome them. Their approach had of course been seen in Ladysmith. Carbineer Veterinary Surgeon Herbert Watkins-Pitchford in a letter to his wife described the arrival of the relief column:

'…someone came running down the road shouting as he passed, "Saddle up at once… Buller's in sight!" Then came the bustle and excitement which you can imagine better than I can describe. The General had seen a body of horsemen advancing over the hills several miles from Ladysmith and as such a sight was a very unusual one for the enemy to present, he had them watched carefully, since it seemed extraordinary that, if they were our people, Long Tom did not open fire on them as they were well within his range.

'As they came nearer, however, it could be seen from their formation that they were not the enemy, so the General wired down to Royston, "British cavalry in sight. Turn your men out to meet them." The Volunteers' horses had fortunately been kept to last, only a few hundreds of our horses and pack ponies having been slaughtered, so that we were able to turn out in some strength – nearly 3 squadrons – while the other cavalry regiments were almost, if not quite, dismounted. Rapidly forming up we galloped across the flats towards the river and down its steep banks into the water, splashing and being splashed until we were drenched. Then a scramble pell mell up the steep and slippery drift on the other side to gain the flat where we had so often fooled Long Tom and his mates in early days, and across the flat stretches, and among the thorn trees as hard as we could gallop. To add to our pleasure, our large 4.7 gun which we had

supposed long dead from want of ammunition, opened fire with a crash and sent his shells whistling and roaring over our heads towards the old enemy on Bulwana which had pounded us so unmercifully during the four previous months. This provoked no answer from the well known spot, and we subsequently learnt that the absence of firing was in consequence of the Boer gunners attempting to remove the gun. This in fact I saw, as soon as I could get a glass to bear on the emplacement.

'Well, across the plain we pelted as hard as we could gallop drawing nearer and nearer each moment to the dark mass of horsemen rapidly advancing toward us. At the end it was like a hostile cavalry charge rather than the meeting of two friendly bodies of men. As we drew within shouting range we yelled and howled like packs of wild dogs. Caps and helmets were waved, guns frantically brandished, horses plunged and bucked with fright, and in a moment the two columns were merged into a struggling mass of horsemen, besieged and deliverers mixed inextricably in one disorderly mass of cheering, laughing, gesticulating, hand-shaking, back-slapping, men. All showed wear and tear. Tattered and lean and brown, the one side with privation and exposure and long anxiety, and the other with hard fighting and desperate derring-do.

'Verney (Veterinary Lieutenant F.A. Verney) was the first man to clasp my hand. He was belted and accoutred like a buccaneer, carrying a long repeating-rifle in a carbine bucket, although he had a star of a lieutenant upon his shoulder. He was very thin, and very vociferous, and seemed unfeignedly glad to see me safe. So back we crowded towards Ladysmith, a noisy shouting rabble, to find the banks of the river on the other side thronged with all the inhabitants of the town who could get down in time. As we plunged and slid down the steep drift to the river the scene was beyond description, the slipping, splashing horses and the excited shouting people on the banks above, mad with delight. It was a picture, my dear, I would not have missed for anything. One's heart was in one's throat all the time to see so much unalloyed human joy. Never this side of heaven can I hope to see such a scene of happiness, and it was all impromptu.'[27]

Of course several of the horses came down in the mêlée, but in the excitement no one worried about any bruises which might be suffered in a tumble from a horse.

In a letter published in the London *Daily Telegraph* on 27 February 1950, Wing Commander WL Shaw, who in 1900 was a 20 year-old trooper with the Carbineers, wrote that when they were half way across the river, 'Major McKenzie touched his famous bay stallion Inspector with his spur. With one leap he was up the river bank and into Ladysmith', the first of the relieving force into the town.[28] For the citizens and Volunteers it was doubly exciting. For four months they had endured a terrible siege, and after so many disappointments, it was their own who had ended their ordeal.

Donald Macdonald had just settled down to a dinner of horseflesh when he heard shouting and above the tumult the cry, 'Buller's cavalry are in sight.' Abandoning their horseflesh, he and his companions ran outside and joined the stream of excited people making their way to the nearest river crossing. They could see horsemen coming towards them and all knew it must be the relief column. It seemed the whole town had come down to the river. Macdonald recorded: 'All the colours and all the nations of earth seemed blended together in a confused throng, all its tongues raised in one exultant din. It was worth having lived and suffered through the siege for that supreme hour.'[29]

He also noticed that many of the sick and wounded from the hospitals had abandoned their beds so that they might welcome the column: 'There were soldiers with white and shrunken faces; men wounded in the legs, who shuffled slowly down the road. One poor young infantry officer had stopped at a deep street channel – he had not the strength to step over it. I lifted him to the other side, but it was no trouble, he was as light as a child. Two other officers drove down in a pony trap, the ghastliness of their faces impressed one, even in that time of wild excitement. They were, in plain and painful truth, living skeletons.'[30]

The relief column was mobbed as it made its way to the centre of town. McKenzie said they '…were pulled about so much that it was difficult to talk to anyone.'[31] People clung to bridles and stirrups as they tried to shake hands or just touch the riders as they came by. Old General White, tired, emaciated, sick and a little bent, rode down to meet them. He had borne a heavy responsibility alone, had been much criticised, but never for a second did he give up, or fail to do what he believed to be right. Now with a fellowship born of their shared suffering, the people crowded round him so he could go no further. He straightened up and attempted to address the crowd. That perceptive witness Donald Macdonald was there:

> '…beginning almost inaudibly (he) thanked them for the loyal way they had, civilian and soldier alike, co-operated with him in defence of the town. Then he struck the keynote that went straight to the hearts of all his people, and roused them to an indescribable enthusiasm "Thank God we kept the flag flying." Such words, spoken with an intensity of solemn feeling, were a match to the mine of human emotion, and what a roar rose in the night air, while the Zulus, knowing not that something fit to be immortal had been said, but inflamed by the infectious joy of the multitude, sprang into the air again, and shouted the war-cry that some few had heard many years ago when Cetewayo's impis swept down upon them. "It cut me to the heart," the General went on, "to reduce your rations as I did." Then his voice faltered and failed him, and it seemed for a moment he would break down altogether. The sympathetic crowd filled in the break, helped him over the crisis with another roar of delight long drawn out, and with the promptness of a soldier he pulled himself together, and mastered his deep feeling. A smile came over his face, and he saved the situation with a laughing. "I promise you, though, that I'll never do it again." The people laughed and cheered.'[32]

Overcome with emotion the General turned his horse away and made his way back to his quarters, and they loved him even more, while those who had so fiercely criticised him, felt ashamed. Spontaneously the crowd, in their many different voices, sang 'God Save the Queen,' before drifting away.

Hubert Gough lost no time in making himself known to General White and joined the 'celebratory' dinner held at Sir George White's residence. In anticipation of this day, two bottles of champagne had been carefully husbanded, there were a few sardines, a piece of horse or mule meat and an army biscuit for each diner.[33] Hubert Gough had by his own admission learnt more in one day with the Carbineers than in ten years in the cavalry. His contribution to the Relief being little more than being present. It was McKenzie and Bottomley who had led the Relieving Force into Ladysmith and yet neither of these officers was invited to headquarters for the celebratory meal.

Whatever was happening at headquarters, it was a great night for the local regiments. The men of the Imperial Light Horse were delighted to be reunited with their 'A' Squadron. Apart from the Carbineers, McKenzie had with him seven members of the Border Mounted Rifles as well as a few troopers from the Natal Mounted Rifles and the Natal Mounted Police. All had much news to exchange and must have talked well into the night before the weary relievers lay down in their greatcoats and, having given away their rations, went supperless to sleep.

As we have seen, Dundonald, with the bulk of the mounted brigade, had been left in the rear by the Carbineers and ILH. At about 3 p.m. he received a note from Gough that the hill in front appeared to be unoccupied. He replied, 'Take your regiment onto the hill and I will support.' The whole brigade then moved forward. A second message from Gough was received to which Dundonald replied, 'Push on towards Ladysmith, I am supporting.'[34] Dundonald and the brigade continued to move forward in support until they were about 6 miles from

Ladysmith. Dundonald now decided that as evening was approaching and their flanks had not been properly scouted, Thorneycroft should take the brigade back to a previously selected position, while he and some of his staff should join the forward regiments. He took with him Major Birdwood, Lieutenant Clowes, Lieutenant W.S. Churchill and some orderlies. This group then set off post haste after the Carbineers and ILH. They reached Ladysmith sometime after the others and made their way to General White's headquarters. The celebratory dinner was already in progress and they were invited to join the other officers. Churchill was a mere lieutenant in a volunteer regiment so his invitation is surprising. He, 'was placed next to Hamilton, who won the fight at Elandslaagte and beat the Boers at Wagon Hill, and next but one to Hunter, whom everyone said was the finest man in the world.'[35]

Churchill appears to have abandoned any notion he might have had of presenting an accurate account of events to his readers, in favour of promoting his personal career as a politician. This is how he described his entry into Ladysmith:

'Presently we arranged ourselves in military order, Natal Carabineers and Imperial Light Horse riding two and two abreast so that there might be no question about precedence and with Gough, the youngest regimental commander in the army, and one of the best, at the head of the column, we forded the Klip River and rode into town.'[36]

Clearly he is misleading his readers into believing that he was with the relief column when it entered Ladysmith, something which would go down well with electors in England. In South Africa it caused a great deal of ill feeling. Many thought Dundonald had claimed to be first into Ladysmith. Dundonald was appalled when he discovered the misinformation being put about. In a letter to Duncan McKenzie he wrote,

'In the same paper it says that I had said I was "first in Ladysmith" – I said, "the Mounted Brigade was first." I did not arrive until 20 minutes after you all had got into town, having naturally the Brigade to attend to, and send back to its bivouac and the Command to give over, when the road was clear, before I could follow... This is all very trifling but it annoyed me as you know what I think of your gallant Squadron and of you my friend.'[37]

Hubert Gough's brother John was among the besieged in Ladysmith, but because of the celebrations at headquarters on the evening of the relief, the brothers arranged to meet at the Klip River bridge at 6 a.m. the next morning. Hubert was there with McKenzie's and Bottomley's squadrons and noticed without recognising an officer with a carefully trimmed naval beard approaching on a grey horse. 'Hello, Hubert,' said the horseman. Hubert recognised his brother's voice at once, and grabbed his hand and shook it violently. Still sitting on the horse, John looked down at his dapper and trim brother. 'Hubert,' he said, 'How fat you have got.'[38]

Shortly afterwards the two squadrons rode back to the Brigade bivouac near Nelthorpe station where they were ordered to cover the left flank and front of Buller's army as it advanced towards Ladysmith. After all the torments of the siege, those in Ladysmith were anxious that the retreating Boers should be attacked in some way. Early that morning Karri Davies took the ILH onto Bulwana hoping to prevent the removal of Long Tom. Unfortunately the Boers had already removed the big gun. Back in town the Natal Volunteer regiments with about 2,500 infantry and artillery set out towards Elandslaagte. The artillery were able to fire a few shots at the retreating Boers before the enterprise was abandoned. They were all too weak to continue. The infantry could not march any distance, the mounted men had used all their own and their horses' energy the previous day, and the artillery horses collapsed in their traces, too weak to draw the cannons. They were however able to forage for food in the deserted Boer camps where much food and other supplies had been abandoned. On the other side of Ladysmith, near Bester's farm, a small party of Natal Police lost one man killed and one wounded in a brush with the enemy.

Ladysmith was again part of the world and throughout the British Empire there was much excitement and celebrating on that first day of March 1900. Newspaper correspondents and the curious flocked to the town. Lt Blake Knox visited Intombi Hospital:

'There were about 800 patients; the features and limbs of one and all showed unmistakably what the ravages of disease and starvation will produce. Thin, gaunt, haggard men, living skeletons met my eyes everywhere, some in beds, others seated, others crawling rather than walking; listless claw fingered beings in ragged hospital clothes, whose only signs of life seemed centred in their large round glistening eyes, set off by pinched, cadaverous, bearded faces. Such was Intombi. The medical staff themselves were almost as bad: one of them, whom I had known as a stout, well groomed man about town, had now a pale emaciated face, his tattered khaki hanging in folds about a wasted frame; he appeared rather a subject for medical aid than one fit to administer it. He pointed out what seemed to me to be a small forest of short white sticks, glistening in the morning sun, between the hospital and Bulwana. I asked him what it was. "It's the graves of 1,600 men." he said. Victims of enteric, dysentery, and wounds. I shuddered.'[39]

When, on the evening of the 28th, the nurses at Intombi realised Ladysmith had been relieved, they were so overcome with joyous emotion that they were unable to speak and carried out their duties as if in a dumb show. The next morning Kate Driver heard a Natal Carbineer asking for her. She looked out of her tent:

'It was young Willy Tanner (in WW1 he served with great distinction in France becoming a Brigadier General), a friend I had known in Maritzburg for some time. He told me of my people, and gave me much news I was hungry to have. He said my young brother had been doing great things. "It was he who volunteered to run down Spion Kop with the message to General Warren for reinforcements, and who had led those reinforcements back up to the top,' he told me. 'Your brother had said when volunteering, that he was less afraid to run down with the messages than to stand there and be shot! He has, however acquired two bullet holes in the flap of his trousers. He is very proud of these two bullet holes."

"But now," said Willie Tanner, diving into his pack, "would you like some rice? And would you like some onions and some stale ginger bread? We came through a deserted farm house and I found these."

'I began to clear a tray of dressings so that he could give these treasures to me. Then suddenly I looked at him. "Ginger bread from a deserted farmhouse. I'm so hungry that I could eat it all this very moment, but somehow specially the ginger bread gives my heart a kind of stab. Being a farmer's daughter, I can so vividly imagine how life went on there before the people had to leave their home."

"Well," he answered quietly, "that is how war goes, doesn't it? But I know how you feel. We have strict orders to commandeer all food and all livestock. A few days ago we came to a dilapidated old farmhouse where there was an old Boer woman alone. She saw us coming and by the time we reached her, she was sitting by her door with her arms round a goose.

She gave a great cry as we came up to her and buried her head in his feathers. We stood still. When she looked up again the tears were streaming down her face, and she said, "Then yes - if you must take my things – take everything, take everything! But leave me my man-goose! Do not kill him! Do not take him from me! Do not hurt my man-goose!"

"There are times when one has to disobey orders," he said. He took my hand
"Goodbye, I must go now. I am glad you are free at last."'[40]

On 3 March, Buller's army made its formal entry into Ladysmith. The long procession met with a reception more subdued than that which had greeted McKenzie's and Bottomley's squadrons a few days earlier. Too much should not be read into this. The spontaneous joy had subsided and now the people just wanted to recover from their ordeal and to resume a normal life. None of the Volunteer regiments participated in the march-past as they were out on patrol. Buller visited Intombi and was appalled by the condition of the patients. He arranged for the immediate transfer of the unpopular Col Exham RAMC to the Cape. Exham's friend, Henry Nevinson, returned to England to write his book, while General Sir Charles Warren was appointed Military Governor of the Cape north of the Orange River, a sparsely populated and arid area.

Though many tried to rush Buller into taking precipitous action against the Boers, he resolutely refused to move until his army was ready.

In the Boer paper, the '*Standard and Digger News*' of 1 March 1900, Gerard Bailey in Dundee was able to read of the 'Glorious Boer Victory' and that, 'Ladysmith is not likely to be relieved.'[41]

CHAPTER TWENTY-THREE

Relief of Mafeking.
Treatment of prisoners by Boers

◆━◆━◆

'They were shopkeepers and farmers and had never taken up arms.
Yet they were held in prison without trial, sleeping on the bare ground,
without shelter and very poorly fed and clothed.'

PLIGHT OF MANY NON-BOER CIVILIANS LIBERATED WHEN THE BRITISH OCCUPIED
PRETORIA. EVIDENCE OF REV GOODMAN AT COMMISSION OF ENQUIRY

SIR REDVERS BULLER has been much criticised for his failure to pursue the Boers while they were withdrawing from the Tugela and Ladysmith. However it should be borne in mind that not only were the defenders of Ladysmith too weak to take part in any military action, but a considerable number were seriously ill, and almost all needed urgent medical attention. This was a priority for Buller and to make and execute the necessary arrangements would take time and effort. In addition, the relieving force had been on the move for more than two and a half months and the men needed rest.

It was not only the men whom Buller had to take into account. To drive the Boers out of Natal, a substantial portion of this force had to be mounted, and of course these men required horses. All 10,000 horses which had been in Ladysmith before the siege had either died, been eaten, or were otherwise no longer fit for service, and therefore had to be replaced. The wastage of horses among his own mounted brigades, the artillery and transport corps had to be made good. Once they arrived, the new horses had to be trained and allocated to units to suit each animal – another time consuming task.

Further, the army, which for so long had been split into 'relievers' and 'defenders', had to be reorganised into one unit. Among those affected were the Carbineers, whose members were to leave Dundonald's Brigade and return to their own regiment. When they paraded before Dundonald for the last time he addressed them as follows:

'Major McKenzie, officers and men of the Natal Carbineers, as you are leaving me today to rejoin your Regiment, I take this opportunity of saying goodbye to you and how sorry I am at losing you from my command. You belong to a regiment whose reputation stands high and you have done much to cover it with honour. For the time I have commanded you, you have had much hard and dangerous work, but I have never feared that however difficult the task set to you to perform, and however dangerous the task, it would be well accomplished, and I may say that were I intending to join any regiment and were it open to me to choose, I would prefer to join the Natal Carbineers. I wish you all goodbye.'[1]

Dundonald had previously commanded the 2nd Life Guards, one of Britain's most famous and prestigious regiments. It was a wonderful and well deserved compliment.

But not everyone had a high opinion of the part played by Dundonald's men in the Relief of Ladysmith. Frederick Tucker was a private in the Rifle Brigade and kept a diary. As a member of the relieving force he had taken part in the fighting on Hart's Hill on 27 February 1900. On the 28th they buried their dead. In his diary he writes,

> 'We had buried our dead so we made ready for the advance which we expected to make, but after waiting for some hours we found to our disappointment that this was not to be. We were reinforced by a strange regiment we had not seen before. In fact we did not even know that they belonged to the Natal Field Force. I suppose that, while we had been fighting every day and having a rough time, they had been living in comfort at the base or Line of Communication, on soft bread and fresh meat. Even the cavalry came across the Tugela and condescended to approve of the way we had twisted the Boers out from Pieter's Hill, but our men didn't want their approval and some of our fellows gave them to understand as much. "There was plenty of work for you fellows." I heard one our men remark to one of the colonial mounted men.
>
> "Yes," he replied, "but our horses wanted rest." I don't know how they got done up for we had not seen them do anything to warrant tiring them. After the guns had crossed the river, the cavalry rode forward to find out if the enemy had gone. They had scarcely gone any distance before they came scampering back as if the devil had them. A few Boers from their rear guard had fired on them and sent them all back to us for protection. However, after being reinforced, they went out again and this time they found nothing. That night they galloped into Ladysmith, and must have snatched all the honours from the papers at home, while we remained on Pieter's Hill for another night in the rain, enjoying the horrid stench of dead horses.'[2]

The Rifle Brigade's response to the unsolicited praise from the Colonials does seem a little ungracious. The strange regiment which Tucker and his comrades saw was almost certainly Thorneycroft's Mounted Infantry. Early on the morning of the 28th it was they who were scouting ahead of the column, made contact with the Boers, and then galloped back with information of the Boer position. When Thorneycroft's men were on Spion Kop desperately needing assistance, Tucker and his mates were busy elsewhere. They spent that momentous day sunning themselves on Mount Alice.

Once it was established that the Boers had retreated behind the Biggarsberg, the Natal Volunteers went to Highlands, near Mooi River. A camp had been set up to rest their horses, while the men were able to take it in turns to go on a few weeks leave. Before he left, General White went to see the Native Scouts who were to be disbanded. Robert Samuelson was present and noted the words of the General:

> 'Simeon Kambule and all you scouts, you have done most useful and important service for Her Majesty the Queen, for which I thank you, on her behalf and on behalf of the Army. I will ever be mindful of your loyalty and services, and when I am over the seas I will look back to you with great pride. I have no doubt you will receive all the rewards that fall due to faithful soldiers of the Queen.'

Colonel William Royston also spoke to the Scouts saying how proud he was of them, that they and their people had proved to be loyal and true at Isandhlwana, and had again displayed these qualities. He went on to say that if he was spared to live, he would persuade the Government to form them into a nucleus of a Native Corps.[3] Reports and despatches often contain phrases such as 'our information is' without giving the source of the information. In many instances this would have been gathered by these scouts who deserved every word of the praise they received from White and Royston.

On 4 March, the Imperial Light Horse, with the exception of Bottomley's squadron, left Ladysmith for three weeks rest and change at Hilton, a village on the hills above Pietermaritzburg. Before they left, Aubrey Woolls Sampson had a long interview with General Buller, who eulogised the regiment, and said that he would do all within reason to help. It was agreed that its strength be increased to 600 men. However, because of the wastage caused by casualties and sickness, the Regiment now needed 300 new recruits to bring it up to strength. Such was the reputation of the ILH that they were to have no trouble signing up good quality recruits, many of whom had been with the Colonial Scouts, a unit which had been raised in Natal and was in the process of being disbanded. Because of the courage they had displayed at Wagon Hill, the Regiment was to be equipped with modern Lee Enfield rifles. (The other volunteer regiments were for the time being to continue using single-shot rifles and it was only much later in the war that these were replaced by rifles equipped with magazines). The Imperial Authorities also agreed to provide them with 400 fresh remounts.[4]

Karri Davies travelled ahead to arrange the camp at Hilton and to buy supplies of fruit and other necessary foods which had been missing from their diet for so long. Those who had not seen Karri since he left for the front in October noted that although he showed the effects of the siege he was 'in fairly good form.' Aubrey Woolls Sampson was still seriously disabled by his wound, and it would be some time before he would have the operation to join his sciatic nerve. Enteric had reduced Charlie Mullins to a living skeleton, hardly able to put one foot in front of the other. Most of the others were still very weak. It was hoped that with better medical care and nutritious food, the health of the whole regiment would soon improve.

The Army Ordnance Department provided uniforms and equipment for the new recruits. On 20 March the Regiment received a telegram enquiring when it would be able to take the field, to which it replied, 'about the first week in April.' Because the Army had to re-equip a large number of troops at the time, it was unable to carry out all its obligations towards the ILH immediately. Anxious to get into the field again with as little delay as possible the ILH applied for and received a loan from Wernher, Beit & Co. as set out in Chapter Five. This enabled them to purchase horses and be ready by the first week of April. There was some talk that they might be transferred to the Cape to take part in the relief of Mafeking.

Karri had taken a couple of weeks recuperative leave, and being anxious to keep up with developments, sent a telegram to the Adjutant: '*Please wire what are your movements?*' To which the Adjutant replied: '*Thanks once daily after breakfast!*'[5] The adjutant was later to become a distinguished general.

Buller was anxious to keep the ILH with his column and on 3 April, the regiment was back in Ladysmith. After a separation of nearly six months it was reunited with 'A' Squadron under Captain Bottomley, whose experienced men would prove a useful leavening for the inexperienced new recruits. Buller's desire to keep the ILH was to be frustrated. On 8 April, the regiment received orders to proceed at once to the Cape and travelled by sea from Durban to Cape Town and then by train to Kimberley, where a column was being assembled to relieve Mafeking. Aubrey Woolls Sampson stayed behind to have his hip operation, while Charlie Mullins, now a Major, had recovered sufficiently to accompany the Regiment.

Command of the Relief Column was entrusted to Colonel Brian Mahon; Colonel Edwards still commanded the ILH, the second in command being Karri Davies. The column consisted of four guns of 'M' Battery RHA and 2 Pom Poms, the Imperial Light Horse, the Kimberley Mounted Corps, a detachment of the Cape Police and some Volunteer infantry – in all about 1,200 men, almost all of whom were Colonials. They were accompanied by 60 mule wagons carrying supplies and baggage. The country they were to traverse was flat semi-desert. For the Natalians this must have been a strange and inhospitable land, added to which the Native peoples had a language and customs very different from those of the Zulu.

On 4 May 1900, they set off for Mafeking, approximately 250 miles north of Kimberley. One mounted regiment would form the advance guard, while the other provided flank and rear guards. The two regiments swapped duties each day. On 10 May, they entered the little town of Vryburg approximately half way to Mafeking. The town had been vacated by the enemy and they were greeted with enthusiasm by local Loyalists. The column was able to wash and eat a prepared meal before setting off again that evening. The sick, and enemy prisoners who had been captured along the way, were left in Vryburg.

On 11 and 12 May, the column continued its advance, though the enemy was reported to be shadowing them. On the 13th a substantial enemy force attacked the ILH in an area where bush provided cover. Firing took place at close range and though outnumbered, the ILH held its ground. However accurate shelling by the artillery forced the Boers to withdraw. In the engagement the ILH lost 6 men killed and 13 wounded. Charlie Mullins was among those wounded and so severe were his injuries that it was thought unlikely he would survive. The wounded were left at Wrights Farm, which would provide more comfort than the ambulance with the column.[6]

Early the next day the column continued its march, hoping to find water at the Maritzani River about 6 miles away. The deep sand they were now traversing made the going tough for all, and especially for the transport wagons. When they arrived at the river it was dry except for a few fetid pools and so long and deep trenches were dug into the sandy riverbed. Potable water seeped into the trenches which was then pumped into canvas troughs. Watering the men and animals by this method took from 8 a.m. to 3.30 p.m. when the column resumed its march. At 8.15 p.m. they stopped for a rest, only to resume the advance at 2.30 a.m.

Just before dawn, fires were seen ahead of them. Patrols were sent out to reconnoitre and soon came back with the news that it was Colonel Plumer's column, which had come down from Rhodesia to join them. Early that morning the two Brigades met at Jan M'sibi, 18 miles west of Mafeking. The rest of the day was spent readying themselves for the final push to relieve the town. Col Mahon, being senior to Plumer, assumed command of their combined forces and Col Edwards took his place as commander of the Kimberley column. Included in Plumer's Brigade was a battery of four 12-pounder guns of the Canadian Artillery and 'D' Squadron of the third Queensland Contingent led by Captain Kellie.

By 7 a.m. the next day the reinforced relief column was on the move again. Colonel Edwards and his Brigade were on the left and Colonel Plumer's Brigade on the right. By noon they were six miles down the road at Sanie's Post where a halt was called to water the horses and give the men an opportunity to have something to eat. At 1 p.m. Edwards saw a column of mounted men moving across their intended line of advance. Higher ground between the two forces appeared to offer a good tactical advantage, so Edwards sought and obtained permission to take it. Taking one ILH squadron with him and collecting two more along the way, they galloped hard and were able to gain possession of the high ground, just before the arrival of the enemy. The ILH dismounted and in the skirmish which followed the Boers were driven back across the valley. The Boers had launched a simultaneous attack on Plumer's force and in the fierce fighting which followed, they had no more success there than they had achieved against the ILH. Finding themselves being steadily driven back, the Boers hurriedly withdrew and in the course of this retirement were badly mauled by the artillery. During the engagement Edwards' command lost 2 men killed and 8 wounded.[7]

Without resting, the column resumed its advance until a rest was ordered at 5.30 p.m. As it was unknown whether any Boer disposition lay between them and Mafeking, Karri Davies with six men went ahead to scout the route into town. They saw no sign of the enemy and rode into the besieged town unmolested. Two of his men, Corporals Warby and Duirs were with Bottomley when Ladysmith was relieved, a remarkable double. Karri returned to base immediately and reported that the road was clear, whereupon Col Mahon decided to ride into Mafeking at once.

At 3.30 a.m. on Wednesday, 17 May 1900, the Relief Column arrived in Mafeking and were warmly welcomed by Colonel Baden-Powell. The men of the Imperial Light Horse, who had had no rest since 6 a.m. the previous day, made their way to a patch of cold bare earth, known as the Market Square, dismounted, loosened girths, lay down in their cloaks by their horses' heads, and fell asleep.[8]

News of the Relief was flashed around the world and Britain, together with much of her Empire, went mad with delight. That morning the Boers launched a surprise attack on the place where the Relief Column had bivouacked the previous evening, and found no one there. Believing their force was not strong enough to engage the combined forces of the Relief Column and the Mafeking garrison, the Boers rode away to the east to join the Commandos defending their Republics.

The Imperial Light Horse had learnt much since that day they had charged up the hill at Elandslaagte behind Col Scott Chisholme waving his little red flag. From the Natal Volunteers they had learnt the value of concealing from the enemy one's position and intentions, and if these elements were combined with speed and decisive action, as at Acton Homes, success could come at little cost.

Far away in Dundee, Gerard Bailey was having his own struggle with the invaders. Once again the town was full of Boers now engaged in fortifying positions on the Biggarsburg. No longer did he hear boasts of 'driving the *rooineks* into the sea.' Instead: '...they tell me they are ready to give back this part of Natal if they can have a guarantee of independence. The Boers are styled Federalists. It is the Federal cause, we are the Imperialists. It is always "Great Federal Victory" – "Federal Forces" – "Rout of the Imperialists" and if there is any interchange of courtesies between our generals and their leaders, such is styled, "The Comity of Nations." There is no small beer about the Boer newspapers.'[9]

The house next door to Bailey's vicarage was owned by a church warden, WH Tatham, who it will be recalled believed the townsfolk had nothing to fear from the Boers, and that in spite of this he was carted off to Pretoria. Possibly because he was a church warden and neighbour of the vicar, Gerard Bailey kept a careful watch over the house, and at the beginning of March it was one of the few premises in Dundee still intact. Gerard now noticed policemen removing furniture from the house. He immediately complained in writing to the *Vrederechter*, however the removals continued. In due course he received a reply to his complaint, the *Vrederechter* stating, '...that in future nothing shall be removed from the premises mentioned by you.' By then the house had been cleaned out, and there was nothing left which could be taken.

Although one could almost stock a library with books about the fate of Boers, both civilian and military, who fell into British hands during the war, little has been written about prisoners taken by them. An exception is the capture, imprisonment, and escape of Winston Churchill, which is one of the best known episodes of the War. However Churchill was the grandson of a Duke, and the treatment accorded to him cannot be compared with that given to other prisoners. During the initial stages of the war, captured British officers were accommodated in the premises of the State Model School in Pretoria. They were allowed considerable freedom, and, if they had the means, were able to supplement their rations, and in other ways make their lives quite comfortable. After the escape of Winston Churchill, security was tightened, and although there was still plenty to complain about and on several occasions prisoners were assaulted, some attempt was made to comply with internationally accepted standards. On 16 March 1900 they were moved to Waterval, about 6 miles from Pretoria. Here the officers were housed in a galvanised shed, 24 feet x 15 feet, with earthen floors and into which twenty-seven beds were crowded. Lunch was the only meal provided by the Transvaal authorities, who thereby compelled the officers to buy their breakfast and supper. Other necessities such as blankets could also be bought at exorbitantly high prices. Outside, a wired off enclosure provided space for exercise.[10]

For the 'other ranks' life was very different. They were detained at Waterval from the beginning and were housed in old corrugated iron sheds which were full of holes and when it rained the roofs leaked profusely. Added to this the earthen floors of the sheds were below the level of the road outside, resulting in rainwater flowing through them. There were no beds with the result that the men were perforce required to lie on the bare earth. Each man was given a blanket but no waterproof sheets were issued. The roads between the shelters were in an 'indescribably filthy condition, rotten animal and vegetable refuse, and even human excrement, lay freely over them.' The latrines consisted of trenches 7 to 8 feet deep situated about 50 yards from the sleeping quarters. Heavy rain filled the trenches causing the contents to float all over the camp. It was the rainy season and the men had to live and sleep with this polluted water around them. By February, the prisoner's clothes were in tatters. Some were without trousers, others without coats or boots. Each man was supposed to receive a pound of meat each week, bread, tea or coffee without milk or sugar, and from time to time *mealie* meal porridge. But often they received nothing at all. Their meat ration was less than a third of the officers' and their food was often of poor quality. The bread was usually sour or stale before it reached them, and other items included in their rations were either reduced or taken off the menu altogether. All this in a city where there was no shortage of food. Not surprisingly, several men collapsed with weakness and typhoid, and dysentery spread rapidly. Drinking and washing water was kept in separate tanks because the latter was unfit for consumption. Yet the same buckets were used indiscriminately to cart both classes of water, thereby introducing another potent system for the spread of disease. During the months they were incarcerated in Pretoria, fifty-six previously healthy men died.[11] Given the conditions under which they lived it is surprising that any survived.

The Transvaal Government established two hospitals for the treatment of sick or wounded prisoners – one at the Pretoria Racecourse and the other near the prison camps at Waterval. The Chief Medical Officer for Military Prisoners was a Dr Veale.

In the middle of December 1899, a conscripted *Uitlander*, Dr Haylett, was instructed to take charge of the Racecourse Hospital, which at that time had about 60 patients. The building was adequate and the patients did have beds with straw mattresses, though there were no sheets and few pillows. There were virtually no medicines or cleaning equipment, and despite numerous requisitions for these necessities, they only dribbled through in totally inadequate quantities, compelling Haylett to rely on decoctions of herbs found nearby. In the first week of January 1900, Haylett was transferred to the hospital at Waterval. A few days later he submitted a report to Dr. Veale, condemning the sanitary arrangements, the water supply, the building and its equipment, all in the strongest possible terms. In the hospital there were more than sixty patients but only 21 beds, 11 mattresses and 49 blankets. The food supply was not only inadequate but irregular.[12] Despite receiving no response, Haylett continued to make written complaints to Veale who either would not or could not do anything to alleviate the situation. By the beginning of February Haylett had begun to wonder whether he had been sent to Waterval to kill or cure the patients, and decided to resign. In his letter of resignation he stated that he wished to serve with the Burghers in the field. No doubt he felt that there his medical skills would at least be used to save lives.

When Veale was finally called to account for his failure to respond to Haylett's reports and requests, he denied having received any letters at all from Dr Haylett. It appears Veale was not prepared to read letters written in English because Dutch was the official language in the

Transvaal. Haylett's requests and reports being in English were therefore set aside unread.[13] Veale, an Englishman and Cambridge graduate, would appear to have come out of the same mould as Ladysmith's notorious Dr Exham.

Haylett was succeeded by a German, Dr Rudolf von Gernet, who on 20 February, went on an inspection tour of the camps with Haylett. Dr von Gernet was appalled by what he saw, and on his return to Pretoria, immediately demanded a meeting with the Committee in Charge of Prisoners of War. As a German, he did of course carry more clout than the Englishman, Haylett. On hearing von Gernet's complaint, the Committee called for Dr Veale and after questioning him decided he should have nothing more to do with the hospital at Waterval, except that the supply of medicines should be administered by him. When von Gernet reported a week later that the supply of medicines was still unsatisfactory, the Committee authorised him to obtain medicines wherever he liked. From this time onwards conditions at the Waterval hospital improved dramatically.[14] In carrying out improvements Dr von Gernet was assisted by J Leigh Wood, manager of the Natal Bank, Pretoria, the Rev Goodwin, a Wesleyan minister, and a businessman, Sammy Marks, who was adept at obtaining funds from donors. Wood subsequently gave evidence about the conditions at the hospitals:

'In the middle of January, I first heard of the condition of the Racecourse hospital, especially as regards the insufficiency of milk. In conjunction with some friends I remedied this as soon as possible. In the middle of February I started a fund to buy medical comforts and food for the sick prisoners at the Racecourse. At this time I had an opportunity of visiting this hospital. Iron bedcots with mattresses were provided, but there were no pillows, sheets and very few blankets. The floor of the rooms in which patients, mostly suffering from enteric and dysentery, were lying, was in an indescribably filthy condition. There were no bedpans or commodes. The resident doctor (Dr Santos) informed me that he had applied repeatedly for scrubbing brushes, soap, soda etc., but without avail. I provided these articles out of my own fund. After this date the Racecourse hospital was greatly improved. In fact, from this date until the British occupation, the complete equipment for some 100 beds, and practically the whole supply of food and ordinary invalid comforts was provided by my fund.

'About eight weeks ago (April 1900) I had the opportunity of seeing the British prisoners, other than soldiers, who were also confined at the Racecourse, but apart from the soldiers. There were 58 of them, and they were sleeping without bedding of any description, on the bare ground, and were in rags. Many of them had been there for several months.

'As regards the Waterval hospital, at the beginning of February 1900, I heard of the terrible state of affairs existing at Waterval. I went to Dr Veale, and three times intimated to him, that if he wanted money to improve the lot of the sick at Waterval hospital, I would guarantee to find it. He did not accept my offers. I endeavoured then to effect my object through the Boer Authorities – the Under Secretary of State, and the Burgomaster – and through them to the Commission. These efforts had no results. As matters seemed to be going from bad to worse, we took the matter into our own hands, and on 20 February, sent out the first consignment of articles for the sick. On 24 February, Dr von Gernet was appointed resident medical officer at Waterval, and henceforth we continued to supply him with all he asked. We fitted out about 200 beds.'[15]

On 18 April 1900, Leigh Wood reported that Dr von Gernet was broken down and seriously ill from overwork. Those who helped Leigh Wood, and by their donations to his fund, saved many lives, were of course *Uitlanders* who had with various excuses obtained permission to remain in the Transvaal.

Soon after the arrival of the first British prisoners of war in Pretoria on 23 October 1899, the Wesleyan minister, the Rev Goodwin, visited them at the Racecourse camp, and when they moved to the Waterval camp he sought permission to visit once a week. He was not the only clergyman seeking permission to visit his congregation. A Baptist minister, a Congregational church minister, and Father de Lacy, a well-known Catholic priest who had been in the Transvaal for more than 30 years, were among those wishing to minister to the prisoners. The Boers, despite their professed Christianity, decided that there would be only one visit by one clergyman per week and that the visit would take place on a Saturday. The result was that the inmates could only see their Pastor on one day each month. Funerals were conducted by a sergeant and many were denied last rites. Father de Lacy was expelled from the Transvaal on 9 April 1900. No reason was ever given for his expulsion. However he had always spoken out fearlessly against the ill-treatment of prisoners and other abuses by the Government.

One clergyman who was not disturbed by the restrictions on visits to the prisoners was the Anglican priest, the Rev J. Godfrey. He was so scandalised by Churchill's escape, that he decided to distance himself from the prisoners and wrote to the incarcerated British officers, *'After what has recently occurred, viz., the escape of Mr. Churchill from confinement, I exceedingly regret that, in consideration of my duty to the Government, I must discontinue such regular ministrations, as I desire to maintain the honour due to my position. Of course I shall always be glad to minister to you in any emergency, with the special permission of the authorities, who will, with their usual kindness, duly inform me.'*[16]

The senior British officers imprisoned in Pretoria, Colonels Hunt, Bullock, Carleton and Moller might have committed some military blunders in Natal, but now they showed a better side of their character. Not only did they complain vigorously about the treatment of their men, but also took notice of, and criticised the treatment meted out to the Colonials. One such complaint followed the death of a Colonial, Lieutenant Tarbutt of the South African Light Horse. He had been captured in Natal and then taken to the Transvaal, where he was held in gaol with common criminals. Here he contracted typhoid and the prison authorities denied him any medical treatment whatsoever until he was at death's door. Only then did they send him to hospital. By this time the disease was so advanced that little could be done to help him and he died shortly afterwards.[17] Another to die in similar circumstances was a doctor, described as 'a native of India,' who died after catching fever at the Racecourse hospital, also having been denied medical attention until it was too late.

In a formal complaint addressed to the Transvaal State Secretary, Lt Col Hunt and his fellow Colonels pointed out that the Colonials were not in any way subjects of the Transvaal Government and continued, 'The distinction therefore made between these prisoners and those belonging to the Imperial Regular forces, seems at variance with recognized International custom, while their treatment does not seem to be that accorded to prisoners of war.'[18]

Another complaint signed by Col Hunt and 80 Officers and civilians stated that,

'…the treatment to which the non-commissioned officers and men at Waterval are subjected, has contributed to the very serious mortality prevalent amongst them. For weeks no soap was issued, so that it was impossible for them to maintain that ordinary cleanliness which is so necessary for health. Many of them are understood to be without boots. The scale of diet is extremely low, and the sanitary conditions generally are very defective, even though some attempts have lately been made to improve them.

'We are never officially informed of the serious illness or death of any of our men. We have a right to demand that this should be done, and that in all cases of serious illness, a man should be attended by a minister of his own religious faith. The provision made for religious services for men are entirely inadequate, and unworthy of a Government professing Christianity.

'We have previously written on the subject of the prisoners of war detained in the civil gaol, and the danger they incur thereby. For many of the deaths which have occurred, both at Waterval and Pretoria, the gravest responsibility rests directly on your officials, whose duty it should be to see to the reasonable comfort, healthy surroundings, and proper medical care of our men. For all this, the Government of the South African Republic is ultimately responsible.'[19]

In reply to the criticism that many men had been kept in gaol without being charged with any offence, the Secretary of the Committee in charge of Prisoners, in an attempt to shift responsibility, stated, 'most of them were received here without any statement of what charge was against them. This was the fault of the Officers at the front who made them prisoners. The Commission did its best to communicate on the subject with the Officers at the front.'[20]

A few further examples illustrate the Boer treatment of, and attitude towards Colonials. The Wesleyan Reverend Goodwin gave this description of the plight of the civilians in the prisoner-of-war camps: 'These prisoners were treated quite differently and with much more severity than the military. They were enclosed in a sort of cattle *kraal*, and complained bitterly to me both of the fact of their being kept as prisoners without trial, and the way in which they were treated. These men were never tried at all. They were mostly shopkeepers and farmers, and had not taken up arms at all. These men had to sleep on the bare ground with nothing but an overhead shelter, and were very poorly fed and clothed.'[21]

C V de V van der Spey left this account of his experiences:

'I was an accountant of the National Bank at Zeerust, and am a British subject. When war broke out the bank manager obtained permits for the bank staff who were British subjects to remain at our posts. Notwithstanding my having this permit, on the 11th December, 1899, I, in the company of six others, was arrested and placed in gaol at Zeerust, without being informed of any charge against me. I made successive applications to General Snyman, the State Attorney, and the American Consul to know the cause of our being imprisoned, but received no reply.

'About the middle of January 1900, we were informed that we could either stay in gaol at Zeerust or be deported across the border, and choosing the latter I was sent to Pretoria. Here I was again lodged in gaol. I wrote again to the State Attorney requesting to be placed across the border as stipulated, and was told in reply that he was unable to comply with our request, and that I must remain in gaol. There were six of us imprisoned at Pretoria. Two were afterwards sent back to Zeerust gaol. One, a land surveyor named Crews, was taken ill with typhoid fever, and put in the prison hospital where there were some 10 or 15 patients. When we asked the chief of the prison, Mr du Plessis, to have Mr Crews removed to a proper hospital, he told us that the Transvaal hospitals were for the sick and wounded burghers, not for us. Eventually Mr Crews was removed, very ill, to the Bourke (Red Cross) hospital, and there he died. Another of us was placed across the border, but Mr van Niekirk and myself were left in gaol until the British arrived. There were as fellow prisoners of ours in Pretoria gaol, Captain Kirkwood, South African Light Horse, and Captain Bates, Cape Police.

'While in Zeerust prison, six of us were confined in one cell which was kept locked all day, except for a quarter of an hour twice a day. Mr van Niekirk and myself were told in Zeerust that if we would take the oath of allegiance to the Transvaal we could be liberated at once.'[22]

The gaoler du Plessis was no doubt the same man who went out of his way to make life unpleasant for Karri and Sambo when they were imprisoned in Pretoria. One particularly unpleasant aspect of life in a Transvaal gaol were the sanitary arrangements: the latrine was a bucket in a corner of the cell regardless of the number of inmates and the hours the cell was kept locked.

After his capture on 27 January 1900, Inspector Landsburg of the Cape Mounted Police was taken to the colonial section of the camp at Waterval. On 7 April, he appealed to the authorities to release him and his fellow inmates into the general compound of the prisoner-of-war camp. He based his request on the following:

1. The place was full of vermin
2. For over three months they had been allowed no exercise (at one time they had been allowed to exercise once a week for an hour very early in the morning when it was bitterly cold)
3. There were no bathing or washing facilities.
4. The place was too small for the number of prisoners kept in it.
5. The den was so enclosed that they never had a breath of fresh air. At times the heat was so intense that they could hardly breathe, while at night it was so cold that they were prevented from sleeping.
6. Since being captured they had received far worse treatment than convicts.
   Inspector Landsburg received no response to his request.[23]

Alex Russell was a clerk employed by the Natal Railways near Glencoe. On 2 November 1899, he was one of the group of approximately 150 residents of Dundee who were put in closed trucks and taken to Pretoria. They arrived at their destination on Sunday, 5 November and were taken to the Racecourse where they were fed and put into tents. The following day they were told to get ready to go back to Natal. The prisoner's goods were searched and a telegram, referring to a military letter, was found in Russell's baggage. He was immediately removed from the group and taken to the gaol where he was placed in a cell and told not to communicate with the other prisoners. He was fed at 6 p.m. and then locked up for the night. At 6 a.m. breakfast was served. This was *mealie* meal porridge without salt, and a little bread. For their midday meal he and the others would receive bread, and twice a week some boiled meat. The water in which the meat was boiled would later be served to them as soup. In the evening they would again receive unsalted *mealie* meal porridge. Most people would regard unsalted *mealie* meal as unpalatable. Pretoria was not short of food and to salt the porridge would have required little effort or expense. The inadequacy of this diet is obvious and many more would have died, had Leigh Wood not arranged for daily meals to be sent to them during the latter stages of their imprisonment.

On 24 April 1900, Russell and four other prisoners were taken to the prison office, and, without ever having been told why they had been held in gaol for so long, were told that they were to be sent across the border. They were taken under guard to the station where they boarded a train which took them and some wounded soldiers to the Portuguese border. From there they made their way to Delagoa Bay where they boarded a ship, arriving in Durban on 3 May 1900.[24]

The group of Dundee residents who travelled with Russell to Pretoria in November 1899, did return to Natal but not to Dundee. Instead they went to Ladysmith which was already under siege. By taking them to Ladysmith, the Boers not only ensured that they continued to be incarcerated, but absolved themselves from the responsibility of feeding and accommodating them, while at the same time providing another drain on the town's medical and food resources. Furthermore, while these unfortunate people were in Ladysmith, the Boers were able to pillage, loot and destroy their farms, businesses and homes without let or hindrance, an opportunity which they exploited to the full.

After the Boers overran the Dundee District in October 1899, they endeavoured to persuade some of the local Dutch to join their invading army. Mr B Liebenberg refused to take up arms against his fellow countrymen with the result that on 18 December 1899, he was arrested and taken to gaol in Pretoria. On 24 April 1900, his wife wrote to the Natal Government begging for help. This is her letter:

> 'Sir, herewith I bring to your notice that my husband B. Liebenberg, of Dundee, has been taken prisoner by the Boers on the 18th December, and sent to Pretoria gaol, where he is still kept and treated most shamefully, the food being very bad, so I was informed by some prisoners since being liberated. My husband was taken prisoner for the simple reason of being loyal to the Queen and Country; he was commandeered to go and fight, which he refused; he said he was a loyal British subject and would not fight, but wished for a passport to go to Durban with his family, which they would not grant him. I myself have been subjected to harsh treatment and rash insults. When they took my husband prisoner, he asked what they intended to do with his wife and family. Then they told him they would give us a passport to go over the border with my wagon and oxen down to Greytown, via Pomeroy. When I got as far as Helpmekaar, by the Boer laager, I was stopped and kept prisoner for three days with guards round my wagon night and day and was threatened to be shot if any of us dared to leave the wagons. On the third day, I was sent back to Dundee, where my eldest boy, a mere lad, was taken and put in gaol and treated as a criminal, having nothing to eat, but the common mealie porridge and dry bread. After 9 days, however, I went to see the Magistrate, and asked him to let my boy off. I asked him, what they got him in gaol for and they told me it was because he said he was a British subject. On the 2nd January, I was sent to Pretoria with my family, and from there to Delagoa Bay, and from there to Durban. I earnestly beg your honourable, Sir, to take notice of this and try to do something towards getting my husband liberated: What they keep him for is quite a mystery, for there is no charge against him; I have spoken myself to the officials in Dundee and they told me that there is no charge against him and that they will soon send him to Delagoa Bay, but it is going on for five months, it is a cruel long time I should think, I am etc.,
>
> Mrs D Liebenberg.'[25]

When the British army finally reached Pretoria on 5 June 1900, its soldiers were shocked by the appearance of the prisoners and appalled by the conditions in which they had been living. A Court of Inquiry was immediately set up to investigate the treatment of prisoners of war by the Transvaal Government. On 24 June 1900, it released its findings. The Court found:

1. That the treatment of the officers of the Imperial Army, who were prisoners of war, appears on the whole to have been fairly good.
2. That the treatment of some of the Colonial prisoners was severe and unjustifiable, inasmuch as they were thrown into a common gaol and not treated as ordinary prisoners of war.
3. That non-commissioned officers and men were very badly fed, and the scale of diet, which was not strictly adhered to, was, in the matter of meat, a starvation ration.
4. That religious ministration was sparingly granted.

5. That the general treatment of sick prisoners was very bad, and has not been exaggerated, and that there is no doubt the prevalence of sickness and many deaths, which occurred amongst the prisoners, were attributable to the gross neglect of most ordinary sanitary precautions.[26]

Although the evidence and findings of the Court of Inquiry held at Pretoria concerned matters of deep and lasting significance to the people of Natal, the writer has been unable to find any reference to this matter in the Natal Archives, which perhaps is not surprising given the British decision to withhold information from Colonials. (see Chapter Three).

CHAPTER TWENTY-FOUR

Invaders chased out
of Natal

•—◆—•

*'Turning round he saw his two companions sitting quietly on their horses
with revolvers drawn, watching the fleeing Boers...'*

THE NATAL CAMPAIGN CONCLUDES WITH A GUNFIGHT, NOT AT THE OK CORRAL,
BUT IN VOLKSRUST MAINSTRAAT

WHILE General Buller was winkling the Boers out of their positions on the Tugela, Lord Roberts was making a spectacular advance from the Cape through the Orange Free State towards Pretoria. On 15 February 1900, the siege of Kimberley was raised. On 27 February, Boer General Cronje surrendered with more than 4,000 men at Paardeberg, and on 13 March, Roberts captured Bloemfontein, the capital of the Orange Free State.

In Natal much had still to be done before any advance could begin. After the Relief, the rail link between Ladysmith and Durban had to be restored. The retreating Boers had wrought considerable damage to the line and many bridges and culverts had been destroyed. In repairing the line one of the unnecessary difficulties faced was that the repair gangs were frequently attacked by the British army, one gang having to deal with three such attacks. These mistakes would seem to have had their origin in the erroneous belief that Natal was inhabited by Boers, and therefore any white man not in British uniform must be a Boer.

Despite the difficulties, the line between Ladysmith and Durban had been repaired by 9 March. On the first train to leave Ladysmith for Durban was General Sir George White. On his arrival at the Station he found his old regiment, the Gordons, formed up outside. He addressed them and then walked onto the platform where he took leave of General Buller, Senior Officers, Mr Farquhar the mayor, and other prominent residents. All noticed how ill and tired he looked. The train pulled out of the station to the swirl of bagpipes and the hurrahs and cheers of all who were privileged to be present. The Australian Donald Macdonald wrote that all who were there, 'will ever have a kind wish for the General, and an affectionate remembrance of the tall soldier who in plain Khaki moved so quietly amongst us.'[1]

On that train with White was one of his staff officers, Col Sir Henry Rawlinson, who during the siege had been critical of Buller's efforts to penetrate the Boer line along the Tugela. From the train he now had a good view of the Boer entrenchments, and wondered how it was Buller had ever broken through to Ladysmith.

One of the issues the British army could no longer shy away from was the arrest and cashiering of Captain CG Willson of the Natal Carbineers. It will be recalled that Willson and the Dundee Squadron of the Carbineers had ridden into Ladysmith on 22 October 1899, several days before the retreating column from Dundee staggered into the town. Not only had the Carbineers arrived safely without any assistance from the Regulars, but they also brought along some Boer prisoners. Given the attitude of some British Officers towards Colonials it is not surprising that they concluded the Carbineers must have ignored orders and run away from the battlefield. Charlie Willson was promptly arrested and word was put about that he was guilty of cowardice and had failed to obey orders. The next day a troop of the 18th Hussars arrived in Ladysmith. Unable to make contact with the British headquarters in Dundee, they too had decided to make their own way to Ladysmith, which for all practical purposes was precisely what Willson had done. Yet the commander of the troop of Hussars was not arrested, neither did he have to suffer the indignity of a Court Martial.

When the bedraggled Dundee column reached Ladysmith on 26 October 1899, it should have been obvious to all that the chain of command had broken down[2] and Willson's decision to retire to Ladysmith was reasonable. However if the Army withdrew the charges it would have resulted in a loss of face, which for some would have been a fate too horrible to contemplate.

On 24 March 1900, Captain Willson appeared before a Court Martial in Pietermaritzburg. An irregularity in the proceedings caused the verdict to be quashed. A fresh Court Martial was convened and on 7 May 1900, he was found guilty of some offence and sentenced to a fine of ten pounds. Charlie Willson said that as he had done nothing wrong, he would not pay the fine. He never paid it and no attempt was ever made to compel payment.

The Record of the Court Martial seems to have disappeared. It should have been sent to the Castle in Cape Town, but no trace of it can be found there; neither is it at the University of Cape Town, where some documents of that period are now housed. In Britain records of Courts Martial prior to 1914 were destroyed in the Blitz, and no mention of it can be found in War Office or Colonial Office papers in the National Archives at Kew, London, or in the Natal Archives. We will probably never know what offence Willson was found to have committed. If it was a failure to obey orders, no conviction should have been possible without Colonel Yule giving evidence, as he was the person responsible for issuing the orders. As we have seen, Yule appears to have suffered some sort of breakdown, and left South Africa in November 1899, never to return.

To add a twist to this tale, Willson was awarded the Volunteer Long Service Medal on 16 January 1900, and later a Queen's South Africa Medal with a bar for the Siege of Ladysmith! Subsequently the Governor appointed him a Justice of the Peace in consideration for his Loyalty, Integrity and Ability.

Was Charlie Willson used by certain elements in the army as a scapegoat to cover up Yule's apparent breakdown and the incompetent handling of the situation in Dundee? The idea of using Colonials as scapegoats was to occur a couple of years later in the notorious 'Breaker Morant' case, in which Australians were sacrificed to promote a British political cause.

For six weeks Colonel W Royston, Commandant of the Natal Volunteers, had been able to fight off a threatening attack of enteric, but a few weeks after the Relief, the fever took a stronger hold. He was taken to hospital in Pietermaritzburg, but died on 6 April 1900. His death was a great loss to Natal. Aware of the threat posed by Boer expansionism, he had ensured that the Volunteers were trained to meet this danger, rather than following standard British military practice. The result was that all his corps were to be more than a match for the Boers throughout the Natal Campaign. He had over the years won the respect of all people in Natal and he was to be much missed in the years to come. John Dartnell, now a Brigadier General, replaced Royston as commandant of the Natal Volunteers.

On 12 May 1900, Buller began his advance to liberate northern Natal. The Boers had concentrated their forces in the Biggarsberg Range, thereby blocking the main road and rail links to the north, and were now well ensconced in their trenches. General Hildyard, who had replaced Warren as commander of the 5th Brigade, was sent forward with his infantry along the railway towards the Biggarsberg Range and Dundee, apparently to drive the Boers out of their fortified positions. Not much attention was paid to Dundonald's Brigade, Dartnell's Volunteers, and some Artillery and Infantry moving south-east on a course roughly parallel to the Biggarsberg. From time to time they were harassed by long-range enemy fire, which the artillery was able to contain. The column made excellent progress and by nightfall was nearing the southern limit of the Biggarsberg, beyond which lay the Pomeroy/Dundee road.

The following day the Mounted Brigade continued its advance until it reached Uithoek Mountain, the southern bastion of the Biggarsberg Range. Uithoek appeared to be unclimbable, however Thorneycroft's MI dismounted and doing as they had done at Spion Kop, scrambled up the precipitous slope towards the summit. However, the mistakes of Spion Kop were not going to be repeated. To support Thorneycroft on the left, Buller ordered three battalions of Lyttelton's infantry to assault the summit from the south-west, while at the same time other units attacked from the south-east. Afraid that their retreat might be cut off, the Boers withdrew from Uithoek.[3] The Biggarsberg line had been turned.

With two squadrons of the Carbineers, McKenzie found himself operating on the flank with units from Dundonald's Brigade. With the consent of Dundonald he attached his squadrons to Dundonald's command for the next stage of the advance.[4] This move brought McKenzie into a position where he would be able to exercise greater influence over military decisions.

The column continued to the Pomeroy/Dundee road where they were joined by the Umvoti Mounted Rifles and Bethune's Mounted Infantry who had come up from the Greytown area. Buller now turned north towards Helpmekaar and Dundee. Several times the Boers attempted to check the advance but each time Dundonald's men would threaten their flanks causing the Boers to retreat. By mid-afternoon Buller decided to call a halt a couple of miles short of Helpmekaar. His force had covered a considerable distance that day, had turned the Boers' defensive position on the Biggarsburg and had received the welcome addition of the two colonial mounted regiments. Added to this, the Boers still did not know whether the main thrust of the British advance would come via Helpmekaar, or follow the railway line through the Biggarsberg towards Dundee?

Before dawn the next day (14 May) the mounted troops had left their bivouacs and had formed up ready to advance. Dundonald's Brigade and the Natal Volunteers immediately set off in pursuit of the Boers. Preceded by scouts, the mounted men swept through Helpmekaar, and deploying across a broad front, chased after the enemy. The Boers attempted to check the advance on various rocky outcrops but as soon as they were spotted, the Colonials would gallop round their flanks causing the Boers to hastily make off. At one *kopje* the Boers showed a little more resolution and tarried a little longer, so the artillery was summoned. The sight of the 7th Battery of the RFA coming up at a gallop, was enough to change Boer minds and away they rode with the Colonials after them. In desperation the Boers set fire to the *veld*, hoping the flames and smoke would check their pursuers. It didn't. Lt Dr Blake Knox, who was following the mounted column that day, recorded his impressions:

'From high ground here and there could be seen masses of horsemen, with our men hot on their heels; then the Boers tried to stem the torrent once more, but in vain, for their flanks were soon turned. Our horsemen strained every nerve, for the word was passed from General to Colonels, and Colonels to officers and men, "Get on, fire away, don't rest or stop, but ride on, on, on!" ... On again swept the cavalry through flame and smoke, the charred veldt grass blowing into men's faces, filling their eyes, mouths and nostrils, singeing the legs of the horses and the hair of the men, and giving the brigade the appearance of an army of demons. Six miles from Dundee the enemy took up a position on the further side of a deep ravine, from the other side of which their artillery came into action with wild fire, which became wilder still when they saw the Irregulars and Natal Volunteers creeping round their flanks.'[5]

As it was getting late, Dundonald received orders to halt. In a despatch to England Buller reported that '... Dundonald's Cavalry pursued the enemy through fire and smoke for 40 miles in a waterless country, I consider his pursuit a very fine performance.'[6]

In the night the Boers slipped away from their position before Dundee and early the next morning the mounted column rode into town. On the 14th Gerard Bailey had heard the sound of the approaching gunfire. He cut down a small tree for a flagstaff and dug a hole for it just behind General Penn Symons' grave. It was nearly seven months since that Union Jack had been used as a shroud for the General. Gerard had hidden the flag which he now took out of its hiding place. He was up early on 15 May, and was out and about by 5.30 a.m. It was a misty morning and all was quiet. An hour later a coloured man came to Gerard with the exciting news that some soldiers had been seen in town. The two men tied the flag to the crude flagstaff which was placed in the prepared hole and raised. It was a still day so there wasn't a flutter from the Union flag, but it was aloft, a symbol of the end of their waiting. A short while later he met the first men to enter Dundee, Major Henderson and two of his guides, Dundee boys Appleby and Cooper. He gave them breakfast and by the time they had finished the South African Light Horse were in town. During the day Gerard met and chatted with some of the leaders, General Buller, Lord Dundonald and Colonel Greene of the Carbineers and many other Natal friends, '...and there was Brigadier-General Dartnell, we Natalians are so proud of. I told him we in Dundee had not got much news of the war, but we had heard of his promotion.'[7] Bailey was once an Englishman and Dartnell a Canadian, but now it was 'we Natalians.'

On the 16th the troops rested, which gave Hildyard's infantry a chance to come up from the Biggarsburg. Initially they had met with determined resistance from the Boers and could make little headway, but once the Boer flank was turned they melted away leaving Hildyard free to advance to Glencoe, Dundee and beyond.

On 17 May, Buller's force continued its advance towards Newcastle and the Transvaal border. Employing the same tactics they had used on the road to Dundee and riding hard, the troops covered the 37 miles to Newcastle that day, and by the 19th they were near Laing's Nek, a further 25 miles closer to the Transvaal border. On their left was Majuba Hill (6,500 ft) and on their right Pogweni Hill (5,400 ft). Between these two hills lay Laing's Nek, heavily fortified with trenches and Artillery. Buller decided to halt the advance and the mounted troops were ordered to withdraw a couple of miles to the northern bank of the Ingogo River. When Dundonald's guns began their retirement large numbers of Boers galloped forward to cut them off. This had been foreseen. McKenzie's men had concealed themselves on one flank while the South African Light Horse were similarly concealed on the other. The advancing Boers rode into the crossfire and quickly abandoned the attack.[8]

Buller decided to wait at the Ingogo River while the railway line was repaired and supplies brought up. In nine days his column had covered 138 miles during which time they had suffered few casualties. The only serious loss had been inflicted on Bethune's MI who had been sent across the Transvaal Border in the direction of Vryheid so as to protect the left of the column. They were ambushed and suffered sixty-eight casualties almost half of whom were killed.[9]

In Newcastle the advancing troops found the same destruction and looting of premises by the Boers which had occurred in other towns they had occupied. They were particularly

After the initial phase of looting in Newcastle the Boer authorities dumped what remained of the resident's possessions in the Town hall for anyone to take what they liked.

vicious in their attack on the Newcastle Catholic Convent, tearing up bibles and other books, smashing pictures and the Sacristy with all its contents, before setting alight to the Chapel. As in Dundee, such furniture as remained in resident's houses after the first wave of looters had had their fill, had been taken to the Town Hall for late comers to choose whatever they wanted.

Always keen to bring the war to an end, Buller, without being authorised to do so, on 30 May, offered peace terms to the Boers.[10] An armistice was agreed until 5 June. In due course the peace terms were rejected, the Boers using the intervening period to strengthen their line.

Buller too had not been idle, Hildyard's Division was sent eastwards across the Buffalo River to the little Transvaal town of Utrecht which was taken without any opposition. Lyttelton's Division was sent north eastwards towards Dornkop which lay just to the east of Laing's Nek and Pogweni Hill. To the Boers it appeared that the British would either attempt a frontal attack on the Nek, or attempt to by-pass it by an eastern route.

When darkness fell on 5 June, Hildyard, without being observed, marched rapidly back to the Newcastle/ Laing's Nek road. On 8 June, Buller launched his attack, not on Laing's Nek, or via some route to the east of it, but westwards via Botha's Pass over the Drakensburg and into the Free State. Hildyard's Infantry, with considerable Artillery support, led the way, while Dundonald's Brigade and Brocklehurst's Regular Cavalry covered the flanks. The attack had not been expected with the result that the defenders, outnumbered and out-gunned, were forced to give way. By nightfall the British had reached the top of the pass. The following day was spent getting supplies up to their camp.

On 10 June, the column set off northwards towards Alleman's Pass which provided a route down the Drakensberg and onto the plain north of Laing's Nek. The South African Light Horse led the way and at times had to fight hard to overcome pockets of resistance; in one skirmish they lost six killed and eight wounded. On the morning of 12 June, they were at the head of Alleman's Pass. The Boers had taken up strong defensive positions on the Pass but were now facing a far wiser enemy. Without cover to conceal their advance, the infantry took note of the wind direction and set fire to the veld. The smoke from the fire not only hid their advance, but the flames drove the Boers out of their concealed positions. With superb support from the Artillery and Dundonald's Brigade on the right flank, the infantry broke through the Boer line. Laing's Nek had been out flanked and the road into the Transvaal was now clear.

On 14 June 1900, Buller's army crossed into the Transvaal. Ahead lay the little town of Volksrust. Corporal Umpleby of the Colonial Guides was sent ahead with two of his men to find out if the town was defended.

From a distance no sign of activity could be seen. Though he had no orders to enter Volksrust, Umpleby decided to ride into town to find out precisely what was happening. Cautiously they entered the town and rode up the main street. In the distance a Swiss ambulance could be seen making its way out of town, but otherwise nothing stirred. All the houses and businesses appeared to be closed or locked and neither man nor beast was seen. Except for the sound of their horses on the road, the silence was all pervasive.

Suddenly horsemen were among them shouting, '*Hande Op*' (Hands up). A man tried to wrest Umpleby's rifle from him, but he was not going to give it up without a struggle. As he and the assailant wrestled for it, both fell from their horses, the Boer shouting as he fell, '*Skiet hom*' (Shoot him). Two shots rang out and Umpleby felt the attacker's grip on his rifle slacken. Scrambling up, he saw a group of Boers galloping away. At his feet lay the wounded leader of the posse, Veldt Cornet Opperman, and a few paces further away lay another wounded Boer. Turning round he saw his two companions sitting quietly on their horses, with revolvers drawn, watching the fleeing Boers.[11]

Postscript

The show is not over until the fat lady sings and her song has some new verses.

WHEN Buller's Army marched out of Natal it left a country which had been devastated by war. The Boers, while rampaging through Northern Natal and the Midlands, had wantonly destroyed towns, villages, businesses and farms, while at the same time carrying off livestock, farm equipment, wagons, furniture and anything else they fancied. One of Natal's greatest assets, the railway system, with its concomitant locomotives, rolling stock, workshops, stations and other equipment had been severely damaged and would take many years to restore to its pre-war condition.

The outbreak of war resulted in almost every man of military age in the Colony enlisting in one of the units fighting the invaders. With their owners and staff away on military service, many businesses closed. For the Government, which relied on trade for its income, this resulted in a drastic decline in its revenue, while at the same time they had the expense of keeping the Volunteers and their supporting units in the field as well as providing for the tens of thousands of penniless refugees crowding into the Colony. As early as December 1899, Natal was bankrupt and was forced to borrow £500,000 at 4% from the Imperial Government to keep its Administration running[1], and this was just a foretaste of the very difficult economic times ahead.

After the invaders were driven out of Natal, almost two years were to elapse before the Boer leaders were prepared to negotiate a peace treaty. As the war dragged on, some British generals applied the lessons learnt in Natal, but for others it was business as usual. Commenting on the repeated failures of the British to capture the elusive Boer General Christiaan De Wet, a Cape colonial volunteer, Major CG Dennison wrote, *'Why did De Wet escape so often? Because of jealousy and incapacity. Why were the colonials never given a chance to capture De Wet independently? Because the military authorities knew too well that the colonials might catch De Wet, and the imperial regular troops would get no kudos. Had a few columns of combined colonial forces, Australians, New Zealanders, Canadians, and South Africans, under their own officers, been given the work to do, De Wet would have been caught, I am confident, without much trouble.'*[2]

Despite the ruling by Sir William Butler that Blacks should not serve against the Boers, they were to play a decisive role in bringing the Boers to the negotiating table. In April 1902, black scouts under Aubrey Woolls Sampson laid the foundation for their comprehensive defeat at Roodevaal in the Western Transvaal. On the other side of the country, in that part of Zululand which had been annexed by the Transvaal in 1884, Boer Kommandos were living off the land, a process which involved helping themselves to food, cattle and livestock belonging to the Zulus. This aggravated the ill-feeling between the Boers and the Zulus and several Boers were killed. Louis Botha, believing members of the Qulusi clan under Chief Sikobobo were responsible, instructed his Kommandos to destroy their settlements and confiscate their livestock.

Acting on Botha's instructions, on 3 May 1902 a Boer Kommando under Jan Potgieter arrived at Chief Sikobobo's *kraal* only to find he was not there. Potgieter laid waste to the *kraal* and drove off three hundred and eighty cattle. He followed up this action by sending a message to the Chief in which he stated that Sikobobo and his people were no better than fowl-lice, and defiantly suggested they come to his laager at Holkrantz to retrieve their cattle. The Chief accepted the challenge, and on the night of 6 May 1902 his impis fell on the Kommando at Holkrantz killing Potgieter and 55 of his men. Only a few Boers escaped, just enough to tell the Boer leadership what had happened. The Qulusi recovered all their cattle and a few more by way of interest, plus all the Boer horses.

This defeat in the East, following on from the defeat at Roodeval in the west, convinced the Boer leadership that the war had been lost, and they were prepared to enter into peace negotiations. Churchill was one of the first to sense that there had been a change in the wind blowing through British politics. In 1899 he had been full of praise for the people of Natal, writing that they were entitled to the general respect and sympathy of all good Englishmen and 'a full indemnity to all individual colonists who have suffered loss, must stand as an Imperial debt of honour.' No sooner had Ladysmith been relieved than he was warning Natal against taking a hard line towards the Boers. By 1902 he had adopted a positively pro-Boer stance. He expressed contempt for those who had opposed the Transvaal's human rights abuses and expansionist aims, and was particularly derisive of the *Uitlanders*, who after all had sought no more than the rights to which it is generally accepted, all men are entitled. The Boers were 'the Rock' on which the new South Africa was to be founded.

Churchill's friend Ian Hamilton, now a General and Lord Kitchener's Chief of Staff, was even more contemptuous of Britain's colonial allies. In his opinion the Boers were 'the best men in South Africa' and in February 1902, he told Churchill, 'Do let us profit by our experience when we smashed the Zulus for the Boers, and not repeat the mistake by annihilating the Boers for the Jewburghers. You have no idea what arrogant insolent devils you will discover as soon as Mr Boer has lost his Mauser.'[3] In making this vicious anti-Semitic statement, Hamilton appears to have forgotten, or perhaps remembered too well, that two years previously the 'arrogant insolent devils' had saved both his and the British army's reputation at Elandslaagte and Wagon Hill.

Churchill and Hamilton had judged the British political mood correctly. Only British and Boer leaders would attend the Peace Conference. Natal, the Cape, the '*Uitlander*' minority in the Transvaal, and all the other peoples of South Africa were denied any say in the proceedings. Predictably, the Conference produced an agreement which would ensure that the Boers, now calling themselves Afrikaners, would exercise exclusive power over all the peoples of South Africa for almost a century.

Churchill was correct about another issue. After the war, Britain did not nationalise, or in any other way attempt to control the gold mines, which continued to be owned by shareholders from all over the world regardless of race, colour, or creed.

When peace came, Robert Samuelson enquired whether his Scouts would receive their medals, and the then Natal Prime Minister, Albert Hime, assured him that they would. When Joseph Chamberlain came to South Africa in December 1902, he saw the leaders of the Scouts and assured them they would get their medals. The Natal Volunteers requested Samuelson to compile a list of the scouts who had served. Assisted by Simeon Kambule and Jabers Molife the list was prepared, and subsequently checked and passed by Colonel Wales of the Volunteers, who strongly recommended that they be granted. However the issue of the medals was vetoed because it was thought that the award might 'offend the Boers.'[4]

A few notes about some of the people we have met in this book

Walter Karri Davies

After the Relief of Mafeking, the role played by Karri in the life of the Imperial Light Horse changed. He continued to serve with the Regiment until the end of the war, being primarily concerned with administrative matters, such as recruiting, the welfare of disabled veterans and the widows and families of those who had been killed. However he was also involved with other matters. Both Lord Roberts and Lord Kitchener recognised his considerable organisational and engineering skills and co-opted him to carry out various important tasks, from ensuring railways were functioning to designing and building bridges. Such was the confidence they had in his ability and integrity that they both gave him a power of attorney, stating, 'All officers of HM Forces, Government Officials and others with whom he may come in contact will do anything he wishes to facilitate his work.' Lord Kitchener appointed him to act as his Representative on several Commissions.

Karri was instrumental in arranging for the future King George V to become Honorary Colonel of the Imperial Light Horse, a position which was retained by succeeding monarchs until South Africa became a republic in 1961. In August 1901, the Prince of Wales visited Natal while returning home after a visit to Australia. He sent a message to Karri expressing his disappointment that they had been unable to meet.[5]

At the end of the War, Karri was offered a knighthood in recognition of the services he had rendered during the conflict. Characteristically he asked to be allowed to decline the honour because he had undertaken to serve King and Country without honour or reward.[6] On the cessation of hostilities, Karri went to Britain where he fell in love with and married an Irish girl, Annie Cochrane, from County Limerick. On his return to South Africa he set up in practice as a Consulting Engineer. Over the following years he was to make a contribution to the future welfare of South Africa which cannot be overestimated. Commissioned to advise on the possibility of establishing irrigation dams in the Orange River Colony, his recommendations were not only carried out but were to form a basis of the great irrigation schemes which were to provide food and water for the expanding mining and industrial conurbations of the Witwatersrand and the Vaal Triangle.

He encouraged the importation by farmers of quality breeding stock, by persuading the government to insert in their mail contracts with shipping lines, a provision that pedigree stock should be carried free. All stock farming benefited, though perhaps none more so than the wool industry where the importation of Merino breeding stock enabled the country to substantially boost its wool production. Thereafter the export of wool was for many years one of the mainstays of the South African economy.

The South African Government also commissioned him to make a Report on the Land Banks and Closer Settlement Systems in Tasmania and New Zealand. This gave him a knowledge of the various methods, both private and government, of settling people on the land and financing them. Out of his report was to come the establishment of the Land Bank of South Africa. Over the years few successful farmers in the country would have succeeded without some help from the Land Bank, which was to play a vital role in the modernisation and development of South African agriculture.

His tact and wisdom enabled him to reconcile parties who had previously been at loggerheads and to persuade parties who appeared to have irreconcilable differences to come to agreement. As an example, shortly after the War, a dispute arose between the Transvaal authorities, the Netherlands Railway Company and the Portuguese at Delagoa Bay. As a result of intervention by Karri, an agreement was reached between the parties which enabled the railways and the harbour to work on amicable terms. During this post-war period Karri worked tirelessly to effect reconciliation between the peoples of South Africa, only to have his illusions shattered in 1914 when several leading Boers rose in armed rebellion against the South African Government.

When his father died in 1913 he returned to Australia, where he remained until the outbreak of war in 1914. Too old to enlist in Australia, he travelled to Britain where he was appointed British Agent on the West Coast of the United States. Based in San Francisco, he soon established a good rapport with the Americans which helped the British, and perhaps more importantly, would have raised the awareness of the Americans to the strategic importance of Australia.

In 1922 he decided that the breech block which had been taken from the Boer gun at Gun Hill, Ladysmith on 7 December 1899, and given to Karri by General Hunter, should be returned to South Africa. It is now housed in the Ladysmith Museum.

Karri died suddenly on 29 November 1926, at Broadstairs in Kent. Had he been willing to compromise his personal integrity, a Knighthood and a Victoria Cross might have been his. No wonder he gained the complete trust of all who knew him. In an obituary published in the London *Times*, an old comrade from his Imperial Light Horse days, Major Percy Greathead, wrote, '*He was the kindest-hearted thing that ever happened. I doubt whether he ever said or thought an evil thing about anybody on earth. He had a fine even temper and a wonderfully stable character. With all that he was a man of iron determination, and altogether a magnificent personality.*'

Aubrey Woolls Sampson

While the ILH was engaged in the Relief of Mafeking, Aubrey Woolls Samson underwent the operation to his thigh. It was successful in the sense that he was able to get about and ride a horse, though he had lost his previous agility and would suffer pain for the rest of his life. At the beginning of July 1900, he replaced Col Edwards as commander of the ILH and joined the regiment at its bivouac near Pretoria. The period during which he commanded the regiment was not a happy time for Aubrey. Of all the people in South Africa, he probably knew more about the country and its peoples than anyone else. He had lived life from the elegant colonial society of the Cape to the rip-roaring goldfields of Barberton, from the dry highveld plains in the west to the rolling green hills of Pondoland and Zululand in the east. He had mingled with wealthy financiers, backveld Dutch farmers and the many different black peoples, learning and absorbing their languages and cultures. In contrast, Kruger and his coterie were only familiar with a small part of southern Africa, the people, languages and cultures of the rest being but dimly known to them. Yet the Boers and the British branded Aubrey an '*Uitlander*,' an outsider, an attitude which caused deep hurt. With a few exceptions he had come to distrust and dislike Imperial officers and resented any interference by them in the affairs of the Regiment. He became uncommunicative and almost fanatical in his desire to finish the war as soon as possible.

On 5 January 1901, near Cyferfontein in the Western Transvaal, he received orders to 'lose no time' and occupy a hill which had that morning been scouted by the 18th Hussars and found to be clear of the enemy. Relying on the information provided by the Hussars, Aubrey ordered his two squadrons of Light Horsemen, in all about 180 men, to occupy the hill. Unknown to him, the Boers had cleverly concealed their movements and had themselves occupied the hill with 700 to 800 men. With little cover the ILH was allowed to approach to within 50 to 100 yards before the enemy opened fire. It was able to retrieve the situation, but not before it had lost 18 killed and 32 wounded. Eighty horses were killed and 20 destroyed later. The British blamed Aubrey for the debacle, resulting in his relinquishing command of the regiment and being transferred to the Intelligence Department.

As an Intelligence Officer, Aubrey was at last able to exercise to the full his vast knowledge of the country. General Sir Ian Hamilton said of him, 'In one leap he became the second figure in the war, second only to Lord Kitchener himself.'[7]

In September 1901, the Boers appeared to be gaining the initiative. Everywhere the British were on the defensive. Louis Botha with 2,000 men appeared to be poised to again invade Natal. To meet this threat the British had assembled 16,000 men with 40 guns under General Lyttelton. On 17 September this column suffered a serious and humiliating setback at Blood River Poort where a battalion led by Hubert Gough was smashed up.

However, things were about to change. Early in September Aubrey was posted as Intelligence Officer to a small column which was stationed at Carolina in the eastern Transvaal, and commanded by Colonel Benson. Though in the heart of enemy territory, and having only 800 men at his disposal, Benson was persuaded to launch a series of night attacks based on information provided by Aubrey. These raids were successfully carried out on 10, 15, 16, and 18 September. Laagers were captured complete with prisoners, wagons, horses and cattle. With his heartland threatened, Louis Botha abandoned his proposed invasion of Zululand and Natal. Though Colonel Benson was killed in an engagement at Bakenlaagte on 30 October 1901, the initiative had passed from the Boers to the British.

After Benson's death, Aubrey joined a column operating in the eastern Transvaal which was commanded by General Bruce Hamilton (no relation of Ian Hamilton) who continued the use of the tactics developed by Benson and Woolls Sampson. Black Scouts would go out in the evening to check the position of any Boers within a 25 mile radius. They would return the next morning and report what they had discovered. After dark the column would leave camp, and riding through the night would attack the Boers at dawn. In eight weeks Hamilton's column had accounted for some 900 Boers and recovered one of Benson's guns without any loss to themselves. Boer resistance in the eastern Transvaal had been broken. Bruce Hamilton was later to write of Aubrey, 'He had an extraordinary sense of what the Boers were likely to do, and over and over again, after marching all night, we would find them at dawn almost exactly where he expected.'[8]

Though Aubrey was on good terms with Bruce Hamilton, his antipathy towards Imperial officers caused him to shun their company, and most of his time was spent with the scouts. Fully aware of the fact that the Boers would shoot any black scouts they captured, he was unceasing in his efforts to ensure their safety and win their confidence while they in turn gave him their absolute loyalty. When the scouts returned from their night-time sorties, Aubrey would spend hours talking to them, encouraging, cross-questioning, and checking all they had told him. He gave great attention to detail and his information was wonderfully accurate. In December 1901, Aubrey moved to the north-eastern Free State to assist General Sir Henry Rawlinson. Here the same pattern of intensive scouting followed by a dawn attack was repeated with success.

Kitchener meanwhile had been relying on an extensive and expensive system of blockhouses and wire fences to defeat the Boers. This system had some limited success in containing the Boers as did a decision to stop bringing woman and children into the concentration camps. In England do-gooders applauded the latter decision thinking it was an act of kindness, whereas in fact it was a necessary military decision. Far more successful than the blockhouses were Aubrey and his scouts. Unable to intimidate the wily General de la Rey in the Western Transvaal, Kitchener sent his Chief of Staff, Ian Hamilton, after him. Ian Hamilton brought Aubrey across as his Intelligence Officer and the intelligence garnered by Aubrey and his scouts set up the defeat of the Boers at Roodeval. Hamilton, who at the best of times was no lover of 'Uitlanders', would not have exaggerated when he wrote of Aubrey, 'In one leap he became the second figure in the war, second only to Lord Kitchener himself.'

To ensure they were effective, the scouts were of necessity drawn from the local community. Near Natal they would have been Zulus, in the eastern Free State Sotho and in the west, Tswana. These people had different languages and customs and Woolls Sampson was one of very few men in the country who were able to converse with all in their own language. Furthermore it was not only the words he understood. He also knew their culture and the way they used words. For example, if a scout referred to an Englishman Woolls Sampson would not assume that the person came from England. It was this understanding of the way they used language which enabled him to obtain such precise knowledge from his scouts of the whereabouts of the Boers and the physical features of the land where they were encamped. Despite their courage and effectiveness, none of Aubrey's black scouts received a war medal.

After the war Aubrey received a knighthood in recognition of his outstanding service as an Intelligence Officer. As Sir Aubrey Woolls Sampson, he practised as an estate agent and subsequently decided to enter politics. He had no trouble getting elected, but apart from this initial success, his foray into politics was a disaster. For him things were either right or wrong, and there was no capacity in his character for the horse-trading which is part and parcel of a politician's lot. He found the debates in Parliament intolerably tedious, except on one occasion when a member challenged his integrity. Grabbing a horsewhip, he chased the offending member out of the parliamentary chamber and down Adderley Street, Cape Town's main thoroughfare. When Sir Percy Fitzpatrick pointed out that this was not the way in which parliamentary debates should be conducted, an unrepentant Aubrey retorted that this was a great pity.

When the First World War broke out Aubrey offered his services to the country, now headed by Louis Botha and Jan Smuts. The two Boer Generals were not prepared to grant any position to the man who had once played such a large part in defeating the Boer Kommandos. His offer was ignored. Aubrey gradually lapsed into a life of quiet retirement in suburban Johannesburg. In 1922 General Sir Henry Rawlinson, (one time Commander of the British Fourth Army in France and from 1920 Commander-in-Chief, India) wrote to Aubrey,

'My dear Woolls Sampson,

After a lapse of more than 20 years I was overjoyed to hear from Walter Bagot that you are still going strong at Johannesburg - and I write this short letter of greeting and good cheer to let you know that my memory of your great self in the trying times of Ladysmith, before, during and after the siege, is as fresh as ever. Much water has flown under the bridge since those days and I have seen something of the wars of nations and the battles of the giants - I look back on them as having taught me that the thing of all others that makes victory certain in the end is that great determination and faith in the cause, of which you were so marked an exponent in Ladysmith. You may not have known it, but as a young staff officer in those days, I have treasured ever since the picture of your lying wounded in a dugout by the Klip River swearing that you would not lose your leg and that you would ride into Pretoria at the head of your Regiment - and you did it - more power and long life to you. In 1914-15 in France when things looked equally black, your example came back many times to my memory and helped much to carry me through the dark days to the sunshine and triumph beyond. Problems of a different character face me to-day but the road which leads to eventual solution is the one you originally indicated to me - unswerving determination to prevail....

Yours ever,
Rawlinson.'[9]

Aubrey died in Johannesburg in 1924, survived by his wife and daughter.

Duncan McKenzie

As the Volunteers had been established solely to defend Natal, once the invaders had been driven out of the Colony, they did not accompany the British troops into the Transvaal and the Free State. Instead, they were deployed along the Natal borders. Buller had wanted Duncan McKenzie with other officers from the Volunteers to join him in the Transvaal, but this move was blocked by Col Greene of the Carbineers obliging them to endure a few frustrating months of inaction conducting guard duties at Dundee. At the end of September 1900, a Composite Regiment was formed from those men from the Natal regiments who volunteered for further service. They received no pay and had to provide their own boots, horses and clothing.[10] Lt Col Robert Evans of the Natal Mounted Rifles was appointed to command this Regiment with McKenzie as his second-in-command. As Colonel Evans had to spend much of his time in Dundee, McKenzie commanded the troops in the field, their principal duty being to escort military convoys in south eastern Transvaal.

On 4 December 1900, Lord Kitchener was travelling by train through Natal on his way to Durban. Stationed at de Jager's Drift, McKenzie received an order to proceed at once to Glencoe as the Commander-in-Chief wished to see him. Riding as hard as he could, Duncan was able to cover the 30 miles to Glencoe just in time to meet the train. He was taken into the C-in-C's saloon carriage, and after the usual polite introductory conversation, Kitchener told McKenzie that a 2nd Regiment of the Imperial Light Horse was to be formed and he would like McKenzie to command it. To encourage acceptance, McKenzie was to be promoted to Lieutenant-Colonel and could choose his own officers.[11]

McKenzie immediately set about organising his new command. From the Composite Regiment he took Capt John ('Galloping Jack') Royston and Capt David Mackay who were both promoted to the rank of Major. He also gave commissions to several men from the ranks, notably B. Nicholson, whom he promoted to Lieutenant in charge of the Regiment's special scouts, sixteen of whom came from the Composite Regiment and were known to be reliable. Col Robert Evans protested that McKenzie was taking all his best men, so McKenzie took no more. With the core of the Regiment established, he moved to Volksrust to meet the men who had been recruited elsewhere.

Unknown to McKenzie, the 1st ILH and the 2nd ILH had the same recruiting officer. Major Karri Davies ensured that the 1st ILH acquired the best recruits, while the rest were sent on to McKenzie. On their arrival at Volksrust it was found that many of the men could not ride or shoot. This provided the officers with a few problems and other ranks a great deal of amusement. An intensive training program began immediately which was far from complete when they were ordered on 19 January 1901 to Pretoria where they were met by Brigadier-General Birdwood, who was on Kitchener's Staff. He invited McKenzie to dine at their Mess. How times had changed! After the meal Birdwood took McKenzie to see Kitchener, who wanted to know all about the Regiment. McKenzie told him that the men needed more training. However Kitchener replied that the shortage of troops was such that he was not able to grant them any further time for training, they were to go to the Eastern Transvaal immediately, where some of the best Boer Kommandos were operating. To comfort McKenzie, Kitchener offered a little advice. He said the Boers had developed a new tactic. On seeing a troop of dismounted men, they would gallop straight at them resulting in the surprised troop mounting and galloping off. Kitchener suggested they lie quiet and shoot the Boers, as this would teach them a salutary lesson. McKenzie replied that if the 2nd ILH dismounted they would have no choice but to lie quiet and shoot, because most were unable to mount their horses.[12] Kitchener laughed. The next day he inspected the Regiment and afterwards it entrained for Wonderfontein on the Pretoria-Delagoa Bay line where the intensive training continued and the Regiment was soon up to standard.

The 2nd ILH was to form part of General Smith-Dorrien's column operating in the eastern Transvaal. McKenzie developed an excellent relationship with his new commander, who gave him a free hand when conducting operations. Duncan applied the same principles which had been so successful in Natal, namely keeping one's whereabouts and intentions hidden from the enemy, careful scouting, avoiding frontal attacks and instead using enveloping flank movements to surprise the enemy. As in Natal he was extraordinarily successful. For example between 9 February and 11 March 1901, the Regiment captured:

> 644 Horses
> 50 Mules
> 9,500 Cattle
> 31,139 Sheep
> 192 Wagons
> 57 Carts
> 20,200 lbs. Mealies(Maize)
> 8,500 lbs. Oat Hay
> 170 Firearms
> 15,050 lbs. Ammunition

In addition:

> 39 Enemy were killed
> 113 Wounded
> 129 Captured
> 30 Surrendered. (Total Boer losses 311 men)

In contrast, the Regiment suffered 2 men killed by lightning, 2 drowned, and one man shot himself in the foot.[13] During this period Duncan received a silver medal from the Royal Humane Society for plunging into a flooded Assegai River to save a drowning British soldier.[14]

Sometimes assisted by Regular units and sometimes on their own, the Regiment continued its successful operations in the eastern Transvaal and Swaziland through the winter of 1901. General Smith-Dorrien was transferred to India at the beginning of May and the 2nd ILH now fell under Duncan's old friend, General Walter Kitchener, who continued the policy of giving Duncan a wide discretion in carrying out his orders, thereby enabling the 2nd ILH to inflict setback after setback on the Boers. For example, at Coalbank they captured 14 Boers and with them over 6,000 cattle, innumerable sheep and about 200 good horses.[15] All captured animals were handed over to the British army who sold them, and kept the proceeds.

The men in the Regiment had signed on for six months which had expired, so it was agreed that they should all have leave. On their return to the Transvaal in November 1901, they were ordered to Harrismith in the Free State where they were to be brigaded with the 1st ILH under General Dartnell. After a few engagements in which the Regiment continued to distinguish itself, the Brigade was ordered to Zululand to counter possible action by Louis Botha. On arrival, they were ordered to return to Harrismith. After the long ride back to the Free State, McKenzie went down with enteric and very nearly died. By the time he had been nursed back to health the war was over.

Starting with a group of men, many of whom could not ride or shoot, McKenzie had welded them into a regiment which was probably the most efficient unit fighting against the Boers. In nineteen months of active service they had not suffered a single reverse of any kind and Lord Kitchener noted that they had taken more prisoners than any other regiment. McKenzie attributed this success to the fact that he had been able to choose his own officers. They all came from Natal.

With the coming of peace in 1902, Duncan McKenzie returned to farming, though he continued his association with the Carbineers. On the retirement of Colonel Greene in 1903, he became commander of the Regiment. Throughout his life he took no interest in politics and played no part in the negotiations and debates in the country which were to lead to the formation of the Union of South Africa. In 1906 a combination of the difficult economic times, the poor recognition they had received for their contribution during the War, and the lack of hope resulting from the peace terms, resulted in unrest and killings in certain districts of Natal and Zululand. Britain decided not to intervene, leaving Natal to deal with the difficulty while at the same time any proposed action was to be cleared by a General Stephenson who held a watching brief on behalf of the Imperial Government. Duncan McKenzie was given the task of quelling the nascent rebellion. As required he submitted his campaign plan to General Stephenson who expressed his approval. Duncan quickly and efficiently brought the rebellion to an end, thereby saving much suffering and loss of life which would have occurred with an extended campaign. The rebels, like the British a few years before, failed to pay due regard to the killing power of the modern rifle, and as a result suffered a disproportionately high number of casualties. After the campaign, Duncan received a long overdue knighthood.

In 1914 Louis Botha, as Prime Minister, took South Africa into the World War alongside Britain. Many former Boer leaders opposed this move and went into armed rebellion. Among the rebels was General Beyers, Kommandant General of South Africa's Defence Force. Botha's first task was therefore to crush the rebellion. Relying principally on loyal Afrikaners, but also with some aid from the Anglo South Africans, Botha inflicted a series of defeats on the rebels and by the end of February 1915, all had surrendered.

With the rebellion over, the next priority was to neutralise the threat posed by German South West Africa which lay to the north-west of the Cape Province. This vast German colony was bounded in the west by the Atlantic, in the north by the Portuguese colony of Angola, in the east by Bechuanaland, and in the south by South Africa. Apart from a strip of savannah in the north, most of the country is sparsely populated semi-desert. Along the Atlantic coast is the Namib, one of the driest places on earth. There were only two harbours of consequence on this treacherous coastline. About 160 miles north of the South African border was Luderitz and another 350 miles further north was Walvis Bay, a small South African enclave on the German Colony's coast. A railway line ran inland from Walvis Bay to the German Colony's capital, Windhoek. Running south from Windhoek the line went down the centre of the country to Seeheim where it was joined by a branch line from Luderitz. From Seeheim it continued southwards to the border where it joined the South African rail network.

It was decided that the South Africans would make a three-pronged attack on the Germans. General Botha, in overall command, would land at Walvis Bay and follow the railway to Windhoek. A second column under McKenzie, now a Brigadier General, would land at Luderitz, proceed east along the railway, and then turn north towards Windhoek. A third column would advance up the railway from the south.

The Germans did not oppose the landings at Luderitz, having decided to rely on the inhospitable terrain for their defence. The railway was blown up, wells poisoned and mines laid. In February 1915, McKenzie's column began its advance east along the railway line. It was a slow process as the railway had to be repaired as the column advanced, while enemy patrols were constantly setting traps. Shortage of water and landmines added to its problems. On 31 March it occupied Aus, 82 miles from Luderitz. Instead of following the railway from Aus to Seeheim, as was generally expected, McKenzie turned north across the desert so as to cut off the main German force retreating along the railway towards Windhoek. He caught the retreating Germans at Gibeon where they were comprehensively defeated.

McKenzie had taken his men over 200 miles of waterless desert and then fought and won a battle. After Gibeon, German resistance in the south of the country came to an end. Louis Botha soon overcame resistance in the north thereby giving the Allies their first real victory in the war. After the capitulation of the Germans in 'South West' McKenzie returned to Natal.

In East Africa a German Column operating out of Tanganyika (Tanzania) provided a constant threat to Uganda and Kenya, the British colonies in the region. To remedy what appeared to be a worsening situation, the British appointed General Smith-Dorrien as commander in East Africa. He cabled an invitation to McKenzie to join him. Before Duncan could accept Smith-Dorrien fell ill so the invitation lapsed.[16] To replace Smith-Dorrien, the British appointed General Jan Smuts commander in East Africa. Smuts was not prepared to share the limelight with a man who had so consistently out-smarted the Boers a few years before. In his selection of senior officers, Smuts ignored Duncan, whose campaigning days were now over.

Towards the end of 1915, Duncan was persuaded to become a non-executive director of a company known as the Smithfield Cold Storage and Exploration Company. Unfortunately the company expanded too quickly and after a couple years was in serious financial difficulty. Most of the other directors cut and ran, but not McKenzie. He believed that many people had been persuaded to invest in the company because he was a director, and therefore he felt morally bound to ensure that all who had invested in it should have their investment refunded. He was told there was no legal liability on him to reimburse them, but he was adamant. He sold assets, mortgaged his property and was finally able to pay out all investors and creditors of the company. The effort brought him close to financial ruin.[17] Today many would regard the decision to ignore his legal rights, and do what he thought correct, foolish. Others might regard it as a most outstanding example of honesty and integrity.

The tension brought into his life by the Cold Storage Company probably contributed to his suffering a stroke from which he never fully recovered. He died on 19 April 1932, and many were the tributes paid to him from people in all walks of life. General Sir Hubert Gough had his faults but he never wavered in his admiration for Duncan McKenzie. In a letter written to Sir Duncan's widow he said,

> '*I am sure you know how really fond I was of your great husband - We had not met often of late years, our paths in life prevented it, but I never forget my admiration for his character - He was a sincere true friend, kind and generous of heart - As a soldier no one had so quick an eye or appreciation of a situation and of the country, a more courageous and resolute will, but he was most balanced and prudent - Many a time has he checked and wisely guided my youthful ardour in those days around Ladysmith. Please accept these very sincere and deep tributes to him and to you and your family in your bereavement - from an old friend, Yours ever, Hubert Gough.*'[18]

The Reverend Gerard Bailey

A few months after the British reoccupied Dundee, Gerard contracted enteric fever and died on 1 December 1900. His published diary of his experiences during the Boer occupation of Dundee should be read by all people interested in those times and it is a wonderful memorial to a kind and perceptive man who was so sadly cut down in his prime of life.

Louis Botha

After the Boers were driven out of Natal, Louis Botha was one of their senior commanders during the two years in which they attempted to wear down the British with guerrilla warfare. With the changes now taking place in South Africa it might be time to re-examine this aspect of the war which might start with two quotations from Louis Botha. On 6 October 1900 at

Roos Senekal he gave the following instruction to his Kommandos: 'Do everything in your power to prevent the burghers laying down their arms. I will be compelled if they do not listen to this, to confiscate everything movable and also to burn their farms.'

On 30 May 1902 General de Wet records General Botha saying: 'We are only too thankful nowadays to know our wives are under English protection.'

After the War he was pre-eminent among Afrikaner politicians and became the first Prime Minister of the Union of South Africa in 1910. He expressed a desire to reconcile the English and Afrikaans sectors of the population, an attitude that resulted in his losing the support of many Afrikaners. He died in 1919.

General Sir Redvers Buller

Having cleared the Boers out of Natal, Buller led his confident army into the Transvaal and linked up with a column under Lord Roberts advancing eastwards from Pretoria. Near Standerton some men from the West Yorkshire Regiment were attempting to lead a span of 18 mules up a ramp onto a wagon. The mules would have none of it kicking and rearing, refusing to be either cajoled or intimidated into going anywhere near the ramp or the wagon. General Buller happened to be riding by, and seeing what was happening dismounted and walking over to the sergeant in charge, smiled and said, 'Let me have a try'. Taking two mules he led them up the ramp and onto the wagon. Two by two the whole span followed him quietly onto the wagon. With the mules safely loaded Buller helped push the wagon onto a railway truck.[19]

When the two British armies met, the half-starved, ragged and exhausted men under Roberts looked at Buller's fit and healthy troops with envy, hoping they might be transferred to his command.[20] But it was not to be. As the war appeared to be almost over, Buller returned to England early in October 1900 to assume command at Aldershot. Sir Redvers received a hero's welcome on his return to England, but the knives of the military establishment were out. Subjected to criticism of the manner in which he had conducted the Natal campaign, he attacked his critics in public and on 23 October 1901 he was relieved of his command at Aldershot. He retired to his family home at Downes in Devon, where he devoted the rest of his life to good works in the local community and was loved by all. He died in 1908 and bore his final illness with his usual fortitude, his last words being, 'I am dying. Well, I think it is about time to go to bed now.'

Despite the criticism which was levelled at him, the men who had served under him never wavered in their loyalty and affection for their former commander.

Dr. Robert Buntine

At the end of the Natal Campaign, Robert Buntine returned to private practice in Pietermaritzburg. During the southern hemisphere summer of 1901–02, he and his wife visited Melbourne to see family and friends. On their return to Natal his wife fell pregnant and tragically died during the birth of their second daughter, Noelle, on Christmas Day 1902. Robert felt he would not be able to bring up two young girls on his own, and arranged for them to be cared for in England.

His pleasing personality enabled him to build up an extensive practice in Pietermartzburg and such was his nature that he would treat the indigent without remuneration. In 1915 he was persuaded to stand for election to Parliament as representative for Pietermaritzburg South. He stood as a supporter of Louis Botha's South African Party, as did his opponent. In colonial Natal they never quite got the hang of party politics. Members always tended to vote on an issue according to their inclination rather than in accordance with party policy. This had its frustrations but it did have one advantage – it worked. With both candidates nominally supporting the South African Party, the election was a test of popularity, a contest which Robert won easily. He had grave doubts about many of Louis Botha's policies, but felt that in those troubled times it would be in the nation's interest to support him. In Parliament he successfully introduced a Bill requiring government support for the development of industry in South Africa. This far-reaching measure was to transform South Africa over the next 75 years into the industrial powerhouse of the continent with its axis on the Durban/Johannesburg corridor.

In 1918 Robert felt he should bring his daughters back to Natal so he went over to England to collect them. He combined this visit with a parliamentary mission which involved meetings with leading British personalities from Prime Minister Lloyd George downwards. It is not known precisely what was discussed, but the probability would have been the post-war investment by British industry in South Africa.

Early in September 1918, Robert Buntine and his two daughters, aged 20 and 15, embarked on the *Galway Castle* for South Africa. While making its way through heavy seas in the Bay of Biscay on 12 September, the passenger steamer was struck by a German torpedo. Women and children were ordered into lifeboats and Robert watched as the lifeboat with his daughters was lowered into the water. Before it could get clear, a large swell dashed it against the ship's bulwarks, tipping its passengers into the ocean. Robert plunged into the sea and managed to save his younger daughter Noelle. He went back to save his older daughter but both she and Robert disappeared. The *Galway Castle* was to remain afloat for another two days during which time the surviving passengers were taken on board ships which answered her distress calls. Noelle eventually made her way to Pietermaritzburg where her two sons still live at the time of writing.[21]

Dr Tommy Crean, VC (1901), DSO (1915)

The wound Tommy sustained at Elandslaagte healed rapidly enabling him to take part in the battle of Wagon Hill and the other engagements in which the ILH was involved while in Ladysmith. As the siege dragged on and additional medical help was required, he joined the medical staff at Intombi where his medical skill and cheerful personality did much to bring new life to the starved, wounded, and fever-stricken patients.

After the siege was raised, he went back to combat duty. He was given command of a Troop and by 1901 he commanded a Squadron. In the middle of that year he gave up combat duties and became Medical Officer to the Regiment. On 18 December 1901, at Tyger Kloof in the Free State, the ILH was heavily engaged by a Boer Kommando. Exposed to close-range enemy fire, Tommy continued to tend the wounded and dress their wounds despite being wounded himself. Only after he had been hit a second time did he desist. Initially it was thought that this second wound would be fatal, the bullet having passed through his stomach, but his youth and strength carried him through. In recognition of his bravery at Tyger Kloof, he was awarded the Victoria Cross. To his disgust, on recovery, he was invalided out of the army. He went to London, where he set up in private practice.

When war broke out in 1914 he went to France as Medical Officer with the 1st Cavalry Brigade which was commanded by General Briggs, who had commanded the ILH in the later stages of the Boer War. Accounts of Tommy's exploits recur in many books and private letters. All tell of his incredible bravery and humane work. On one occasion a General and his Staff were sheltering from a heavy bombardment when they saw Tommy walking by as if on a Sunday morning stroll. The General, a well known martinet, told him to take cover which Tommy declined to do, saying all his stretcher-bearers had been killed or wounded and he must attend to his men. Unaccustomed to having his orders queried, the General ordered him to take cover immediately. The Staff looked on in horror as Tommy smiled and, putting his arm around the General's shoulders, said, 'General darling, 'Tis written that I'm to die in my bed. The boys need me. Go I must.' So saying he left to look for the wounded. Those too badly wounded to be moved had their wounds dressed and their position marked. Others he tenderly put across his broad back and carried to safety. For long hours he carried on, paying no regard to the ghastly inferno raging about him, until nightfall and exhaustion finally forced him to rest.

He survived the war, but his health had been ruined and he died in his bed, as prophesied, in 1925.[22] How could Lord Salisbury, or anyone else, despise such people?

Nurse Kate Driver

After the siege Kate married Dr J Boyd whom she had met before the war at Grey's Hospital. In pre-war days the nurses, including Kate, loved to watch the Doctor's attempts to mount and ride a horse. After the siege she came to love him dearly and theirs was to be a long and happy marriage. While in Ladysmith, Kate had made notes of her experiences. Three years later her husband encouraged her to write her story drawn from these contemporaneous notes. If some facts seem a little strange and fudged it can be attributed to her desire to be tactful while at the same time leaving a memorial to the young Light Horseman who had meant so much to her. Sixty years and two world wars later, Kate was to write that the 120 days of the siege were still 'drawn out long and very taut' and that time had not 'dulled the high strung feel of them… The sharp anxiety of those who wait for news is the same individual experience always, and the loss of snapped-off lives is bitter, bitter loss whether in the hearts of a few thousand or of world-wide millions.'

Lord Dundonald

On the conclusion of the Natal Campaign, Dundonald returned to England where his poor health ensured his campaigning days were over. However his efforts to improve marksmanship in the Army together with the success of the Colonial Volunteers under his command, must have been a major influence in persuading the Army to place more emphasis in training on shooting skills. But for this, in the Reteat from Mons in August 1914, the British Expeditionary Force would in all probability have been overwhelmed by the numerical superiority of the Germans, whose casualties from rifle fire were more than twice that of the British.[23]

Lt Col Robert Evans and his son Trooper A. W. Evans, both of the NMR

On 20 February 1902, Col Evans, in command of the Composite Regiment, was killed when he approached a farmhouse to accept its surrender. It will be recalled that his son, while serving in General White's bodyguard, had been awarded a DCM for the rescue of a comrade in a skirmish on 23 October 1899. At the end of the war, he was awarded a scholarship to Columbia University. After graduating he moved with his young bride to New Zealand to take up a post as Resident Engineer of a mining company. On the outbreak of war in 1914, he raised the 3rd Battalion of the New Zealand Rifle Brigade, which he commanded with the rank of Lieutenant Colonel in France. He received a DSO, the citation stating '…*he showed the greatest coolness and energy inspiring all ranks by his magnificent personal example and never sparing himself to make the operation of his battalion the success which it was.*' He was wounded and died at Passchendaele on 13 October 1917.

MK Gandhi

Mohandas Gandhi was to achieve many things in his life, however through no fault on his part, his contribution to the Boer War was very small. To exaggerate his achievements in the war does his reputation no favour and would have caused him considerable embarrassment. He was to play a greater part serving with the Natal forces in the disturbances in Natal in 1906.[23]

Major Hubert Gough (later General Sir Hubert Gough)

An enigmatic character, he held Duncan McKenzie in awe, and was one of the first to recognize the outstanding quality of the Natal regiments. An ambitious man, he carried the burden of having a father, an uncle and a brother who had won the Victoria Cross. The impossibility of matching their achievements might account for a certain meanness of character. After Dundonald left South Africa in 1900, the SA Light Horse suffered a setback. Gough sent a description of the engagement to Dundonald, which concluded with the statement that, 'The only laughable thing about it was that the Natal Volunteers were in charge of the line and of the country – whose prudence, slimness and invariable watchfulness have so aggressively been held up as patterns to the Regular soldiers in all the papers.'[24]

Whether or not the colonials of the SALH thought the disaster suffered by Gough's column at Blood River Poort in September 1901, was 'laughable,' is unknown, however they might have thought it served him right. On that occasion Colonial scouts warned him the Boers were present in considerable numbers. Like Penn Symons, Gough dismissed the information as colonial exaggeration, and his men paid the penalty. During the engagement Gough became detached from his unit, and had a humiliating time hiding from the Boers, who eventually caught him, stripped of him of clothes, and let him loose.

It seems he resented the success achieved by the one time commander of the mounted Volunteers. Writing many years after the Boer War, when Dundonald and his contemporaries were long dead, Gough described Dundonald as, '...another of Buller's weak subordinates. Known among us as Dundoodle, he was hesitating, vacillating and vain. Mistakenly over-praised by a not well-informed Press, he was known to the people at home as "the stormy petrel." The fact behind this soubriquet was that he had men under him of independent character and initiative, whose every act was credited to Dundonald. Such men were Thornycroft, Bethune, Byng, and perhaps pre-eminently Duncan McKenzie of the Natal Carbineers.'

This attack on a man who had done much to promote his career and whom Gough treated as a confidant shows a remarkable lack of loyalty. It also shows that he did not know what happened to men who lived in glass houses. He became known in the ranks as 'Bumface' apparently because of a cleft down the middle of his nose.

Gough's name will forever be linked to the slaughter in the bloody battle of Passchendaele in 1917. Total losses on the British side were in the region of 250,000, killed, wounded, and missing, a substantial portion of whom were Colonials. Subsequently Gough was blamed, perhaps unfairly, for the German breakthrough in the spring of 1918 and dismissed from his command.

General Sir Ian Hamilton

He was in command at Gallipoli, one the most disastrous and bloody campaigns of the First World War. He died in 1947 and was a prolific writer on military matters.

Dr. Leander Starr Jameson

Once Dr Jameson had recovered from the enteric he had contracted in Ladysmith he entered Cape politics and was elected to the Cape Legislative Assembly as member for Kimberley.

In his maiden speech to the Legislature in August 1902, he asked that the 1895 Raid might be forgotten. He was elected leader of the new Progressive Party which he led to victory in the 1904 general election, and was duly appointed Prime Minister, retaining for himself the position of Minister of Native Affairs. He showed especial interest in the recommendations of the South African Native Affairs Commission 1903-1905. He firmly believed that higher education should be available to all and he was the initial driving force behind the formation of the University of Fort Hare, which was to open in 1916. Situated at Alice in the Eastern Cape, it was the first university in sub-Saharan Africa to attend to the needs of Black students.[25] These well documented facts should dispel forever the modern theory that the Boer War was fermented by Milner, Jameson and the *Uitlanders* to oppress the Blacks.

Jameson lost the premiership in 1908 and subsequently served as leader of the Unionist Party (South Africa). He returned to England in 1912 and died in 1917.

J. S. Marwick

Early in December 1899, Sydney Marwick enlisted and was posted to the Intelligence Corps. Because of his knowledge of Zulu, Marwick was assigned to the Natal Labour Corps, which served in a non-combatant role digging trenches, transporting goods and other fatigue duties. Its members received a reasonable wage which provided some compensation for the loss of income from the mines. At the end of the War, Marwick was appointed Native Commissioner in Johannesburg. A few years later he was elected Member of Parliament for Illovo in Natal and when that constituency was abolished he was elected as MP for Pinetown near Durban. When he died in 1958, Zulus came from far and wide to pay their last respects to him.

Sir Alfred Milner

After the war Milner was to prove a diligent Governor whose principal legacy to South Africa was the establishment of an efficient and incorruptible Civil Service. His arrogance ensured that he would never be popular and in 1906 the British parliament passed a motion of censure on him, resulting in his resignation. By December 1916 he was once more back in favour. Aware of his organisational skills, Prime Minister Lloyd George brought him into the War Cabinet. He died in 1924 after contracting malaria while on a visit to South Africa.

Charles Herbert Mullins, VC, CMG

We left Charlie Mullins lying wounded at Wright's Farm on the road to Mafeking. His body was riddled with bullets and no one thought he would survive, but survive he did. His most serious wound was an injury to his spine which left him crippled for life and able only to get around with crutches. Added to this he had to endure constant pain and bouts of illness. He resumed practice as a lawyer in Johannesburg, a difficult task given his disabilities. A devout Anglican, he was indefatigable in the support he gave to the Church as it revived after the war. He also maintained a constant interest in the ILH which he had helped to found and make famous. He died on 24 May 1916, aged 46, and was buried in Grahamstown, Eastern Cape, in the town's Old Cemetery. He was survived by his wife and two sons.

Teise Ndlovu

Despite his Zulu surname, Teise was a Sotho and when the British army moved into the Free State, which bordered Lesotho, he joined it. So excellent was his service that the army used him to check the reports of other scouts. In due course he was sent out to check a report that the Boers had set an ambush on a particular ridge. While reconnoitring the position, Teise must have been seen by the Boers who opened fire on him, hitting him in several places. Realising that the element of surprise had been lost, the Boers abandoned their proposed ambush and galloped off.

Teise died the next day. Robert Samuelson applied to the Natal government for an allowance for his widow and free schooling for his children. From Natal his widow received a gratuity of £10, quite a large sum in those days (for example a widow of a Volunteer killed on duty received a gratuity of £5). As Teise was killed while serving with the Imperial Army and he came from the Free State, any other benefits due to him should have come from the Free State or Britain.

Deneys Reitz

In his much quoted book '*Commando*' which relates his youthful experiences with a Boer Kommando, Reitz makes no mention of the Colonials in Natal except for his admission that he enjoyed looting Dundee. Perhaps he realised that whatever quarrels the Boers had with Britain, there was no excuse for the invasion of Natal or the manner in which it was smashed up by the Boers, and any mention of this topic could be embarrassing for himself and his people.

Returning to South Africa in 1906 after four years of self-imposed exile, he was prominent among those Afrikaners who sought harmony between English and Afrikaans South Africans. He took part in the campaigns in South West Africa and in East Africa. During the later stages of World War One, he served in France as commander of the Royal Scots Fusiliers and was wounded in 1918. In defiance of a campaign to demonise the Imperial Light Horse he became a Colonel of that regiment and was a staunch opponent of the Broederbond and Ossewa Brandwag, organisations which sought and achieved exclusive control by Afrikaners of all aspects of South African life. He entered politics and became a Member of Parliament supporting Smuts. When Smuts became Prime Minister in 1939, Deneys was appointed Deputy Prime Minister until he was appointed South African High Commissioner to London in 1944. He died later that year.

JR 'Galloping Jack' Royston, DSO

In April 1901 Jack Royston was promoted to Lieutenant Colonel and left the 2nd ILH to take command of the 5th and 6th West Australian Mounted Infantry contingents which had recently arrived in the country. Serving first under General F.W. Kitchener and later under General Bruce Hamilton, they took part in many of the successful operations in the Eastern Transvaal which eventually led to the military defeat of the Boers. During this period Royston was awarded the DSO. He raised a mounted regiment known as 'Royston's Horse' for service in the 1906 unrest and in 1914 raised the Natal Light Horse, which served first under Louis Botha in putting down the Afrikaner Rebellion, and later under McKenzie in German South West.

In 1916 Royston was able to obtain a posting to the Australian Light Horse, then engaged in keeping the Turks away from the Suez Canal. Now a Brigadier General, he commanded the 3rd Brigade of the ALH.

Banjo Paterson, the Australian poet and journalist, was a major serving with the Australian Remount Depot in Egypt. Here he met Royston, and left this description of him: '…a square-built energetic man always doing something, a sort of prototype of "Teddy" Roosevelt when the latter was the colonel of the rough-riders. It is said that there were sixty generals at one time quartered in Shepheard's Hotel (in Cairo). But Royston was not the Shepheard's Hotel brand of general – far from it. He had been given command of a brigade of Australian light horse. While it is altogether an admirable thing for a general to set his troops a good example by showing a contempt for danger, it must be admitted that Royston rather over did it; and his troops alternately admired and cursed him. It was not that he wanted to show off – he was not that sort of man – but when he got anywhere near a fight, a sort of exaltation seemed to seize him, and he took no more account of bullets than of so many house flies.

"When I'm running a show, Paterson," he said to me. "I stick my lance in the ground; leave Dangar (his brigade major) in charge, and I go off to see how the boys are getting on."

'Poison gas had been used by the Germans and experiments were being made with it on the Palestine front. Nothing would do for Royston, but that he must have a sniff of it. He was one of those men who would try anything once. He was warned against it, but no, he must have just one sniff of it so that he might be able to recognize it if it should ever be used against his troops. The result was that I found him in a hospital, a badly shaken man, passing green urine, and ordered away for long leave. But nothing would daunt him and he spoke most cheerfully of the day he would come back.'[26]

He never did get back. By the time he had recovered, the war was over and he had returned to his farm at Umtentweni on the Natal South Coast, where his neighbour was his old friend, Lieutenant Colonel JF Rethman. In 1934 Jack Royston visited Australia and was feted wherever he went. In five weeks he attended no fewer than fifty dinners, balls and official functions as a guest of Governments and public bodies. He regretted that his schedule did not enable him to visit his friends in Queensland, Tasmania and New Zealand.

Two incidents might explain why, in contrast to the British, he was so successful with Australian units. At Deir el Belah a young trooper was found guilty of sleeping on duty, a serious offence which in many armies would have resulted in the offender being shot. He was found guilty by a Court Martial. The Brigade was drawn up in a hollow square to hear the sentence imposed on the prisoner, who stood between two escorts. When the sentence, 90 days in the Cairo citadel, was passed, the young man went pale but otherwise did not flinch. Royston then addressed the Brigade: 'Our young comrade here is going to pay the penalty for sleeping at his post. In future we will guard against this by doubling the men at each outpost. Until now our comrade has been a good soldier. When he comes out of the citadel I shall be proud to have him back under my command.' Turning to the prisoner, he said: 'When you are in the citadel son, keep your head up.'

Concerts were arranged to entertain the men from time to time. One such concert was held on the beach at El Arish, where the stage consisted of planks laid across bales of hay. Among the entertainers was the double act of the Australian, General Granville Ryrie and Jack Royston, whose combined weight at the time would have been about 225 kilograms. To roars of delight they entertained the troops with an exhibition of tap-dancing![27]

When the Italian dictator Mussolini invaded Ethiopia in 1935, Royston was so outraged that he wrote to the Emperor Hailie Selassie offering his assistance. He was 75 at the time. He died at Durban in 1942.

Freda Schlosberg

The young girl who left such a vivid description of life behind the Boer lines, drowned with her husband near Pretoria in 1922 when their car was swept away in a flash flood.

Peter Smith

After the retreat of the Boers from Dundee, Peter and Ann Smith returned to their farm on Talana Hill. They had spent nine wretched months living in the outhouses of the Oaks Hotel in Pietermaritzburg where there were 'no conveniences.' On arrival, they found their home had been shattered by shell fire, the thatched roof had fallen in and was rotting on the floor which had been stained by blood of the dead and wounded. Under the eucalyptus trees near their home were the graves of British soldiers who had died there nine months before. Apart from the hardships endured and financial loss suffered, they had the grief of losing their grandson, who had been killed by the shell which struck the Carbineers' camp in Ladysmith on 18 December 1899. Across the valley, the town of Dundee, which had once supplied the community with its needs, was devastated, and its inhabitants were only just beginning to dribble back to their wrecked homes. Now in their late seventies, the old couple set about rebuilding their lives. Their cottage was refurbished with a new iron roof and veranda, the trees in the orchard were pruned and fertilized, the vegetable garden re-established and the ducks and geese which had been stolen were replaced. Visitors once again called at the farm where they were welcomed with the kindly hospitality which had always been shown to one and all. On leaving, visitors would receive a jar of Ann's special crab apple jelly. Peter and Ann lie buried next to each other in the family graveyard near the farmhouse which they had made their home so many years before. It is sad that a Boer, Piet Smit, is now being put forward as the owner of Talana on the day of the famous battle.[28]

Field Marshal Jan Christiaan Smuts

The peace negotiations in 1902 were the start of a love affair between Smuts and the British who were so love-struck that they made no attempt to compel the Boers to account for any of their actions during the war. Even allegations of atrocities against Black people by Smuts' *Kommando* were brushed aside.

In 1915 the British colonies in East Africa were struggling to contain the Germans under their astute commander, Colonel von Lettow-Vorbeck, who had under his command 3,500 Germans and about 12,000 black Askaris. Smuts was asked to take command of the campaign and arrived in Kenya in February 1916. By the beginning of April he had reorganized the force into three Divisions with a total complement 130,000 men. The 1st Division was commanded by Major-General Hoskins and was comprised of a mixed bag of Rhodesians, Punjabis, Baluchis, Pathans, Kashmiris, Royal Fusiliers, King's African Rifles, the Cape Corps (Coloured South Africans) and the 5th Battery of the SA Field Artillery. The 2nd and 3rd Divisions were commanded by Major-General van Deventer and Major-General Brits respectively, both were Afrikaners, as were most of their senior officers, while the rank and file were almost exclusively Anglo South Africans. Backed by his army of 130,000 men Smuts attacked the Germans with all the vigour which Lord Roberts had displayed in South Africa. Victories were gained here and there, though there were little slip-ups from time to time, these could be explained away. The British were thrilled. On 20 January 1917, Smuts left Dar-es-Salaam to attend an Imperial War Conference in London, after which he became a member of the British War Cabinet. In Africa, Colonel von Lettow-Vorbeck with his little force held at bay the Allied army of 130,000 men and when peace came on 11 November 1918 his column, though depleted, was still in the field. Smuts later received a Field Marshal's baton from the grateful British.

When Louis Botha died in 1919, Smuts took over as Prime Minister. Though defeated in an election in 1924 he was returned to power in 1939 when he took South Africa into the Second World War on the Allied side. Smuts died in 1950. He never had any empathy with any of the peoples in Natal.

Natal Carbineer Lt William Tanner

This friend of the Driver family was promoted regularly over the years and in 1916 he was in command of the 2nd Infantry Regiment (Natal) of the SA Brigade in France. With the Somme offensive underway on 15 July 1916, orders were received to capture and hold Delville Wood. Tanner, now a Lieutenant Colonel, was in command in the wood which was captured and held. When his regiment was relieved six days and five nights later, of the 3,155 men who had entered the wood only 143 staggered out for the roll call. Other groups which had become isolated were subsequently found, the final tally of casualties being 2,435 and this was only the beginning. Tanner was wounded, recovered, and was promoted to Brigadier General serving with distinction until the Armistice.

William Watson

He died in 1906. He was never able to re-establish his beloved grove of trees and bird sanctuary. His quotation from Byron is as relevant today as it was in 1900.

Charlie Willson

Once his Court Martial had been finalised, he returned to Dundee where he was elected Chairman of the Town Board and Commander of the Town Guard. He organised the Guard into an efficient unit and the Boers never dared to launch another attack on the town. Perhaps to avoid British interference, he made no attempt to be restored to his former position in the Carbineers. He died in 1912. Two years later his son was killed in action while serving with the British Expeditionary Force in France.

Before, during and after the Boer War many myths were created and facts hidden to suit political ends. The result was that many of the lessons which should have been learnt were never adequately understood.

Kodwa thina sizonihalalisa
Koze kuwe ilanga.

(We will forever recount your deeds
until the falling of the sun.)
From a praise song in Zulu to honour Natal pioneer, Dick King

APPENDICES

APPENDIX 1

GRANT

I, Inguos (Inkosi) Chaka, King of the Zulus, and the country of Natal, as well as the whole of the land from Natal to Delagoa Bay, which I have inherited from my father, for myself and heirs, do hereby, on the seventh day of August, in the year of our Lord eighteen hundred and twenty-four, in the presence of my Chiefs, and of my own free will, and in consideration of diverse goods received, grant, make over, and sell unto, F.G. Farewell and Company,

The entire and full possession in perpetuity to themselves, heirs, and executors, of the Port or Harbour of Natal, known by the native name 'Bubolongo,' together with the Islands therein and the surrounding country, as herein described, viz. The whole of the neck of land or peninsula in the south-west entrance, and all the country ten miles to the southern side of Port Natal, as pointed out, and extending along the sea-coast to the northward and eastward as far as the river known by the native name, 'Gumgelote,' and now called 'Farewell's River,' being about twenty-five miles of sea coast to the north-east of Port Natal, together with all the country inland as far as the nation called by the Zulus 'Gowagnewkos,' extending about one hundred miles backward from the sea-shore, with all the rights to the rivers, woods, mines and articles of all denominations contained therein, the said land and appurtenances to be from this date for the sole use of the said Farewell and Company, their heirs and executors, and to be by them disposed of in any manner they think best calculated for their interests, free from any molestation or hindrance from myself or subjects. In witness whereof, I have placed my hand, being fully aware that the so doing is intended to bind me to all the articles and conditions that I, of my own free will and consent, do hereby, in the presence of the undermentioned witnesses, acknowledge to have fully consented and agreed to on behalf of F.G. Farewell as aforesaid, and perfectly understand all the purport of this document, the same having been carefully explained to me by my interpreter, Clambamarnze, and in the presence of two interpreters, Coliat and Frederick, before the said F. G. Farewell, whom I hereby acknowledge as the Chief of the said country, with full power and authority over such natives that like to remain there after this public grant, promising to supply him with cattle and corn, when required, sufficient for his consumption, as a reward for his kind attention to me in my illness from a wound.

Chaka signified his acceptance by making a mark.

Four witnesses, Umbequarn (Chaka's uncle), Umsega, Euntclope, and Chaka's Interpreter Clambermarnze added their marks to the grant.

7th August, 1824.

....

APPENDIX 2

MISSION TO HIS BRITANNIC MAJESTY

I, Chaka, King of the Zulus, do in the presence of my principal chiefs now assembled, hereby appoint and direct my friend, James Saunders King, to take under his charge Sotobi, one of my principal chiefs, whom I now create of the 'Tugusa' kraal, Kati, my body-servant, Jacob, my interpreter, and suite. I desire him to convey them to H. M. George's dominions, to represent that I send them on a friendly mission to King George the Fourth; and after offering him assurances of my friendship and esteem, to negotiate with His Britannic Majesty on my behalf, with my chief Sotobi, a treaty of friendly alliance between the two nations, having given the said J.S. King and Sotobi full instructions and invested with full power to act for me in every way as circumstances may seem to them most beneficial and expedient. I require my friend King to pay every attention to the comforts of my people entrusted to his care, and solemnly enjoin him to return with them to safety to me, and to report to me faithfully such accounts as they may receive from King George.

I hereby grant him, my said friend J. S. King, in consideration of the confidence I repose in him, of various services he has already rendered me, presents he has made, and above all the obligations I am under to him for his attention to my mother in her last illness, as well as having saved the lives of several of my principal people, the free and full possession of my country near the sea-coast and Port Natal, from Natal head to the Stinkein River including the extensive grazing flats and forests, with the islands in the Natal harbour, and the Matabana nations, together with the free and exclusive trade of all my dominions; I hereby also confirm all my former grants to him.

Note: Shaka scribbled all over the paper saying that as he was a great king he should make a great show. Two witnesses made the more simple conventional mark. N.J. Issacs signed as a witness. February, 1828.

Appendix 3

Port Natal

At a greater distance from the eastern frontier another body of British subjects have, it appears, settled themselves at Port Natal, influenced by the wish to diffuse religious knowledge and principles amongst the natives. It is impossible to contemplate without serious distrust the attempt to combine European colonisation with plans for the conversion of natives to Christianity. The allurements to deviate to the pursuit of secular and selfish ends are many and powerful, and although they may be counteracted at first by the principles and character of the settlers, yet no permanent and effective restraint on their cupidity appears to have been devised. It will be the duty of the Government at the Cape of Good Hope to maintain, as opportunity offers, a vigilant superintendence over the growing settlement of Port Natal, so that any injuries done to the tribes may be arrested and punished before they assume the form of actual hostility.

....

Appendix 4

TO THE HONOURABLE THE COMMONS OF THE UNITED KINGDOM OF GREAT BRITAIN AND IRELAND, IN PARLIAMENT ASSEMBLED.

THE PETITION OF THE UNDERSIGNED MERCHANTS, AND OTHERS, INTERESTED IN THE PROSPERITY AND CIVILIZATION OF SOUTHERN AFRICA,

Humbly Sheweth, – That many of your petitioners have had much experience in the colonisation of Southern Africa, and that all of them take a warm interest in the various settlements, and in the happiness and civilization of the native tribes.

And petitioners, while they lament the difficulties and misfortunes which have too often impeded the progress of the settlements already established, especially the frequent sanguinary conflicts with the natives, submit, that such are attributable to the want of a proper system of Colonial Government, and not an impossibility of conciliating the interests of the white and coloured races.

And petitioners therefore submit to your honourable House, that it is advisable to found, in Southern Africa, a new Colony, by which not only the interests of settlers, and of Great Britain, will be honourably promoted, but also those of the natives secured, and their civilization advanced: and your petitioners show, that the country in which such a Colony can be established is Port Natal in South Eastern Africa, containing more than 15,000,000 acres of land, nearly depopulated by native conquerors, almost unoccupied, and well known to be healthy and fertile, both in the interior and coastwise. It lies between the latitudes of 29 degrees and 31,30 south and longitude 27,30 and 30,31 east beginning at the Umzimvoobo (Ivory), or St. John's River, and extending about 300 miles along the coast to the Tugela, about 70 miles to the north east of Port Natal, and running inland between 60 and 100 miles to the Quathlamba Mountains.

Your petitioners possess the means of proving, by witnesses, who have visited the country in question, all the allegations contained in this petition: showing that among the advantages which may be secured by founding a Colony of Natal, are the following :- Advancing the security of the Cape of Good Hope, by promoting the civilization of the native tribes; affording a powerful aid towards abolishing the East African slave trade, by the introduction of legitimate commerce in its place; extension of religious missions; and protection for the interior trade.

Your petitioners are also able to prove, to the satisfaction of your honourable House, that the few natives dispersed within, and the populous tribes beyond the borders of the proposed Colony, have long evinced themselves anxious to have a British Colony established at Natal, and to hold friendly intercourse with white people; that large grants of the above mentioned territory have been already made by native chiefs to British subjects in the course of the last fourteen years; that during that period a number of English settlers have resided there, generally in safety, until the late unhappy events, which, from the great respect always manifested by the present Zoola chief and his predecessor to legitimate British authority, could not have occurred had a British Colony been established on a sound system.

Your petitioners also submit that, as a considerable number of other British subjects, Cape Dutch farmers, with their families and property, have lately emigrated to Natal, by the adoption of wise measures they will become valuable members of the new Colony, and greatly promote its interests.

It will not be unknown to many members of your honourable house, that, during the last fourteen years, various applications have been made to the Crown to found a Colony at Natal, and that the several governors at the Cape of Good Hope have either warmly supported the said applications, or have not disapproved of them; particularly in 1834, when a large number of the merchants, and other inhabitants of the Cape of Good Hope, represented to the Government that such a Colony was highly desirable; and your petitioners submit, that the objections then made on the score of expense, which at that period led the Government to refuse acquiescence in such applications, no longer exist, inasmuch as the self-supporting principle of selling the freehold of soil having been tested by experience, is now more fully understood; and is so available at Natal that the British Treasury will not be called upon to advance one shilling towards the establishment of the Colony.

Your petitioners submit, that it is impossible to procure the funds necessary for carrying into effect the proposed important objects if land-selling principle be not adopted; they, therefore humbly suggest, that the South Australian plan as respects the sale of land, may be employed at Natal, but with this variation, that a portion only of the money obtained by such sales shall be applied to defray the expense of the emigration of labourers - mechanics being chiefly wanted, in as much as free★ native labour may be easily obtained when the Colony is established - the remaining portion of the money so raised is to be applied to the purposes of surveys, the formation of roads, bridges, and the general expenses of Government, including the protection of the natives, their proper restraint by a good police, and their moral and religious improvement.

Your petitioners further submit, that a colony based upon sound principles of political and social liberty, guaranteed to all denominations of men, and properly guarded against abuse and license, will secure the confidence of capitalists, lead to a profitable investment of money, and obtain for free labourers of all classes and colours ample remuneration, with the prospect of steadily bettering their conditions; and that such a system, if established at the same time with the principle of selling the Crown lands, and applying the proceeds to public colonial objects alone, will lay a firm foundation for great improvements in the condition of large masses of men in Southern Africa.

Your petitioners likewise submit to your honourable House that the establishment of a just and well-matured system of colonial government and administration under the crown, with constitutional guarantees, is beyond all comparison preferable to the plan recently proposed for substituting the political agency of missionaries, in place of the power and influence of regular British government, wherever the fair interests and just activity of British subjects may in future carry them; your petitioners, on the contrary, submit that, whilst missionaries ought to be supported and multiplied to the utmost need by all possible means, actual experience proves that their efficiency becomes deteriorated by unnecessary political agency.

Your petitioners therefore humbly pray that the foregoing allegations may be inquired into by your honourable House, and that your honourable House, will address her Majesty not only to adopt the acquisitions already made by British subjects at Natal, but also to cause the remaining portions of the depopulated country to be acquired by treaty with the chiefs who own it. Your Petitioners likewise pray, that a colony may be established there on a new and just system with regard to the natives, and upon the principle of selling Crown lands according to a plan to be settled by Act of Parliament, so as to furnish competent means for carrying such a good system into effect for the equal benefit of all classes of men.

And your petitioners pray that the Act of Parliament may vest the government of the proposed colony in the crown, and independently, of the Cape of Good Hope, and appoint commissioners in London to sell the lands. That provision be made in the Act of Parliament to guarantee all existing rights; and that all details be also introduced into the said Act for the establishment of a steady system of just and safe intercourse with the neighbouring tribes; and for the equal protection of the coloured as well as white people within the colony; likewise that a loan of sufficient amount, according to an estimate of all the public wants of the colony, for a certain number of years may be authorized to be raised under the Act upon the security of a competent portion of the land to be sold, – And petitioners, as in duty bound, shall ever pray.

22.3. 1839

Note: By free labour it is meant that free men, as distinct from slaves, should provide labour.

CHAPTER NOTES

Abbreviations
UKNA = National Archives, Kew, London
LHS = Ladysmith Historical Society

Chapter One
1. UKNA, CO179/207 and Marwick Papers, Killie Campbell Museum, Durban

Chapter Two
1. Extract from the much quoted Manifesto of Voortrekker leader Piet Retief.

Chapter Three
1. Sampson, V and Hamilton I, 96/97.
2. Julius, Anthony, 269-276.

Chapter Four
1. Mackeurton, G, p63.
2. Ibid, 66.
3. Ibid, 67.
4. Ibid, 72/73.
5. Ibid, 69.
6. Ibid, 65.
7. Diary of HF Fynn, 234
8. Ibid, 234
9. Mackeurton, G, 154.
10. Gardiner, 11.
11. Ibid, 183/184.
12. Mackeurton, G, 189/190.
13. Ibid, 188.
14. Chase, JC, Part 1, 132.
15. Ibid, Part, 1 131/132, and Part 2, 71/72.
16. Ibid, Part 2, 8/9
17. Mackuerton, G, 225/226.
18. Ibid, 228/229.
19. Goetzche, E, *Father of a City*, 30/31.
20. Lugg, HC, 45.
21. Mackuerton, G. 239.
22. Ibid, 240/241.
23. Ibid, 241/142.
24. Ibid, 252.
25. Chase, Part 2 p119.
26. Mackuerton, 256/257, and Chase, Part 2, 122/123.
27. Chase, Part 2, 127/128.
28. Ibid, 129.
29. Ibid, 118.
30. Ibid, 59/160.
31. Ibid, 190.
32. Ibid. 209.
33. Ibid, 209.
34. Ibid, 214,
35. Ibid, 215/216.
36. Goetzche, E., *Father of a City*, 42.
37. Chase, Part 2, 217/218.
38. Lugg, H.C. 51.
39. Mackueton, 278/280.
40. Ibid, 281.

41. Ibid, 281/282.
42. Ibid, 282.
43. Goetzche, *Father of a City* 47/48.
44. Chase, Part 2, 224.
45. Ibid, 237/239.
46. Bazley, D, 16.
47. McKenzie, Col AG, 153
48. Inter alia, *The Curling Letters of the Zulu War*, 50.
49. Diary Trooper F.Symons quoted in *Pro Patria* by Mark Coglan page 7.
50. Samuelson, RCA, 218.
51. Ibid, 228.

Chapter Five
1. May, HJ 30/31.
2. Amery, LS, Vol. II., 68-70.
3. Samuelson, RCA, 160/161.
4. Bazley, D, 63-69.
5. Statement made by Mehlokazulu after capture later in the war. Various sources.
6. David, S, 146/147.
7. Goetzche, E, *Rough but Ready*, 122.
8. LHS *Diary of a Siege No. 4* (Lt Col B.W. Martin), 27/28 and other sources.
9. Lugg, H.C., *A Natal Family Looks Back*, 38/39.
10. Reminiscences Lt Col J.F Rethman.
11. Amery, LS, Vol. II, 32-37
12. Evidence of General Sir Archibald Hunter to the Commission on the War in SA.
13. Amery, LS, Vol. II., 75.
14. Conditions of establishment of ILH.
15. Ibid.
16. Correspondence contained in ILH papers in African Studies Library, Johannesburg.
17. Ibid.
18. Ibid.
19. Gibson, G.F, 23.
20. Ibid, 22.
21. McKenzie, Col AG, 156.
22. Dennison, C.J, 204.

Chapter Six
1. Amery, LS, Vol. II, 141.
2. Doyle, A.C, 70.
3. Reitz, D, 15.
4. Samuelson, RC, 142.
5. May, HJ, 17.
6. Reitz, D, 23.
7. Lugg, HC, 92.
8. The writer's father worked for fourteen years before he could afford a home of his own, which was constructed of wood and corrugated iron (not only the roof, but the walls as well) – a great social gaffe one gathers from the writings of some British war correspondents. Across the road from this house was a substantial brick building which, two or three times a week, provided overnight accommodation for men going to the mines.

At night they would sing. Such was the beauty of their singing that the best Welsh choirs would have had difficulty matching them, and it was all unpremeditated – words, melody and harmonies. Today, Ladysmith Black Mambaso produce music similar to that which was once heard so often.

9. Marwick Papers.
10. McFadden, Pam, *Khaki Cameos*
11. *Natal Mercury*, 10 July, 1900.

Chapter Seven
1. Samuelson, RC, 138-141.
2. Gordon, Dr R, 258/259.
3. Reminiscences, Lt Col JF Rethman.
4. Hattersley, *History of the Royal Natal* Carbineers, 36/37 and others.
5. Unisa Archives, Diary of Lt D Howard Gill RFA.

Chapter Eight
1. May, HJ, *Music of the Guns* 19.
2. Reitz, D, 26.
3. Ibid, 27.
4. Amery, LS, Vol. II, 152.
5. Bailey, GC, 52.
6. Ibid, 28.
7. Ibid, 46/47.
8. Marling, Col Sir Percival, *Rifleman and Hussar.*

Chapter Nine
1. Letter dated 27 Sept. 1899 with ILH papers in the African Studies Library, Jhbg.
2. Gibson, GF, 39.
3. Schiel, Col A, *Twenty-three years of Storm and Sunshine in South Africa.*
4. Ibid.
5. Ibid.
6. Ibid.
7. Stirling, J, 30.
8. Schiel, Col A,
9. Diary in ILH papers at the African Studies Library. Jhbg.
10. Information from Douglas Campbell, grandson of Lt Douglas Campbell ILH.
11. Sampson, V and Hamilton, I, 113.
12. Schiel, Col A,
13. Ibid.
14. Ibid.
15. Ibid
16. Gibson, GF, 35.
17. Diary in ILH papers in African Studies Library, Jhbg.
18. Ibid.
19. Sampson, V and Hamilton, I, 116.
20. Pakenham 1979 Edition, 140, Illustrated Edition 1993, 78.
21. Schiel, Col A.
22. Ibid.
23. Diary JC Burton. For corroboration Mead, G, 109

Chapter Ten
1. LHS. *Diary No. 6*, (Nurse Kate Driver), 3/4. No Australians or ILH members ought have been on the train with the diarist, however, for reasons suggested later, she might have transposed an incident in Maritzburg to the train journey.
2. Ibid, 4.
3. Ibid, 5.
4. Gibson, GF, 39. See also Bridgland, A, *Field Gun Jack*, 45.
5. Goetsche, E., *Rough but Ready*, 55: also Stirling, J. *Colonials in Natal*, 30.
6. Gibson, G.F. 39/40.
7. ILH papers in African Studies Library, Jhbg.
8. Newspaper reports in Talana Museum.

Chapter Eleven
1. Brooking, Lt Hugh, Diary. African Studies Library.
2. Ibid.
3. Goetsche, E, *Rough but Ready*, 57/58.
4. Samuelson, RC 158
5. Steevens, WG, 89; inter alia
6. Slirling, J, 31.
7. Macdonald, D, 17.
8. Watkins-Pitchford, H, 14/15.
9. Reitz, D, 32/33.
10. Bailey, GC, 69-71.
11. Steevens, WG, 66-68.

Chapter Twelve
1. Nevinson, HW, 6.
2. Ibid, 17.
3. Ibid, 8.
4. Ibid, 18.
5. Sampson, V. and Hamilton I, 116.
6. Nevinson, HW, 9.
7. LHS *Diary No. 4*, (Letters), 2/3.
8. Ibid, No. 7, (Watson), 7.
9. Bridgland, Tony, 6.
10. Ibid, 20.
11. Ibid, 20
12. Samuelson, RC, 151.
13. Brooking, Lt Hugh, Diary.
14. Stirling, John, 32.

Chapter Thirteen
1. Reminiscences Lt Col JF Rethman.
2. Diary Gen Ian Hamilton.
3. LHS, *Diary No. 6* (Nurse K. Driver), 6.
4. Ibid, 7.
5. Ibid, 9.
6. Pearse, HHS, 20.
7. LHS, *Diary No. 1* (G. Tatham), 1.
8. LHS, *Diary No. 7* (W. Watson), 2.
9. Gordon, Dr R, 261.
10. Commission of Enquiry into the War in South Africa.
11. Ibid.
12. Ibid.
13. Watkins-Pitchford, H, 20.

14. Gibson, GF, 50.
15. Ibid, 53. Quoting G.W. Steevens in the London *Daily Mail*.
16. Ibid, 54.
17. Goetsche, *Rough but Ready*, 79.
18. Macdonald, D, 147.
19. Gibson, GF, 56.

Chapter Fourteen
1. McKenzie, Col AG, 154.
2. Ibid, 154.
3. Stirling, J, 46.
4. Churchill, W.S., *London to Ladysmith*, 20.
5. Ibid, 20.
6. Ibid, 21.
7. Ibid, 21.
8. Ibid, 21.
9. *South African Military History Society Journal*, Vol.2, No. 2.
10. Churchill, W.S., *London to Ladysmith*, 28/29.
11. Ibid, 30/31.
12. Creswicke, L, *South African and Transvaal War Vol I*, 40/41.
13. Chisholme, R, 82.
14. UKNA CO/179. Affidavit received by Colonial Office, 26.12.1899.
15. McKenzie, Col AG, 154/155.
16. Amery, L, Vol. II, 305/308.
17. Griffith, K, 130.
18. Amery, S, Vol II 305/308.
19. Pakenham, T. *The Boer War*, 172.
20. McKenzie, Col AG, 155/156 also Stirling, J, 38/39 and Amery as in 16 above.
21. Riall, N., Editor, *The Boer War, Letters and Photographs of Malcolm Riall*.
22. Mc Kenzie, Col A.G, 157.
23. Ibid, 159.
24. EH Carrick: papers in possession of his granddaughter.
25. McKenzie, Col AG, 157.
26. Ibid, 157-161.
27. Stirling, J, 10.
28. McKenzie, Col AG, 161-162.
29. Dundonald, Lt Gen the Earl of, 99. On this subject see also Smith-Dorien, 398
30. Ibid, 81.
31. Ibid, 97. See also Treves, Dr Frederick, 13.
32. Gough, Gen Sir Hubert, 66/67.
33. Stirling, J, 41 and Amery Vol II, 319.

Chapter Fifteen
1. Churchill, WS, London to Ladysmith, 52-54.
2. Ibid, 60.
3. LHS, *Diary No.6* (Kate Driver), 11.
4. Ibid, 14/15.
5. Ibid, 16/17.
6. LHS, *Diary No. 4* (Reverend Mother Marie), 22/23.
7. Ibid, 23.
8. Nevinson, HW, 33.

9. Pearse, HSS, 38.
10. LHS, *Diary No.4* (Reverend Mother Marie), 23/24.
11. Ibid, 23.
12. Gibson, GF, 52.
13. Macdonald, D, 253/254.
14. Nevinson, HW, 42.
15. Pearse, HSS, 49/50.

Chapter Sixteen
1. McKenzie, Col AG, 162/163.
2. Dundonald, Lt Gen the Earl of, 98.
3. McKenzie, Col AG, 164. See also O'Mahony, CJ, 192/193.
4. Ibid, 164.
5. Ibid, 145.
6. Ibid, 166.
7. Wasserman and Kearney, Eds. *A Warriors Gateway*, 212-214.
8. McFadden, P, *Khaki Cameos*.
9. Stanford, Sir Walter, 208-210.
10. UKNA, CO179/209.

Chapter Seventeen
1. Pearse, HHS, 28.
2. Ibid, 69.
3. Macdonald, D, 129.
4. Gibson, GF, 117/118.
5. Pearse, HHS, 82.
6. LHS *Diary No.6* (Kate Driver), 23.
7. Gibson, GF, 81/82.
8. Ibid, 83.
9. Ibid, 85.
10. Ibid, 87.
11. Ibid, 87.
12. Ibid, 88/89.
13. Ibid, 104.
14. Ibid, 90.
15. Ibid, 91.
16. Pearse, HSS, 96.
17. Gibson, GF, 92/93.
18. LHS, *Diary No.4* (Memoirs Lt Col BN Martin.)
19. Macdonald, D, 165.
20. Ibid, 184.
21. LHS, *Diary No.3* (Maj Gen CW Park), 22/23.
22. Gibson, GF, 111.
23. Macdonald, D, 167.
24. Gibson, G.F, 106.

Chapter Eighteen
1. Sampson, V and Hamilton, I, 122.
2. Nevinson, HW, 68.
3. Ibid, 73.
4. Ibid, 73.
5. LHS *Diary No. 6* (Kate Driver), 18.
6. Samuelson, RC 163.
7. Ibid, 165.
8. Ibid, 141.
9. Ibid, 152.
10. Ibid, 154.

11. Bailey, Rev GC, 72-73.
12. Ibid, 74, see also the Irish writer T. Pakenham who states that the looting in Natal was 'good-humoured', *The Boer War* 1979 edition, 210.
13. Ibid, 82.
14. Ibid, 84.
15. Ibid, 88.
16. Ibid, 96.
17. UKNA, CO179/209.

Chapter Nineteen

1. Dundonald, Major-General The Earl of, 112, and McKenzie, Col AG, 167.
2. Gibson, GF, 154/155.
3. Churchill, WS in a much quoted despatch to the *Morning Post*.
4. Blake Knox, Lt Dr, 6.
5. Dundonald, Major-General The Earl of, 116/117.
6. Ibid, 118/119.
7. Mc Kenzie, Col AG, 166-167 and inter alia Natal Carbineers Record for 17 Jan 1900.
8. Dundonald, Major-General the Earl of, 123/124.
9. McKenzie, Col AG, 167.
10. Ibid, 167/169.
11. Greening Diary quoted by M.Coglan in *Defending the Home Front*.
12. Written statement by General Sir Charles Warren to supplement his evidence given to the Commission on the War in South Africa.
13. Dundonald, Major-General The Earl of, 128.
14. Romer & Mainwaring, *2nd Battalion Royal Dublin Fusiliers in SA War*, 47.
15. Much quoted evidence by Gen Buller to the Royal Commission on the War.

Chapter Twenty

1. Churchill, WS, *London to Ladysmith*, 142/143.
2. Ibid, 143,
3. Ibid, 143/146.
4. Symons, J, 201, and UKNA, Spion Kop Despatches.
5. Blake Knox, Lt Dr E, 30/31.
6. O'Mahony, CJ, 147/148.
7. Churchill, WS, *London to Ladysmith*, 143/144.
8. UKNA, National Army Museum Templer Study Centre, 7101/23/192/19 'Spion Kop Despatches'.
9. Symons, J., 210/211 quoting comment by Buller to a Staff Officer Lt Col a'Court.
10. Gibson, GF, 151/152.
11. Symons, J, 213.
12. Ibid, 216.
13. UKNA, National Army Museum Templer Study Centre, 7101/23/192/19 'Spion Kop Despatches'.
14. Ibid.
15. Griffith, K, 267.
16. UKNA, National Army Museum Templer Study Centre, 7101/23/192/19 'Spion Kop Despatches'.

17. Ibid.
18. Blake Knox, Lt Dr E, 52.
19. Stirling, J, 83-86.
20. Ibid, 85.
21. Ibid, 85/86.
22. Blake Knox, Lt Dr E, 50.
23. Ibid, 50.
24. Griffith, K, 275.
25. Dundonald, Lt Gen The Earl of, 133.
26. Wasserman and Kearney, 214/218.
27. Treves, Dr F, 77.
28. LHS *Diary No. 6* (Nurse K. Driver) 30.
29. Incident related to the writer by Major Keith Archibald Natal Carbineers.

Chapter Twenty-One

1. Macdonald, D, 220.
2. Pearse, HHS, 107.
3. LHS *Diary No. 7* (William Watson)16-19.
4. Ibid, 30
5. Macdonald, D, 235.
6. Ibid, 205.
7. Ibid, 232.
8. Ibid, 227.
9. LHS *Diary No, 2*, (Bella Craw), 41.
10. Ibid, 47/48.
11. UKNA CO179/212.
12. Ibid
13. Coulson, C, 105.
14. UKNA CO179/212.

Chapter Twenty-Two

1. Dundonald, Maj Gen The Earl of, 140.
2. McKenzie, Col AG, 171.
3. Much quoted passage from Lt Gen Sir Charles Warren's account of events of that time. e.g. Coetzer, Owen, 220.
4. Ibid.
5. Blake Knox, Lt Dr E, 152.
6. McKenzie, Col AG, 171.
7. Dundonald, Maj Gen The Earl of, 141.
8. Ibid, 141
9. Churchill, WS, *London to Ladysmith* 174/175.*
10. Dundonald, Maj Gen The Earl of, 144.
11. Ibid, 143.
12. Blake Knox, Lt Dr E, 148.
13. Ibid, 152.
14. McKenzie, Col AG, 172.
15. Blake Knox, Lt Dr E, 163.
16. Ibid, 174.
17. Stirling, J, 87-89.
18. Blake Knox, Lt Dr E, 102.
19. Ibid, 104.
20. Symons, J, 268.
21. Dundonald, Maj Gen The Earl of, 149.
22. Ibid, 147.
23. Ibid, 149.
24. McKenzie, Col AG, 173.
25. Ibid, 174.
26. Ibid, 174.

27. Watkins-Pitchford, H, 120–122.
28. Mckenzie, Col AG, 176–178.
29. Macdonald, D, 262.
30. Ibid, 264.
31. McKenzie, Col AG, 174.
32. Macdonald, D, 266.
33. Gough, Gen Sir Hubert, 79.
34. Dundonald, Maj Gen The Earl, 151.
35. Churchill, WS, *London to Ladysmith*, 210.
36. Ibid, 209/210.
37. McKenzie, Col AG, 189/190.
38. Gough, Gen Sir Hubert, 78.
39. Blake Knox, Lt Dr E, 237.
40. LHS *Diary No.6* (Nurse Kate Driver), 35/36.
41. Bailey, the Rev GC, 107.

Chapter Twenty-Three

1. McKenzie, Col AG, 185
2. Tucker, Private F, 82/83.
3. Samuelson, R.C, 147.
4. Gibson, F, 164.
5. Ibid, 164.
6. Ibid, 171/172.
7. Ibid, 173/174.
8. Ibid, 175–177.
9. Bailey, Rev GC, 109.
10. UKNA WO108, Letter from Lt Col H.V. Hunt, RFA senior Officer of British Prisoners of War.
11. Ibid.
12. UKNA WO108, Court of Inquiry into the treatment of British prisoners, pages 3/4.
13. Ibid, 4.
14. Ibid, 5/6.
15. Ibid, 4/5.
16. Ibid, 2 and Appendix 1.
17. Ibid, Appendix VI.
18. Ibid, Appendix II,
19. Ibid, Appendix II.
20. Ibid, 9.
21. Ibid, 7.
22. Ibid, 11/12
23. Ibid, Appendix IX.
24. UKNA CO 179/212.
25. UKNA CO 179/211
26. UKNA WO108, Court of Inquiry as above. Page 12. See also Pretoria from Within by H.J. Batts.

Chapter Twenty-Four

1. Macdonald, D, 268.
2. see Chapter 8.
3. Dundonald, Maj Gen The Earl of, 157.
4. McKenzie, Col AG, 194.
5. Blake Knox, Lt Dr E, 138
6. Stirling, J, 55
7. Bailey, The Rev GC, 111–112.
8. Dundonald, Maj Gen The Earl of, 160.
9. Stirling, J, 64/65.
10. Dundonald, Maj Gen The Earl of, 160.
11. Blake Knox, Lt Dr E, and newspaper reports in Brenthurst Library.

Postscript

1. Child, Daphne, 183.
2. Dennison, Maj CG, 204.
3. I. Hamilton Papers, King's College, London
4. Samuelson, RC, 148.
5. Letter dated 23.8.01 from Alexander George of Tech, brother of the future Queen Mary, African Studies Library. Jhbg.
6. Obituary published in the London *Times* with a copy in the *Johannesburg Star*, 30.11.1926.
7. Sampson, V. and Hamilton, I., *Anti-Commando*
8. Ibid, 152
9. Gibson, GF, 265.
10. Hattersley, AF, *History of the Royal Natal Carbineers*, 45
11. McKenzie, Col AG, 200.
12. Ibid, 201.
13. Ibid, 206–220.
14. Smith-Dorien, Lt Gen Sir Horace, 310
15. McKenzie, Col AG, 227–229
16. Ibid, 330.
17. Ibid, 330–333.
18. Ibid, 358/359.
19. O'Mahony, CJ 201
20. Ryall, N., 105
21. Information supplied by Dr Buntine's grandson, R Lewis.
22. Gibson, GF, 320–325.
23. David S, *100 Days to Victory*, 36/37
24. see Natal Indian Opinion 9.9.05.
25. Dundonald Papers, Talana Museum.
26. Stanford Reminiscences, Vol. 2, 242
27. Paterson, AB, *Happy Despatches*, Lansdowne Press Reprint, 119–127.
28. Devitt, N, 107.
29. Pakenham, T, *The Boer War*, 126 (Illustrated Edition, 70)

SOURCES AND SELECT BIBLIOGRAPHY

Archives, Museums, Collections and Unpublished Material

The National Archives at Kew, London:

    Colonial Office Papers, CO179/206-214.

    War Office Papers WO105 to 137. Evidence given to the Royal Commission on the War in South Africa. Report of and Evidence given to the House of Commons Aborigines Committee, 1836.

Brenthurst Library, Johannesburg: AA Kelsey Papers (Secretary, Reform Committee), newspaper clippings and other data relevant to the War.

Ladysmith Siege Museum, Ladysmith: Diaries and Photographs.

African Studies Library, Johannesburg: eight boxes and five scrapbooks relevant to the Imperial Light Horse.

Talana Museum, Dundee, South Africa: Dundonald Papers and various documents relating to local history.

Killie Campbell Museum, Durban: Marwick Papers, diary of Dr. Sam Campbell, and documents relating to the abuse by Boers of Black refugees.

Natal Archives, Pietermaritzburg, South Africa: Correspondence between the Natal Government, the Governor and the British Military, September 1899-May 1902.

The South African Museum of Military History, Johannesburg: various papers and files.

Reminiscences of Lt Col JF Rethman (unpublished).

King's College, London: Papers of Ian Hamilton.

Natal Carbineers Museum, Pietermaritzburg, South Africa: Diaries of Carbineers during Boer War.

Old Fort Museum, Durban: Exhibits covering Durban's Military History.

Natal Society Library, Pietermaritzburg, South Africa: Newspaper reports and correspondence during the Boer War.

Natal Mounted Rifles Museum, Durban.

Diaries and Photographs in private possession.

Books

Amery, LS (ed) *The Times History of the War in South Africa*, 7 Vols., Sampson, Low & Co. London, 1907.

Anglo African Who's Who, (ed Walter H. Wells) L Upcott Gill, London 1907.

Attwood, R, *Roberts and Kitchener in South Africa 1900-1902*, Penn & Sword Military, Barnsley, 2011.

Australian Military Contingents to the War in South Africa, ed Lt Col PL Murray RAA (retd) Melbourne, 1911.

Bailey, Gerard C, *Seven Months Under Boer Rule*, RA Burns & Co. Pty, Ltd, Dundee, 1999.

Baker, A, *Battle Honours of the British and Commonwealth Armies*, Ian Allan Ltd. London, 1986.

Barthorpe, Michael, *The Zulu War*, Blandford Press Ltd, Poole, Dorset, 1980.

Batts, HJ, *Pretoria from Within during the War*, F Shaw & Co London, 1901.

Bazley, D, *Nil Desperandum*, The Royale Trust, Kloof. 2000.

Beckett, Dr Ian F.W., *The Judgment of History, Sir Horace Smith Dorrien, Lord French and 1914*, Tom Donovan, London, 1993.

Binns, CT, *The Last Zulu King*, London, 1963.

Brigland, Tony, *Field Gun Jack v The Boers*, Leo Cooper, Barnsley, 1998.

Brink, Elsabe, *The Long Walk Home*, Kwela Books, 1999.

Carver, Field Marshal Lord, *The Boer War*, Sidgwick & Jackson, London, 1999.

Castle, I, *Zulu War – Volunteers, Irregulars & Auxiliaries*, Osprey, 2003.

Chase, John Centlivres, *The Natal Papers*, R. Godlonton, Grahamstown, 1845.

Child, D, *Charles Smythe*, C. Struick (Pty) Ltd, Cape Town, 1973.

Child, D, *Portrait of a Pioneer*, Macmillan SA (Pty) Ltd Johannesburg, 1980.

Childs, L, Ladysmith, *Colenso/Spion Kop/Hlangwane/Tugela* Leo Cooper, Barnsley, 1998.

Childs, L, Ladysmith, *The Siege*, Leo Cooper, Barnsley, 1999.

Chisholme, R, *Ladysmith*, Osprey, 1979.

Churchill, Winston S, *London to Ladysmith*, Longmans, London 1900.

Coetzer, O, *The Anglo-Boer War – The Road to Infamy*, Waterman, Rivonia, 1996.

Coglan, Mark, *Pro Patria*, Natal Carbineer Trust, Pietermaritzburg, 2000.

Coglan, Mark, *Defending the Home Front – The Natal Volunteers*, Brenthurst Library.

Coulson, Charmian, *Richmond Natal – Its People and History*, 1986, Richmond Women's Institute, 1986.

Craw, Bella. *Diary 27.10.1899 to 23.3.1900*, Ladysmith Historical Society, 1970.

Creswicke, L, *South African and Transvaal War* 7 Vols., London, 1900-1902.

Crisp, R, *The Outlanders*, Peter Davies Ltd., London 1964.

Crosby, AJ, *Extract from notes 1899-1900*, Ladysmith Historical Society 1976.

Crowe, Brig Gen JH, *Gen Smuts' Campaign in East Africa, 1918*, Naval and Military Press, Reprint.

Cullinan, Patrick. *Robert Jacob Gordon*, Struick Winchester, Cape Town 1992.

David, Saul, *Zulu Heroism & Tragedy in the Zulu War*, Viking, London, 2004.

David, Saul, *100 Days to Victory*, Hodder & Stoughton, London, 2013.

Davies, HE, Ed., *Landmarks of Old Durban*, Durban 1948.

Davis, RH, *With both armies in South Africa*, Charles Scribners & Son, 1900.

Dennison, Maj CJ, *A Fight to the Finish*, Longmans Green & Co, London 1904.

des Anges, Rev Mother Marie, *Letters*, Ladysmith Historical Society, 1970.

Devitt, Napier, *Galloping Jack, Reminiscences*, Brig Gen JR Royston, London, 1937.

Digby, PKA, *Pyramids and Poppies*, Ashanti Publishing, Rivonia, 1993.

Dixon, Capt CM, *The Leaguer of Ladysmith*, Eyre & Spottiswoode, London, 1900.

Driver, Nurse Kate, *A Nurse Looks Back*, Ladysmith Historical Society, 1994.

Doyle, A Conan, *The Great Boer War*, Smith Elder & Co, London 1900.

Dundonald, Lt Gen the Earl of, *My Army Life*, Edw Arnold & Co, London 1926.

Featherstone, D, *Victorian Colonial Warfare, Africa*, Blandford & Cassel, 1993.

Gardiner, The Reverend Capt AF, *Narrative of a Journey to the Zoolu Country in South Africa*, William Crofts, London, 1836.

Gibson, G.F, *The Story of the Imperial Light Horse*, G.D. & Co, London, 1937.

Goetsche, Eric, *Father of a City*, Shuter & Shooter, Pietermaritzburg, 1966.

Goetsche, Eric, *History of the Natal Mounted Rifles*, Durban, 1971.

Gordon, Dr Ruth, Ed., *Honour Without Riches*, TW Griggs & Co, Durban, 1978.

Gough, Gen Sir Hubert, *Soldiering On*, Arthur Baker Ltd, London 1954.

Greaves & Best (eds.), *The Curling Letters of the Zulu War*, Pen & Sword Books, Barnsley, 2001.

Griffith, K, *Thank God We Kept the Flag Flying*, Viking Press, New York, 1974.

Hackett, RG, *South African War Books*, Privately Printed, London 1994.

Hattersley, AF, *More Annals of Natal*, Shuter & Shooter, Pietermaritzburg, 1936.

Hattersley, AF, *History of the Royal Natal Carbineers*, Gale & Plodden Ltd, Aldershot, 1950.

Hurst, Col GT, *History of the Natal Mounted Rifles*, 1935, Durban

Inniskilling Diaries, (ed.), Martin Cassidy, Leo Cooper, Barnesley, 2001.

Jackson, Stanley, *The Great Barnato*, Heineman, London, 1970.

Jackson, Tabitha, *The Boer War*, Channel 4 Books, London, 1999.

Jameson Raid, A Centennial Retrospective, Brenthurst Press, 1966.

Julius, Anthony, *Trials of the Diaspora*, Oxford University Press, 2010.

Klein, H, *Light Horse Cavalcade 1899-1961*, H Timmins, Cape Town, 1969.

Knight, Ian, *Boer Commando 1876-1902*, Osprey, London.

Knox, Lt Dr E Blake, *Buller's Campaign with the Natal Field Force*, Brimley Johnson, London, 1902.

Kruger, Rayne, *Goodbye Dolly Grey*, Cassel, 1959.

Le Vaillant, Francois, *Travels into the Interior Parts of Africa* (3 Vols.), AG Robinson, London 1796.

Lines, GW, *The Ladysmith Siege*, London, 1900.

Lugg, HC, *A Natal Family Looks Back*, TW Griggs, Durban 1970.

Macdonald, Donald, *How We Kept the Flag Flying*, Ward Lock & Co Ltd, Melbourne, 1900.

Mackeurtan, Graham, *The Cradle Days of Natal (1497-1845)*, Longman's Green & Co., London. 1930.

Maclean, CR, *The Natal Papers of "John Ross"*, Ed. S Gray, Killie Campbell Africana Library, Pietermaritzburg, 1992.

Martin, Col AC, *The Concentration Camps 1900-1902*, Facts Figures and Fables, Cape Town, 1957.

Martin, Lt Col BW, *Memoirs of the Siege of Ladysmith*, Ladysmith Historical Society, Ladysmith. 1970.

Marling, Col Sir Percival, *Rifleman and Hussar*, John Murray, London, 1931.

Maurice, Sir Frederick, Editor, *Official History of the War in South Africa 1899-1902*, Vols. 1 and 2, Hurst & Blackett Ltd. London 1906-1910.

May, HJ, *Music of the Guns*, Hutchinson, Johannesburg, 1970.

Mead, G, *The Good Soldier: The Biography of Douglas Haig*, Atlantic Books, London 2007.

Men of the Times, Eyre & Spottiswood. London 1905.

Mills, G and Williams, D, *Seven Battles that shaped South Africa*, Tafelberg Publishers, Cape Town, 2006.

Mitford, Bertram, *Through the Zulu Country*, Kegan Paul Trench & Co, London, 1883.

Morris, Donald, *The Washing of Spears*, Pimlico London 1965.

McFadden, Pam, *Khaki Cameos*, KZN Battlefield Promotions 1999.

McFadden, Pam, *Elandslaagte*, Raven Press, Randburg, 1999.

McKenzie, Col AG, *Delayed Action, a biography of the life of Brig Gen Sir Duncan McKenzie KCMG CB DSO VD, Legion d'Honeur*, Privately printed 1964.

Nevinson, HW, *Ladysmith, Diary of a Siege*, Methuen & Co, 1900.

O'Mahony, CJ, *A Peep over the Barleycorn*, Dublin, 1911.

Pakenham, T, *The Boer War*, Weidenfield & Nicholson Ltd, London, 1979.

Pakenham, T, *The Boer War, Abridged Illustrated edn.*, Weidenfield & Nicholson Ltd, 1993.

Park, Maj Gen CW *Correspondence*, Ladysmith Historical Society, 1972.

Paterson, AB (Banjo), *Happy Dispatches*, Angus & Robertson. Sydney 1934.

Pearse, HSS, *Four Months Besieged*, Macmillan, London, 1900.

Pollock J, *Kitchener: The Road to Omdurman*, Constable & Co Ltd, London, 1998.

Portsmouth, H, *The Story of Wyford*, Osborne Literary Services. Westville, 2010.

Reitz, Deneys, *Commando*, Faber & Faber, London, 1929.

Riall, N. ed, *Letters and Photographs of Malcolm Riall*, Brassey's, London, 2000.

Ritter, EA, *Shaka Zulu*, London 1957.

Romer, Maj CF & Mainwaring Maj AE, *The Second Battalion Royal Dublin Fusiliers in the South African War*, A.L. Humphreys, London, 1908.

Russell, George, *A History of Old Durban*, P Davis & Sons, Durban, 1899.

Russell, Robert, *Natal – The Land and its Story*, P Davis & Sons, Maritzburg, 1903

Sampson, V, and Hamilton, I, *Anti-Commando*, 1931.

Samuelson, RCA, *Long Long Ago*, Knox Printing and Publishing, Durban, 1929.

Sandys, Celia, *Churchill Wanted Dead or Alive*, Harper Collins, London, 1999.

Schiel, Col Adolf, *Twenty-three years of Storm and Sunshine in South Africa*, Leipzig 1902.

Smail, GS, *Historical Monuments and Battlefields in Natal and Zululand*, Howard Timmins, Cape Town, 1965.

Spiers, EM, ed, *Letters from Ladysmith*, Jonathon Ball, Jeppestown, 2010.

Smith-Dorrien, Lt Gen Sir Horace, *Isandlwhana to the Great War*, Oakpast Ltd, London 2009

Stafford and Franklin, *Principles of Native Law*, Shuter & Shooter, Pmb, 1950.

Stanford, Sir Walter, *Reminiscences*, van Riebeeck Society, Cape Town, 1962.

Stalker, J, *The Natal Carbineers 1855-1911*, P Davies & Son, Pmb, 1912.

Steevens, GW, *From Cape Town to Ladysmith*, William Blackwood & Sons, London, 1900.

Stirling, J., *The Colonials in South Africa*, Wm Blackwood & Sons, London, 1902.

Stott, Clement H, *The Boer Invasion of Natal*, SW Partridge & Co, London, 1900.

Stuart, J, & Malcolm D. McK., Eds. *Diary of H. Fynn*, 1950 reprint.

Strydom, Hans, *For Volk and Fuhrer*, Jonathon Ball, Jeppestown, 1982.

Symons, Julian, *Buller's Campaign*, The Cresset Press, London, 1963.

Tatham, George F, *Diary No 1*, Ladysmith Historical Society, 1970.

Treves, Dr Frederick, *The Tale of a Field Hospital*, Cassell & Co Ltd, London, 1900.

Tucker, Private Frederick, *Diary*, Elmtree Books, London. 1980.

Union of South Africa, *Official History of the Great War 1914-1918*, Imperial War Museum and Naval and Military Press, Uckfield, UK.

War Services of Military Officers 1899-1902, Savannah Publications, London, 1998.

Wasserman & Kearney (Eds), *A Warrior's Gateway*, Protea Book House, Pretoria, 2002.

Watkins-Pitchford, H, *Besieged in Ladysmith*, Shuter & Shooter, Pmb., 1964.

Watson, William, *Diary No. 7*, Ladysmith Historical Society, 1989.

Whitton, Lt George, *Scapegoats of the Empire*, first published in Australia 1907, subsequently by Angus & Robertson in Britain in 1982.

Williams, WA, *Commandant of the Transvaal*, Bridge Books, Wrexham, 2001.

Willis, GW, Letter, *Booklet No. 4*, Ladysmith Historical Society, 1970.

Wilson, H.W, *With the Flag to Pretoria*, Vols. 1 and 2, Harmsworth, London 1901.

Index